Inventions of Enlightenment since 1800
Concepts of Lumières, Enlightenment and Aufklärung

INVENTIONS OF ENLIGHTENMENT
SINCE 1800
CONCEPTS OF LUMIÈRES,
ENLIGHTENMENT AND AUFKLÄRUNG

Edited by

NICHOLAS CRONK

and

ÉLISABETH DÉCULTOT

Published by Liverpool University Press on behalf of
© 2023 Voltaire Foundation, University of Oxford
ISBN 978 1 80207 876 3
Oxford University Studies in the Enlightenment 2023:11
ISSN 2634-8047 (Print)
ISSN 2634-8055 (Online)

Voltaire Foundation
99 Banbury Road
Oxford OX2 6JX, UK
www.voltaire.ox.ac.uk

A catalogue record for this book is available from the British Library

The correct style for citing this book is
Nicholas Cronk and Elisabeth Décultot, eds, *Inventions of Enlightenment
since 1800: concepts of* Lumières, *Enlightenment and* Aufklärung
Oxford University Studies in the Enlightenment
(Liverpool, Liverpool University Press, 2023)

Cover illustration: *Le Tombeau de Voltaire foudroyé* by Charles François
Le Tellier. Philadelphia Museum of Art: Gift of Mrs. John D. Rockefeller,
Jr., 1946, 1946-51-252.

Printed and bound by CPI Group (UK) Ltd, Croydon CR0 4YY

Oxford University Studies in the Enlightenment

INVENTIONS OF ENLIGHTENMENT SINCE 1800
CONCEPTS OF LUMIÈRES, *ENLIGHTENMENT* AND AUFKLÄRUNG

Enlightenment values, including an emphasis on human rights and belief in rationalism and progress, aspire to be universals, yet at the same time they are concepts grounded in the eighteenth century. Since the French Revolution we have grappled with the ideas of *Lumières*, Enlightenment and *Aufklärung*, in an attempt to understand how these eighteenth-century concepts continue to shape and influence modern notions of liberal culture.

This collection of articles approaches these important questions in a resolutely European and multi-lingual perspective. Ranging from Victor Cousin to Peter Gay, different contributions consider Tocqueville and the Hegelian school (Bruno Bauer, David Friedrich Strauss, Hermann Hettner), the intellectual currents in Europe around 1900 (Wilhelm Dilthey, Gustave Lanson), the thinkers of the Weimar Republic (Ernst Cassirer) and of the Frankfurt School (Max Horkheimer, Theodor W. Adorno), and the debates after the Second World War (Franco Venturi). While the principal focus is on writing in French, German and English, the book also treats the Russian- and Italian-speaking worlds.

This important contribution to the history of ideas helps us to redefine the Enlightenment. These articles do not merely describe historical assessments of an eighteenth-century movement of ideas: they contribute to the ongoing debate about the very nature of the concept of Enlightenment.

Contents

List of figures   ix

Preface   xi

NICHOLAS CRONK *and* ÉLISABETH DÉCULTOT, Introduction:
les Lumières après les Lumières? Pourquoi une histoire des
notions de Lumières, d'*Enlightenment* et d'*Aufklärung* entre
1800 et 1980   1

CHRISTIAN HELMREICH, Victor Cousin et la philosophie
des Lumières   5

ÉLISABETH DÉCULTOT, Alexis de Tocqueville et Hermann
Hettner, 1856: deux historiens face au dix-huitième siècle   21

DANIEL WEIDNER, Unveiling or inventing the Enlightenment?
Bruno Bauer, the political theology of radical critique and the
construction of Enlightenment in the *Vormärz* epoch   37

FRANCESCA IANNELLI, Understanding, radicalising and
illuminating the Enlightenment: Hegel's use of *Lumières* and
Aufklärung for an enlightened philosophy   57

STÉPHANE ZÉKIAN, Les Lumières à l'épreuve des concours:
le cas du prix d'éloquence à l'Académie française (1831-1904)   81

BRIAN W. YOUNG, After Carlyle: 'Enlightenment' in
Victorian Britain   101

AVI LIFSCHITZ, Germanising the Enlightenment: Wilhelm
Dilthey's *Aufklärung*   119

NICHOLAS CRONK, *Lumières* in France: the contribution of
Gustave Lanson and his pupils   141

ANDREW KAHN, The theme of Enlightenment in Russian
historiography, 1860-1900   155

MIKE ROTTMANN, The dilemma of Enlightenment: German,
Jewish and antisemitic constructions of *Aufklärung* in the
nineteenth century   185

JAMES SCHMIDT, Nihilism, Enlightenment and the 'new
failure of nerve': arguments about Enlightenment in New York
and Los Angeles, 1941-1947   223

RUGGERO SCIUTO, Ideas in action: Franco Venturi's *Settecento*   241

GREGORY S. BROWN, The question of Peter Gay's
Enlightenment: between 'heavenly city' and the 'brute facts of
political life' (1948-1956)   257

DANIEL FULDA, 'Die Zeit der Aufklärung ist wieder da':
activist appropriations of the Enlightenment in the Hegelian
Left and in eighteenth-century studies in the GDR   285

Bibliography   307

Index   345

List of figures

Figure 1: Cover page from Dr. S[imon]. Bernfeld, *Am Ende des Jahrhunderts: Rückschau auf 100 Jahre geistiger Entwicklung*, vol.3: *Juden und Judentum im neunzehnten Jahrhundert* (Berlin, 1898). © Freimann-Sammlung. Universitätsbibliothek Johann Christian Senckenberg, Goethe-Universität Frankfurt am Main.   191

Figure 2: Cover page from *Lessing-Mendelssohn-Gedenkbuch: zur hundertfünfzigjährigen Geburtsfeier von GOTTHOLD EPHRAIM LESSING und MOSES MENDELSSOHN, sowie zur Säcularfeier von Lessing's 'Nathan'*, ed. Deutsch-Israelitischer Gemeindebunde (Leipzig, 1879). © Bayerische Staatsbibliothek München.   193

Figure 3: 'Billige Flugblätter zur Aufklärung über die jüdische Mißwirthschaft', advert in *Statistik des Judenthums: Sonder-Abdruck aus dem Antisemiten-Katechismus von Theodor Fritsch (Thomas Frey)* (Leipzig, 1892). © Freimann-Sammlung. Universitätsbibliothek Johann Christian Senckenberg, Goethe-Universität Frankfurt am Main.   194

Figure 4: 'Antisemiten-Katechismus', advert in *Statistik des Judenthums: Sonder-Abdruck aus dem Antisemiten-Katechismus von Theodor Fritsch (Thomas Frey)* (Leipzig, 1892). © Freimann-Sammlung. Universitätsbibliothek Johann Christian Senckenberg, Goethe-Universität Frankfurt am Main.   194

Figure 5: 'Deutsch-soziale Blätter', advert in *Antisemiten-Katechismus: eine Zusammenstellung des wichtigsten Materials zum Verständnis der Judenfrage von Theodor Fritsch*, 25th edn (Leipzig, 1893). © Freimann-Sammlung. Universitätsbibliothek Johann Christian Senckenberg, Goethe-Universität Frankfurt am Main.   195

Figure 6: Title page of [Nicolaus Hieronymus Gundling], *Gundlingiana, darinnen allerhand zur Jurisprudentz, Philosophie, Historie, Critic, Litteratur und übrigen Gelehrsamkeit gehörige Sachen abgehandelt werden*, vol.1-45 (Halle, Rengerische Buchhandlung, 1715-1732), vol.1. Source: Universitäts- und Landesbibliothek Sachsen-Anhalt, Halle (Saale).   288

Preface

A well-known engraving, *Le Tombeau de Voltaire*, published in 1779, the year after Voltaire's death, depicts three men and a woman paying hommage to Voltaire's tomb while defending it from the dark forces of unreason. The picture on the cover of this volume is of another polemical print, *Le Tombeau de Voltaire foudroyé*, engraved by Charles François Le Tellier, after a drawing by Claude Louis Desrais based on an idea of Charles François Gabriel Levachez, and published by Levachez between 1779 and 1790 as a reply to the first; in it we see Jean-Jacques Rousseau's tomb on the horizon, while the tomb of Voltaire is placed front and centre. The forces of Christianity defiantly dominate Voltaire's monument, confounding the prestigious group of enlightened protesters to the right: D'Alembert, Catherine the Great, Prince Oroonoko and Benjamin Franklin, representing respectively the four continents of Europe, Asia, Africa and America. The legacy of the Enlightenment is here depicted as a global one, already at the end of the eighteenth century. As this volume demonstrates, in a series of articles examining a cross-section of European and American responses to the concepts of *Lumières*, Enlightenment and *Aufklärung*, that struggle continues in the years after 1800.

We are very grateful to all the colleagues in Halle and Oxford who have assisted both in the preparation of this book and in the organisation of the meetings which led to it. We thank in particular Mike Rottman and Aleksandra Ambrozy, both from Halle, who took on the patient work of preparing the manuscript, and Dominique Lussier, from Oxford, who compiled the index.

Greg Brown encouraged this project at every stage of its development, and our sincere thanks go to him, and also to the two anonymous readers of our manuscript for their helpful and judicious comments.

We also express our sincerest gratitude to Leah Morin, whose expert copy-editing has made an enormous contribution to the quality and cohesion of this volume.

The planning of this project was made more complicated by the health crisis that prevented our planned in-person meetings, and we most of all thank our contributors for their forbearance and enthusiasm.

The publication of this book marks an important step in the growing collaboration between the Interdisziplinäres Zentrum für die Erforschung der Europäischen Aufklärung (IZEA) in Halle and the Voltaire Foundation (VF) in Oxford: we hope this volume will be the first of many such collaborative projects.

Nicholas Cronk, Elisabeth Décultot

Introduction: les Lumières après les Lumières? Pourquoi une histoire des notions de Lumières, d'*Enlightenment* et d'*Aufklärung* entre 1800 et 1980

Nicholas Cronk

University of Oxford

Élisabeth Décultot

Martin-Luther-Universität Halle-Wittenberg

L'objet du présent ouvrage est d'esquisser l'histoire des notions de Lumières, d'*Enlightenment* et d'*Aufklärung* entre 1800 et 1980, c'est-à-dire *après* le dix-huitième siècle, au fil d'une enquête qui traverse les espaces francophones, germanophones et anglophones, en y associant quelques aperçus sur les mondes russophones et italianophones. Ce parcours européen mène de Victor Cousin à Peter Gay, en passant par Tocqueville et l'école hégélienne (Bruno Bauer, David Friedrich Strauss, Hermann Hettner), puis par les courants intellectuels de l'Europe de 1900 et d'avant la première guerre mondiale (Wilhelm Dilthey, Gustave Lanson), avant d'aborder le vingtième siècle avec les penseurs de la République de Weimar (Ernst Cassirer, Hannah Arendt, Gershom Scholem), de l'Ecole de Francfort (Max Horkheimer, Theodor W. Adorno) et de l'après seconde guerre mondiale (Franco Venturi).

Pourquoi cette focalisation sur l'histoire de ces notions aux dix-neuvième et vingtième siècles? La raison, interne au discours scientifique, est tout d'abord que nous entendons contribuer par là à combler une importante lacune de la recherche. Si l'histoire des notions de Lumières, d'*Enlightenment* et d'*Aufklärung* est assez bien connue pour le dix-huitième siècle, elle l'est beaucoup moins pour les

1

siècles ultérieurs.[1] Il existe certes d'éclairantes études touchant à la formation et à l'usage de ces notions aux dix-neuvième et vingtième siècles,[2] mais d'importantes zones d'ombre persistent. S'il nous a paru utile de faire porter nos travaux sur cette période, c'est en outre qu'elle est doublement centrale – à la fois pour l'histoire des concepts de Lumières, d'*Enlightenment* et d'*Aufklärung* et pour l'histoire de la pensée de nombreuses figures intellectuelles de ces deux siècles.

Notre but n'est bien sûr pas l'exhaustivité, objectif trop ambitieux pour un seul volume et d'ailleurs sans doute vain pour un sujet aussi ample. Il s'agit plutôt d'analyser un ensemble cohérent de figures et de constellations exemplaires, à partir desquelles nous développons un arsenal de questions transversales, essentiellement organisées autour de trois axes: (1) acteurs et contextes; (2) échelle géographique; (3) synergies et décalages. Plus précisément, il s'agit d'identifier certains acteurs, groupes d'acteurs et contextes ayant encouragé l'émergence, durant la période considérée, des notions de Lumières, d'*Enlightenment* et d'*Aufklärung* comme catégories historiographiques. L'enjeu est aussi de s'interroger sur la dimension – locale, régionale, nationale, européenne – de cette émergence et sur les décalages qui s'esquissent entre les différentes aires linguistiques européennes dans l'acception de ces notions. Autrement dit, les termes de Lumières, d'*Enlightenment* et d'*Aufklärung* ont-ils des significations et des fonctions comparables

1. Parmi les nombreux travaux sur l'histoire de ces notions, citons, dans un aperçu nécessairement très lacunaire, par exemple: Karin E. Becker, 'Licht – (L) lumière(s) – siècle des Lumières: von der Lichtmetapher zum Epochenbegriff der Aufklärung in Frankreich', thèse de doctorat, Université de Cologne, 1994; Jonathan C. D. Clark, 'The Enlightenment: catégories, traductions et objets sociaux', *Lumières* 17/18 (2011), numéro thématique: *Les Lumières dans leur siècle*, éd. Didier Masseau et Gérard Laudin, p.19-39; Michel Delon, 'Les Lumières: travail d'une métaphore', *SVEC* 1552 (1976), p.527-41; Dan Edelstein, *The Enlightenment: a genealogy* (Chicago, IL, 2010); Vincenzo Ferrone, *The Enlightenment: history of an idea* (Princeton, NJ, et Oxford, 2017); Rainer Godel *et al.*, 'Aufklärungen', dans *Handbuch Europäische Aufklärung: Begriffe – Konzepte – Wirkung*, éd. Heinz Thoma (Stuttgart, 2015), p.86-122; Fritz Schalk, 'Aufklärung', dans *Historisches Wörterbuch der Philosophie*, éd. Joachim Ritter, t.1 (Bâle, 1971), col.620-33; Heinz Thoma, 'Aufklärung', dans *Handbuch Europäische Aufklärung*, éd. H. Thoma, p.67-85.
2. *Lumières* 8 (2006), numéro thématique: *Foucault et les Lumières*, éd. Fabienne Brugère *et al.*; Antoine Lilti, *L'Héritage des Lumières: ambivalences de la modernité* (Paris, 2019); *Historiographie et usages des Lumières*, éd. Giuseppe Ricuperati (Berlin, 2002); Franck Salaün et Jean-Pierre Schandeler, *Enquête sur la construction des Lumières* (Ferney-Voltaire, 2018).

dans les espaces francophones, anglophones et germanophones durant la période 1800-1980? Ces sujets sont particulièrement importants dans le contexte des débats actuels sur le dix-huitième siècle, car ils permettent d'aborder la question centrale de la relativité et de la diversité des Lumières, notamment débattue dans les études post- et décoloniales, en reconstituant, à l'échelle intra-européenne, l'évolution progressive de l'entité historiographique du 'siècle des Lumières' et de ses équivalents européens à partir du dix-neuvième siècle.

Les notions de Lumières, d'*Enlightenment* et d'*Aufklärung* présentent aujourd'hui la particularité d'être utilisées dans une double acception. Elles renvoient d'une part à un certain nombre d'idées, de phénomènes ou de valeurs – autonomisation du sujet, reconnaissance juridique et politique des droits de l'individu, rationalisation, progrès – qui ont une prétention, une visée universelle. Dans cette acception, que l'on pourrait qualifier pour plus de commodité d'axiomatique, ces notions sont déconnectées de tout contexte historique ou géographique précis, c'est-à-dire qu'elles sont en principe actualisables à tout moment et en tout lieu du globe, ou encore qu'elles sont généralisables à l'ensemble de l'humanité, hier, aujourd'hui et demain. Mais ces notions désignent aussi, dans une acception inséparable de cette première signification, l'époque où ces idées et valeurs ont été élaborées et débattues, à savoir un dix-huitième siècle plus ou moins largement conçu – les limites chronologiques des Lumières comprises comme époque historique faisant l'objet de nombreuses discussions.[3] Cette double acception – axiomatique et historique – n'a certes rien de spécifique aux notions de Lumières, d'*Enlightenment* et d'*Aufklärung*: elle se retrouve dans de nombreux termes désignant à la fois une époque et un courant intellectuel ou artistique, tels que les notions de classicisme ou de romantisme.[4] La spécificité des notions de Lumières, d'*Enlightenment*

---

3. Certains font commencer la période des Lumières dès le dix-septième siècle, avec Spinoza, tel Jonathan Israel, *Radical Enlightenment: philosophy and the making of modernity, 1650-1750* (Oxford, 2001), ou encore, selon une tradition historiographique bien établie, avec Bayle et Fontenelle. D'autres la cantonnent au dix-huitième siècle et voient dans toute application de la notion de Lumières à des périodes ultérieures un anachronisme, comme Andreas Pečar et Damien Tricoire, *Falsche Freunde: war die Aufklärung wirklich die Geburtsstunde der Moderne?* (Francfort-sur-le-Main et New York, 2015).

4. Fernand Baldensperger, 'Romantique, ses analogues et ses équivalents: tableau synoptique de 1650 à 1810', *Harvard studies and notes in philology and literature* 19 (1937), p.13-105; *Romantic and its cognates: the European history of a word*, éd. Hans Eichner (Toronto, 1972); Arthur O. Lovejoy, 'The meaning of "romantic"

et d'*Aufklärung* est que cette articulation entre l'acception historique et axiomatique de ces termes fait problème et est au cœur même de débats touchant à leur signification. Or c'est à partir du dix-neuvième siècle, au moment où émergent les grands récits retraçant l'histoire du dix-huitième siècle, que cette double potentialité sémantique se dessine et s'établit réellement. Faire l'histoire des concepts de Lumières, d'*Enlightenment* et d'*Aufklärung* aux dix-neuvième et vingtième siècles, ce n'est donc pas faire une histoire des Lumières *après* les Lumières, mais c'est bien faire une histoire du concept de Lumières tout court.

───────────

in early German Romanticism', *Modern language notes* 31 (1916), p.385-96, et 32 (1917), p.65-77; Wilhelm Vosskamp, 'Klassisch/Klassik/Klassizismus', dans *Ästhetische Grundbegriffe: historisches Wörterbuch in sieben Bänden*, éd. Karlheinz Barck *et al.*, 7 vol. (Stuttgart et Weimar, 2001-2005), t.3, p.289-305; René Wellek, 'The term and concept of classicism in literary history', dans *Discriminations: further concepts of criticism* (New Haven, CT, et Londres, 1970), p.55-89.

Victor Cousin et la philosophie des Lumières

Christian Helmreich

Martin-Luther-Universität Halle-Wittenberg

Ouverture

De plus en plus on devait reconnaître, dans le philosophe qui avait fait naître tant d'espérances, un orateur auquel, comme aux orateurs en général, s'il faut en croire Aristote, le vraisemblable, à défaut du vrai, suffisait. Là où l'on s'était cru convaincu, on avait cédé le plus souvent à la séduction, plus puissante peut-être à l'époque où l'éclectisme s'était produit, de la parole ou du style. D'autres temps étaient venus; on eût préféré désormais sous des formes moins brillantes, s'il le fallait, un fond plus riche, moins de littérature peut-être, et plus de doctrine.[1]

Voilà comment, dès 1868, dans des pages célèbres, Félix Ravaisson critique sévèrement, au moment même où disparaît Victor Cousin (1792-1867), la philosophie de celui qui, d'une certaine façon, fut son maître, comme il fut le maître de presque tous les philosophes français de la première moitié du dix-neuvième siècle. De fait, d'un point de vue purement philosophique, la cause semble entendue: il n'y a pas lieu d'étudier la pensée de Cousin. Ce jugement sévère n'a pas vraiment été révisé depuis la seconde moitié du dix-neuvième siècle. Quand, du coup, on s'intéresse à Victor Cousin, ce n'est pas sans s'en excuser, comme s'il s'agissait d'un sujet en quelque sorte honteux.[2] Cela dit, Ravaisson n'en souligne pas moins l'importance

---

1. Félix Ravaisson, *La Philosophie en France au XIXᵉ siècle* (Paris, 1868), p.31-32.
2. Sur Victor Cousin, on consultera en particulier Paul Janet, *Victor Cousin et son œuvre* (Paris, 1885); Jules Simon, *Victor Cousin* (Paris, 1887); Jean Pommier, 'L'évolution de Victor Cousin', *Revue d'histoire de la philosophie* [1ʳᵉ série] (1931), p.172-203; Pierre Macherey, 'Les débuts philosophiques de Victor Cousin', *Corpus: revue de philosophie* 18 (1991), p.29-49; Patrice Vermeren, *Victor Cousin: le jeu de la philosophie et de l'Etat* (Paris, 1995); *Victor Cousin, homo théologico-politicus:*

de Cousin dans le paysage intellectuel français du dix-neuvième
siècle. Figure institutionnellement puissante, Cousin a profondément
marqué ses successeurs immédiats. Mais, de manière subliminale,
la figure de Cousin est encore présente de nos jours. En France, sa
conception de l'enseignement philosophique (le fait, notamment,
pour toute question philosophique, de présenter un panorama
historique des doctrines préexistantes) a cours encore de nos jours.
A en croire Pierre-François Moreau, 'il a mis en place notre façon
de nous rapporter à la philosophie, avec ses avantages, avec aussi ses
difficultés.' Nous vivons aujourd'hui encore 'sur l'apport de Cousin,
mais sans le savoir'.[3]

Dans les développements qui suivent, nous ne nous intéresserons
en premier lieu ni au contenu philosophique des œuvres de Cousin,
ni à son importance institutionnelle, mais à la manière dont Cousin,
au début du dix-neuvième siècle, analyse et décrit la philosophie
du siècle précédent. Nous nous sommes concentrés sur les célèbres
cours que Victor Cousin donne à la Sorbonne dans les années qui
précèdent immédiatement la révolution de juillet 1830: dans le *Cours
de 1828* (*Introduction à l'histoire de la philosophie*), une place importante
est ménagée au dix-huitième siècle; quant au Cours de 1829, il est
consacré à l'*Histoire de la philosophie du XVIII*e siècle. Cette histoire
est certes fragmentaire, du fait des circonstances historiques. La
révolution de 1830 a en quelque sorte empêché que le projet soit
mené à son terme, Cousin ayant été appelé à d'autres fonctions
dans le système éducatif français, notamment en tant que membre
du Conseil royal de l'Instruction publique. Ainsi, l'*Histoire de la
philosophie* de 1829 nous présente dans un premier tome un panorama
historique de toute la philosophie européenne, avant, dans un second
tome, de s'intéresser spécifiquement à la philosophie de Locke et de
ses successeurs. Malgré l'inachèvement de ce vaste panorama de la
philosophie du dix-huitième siècle, qui aurait peut-être rempli six
ou huit tomes au lieu des deux tomes existants, le texte de Victor
Cousin est un document tout à fait central lorsqu'on s'intéresse à la
réception de la philosophie des Lumières. La lecture cousinienne de
la philosophie du dix-huitième siècle montre de façon exemplaire les

---

philologie, philosophie, histoire littéraire, éd. Eric Fauquet (Paris, 1997); Lucie
Rey, 'Victor Cousin et l'instrumentalisation de l'histoire de la philosophie', *Le
Télémaque* 54:2 (2018), p.43-55.

3.   Pierre-François Moreau, 'Victor Cousin, la philosophie et son histoire', *Le
Télémaque* 54:2 (2018), p.57-66 (65).

enjeux, mais aussi les limites, de la réception des Lumières au début du dix-neuvième siècle. Pour la génération qui se retrouve sur le devant de la scène à partir de 1815 ou 1820, à un moment où, dans bien des disciplines, après les bouleversements matériels, institutionnels et idéologiques de l'épisode révolutionnaire et napoléonien, il s'agit de repartir sur de nouvelles bases, le dix-huitième siècle est quelque peu 'encombrant'.

Comme bien des auteurs de son époque, Cousin sent que, après l'accélération du cours de l'histoire, il est nécessaire de s'arrêter, de prendre en quelque sorte le temps de regarder en arrière avant de repartir. Après un temps qui, surtout en France, semble avoir sapé bien des fondements, il faut savoir quels sont les appuis sur lesquels il est possible de compter. Le réflexe historique (ou historicisant), si puissant dans la France de la Restauration, s'explique notamment par le besoin de donner un sens à ce qui vient de se passer, et de réfléchir à ce qu'il convient, très concrètement, de faire. Il apparaît clairement, en 1820, qu'il n'est pas possible de faire comme si 1789 n'avait pas eu lieu (c'est-à-dire de considérer la Révolution comme une 'parenthèse', comme le font certains ultra-royalistes);[4] en même temps, rares sont ceux qui se réclament ouvertement de cette révolution accusée d'avoir causé bien des troubles et bien des excès, des guerres civiles meurtrières et des guerres extérieures qui, *in fine*, ont été perdues et qui, dans la perception des contemporains, ont eu pour le pays des conséquences humaines, économiques et politiques très couteuses. Dans le domaine philosophique, Cousin cherche lui aussi à faire en quelque sorte l'inventaire, et c'est dans cette optique qu'il s'intéresse au dix-huitième siècle.

Faire inventaire, ou justification de l'éclectisme

Avant de jeter notre regard sur l'analyse que Cousin fait du dix-huitième siècle philosophique, il convient d'examiner d'un peu plus près ce qui fonde son regard sur l'histoire de la philosophie. Pour Cousin, un certain nombre de raisons expliquent pourquoi il est nécessaire de faire inventaire.

---

4. On connaît la réaction de François Guizot face aux déclamations des ultra-royalistes: 'Il est impossible d'entendre sans effroi tant de gens répéter: "la révolution est finie"', écrit-il en 1816. 'Comme si une révolution pouvait finir à jour fixe et par l'effet magique d'un seul événement!' Cité par Laurent Theis, *François Guizot* (Paris, 2008), p.307.

'La philosophie n'est pas à chercher, elle est faite'

D'abord, il semble inutile et d'ailleurs présomptueux, dans l'esprit de Cousin, d'inventer une nouvelle philosophie – il faut commencer par répertorier l'existant. 'Je l'ai dit il y a déja long-temps, la philosophie n'est pas à chercher, elle est faite. Si elle n'est pas faite, vous la cherchez en vain; vous ne la trouverez pas', écrit-il dans son *Cours* de 1829, et il poursuit:

> Ne serait-il pas absurde, en effet, qu'ici, en 1829, je vinsse me porter pour avoir découvert, enfin, dans ce point du temps et de l'espace, et vous enseigner la vérité qui aurait échappé à trois mille ans de recherches infructueuses, et à tant de générations d'hommes de génie? La prétention est insensée, et toute philosophie qui procède ainsi est une philosophie qu'il est aisé de confondre, même avant d'avoir entendu les révélations qu'elle promet. Si au contraire, sous toutes les erreurs, dans l'histoire de la philosophie comme dans l'esprit humain lui-même, est une philosophie toujours subsistante, toujours ancienne et toujours nouvelle, alors il ne s'agit pas de faire la philosophie, mais de la constater; car elle est.[5]

Ainsi, la méthode éclectique cherche-t-elle dans la diversité des systèmes ce que Cousin, dans un passage voisin de celui que nous venons de citer, nomme, en reprenant une expression trouvée chez Leibniz, une *perennis philosophia*, 'une philosophie immortelle, cachée et non perdue dans les développemens excentriques des systèmes'. D'aucuns pourront voir dans cette méthode une manière commode de développer une pensée philosophique sans se donner la peine d'en produire une soi-même. Dans un article du *Globe*, Théodore Jouffroy souligne discrètement le problème dès les années 1820: 'M. Cousin a rendu plus de services à la philosophie en faisant connaître les grands systèmes qu'en y ajoutant lui-même un système de plus.'[6] Cousin lui-même note à la fin de son cours sur Locke: 'Ce que je professe avant tout, ce que j'enseigne, ce n'est pas telle ou telle philosophie, mais la philosophie elle-même; ce n'est pas l'attachement à tel ou tel

---

5. Victor Cousin, *Cours de l'histoire de la philosophie: histoire de la philosophie du XVIIIᵉ siècle*, 2 vol. (Paris, 1829), t.2, p.29.
6. Cité par Janet, *Victor Cousin et son œuvre*, p.167. Alors qu'il cherche à 'exposer avec impartialité et équité la grande œuvre de restauration philosophique que le célèbre Victor Cousin avait accomplie' (p.v), Paul Janet n'en souligne pas moins que Cousin n'a pas été 'un métaphysicien créateur comme Descartes, Kant ou Hegel' (p.166).

système, si grand qu'il puisse être, l'admiration de tel ou tel homme, quelqu'ait été son génie, mais l'esprit philosophique.'[7] Dans l'esprit de Cousin, l'étude de l'histoire de la philosophie est un travail philosophique, et il l'est d'autant plus qu'il n'y a pas, selon lui, de système philosophique complètement fautif, parce qu'il est impossible qu'une pensée soit parfaitement absurde.[8] Ainsi donc, 'l'histoire de la philosophie contient une philosophie vraie.'[9] Il suffit, écrit-il, 'de dégager ce fond immortel des formes défectueuses et variables qui l'obscurcissent à la fois et le manifestent dans l'histoire, pour atteindre à la vraie philosophie'.[10] En d'autres termes, il faut faire le tri, séparer le bon grain de l'ivraie. Cousin lui-même utilise une autre métaphore – une image qui, comme celle de l'inventaire que nous avons employée, est empruntée au domaine du commerce et de la comptabilité (ce qui est peut-être un hommage involontaire que le professeur de philosophie rend à l'esprit marchand qui se développe au cours du dix-neuvième siècle):

> Toute grande époque de l'histoire de la philosophie a pour ainsi dire un résultat net, qui se compose, d'une part, de toutes les erreurs, de l'autre, de toutes les vérités qui sont dûes à cette époque; c'est là le legs qu'une époque fait à celle qui la suit. Le dix-huitième siècle a aussi son résultat net; il a un legs à faire au dix-neuvième siècle. C'est ce legs qu'il s'agit de dégager et d'épurer, et de présenter à la génération qui s'avance comme son patrimoine, et le fond sur lequel elle doit travailler.[11]

De façon intéressante, la métaphore capitalistique du 'résultat net' est rapidement remplacée par le champ lexical de l'héritage: dans le regard diachronique qui est celui de Victor Cousin, le capital se présente sous la forme du legs. Ce qui, en revanche, est escamoté dans l'emploi de ces métaphores économiques, c'est la question de savoir *qui* évalue le résultat net ou l'héritage qui nous a été donné: s'il y a un tri à faire, s'il faut débarrasser la vérité des scories inutiles qui encombrent

---

7. Cousin, *Cours de l'histoire de la philosophie*, t.2, p.558.
8. 'L'absurdité complète n'entre pas dans l'esprit de l'homme; c'est la vertu de la pensée de n'admettre rien que sous la condition d'un peu de vérité, et l'erreur absolue est inintelligible [...]. L'erreur absolue est inintelligible; donc elle est inadmissible, donc elle est impossible.' Cousin, *Cours de l'histoire de la philosophie*, t.1, p.168.
9. Cousin, *Cours de l'histoire de la philosophie*, t.2, p.28.
10. Cousin, *Cours de l'histoire de la philosophie*, t.2, p.28.
11. Cousin, *Cours de l'histoire de la philosophie*, t.2, p.30-31.

ou rendent problématiques les philosophies du passé, il faut une instance à laquelle cette évaluation est confiée. Cette fonction revient à celui qui se charge de faire histoire de la philosophie, c'est-à-dire à Cousin lui-même.

Le 'besoin de reconstruire'

Cette méthode prudente qui cherche non pas à partir de zéro, mais à faire fond sur ce qui existe, est de façon évidente liée à la conjoncture historique que nous avons esquissée tout à l'heure. L'idée de faire table rase n'est pas très porteuse en 1820 (ni d'ailleurs dans les décennies qui suivent). En 1826, dans la préface de son recueil de *Fragmens philosophiques*, Cousin propose une description saisissante de son époque: 'Examinons-nous bien nous autres hommes et surtout Français du dix-neuvième siècle. L'esprit d'analyse a beaucoup détruit autour de nous. Nés au milieu de ruines en tout genre, nous sentons le besoin de reconstruire; ce besoin est intime, pressant, impérieux; il y a péril pour nous dans l'état où nous sommes.'[12] Inutile, dans une période agitée comme l'est le début du dix-neuvième siècle, d'ajouter du désordre au désordre: il convient de stabiliser les choses. Ce qui, d'une certaine façon, revient à valoriser l'existant et à déprécier l'idée que l'on puisse apporter des choses neuves. L'éclectisme de Victor Cousin s'accompagne d'une forme de scepticisme, de mélancolie ou de lassitude historique (ce dont témoigne d'ailleurs la métaphore des 'ruines'): fatiguée par les soubresauts capricieux et par les désordres de l'histoire, la génération de 1820 préfère réparer ce qui a été maltraité par les tempêtes du passé plutôt que d'initier de nouveaux bouleversements et de provoquer de nouvelles tourmentes. Dans un autre passage de ses *Fragmens philosophiques*, Cousin convoque là encore la métaphore des ruines:

> Les anciens n'avaient point assez vu, pour être importunés de la fatigante mobilité du spectacle, et de la stérile variété de ces fréquentes catastrophes, qui ne paraissent avoir d'autre résultat qu'un changement inutile dans la face des choses humaines. [...] Pour nous, qui avons vu passer cette noble antiquité, et que la tempête perpétuelle des révolutions a précipités tour à tour dans des situations si diverses; qui avons vu tomber tant d'empires, tant de sectes, tant d'opinions; qui ne nous sommes traînés que de ruines en ruines vers celles que nous habitons aujourd'hui sans pouvoir nous y reposer;

12. Victor Cousin, *Fragmens philosophiques* (Paris, 1826), p.vi.

nous sommes las, nous autres modernes, de cette face du monde qui change sans cesse.[13]

Les Lumières

Dans cette constellation, quelle est donc la place de la philosophie des Lumières? Une première remarque s'impose: si Victor Cousin traite assez fréquemment de la philosophie du dix-huitième siècle, il n'utilise pas le terme de 'Lumières', pas plus d'ailleurs qu'il ne parle des 'philosophes' lorsqu'il s'agit de désigner par exemple le groupe des encyclopédistes. Le siècle des Lumières ne porte pas chez Cousin le nom que nous lui donnons aujourd'hui. De façon significative, les deux cours spécifiquement consacrés au siècle de Voltaire, de Rousseau et de Kant portent des titres sobres: celui de 1819/1820, édité en 1839, est intitulé *Cours d'histoire de la philosophie morale au XVIIIe siècle*,[14] celui de 1829 (imprimé cette année même) *Histoire de la philosophie du XVIIIe siècle*.

Ombres et lumières des Lumières

Dans ces textes, les références à la philosophie du dix-huitième siècle ne sont jamais neutres. En 1829, Cousin donne son cours d'histoire de la philosophie dans un contexte particulier. Avec ses collègues Villemain et Guizot, il apparaît comme l'un des porte-étendards des libéraux.[15] Les cours de ces trois professeurs avaient été suspendus au début des années 1820,[16] au moment où, après l'assassinat du duc de Berry, les ultra-royalistes étaient arrivés au pouvoir. En 1828, le ministère Martignac rétablit leurs cours, et ce geste est perçu par l'opinion publique comme une petite victoire pour l'opposition libérale. Ainsi, les cours de ce 'triumvirat' constitué d'un professeur d'histoire, d'un

---

13. Cousin, *Fragmens philosophiques*, p.202-203.
14. Victor Cousin, *Cours d'histoire de la philosophie morale au dix-huitième siècle professé à la Faculté des lettres en 1819 et 1820*, 4 vol. (Paris, 1839-1842).
15. Voir Alan B. Spitzer, *The French generation of 1820* (Princeton, NJ, 1987); Xavier Landrin, 'Genèse et activités du groupe doctrinaire (1815-1821): contribution à une sociologie historique du libéralisme', dans *Les Formes de l'activité politique: éléments d'analyse sociologique (18e-20e siècle)*, éd. Antonin Cohen, Philippe Riutort et Bernard Lacroix (Paris, 2006), p.211-26; Francis Demier, *La France de la Restauration (1814-1830)* (Paris, 2012).
16. Celui de Cousin est suspendu à la fin de l'année 1820, ceux de Guizot et de Villemain en 1822.

professeur de philosophie et d'un professeur de littérature française
sont souvent présentés comme un bloc plus ou moins indissociable qui
fait souffler un vent de liberté à la Sorbonne.[17] Les trois professeurs en
question cultivent d'ailleurs cet effet de groupe.

Les cours de Victor Cousin sont donc philosophiques, mais ils
ont une teneur politique évidente qu'il est possible de mesurer en
observant les références à la Charte constitutionnelle de 1814 – qui
n'est pas un texte philosophique du dix-huitième siècle, mais l'un
des documents politiques les plus discutés de la Restauration.[18] On
entend dans les cours de Cousin (comme dans ceux de Villemain et de
Guizot) des échos à peine atténués des débats enflammés qui agitent
Paris à la veille de la révolution de 1830.

C'est dans ce cadre que Cousin fait l'éloge de la philosophie du
dix-huitième siècle qui, comme il l'indique dans la première séance de
son *Cours* de 1829, se caractérise par 'la généralisation et la diffusion
du principe de liberté'.[19] Ainsi peut-on lire la remarque suivante,
dans une tonalité qui est assez proche de celle de Villemain et de
Guizot[20] (à cela près que Guizot voit non pas dans le cartésianisme

17. On trouve la trace de cet enthousiasme et de cette étroite association des trois
     noms jusque dans les *Entretiens de Goethe et d'Eckermann*. Eckermann rapporte
     à la date du 27 février 1829 les propos suivants: 'Das Gespräch lenkte sich
     auf die Franzosen, auf die Vorlesungen von Guizot, Villemain und Cousin,
     und Goethe sprach mit hoher Achtung über den Standpunkt dieser Männer
     und wie sie alles von einer freien und neuen Seite betrachteten und überall
     grade aufs Ziel losgingen. "Es ist", sagte Goethe, "als wäre man bis jetzt in
     einen Garten auf Umwegen und durch Krümmungen gelangt; diese Männer
     aber sind kühn und frei genug, die Mauer dort einzureißen und eine Tür an
     derjenigen Stelle zu machen, wo man sogleich auf den breitesten Weg des
     Gartens tritt.' Johann Peter Eckermann, *Gespräche mit Goethe in den letzten
     Jahren seines Lebens* (Berlin, 1982), p.274.
18. Nous reviendrons sur ce point dans la suite de cette contribution.
19. Cousin, *Cours de l'histoire de la philosophie*, t.1, p.1. La citation est reprise du
     résumé imprimé en tête de la leçon; si ce résumé n'est pas de la main de Cousin,
     il en restitue parfaitement le propos.
20. On a presque l'impression que les Villemain, Cousin et Guizot se sont concertés
     avant de décrire le dix-huitième siècle. Mais la concordance de leurs vues
     tient de toute façon à leur proximité idéologique, aux échanges qu'ils ont pu
     avoir avec les autres figures qui appartenaient au groupe des 'Doctrinaires',
     ou qui en étaient proches. Villemain écrit: 'Le génie littéraire du XVIIe siècle
     s'était formé sous trois influences, la religion, l'antiquité, la monarchie de
     Louis XIV. [...] Les influences qui dominent la littérature du XVIIIe siècle sont,
     au contraire, la philosophie sceptique, l'imitation des littératures modernes, et
     la réforme politique. Rien de plus opposé, et pourtant rien de plus lié que ces

mais dans la Réforme l'une des premières manifestations de l'esprit d'indépendance):[21]

> Le dix-huitième siècle a fait en philosophie ce qu'il a fait dans tout le reste. La scolastique étant abattue, le principe du cartésianisme, savoir, l'esprit d'indépendance, se trouvait face à face avec le principe d'autorité. De là, la lutte nécessaire du principe général de la liberté contre le principe général de l'autorité, sans aucun intermédiaire; telle était la mission, telle a été l'œuvre du dix-huitième siècle. En effet, il a généralisé le principe de la révolution cartésienne, et l'a élevé à toute sa hauteur; de plus, il a propagé et répandu ce principe, d'abord dans toutes les classes de la société, puis dans tous les pays de l'Europe.[22]

Ce tableau positif est encore réaffirmé dans la conclusion de cette leçon:

> Concluons, Messieurs, que tous les philosophes du dix-huitième siècle ont mis la main dans la révolution de l'indépendance philosophique que le dix-huitième siècle a généralisée, répandue, consommée. Ce siècle s'est appelé le siècle de la philosophie, et après tout la postérité ratifiera ce titre; car c'est un fait incontestable que c'est du dix-huitième siècle que date l'avénement de la philosophie dans le monde sous son nom propre, avec les caractères qui lui appartiennent, tandis qu'auparavant elle était réduite à se cacher sous le manteau de la

deux époques: la grandeur et les abus de la première devaient enfanter l'autre.' Abel-François Villemain, *Cours de littérature française: tableau du XVIIIᵉ siècle*, 4 vol. (Paris, 1838), t.1, p.2-3. Quant à Guizot: 'Que l'élan de l'esprit humain, que le libre examen soit le trait dominant, le fait essentiel du dix-huitième siècle, ce n'est pas la peine de le dire. Déjà, Messieurs, vous en avez beaucoup entendu parler dans cette chaire; déjà, par la voix d'un orateur philosophe [Villemain] et par celle d'un philosophe éloquent [Cousin], vous avez entendu caractériser cette époque puissante.' François Guizot, *Cours d'histoire moderne: histoire générale de la civilisation en Europe, depuis la chute de l'empire romain jusqu'à la Révolution française* (Paris, 1828), leçon 14, p.33-34.

21. Voici à titre d'exemple ce qu'on lit dans la douzième leçon du *Cours d'histoire moderne* que Guizot consacre en 1828 à l'*Histoire générale de la civilisation en Europe, depuis la chute de l'empire romain jusqu'à la Révolution française* (voir note précédente), p.24: 'Au seizième siècle, dans le sein de la société religieuse, une insurrection éclate contre le système de la monarchie pure, contre le pouvoir absolu dans l'ordre spirituel. Cette révolution amène, consacre, établit en Europe le libre examen. De nos jours nous avons vu, dans l'ordre civil, un même événement. Le pouvoir absolu temporel est également attaqué, vaincu.'

22. Cousin, *Cours de l'histoire de la philosophie*, t.1, p.70-71.

théologie, ou de quelque autre science, et n'osait pas se montrer à
visage découvert.[23]

Le dix-huitième siècle philosophique, dans cette perspective, est
présenté de façon éminemment positive – et la critique sous-jacente du
catholicisme est relativement audacieuse, alors que, dans la première
moitié du dix-neuvième siècle, le pouvoir de l'Eglise (et notamment
son influence sur tout ce qui touche à l'enseignement) est loin d'être
négligeable. Les philosophes du dix-huitième siècle sont, dans l'esprit
de Cousin, ceux qui ont achevé de conquérir pour la philosophie
l'indépendance et l'autonomie; à eux revient le mérite de 'détruire
en matière philosophique, le principe de l'autorité et [de] resserrer la
théologie dans son domaine propre'.[24]

Cet éloge du dix-huitième siècle est cependant agrémenté de
réserves: d'abord, les Lumières se situent dans la continuité de ce qui
a été achevé au cours des siècles précédents. Pour Cousin, le véritable
héros de l'époque moderne, c'est Descartes. En mettant en avant la
nécessité de tout soumettre à une critique serrée, le siècle des Lumières
s'est contenté de poursuivre le chemin ouvert par l'auteur du *Discours
de la méthode* et des *Méditations métaphysiques*. Par ailleurs, l'action et la
'mission' du dix-huitième siècle sont entièrement négatives: sa 'mission
philosophique' a été 'd'en finir avec le moyen âge en philosophie'.[25]
Cousin ne précise pas (mais ses auditeurs et lecteurs le comprennent
immédiatement, préparés d'ailleurs par des passages plus explicites
concernant la Révolution française que l'on trouve dans la première
leçon du *Cours* de 1829) que les propos ici appliqués à l'histoire
philosophique peuvent aussi être appliqués à l'histoire politique.
Et c'est sans doute ce qui explique que Cousin puisse qualifier de
'tragique' la mission philosophique du dix-huitième siècle: ce qui est
tragique, c'est ce que Cousin, comme nombre de ses contemporains (et
notamment les penseurs libéraux), appelle les excès[26] de la Révolution

---

23. Cousin, *Cours de l'histoire de la philosophie*, t.1, p.77-78.
24. Cousin, *Cours de l'histoire de la philosophie*, t.1, p.75.
25. Cousin, *Cours de l'histoire de la philosophie*, t.1, p.75. L'idée revient souvent, et le
    terme de mission est présenté dès la première leçon du *Cours* de 1829.
26. Un exemple parmi d'autres: 'Aux aveugles adversaires du dix-huitième siècle et
    du grand événement qui s'offre à eux sous de si affreuses couleurs, je pourrais
    proposer ce dilemme qui renferme le résumé de cette leçon: Laissez-là, leur
    dirais-je, les excès qui vous révoltent et qui me révoltent autant que vous:
    considérez dans la révolution française ses principes et ses résultats.' Cousin,
    Cours de l'histoire de la philosophie, t.1, p.36.

française. On a l'impression que, comme la philosophie et la politique marchent de conserve, le tragique politique est transféré dans le champ philosophique. Quoi qu'il en soit, de même que dans l'esprit de Cousin, le dix-neuvième siècle doit dépasser la Révolution française, il doit en philosophie aussi dépasser (en en gardant les acquis positifs) la philosophie du siècle précédent:

> En dernière analyse, tout examiné et pesé, la part du bien et la part du mal équitablement faite, il me semble, et je n'hésite pas à conclure, avec mes deux honorables collègues et amis M. Guizot et M. Villemain, que le dix-huitième siècle en masse est un des plus grands siècles qui aient paru dans le monde. La mission que lui imposait l'histoire était d'en finir avec le moyen âge; il a rempli cette *tragique mission*; il n'a rempli que celle-là: un siècle, un seul siècle n'est guère chargé de deux missions à la fois; il a détruit, il n'a rien élevé: il ne pouvait faire davantage. Sur l'abîme de l'immense révolution qu'il a ouverte et qu'il a fermée, le dix-huitième siècle n'a guère laissé que des abstractions; mais ces abstractions sont des vérités immortelles qui contiennent l'avenir. Le dix-neuvième siècle les a recueillies; sa mission est de les réaliser en leur imprimant une organisation vigoureuse.[27]

Des Lumières 'réduites'

On peut se demander quels sont les auteurs et les textes auxquels Cousin pense lorsqu'il brosse le tableau de la philosophie du dix-huitième siècle. La question est d'autant plus légitime que l'on trouve bien peu de références concrètes à Montesquieu, Voltaire, Diderot, Rousseau.

---

27. Cousin, *Cours de l'histoire de la philosophie*, t.1, p.77 (je souligne). Cette même idée est répétée à la fin de la leçon suivante (p.130): 'Reconnaissons, Messieurs, l'état présent des choses; rendons-nous compte de ce qu'a fait le dix-huitième siècle, et de ce qui nous reste à faire à nous-mêmes. La mission politique du dix-huitième siècle était d'en finir avec le moyen âge; sa mission générale, en philosophie, était d'en finir avec l'autorité; sa mission plus spéciale, en fait de méthode, était d'en finir avec l'hypothèse. Telle était la mission du dix-huitième siècle, il l'a accomplie dans la méthode comme dans tout le reste. Aujourd'hui la liberté politique est assez forte pour n'avoir plus besoin de détruire: elle commence à organiser. Aujourd'hui l'indépendance philosophique est assez assurée pour qu'il soit temps de cesser d'inutiles et imprudentes hostilités, et la philosophie doit enfin donner la main à la religion, avec respect comme avec indépendance. De même, l'analyse que le dix-huitième siècle a léguée au dix-neuvième doit être assez puissante, assez sûre d'elle-même pour regarder en face la synthèse, et ne s'en plus laisser effrayer.'

Ces auteurs sont rarement cités; lorsqu'ils le sont, ils sont (sauf dans le cas de Montesquieu) en général critiqués, dans un mouvement sans doute dicté en partie au moins par une forme de prudence politique. Ainsi, lorsqu'il souligne que 'l'Europe a applaudi [...] aux plaisanteries de Voltaire', Cousin s'empresse de souligner qu'il est 'loin de vouloir [les] entièrement absoudre'.[28] De façon générale, la philosophie politique n'est guère détaillée par Cousin, ce qui explique sans doute la timidité de ses références, ce dont pâtit aussi l'œuvre philosophique de Condorcet, dont l'*Esquisse d'un tableau historique des progrès de l'esprit humain* est critiquée sans ménagement ('quelques idées sans étoffe').[29] Le peu de place accordée par Cousin à la philosophie politique ou à la philosophie de l'histoire produite au dix-huitième siècle est certainement due à sa prudence. Il est problématique de s'intéresser à des auteurs qui, pour certains, ont la réputation d'avoir été en quelque sorte intellectuellement responsables de la Révolution et de ses 'excès'.

Une autre raison explique encore la parcimonie des références cousiniennes aux auteurs que nous venons de citer. C'est que, d'une certaine façon, ce ne sont pas vraiment des auteurs de textes philosophiques dans la définition que Cousin donne au terme de philosophie. Cousin se concentre en effet sur la philosophie du moi, sur la philosophie de la connaissance, sur la métaphysique et sur la morale (à peu près dans cet ordre) – la philosophie de l'histoire et la philosophie politique (champs d'ailleurs plus 'dangereux') ne sont donc guère que des domaines périphériques.[30] Voilà ce qui explique pourquoi Cousin, de longue date, s'intéresse avant tout aux travaux philosophiques de Condillac. 'Condillac', explique-t-il en 1816, 'représente en France la philosophie du dix-huitième siècle, comme Descartes représente celle du dix-septième.'[31] Douze ans plus tard, Condillac occupe une place plus importante encore. Il est, dans la présentation que Cousin en fait en 1828, le véritable penseur de la philosophie de Locke. Puisque, comme le prouve l'histoire, l'Angleterre manque de 'cette puissance de généralisation et de déduction qui seule pousse une idée, un

---

28. Cousin, *Cours de l'histoire de la philosophie*, t.1, p.18.
29. Victor Cousin, *Cours de philosophie: introduction à l'histoire de la philosophie* (Paris, 1828), leçon 11, p.33.
30. Voir à ce propos les judicieuses remarques de L. Rey, 'Victor Cousin et l'instrumentalisation de l'histoire de la philosophie', p.45.
31. Victor Cousin, *Cours d'histoire de la philosophie moderne pendant les années 1816 et 1817* (Paris, 1841), leçon 17, p.163.

principe à son entier développement', il a fallu que 'la philosophie de Locke passât en France'. En effet,

> la philosophie de la sensation est encore incertaine dans Locke: le philosophe anglais fait jouer à la sensation un grand rôle, mais il a une place aussi pour la réflexion. Ce fut un Français [Condillac], qui donna à la philosophie de Locke son vrai caractère et son unité systématique, en supprimant le rôle insignifiant et équivoque que Locke avait laissé à la réflexion.[32]

Or, de même que Cousin cherche à réfuter ce que, après d'autres historiens de la philosophie,[33] il nomme le 'sensualisme' de Condillac, de même cherche-t-il d'emblée à saper ce qui, selon lui, est la conséquence nécessaire de la pensée de Locke et de Condillac, à savoir le matérialisme d'Helvétius, qu'il appelle aussi la 'philosophie de l'égoïsme'.[34] Quand, dans son *Cours* de 1829, Cousin examine l'*Essai sur l'entendement humain* de Locke, il en donnera une analyse assez détaillée, sans toutefois cacher les réserves que lui inspirent les théories du philosophe anglais, qui, à l'en croire, mettent en péril l'idée de liberté (fatalisme), celle de l'immatérialité de l'âme (matérialisme) et la certitude de l'existence de Dieu (athéisme) – trois tendances que l'on est obligé,[35] lorsqu'on donne un cours public dans la Sorbonne des années 1820, de condamner fermement:

---

32. Cousin, *Cours de philosophie*, leçon 14, p.23-24. A noter que cette déclaration s'accorde mal avec la suite que Cousin donnera lui-même à son cours, puisqu'il ménagera une place importante à l'analyse détaillée de la philosophie de Locke, qui occupe onze des vingt-cinq leçons du *Cours* de 1829.
33. Sur la genèse du concept de sensualisme (et sur le rôle de Victor Cousin dans sa diffusion), voir l'étude détaillée de Pierre F. Daled, *Le Matérialisme occulté et la genèse du sensualisme: écrire l'histoire de la philosophie en France* (Paris, 2005).
34. 'Comme il n'y a rien dans la pensée qui ne soit venu par les sens, et que toutes nos idées en dernière analyse se réduisent à des sensations; de même dans les motifs déterminans de nos actions, il n'y en a point qui ne puisse se ramener à un motif intéressé, à l'égoïsme.' Cousin, *Cours de philosophie*, leçon 3, p.26-27.
35. Sans doute ne faut-il pas exagérer ce qui revient au calcul politique dans le positionnement de Cousin. Certes, il entre de l'opportunisme dans les positions philosophiques de Cousin, et, comme il a déjà maille à partir avec le parti ultra-royaliste et avec les défenseurs de l'orthodoxie catholique, il lui serait particulièrement difficile de se faire le défenseur du 'matérialisme' des Lumières. Cependant la pensée matérialiste lui est elle aussi antipathique. Editeur de Platon et de Descartes, Cousin a des préférences évidentes pour la pensée de ces auteurs-là. De façon générale, le matérialisme semble passé de mode en 1820; d'autres conjonctures lui seront plus favorables.

Le caractère essentiel du sensualisme est, nous l'avons vu, la négation de toutes les grandes vérités qui échappent aux sens et que la raison seule découvre, la négation du temps et de l'espace infini, du bien et du mal, de la liberté humaine, de l'immatérialité de l'âme et de la divine Providence; et, selon les temps et le plus ou moins d'énergie de ses partisans, il affiche ouvertement ces résultats, ou il les voile par la distinction souvent sincère, souvent fictive de la philosophie et de la théologie.[36]

En guise de conclusion: politique et philosophie

Lorsqu'il s'intéresse à la philosophie du dix-huitième siècle, Cousin s'intéresse avant tout à son versant sceptique, c'est-à-dire à la critique, par les auteurs du dix-huitième siècle, des courants idéalistes. A défaut de laisser dans son histoire de la philosophie une place à la philosophie politique du dix-huitième siècle, Victor Cousin ne cesse, dans ses textes philosophiques, de faire de la politique. De façon étonnante, on trouve dans les cours de philosophie de Cousin des éloges appuyés de la Charte ou encore, après 1830, de la monarchie de Juillet. La monarchie constitutionnelle française est l'équivalent politique de l'éclectisme, de même que l'éclectisme est, en philosophie, un reflet de la Charte.[37]

Par là, Cousin tente de se situer dans un juste milieu également éloigné des désordres démocratiques et révolutionnaires que du retour intempestif à un absolutisme rétrograde. En 1833, dans la préface à la seconde édition de ses *Fragments philosophiques*, il fait lui-même le parallèle entre philosophie et politique, lorsqu'il décrit comment, à la fin des années 1820 (c'est-à-dire aussi au moment de prononcer

---

36. Cousin, *Cours de l'histoire de la philosophie*, t.2, p.548-49. Voir aussi p.551-52: 'Toutes ces théories sur lesquelles je vous ai si long-temps arrêtés [...] vont, avec le temps, en moins d'un demi-siècle, grandir, s'étendre, se régulariser, et devenir entre les mains hardies des successeurs de Locke des théories fermes et précises, qui obtiendront, dans plus d'un grand pays de l'Europe, une autorité presque absolue, et y sembleront le dernier mot de la pensée humaine. Ainsi la théorie de Locke sur la liberté tendait au fatalisme; cette théorie développée y arrivera. Locke ne semblait pas trop redouter le matérialisme; ses élèves l'accepteront et le proclameront. Bientôt, le principe de causalité, n'étant plus seulement négligé, mais repoussé et détruit, la preuve *a posteriori* de l'existence de Dieu manquera de base, et le théisme naturaliste du sensualisme indécis de Locke finira par un panthéisme avoué, c'est-à-dire par l'athéisme.'
37. Ce point a déjà été souligné par L. Rey, 'Victor Cousin et l'instrumentalisation de l'histoire de la philosophie'.

les cours dont nous avons cherché à retracer l'orientation) il était en butte à l'hostilité de deux écoles philosophiques, lesquelles correspondaient à deux tendances politiques 'extrêmes' (les révolutionnaires et les ultras): 'J'ai eu l'avantage de tenir unies contre moi, pendant plusieurs années, et l'école sensualiste et l'école théologique. En 1830, l'une et l'autre école sont descendues dans l'arène politique. L'école sensualiste a produit tout naturellement le parti démagogique, et l'école théologique est devenue tout aussi naturellement l'absolutisme.'[38] L'idée se trouvait déjà dans des textes des années 1820, notamment dans une page qui n'est pas signée par Cousin, mais qui, si elle n'est pas de sa main, reflète assez fidèlement sa position. Il s'agit de l'Avis des éditeurs' placé en tête de son *Cours* de 1828:

> Après avoir démontré l'insuffisance des deux écoles qui se sont partagé le dix-huitième siècle, savoir, le sensualisme en France, représenté par Condillac et ses disciples, l'idéalisme en Allemagne, représenté par Kant et Fichte, M. Cousin établit que l'œuvre de la philosophie nouvelle sera de chercher la conciliation de ces deux écoles. Cet éclectisme, traité de paix entre les élémens divers de la philosophie contemporaine, M. Cousin le reconnaît et le suit dans toutes les parties de l'ordre social actuel. En politique, par exemple, la Charte est une transaction entre le passé et la société nouvelle, entre l'élément monarchique et l'élément populaire. En littérature, c'est l'accord de la légitimité classique avec l'innovation romantique.[39]

Dans les textes plus tardifs, on assiste à un net raidissement de Victor Cousin qui signale clairement son opposition à la 'déplorable' philosophie du dix-huitième siècle français, tout en exagérant l'ancienneté de cette position. Dans ses premiers textes en effet, on trouve une tonalité bien moins critique que dans les années 1840 ou 1850. 'L'avantage' de l'éclectisme et de sa rhétorique du juste milieu, c'est qu'il suffit de modifier un peu la part de critique et d'éloge: en déplaçant légèrement son discours, il est toujours possible de délivrer une parole qui soit au goût du jour. C'est bien ce que fait Cousin, qui, dans les années 1830, 1840 et 1850, rectifie constamment ses textes anciens. En 1855, Cousin décrit sa philosophie comme une philosophie

---

38. Victor Cousin, *Fragmens philosophiques*, 2e éd. (Paris, 1833), p.lviii.
39. 'Avis des éditeurs', dans Cousin, *Cours de philosophie*, p.vii. L'idée d'une nécessaire paix à conclure entre les diverses factions philosophiques qui instaure l'historien de la philosophie en position de médiateur se trouve déjà dans l'*Histoire comparée des systèmes de philosophie* (1804) de Degérando. Sur ce point, voir P. F. Daled, *Le Matérialisme occulté et la genèse du sensualisme*.

'radicalement opposée à la philosophie de la sensation, qui domina en France pendant le dix-huitième siècle, et que, dans les commencements du dix-neuvième, nous avons rencontrée toute-puissante encore'. Et il poursuit:

> En même temps que nous rompons hautement ici avec cette déplorable philosophie, où tant de fois nous avons signalé la racine des malheurs de la patrie, parce qu'en répandant de proche en proche, pendant de longues années, dans toutes les classes de la société française, le scepticisme et le matérialisme, elle a ôté d'avance les fondements nécessaires de la vraie liberté, nous ne donnons point à la philosophie nouvelle des guides étrangers, fût-ce même le sage Reid ou le profond et vertueux philosophe de Kœnigsberg: de bonne heure nous l'avons placée sous l'invocation de Descartes.[40]

---

40. Victor Cousin, *Premiers essais de philosophie*, 3ᵉ éd. (Paris, 1855), p.ix. En fait, ces 'premiers essais' sont en quelque sorte la troisième édition du *Cours d'histoire de la philosophie moderne pendant les années 1816 et 1817* dont deux éditions avaient été publiées en 1841 et 1846.

Alexis de Tocqueville et Hermann Hettner, 1856: deux historiens face au dix-huitième siècle

ÉLISABETH DÉCULTOT

Martin-Luther-Universität Halle-Wittenberg

Les notions de Lumières, d'*Enlightenment* et d'*Aufklärung* sont, comme esquissé dans l'introduction au présent volume, travaillées en profondeur par une tension fondamentale entre deux acceptions, deux potentialités sémantiques qui sont à la fois inextricablement liées l'une à l'autre dans l'histoire de ces mots et de leur usage, mais aussi sémantiquement distinctes. Dans une acception d'ordre normatif ou axiomatique, ces notions renvoient d'une part à un certain nombre d'idées, de phénomènes ou de valeurs à visée universelle et de dimension an- ou transhistorique, parmi lesquels la promotion de l'examen critique et le respect fondamental de l'autonomie du sujet. Dans cette acception, la notion de Lumières est d'abord saisie non pas comme se référant à un contexte historique et géographique précis, mais comme un principe actualisable en tout temps et en tout lieu. D'autre part, cette notion désigne aussi, et de façon indissociable de cette première signification, l'époque où ces concepts et valeurs sont supposés avoir été élaborés, discutés et/ou transposés en réalités politiques et sociales, à savoir une période large dont le centre de gravité est généralement situé au dix-huitième siècle. Dans cette seconde acception, la notion de Lumières revêt une signification historique et historiographique: historique, en ce qu'elle est considérée par certains comme un ensemble de faits ou de phénomènes advenus à une époque, à un moment précis de l'Histoire; historiographique, en ce qu'elle est une catégorie utile aux historiens pour découper dans le continuum temporel un segment précis de l'Histoire. Pour résumer, on peut donc dire que la notion de Lumières possède une double dimension: hors de l'Histoire (ou hors de toute perspective historique) comme ensemble de concepts,

21

phénomènes ou valeurs universels et atemporels touchant au statut de l'être humain en général; et dans l'Histoire, comme catégorie désignant un développement particulier survenu à un moment précis et, par métonymie, comme nom désignant l'époque où ce développement s'est manifesté. Cette tension fondamentale entre le particulier et l'universel, le local et le global, l'historique et l'anhistorique fait la difficulté, mais aussi la singularité, des notions de Lumières, d'*Enlightenment* et d'*Aufklärung*. Cette double virtualité sémantique existe certes dès le dix-huitième siècle: elle affleure par exemple dans la manière dont D'Alembert pense le dix-huitième siècle dans l'Histoire, entre le 'Discours préliminaire' à l'*Encyclopédie* de 1751[1] et le 'Tableau de l'esprit humain au milieu du dix-huitième siècle' de 1759.[2] De nombreux historiens – parmi lesquels Wilhelm Dilthey, Werner Krauss, Reinhardt Koselleck ou Hans Blumenberg – ont vu d'ailleurs dans l'émergence de cette conscience historique

1. D'Alembert se voit lui-même comme le témoin et l'acteur d'un siècle nouveau dans l'histoire de l'humanité, un siècle dont la marque singulière est d'être 'de lumière', selon sa formule du 'Discours préliminaire' à l'*Encyclopédie* (1751), par opposition notamment au Moyen Age, considéré comme un 'long intervalle d'ignorance'. Voir [Jean D'Alembert], 'Discours préliminaire des éditeurs', dans *Encyclopédie, ou Dictionnaire raisonné des sciences, des arts et des métiers*, éd. Denis Diderot et Jean D'Alembert, t.1 (Paris, Briasson, David l'aîné, Le Breton, Durand, 1751), p.i-xlix (xix-xx).
2. Jean D'Alembert, 'Essai sur les élémens de philosophie, ou sur les principes des connaissances humaines, avec les éclaircissemens', dans *Œuvres complètes* (1821-1822), 5 vol. (Genève, 1967), t.1, p.115-348 (121-22): 'Il semble que depuis environ trois cents ans, la nature ait destiné le milieu de chaque siècle à être l'époque d'une révolution dans l'esprit humain. La prise de Constantinople, au milieu du quinzième siècle, a fait renaître les lettres en Occident. Le milieu du seizième a vu changer rapidement la religion et le système d'une grande partie de l'Europe; les nouveaux dogmes des réformateurs, soutenus d'une part et combattus de l'autre avec cette chaleur que les intérêts de Dieu bien ou mal entendus peuvent seuls inspirer aux hommes, ont également forcé leurs partisans et leurs adversaires à s'instruire [...]. Enfin Descartes, au milieu du dix-septième siècle, a fondé une nouvelle philosophie, persécutée d'abord avec fureur, embrassée ensuite avec superstition, et réduite aujourd'hui à ce qu'elle contient d'utile et de vrai. Pour peu qu'on considère avec des yeux attentifs le milieu du siècle où nous vivons, les événemens qui nous agitent, ou du moins qui nous occupent, nos mœurs, nos ouvrages, et jusqu'à nos entretiens, il est difficile de ne pas apercevoir qu'il s'est fait à plusieurs égards un changement bien remarquable dans nos idées; changement qui, par sa rapidité, semble nous en promettre un plus grand encore. C'est au temps à fixer l'objet, la nature et les limites de cette révolution, dont notre postérité connaîtra mieux que nous les inconvéniens et les avantages.'

le début des temps 'modernes' en Histoire: l'homme moderne se penserait d'abord dans l'Histoire et penserait ce temps qui est le sien comme une entité chronologique différente de l'avant, riche de qualités nouvelles et porteuse d'un avenir ouvert.[3] Ce que nous appelons la Modernité ne serait autre que l'émergence de ce nouveau régime de conscience historique.

Cependant, ce n'est qu'avec le dix-neuvième siècle, au moment où émergent les grands récits historiques sur le dix-huitième siècle – en histoire politique, intellectuelle et culturelle comme en histoire des disciplines et du savoir – que cette tension entre les deux acceptions sémantiques des notions de Lumières, d'*Enlightenment* et d'*Aufklärung* s'établit réellement. Quelles sont la place et la signification des notions de Lumières, d'*Enlightenment* et d'*Aufklärung* dans les récits historiques retraçant au dix-neuvième siècle l'histoire du dix-huitième siècle? Qu'en est-il dans ces travaux de l'articulation entre la dimension normative, axiomatique des 'idées' des Lumières et des Lumières comme 'idée' d'une part et leur dimension historique d'autre part? Pour répondre à ces questions, nous avons choisi de nous intéresser à Alexis de Tocqueville et Hermann Hettner, deux historiens qui publient exactement la même année, en 1856, deux importantes études sur le dix-huitième siècle.

Le dix-huitième siècle selon Tocqueville

Tocqueville n'emploie jamais le terme de 'siècle' ou d''époque' des 'Lumières' pour désigner le dix-huitième siècle. Il faut voir dans ce phénomène l'effet d'une utilisation longtemps agonale et polémique de l'expression 'siècle des Lumières' dans la langue française.[4] Au

---

3. Wilhelm Dilthey, 'Das achtzehnte Jahrhundert und die geschichtliche Welt', dans *Wilhelm Diltheys gesammelte Schriften*, t.3 (Leipzig et Berlin, 1927), p.209-75; Werner Krauss, 'Der Jahrhundertbegriff im 18. Jahrhundert: Geschichte und Geschichtlichkeit in der französischen Aufklärung', dans *Die Innenseite der Weltgeschichte: ausgewählte Essays über Sprache und Literatur*, éd. Helga Bergmann (Leipzig, 1983), p.109-54; Werner Krauss, '*Siècle* im 18. Jahrhundert', *Beiträge zur romanischen Philologie* 1 (1961), p.83-98; Reinhart Koselleck, 'Das 18. Jahrhundert als Beginn der Neuzeit', dans *Epochenschwelle und Epochenbewußtsein*, éd. Reinhart Herzog et Reinhart Koselleck (Munich, 1987), p.269-82; Hans Blumenberg, *Aspekte der Epochenschwelle: Cusaner und Nolaner* (Francfort-sur-le-Main, 1976), p.19.
4. Voir Fritz Schalk, 'Aufklärung', dans *Historisches Wörterbuch der Philosophie*, éd. Joachim Ritter, t.1 (Bâle, 1971), col.620-33, notamment col.621.

début du dix-neuvième siècle, cette formule se retrouve par exemple fréquemment sous la plume de Louis de Bonald, l'un des adversaires les plus fervents des idées des philosophes, grand contempteur de la Déclaration des droits de l'homme et du *Contrat social* de Rousseau, pour désigner le siècle précédent. Dans ses analyses détaillées des causes qui ont conduit à ce qui était à ses yeux le désastre de la Révolution française, Bonald incrimine volontiers les 'erreur[s] du siècle de lumière' ou ironise sur 'cette bienheureuse époque, pompeusement décorée du nom de *siècle des lumières*'.[5] La notion de 'siècle des Lumières' se trouve ainsi fréquemment réinvestie ou captée – plus que réellement inventée, comme on a pu l'écrire[6] – par les ennemis déclarés des Lumières à l'aube du dix-neuvième siècle. L'expression 'siècle des Lumières' reste cependant peu employée dans ce sens historiographique rétrospectif tout au long du dix-neuvième siècle, comme en témoigne par exemple l'usage très restreint et explicitement distant qu'en fait Hippolyte Taine dans *Les Origines de la France contemporaine*.[7] A la fin du dix-neuvième siècle encore, la dénomination 'siècle des Lumières' n'est pas perçue comme une catégorie historiographique neutre. Elle reste normative – que cette norme soit jugée favorablement ou défavorablement – et par là sujette à polémique. Ce n'est finalement que dans la seconde moitié du vingtième siècle qu'elle s'impose dans une acception historiographique. A partir de 1950, le terme d'étude sur les Lumières devient courant dans la littérature

5.   Louis de Bonald, 'De la chrétienté et du christianisme', dans *Œuvres de M. de Bonald*, t.12 (Paris, 1830), p.317-48 (343); Louis de Bonald, 'Démonstration philosophique du principe constitutif de la société', dans *Œuvres de M. de Bonald*, t.12, p.1-254 (75).

6.   Fritz Schalk avance l'idée que la notion historiographique de 'siècle des Lumières' comme désignant une époque serait une invention tardive, datant du début du dix-neuvième siècle et notamment propagée par les adversaires des idées des Lumières. Schalk, 'Aufklärung', col.621. Cette lecture a été contestée, à bon droit comme il nous semble, par Karin Elisabeth Becker, qui souligne que cet usage historiographique du terme a une origine beaucoup plus ancienne, dans les textes des philosophes des Lumières, au dix-huitième siècle même. Voir Karin E. Becker, 'Licht – (L)lumière(s) – siècle des Lumières: von der Lichtmetapher zum Epochenbegriff der Aufklärung in Frankreich', thèse de doctorat, Université de Cologne, 1994, p.277-78.

7.   Hippolyte Taine, *Les Origines de la France contemporaine*, t.1: *L'Ancien Régime* (Paris, 1875), p.266 (cité d'après l'édition de 1876): 'Aux approches de 1789, il est admis que l'on vit "dans le siècle des lumières", dans "l'âge de raison", qu'auparavant le genre humain était dans l'enfance, qu'aujourd'hui il est devenu "majeur".'

scientifique de langue française comme dénomination des recherches
touchant au dix-huitième siècle.[8]

L'ouvrage de Tocqueville intitulé *L'Ancien Régime et la Révolution*
poursuit une ambition très vaste, qui dépasse l'analyse du seul
dix-huitième siècle.[9] Il s'agit pour l'historien d'expliquer la rupture
fondamentale de la Révolution française en l'insérant dans une vaste
histoire des structures politiques, sociales et intellectuelles de la France
depuis le Moyen Age, structures qu'il compare par endroits avec celles
de pays voisins tels que la Grande-Bretagne et l'Allemagne. Si, comme
nous l'avons mentionné, Tocqueville ne recourt pas une seule fois à
l'expression 'siècle des Lumières' ou même au mot 'Lumières' dans un
sens historiographique et/ou axiomatique,[10] le dix-huitième siècle fait
néanmoins figure de période singulière et matricielle pour certaines
transformations majeures survenues dans le temps long d'environ six
siècles qu'embrasse l'ouvrage.

Parmi ces transformations figure l'émergence d'un groupe de 'gens
de lettres', encore désignés comme 'écrivains', qu'une historiographie
plus tardive subsumera sous le nom de philosophes des 'Lumières'.[11]
Deux attributs caractérisent ce groupe selon Tocqueville: son
rapport au pouvoir d'une part et sa relation à la religion d'autre
part. Dans un chapitre central de son ouvrage, l'historien donne
du premier point une analyse structurelle. La France, 'depuis
longtemps [...] la plus littéraire' de 'toutes les nations de l'Europe',
voit cette qualité 'littéraire' se transformer en structure sociale au
dix-huitième siècle et s'établir un groupe puissant de 'gens de lettres',
dont l'influence repose sur un positionnement singulier par rapport
au pouvoir.[12] Si ce positionnement peut être qualifié de singulier,
c'est qu'il s'appuie sur une distinction sans pareille en Europe entre
d'une part la pratique du pouvoir et d'autre part la réflexion critique

8. K. E. Becker, 'Licht – (L)lumière(s) – siècle des Lumières', p.281-86; John
Lough, 'Reflections on *Enlightenment* and *Lumières*', *British journal for eighteenth-century studies* 8:1 (1985), p.1-15.
9. Alexis de Tocqueville, *L'Ancien Régime et la Révolution*, éd. J.-P. Mayer (Paris, 1967).
10. Le terme 'lumières' (avec minuscule) revient en revanche de façon récurrente pour désigner les 'connaissances'. Ainsi dans cette phrase de l'avant-propos: 'Les procès-verbaux des assemblées d'états, et plus tard des assemblées provinciales, m'ont fourni sur ce point beaucoup de lumières.' Tocqueville, *Ancien Régime*, p.45.
11. Tocqueville, *Ancien Régime*, notamment p.229-41.
12. Tocqueville, *Ancien Régime*, p.229.

sur celui-ci. Dans une description succincte, mais très plastique, Tocqueville dresse le portrait de ces hommes de lettres qui, tout en faisant de l'analyse du pouvoir en général et du pouvoir politique en particulier un objet – si ce n'est même l'objet – central de leur réflexion, se tiennent volontairement et scrupuleusement loin de l'exercice du pouvoir:

> Ils n'étaient point mêlés journellement aux affaires, comme en Angleterre; jamais, au contraire, ils n'avaient vécu plus loin d'elles; ils n'étaient revêtus d'aucune autorité quelconque, et ne remplissaient aucune fonction publique dans une société déjà toute remplie de fonctionnaires.
>
> Cependant ils ne demeuraient pas, comme la plupart de leurs pareils en Allemagne, entièrement étrangers à la politique, et retirés dans le domaine de la philosophie pure et des belles-lettres. Ils s'occupaient sans cesse des matières qui ont trait au gouvernement; c'était là même, à vrai dire, leur occupation propre. On les entendait tous les jours discourir sur l'origine des sociétés et sur leurs formes primitives, sur les droits primordiaux des citoyens et sur ceux de l'autorité, sur les rapports naturels et artificiels des hommes entre eux, sur l'erreur ou la légitimité de la coutume, et sur les principes mêmes des lois.[13]

Autrement dit, les philosophes français des Lumières se définissent selon Tocqueville par le fait que, à la différence de leurs homologues allemands, ils réfléchissent prioritairement sur le pouvoir, mais, à la différence de leurs homologues britanniques, sans l'exercer directement.[14] Par là, ces 'hommes de lettres' se distinguent non seulement par le rapport qu'ils entretiennent en tant que personnes à la pratique du pouvoir d'une part et à l'observation critique de cette pratique d'autre part, mais aussi par la relation forte qu'ils établissent entre ces deux pôles: pour être efficace, l'observation critique de la pratique du pouvoir doit être la plus déconnectée possible de l'exercice même du pouvoir. Ce que Tocqueville décrit ainsi, c'est donc l'autonomisation d'un groupe dont la fonction sociale, le 'métier', est d'observer et de critiquer le pouvoir, à côté des gouvernants, parfois

---

13. Tocqueville, *Ancien Régime*, p.229-30.
14. Sans doute cette définition de l'homme de lettres français du dix-huitième siècle ne résiste-t-elle que partiellement à l'examen des faits, si l'on songe par exemple au cas de Montesquieu, conseiller, puis président à mortier du parlement de Bordeaux. La description de Tocqueville s'applique davantage à la figure de Diderot et, dans une certaine mesure seulement, à celle de Voltaire et de Rousseau.

contre eux, mais sans jamais vouloir se substituer à eux dans l'exercice de l'art de gouverner.[15]

Le second caractère distinctif des 'gens de lettres' du dix-huitième siècle réside selon Tocqueville dans leur rapport à la religion. Par là, l'historien s'inscrit certes dans une tradition interprétative ancienne, développée par plusieurs acteurs du dix-huitième siècle eux-mêmes, parmi lesquels Voltaire, et repris rapidement dans le discours historique sur le dix-huitième siècle au dix-neuvième siècle. En 1808, le catholique Félicité de Lamennais décrivait ainsi le combat acharné que la 'religion philosophique' des Lumières avait mené contre le christianisme: 'La philosophie du dix-huitième siècle a eu des effets terribles; elle a renversé à-la-fois la Religion et l'Etat, qui s'ébranlent toujours ensemble, parce qu'ils reposent sur la même base.'[16] Tocqueville reprend certes le schéma d'un combat bipartite entre 'philosophie' et religion, mais lui apporte un tour moins agonal, qui marque un tournant important dans l'interprétation de la période. Il commence par identifier l'incrédulité ou encore 'l'irréligion' comme un caractère propre, à des degrés divers, aux élites européennes du dix-huitième siècle en général: Si les 'classes moyennes' et le 'peuple' restent généralement croyants et fidèles à l'institution religieuse, les aristocrates européens, et les élites ecclésiastiques elles-mêmes, 'délaissent' volontiers la religion, constate-t-il.[17] Pour répandu qu'il soit dans les classes supérieures européennes, cet éloignement par rapport à la chose religieuse se dote néanmoins d'une qualité particulière en France:

> En France, on attaqua avec une sorte de fureur la religion chrétienne, sans essayer même de mettre une autre religion à sa place. On travailla ardemment et continûment à ôter des âmes la foi qui les avait remplies, et on les laissa vides. Une multitude d'hommes

---

15. Pour une analyse de cette constellation, voir Roger Chartier, *Les Origines culturelles de la Révolution française* (Paris, 2000), p.13-36.

16. Félicité de Lamennais, *Réflexions sur l'état de l'Eglise en France pendant le dix-huitième siècle, et sur sa situation actuelle* (Paris, 1808), p.vii. Voir également Félicité de Lamennais, 'Influence des doctrines philosophiques sur la société' (1815), dans *Œuvres complètes de F. de Lamennais*, 12 vol. (Paris, 1836-1837), t.6, p.119-52 (132): 'Lisez ces nombreux pamphlets qu'enfante chaque jour le délire philosophique; toutes les rêveries antisociales y sont renouvelées, exaltées, consacrées sous le nom d'*idées libérales*, expression sacramentelle, dont l'obscurité réfléchie cache aux yeux du vulgaire l'obscurité redoutable de la religion philosophique.' Voir Darrin McMahon, *Enemies of the Enlightenment: the French counter-Enlightenment and the making of modernity* (Oxford et New York, 2002), p.164.

17. Tocqueville, *Ancien Régime*, p.242.

s'enflammèrent dans cette ingrate entreprise. L'incrédulité absolue en matière de religion, qui est si contraire aux instincts naturels de l'homme et met son âme dans une assiette si douloureuse, parut attrayante à la foule. Ce qui n'avait produit jusque-là qu'une sorte de langueur maladive engendra cette fois le fanatisme et l'esprit de propagande.[18]

Pour mieux souligner la spécificité du cas français, Tocqueville, en s'appuyant sur Mirabeau et son tableau du royaume de Prusse de 1788, dément le 'préjugé répandu généralement en Allemagne [...] que les provinces prussiennes sont remplies d'athées. La vérité est que, s'il s'y rencontre quelques libres penseurs, le peuple y est aussi attaché à la religion que dans les contrées les plus dévotes, et qu'on y compte même un grand nombre de fanatiques'.[19] Nulle part ailleurs, donc, 'l'irréligion n'était encore devenue une passion générale, ardente, intolérante ni oppressive, si ce n'est en France'.[20]

Tocqueville n'en reste cependant pas à ce constat d'une incompatibilité de nature quasi passionnelle entre l'esprit des élites françaises au dix-huitième siècle et la religion. Dans le titre même d'un chapitre central de son ouvrage, il soutient d'emblée la thèse que 'l'objet fondamental et final de la Révolution n'était pas, comme on l'a cru, de détruire le pouvoir religieux et d'énerver le pouvoir politique.'[21]

---

18. Tocqueville, *Ancien Régime*, p.243-44.
19. Tocqueville, *Ancien Régime*, p.243; comte de Mirabeau, *De la monarchie prussienne sous Frédéric le Grand*, 8 vol. (Londres, s.n., 1788), t.5, p.22-23: 'M. Nicolaï, libraire de Berlin, et savant très-distingué (réunion infiniment rare, bien qu'elle dût être commune), a peint Berlin avec une grande vérité, sous cet aspect, dans un roman (1) [en note (1): *Das Leben des Sebaldus Nothanker*] qui donne d'excellentes notions sur les mœurs de l'Allemagne. En général, il y a montré que s'il est quelques francs-penseurs dans les provinces prussiennes, le peuple y est aussi attaché à sa religion que dans les contrées les plus dévotes et qu'on y compte même un grand nombre de ces fanatiques connus en Allemagne sous le nom de *piétistes* (2) [en note (2): Les gens du monde donnent le nom de *piétistes* en général à tous les frères Moraves, Quakers, Anabaptistes etc.; et en effet en Allemagne, toutes ces sectes sont unies d'un lien secret, parce que dans la plupart des dogmes, elles se trouvent d'accord. Mais il y a pourtant une secte particulière, qui se nomme ainsi, et dont le père ou le principal arc-boutant a été un certain *Spener*, ministre de la parole de Dieu, à Francfort. Ils se distinguent par un éloignement de toutes les jouissances mondaines, et une illumination particulière de l'esprit divin, qui opère soudainement sur le cœur d'une façon surnaturelle et sensible. Ils nomment cela, *der Durchbruch*.].'
20. Tocqueville, *Ancien Régime*, p.243.
21. Tocqueville, *Ancien Régime*, p.62.

Chez les philosophes français du dix-huitième siècle et dans la Révolution elle-même, il discerne non une opposition fondamentale à la religion, mais bien plutôt une complémentarité, qui repose sur l'affinité profonde entre démocratie et christianisme: 'Croire que les sociétés démocratiques sont naturellement hostiles à la religion est commettre une grande erreur: rien dans le christianisme, ni même dans le catholicisme, n'est absolument contraire à l'esprit de ces sociétés, et plusieurs choses y sont très-favorables.'[22] Autrement dit, la pensée politique des Lumières, qui a sous-tendu l'avènement de la démocratie, rejoint le christianisme par sa dimension universaliste. Comme la religion chrétienne, la philosophie des Lumières et la Révolution qui s'en réclame s'adressent à tout homme, sans considération de son origine nationale, sociale ou ethnique:

> Toutes les révolutions civiles et politiques ont eu une patrie et s'y sont renfermées. La révolution française n'a pas eu de territoire propre; bien plus, son effet a été d'effacer en quelque sorte de la carte toutes les anciennes frontières. On l'a vue rapprocher ou diviser les hommes en dépit des lois, des traditions, des caractères, de la langue, rendant parfois ennemis des compatriotes, et frères des étrangers; ou plutôt elle a formé, au-dessus de toutes les nationalités particulières, une patrie intellectuelle commune dont les hommes de toutes les nations ont pu devenir citoyens.[23]

Dans son esprit même, donc, le mouvement révolutionnaire de 1789 ne diffère en rien des grandes religions, et notamment de la religion chrétienne, dont le 'caractère habituel' est 'de considérer l'homme en lui-même, sans s'arrêter à ce que les lois, les coutumes et les traditions d'un pays ont pu joindre de particulier à ce fonds commun'.[24] A la différence de Bonald, donc, qui, au début du dix-neuvième siècle, voyait dans l'esprit des Lumières l'expression d'un processus de dissociation entre la religion et la société et dans la Révolution un point d'orgue de ce phénomène, Tocqueville discerne cinquante ans plus tard dans l'histoire du dix-huitième siècle français un processus de fusion entre religion et société, au cours duquel des schémas profonds de saisie religieuse du monde se trouvent appliqués à une sphère politique en apparence sécularisée.

---

22. Tocqueville, *Ancien Régime*, p.64.
23. Tocqueville, *Ancien Régime*, p.68.
24. Tocqueville, *Ancien Régime*, p.69-70.

Le dix-huitième siècle européen de Hermann Hettner

En 1856, l'année même de la publication de *L'Ancien Régime et la Révolution* par Tocqueville, l'historien allemand Hermann Hettner fait paraître de son côté le premier volume de son histoire littéraire du dix-huitième siècle (*Literaturgeschichte des 18. Jahrhunderts*, 1856-1869), le terme 'littéraire' étant à comprendre, conformément à l'acception allemande du mot 'Literatur', dans le sens large d'une histoire intellectuelle embrassant l'ensemble des sciences humaines, depuis les belles-lettres jusqu'à la philosophie, en passant par l'histoire, la théologie, l'esthétique ou encore la pensée sociale et politique.[25]

Après des études de philosophie, de philologie, d'histoire de l'art et d'esthétique à Berlin, Heidelberg et Halle, l'historien Hermann Julius Theodor Hettner (1821-1882) obtient le titre de professeur extraordinaire à l'université d'Iéna en 1851, où il enseigne l'esthétique, l'histoire de l'art et la littérature, avant d'être nommé en 1855 directeur de la collection royale des antiquités de Dresde et professeur d'histoire de l'art à l'Académie des beaux-arts de cette ville. Libéral engagé à gauche, il est proche de la mouvance des jeunes hégéliens, ce qui se traduit aussi bien politiquement que philosophiquement dans sa production intellectuelle : en 1844, il fait paraître une défense de la pensée de Ludwig Feuerbach et se réclame au plan esthétique de la tradition sensualiste. En 1850, il se fait remarquer par une première publication d'histoire littéraire touchant à l'école romantique allemande et au classicisme weimarien, dans lesquels il voit – contrairement aux positionnements affichés par les acteurs de ces mouvements eux-mêmes – une réaction non pas divergente, mais convergente, au contexte social, culturel et politique de l'époque contemporaine.[26]

---

25. Hermann Hettner, *Literaturgeschichte des 18. Jahrhunderts: in drei Theilen* (Braunschweig, 1856-1869), t.1: *Geschichte der englischen Literatur von der Wiederherstellung des Königthums bis in die zweite Hälfte des achtzehnten Jahrhunderts, 1660-1770* (1856); t.2: *Geschichte der französischen Literatur im achtzehnten Jahrhundert* (1860); t.3.1: *Geschichte der deutschen Literatur im achtzehnten Jahrhundert: erstes Buch. Vom Westfälischen Frieden bis zur Thronbesteigung Friedrichs des Großen, 1648-1740* (1862); t.3.2: *Geschichte der deutschen Literatur im achtzehnten Jahrhundert: zweites Buch. Das Zeitalter Friedrich's des Großen* (1864); t.3.3: *Geschichte der deutschen Literatur im achtzehnten Jahrhundert: drittes Buch. Das klassische Zeitalter der deutschen Literatur* (1869). Toutes nos citations se réfèrent à la quatrième édition augmentée (Braunschweig, 1881) et sont traduites par l'auteure de la présente contribution.
26. Hermann Hettner, *Die romantische Schule in ihrem inneren Zusammenhange mit Göthe und Schiller* (Braunschweig, 1850), p.10-11.

Le classicisme et le romantisme allemands sont pour Hettner des mouvements complémentaires, voire similaires, dans la mesure où leurs représentants respectifs ont en commun de se détourner du présent pour situer leur point de référence historique dans un passé idéalisé. Certes, cet étalon historique varie, les uns se réclamant de l'Antiquité, les autres du Moyen Age. Mais classiques et romantiques participent par là d'un même 'faux idéalisme' ('falscher Idealismus'), fondé sur une aspiration profonde à échapper à ou lutter contre la réalité historique du temps présent.[27]

Avec sa *Literaturgeschichte des 18. Jahrhunderts*, Hettner complète ce tableau du début du dix-neuvième siècle par une fresque du dix-huitième siècle, auquel il attribue des caractéristiques bien différentes de celles du romantisme et du classicisme. De façon générale, l'ouvrage de Hettner marque un moment important dans l'histoire de la notion d'*Aufklärung* en Allemagne, en raison de l'ampleur et de la signification tout à la fois intellectuelle, géographique et nationale qu'il donne à cette période, mais aussi par la fonction historiographique qu'il lui confère.[28] Cette histoire du dix-huitième siècle contribue fortement à établir la notion d'*Aufklärung* comme catégorie chronologique désignant une vaste période de l'histoire intellectuelle, autrement dit comme mesure du temps historiographique, au même titre que les notions de 'Romantik' ou de 'Klassik', que Hettner avait traitées dans son ouvrage précédent.[29]

Hettner était tout à fait conscient de son rôle pionnier, qui souligne dans sa préface que seuls deux historiens se sont avant lui consacrés à une histoire de l'*Aufklärung*: Abel-François Villemain[30] et Friedrich Christoph Schlosser.[31] Mais, insiste Hettner, ces deux précurseurs

---

27. Hettner, *Die romantische Schule*, p.12-13.
28. Hettner ouvre son ouvrage par une introduction générale intitulée 'Die Kämpfe der Aufklärung'. Hettner, *Literaturgeschichte des 18. Jahrhunderts*, t.1, p.3-10.
29. Werner Krauss, 'Zur Periodisierung Aufklärung, Sturm und Drang, Weimarer Klassik', dans *Sturm und Drang*, éd. Manfred Wacker (Darmstadt, 1985), p.67-95, paru d'abord dans *Sinn und Form* 12:1-2 (1961), p.376-99; Dieter Borchmeyer, *Weimarer Klassik: Portrait einer Epoche* (1994; Weinheim, 1998), p.13-63.
30. Abel-François Villemain, *Tableau de la littérature au XVIIIe siècle*, 2e éd., 4 vol. (Paris, 1840). L'ouvrage fait partie du *Cours de littérature française* paru pour la première fois en cinq tomes en 1828-1829 et maintes fois réédité et augmenté.
31. Friedrich Christoph Schlosser, *Geschichte des achtzehnten Jahrhunderts in gedrängter Uebersicht: mit steter Beziehung auf die völlige Veränderung der Denk- und Regierungsweise am Ende desselben*, 2 vol. (Heidelberg, 1823); Friedrich Christoph Schlosser, *Geschichte des achtzehnten Jahrhunderts und des neunzehnten bis zum Sturz des französischen Kaiserreichs: mit besonderer Rücksicht auf geistige Bildung*, t.1 (Heidelberg,

avaient une tout autre ambition, Villemain laissant complètement de côté la littérature allemande dont il ne maîtrisait pas la langue, et Schlosser s'intéressant essentiellement à l'histoire politique, ce qui le conduisit à négliger l'histoire littéraire au sens spécifique du terme:

> Comme c'est étrange! Jusqu'à présent, seuls deux historiens se sont attelés en ce sens à cette grande tâche: Villemain chez les Français et F. Ch. Schlosser chez les Allemands. Tous deux ont reçu pour cela de toute part la reconnaissance la plus méritée; mais Villemain exclut complètement la littérature allemande de son ouvrage en raison de son ignorance de la langue allemande, et Schlosser, qui, conformément au projet de sa célèbre histoire du dix-huitième siècle, devait donner aux événements politiques plus de place qu'aux événements littéraires, se contente généralement dans ses considérations sur la littérature d'indices et d'allusions.[32]

De fait, Hettner est le premier à proposer une aussi vaste histoire du dix-huitième siècle, englobant en trois larges sections les espaces littéraires anglais, français et allemands, l'Allemagne occupant à elle seule une bonne moitié de l'ensemble.

Cette construction reflète les deux caractéristiques principales du mouvement de l'*Enlightenment*, des Lumières et de l'*Aufklärung* selon Hettner. En premier lieu, il s'agit là pour lui d'un mouvement européen et par là d'un phénomène dont seule une perspective supra- ou transnationale peut rendre compte – position clairement défendue en préface de l'ouvrage: 'Parce que la littérature des Lumières n'appartient pas exclusivement à tel ou tel peuple, mais est, selon une expression bien connue de Goethe, une littérature absolument mondiale, une histoire des Lumières ne peut être que générale, c'est-à-dire une histoire littéraire du dix-huitième siècle englobant de la même manière les actions et réactions de tous les

---

    1836), multiples rééditions augmentées, par exemple: 4e éd., 8 vol. (Heidelberg, 1853-1860).

32. Hettner, *Literaturgeschichte des 18. Jahrhunderts*, t.1, p.9: 'Seltsam genug! Bisher haben sich in diesem Sinn nur zwei Geschichtsschreiber dieser großen Aufgabe unterzogen. Villemain unter den Franzosen, und F. Ch. Schlosser, unter den Deutschen. Beide haben dafür überall die verdienteste Anerkennung gefunden; aber Villemain schließt aus Unkenntniß der deutschen Sprache die deutsche Literatur ganz und gar aus, und Schlosser, der nach der ganzen Anlage seiner berühmten Geschichte des achtzehnten Jahrhunderts den politischen Ereignissen mehr Raum geben mußte als den literarischen, begnügt sich in seiner Literaturbetrachtung meist nur mit Winken und Andeutungen.'

peuples occidentaux.'[33] Si transnationale soit elle, cette géographie intellectuelle de l'Europe du dix-huitième siècle n'ignore cependant nullement différences, limites et hiérarchies nationales. Ainsi Hettner place-t-il la France des Lumières, dont Tocqueville s'emploie au même moment à souligner l'absolue singularité, résolument *entre* l'Angleterre et l'Allemagne. Plus qu'un rôle de pionnier, il lui attribue avec insistance un caractère d'hybridité, voire d'épigonalité, et un simple rôle de 'passeur': les Lumières françaises sont pour Hettner d'abord l'''interprète' ('Dolmetscher') de l'*Enlightenment* britannique sur le continent, selon une métaphore empruntée à Macaulay:

> Macaulay, dans son traité sur Walpole, dit admirablement: 'La littérature française est devenue pour l'anglaise ce qu'Aaron était pour Moïse: les grandes découvertes de la physique, de la métaphysique et de la science politique appartiennent aux Anglais; mais aucun autre peuple que la France ne les a reçues directement d'Angleterre; l'Angleterre était trop isolée par sa situation géographique et ses coutumes pour cela; la France a servi d'interprète entre l'Angleterre et l'humanité.'[34]

A ce titre, Hettner n'hésite pas à reprocher aux écrivains français de cette époque d'être peu 'créatifs et originaux', notamment au regard des Anglais, auxquels ils auraient beaucoup emprunté. La conclusion est sévère: le 'bénéfice strictement scientifique des Lumières françaises' n'est finalement à ses yeux que secondaire; les Lumières ont produit peu d'œuvres 'durables', mais quantité d'ouvrages 'sec[s] et étriqué[s]', la plupart du temps portés par l'intention appuyée d'instruire:

> Le bénéfice strictement scientifique des Lumières françaises n'est pas significatif. Peu de ces écrivains sont créatifs et originaux; tout le

---

33. Hettner, *Literaturgeschichte des 18. Jahrhunderts*, t.1, p.8: 'Weil die Literatur der Aufklärung nicht ausschließlich diesem oder jenem Volk zufällt, sondern nach einer bekannten Bezeichnung Goethe's durchaus Weltliteratur ist, so kann eine Geschichte der Aufklärung nur eine allgemeine, d. h. eine die Wirkungen und Gegenwirkungen aller abendländischen Völker in gleicher Weise umfassende Literaturgeschichte des achtzehnten Jahrhunderts sein.'

34. Hettner, *Literaturgeschichte des 18. Jahrhunderts*, t.1, p.4: 'Macaulay sagt in seiner Abhandlung über Walpole vortrefflich: "Die französische Literatur ist für die englische geworden, was Aaron für Moses war: die großen Entdeckungen in Physik, Metaphysik und Staatswissenschaft gehören den Engländern an; kein Volk außer Frankreich aber hat sie von England unmittelbar empfangen; dazu war England durch seine Lage und Gebräuche zu vereinsamt; Frankreich ist der Dolmetscher zwischen England und der Menschheit gewesen."'

monde le voit, et eux-mêmes admettent ouvertement qu'ils ont surtout emprunté leurs opinions et leurs dispositions aux savants et penseurs anglais. Les uns se contentent d'emblée du trésor hérité, dans son ampleur et ses limites, et le mettent en circulation facile et efficace sous forme de petite monnaie; les autres, au contraire, essaient de l'accroître et de le développer de manière indépendante, mais ceux-ci aussi ne produisent que des idées pleines d'esprit plutôt que des faits et des corps de pensées vraiment définitifs. On comprend dès lors que l'histoire de la philosophie accorde peu d'attention à ces tentatives, quoiqu'il eût été préférable pour elle de les accepter et de les présenter avec impartialité plutôt que de les dénoncer avec une suffisance arrogante et en toute ignorance.

On peut citer peu d'œuvres d'art durables. Les limites du classicisme français sont dépassées, un art et une poésie plus neufs et plus populaires s'éveillent. Mais le contenu reste majoritairement sec et étriqué, intentionnel et didactique.[35]

Les Lumières françaises se sont, caractère aggravant, tout spéciale-ment montrées dépourvues de sens 'du passé et du développement historique' ('Sinn [...] für die Vergangenheit und die geschichtliche Entwicklung') et de respect de l'Etat, dans lequel elles n'ont vu qu'un 'contrat contingent' ('einen zufälligen Vertrag').[36]

En cela, le rapport de Hettner aux Lumières françaises paraît très marqué par des représentations et jugements de valeur empruntés à la philosophie hégélienne. C'est d'ailleurs aux leçons de Hegel sur

---

35. Hettner, *Literaturgeschichte des 18. Jahrhunderts*, t.2, p.543: 'Der rein wissen-schaftliche Ertrag der französischen Aufklärung ist nicht bedeutend. Nur wenige unter diesen Schriftstellern sind schöpferisch und ursprünglich; Jedermann sieht es und sie selbst bekennen es offen, daß sie ihre Meinungen und Gesinnungen meist den englischen Forschern und Denkern entlehnt haben. Die Einen begnügen sich von vornherein mit dem Maß des überkommenen Schatzes und setzen ihn in kleiner Münze in bequemen und wirksamen Umlauf; die Anderen allerdings suchen ihn zu vergrößern und selbständig fortzubilden, aber auch diese geben mehr nur geistreiche Anregungen als wirklich abschließende Thatsachen und Gedankenreihen. Es ist daher erklärlich, wenn die Geschichte der Philosophie auf diese Bestrebungen jetzt wenig einzugehen pflegt, obwohl es ihr immerhin besser anstehen würde, sie unbefangen anzunehmen und darzustellen, statt mit vornehmer Selbstgenügsamkeit kenntnißlos über sie abzusprechen.
      Ebensowenig sind viele bleibende künstlerische Werke aufzuweisen. Die Schranken des französischen Klassicismus werden durchbrochen, es regt sich eine frischere und volkstümlichere Kunst und Dichtung. Aber der Inhalt bleibt meist trocken und dürftig, absichtlich und lehrhaft.'
36. Hettner, *Literaturgeschichte des 18. Jahrhunderts*, t.2, p.546.

l'histoire de la philosophie qu'il emprunte une longue citation pour expliquer le rapport des philosophes français à la religion, dans laquelle ces derniers ne voyaient que 'la ruse d'ecclésiastiques avides de pouvoir' ('herrschsüchtige Priesterlist'):[37]

> On a beau jeu de blâmer les Français pour leurs attaques contre la religion et l'Etat. Il faut cependant se représenter l'horrible état de la société, la misère, la bassesse en France, pour apprécier le mérite qu'ils avaient. Que l'hypocrisie, la bigoterie, la tyrannie, qui se voit dépouillée de ses rapines, que l'idiotie dise qu'ils ont attaqué la religion, l'Etat et les mœurs. Et quelle religion! Non pas celle purifiée par Luther – mais la superstition la plus honteuse, le clergé calotin, la stupidité, la confusion d'esprit, et surtout le gaspillage des richesses et le prélassement dans une abondance de biens temporels au milieu de la misère publique! Et quel Etat! La domination la plus aveugle des ministres et de leurs catins, de leurs femmes, de leurs valets, de sorte qu'une vaste armée de petits tyrans et d'oisifs considérait comme un droit divin le fait de piller les recettes de l'Etat et d'exploiter la sueur du peuple.[38]

Dans cette histoire des *Aufklärungen* européennes, c'est bien évidemment la dernière venue, l'allemande, qui, dans le schéma hégélien de Hettner, surpasse les deux autres: 'Entre-temps, l'Allemagne aussi s'était relevée après une longue stagnation. Bientôt même, elle prend la tête et donne le ton. Avec une rapidité vraiment merveilleuse, elle

---

37. Hettner, *Literaturgeschichte des 18. Jahrhunderts*, t.2, p.546.
38. Hettner, *Literaturgeschichte des 18. Jahrhunderts*, t.2, p.548. Hettner cite ici mot pour mot le passage suivant de Hegel sur les Lumières françaises: Georg Wilhelm Friedrich Hegel, *Vorlesungen über die Geschichte der Philosophie III*, éd. Eva Moldenhauer et Karl Markus Michel, dans *Werke in zwanzig Bänden: auf der Grundlage der Werke von 1832-1845 neu edierte Ausgabe*, t.20 (Francfort-sur-le-Main, 1979), p.295: 'Wir haben gut den Franzosen Vorwürfe über ihre Angriffe der Religion und des Staats zu machen. Man muß ein Bild von dem horriblen Zustand der Gesellschaft, dem Elend, der Niederträchtigkeit in Frankreich haben, um das Verdienst zu erkennen, das sie hatten. Jetzt kann die Heuchelei, die Frömmelei, die Tyrannei, die sich ihres Raubes beraubt sieht, jetzt kann der Schwachsinn sagen, sie haben die Religion, Staat und Sitten angegriffen. Welche Religion! Nicht durch Luther gereinigt, – der schmählichste Aberglaube, Pfaffenthum, Dummheit, Verworrenheit der Gesinnung, vornehmlich das Reichthumverprassen und Schwelgen in zeitlichen Gütern beim öffentlichen Elend! Welcher Staat! Die blindeste Herrschaft der Minister und ihrer Dirnen, Weiber, Kammerdiener, so daß ein ungeheures Heer von kleinen Tyrannen und Müßiggängern es für ein göttliches Recht ansah, die Einnahme des Staats und den Schweiß des Volks zu plündern.'

surpasse l'Angleterre et la France, sinon en puissance extérieure et en
liberté, du moins en éducation intérieure, en art et en science. L'élève
devient le maître.'[39]

Ainsi, avec Hettner, le mot *Aufklärung* devance largement le mot
français 'Lumières' et ses équivalents européens dans un emploi
prioritairement chronologique et/ou historiographique pour désigner
un segment du continuum temporel. Le terme de 'Lumières',
normativement connoté, est absent de l'ouvrage de Tocqueville et
le restera longtemps des discours français sur le dix-huitième siècle
à ambition historiographique. Longtemps encore, en l'absence de
terme à usage véritablement similaire, le vocable allemand sera même
utilisé hors d'Allemagne par des historiens des idées travaillant sur
des objets italiens, anglais ou français. C'est par exemple encore le
cas en 1946 chez Paul Hazard, qui, dans son ouvrage sur *La Pensée
européenne au XVIIIᵉ siècle de Montesquieu à Lessing*, utilise le terme
d'*Aufklärung* pour désigner non seulement un mouvement porté par
un auteur allemand comme Kant, mais aussi le mouvement plus
général des Lumières européennes.[40] Néanmoins, lorsque l'ouvrage
de Ernst Cassirer intitulé *Die Philosophie der Aufklärung* (1932) est
traduit par Pierre Quillet en français en 1966, on choisit de lui donner
pour titre *Philosophie des Lumières*.[41] Si l'usage que Hettner fait de la
notion d'*Aufklärung* se veut essentiellement historiographique, il reste
néanmoins, comme on l'a vu, fortement indexé par des représentations
normatives à la fois quant à la 'valeur' de ce mouvement et quant à la
'qualité' de ses variantes nationales.

---

39. Hettner, *Literaturgeschichte des 18. Jahrhunderts*, t.1, p.6: 'Inzwischen war auch
    Deutschland nach langer Erschlaffung wieder erstanden. Bald sogar wird es
    anführend und tonangebend. Mit wahrhaft wunderbarer Raschheit überflügelt
    es, wenn auch nicht durch äußere Macht und Freiheit, so doch durch innere
    Bildung, durch Kunst und Wissenschaft, England und Frankreich. Aus dem
    Schüler wird es zum Lehrer.'
40. Paul Hazard, *La Pensée européenne au XVIIIᵉ siècle de Montesquieu à Lessing*, 3 vol.
    (Paris, 1946), t.1, p.43-44, 299; t.2, p.12; t.3, p.29-30.
41. Ernst Cassirer, *Die Philosophie der Aufklärung*, 2 vol. (Tübingen, 1932); Ernst
    Cassirer, *La Philosophie des Lumières*, éd. et traduit par Pierre Quillet (Paris,
    1966).

Unveiling or inventing the Enlightenment? Bruno Bauer, the political theology of radical critique and the construction of Enlightenment in the *Vormärz* epoch

Daniel Weidner

Martin-Luther-Universität Halle-Wittenberg

On 17 August 1842, Bruno Bauer, having just been expelled from Bonn University for his radical critique of the Gospels, writes to his friend Arnold Ruge from his new home Berlin:

> Here I found a delicious library of Enlightenment books from the previous century, and I will describe the most notable ones for your journal. This material is completely unknown to us, but is excellent and contains a lot of good things. Some of it is so correct and conforms with the most recent findings and theories that it only needs a translation into modern language.[1]

Indeed, this project will become a major occupation of Bauer as well as of his brother Edgar in the years to come. Bauer writes *Christianity revealed* (*Das entdeckte Christentum*, 1843) on Johann Christian Edelmann, which is immediately censored, and a *History of politics, culture and Enlightenment of the eighteenth century* (*Geschichte der Politik, Cultur und Aufklärung des achtzehnten Jahrhunderts*) that

---

1. 'Ich habe jetzt eine köstliche Bibliothek von der Aufklärungsliteratur des vorigen Jahrhunderts vorgefunden und werde der Reihe nach für die Jahrbücher die merkwürdigsten Erscheinungen charakterisieren. Die Sachen sind uns ganz unbekannt, aber trefflich und enthalten viel Gutes. Manches bedarf bloss einer Übersetzung in die moderne Sprache, so richtig ist es und stimmt mit den neuesten Entdeckungen und Sätzen überein.' Bruno Bauer to Ernst Ruge, 17 August 1842, quoted by Ernst Barnikol, *Bruno Bauer: Studien und Materialien* (Assen, 1972), p.69. All translations in this article are my own unless otherwise indicated.

he manages to publish in four volumes (1843-1845). Edgar Bauer publishes five volumes of a *Library of German enlighteners of the eighteenth century* (*Bibliothek der deutschen Aufklärer des achtzehnten Jahrhunderts,* 1846/1847) and four volumes of *The Political literature of the Germans in the eighteenth century* (*Die politische Literatur der Deutschen im achtzehnten Jahrhundert,* 1847).

Enlightenment became a major occupation of the 'Left Hegelians' who, as Bauer's letter reveals, feel a certain elective affinity to it. In part, this corresponds to the political restoration in Germany after 1815, when feudalism is reestablished, including the institution of censorship, and movements like Romanticism seem to revive the past. However, history never repeats itself, nor are 'translations' ever simple. Indeed, the period of the 1840s, the so-called *Vormärz* epoch, also differs radically from its chosen parallel century, first on account of the memory of the French Revolution, second because of a new understanding of philosophy that has changed its claim and social role since Kant and Hegel, and third due to the emergence of what is already seen as classical German literature, namely the writings from Lessing to Goethe.

The retrospective construction of the Enlightenment in the *Vormärz* is thus characterised by a complex movement of recognition and projection that can be figured as an anachronistic move 'back to the future', as Wolfgang Bunzel put it: expectations for the immediate future are projected back into the past to figure one's present as a 'second Enlightenment'.[2] This construction is an early attempt both to understand the role of Enlightenment in history and to continue it as a task yet unfulfilled, thus oscillating between a historical and a normative understanding of the Enlightenment – an ambiguity that arguably is central to any discourse on the Enlightenment up to the present day. Moreover, as we will see, Bauer's account of the Enlightenment manoeuvres through a series of tensions that the idea and the epoch of Enlightenment pose for him and perhaps still pose today, such as the tension between the ambition and the reality of the Enlightenment, the tension between power and truth, and between the state, the Church and the enlightened critic.

---

2.   Wolfgang Bunzel, 'Zurück in die Zukunft: die Junghegelianer in ihrem Verhältnis zur Aufklärung', in *Der nahe Spiegel: Vormärz und Aufklärung*, ed. Wolfgang Bunzel, Norbert Otto Eke and Florian Vaßen (Bielefeld, 2008), p.31-49. The figure of a second Enlightenment is already prominent in Arnold Ruge; see the contribution by Daniel Fulda in this volume.

This latter tension will prove central for Bauer's argument and his account of Enlightenment not only because, historically, the German Enlightenment did have a special and ambivalent relation to matters of religion but also because of the situation in which Bauer writes his history of the Enlightenment, immediately after being expelled from the university on the initiative of the Church. This situation, I will argue, leads Bauer to a repositioning of his critique that breaks away from the imagined coalition between critique and the state towards a new discursive politics that radically affirms the position of the individual critic as an outsider. This move in turn leads him to invent a different tradition of radical Enlightenment critics and especially critics of religion, as we see in the letter quoted above. Thus, what can be called the political theological predicament of the Enlightenment, the mutual and triangular tension between the state, the Church and *Wissenschaft*, can be seen in Bauer's account in all its ambiguities.

To unpack the ambiguities of this position, I will focus on one text in particular, namely Bauer's *History of politics, culture and Enlightenment of the eighteenth century*. Even though Bauer's writings are dispersed, idiosyncratic and closely related to the extremely dense debates in the left-wing Hegelian circles to which Bauer belongs, this text permits a focused reading of several of the issues mentioned, namely (1) the question of religion, (2) the position of the critic, (3) the role of culture in Bauer's account and (4) the function of its telos, the French Revolution, for the narrative of the eighteenth century.

Religion

Bruno Bauer (1808-1882) is one of the most eccentric intellectuals of the nineteenth century.[3] A learned theologian, he began as a right-wing Hegelian; he defended speculative theology against the historical criticism of David Friedrich Strauss from 1835, and edited Hegel's posthumous *Lectures on the philosophy of religion*. But soon he developed a substantial critique of the Gospels in four volumes published from 1840 to 1842, which is in many ways more radical (and arguably less historical) than that of Strauss, and which led to

---

3. The most substantial account of Bauer is still Barnikol, *Bruno Bauer*. For a more recent overview, see also Massimilano Tomba, *Krise und Kritik bei Bruno Bauer* (Frankfurt am Main, 2005), and Douglas Moggach, *Philosophie und Politik bei Bruno Bauer* (Frankfurt am Main, 2009).

the revocation of his *venia legendi* for theology. Bauer now became a
leading figure of left-wing Hegelianism and one of the most notorious
critics of religion, leading numerous public controversies, among
others with Ludwig Feuerbach and Marx and Engels. After the failed
revolution of 1848, Bauer changed sides again. He became a regular
contributor to conservative journals and newspapers, increasingly
also adopting anti-Jewish positions and continuing to write popular
historical books that now focused on the Caesarism of great men such
as Napoleon or the Russian tsar Peter the Great.

Bauer's *History* is a typical book of this strange author. It suffers
from a major imbalance, since the first volume covers the first half
of the eighteenth century, while the second one jumps to the French
Revolution and the German reactions to it, which are dealt with in
volumes 2 to 4. Moreover, in its composition, it is to a large extent
the book of an autodidact presenting an odd mixture of minute
factual and often anecdotal accounts on the one hand and very
broad generalisations on the other. Whereas Bauer eclectically uses
historical sources and contemporary chronicles for his narrative
without treating those materials critically, his general judgements are
inspired by a Hegelian view of history, or at least what Bauer took to
be such a view. In both respects, the book is somewhat untimely in the
period of the emerging historicist writing of history that would try to
give a coherent account based on the critical use of all contemporary
sources and refrain from general judgements altogether. But precisely
these oddities and the deviation from the historicist mainstream make
Bauer an interesting case that reveals how difficult it was to integrate
the Enlightenment into this mainstream which would soon turn into
the dominant form of national history.

The first volume of Bauer's *History* starts with a story of decay.
Over 150 pages, he describes how the old German Empire disinte-
grated and how the particular interests of the different members
of the Empire overruled any general interest. Countless political
intrigues as well as the superficiality of courtly life and the poverty
of bourgeois culture reveal that there was no 'whole' anymore, as
Bauer states.[4] Only rare moments point to a different future, such
as when the Prussian king Friedrich Wilhelm I expelled the useless
opera and followed the principles of utility and common sense. In
Bauer's narrative, we can discern elements of a later national-liberal

---

4. Bruno Bauer, *Geschichte der Politik, Cultur und Aufklärung des achtzehnten
    Jahrhunderts*, 4 vols (Berlin, 1843-1845), vol.1, p.99.

view that foregrounds the rise of bourgeois society and focuses on Prussia, but Bauer is far from the glorification of Prussian expansion that will orient later national histories. The most important impulse for development is, according to Bauer, neither political nor cultural, but religious: 'It was not until Pietism gained influence over the people that it was able to combine the achievements of the previous endeavours into a whole, and worked the people in such a way that from then on it was able to follow every new current of the spirit of the age.'[5] It was the emergence of Pietism as a mass movement, rather than either Frederick the Great or Lessing, that transformed the different histories into one German history. In Bauer's narrative, Pietism brings about a people able to follow the spirit of the age, which is a precondition to create unity otherwise lost at the political level. Thus, in a certain sense, Bauer's argument seems to prefigure the idea of an indirect, and in fact involuntary, 'secularising' effect of Pietism that would be similar to the famous idea of a Protestant genealogy of modernity developed by Max Weber.[6] However, despite the historical role Bauer ascribes to Pietism, he remains highly critical of it, highlighting the narrow-mindedness, pettiness and especially hypocrisy of this movement: Bauer compares it to a 'weak old man', in that it does not act seriously but mostly chatters about itself and its private experience: 'The chieftains of Pietism did nothing for the expansion of the people's consciousness or for the progress in the sciences.'[7] Even though Pietism was critical of Lutheran orthodoxy, it did not dare to openly proclaim this opposition and thus remained compromised, leading Bauer to sharply criticise any form of religious enlightenment:

5. 'Erst der Pietismus [...] bekam auf das Volk Einfluß, war im Stande, den Gewinn der vorhergehenden vereinzelten kritischen Bestrebungen in ein Ganzes zusammen zu fassen, und bearbeitete das Volk so weit, daß es von nun an jeder neuen Strömung des Zeitgeistes folgen konnte.' Bauer, *Geschichte*, vol.1, p.151-52.

6. For such a reading, see Ernst Barnikol, 'Bauers Kulturgeschichte des 18. Jahrhunderts und seine These von der Säkularisation des Pietismus', in *Bruno Bauer*, p.274-90.

7. 'Der Pietismus kam altersschwach auf die Welt und sein Betragen war auch danach. Eine Sache ernsthaft angreifen und behandeln war ihm unmöglich; er konnte nur pretentiöse Fingerzeige geben, gegen die Welt poltern, oder mit selbstgefälliger Schwatzhaftigkeit [...] seine kleinlichen Erfahrungen der Gnade Gottes vortragen. Für die Erweiterung des Volksbewußtseyns oder für den Fortschritt in den Wissenschaften haben die Häuptlinge des Pietismus Nichts gethan.' Bauer, *Geschichte*, vol.1, p.163.

Every progress that is attempted or actually made in the religious way soon betrays itself as a step backwards into a deeper darkness than ever existed before. The closer the time comes when the cause of religion will be decided, the more the men of 'religious progress' turn into evil spirits [...]. But the deeper darkening of the spirit compels mankind to more thorough effort, and the displeasure at the growing hypocrisy of egoism at last awakens the men who take up the struggle against all evil spirits.[8]

In a typical dialectical mode, Bauer argues that any attempt to treat religion progressively turns into a reaction, until the very moment religion as such envisions its final crisis. Even those enlightened theologians who stress the reasonableness of Christianity have produced unfree consciousness in the end:

Those men have created the form of religious consciousness that is today the enemy of manhood and bravery and the adversary of freedom. When they appeared to teach the enlightened and refined the form of religion their time asked for, they were men of progress, but their successors today make up the mass on which the reaction against progress can rely.[9]

Again, Bauer argues dialectically that formerly progressive forces can evolve into forces of reaction. The reference to 'today' reveals that Bauer's argument about Pietism and other forms of religious 'progress' in the Enlightenment is not merely historical but has a present situation in mind, and a very personal one, namely the conflicts over the relation between state and Church as well as over the freedom

8. 'Jeder Fortschritt, der auf religiösem Wege versucht oder auch wirklich gethan wird, verräth sich bald als der Rückschritt in eine tiefere Verfinsterung, als wie sie jemals vorher da gewesen war. Je näher nun gar die Zeit ist, welche die Sache der Religion entscheiden wird, um so mehr sind die Männer des religiösen Fortschritts, die zehnmal ärgeren Geister [...]. Aber die tiefere Verfinsterung des Geistes zwingt die Menschheit zu gründlicherer Anstrengung und der Unwille über die wachsende Heuchelei des Egoismus erweckt endlich die Männer, die den Kampf mit allen böse Geistern auf sich nehmen.' Bauer, *Geschichte*, vol.1, p.174-75.
9. 'Diese Männer [...] haben die Form des religiösen Bewußtseyns geschaffen, die in unserer Zeit der Feind der Männlichkeit und Tapferkeit und der Widersacher der Freiheit ist. Als sie auftraten, um die aufgeklärte und geläuterte Religiosität zu lehren, nach welcher ihre Zeit verlangt, waren sie die Männer des Fortschritts; ihre jetzigen Nachfolger bilden die furchtbare Masse, auf welche sich jede Reaction gegen den Fortschritt stützen und verlassen kann.' Bauer, *Geschichte*, vol.1, p.253.

of the university that lead to Bauer's dismissal from the university.[10] As mentioned, Bauer had consciously staged this conflict as a major battle between progress and reaction and also between *Wissenschaft* and superstition in order to ensure he received the support of the Prussian state. He had even written an anonymous pamphlet, 'The trumpet of the Last Judgement on Hegel: an ultimatum' ('Die Posaune des Jüngsten Gerichts über Hegel, den Atheisten und Antichristen: ein Ultimatum', 1841), arguing in a feigned Pietist voice full of religiosity that Hegel's philosophy effectively denied religion, identifying it with self-consciousness:

> This is the horrible, shuddering kernel of the system that kills all piety and religiosity. Whoever has enjoyed this kernel is dead to God, for he thinks God is dead; whoever eats this kernel has fallen lower than Eve, since she ate the apple and Adam was seduced by her, so the follower of that system lacks even this – albeit sinful arrogance, he no longer even wants to become like God, he only wants to be the I and to gain and enjoy the blasphemous infinity, freedom and self-sufficiency of self-consciousness.[11]

Bauer's mockery – a typical gesture of Enlightenment criticism that reminds us of Voltaire – reveals a typical paradox of the critique of religion that quite often adopts the very rhetoric of the religion criticised. As Wolfgang Essbach has shown in a magisterial study on the 'sectarian' group sociology of the Left Hegelians, they develop a manifest 'gnostic' and 'eschatological' habitus, claiming to be in the

10. See Arnulf von Scheliha, 'Der Entzug von Bruno Bauers *venia docendi* und die Argumente der gutachtenden theologischen Fakultäten', in *Bruno Bauer: ein 'Partisan des Weltgeistes'?*, ed. Klaus-Michael Kodalle and Tilman Reitz (Würzburg, 2010), p.63-73.
11. 'Das ist der entsetzliche, schaudererregende, alle Frömmigkeit und Religiosität ertötende Kern des Systems. Wer diesen Kern genossen hat, ist für Gott tot, denn er hält Gott für tot, wer diesen Kern ißt, ist tiefer gefallen als Eva, da sie den Apfel aß und Adam von ihr verführt wurde, so fehlt dem Anhänger jenes Systems sogar dieser – wenn auch sündhafte Hochmut, er will gar nicht mehr werden wie Gott, wer will nur Ich-Ich sein und die blasphemische Unendlichkeit, Freiheit und Selbstgenügsamkeit des Selbstbewusstseins gewinnen und genießen.' Bruno Bauer, 'Die Posaune des Jüngsten Gerichts', in *Die Hegelsche Linke: Dokumente zu Philosophie und Politik im deutschen Vormärz*, ed. Heinz and Igrid Pepperle (Leipzig, 1985), p.235-372 (273-74). On this text, see Jean-Claude Wolfe, 'Bruno Bauers Posaune des Jüngsten Gerichts', in *Utopie und Apokalypse in der Moderne*, ed. Stefan Bodo Würffel *et al.* (Paderborn, 2010), p.119-28.

know and expecting an imminent decision of the cause of religion.[12]
The result of this turn is not only that the critique of religion is
positioned in the very core of Enlightenment but that this critique
is also associated with strong Hegelian connotations of 'overcoming'
false consciousness by the famous *Aufhebung*. For Bauer, however, after
his disappointment with the university, this overcoming is no longer
the task of the state or of the university, but that of the critic.

The critic

As we have seen, according to Bauer, religious progress leads to
hypocrisy – but this hypocrisy in turn leads some individuals to take
up the struggle against it. The description of the spiritual void of the
eighteenth century that makes up the first volume of Bauer's *History*
is interwoven with portraits of individual critics that stand out from
their miserable century, such as Martin Knutzen, Balthasar Becker,
Anton van Dale, Hermann von Hardt and others. However, they all
remain isolated and thus are only intermittently effectual. Again, it is
only later, after Pietism has prepared a new sensibility in the people,
that critics become more influential. This applies to Johann Conrad
Dippel and Johann Christian Edelmann, whom Bauer calls the 'true
successors of the work begun by Pietism';[13] Edelmann in particular is
portrayed in great detail in the longest chapter of the work.

As Ernst Barnikol has shown, Bauer figured himself as an
Edelmann redivivus precisely by misreading the latter, who was a
deist rather than an atheist.[14] The parallel is very clear in the way
he posits Edelmann in the history of philosophy. Whereas Spinoza
criticised religion in general, Edelmann did so in detail; whereas
reformers are always compromising, Edelmann understands himself
as a partisan of critique who does not want to repair or build new

12. See Wolfgang Essbach: *Die Junghegelianer: Soziologie einer Intellektuellengruppe*
    (Munich, 1988), esp. part 4. On the 'hegemonic function' of the eschatological
    rhetoric of the Young Hegelians, see also Olaf Briese, 'Vom Gottesgericht zum
    Weltgericht: apokalyptische Motive in Aufklärung und Vormärz', in *Der nahe
    Spiegel*, ed. W. Bunzel *et al.*, p.51-78 (77).
13. 'Dippel, Edelmann und alle die folgenden Aufklärer sind daher die wahren
    Fortsetzer des Werkes, welches der Pietismus begonnen hatte.' Bauer, *Geschichte*,
    vol.1, p.181.
14. See Ernst Barnikol, *Das entdeckte Christentum im Vormärz: Bruno Bauers Kampf
    gegen Religion und Christentum und Erstausgabe seiner Kampfschrift* (Jena, 1927),
    esp. ch.5.

sects: 'My only task now is, like Jeremiah's, to root out, break, destroy and ruin.'[15] Edelmann is a man beyond compromise, as Bauer figures himself, thus his deist inclinations have to be downplayed.

Bauer's reading also reflects the repositioning of the critic after his expulsion from the university. For, as other Hegelians, Bauer at first conceived himself to be not an isolated, subjective critic but rather an official representative of philosophy employed by the state, following the Hegelian alliance of Prussia and the *Weltgeist*. Bauer's first publication actually concerned issues of religious politics, namely the Prussian union of the Reformed and Lutheran confessions or the pleas of Prussian Catholics for emancipation – cases in which Bauer would rigorously defend the right of the state to administer religion. In his own case, when accused of atheism, Bauer expected for a long time that the state would defend him, and freedom of investigation generally, against the allegation of the Church. He even tends to present himself as a sort of martyr for the good cause of freedom and philosophy. Finally, being expelled nonetheless, he redefines the situation and his own position as a subjective, individual critic. In a letter to his brother Edgar dated 4 February 1844, he uses the image of Prometheus:

> Prometheus in chains was freer than when he had walked around and taught man to sacrifice. This free Prometheus, as we know, had been a sophist in his doctrine of sacrifice, but in the pain of his bonds he stood out above all powers. *Wissenschaft*, being rejected, is left to itself. One no longer wants it, good! So it is emancipated, and I am also free, insofar as I serve the outcast. I have never felt so happy, so free...[16]

It is in this moment of subjective individual freedom that Bauer looks for new company no longer among his contemporaries, but

---

15. 'Jetzt habe ich, wie Jeremias, keinen andern Beruf, als daß ich ausreißen, zerbrechen, zerstören und verderben soll.' Johann Christian Edelmann, quoted by Bauer, *Geschichte*, vol.1, p.215.

16. 'Der gefesselte Prometheus war als solcher freier als damals, da er noch frei umherging und die Menschen opfern lehrte. Der Freie Prometheus war bekanntlich in seiner Opferlehre ein Sophist, aber im Schmerz seiner Fesseln war er über alle Mächte erhaben. Indem die Wissenschaft verstoßen wird, ist sie sich selbst überlassen. Man will sie nicht mehr, gut! So ist sie emanzipiert und ich bin auch frei, soweit ich der Verstoßenen diene. Ich habe mich noch nie so glücklich, so frei gefühlt...' Bruno Bauer, *Briefwechsel zwischen Bruno Bauer und Edgar Bauer während der Jahre 1839-1842* (Berlin, 1844), p.36-37.

in the past – he invents his own tradition of radical critique. When he comes across the writings of Edelmann, he decides to rescue his forerunner from oblivion through a booklet in 1843, which was, as mentioned, initially confiscated by censorship, entitled *Christianity revealed: a recollection of the eighteenth century and a contribution to the crisis of the nineteenth* (*Das entdeckte Christentum: eine Erinnerung an das achtzehnte Jahrhundert und ein Beitrag zur Krisis des neunzehnten*). The title epitomises Bauer's project in all its ambiguities. *Christianity revealed* echoes both *Christianisme dévoilé* (1766), a radical reduction of Christian faith to the trickery of priests, and Johann Andreas Eisenmenger's infamous *Judaism revealed* (*Entdecktes Judentum*, 1700), an anti-Jewish pamphlet, and more generally a hermeneutic that claims to undo the mysteries of faith by simple arguments. The subtitle, which makes the recollection of the past a moment of critique of the present, spells out the move back into the future so typical of the *Vormärz* Enlightenment. In a similar vein, Bauer claims in his *History* that Edelmann must be remembered today as part of a counter-tradition: '[H]e was only forgotten because his opposition [...] almost completely disappeared from memory in the following period and the world view changed completely even within the theological systems. He was forgotten because the following period appropriated not his strength but his weakness, his lack of clarity.'[17]

Here again, history proceeds dialectically: just as Pietism first acted progressively but turned to reaction due to its compromising with the Church, Edelmann's radical thought has been forgotten but can be remembered today and help bring about the final crisis of religion. Again, this argument was not easy to pursue for Bauer: as with the booklet, censorship intervened and Bauer had to engage in a long dispute and omit a series of passages from the manuscript, but he was finally able to publish the book with those passages omitted – a process that he comments upon in another volume, *Documents on the negotiations on the confiscation of the 'History of politics, culture and Enlightenment of the eighteenth century'* (*Aktenstücke zu den Verhandlungen über die Beschlagnahme der 'Geschichte der Politik, Kultur und Aufkärung des achtzehnten Jahrhunderts'*), which includes the long

---

17. 'Allein er ward nur vergessen, weil sein Gegensatz [...] der folgenden Zeit fast ganz aus dem Gedächtniß verschwand und die Weltanschuuung [*sic*!] auch innerhalb der theologischen Systeme sich vollständig veränderte. Er wurde vergessen, weil die folgende Zeit nicht seine Stärke, sondern seine Schwäche, seine Unklarheit sich aneignete.' Bauer, *Geschichte*, vol.1, p.236.

and often tiring exchange of orders, petitions and protest.[18] But despite these – still visible! – omissions, Bauer's *History* also contains a portrait of the critic as a solitary protester who becomes quite representative at least of a certain type of Enlightenment historiography: a sort of hidden and suppressed intellectual heroism that is ever more radical than we can imagine. In Bauer, we can see how this radical Enlightenment emerges hand in hand with a shift of the enunciative position. For it is no longer state-sponsored *Wissenschaft* that speaks and performs the critique, but the individual – even the outsider who now projects him- or herself back into the past to find a community of outsiders, a tradition of the suppressed that must be unearthed or unveiled.

Culture

Bauer's *History of politics, culture and Enlightenment of the eighteenth century* covers not only religion and philosophy, but also 'culture', namely the development of literature and the arts. This is not particularly remarkable, since most accounts of eighteenth-century history written in the first half of the nineteenth century are oriented towards culture rather than politics. As historiography became a *wissenschaftliche* discipline in these years, it focused on political history but also on past history, Antiquity, the medieval epoch and the Reformation, whereas the more recent *Zeitgeschichte*, the history of the immediate past, became the domain of journalistic or autodidactic accounts, such as Karl Biedermann's *Germany in the eighteenth century* (*Deutschland im achtzehnten Jahrhundert*), published in 1854. Implicit in this division of labour is the assumption that only temporal distance can grant objectivity, while issues that are still politically contested resist becoming history. At the same time, with the construction of a 'classical' German literature of the 'Goethe period', eighteenth-century literary history becomes the prefiguration of that German national literature, as in Gottfried Gervinus' and in Hermann Hettner's literary histories.[19] Often, these accounts implied that this German classical literature, as well as German philosophy, should somehow replace political history and namely the Revolution – be it affirmatively, as with most national liberal historians, or critically,

18. This volume was published in Copenhagen in 1844. See Barnikol, *Bruno Bauer*, p.274-80.
19. On Hettner, see the contribution by Elisabeth Décultot in this volume.

as with those writers of the *Vormärz* arguing that German literature should transcend aesthetic classicism and turn towards the political. Thus, for example, Heinrich Heine argues in his 1835 essay *On the history of religion and philosophy in Germany* (*Zur Geschichte der Religion und Philosophie in Deutschland*) that classical and romantic German art did not so much replace religion as prefigure a revolution to come.

Bauer's account of eighteenth-century literary history is situated in these *Vormärz* debates about politics and aesthetics.[20] He shares the critique of the *Vormärz*, that German classical literature resulted in a flight from political activity. The Germans 'were not yet destined to enter the circle of the people who make their history. Beauty, if it becomes the primary occupation of a nation, educates, weakens and unnerves it, and finally leads to a general atony, since it presents the ideas – be they ever so revolutionary – in a sensual cover.'[21] As a result, Bauer treats most literature of the eighteenth century quite critically. He appreciated the Gottschedian reform and considered the controversy of Gottsched with Bodmer and Breitinger as a necessary stage of German literature, but generally did not value very highly the German literature of the first half of the eighteenth century. German authors remained isolated and dispersed, lacking the courtly life of other nations such as France, thus expressing the poverty of German life. 'They have not transcended the barbarism of their time but are themselves barbaric in their sentimentalism.'[22] The best writers turned to satire, but their writings 'did not help a lot and were only perceptible to a few due to the general lack of understanding. Anyway, satire and irony are usually symptomatic of the fact that their object is already in decay.'[23] The decay of German

20. On the relation of his aesthetics to Hegel's thesis of the end of art, see Ernst Müller, *Kunstreligion und ästhetische Religiosität* (Berlin, 2004), p.245-53.

21. 'Sie waren noch nicht dazu bestimmt, in den Kreis der Völker einzutreten, die Geschichte machen und die neuere Geschichte wirklich gemacht haben. Das Schöne, wenn es das vorwiegende Interesse einer Nation bildet, schwächt, entnervt und hat endlich eine allgemeine Erschlaffung zur Folge, da es die Ideen – und wären sie noch so revolutionär – in einer sinnlichen Hülle darstellt.' Bauer, *Geschichte*, vol.1, p.285.

22. 'Die Barbarei des damaligen Lebens haben sie nicht überwunden, in ihrer Sentimentalität sind sie vielmehr selbst barbarisch.' Bauer, *Geschichte*, vol.1, p.297.

23. 'halfen jetzt nicht und waren bei der herrschenden Gefühllosigkeit nur Wenigen empfindlich und fühlbar. Ohnehin ist die Satire und Ironie wohl ein Beweis, daß der Zustand, den sie trifft, sich in der Auflösung befindet.' Bauer, *Geschichte*, vol.1, p.282.

literature thus reflects the general decay of German life during the eighteenth century. And this is particularly true at the end of the eighteenth century: where historians of national literature saw a specifically German literature emerging out of the Enlightenment, namely the sentimentalism of the 1770s and 1780s, Bauer sees an even deeper lapse into the sensual, an even weaker conception of man who now becomes an object of psychology and degenerates into the role of hero of the novel. 'The vagabonds and heroes of the novel of the eighteenth century were the last knights of the Enlightenment.'[24] The novels of Jean Paul, August Lafontaine and Goethe represent private conflicts of small heroes who, in the end, 'as compensation for their lack of countenance are being engaged with their last lover'. Echoing Hegel's critique of the *Bildungsroman*, Bauer complains that the meaning of life is confused with private happiness and that the self-consciousness of the subject is in fact undercut by the rule of another instance, as the secret society of the tower in Goethe's *Wilhelm Meister* that constantly directs the protagonist: 'Since these poor heroes think themselves lost in a dead end at every step, they are always in need of a mediator risen above the human, watching the heroes' goings-on in a calmness that is almost divine, who steps out of his sanctuary now and then with a wise saying, offering the lost human child a hand.'[25] This kind of literature does not present a heroic, sovereign and manly subject, but one poor and confused, ready to submit to the rule of others.

For Bauer, literature does not present an 'ideal' or 'philosophical' alternative to politics, nor does it point to a better political future. As in the realm of religion, culture and literature are rather expressions of decay that point to the future only indirectly, since the deepest decay will at some point turn into its opposite, as Bauer argues in a passage that summarised the poverty of eighteenth-century culture:

> At the moment when, as a result of the literary period up to now, meanness and dissolution have reached the point which they cannot

24. 'Die Vagabonden und Romanhelden des achtzehnten Jahrhunderts waren die letzten Ritter der Aufklärung.' Bauer, *Geschichte*, vol.2, p.9.
25. 'Da diese armen Helden bei jedem Schritte sich in eine Sackgasse verlaufen zu haben glauben, so bedürfen sie immer einer Mittelsperson, die über das Menschliche hinausragt, in einer Ruhe, die fast göttlich ist, dem Treiben der Helden zusieht, ab und zu mit einem weisen Spruche aus ihrem Heiligthum heraustritt und dem verirrten Menschenkind die Hand bietet.' Bauer, *Geschichte*, vol.2, p.11.

possibly exceed, the ideas which can inflame to historical deeds
have also emerged among the Germans in a purity which they
have never reached before among any people – it has come to the
question (which will perhaps be decided tomorrow, today) whether
the Germans should cease to be a mere mass or whether those
bourgeois are right who declare the determination of the spirit to be
wrong and an outrage against German innocence.[26]

Here again, the past is conceived from the viewpoint of a present
that will – tomorrow or even today – decide whether the malaise
of German culture will finally lead to liberation or is just a story
of decay. Inside the historical account, however, literature does not
present an alternative nor does it lead into a different realm. This role
is rather reserved for a different art, namely music, for which Bauer
reserves the ultimate chapter of his first volume: 'As long as a people
lives in so constrained a way that it does not have public general
affairs, it possesses one sanctuary wherein, surreptitiously or protected
and supported by its masters, it stretches its chest and clears itself
from the dirt of its slavery.'[27] This sanctuary is no longer religion and
not yet philosophy or literature, but music, namely that of Bach and
Handel, whose temper expresses the feeling of the time.

Bauer's *History of politics, culture and Enlightenment of the eighteenth
century* sees culture in the context of politics, or, in a word that he
rarely uses, as a public affair. As with other *Vormärz* writers, this makes
him highly critical of the achievements of classical literature and the
rising narrative of a German national literary history culminating in
Goethe and Schiller. This scepticism will last until late in his life: his

26. 'In dem Augenblick, wo das Resultat der bisherigen literarischen Periode, die
    Gemeinheit und Zerflossenheit den Punkt erreicht haben, den sie unmöglich
    noch übersteigen können, sind auch die Ideen, die zu geschichtlichen Thaten
    inflammiren können, in einer Reinheit unter den Deutschen hervorgetreten,
    die sie vorher noch nie, unter keinem Volke erreicht haben, – es ist zur Frage
    gekommen, (die morgen, heute vielleicht schon entschieden wird), ob die
    Deutschen aufhören sollen, eine bloße Masse zu seyn, oder ob jene Bieder-
    männer Recht behalten, welche die Entschiedenheit des Geistes für Unrecht
    und einen Frevel gegen die deutsche Unschuld erklären.' Bauer, *Geschichte*, vol.1,
    p.286.
27. 'So lange ein Volk noch so eingeengt lebt, daß es keine eigene öffentliche
    allgemeine Angelegenheit hat, besitzt es immer ein Heiligthum, in dem es
    sich verstohlener Weise oder auch unter dem Schutz und der Begünstigung
    seiner Herrn einmal die Brust ausweitet und vom Schmutz seiner Knechtschaft
    reinigt.' Bauer, *Geschichte*, vol.1, p.314.

final publication is an essay from 1882 on Karl Philipp Moritz whose *Anton Reiser* Bauer considers much superior to Goethe's *Werther's sorrows*.[28] Once more, this is an attempt to rescue an outsider, and, again, it is a character situated somewhere between Protestant sectarian piety and rebellion that Bauer finds appropriate to become the new German classic.

Revolution and reaction

The French Revolution is the clear telos of Bauer's book, which dedicates no fewer than three of its four volumes to the description of German reactions to the Revolution. Bauer simultaneously published numerous journal articles on the history of the French Revolution itself, and in 1846 he continued his historiographical project with a two-volume *History of Germany and of the French Revolution under the rule of Napoleon* (*Geschichte Deutschlands und der französischen Revolution unter der Herrschaft Napoleons*) and, in 1847, a three-volume *History of the French Revolution until the founding of the Republic* (*Geschichte der französischen Revolution bis zur Stiftung der Republik*), co-authored with his brother Edgar and Ernst Jungnitz.[29] In Bauer's account of the eighteenth century, the Revolution is the second central turning point of his narrative and, besides the essentially biographical crisis that functions as the 'now' of Bauer's text, it is also the point of decision where the preceding history – the achievements of the Enlightenment – is put to a historical test. Here, Bauer follows the Hegelian interpretation of the French Revolution as the result and climax of the Enlightenment, but, for him, it is not the radical French Enlightenment that faces its consequences in the Terror, but the half-hearted German attempts that lead to the reaction, as Bauer states at the beginning of volume 2:

> When the Germans, after the Sturm period of their literary movement and after the decline of the Enlightenment, had arrived in the void of this novel-world, they received the news of the outbreak of the French Revolution. The further development of their consciousness was

28. See Barnikol, *Bruno Bauer*, p.447-54.
29. See Massimilano Tomba, 'Bruno Bauers kritische Auseinandersetzung mit der französischen Revolution: Historiographie, Politik, Geschichtsphilosophie', in *Bruno Bauer*, ed. K.-M. Kodalle and T. Reitz, p.251-62. See also on similar contemporary accounts Lars Lambrecht, 'Zur Rezeption der Französischen Revolution bei den Junghegelianern', in *Der nahe Spiegel*, ed. W. Bunzel *et al.*, p.205-18.

determined almost solely by the relationship they gave themselves to this event and were able to give themselves to it.[30]

The account of the Revolution and the German reactions towards it is even less structured than the first volume of Bauer's work. Not only does he leap over nearly fifty years from the middle of the eighteenth century to its end, but the descriptions Bauer gives of the Revolution and the reactions to it are also piecemeal, at times confused, and full of details that there is no space to discuss here. In general, he sympathises with the Jacobins who want to transform the French people into a political commonwealth, and laments the outcome of the Revolution, namely the bourgeois directory, which is nothing but the triumph of private and particular interest.

As for German reactions, Bauer emphasises that the Enlightenment public at first welcomed the Revolution but quickly turned much more sceptical towards its violent moments. The 'veterans of the Enlightenment' ('Veteranen der Aufklärung'), Bauer ironically stated, saw themselves and their slogans confirmed by the Revolution, but 'their time was over' ('Ihre Zeit war vorüber').[31] In some detail he describes the reactions of writers such as Kotzebue, Iffland or Lafontaine, who do not have a proper standpoint, or of Goethe, whose reduction of the Revolution to the necklace affair Bauer considers poor. He considers Wieland, one of the earliest supporters turned critic, as naive and as having no 'experience of the real world':

> In his good-natured enthusiasm for the French movement, he expressed the views and feelings of the middle class of his people, who, beyond the limited scope of their family, knew only the world of novels and regarded the spectacle of the Revolution simply as a novel, and were not prepared for the fact that the world's affairs demanded a solution of a completely different kind.[32]

30. 'Als die Deutschen nach der Sturm-Periode ihrer literarischen Bewegung und nach dem Verfall der Aufklärung in der Leere dieser Romanenwelt angelangt waren, erhielten sie die Kunde von dem Ausbruch der französischen Revolution. Die weitere Entwickelung ihres Bewusstseyns war fast einzig und allein durch das Verhältniß bestimmt, welches sie sich zu dieser Begebenheit gaben und zu geben vermochten.' Bauer, *Geschichte*, vol.2, p.13.
31. Bauer, *Geschichte*, vol.2, p.14-15.
32. 'In seinem gutmüthigen Enthusiasmus für die französische Bewegung sprach er die Ansichten und Empfindungen der mittleren Klasse seines Volks aus, die außer dem beschränkten Umfang ihrer Familienstube nur die Romanenwelt kannte, das Schauspiel der Revolution auch nur wie einen Roman betrachtete

Bauer also criticised those who argued that the Enlightenment was already about to achieve what the French Revolution demanded – because they did not understand that the achievements of the Enlightenment were only a new polishing of old ideas: 'They had no clue of the courage a nation must have that feels that its fate and future depend on its own conduct.'[33]

The reactions of German intellectuals to the French Revolution, ranging from the reluctant to the hostile, once more underline the limited nature of the German Enlightenment that 'had stopped in front of certain statutes and meanings, therefore one only carried out its own will when one closed the barriers completely. [...] It was fundamentally in agreement with the spiritual world which it fought against: it is thus only natural that it was forced to completely submit to the laws of this world.'[34] The reactionary turn of German intellectuals is thus less an act of counter-Enlightenment than the consequence of a half-hearted Enlightenment: a consequence of the lack of principles, of a limited understanding of man as in the anthropological pessimism of the late Enlightenment, a consequence of lack of courage. In this respect, the Enlightenment is not a general but unfulfilled project, rather a historical epoch that came to an end with the Revolution, or, in Bauer's words: 'The Enlightenment was finished – its opposition to the system it had fought so hard against had collapsed.'[35] Finished, *fertig* in German, is neither fulfilled nor failed. In Bauer's account, the Revolution is neither the logical outcome of the Enlightenment nor its tragic failure into something completely different. Rather, it is the final crisis, or a historical test of the Enlightenment: the moment that reveals the limits of that movement and brings it to an end.

---

und nicht darauf gefaßt war, daß die Welthändel eine Lösung ganz anderer Art verlangten.' Bauer, *Geschichte*, vol.2, p.44.

33. 'Sie hatten also keine Ahnung von dem Muth, den eine Nation haben mußte, die sich mit dem Bewußtseyn erhob, daß von ihrer Haltung und Ausdauer das Schicksal und die Zukunft von dem ganzen Gewinn ihres Jahrhunderts abhänge.' Bauer, *Geschichte*, vol.2, p.55.

34. 'Die Aufklärung war vor bestimmten Satzungen und Meynungen stehen geblieben: man vollzog daher nur ihren eigenen Willen, wenn man die Schranken vollends schloß. [...] Sie stimmte im Grunde mit der geistigen Welt, die sie bekämpfte, überein: es kann also nur recht genannt werden, daß man sie zwang, sich den Gesetzen dieser Welt wieder vollends zu unterwerfen.' Bauer, *Geschichte*, vol.2, p.6.

35. 'Die Aufklärung war fertig – ihr Gegensatz zu dem System, welches sie bisher bekämpft hatte, war zusammengefallen.' Bauer, *Geschichte*, vol.2, p.7.

Conclusion

Bauer's *History of politics, culture and Enlightenment of the eighteenth century* is an ambivalent account. Though it sympathises with the emancipatory tendencies of the Enlightenment, it constantly highlights the weakness and the limitations of the German Enlightenment, which become manifest at its end, particularly in its reaction to the French Revolution. In fact, this ambivalence is already expressed in the preface of the first volume. On the one hand, Bauer claims that his object, the history of the eighteenth century, has universal meaning: 'There is a Greek history, a Roman history, a history of the Christian world, but the history of humanity, the history that generates the idea of humanity and has set itself the task of founding a human society, only begins with the eighteenth century of our era.'[36] The *History of culture, politics and Enlightenment in the eighteenth century* is the history of humanity; it allows a combination of these different aspects of human life into one process, namely into the dawn of humanity's self-consciousness. On the other hand, however, this history has not even begun:

> The eighteenth century attempted to bring the new thought to recognition on the ground and within the confines of the traditional customs and ideas – an attempt that necessarily had to fail, and whose outcome was either tragic (when a pure will and an enthusiasm hithterto unknown to humanity guided the experiment) or repugnant (when an old prerogative hypocritically sought to settle for the better conviction), or resembled an unsuccessful theatrical coup (where the new principle had to outwit [...] the nonsense and selfishnes of the old in order to prevail).[37]

36. 'Es giebt eine griechische, eine römische Geschichte, eine Geschichte der christlichen Welt; – die Geschichte der Menschheit, die Geschichte welche den Gedanken der Menschheit erzeugt und die Stiftung einer menschlichen Gesellschaft sich zur Aufgabe gesetzt hat, beginnt erst mit dem achtzehnten Jahrhundert unserer Zeitrechnung.' Bauer, *Geschichte*, vol.1, p.ix.

37. 'Das achtzehnte Jahrhundert hat den Versuch gemacht, den neuen Gedanken auf dem Boden und innerhalb der Schranken der hergebrachten Ueberlieferungen und Vorstellungen zur Anerkennung zu bringen – ein Versuch, der nothwendig scheitern mußte und dessen Ausgang da, wo ein reiner Wille und eine bisher der Menschheit fremd gewesene Begeistrung das Experiment leitete, tragisch, wo ein altes Vorrecht mit der bessern Ueberzeugung sich heuchlerisch abzufinden suchte, widerlich, und wo das neue Prinzip um sich durchzusetzen [...] den Blödsinn und die Selbstsucht des Alten überlisten mußte, ein erfolgloser Theatercoup war.' Bauer, *Geschichte*, vol.1, p.ix.

Here, the very same history is unfolded into three interpretations. The history of Enlightenment failed, and its failure is at times tragic, at times repugnant, at times a coup de théâtre, a farce. Enlightenment, if you will, thus suggests a true human history and denies it at the same time – a tension that remains instructive for ambitious interpretations of the Enlightenment, which must all balance the promise of the Enlightenment and its reality. Bauer's construction of the Enlightenment displays this tension in a most extreme way, and even the fact that he does not end upon one interpretation of failure but gives three underlines the disparity between the Enlightenment's promise and its actual result.

Other tensions, ambiguities and contradictions marking Bauer's narrative are probably less specific for the eighteenth century than for the *Vormärz* period. Most prominent among these is a certain shaping of the question of Enlightenment, religion and politics that one could describe as the political theological predicament of the Enlightenment. By modelling critique in general on the critique of religion, but at the same time directing this critique beyond religion proper to the critique of bourgeois culture and of the state, Bauer not only imagines a critique that is universal and omnipotent, but, consciously or not, claims a transcendent authority for the critique for the critic, namely for himself. Thereby, the theological-political constellation of the *Vormärz* brings about the idea that philosophy falls into different more or less orthodox and heretical schools which are judged the more truthful the more radical they are. This move fosters the eschatological and gnostic habitus that Bauer acts out so radically, and informs an understanding of the 'power of truth' which can then be projected back into the Enlightenment of the eighteenth century.

Understanding, radicalising and illuminating the Enlightenment: Hegel's use of *Lumières* and *Aufklärung* for an enlightened philosophy

Francesca Iannelli

Università Roma Tre

Hegel in Stuttgart: a young, convinced enlightener

Let us begin with an assessment, namely that the German term *Aufklärung* is a neologism[1] that German philosophers coined at the end of the eighteenth century to translate a philosophical-political programme that they received through the political struggles of France, and that Germany tended to conceptualise, understand and overcome. In the essay 'Über die Frage: was heisst aufklären?', published in September 1784 in the *Berlinische Monatsschrift*, Moses Mendelssohn discussed it as a circumscribed and technical term scarcely naturalised in the German language,[2] which Kant, in his article 'Beantwortung der Frage: was ist Aufklärung?' – published in December of the same year in the same journal and destined to become famous – would help to define. At the time of the publication of Kant's essay, Hegel (1770-1831) was only fourteen years old and was passing through an extremely delicate and

---

1. While Horst Stuke, 'Aufklärung', in *Geschichtliche Grundbegriffe: historisches Lexikon zur politisch-sozialen Sprache*, ed. Otto Brunner, Werner Conze and Reinhart Koselleck, vol.1 (Stuttgart, 1972), p.243-342 (247), insists on the status of a neologism, but believes that the history of the term begins even before 1700, Pascal David, 'Lumière', in *Vocabulaire européen des philosophies: dictionnaire des intraduisibles*, ed. Barbara Cassin (Paris, 2004), p.742-46, circumscribes this introduction to the second half of the eighteenth century.
2. Mendelssohn considered the terms 'Aufklärung', 'Kultur' and 'Bildung' as 'neue Ankömmlinge'. Moses Mendelssohn, 'Über die Frage: was heißt aufklären?', *Berlinische Monatsschrift* 4 (1784), p.193-200 (193).

mournful period of his life following the sudden death of his mother Maria Magdalena Louisa Fromm due to a typhus epidemic.[3] Against this dark existential background, from the summer of 1785 Hegel took refuge in the *Bildung*[4] that his mother had disclosed to him,[5] in the purchase of books[6] and in the readings conducted in the ducal library.[7]

For the first time at the Gymnasium illustre in Stuttgart, Hegel familiarised himself with Enlightenment readings,[8] an influence from which he would never completely free himself.[9] Alongside the classics of Greek and Latin literature, he focused on the German *Aufklärungsphilosophie*: in 1785 he read *Phädon oder über die Unsterblichkeit der Seele, in drey Gesprächen* by Moses Mendelssohn,[10] while the 'Exzerpte' of the three-year period 1785-1788 testify to

3. On the emotional trauma due to the death of his mother, see Terry Pinkard, *Hegel: a biography* (Cambridge, 2000), p.3.
4. On the compensatory and consolatory value of education, Hegel expressed himself in a passage of his *Tagebuch* in memory of the late beloved teacher Loeffler. Georg Wilhelm Friedrich Hegel, *Frühe Schriften I*, ed. Nicolin Friedhelm and Gisela Schüler, in *Gesammelte Werke* (henceforth *GW*), vol.1 (Hamburg, 1989), p.8. More generally, on the immense value attributed by Hegel to *Bildung*, see Georg Wilhelm Friedrich Hegel, *Grundlinien der Philosophie des Rechts*, ed. Klaus Grotsch and Elisabeth Weisser-Lohmann, in *GW*, vol.14.1 (Hamburg, 2009), p.164. For a better contextualisation, see my 'Die Kunst der ästhetischen Bildung bei Hegel', in *Objektiver und absoluter Geist nach Hegel*, ed. Thomas Oehl and Arthur Kok (Leiden, 2018), p.481-503, and the critical literature indicated there.
5. Klaus Vieweg, *Hegel: der Philosoph der Freiheit* (Munich, 2019), p.37.
6. Vieweg, *Hegel*, p. 41.
7. Hegel, *Frühe Schriften I*, p.9. See also Pinkard, *Hegel*, p.5. The first volume the young Hegel reads in the ducal library is a text destined to become a classic of Enlightenment aesthetics, namely the *Einleitung in die Schönen Wissenschaften: nach dem Französischen des Herrn Batteux, mit Zusätzen vermehret von Karl Wilhelm Ramler* (in the 1770 edition).
8. From 1784 to 1788 Hegel attended the *Obergymnasium*. This phase represents a period of intellectual initiation, the 'Eintritt in die intellektuelle Welt'. Vieweg, *Hegel*, p.41.
9. See José Maria Ripalda, 'Aufklärung beim frühen Hegel', in *Der Weg zum System: Materialien zum jungen Hegel*, ed. Christoph Jamme and Helmut Schneider (Frankfurt am Main, 1990), p.112-29 (126-27).
10. Hegel, *Frühe Schriften I*, p.10.

his close reading of Sulzer,[11] Nicolai,[12] Feder,[13] Garve,[14] Campe[15] and Eberhard.[16]

As attested in Karl Rosenkranz's famous biography, Hegel also approached the Scottish Enlightenment by reading, among others, Adam Ferguson.[17] This is particularly the case with Garve's translation of *An Essay on the history of civil society* (1767), which was published in Germany in 1768 under the title *Versuch über die Geschichte der bürgerlichen Gesellschaft*.[18] This youthful study would have a lasting influence on Hegel both for its condemnation of despotism and for its insights into the inescapability of the economic-political dimension within society. In addition to that of Adam Smith, the influence of Ferguson will also be evident in the *Grundlinien der Philosophie des Rechts* (1820). Another fundamental reading will be that of Lessing's *Nathan*, whose

11. See Georg Wilhelm Friedrich Hegel, *Frühe Exzerpte*, ed. Friedhelm Nicolin, in *GW*, vol.3 (Hamburg, 1991), p.115. Excerpts from: Johann Georg Sulzer, *Kurzer Begriff aller Wissenschaften* [...]: *zweyte ganz veränderte und sehr vermehrte Auflage* (Leipzig, bey Johann Christian Langenheim, 1759).

12. See Hegel, *Frühe Exzerpte*, p.177-79. Hegel makes excerpts from the fourth (1784) and fifth (1785) volumes of Friedrich Nicolai's *Beschreibung einer Reise durch Deutschland und die Schweiz, im Jahre 1781: nebst Bemerkungen über Gelehrsamkeit, Industrie, Religion und Sitten*, 12 vols (Berlin and Stettin, Friedrich Nicolai, 1783-1796).

13. See Hegel, *Frühe Exzerpte*, p.6-73. Hegel makes a very long excerpt from the work of Johann Georg Heinrich Feder, *Der neue Emil oder von der Erziehung nach bewährten Grundsätzen*, 2 vols (Erlangen, Walther, 1768-1775).

14. See Hegel, *Frühe Exzerpte*, p.126-62. An extensive excerpt is made by Hegel from 14 to 18 March 1787 from the work of Christian Garve, 'Versuch über die Prüfung der Fähigkeiten', *Neue Bibliothek der schönen Wissenschaften und der freyen Künste* 8:1 (1769), p.1-44. The reading of Garve's works also influenced the writing of the texts 'Ueber einige charakteristische Unterschiede der alten Dichter' (1787) and 'Über einige Vortheile, welche uns die Lektüre der alten klassischen Griechischen und Römischen Schriftsteller gewährt' (1788).

15. See Hegel, *Frühe Exzerpte*, p.100-107. In October 1786 he made an excerpt from Joachim Heinrich Campe's *Kleine Seelenlehre für Kinder* of 1784.

16. See Hegel, *Frühe Exzerpte*, p.175-76. This is an undated excerpt from pages 23-25 of Johann August Eberhard, 'Vermuthungen über den Ursprung der heutigen Magie: ein historischer Versuch', *Berlinische Monatsschrift* 10 (1787), p.6-33.

17. See Karl Rosenkranz, *Georg Wilhelm Friedrich Hegel's Leben* (Berlin, 1844); Pinkard, *Hegel*, p.12; Vieweg, *Hegel*, p.46.

18. On Garve's influence as a translator and disseminator of the Scottish Enlightenment in Germany, see Norbert Waszek, 'The Scottish Enlightenment in Germany, and its translator Christian Garve (1742-1798)', in *Scotland in Europe*, ed. Tom Hubbard and R. D. S. Jack (Amsterdam and New York, 2006), p.55-71.

powerful message of religious tolerance will resonate particularly in the writings of Bern. As Terry Pinkard notes:

> Hegel's diary entries, his excerpts, and the essays of his school days in Stuttgart display a keen young mind that is throwing around a lot of thoughts without coming down to anything like a settled position on things. He reveals himself as 'for' the Enlightenment in the sense of an unbiased, critical approach to things; he is 'for' religion, especially a religion that actually claims the hearts of people and can make equal claim to being 'enlightened'; he is 'against' dry abstract reason and 'mere' book learning [...]; he is 'for' progress; and, like any good young Rousseauian, he is 'for' learning from 'experience', from 'life', from 'activity'. He seems to have fully absorbed the emerging German ideal of *Bildung* [...] which people such as the revered Moses Mendelssohn had identified with Enlightenment itself.[19]

Thanks to his friendship with the theologian and philosopher Jacob Friedrich Abel, professor at the Karlsschule in Stuttgart, Hegel indirectly approached Scottish Common-Sense Philosophy and Kantian Criticism, and then detached himself from Abel's overtly metaphysical teachings[20] and immersed himself in the reading of Rousseau and Schiller, who, thanks to their philosophical battles for freedom, became in his young eyes *Haupthelden*.

Relevant in this context is that this young gymnasium student, in his own manner, faced the most ambitious questions in the philosophy of the time, as evidenced by the fragment of 22 March 1786, in which Hegel himself intended to give an answer to the fateful question: what is the Enlightenment?

> All people want to make themselves happy. With a few rare exceptions, there are those who, in order to make others happy, possessed so much sublimity of soul as to sacrifice themselves. But these individuals, I believe, did not sacrifice true happiness, but only temporal advantages, temporal luck, even life.
>
> So these individuals make no exception here. But first I must define the concept of happiness; so that I understand it as a concept to be put down on paper here, I have to first specify what I understand by Enlightenment. I am talking here only about Enlightenment through science and the arts. It is thus limited only to the state of the learned. For to make a draft of an Enlightenment of the common

---

19. Pinkard, *Hegel*, p.15-16.
20. Vieweg, *Hegel*, p.50.

human being I consider partly very difficult for most of even the most learned people, but partly also much more difficult especially for me, since I have not yet studied history philosophically and thoroughly at all. Otherwise, I also believe that this Enlightenment of the common human being has always been directed according to the religion of his time, and it extends in general only to the Enlightenment by craftsmen and convenience of life. So I speak here [according to my intention] only of the sciences and arts. With regard to these, I am of the opinion that they first flourished in the Orient and the South and then migrated from there more and more to the West. Although nowadays, at least with regard to philosophy, the great fame of the erudition of the Egyptians is rightly diminished, so much remains certain, since at least with regard to the mechanical and fine arts, they had reached such a degree of perfection that even now the ruins of their works of art are admired, and it is very likely that the great and extensive practical knowledge has already been brought into a more precise theory.[21]

21. Hegel, *Frühe Schriften I*, p.29-30: 'Alle Menschen haben die Absicht sich glüklich zu machen. Von einigen seltenen Ausnahmen [abgesehen], die um andre glüklich zu machen so viel Erhabenheit der Sele besassen, sich aufzuopfern. Doch diese haben, glaub' ich nicht wahre Glükseeligkeit aufgeopfert, sondern nur zeitliche Vortheile, zeitliches Glük, auch Leben. Diese machen also hier keine Ausnahme. Doch zuerst muss ich den Begriff von Glükseeligkeit festsezen, ich verstehe naemlich darunter einen hier zu Papier bringe, muß ich vorher vorausschiken, was ich unter Aufklärung verstehe. Ich rede naemlich also hier nur von der Aufklärung durch Wissenschaften und Künste. Sie schränkt [sich] also blos auf den Stand der Gelehrten ein. Denn einen Entwurf von einer Aufklärung des gemeinen Mannes zu machen halte ich teils für die meisten auch gelehrtesten Leuten für sehr schwer, teils aber auch besonders für mich noch viel schwerer, da ich überhaupt die Geschichte noch nicht philosophisch und gründlich studiert habe. Sonst glaube ich auch, diese Aufklärung des gemeinen Mannes habe sich immer nach der Religion seiner Zeit gerichtet, und sie erstreke sich überhaupt nur auf die Aufklärung durch Handwerker und Bequemlichkeit des Lebens. Ich spreche hier also meiner Absicht [gemäß] blos von den Wissenschaften und Künsten. In Ansehung dieser bin ich also der Meinung sie haben zuerst im Orient und Süden geblüht und seyen dann von da aus immer mehr nach Westen gewandert. Sosehr man nun heutzutag wenigstens in Ansehung der Philosophie das Grosse Rühmen von der Gelehr-samkeit der Ägypter mit Recht vermindert, so bleibt doch so viel gewiß, da sie es wenigstens in Ansehung der Mechanischen und bildenden Künsten zu einem solchen Grad der Vollkommenheit gebracht haben, da noch jezt die Trümmer ihrer Kunstwerke bewundert werden, und es ist sehr wahrscheinlich, da die grosse und weitläufige praktische Kenntnisse auch schon in eine genauere Theorie gebracht worden seyen.' All translations in this article are my own unless otherwise indicated.

This is an incomplete text that nevertheless finds an adolescent Hegel engaged in an ambitious attempt, which is quite extensive and articulate, to define Enlightenment. On the one hand, Hegel distinguished between an Enlightenment of the intellectuals and the cultured – which takes place through art and science and which concerns every epoch,[22] so much so that here Hegel even referred to ancient Egypt – and an Enlightenment of the common human being, which is limited to the professions and the comforts of life, and which the young student does not believe he has the hermeneutical and historical-philosophical tools to adequately deal with. On the other hand, in a previous diary entry dating back to 11 March 1786, in harmony with the essays of Kant and Mendelssohn published in the *Berlinische Monatsschrift*, the young Hegel reflected ironically on his epoch, which should be indicative par excellence of an *aufgeklärte Zeit*, especially with respect to Antiquity, but which instead seemed not to be so because of widespread superstition: 'It often occurs to me, reflecting on our enlightened times, to think of the insults of superstition and illusion that we have addressed to the various errors of the pagans and, in general, to the manners and opinions established since antiquity by all ancient human beings.'[23]

In this sense, in the late eighteenth century the extraordinary *Zeitalter der Aufklärung* was not yet fully an *aufgeklärtes Zeitalter*. With Kant, Hegel thus seemed to view the Enlightenment as a challenge for humanity, as a long-term project whereby each epoch would have the degree of Enlightenment (or lack thereof) that it has earned; thus, one could rightly express this ambivalent term in the plural sense of *Aufklärungen* that runs through Hegel's thought: that of the elites and that of the masses, the historical and the retrospective, the one to come and the one that will never happen, but also above all the German and the French, the English and the Scottish.[24]

---

22. This retrospective use of the term continues to the present day, for example in relation to the Middle Ages. See Marcel Bubert, 'Aufklärerisches Denken im Mittelalter? Alteuropäische Anläufe zu Differenzierung, Vernunftkult und Religionskritik', in *Bildung als Aufklärung: historisch-anthropologische Perspektiven*, ed. Anne Conrad, Alexander Maier and Christoph Nebgen (Vienna, 2020), p.159-74.

23. Hegel, *Frühe Schriften I*, p.28: 'Saepe mihi de collustratis nostris temporibus cogitanti incurrit et in animum, saepe a nobis convicia et illusiones jaci in varios errores pagano rum et omnino in omnium priscorum mores et vetustate firmatas opinions.'

24. On Hegel's awareness of the different national profiles of the Enlightenment

The young Hegel was therefore trained in Stuttgart in the midst of Enlightenment, so that his biographer Karl Rosenkranz could later write in his successful *Hegel's Leben* of 1844 that the philosopher was imbued with it. Pinkard masterfully summarised the situation at the conclusion of his studies at the gymnasium in this way:

> Hegel had firmly allied himself with the Enlightenment, at least as he understood it, and the future he ambitiously imagined for himself as a young man had him playing a role in continuing that progress promised by more Enlightenment. The issue of what was genuinely modern and of how to bring the past up to date, make things more enlightened, formed the hazy edges of the future he was beginning to envision for himself.[25]

Hegel from Tübingen to Frankfurt: how to radicalise the Enlightenment?

In the period he spent at the Stift in Tübingen (1788-1793) – which coincided with the heroic years of the French Revolution – Hegel continued, with his friends Schelling and Hölderlin, to read Rousseau and clandestine French pamphlets, as well as the German periodical *Minerva*. He was also part of a political circle[26] and stood out as one of the prominent figures among the young sympathisers of the French Revolution in Württemberg.[27] In the following years, he would even go so far as to play the clandestine role of letter courier (*Briefkurier*), smuggling letters to support communication among Württemberg's revolutionaries, and to actively share such ideals with his sister Christiane Louise.[28]

Towards the end of his Tübingen years, in the summer of 1793, during a period of convalescence spent at his home in Stuttgart, Hegel concluded the so-called *Tübinger Fragment*,[29] an essay that he never published, but which represents an early attempt to draft a critical

---

and his hostility against the German Enlightenment, see Norbert Waszek, *The Scottish Enlightenment and Hegel's account of civil society* (Boston, MA, and London, 1988), p.19.

25. Pinkard, *Hegel*, p.17.
26. Vieweg, *Hegel*, p.67-68.
27. Vieweg, *Hegel*, p.73.
28. Alexandra Birkert, *Hegels Schwester: auf den Spuren einer ungewöhnlichen Frau um 1800* (Ostfildern, 2008), p.111-14; Vieweg, *Hegel*, p.72.
29. Hegel, *Frühe Schriften I*, p.83-114.

paper in the style of the French *philosophes*, in which he attacked the
'Enlightenment of the intellect' ('Aufklärung des Verstandes') – a
(pseudo-)enlightened attitude that can make one more circumspect
('klüger'), but not better,[30] because it is so abstract as to be ineffective.
Against this polemical backdrop, he targeted the critique of purely
abstract and (pseudo-)enlightenment religion, seeing instead in
subjective religion a means of overcoming fragmentation.

Hegel's aim was 'to make Enlightenment common' ('die Aufklärung
allgemein zu machen').[31] In order to do this, he intended to revisit the
Enlightenment ideal of reason in relation to Kantian moral doctrine,
considering the authentic Enlightenment as the affirmation of reason
in a collective and social sphere that thus allows for the overcoming
of the split between the learned few and the popular masses.[32] He
therefore asked: How can rational morality become public moral
religion? Hegel, that is, continued to reflect on the Enlightenment of
the common human being that in Stuttgart he believed he did not
yet have the resources to deal with and that he now approached with
more sophisticated Kantian speculative tools. What Hegel deplored
was 'printed' and bookish morality (e.g. of Campe's *Theophron*),[33]
that is, the rhetoric of Enlightenment that creates separations and
divisions without affecting real life. Hegel proposed the example
of the inexperienced young man, who – in such bookish times ('in
unseren vollgeschriebenen Zeiten')[34] – seeks enlightenment in the
written world without finding it, remaining inhibited and inadequate.
He noted:

> Joyfulness is a main trait in the character of a well-disposed young
> man; if circumstances prevent him from doing so, since he must turn
> more to himself, and he almost makes up his mind to form himself
> into a virtuous man, and has not yet enough experience in doing so,
> since books cannot make him so – he may take Campe's *Theophron*
> into his hands –in order to make these teachings of wisdom and
> prudence the guiding principle of his life – he reads a passage from

---

30. Hegel, *Frühe Schriften I*, p.94.
31. Christoph Jamme, '"Jedes Lieblose ist Gewalt": der junge Hegel, Hölderlin
    und die Dialektik der Aufklärung', in *Der Weg zum System*, ed. C. Jamme and
    H. Schneider, p.130-70 (141).
32. Italo Testa, *Hegel critico e scettico: Illuminismo, repubblicanesimo e antinomia alle
    origini della dialettica* (Padua, 2002), p.56-58.
33. Hegel, *Frühe Schriften I*, p.94.
34. Hegel, *Frühe Schriften I*, p.98.

it in the morning and in the evening, and thinks about it all day long – what will be the result? Real perfection, perhaps? This requires years of practice and experience – but the meditations on Campe and the Kampian ruler will be too much for him in eight days! He goes into society gloomy and anxious, where only those are welcome who know how to cheer themselves up, shyly he enjoys a pleasure that only tastes good to those who are there with a happy heart – imbued with the feeling of his imperfection, he resents everyone – contact with women does not cheer him up, because he fears – a slight touch of some maiden might pour a kindling fire through his veins – and this gives him a clumsy, stiff appearance – but he will not endure it long, but soon shakes off the supervision of this sullen *Hofmeister*, and will be in a better state.[35]

True Enlightenment should also have, according to the young Hegel, a tangible social impact on interpersonal and emotional relationships; that is, it should be 'praktische Weisheit',[36] namely practical wisdom.

A few years later,[37] in Frankfurt, Hegel, Schelling and Hölderlin[38] would articulate the programme of an aesthetic revolution

---

35. Hegel, *Frühe Schriften I*, p.97-98: 'Frohseyn ist in dem Charakter eines gutgearteten Jünglings ein Hauptzug; verhindern ihn Umstände daran, da er sich auf sich selbst mehr zurükziehen mus, und er fast den Entschlus sich zu einem tugendhaften Menschen zu bilden, und hat dabei noch nicht Erfahrung genug, da Bücher ihn nicht dazu machen kennen – so nimmt er vielleicht Campe's *Theophron* in die Hände – um sich diese Lehren der Weisheit und Klugheit zur Richtschnur seines Lebens zu machen – er liest morgens und abends einen Abschnitt daraus, und denkt den ganzen Tag daran – was wird die Folge seyn? Etwa wirkliche Vervollkommnung? zu dieser gehört jahrelange Übung und Erfahrung – aber die Meditationen über Campe und das Kampische Lineal warden ihm in 8 Tagen entleiden! Düstern und ängstlich geht er in die Gesellschaft, wo nur derjenige willkommen ist, der sie aufzuheitern weis, schüchtern geniest er ein Vergnügen, das nur dem schmekt, der mit frohem Herzen dabei ist – vom Gefühl seiner Unvollkommenheit durchdrungen bükt er sich gegen jedermann – Umgang mit Fraunzimmen heitert ihn nicht auf, weil er da fürchtet – eine leise Berührung irgendeines Mähdchens möchte ein entzündendes Feuer durch seine Adern giessen – und diß gibt ihm ein linkisches, steifes Ansehen – er wird es aber nicht lange aushalten, sondern schüttelt bald die Aufsicht dieses mürrischen Hofmeisters ab, und wird sich besser dabei befinden.'
36. Hegel, *Frühe Schriften I*, p.97.
37. There are several possible dates for the manuscript. Here we follow the date proposed by Otto Pöggeler, 'Hegel, der Verfasser des ältesten Systempro-gramms des deutschen Idealismus', *Hegel-Studien* 4 (1969), p.17-32.
38. The authorship of the text has been much debated. Here, too, we follow the Hegelian attribution claimed by Pöggeler, 'Hegel'.

enshrined in the manifesto known as *Das älteste Systemprogramm des deutschen Idealismus*, according to the title of Franz Rosenzweig who found the manuscript and published it in 1917. Beyond the attribution of the text, the intention of the three young friends was to continue the programme of the Enlightenment and to strengthen its regenerative force through an aestheticisation of reason that would benefit both *Aufgeklärte* and *Unaufgeklärte*, that is, those who had lived up to the Enlightenment ideals – as the three former *Stiftler* themselves had done – as well as the popular masses. It would be essential to make the ideas aesthetic in order to capture the people and to offer a sensitive terrain for the speculations of philosophers so that they would not get lost, like the Enlightenment itself, in abstractions. Therefore, it was not intended to limit the renewal advocated by the Enlightenment, but rather the question was how to make the Enlightenment practical and effective, how to give art a political relevance such as to impact concretely and pervasively on society.[39]

It should come as no surprise that the first writing Hegel published in 1798 was a translation from the French *Lettres de Jean-Jacques Cart a Bernard Demuralt, trésorier du pays de Vaud, sur le droit public de ce pays, et sur les événemens actuels* by Jean-Jacques Cart, a Girondin text whose translation had been initiated in Switzerland and printed anonymously by Hegel in Frankfurt as *Vertrauliche Briefe über das vormalige staatsrechtliche Verhältnis des Waadtlandes (Pays de Vaud) zur Stadt Bern*.[40] This political pamphlet on the French Revolution, which appeared at the time of those events, is of particular interest. First, it should be made clear that the young Hegel's political interest in Cart's *Lettres* was prompted by a 'pilgrimage trip' dating back to 1795 to Geneva, Rousseau's hometown, where the young philosopher visited former *Stiftler* Christoph August Klett. Little attention has been paid by the *Hegel-Forschung* to the fact that Hegel's first publication, although anonymous for security reasons, is precisely a translation from French, the language he had been taught by his beloved and cultivated mother at an early age, and that this translation concerns

39. In the *Systemprogramm*, therefore, a continuation of the Enlightenment project is outlined, so that philosophy becomes practical through an ethical-aesthetic synergy. On this synergy, see Annemarie Gethmann-Siefert, 'Arte e religione: un effetto sinergetico nella questione "Illuminismo"', in *Arte, religione e politica in Hegel*, ed. Francesca Iannelli (Pisa, 2013), p.59-68.
40. Georg Wilhelm Friedrich Hegel, *Frühe Schriften II*, ed. Walter Jaeschke, in *GW*, vol.2 (Hamburg, 2014), p.387-581.

a pamphlet of Girondin orientation. Together with the reading of Ferguson, begun in Stuttgart, and Georg Forster, dating back to Bern,[41] this pamphlet undoubtedly contributes to defining the importance of the political-economic dimension in society.[42] This constellation, if better investigated and contextualised, could lead to original research perspectives, confirming that famous position of Ritter[43] for which Hegelian philosophy is, par excellence, a philosophy of revolution, but also opening up the possibility of viewing Hegel's philosophy as a 'translative' (in a broad sense) and productive dialectical practice, as has been highlighted in recent years.[44]

In this regard, the translation of the *Vertrauliche Briefe* could be taken as symbolic of the Hegelian Critical Enlightenment since the 'translator Hegel' does not conform to the translational ideal of the 'domestication' of the *Lumières* (whereby the translator must please the reader-recipient),[45] nor of 'estrangement' in the German sense (which will be realised shortly thereafter by Schleiermacher and later by Heyne), but pursues his own personal approach to translation[46] that will lead him to Jena, even speculatively beyond the *Aufklärung*, albeit in a perpetual recognition of that dawn of freedom that was the French Revolution, of which he never denied the need. In this sense, the testimony of Victor Cousin (1792-1867) can be valuable; he met Hegel in 1817 and befriended the philosopher to contribute significantly to the spread of Hegelian philosophy in France once he became the most influential French intellectual of the time. In the essay *Fragments et souvenirs*, we find a precious personal memory:

M. Hegel aimait la France, il aimait la révolution de 1789, et, pour

41. Hegel, *Frühe Exzerpte*, p.217-18.
42. Vieweg, *Hegel*, p.178.
43. Joachim Ritter, *Hegel und die Französische Revolution* (Cologne and Opladen, 1957), p.40.
44. See e.g. Elena Nardelli and Saša Hrnjez, 'Is it possible to speak about a Hegelian theory of translation? On Hegel's *Übersetzungsbegriff* and some paradigmatic practices of translation', *Verifiche* 49:1-2 (2020), p.v-xxvii.
45. See François Thomas, 'Introduire le sauvage allemand dans le beau monde parisien: l'enjeu éthique et politique de la traduction dans le débat entre les Lumières et le romantisme allemand', in *La Traduction: philosophie et traduction – interpréter/traduire*, ed. Christian Berner and Tatiana Milliaressi (Villeneuve d'Asc, 2011), p.148-62 (150).
46. On this, see Francesca Iannelli and Alain P. Olivier, 'En traduisant Hegel – traducendo Hegel: aesthetic theory and/in translation practice', *Studi di estetica* 1 (2022), p.157-98.

me servir d'une expression de l'empereur Napoléon, que M. Hegel
me rappelait souvent, lui aussi il était Bleu. Il était à la fois très libéral
et très monarchique, et ces deux sentiments sont aussi au plus haut
degré et dans mon cœur et dans ma raison. Il connaissait parfaitement
l'histoire de la révolution française, qui m'était familière, et nous
en parlions perpétuellement. J'étais charmé de trouver dans un
homme de son âge et de son mérite mes sentiments les plus intimes;
et lui, déjà vieux, semblait comme réchauffer son âme au feu de la
mienne. Et puis M. Hegel était un esprit d'une liberté sans bornes. Il
soumettait à ses spéculations toutes choses, les religions aussi bien
que les gouvernements, les arts, les lettres, les sciences; et il plaçait
au-dessus de toute la philosophie. Il me laissa voir pour ainsi dire
le fantôme d'idées grandes et vastes; il me présenta, dans le langage
un peu scholastique qui lui était propre, une masse de propositions
générales plus hardies et plus étranges les unes que les autres, et qui
firent sur moi l'effet des ténèbres visibles du Dante. Tout ne m'y était
pas entièrement inintelligible, et ce que j'en saisissais me donnait
un ardent désir d'en connaître davantage. Il y avait du moins entre
Hegel et moi quelque chose de commun, une foi commune dans la
philosophie, une commune conviction qu'il y a ou qu'il peut y avoir
pour l'esprit humain une science vraiment digne de ce nom qui
n'atteint pas seulement l'apparence, mais la réalité des choses, qui
n'exprime pas seulement les rêves mobiles de l'imagination humaine,
mais les caractères intrinsèques des êtres.[47]

The young Hegel, like the more mature Hegel, was and remained
therefore a philosopher of revolution, given that French political
events would continue to interest him until the end of his life.[48]
He participated indeed in the July Revolution of 1830, though
not without fear for the risk of the reappearance of terror in new
forms.[49] Similarly, Hegel, while aware that some Enlightenment ideas,
motifs and tendencies could not be shared, proposed to enhance and
intensify the Enlightenment project. As Brauer has argued, Hegel
never rejected or disavowed the Enlightenment *as such* ('Aufklärung
als solche'),[50] so much so that some of the political and legal concepts
in his philosophy of right are indebted to the Enlightenment, but

47. Victor Cousin, *Fragments et souvenirs*, 3rd edn (Paris, 1857), p.79-80.
48. See Norbert Waszek, '1789, 1830 und kein Ende: Hegel und die Französische
     Revolution', in *Französische Revolution und Pädagogik der Moderne*, ed. Ulrich
     Herrmann and Jürgen Oelkers (Weinheim and Basel, 1989), p.347-59.
49. Vieweg, *Hegel*, p.669.
50. Oscar Daniel Brauer, 'Hegels Aufklärung der Aufklärung', in *Hegels Phänome-
     nologie des Geistes: ein kooperativer Kommentar zu einem Schlüsselwerk der Moderne*,

Hegel certainly does not share the epistemic assumptions of the Enlightenment as is evident in Jena, and more implicitly already in the above-mentioned *Tübinger Fragment* of 1793.

Hegel from Jena to Berlin: how to enlighten the Enlightenment?

The youthful immersion in Enlightenment culture that had seen the young Hegel express enthusiasm for the French Revolution would gradually see him critically confronted with a political-cultural programme in which he would identify deep contradictions and lacunae. In this sense, Hegel is positioned on a line of interpretation that comes down to our time. In fact, one of the many recent criticisms that has been levelled at the Enlightenment concerns primarily its incompleteness and fragility.[51] Hegel's criticism, as we shall see, is no less radical.

In Jena, Hegel became increasingly aware that *Lumières* and *Aufklärung* were not overlapping movements, and that the most influential German intellectuals of the eighteenth century – from Lessing to Kant – were heirs of the *Lumières* and not of the German *Aufklärung* with which they had always been in contact, albeit with a critical distance.[52] In this sense, as has been noted,[53] in many pre-phenomenological Jenaean essays, Hegel refers to the works of French philosophers, such as d'Holbach,[54] Voltaire[55] or Montesquieu,[56]

---

ed. Klaus Vieweg and Wolfgang Welsch (Frankfurt am Main, 2008), p.474-88 (486).

51. Jürgen Habermas, *Die Moderne – ein unvollendetes Projekt: philosophisch-politische Aufsätze 1977-1990* (Leipzig, 1990), p.41-42.

52. In this regard, consider the 'Spinoza controversy' (*Spinozastreit*), which found Moses Mendelssohn and Jacobi in opposition, and which involved Kant after the death of Mendelssohn in 1786 with the essay 'Was heißt: sich im Denken orientieren?', attacking both Mendelssohn's dogmatic Enlightenment rationalism and Jacobi's fideism. See Immanuel Kant, 'What is orientation in thinking?', in *Critique of practical reason and other writings in moral philosophy*, ed. and translated by White Beck Lewis (Chicago, IL, 1949), p.295-305.

53. See Jamila Mascat, *Hegel a Jena: la critica dell'astrazione* (Lecce, 2011), p.113-29.

54. Georg Wilhelm Friedrich Hegel, *Jenaer kritische Schriften*, ed. Otto Pöggeler and Hartmund Buchner, in *GW*, vol.4 (Hamburg, 1968), p.80. On Hegel and d'Holbach, particularly on the *Système de la nature*, see Jean-Claude Bourdin, *Hegel et les matérialistes français du XVIIIe siècle* (Paris, 1992), p.144-71.

55. Hegel, *Jenaer kritische Schriften*, p.405.

56. Hegel, *Jenaer kritische Schriften*, p.481.

to highlight the limitations of contemporary German dogmatic philosophy. In §15 of the Jenaean wastebook, he differentiates well between the 'genuine common sense' ('echte gesunde Menschenverstand') of the French – exemplified by Voltaire or Helvétius,[57] who expressed himself through 'experience, reasoning, wit' ('Erfahrung, Raisonnement, Witz')[58] – and the supposed 'healthy common sense' ('gesunder Menschenverstand') of the Germans.[59] While in Berlin, Hegel distinguished the German *Aufklärer*, including, for example, Tetens, Eberhard or Friedrich Nicolai, all of whom he considered boring, uncertain and ambiguous,[60] from the far more vital and original French *Lumières*, to whom the critical-sceptical intellectual attitude and *Weltweisheit* should be attributed.[61]

Hegel's best-known criticism of the Enlightenment is, however, in the *Phänomenologie des Geistes* (1807), in which he treasured the Enlightenment position and brought it to completion by contextualising it within the same phenomenological 'voyage of discovery' (*Entdeckungsreise*): so that the real exit from the state of minority, which Kant spoke of in his famous essay of 1784,[62] is due to the 'absolute knowledge' ('absolutes Wissen'), understood as a post-revolutionary historical-speculative achievement of the philosophy of German Idealism.[63]

57. On Hegel and Helvétius, see Bourdin, *Hegel et les matérialistes français*, p.171-84.
58. As Bourdin, *Hegel et les matérialistes français*, p.44-45, notes, it is significant that in this aphorism Hegel uses the French term *raisonnement*, instead of the German *Räsonnement* – which is instead linked to the German *Aufklärung* in the so-called *Tübinger Fragment* (Hegel, *Frühe Schriften I*, p.97) – or the German *räsonnieren*, criticised in the *Vorrede* to the *Phenomenology* (Georg Wilhelm Friedrich Hegel, *Phänomenologie des Geistes*, ed. Wolfgang Bonsiepen and Reinhard Heede, in *GW*, vol.9, Hamburg, 1980, p.41).
59. Georg Wilhelm Friedrich, *Jenaer Schriften, 1801-1807*, ed. Eva Moldenhauer and Karl Markus Michel, in *Werke in zwanzig Bänden: auf der Grundlage der Werke von 1832-1845 neu edierte Ausgabe*, vol.2 (Frankfurt am Main, 1970), p.543-44.
60. Georg Wilhelm Friedrich Hegel, *Vorlesungen über die Geschichte der Philosophie III*, ed. Eva Moldenhauer and Karl Markus Michel, in *Werke in zwanzig Bänden*, vol.20 (Frankfurt am Main, 1971), p.308-10.
61. For a more adequate contextualisation, I refer to Mascat, *Hegel a Jena*, p.129-33.
62. 'Enlightenment is man's emergence from his self-incurred immaturity.' Immanuel Kant, 'An answer to the question: what is Enlightenment?', in *Kant's political writings*, ed. Hans S. Reiss, translated by Hugh Barr Nisbet (Cambridge, 1970), p.54-60 (54).
63. On this point, we fully agree with Francesco Valentini, 'Hegel critico dell'Illuminismo', in *Individuo e modernità: saggi sulla filosofia di Hegel*, ed. Marcella D'Abbiero and Paolo Vinci (Milan, 1995), p.63-74.

More specifically, in section B, 'Der sich entfremdete Geist; die Bildung', of the sixth chapter of the *Phänomenologie*, Hegel addressed the opposition between faith and Enlightenment, interpreting it as the result of the process that led from the actual consciousness of the world of wealth (*Reichthum*) to pure consciousness, which has in itself the moment of identity and that of difference, but is not aware of it because it belongs to the world of the alienated spirit and, therefore, splits them into faith (*Glauben*) and pure insight (*reine Einsicht*). As Hinchman noted: 'He is not satisfied simply to show that faith and Enlightenment share some points in common. More ambitiously, he wishes to argue that they are two aspects of a selfsame, transindividual spirit, different yet also identical.'[64]

Faith is not understood here as irrational faith; it is justified by thinking and conceived in opposition to the insight of knowing. However, for Hegel, this world of faith is nothing but an escape from the real world which, therefore, ends up reproducing its structures. This faith is opposed precisely to pure insight, which will show its fatuity of reflection that touches the object, but which does not come to understand it. Thus, what destroys is not faith, but superstition – that is, what was already destroyed in itself. The opposition between faith and pure insight has, therefore, its root in the fact that neither understands its one-sidedness and, therefore, the other. In a very powerful and evocative passage, Hegel makes a lucid and merciless diagnosis: 'The Enlightenment itself [...] is no more enlightened about itself.'[65]

The apparent winner is also the Enlightenment movement, which nevertheless splits into materialism (by d'Holbach) and deism (by Robinet and Voltaire). Pure matter and pure thinking are, however, both pure abstractions. Enlightenment culture therefore arrives and is fulfilled in utility (*das Nützliche*), which in turn passes into the absolute freedom of the general will of Rousseau's memory. The latter, however, needs a particular will in order to be realised, which it can only accept as a betrayal of its universality; hence its 'fury of disappearing' ('Furie des Verschwindens'),[66] which seeks to eliminate the particular that it

---

64. Lewis P. Hinchman, *Hegel's critique of the Enlightenment* (Gainesville, FL, 1984), p.126.
65. Georg Wilhelm Friedrich Hegel, *The Phenomenology of spirit*, translated by Terry Pinkard (Cambridge, 2018), p.328; Hegel, *Phänomenologie*, p.306: 'Die Aufklärung selbst aber [...] ist eben so wenig über sich selbst aufgeklärt.'
66. Hegel, *Phenomenology*, p.343; Hegel, *Phänomenologie*, p.319.

itself has posited. We have thus arrived at the Self of Kant's critical philosophy, as pure and self-conscious knowledge, but we still must experience the forgiveness of evil and symmetrical recognition in order to arrive at the absolute spirit and then at absolute knowledge. As a first essential contribution to the completion of the Enlightenment, in Jena, Hegel therefore traced his own philosophy, which contributes to 'enlighten' the Enlightenment, through the steps of the phenomenological ascensional path culminating in a transparent and 'conceptual knowledge' ('das begreiffende Wissen').[67] It would then be through other emancipatory instances – such as the notion of *Bildung* and *Anerkennung* – present in his thought, especially in his Berlin period (1818-1831), that Hegel would contribute to illuminating the shadows of the Enlightenment, as we will see in more detail in the final section of this article.

The *Phenomenology*, however, is only one step in Hegel's lifelong effort to come to terms with the legacy of the Enlightenment, with its achievements and its degeneration. That 'conscious influence' of the Enlightenment, which can be traced in Hegel's youth, would turn with time into a more hidden 'subterranean current'[68] with its dangers and ghosts that Hegel was not afraid to confront. This is especially evident in the *Grundlinien*. In the introduction,[69] Hegel thematised the negative and empty freedom, abstracted from all content, which characterised the dictatorship at the time of the French Revolution, and which marked radical and fanatical political-religious phenomena that easily cross the border into terrorism. Thus –in both the religious and the political spheres – genuine tyrannies are generated in which *Polyreligiosität* and *Polykulturalität* are annihilated and in which the destructive fury ('Furie des Zerstörens')[70] of every *Besonderung* and *Besonderheiten* reappears, which Hegel identifies exemplarily, first of all, in the Jacobin dictatorship.[71]

---

67. Hegel, *Phenomenology*, p.460; Hegel, *Phänomenologie*, p.427.
68. Waszek, *The Scottish Enlightenment*, p.17.
69. Hegel, *Grundlinien*, §5, p.32-33.
70. Hegel, *Grundlinien*, p.33.
71. On the intertwining of logical figures and practical-philosophical topics, see Erzsébet Rózsa, 'Besonderheit und Selbstbestimmung: einführende Gedanken in Hegels Grundlegung seiner Theorie der modernen Freiheit in der *Einleitung* zur *Rechtsphilosophie* von 1820', in *Hegel's logic and politics: problems, legacies, and perspectives*, ed. Gregor Schäfer (Lanham, MD, in press).

How enlightened is Hegel's philosophy?

The question now arises: if Hegel intended to enlighten the Enlightenment, how enlightened is his own philosophy to undertake this ambitious task? In order to answer this question, it is sufficient to recall that on the occasion of the 250th anniversary of the philosopher's birth in 2020, which coincided with one of the darkest and most troubled periods in recent history, numerous assessments were carried out on the relevance of Hegelian thought and on the presence, more or less underground, of Hegelian figures and paradigms that are still pertinent in our time.[72] Obviously, these assessments imply an evaluation of the greater or lesser degree of 'Enlightenment' of Hegel's philosophy as a progressive philosophy, and must reckon with a series of legends, accusations and stereotypes that are not possible to consider here in detail, and which see Hegel from time to time labelled as the representative of a reactionary, capitalist, racist and chauvinist philosophy,[73] about which everything and its opposite has been said.

In this section, therefore, we will instead assess the 'Enlightenment' of Hegelian philosophy from a particular observational point, that of the feminine, in order to reflect more generally on the emancipatory potential of Hegelian thought, not only as the last great philosophical system, but also as an expression of 'practical wisdom'. The young Hegel, moreover, already identified the Enlightenment's inability to have a concrete impact on interpersonal relations as a serious deficiency. One of the greatest weaknesses of the Enlightenment project undoubtedly relates to its lack of inclusiveness, if not outright discrimination, in a project claiming freedom and liberation from the chains of ignorance, but which seems to be insensitive to gender differences. Certainly, women were not excluded from Enlightenment discourse, some were true Maecenas, such as Marie-Thérèse Geoffrin (1699-1777), but their theoretical contribution was mainly circumscribed to specific educational issues or confined, mostly, to the roles of translator and educator.[74]

---

72. See e.g. Francesca Iannelli, 'Die Omnipräsenz von Hegels Philosophie und insbesondere seiner Ästhetik: ein Kabinett hegelianischer Kuriositäten', in *Das Beste von Hegel*, ed. Klaus Vieweg (Berlin, 2023), p.307-26.
73. See e.g. Waszek, '1789, 1830 und kein Ende'; M. A. R. Habib, *Hegel and the foundations of literary theory* (Cambridge, 2019); Klaus Vieweg, 'Warum Hegel kein Rassist war', *Die Welt* (24 December 2020), p.28.
74. See *Frauen in der Aufklärung: '... ihr werten Frauenzimmer, auf!'*, ed. Iris

Against this complex backdrop lies Hegel's relationship with the female universe, which –both in his private existence and in his philosophy – is highly complex and articulate. Indeed, it should be noted that Hegel's private life was constantly marked by the presence of educated women who were sensitive to *Bildung*, from his mother to his sister and his wife. To his mother Maria, Hegel owed his passion for *Bildung*; with his sister Christiane Louise (1773-1832), he shared the early stages of education; and he was united by a passion for art and beauty to his wife, Marie. The three stars that illuminate the private constellation of the Hegelian feminine are certainly all unusual figures for their times. His mother, Maria Magdalena Louisa Fromm, was in fact 'an educated woman' ('eine Frau von Bildung'), as Christiane Louise stated in a letter dated 1 January 1832 and addressed to Marie, Hegel's widow, a few weeks after the sudden death of her brother.[75] Maria Magdalena Louisa died prematurely of typhus in 1783 at the age of forty-two, when Wilhelm, who had fallen ill with the same infectious disease, was only thirteen years old and at risk of death. Up to that point, she had been the young man's most important orientation person (*Orientierungsperson*), and throughout his life Hegel would remain devoted to the figure of his mother, such an uncommon woman, as she was his first teacher of Latin and French.[76] As the daughter of a lawyer, it was in the family context that Hegel's mother received an atypical education for her time. However, she was indebted in this not to her natural mother, whom she lost at an early age, but to her stepmother Charlotte Wilhelmine von Hermersdorf.[77] The maternal figure, therefore, represented for Hegel the first guardian of *Bildung*, which every woman will embody according to her talents and possibilities before entrusting her children to the school, the place where a secular transfiguration of the individual takes place in rising to the universality of knowledge.[78] In full harmony with this formative trust in the maternal figure, it is not surprising that it would

Bubenik-Bauer and Ute Schalz-Laurenze (Frankfurt am Main, 1995); Anne Conrad, 'Aufklärung(en), Bildung, Religion – und Gender?', in *Bildung als Aufklärung*, ed. A. Conrad *et al.*, p.379-402; *Gelehrte Frauen der Frühaufklärung: einsame 'Wunderthiere' oder vernetzte Akteurinnen?*, ed. Corinna Dziudzia and Sonja Klimek (Berlin, 2022).

75. *Hegel in Berichten seiner Zeitgenossen*, ed. Friedhelm Nicolin (Hamburg, 1970), p.563.
76. Vieweg, *Hegel*, p.37.
77. See Birkert, *Hegels Schwester*, p.32.
78. Georg Wilhelm Friedrich Hegel, *Vorlesungen über die Philosophie des subjektiven*

be another woman, one of Hegel's first followers in America, Susan E. Blow (1843-1916), who a few decades later would draw inspiration from Hegel's reflections that education begins at home, and combine them with the theories of the German pedagogue Friedrich Wilhelm August Fröbel (1782-1852), Pestalozzi's pupil and kindergarten pioneer in Germany. Hegel's sister, Christiane Louise, was also an educated woman, fluent in Latin and French, who in her youth sympathised with revolutionary ideas and had contact with many renowned personalities of her time, including those intellectuals who struggled for women's education (*Frauenbildung*) in Stuttgart.[79] Christiane dedicated a significant part of her life to *Bildung*, becoming in turn an educator for the Berlichingen family (1801-1814), before being struck by psychotic crises from the mid-1810s onwards, which presumably led her brother to pay particular attention to the main medical theories of the time, from Pinel's positions to the theses of mesmerism, developing a particular interest in the theme of madness and of the unconscious,[80] which would later be widely explored and thematised in the *Vorlesungen über die Philosophie des subjektiven Geistes* and in the additions to the *Encyclopaedia*.[81]

The relationship with Marie Helena Susanne von Tucher (1791-1855), whom the philosopher married on 16 September 1811 in Nuremberg, is worthy of mention and further analysis, given that Hegel shared with his wife an interest in art, especially in painting and music, and that his wife actively participated in the cultural life of the time; for example, she attended Alexander von Humboldt's Berlin lectures.[82] Marie von Tucher, moreover, would not only gradually replace the dedication of his sister Christiane Louise in Hegel's life, but also lead Hegel to reconsider the figure of Antigone as a heroic

---

Geistes I: Nachschriften zu den Kollegien der Jahre 1822 und 1825, ed. Christoph Johannes Bauer, in *GW*, vol.25.1 (Hamburg, 2008), p.39.

79. See Birkert, *Hegels Schwester*, p.126.
80. See Stefania Achella, 'The dark side of thought: the body, the unconscious and madness in Hegel's philosophy', in *The Owl's flight: Hegel's legacy to contemporary philosophy*, ed. Stefania Achella *et al.* (Berlin, 2021), p.23-36; Giulia Battistoni, 'Implications of mental derangement in moral and juridical context starting from Hegel', in *Philosophy and madness from Kant to Hegel and beyond*, ed. Francesca Iannelli and Mariannina Failla (Milan, in press).
81. The additions are published in Georg Wilhelm Friedrich Hegel, 'Sekundäre Überlieferungen', in *GW*, vol.25.2, ed. Christoph Johannes Bauer (Hamburg, 2011), p.919-1117; see e.g. the addition to §408, p.1045-54.
82. *Hegel: the letters*, translated by Clark Butler and Christiane Seiler (Bloomington, IN, 1984), p.666.

female model, by virtue of a more equal and exchangeable sentimental relationship and a realistic vision of marriage.[83] Unlike Kant, who in the *Metaphysik* had expressed a crude view of marriage,[84] the Berlin Hegel was well aware, also and above all from personal experience, that marriage is an institution as basic as it is frail, marked by the incessant need for adaptation.[85]

To this private constellation is added the public constellation of the Hegelian feminine, which is equally varied and suggestive.[86] Suffice it to recall that Hegel knew (in some cases personally) several prominent female figures, such as Mme de Staël (1766-1817), Karoline von Günderrode (1780-1806), Bettina von Arnim (1785-1859) and Caroline Michaelis-Schlegel-Schelling (1763-1809), to name but a few of the most exceptional women of his time. In addition, as we shall see in more detail, he admired and followed with great interest the artistic activities of renowned singers and artists of the time. He was friendly with brilliant translators such as Meta Dorothea Forkel-Liebeskind, a cultured woman who translated Volney's *Ruines* in 1792 and represented the so-called *Universitätsmamsellen*, a group of five young women who were daughters of academics at the University of Göttingen, together with Philippine Engelhard, Caroline Michaelis-Schlegel-Schelling, Therese Huber and Dorothea Schlözer. In addition, it should not be forgotten that Hegel particularly appreciated the literature of Theodor Gottlieb Hippel, the author of the 1792 essay *Über die bürgerliche Verbesserung der Weiber* in support of women's emancipation.[87]

83. Erzsébet Rózsa, 'Von Antigone zur anständigen Frau: Hegels Frauenbild im Spannungsfeld zwischen der Phänomenologie des Geistes und der Rechtsphilosophie von 1820', in *The Owl's flight*, ed. S. Achella *et al.*, p.259-76.

84. On the embarrassing conception of the role of women and marriage in Kant's political philosophy and anthropology, see Norbert Waszek, 'Zwischen Vertrag und Leidenschaft – Hegels Lehre von der Ehe und die Gegenspieler: Kant und die Frühromantiker (Schlegel, Schleiermacher)', in *Gesellschaftliche Freiheit und vertragliche Bindung in Rechtsgeschichte und Philosophie*, ed. Jean-François Kervégan and Heinz Mohnhaupt (Frankfurt am Main, 1999), p.271-99.

85. Georg Wilhelm Friedrich Hegel, *Grundlinien der Philosophie des Rechts: Beilagen*, ed. Klaus Grotsch and Elisabeth Weisser-Lohmann, in *GW*, vol.14.2 (Hamburg, 2010), p.737.

86. For a better contextualisation, see Francesca Iannelli, 'Hegel's constellation of the feminine between philosophy and life: a tribute to Dieter Henrich's *Konstellationsforschung*', in *The Owl's flight*, ed. S. Achella *et al.*, p.239-55.

87. Rachel Falkenstern, 'On the uses and abuses of doing feminist philosophy with Hegel', *Verifiche* 2 (2021), p.111-32.

In this context, important acknowledgements by Hegel of the talent of famous European women of his time, expressed during the Berlin course on the philosophy of art in 1820-1821,[88] cannot be neglected, where Hegel mentioned the contralto Gentile Borgondio (1780-1830), who trained at the school of Andrea Costa, and the world-famous soprano Angelica Catalani (1780-1849). What is remarkable is that Heinrich Gustav Hotho, auditor of the *Vorlesungen* and then editor of the *Ästhetik* (1835-1838; 1842) after the master's sudden death in 1831, did not take these female figures into account for his posthumous edition – which has been the reference text of the most important translations of Hegel's *Aesthetics* worldwide in the nineteenth, twentieth and in some cases still twenty-first century – thereby contributing to the reputation of a 'sexist' Hegel. What is more, Hotho's edition does not mention any living woman whatsoever.

Furthermore, the great compensatory value of art and music in Berlin during the reign of Frederick of Prussia (1797-1840) should be acknowledged. On the one hand, as influential public figures, the presence or absence of these women in European capitals, salons and international festivals exerted an obvious form of political 'soft power'; on the other hand, Hegel's admiration for the great female performers of Rossini's music, with its impotent, cynical and comic figures, which was highly discredited in Germany at the time, represents an alternative proposal for an anti-romantic and innovative *Bildung*.

In reconstructing the artistic constellation of the Hegelian feminine, further social and intellectual interactions with talented and progressive women of his time cannot be disregarded, including first and foremost with the novelist Caroline Paulus,[89] the soprano Henriette Sontag, the Swabian actress Friederike Robert and the pianist Fanny Mendelssohn, sister of Felix, who attended Hegel's last lecture on aesthetics in Berlin in 1828-1829. Last, we must mention another artist for whom Hegel nurtured immense admiration: the legendary Pauline Anna Milder-Hauptmann, acclaimed throughout Europe, whom even Hegel applauded with great enthusiasm in Berlin in the role of Antigone and whom he frequented in the salons of Berlin. A pupil of Salieri, she worked with Haydn, and Beethoven

---

88. Georg Wilhelm Friedrich Hegel, *Vorlesungen über die Philosophie der Kunst I: Nachschriften zu den Kollegien der Jahre 1820/21 und 1823*, ed. Niklas Hebig, in *GW*, vol.28.1 (Hamburg, 2015), p.181 and 163.

89. See Habib, *Hegel and the foundations of literary theory*, p.292-94; Vieweg, *Hegel*, p.320.

composed the role of Leonore for her in *Fidelio*, as Napoleon tried in vain to convince her to join him in Paris.

The question then arises whether there is any synergy between life (private and public) and speculation. At first it would seem not, since Hegel was a child of his time, in which most women, except for a few exceptional cases,[90] were mostly restricted to the domestic sphere. In his own philosophical reflection, however, one gradually notices an openness that – from Jena to Berlin – led Hegel to go beyond the limits of his time and to reject those preconceptions about female frivolity that still applied to Kant. While Hegel certainly does not stand out as an 'enlightened' defender and spokesman for female emancipation, for him, despite the recurring plant metaphor,[91] women are legal subjects like men, and marriage must be based on love and the free decision of both subjects,[92] even to the extent of admitting divorce, should the differences between the spouses reach the limit of total *Entfremdung*.[93] The Nuremberg letters to his fiancée and future wife Marie hint at this equality in diversity and in many respects also at the emotional superiority of women, beyond the traditional gender roles that Hegel nonetheless accepted.[94]

It would therefore be short-sighted to continue to view Hegel as the patriarchal philosopher of phallologocentrism or as the 'unenlightened' persecutor of the feminine, worthy of being spat upon in the spirit of Carla Lonzi's *Sputiamo su Hegel* (1970). In fact, in recent years there has been no lack of significant reevaluations of the Hegelian heritage, starting from a central notion such as *Anerkennung*, both for feminist thought and for a broader reflection on love, family and marriage,[95]

90. Seyla Benhabib, 'Hegel, die Frauen und die Ironie', in *Denken der Geschlechterdifferenz*, ed. Herta Nagl-Docekal and Herlinde Pauer-Studer (Vienna, 1990), p.19-36 (32-36).

91. Hegel, *Grundlinien der Philosophie des Rechts: Beilagen*, p.747; Georg Wilhelm Friedrich Hegel, *Grundlinien der Philosophie des Rechts: Anhang*, ed. Klaus Grotsch and Elisabeth Weisser-Lohmann, in *GW*, vol.14.3 (Hamburg, 2011), p.1012-13.

92. See Hegel, *Grundlinien*, §162, p.145.

93. See Erzsébet Rózsa, 'Liebe und Freiheit bei Hegel', in *Morale, etica, religione tra filosofia classica tedesca e pensiero contemporaneo*, ed. Luca Illetterati *et al.* (Padua, 2020), p.365-77; Vieweg, *Hegel*, p.501-503, 766.

94. See Joanna Hodge, 'Women and the Hegelian state', in *Women in Western political philosophy*, ed. Ellen Kennedy and Susan Mendus (New York, 1987), p.127-58.

95. See e.g. Klaus Vieweg, *Das Denken der Freiheit* (Munich, 2012); Paul Kottman, *Love as human freedom* (Stanford, CA, 2017).

and much remains to be done to adequately assess the Enlightenment of Hegelian philosophy, even in other areas.

Therefore, it will be valuable to evaluate whether Hegel's Idealism can be the matrix for a counter-narrative that can recognise and enhance the role of the above-mentioned women and artists and go in search of the most innovative aesthetic-philosophical resonances advanced at the time in order to assess their potential application in the contemporary world. Hegel, as the philosopher of *Bildung*, freedom and recognition, is still reckoned today as an important theorist for the rights of all diversities, as Hegelian philosophy continues to enhance precisely that *Besonderheit* which the fury of destruction erased. Hegel practised, privately and publicly, the recognition of the value of the feminine while speculatively laying the foundations for a plural recognition of all diversity and otherness. As Alison Stone puts it, 'without Hegel we couldn't even formulate the notion of a politics of recognition. Indeed, based on Hegel's account it can be argued that cultural recognition is just as vital as economic justice.'[96]

Therefore, if on the one hand it is true that Hegel understood philosophy as its own time apprehended in thoughts ('so ist auch die Philosophie, ihre Zeit in Gedanken erfaßt'),[97] and that it would be inconsistent to ask it for a prophetic and visionary capacity, on the other hand, the greatness of the 'enlightened' Hegelian philosophy resides in its constant global and encyclopaedic view and in its ability to identify and define the speculative pillars of the contemporary – *Bildung*, freedom, recognition – and lay the foundations, albeit often in embryonic form, for imagining the future[98] and other *aufgeklärte Zeiten*. Hegel's philosophy, then, however complex and at times difficult to decipher, always remains a *Weltweisheit* that can help us to orient ourselves in our own time, itself not fully enlightened, in search of new enlightening hermeneutical principles.

96. Alison Stone in Nancy Bauer *et al.*, 'Debating Hegel's legacy for contemporary feminist politics', in *Hegel's philosophy and feminist thought: beyond Antigone?*, ed. Kimberly Hutchings and Tuija Pulkinnen (New York, 2010), p.233-52 (234).
97. Hegel, *Grundlinien*, p.15.
98. See e.g. Slavoj Žižek, *Hegel in a wired brain* (London and New York, 2020); Alexander Schubert, *Phänomenologie des Zeitgeistes: mit Hegel durchs 21. Jahrhundert* (Vienna, 2022).

Les Lumières à l'épreuve des concours: le cas du prix d'éloquence à l'Académie française (1831-1904)

STÉPHANE ZÉKIAN

CNRS / Lyon 2

Il y a près de cinquante ans, Roger Fayolle appelait à 'examiner de près les différents visages qu'a pu prendre le "Siècle des Lumières", depuis bientôt deux siècles qu'on l'interroge et qu'on le sollicite selon les variations de l'idéologie'.[1] Joignant le geste à la parole, il montrait l'exemple en retraçant l'histoire mouvementée d'un concours académique organisé sous le Premier Empire (*Le Tableau littéraire de la France au XVIIIe siècle*). Je me propose de reprendre ici le questionnement préconisé par Fayolle, en demeurant sur le même terrain que le sien, celui des concours académiques du dix-neuvième siècle. Au-delà du choix des étiquettes et des catégories historiographiques, je voudrais déterminer quelle vision des Lumières l'Académie française entend promouvoir et diffuser à travers les récompenses qu'elle distribue tout au long du siècle. Pour ce faire, je m'attarderai sur son concours à la fois le plus ancien et le plus commenté à l'époque, à savoir son prix d'éloquence.

Depuis une réforme menée dans les années 1750, les programmes du concours d'éloquence étaient des monographies individuelles, le plus souvent libellées sous la forme d'un 'éloge des grands hommes' (ou, quand le sujet semblait trop sulfureux, d'un simple 'discours' sur les grands hommes). Eloge ou discours, c'est un auteur du passé qui, dans tous les cas, se trouvait mis à l'honneur. D'un sujet à l'autre, au rythme d'une session en moyenne tous les deux ans, c'est donc une sorte de panthéon immatériel que l'Académie édifie par le truchement

---

1. Roger Fayolle, 'Le XVIIIe siècle jugé par le XIXe: à propos d'un concours académique sous le premier Empire', dans *Approches des Lumières: mélanges offerts à Jean Fabre* (Paris, 1974), p.181-96 (196).

de ce concours. Quelle place le dix-huitième siècle occupe-t-il dans ce panthéon? Entre la monarchie de Juillet et la fin du Second Empire, sont successivement honorés Malesherbes (1831), Voltaire (1844), Turgot (1846), Bernardin de Saint-Pierre (1852), Vauvenargues (1856) et Jean-Jacques Rousseau (1868). Au début de la Troisième République, la cadence augmente avec trois sessions sur Buffon, Marivaux et Beaumarchais entre 1878 et 1886. Autour de 1900, André Chénier et surtout Fontenelle ont à leur tour les honneurs du programme académique.

Ces concours, dans leur écrasante majorité, sont tombés dans l'oubli. Même la mémoire universitaire ne s'y est guère attardée. Tout se passe comme si la mémoire académique des Lumières avait été épuisée par le fameux *Tableau littéraire de la France au XVIII* siècle* auquel non seulement Roger Fayolle mais Roland Mortier, Heinz Thoma et Jean-Claude Bonnet ont consacré des analyses détaillées. Il est vrai que ce concours fit date, à la fois comme premier bilan d'envergure et comme plaidoyer en faveur des Lumières: dans un contexte de réaction doctrinale, l'Académie, où siégeaient encore des figures comme Naigeon, Suard, Morellet, Garat, Volney, Marie-Joseph Chénier et Parny, s'efforçait en effet de compenser l'abondante littérature dénigrant l'héritage intellectuel et politique du dix-huitième siècle. En dépit d'un impressionnant écho médiatique, les résultats officiels ne furent pas à la hauteur des attentes. Après plus de cinq années de controverses, la longue séquence du *Tableau* fut en effet tranchée 'par lassitude plutôt que par enthousiasme'.[2] Elle s'acheva 'dans la grisaille',[3] par le couronnement de deux manuscrits finalement assez convenus, et qui s'effacèrent bientôt de toutes les mémoires, contrairement à la contribution de Barante, non couronnée dans l'immédiat, mais promise à une longue postérité.[4]

Une telle issue peut expliquer la désaffection dont firent l'objet les sessions ultérieures du concours. Car ce précoce effort de synthèse sur le dix-huitième siècle n'engendra, en définitive, que de la frustration. Un demi-siècle plus tard, en plein Second Empire, Eugène Despois,

---

2. Roland Mortier, *Le 'Tableau littéraire de la France au XVIII* siècle': un épisode de la 'guerre philosophique' à l'Académie française sous l'Empire, 1804-1810* (Bruxelles, 1972), p.85.

3. Mortier, *Le 'Tableau littéraire de la France au XVIII* siècle'*, p.87.

4. Jean-Noël Pascal, 'Les débuts du procès des Lumières: Barante et son *De la littérature française pendant le XVIII* siècle* (1809)', *Orages: littérature et culture 1760-1830* 2 (2003), p.177-90.

historien de la littérature aux convictions républicaines, ne s'en souvient que pour brocarder ce qu'il nomme l''admiration peureuse' de l'Académie pour le dix-huitième siècle:

> En 1806 [*sic*], l'Institut se hasardait même à mettre au concours un *tableau du dix-huitième siècle*; mais il avait grand soin de spécifier qu'il ne demandait qu'un ouvrage de critique littéraire, invitant ainsi à admirer la forme nouvelle qu'avait pu revêtir la pensée humaine, sans permettre d'examiner cette pensée même et ses progrès. Cette admiration peureuse ressemblait à un désaveu: autant valait se taire; mais l'Institut, en laissant entrevoir ses véritables sympathies, était déjà sans doute épouvanté de son audace. Les académies ne se sont jamais permis que des témérités de ce genre-là.[5]

Quand il fustige ainsi la frilosité de l'Institut, sa 'façon mesquine d'envisager le dix-huitième siècle',[6] Despois ne vise pas seulement le concours du Premier Empire. Ce qu'il laisse entendre de manière assez transparente, c'est que les hommages officiels offrent *en général* un moyen commode de neutralisation doctrinale. Sous les dehors trompeurs d'une certaine audace, l'Académie désarmerait en réalité ce qu'elle fait mine de célébrer. Et l'interprétation littéraire du dix-huitième siècle serait un vecteur privilégié de cette neutralisation: les académiciens, insiste l'historien, 'traitaient Voltaire et Rousseau comme des gens de lettres; c'était méconnaître la grandeur de leur rôle, c'était surtout dénaturer étrangement la véritable physionomie du dix-huitième siècle, ce siècle où la pensée s'élève à la hauteur de l'action'.[7] Dans quelle mesure ce jugement sans appel s'applique-t-il aux nombreuses sessions qui, jusqu'à la fin du siècle, portèrent sur des figures individuelles du dix-huitième siècle?

Avant d'en venir aux discours des lauréats, l'accent doit être mis sur les contraintes inhérentes à l'éloquence du concours. La première est liée à la tradition du genre épidictique, dans laquelle s'inscrit évidemment le discours de l'éloge, et que le rite académique, s'attirant par là-même des accusations d'anachronisme,[8] prolonge obstinément pendant presque tout le dix-neuvième siècle. Il existe une tension

5. Eugène Despois, *Les Lettres et la liberté* (Paris, 1865), p.170.
6. Despois, *Les Lettres et la liberté*, p.170.
7. Despois, *Les Lettres et la liberté*, p.169.
8. Pour plus de précisons, voir Stéphane Zékian, 'Vie et mort d'un concours: le prix d'éloquence à l'Académie française (XIXᵉ-XXᵉ siècle)', *Recherches & travaux* 99 (2001), http://journals.openedition.org/recherchestravaux/4082 (date de dernière consultation le 20 avril 2023).

entre la fonction traditionnellement assignée au genre épidictique et
le potentiel subversif des auteurs du dix-huitième siècle, quel que soit
par ailleurs le nom attribué au mouvement philosophique de cette
époque. On a de fait longtemps cantonné les discours d'éloge à un
rôle de consolidation morale et idéologique. Les candidats aux lauriers
académiques s'inscrivent dans la tradition d'une éloquence vouée, pour
reprendre la formule de Hans Ulrich Gumbrecht, à 'persuader ceux qui
pensent comme vous'. Parce qu'il 'consolide le savoir antérieurement
acquis de ses auditeurs (sans en changer le contenu), qu'il renforce le
sentiment de groupe (sans entraîner d'actions de ce groupe)',[9] l'éloge
remplit une mission de stabilisation et d'affermissement. Son office
n'est pas d'inquiéter mais de conforter. Sa visée ne serait au fond que
'd'accroître l'intensité d'adhésion aux valeurs communes de l'auditoire
et de l'orateur'.[10] En ce qu'il vise moins 'à un changement dans les
croyances qu'à une augmentation de l'adhésion à ce qui est déjà
admis',[11] l'orateur du genre épidictique, Perelman y insiste, tourne *a
priori* le dos à toute visée révolutionnaire: 'La conception même de ce
genre oratoire [...] le fera pratiquer de préférence par ceux qui, dans
une société, défendent les valeurs traditionnelles, les valeurs admises,
celles qui sont l'objet de l'éducation, *et non les valeurs révolutionnaires, les
valeurs nouvelles qui suscitent des polémiques et des controverses.*'[12] Dans ces
conditions, que reste-t-il de l'héritage inflammable du dix-huitième
siècle une fois coulé dans le moule refroidissant du genre épidictique?

Une seconde contrainte tient au périmètre des sujets inscrits
au programme. Les archives académiques attestent, au cours du
dix-neuvième siècle, plusieurs propositions de réforme visant à
moderniser le concours en promouvant des sujets thématiques ou
historiques. Toutes restèrent lettres mortes. En ne renonçant jamais
à une focale étroitement monographique, l'Académie privilégie le
portrait au lieu du récit; elle invite à camper des personnages, non
à déployer une fresque. L'insertion du dix-huitième siècle dans un
dessein plus vaste n'est donc pas à l'ordre du jour. Considéré en bloc,
l'ensemble des sessions n'offre pas une histoire du dix-huitième siècle
mais, sous formes d'éclats, les éléments disjoints mais cohérents d'un
puzzle doctrinal qu'il n'est pas vain de reconstituer.

---

9. Hans Ulrich Gumbrecht, 'Persuader ceux qui pensent comme vous: les fonctions
    du discours épidictique sur la mort de Marat', *Poétique* 79 (1979), p.363-84 (366).
10. Chaïm Perelman et Lucie Olbrechts-Tyteca, *La Nouvelle Rhétorique: traité de
    l'argumentation*, t.1 (Paris, 1958), p.69.
11. Perelman et Olbrechts-Tyteca, *Nouvelle Rhétorique*, p.72.
12. Perelman et Olbrechts-Tyteca, *Nouvelle Rhétorique*, p.67-68 (je souligne).

Les noms du siècle

Les modes de nomination du siècle offrent un premier indicateur des jugements portés sur le mouvement philosophique et sur le bien-fondé de sa catégorisation sous le seul signe des Lumières. Dans l'ensemble, les discours des lauréats confirment les tendances mises au jour par Diego Venturino dans son étude sur l'émergence de l'expression 'siècle des Lumières' dans l'historiographie postré-volutionnaire.[13] A l'évidence, 'siècle des Lumières' n'est pas, au dix-neuvième siècle, une catégorie opératoire pour désigner positivement l'apport intellectuel et politique du dix-huitième siècle. Auteur d'une volumineuse histoire de la France au dix-huitième siècle souvent rééditée sous la Restauration, l'académicien Charles Lacretelle illustre cette réticence dans son *Testament philosophique* paru en 1840. La tendance commune à n'user du syntagme que de manière ironique, pour ainsi dire oblique, transparaît clairement dans cette exclamation: 'Un règne de la terreur était donc venu terminer le siècle des lumières et couronner l'âge de la philan-thropie!'[14] L'étendard philosophique est repris, mais de manière si dérisoire que son acception en est retournée. Quant aux croyances relatives à la propagation naturelle des connaissances à travers toutes les couches de la société, Lacretelle en pointe le caractère naïvement magique:

> L'imagination semblait avoir fait des *lumières du siècle* un fluide réel et non métaphorique, un fluide d'une élasticité merveilleuse et d'une propagation presque aussi rapide que celle de la lumière du soleil; les intelligences les plus grossières seraient amenées par degrés au niveau des intelligences supérieures, grâce à la logique de Condillac, à un certain catéchisme de morale auquel on travaillait, et à une bonne déclaration des droits de l'homme.[15]

De manière prévisible, cette froideur à l'égard d'un certain optimisme philosophique est de mise quand on recherche l'adoubement de l'Académie. De la session sur Malesherbes en 1831 à celle sur

---

13. Diego Venturino, 'L'historiographie révolutionnaire française et les Lumières, de Paul Buchez à Albert Sorel: suivi d'un appendice sur la genèse de l'expression "siècle des lumières" (XVIIIᵉ-XXᵉ siècles)', dans *Historiographie et usage des Lumières*, éd. Giuseppe Ricuperati (Berlin, 2002), p.21-84. Lacretelle est absent du vaste corpus exploité par Venturino.
14. Charles Lacretelle, *Testament philosophique et littéraire*, t.1 (Paris, 1840), p.360.
15. Lacretelle, *Testament philosophique*, p.326-27 (c'est Lacretelle qui souligne).

Fontenelle en 1904, aucun des lauréats n'identifie spontanément le dix-huitième siècle à un supposé 'siècle des Lumières'.

Plus généralement, on observe un flottement durable quand il s'agit de nommer le dix-huitième siècle qui, de fait, ne reçoit ici aucune appellation stabilisée. A titre d'exemple, le lauréat de 1844 (session sur Voltaire) multiplie les formules, depuis le 'siècle philoso-phique' jusqu'à 'l'âge critique de la France'[16] en passant par 'ce siècle de nouveautés'.[17] Mais de 'siècle des Lumières' proprement dit, aucune trace. Constat similaire en 1846: Turgot vécut dans 'ce siècle de grandeur et de faiblesse, d'analyse et de rêves',[18] c'est-à-dire au cœur d'"un temps qui mêla jusqu'à les confondre le mal au bien et l'erreur à la vérité!'[19] Le dix-huitième siècle fut 'une époque hardie',[20] mais avant tout 'un siècle sceptique'.[21] Devant un jury où dominent les influents ministres de Louis-Philippe que sont François Guizot, Victor Cousin, Abel-François Villemain ou Narcisse-Achille de Salvandy, on conçoit que la prudence ait été de mise. La réticence à parler sans réserve d'un 'siècle des Lumières' n'obéit pourtant pas à des ressorts conjoncturels. A considérer l'ensemble du siècle, on constate que les régimes politiques n'offrent pas un critère pertinent pour apprécier la marge de manœuvre laissée aux concurrents. Ainsi, même l'avènement de la République en 1870 (puis sa consolidation à partir de 1877) n'affecte pas fondamentalement les pratiques lexicales des candidats primés. En 1878, les deux lauréats du concours sur Buffon s'inscrivent dans le droit fil de leurs prédécesseurs: le naturaliste est replacé dans une 'époque d'effervescence universelle',[22] une 'époque aventureuse, où tout est affirmé et nié avec la même assurance'.[23] Les lauréats évoquent tour à tour 'l'esprit des temps nouveaux',[24] 'l'esprit de son siècle',[25] 'l'esprit du XVIIIe siècle'[26] ou

---

16. Charles-Jean Harel, *Discours sur Voltaire, qui a remporté le prix d'éloquence décerné par l'Académie française, dans sa séance publique du jeudi 29 août 1844* (Paris, 1844), p.4.
17. Harel, *Discours sur Voltaire*, p.13.
18. Henri Baudrillart, 'Turgot', *Revue des deux mondes* 15:6 (1846), p.1019-49 (1020).
19. Baudrillart, 'Turgot', p.1021.
20. Baudrillart, 'Turgot', p.1026.
21. Baudrillart, 'Turgot', p.1032.
22. Félix Hémon, *Eloge de Buffon* (Paris, 1878), p.1.
23. Hémon, *Eloge*, p.35.
24. Narcisse Michaut, *Eloge de Buffon, précédé d'une notice par M. Emile Gebhart* (Paris, 1878), p.40.
25. Michaut, *Eloge de Buffon*, p.189.
26. Michaut, *Eloge de Buffon*, p.212.

bien encore 'la philosophie de son temps'.[27] Toujours pas de 'siècle des Lumières' à l'horizon.

La notion de 'lumières' n'est toutefois pas absente du corpus. Toujours sans majuscule, on la trouve dans son acception originaire de 'connaissance en général' (les ouvrages de Voltaire 'ont répandu partout la lumière')[28] comme dans celle, plus récente, de 'diffusion des connaissances'. Ce dernier usage tend à l'emporter, privilégiant donc un sens processuel et dynamique plutôt qu'un acquis. Pour Malesherbes, il est bon que la littérature s'occupe 'd'instruire les hommes, d'*éclairer* leur raison, de les rendre meilleurs ou plus heureux'.[29] C'est bien d'un mouvement qu'il s'agit ici, d'une maturation à l'œuvre bien plus que d'une maturité déjà atteinte. Dans les années 1880, le discours sur Beaumarchais décrit encore la diffusion de 'cette lumière maligne, rude aux yeux des puissances, douce aux yeux des foules, parce qu'elle dévoile les abus et annonce les réformes, parce qu'elle brûle autant qu'elle éclaire, qu'elle échauffe les idées et enflamme les passions'.[30]

La fréquence du mot 'lumières' et de son réseau sémantique ne va pas sans de sévères précautions d'emploi. Au lieu d'une identification spontanée du mouvement philosophique à l'image rayonnante des lumières en marche, on ne voit que doutes et restrictions. Encore en 1904, dans son épais manuscrit sur Fontenelle, le lauréat Auguste Laborde-Milaà fait du mot 'lumières' un emploi qui, tout en en suggérant la banalisation, trahit un vieux reste de réticence: 'Les lumières, *comme on dit*, qui se composent de notions plus exactes sur la nature humaine et sur le système du monde, d'une observation plus attentive et d'une intelligibilité plus complète des phénomènes, c'est-à-dire d'une connaissance plus scientifique de ce perpétuel enchaînement de causes et d'effets qu'est l'univers, – les lumières augmentaient.'[31] Cette incise en début de phrase ('les lumières, comme on dit') relève de ce que les linguistes appellent, par opposition à

---

27. Michaut, *Eloge de Buffon*, p.189.
28. Harel, *Discours sur Voltaire*, p.36.
29. Anaïs Bazin, *Eloge historique de Chrétien-Guillaume Lamoignon de Malesherbes: discours qui a remporté le prix d'éloquence décerné par l'Académie française, dans sa séance du 9 août 1831* (Paris, 1831), p.21(je souligne).
30. Adolphe de Lescure, *Etude sur Beaumarchais: discours qui a obtenu le prix d'éloquence décerné par l'Académie française dans sa séance publique annuelle du 25 novembre 1886* (Paris, 1887), p.10.
31. Manuscrit d'Auguste Laborde-Milaà, 'Fontenelle', Paris, Archives de l'Institut (désormais AI), 2D102, Ms.6, f.47 (je souligne), passage repris avec variantes dans Auguste Laborde-Milaà, *Fontenelle* (Paris, 1905), p.118.

l'emploi en usage, un emploi en mention. Le mot est bel et bien employé, mais sans transparence aucune: il est avant tout mis en relief, exhibé en tant que tel, comme pour en souligner l'étrangeté. La suite aide à saisir les motifs de cette prise de distance: 'c'est que, pour la postérité qui ne regarde jamais les choses qu'en gros et ne s'attache dans le passé qu'aux zones lumineuses, Fontenelle se trouve perdu et comme noyé d'ombre entre deux grandes périodes très éclairées, la grande époque classique et le vrai dix-huitième siècle, qui ne commence guère avant 1750.'[32] La contribution du dix-huitième siècle au progrès et à la diffusion des connaissances (en particulier scientifiques) n'est aucunement niée. Elle est au contraire illustrée et même célébrée. Mais cette œuvre, le lauréat y insiste, ne saurait être versée au crédit d'une période unique. Il faudrait ici reprendre la distinction proposée par Diego Venturino entre '*un* siècle *de* lumière', simple chaînon au sein d'une série, et '*le* siècle *des* lumières' qui opère un coup de force en concédant à une époque particulière le monopole d'un travail en réalité multiséculaire. En somme, le terme 'lumière' est crédité d'une valeur descriptive, mais sa vertu périodisante est encore à prouver.

Au-delà des questions de périodisation, le champ sémantique des lumières soulève une autre difficulté à laquelle se heurtent les lauréats. Il s'agit non plus de l'assignation chronologique des Lumières, mais de leur localisation sociale. En 1846, l'*Eloge de Turgot* témoigne d'une tension dont on prend la mesure en confrontant ces deux passages: 'Au dix-huitième siècle, écrit d'une part Baudrillart, la nation était supérieure à ses chefs pour les mœurs et pour les lumières.'[33] Mais que désigne, au juste, cette nation des lumières dont l'esprit clairvoyant devait inspirer tant de réformes salutaires? A quelles réalités sociales la formule réfère-t-elle vraiment? Quelques pages plus haut, l'auteur avait pris soin d'en restreindre le champ d'application, de manière à désamorcer par avance tout malentendu. Turgot, précisait-il, s'est dressé avec courage 'contre la souveraineté du nombre, cette doctrine matérialiste qui substitue, sous une noble apparence, la puissance matérielle aux lumières et à la justice'.[34] Les lumières, c'est la nation sans le peuple; ce sont les élites urbaines, ce ne saurait être le grand nombre.

---

32. Laborde-Milaà, 'Fontenelle', f.62, passage repris avec variantes dans Laborde-Milaà, *Fontenelle*, p.167.
33. Baudrillart, 'Turgot', p.1038.
34. Baudrillart, 'Turgot', p.1032.

Loin du siècle

Cette prudence dans la caractérisation et la nomination du dix-huitième siècle nous renseigne sur l'enjeu principal des concours. L'objet des joutes académiques, en effet, n'est pas d'honorer en bloc toute une époque qu'il serait loisible d'unifier sous une appellation globale. A travers sa politique des prix, l'institution s'attache plutôt à séparer, à différencier les éléments d'un héritage trop connoté pour ne pas être encombrant. Dans cette perspective, le rôle des grands hommes ne saurait être d'illustrer l'esprit philosophique. De manière significative, les discours récompensés ne débouchent d'ailleurs pas sur un portrait de groupe, ni sur une fresque qui, par définition, aurait la dimension d'une geste collective. L'héroïsation des sujets, quand elle a lieu, ne se déploie ici qu'à l'échelle individuelle. Et ce qui se joue à cette échelle réduite, c'est le plus souvent une action de contrepoids, une œuvre de compensation, un travail de modération venant nuancer voire contre-carrer le mouvement général du dix-huitième siècle. Selon l'historien Julien Vincent,

> Le régime d'historicité libéral qui s'affirme sous la monarchie de Juillet [...] n'accepte les idéaux de la Révolution française que pour les repousser dans un avenir lointain et indéfini. Tout en affirmant vouloir renouer avec l'héritage révolutionnaire, la monarchie de Juillet inaugure un rapport au passé dans lequel la prise en compte des discordances entre divers processus historiques permet de justifier le conservatisme croissant du régime.[35]

Le concours d'éloquence apparaît comme un lieu privilégié de cet inventaire avant liquidation. Autant dire qu'on chercherait en vain, dans ces éloges des grands hommes du dix-huitième siècle, un éloge du dix-huitième siècle lui-même.

C'est une différence majeure avec les concours portant sur le dix-septième siècle: les grands hommes du 'siècle de Louis XIV' passent pour représenter leur temps, ils en sont les produits et cette qualité motive leur inscription au programme. Leur œuvre, parfois même leur existence, y apparaît comme la vitrine lumineuse de leur époque. Les grands hommes du dix-huitième siècle, à l'inverse, sont

---

35. Julien Vincent, '"Maudit soit le talent qui n'a pas la vertu pour compagne": l'abbé Grégoire face à la lâcheté des hommes de lettres (1789-1839)', dans *'La Modernité dure longtemps': penser les discordances des temps avec Christophe Charle*, éd. François Jarrige et Julien Vincent (Paris, 2020), p.19-41 (41).

valorisés pour tout ce qui, en eux, résiste aux emportements, aux engouements collectifs de leur temps. Ce travail de désolidarisation ne va pas jusqu'à une complète dissociation, mais il y a décidément, dans les hommages qui leur sont rendus sous la Coupole, du frottement, de la résistance, de la contradiction entre ces hommes et leur temps. Et c'est dans ces complications, souterraines ou éclatantes, que l'Académie veut trouver la matière d'une leçon à méditer, d'un héritage à endosser.

Cette désolidarisation peut reposer, les *Eloges de Buffon* en offrent un bon exemple, sur des observations d'ordre psychologique. Du naturaliste, on affirme qu'il 'est éloigné des philosophes beaucoup moins par sa doctrine que par son caractère'.[36] Sur une toile de fond agitée, tourmentée même, se détache sa silhouette apaisée autant qu'apaisante. Alors que tout s'emportait autour de lui, 'il a su être calme'.[37] Buffon est volontiers dépeint comme planant au-dessus de la mêlée: 'le bruit des jalousies, des querelles du dehors ne montait pas jusqu'à lui';[38] en un mot, 'il n'a point connu de partis'[39] et ne ressent que 'mépris pour les coteries'. C'est pourquoi il demeure volontiers 'à l'écart'[40] du monde, mot décisif tant cet éloge se déploie de manière systématique sous le signe de l'*écart*. Buffon est bien sûr qualifié de philosophe, mais on s'empresse d'ajouter, comme par crainte d'un rapprochement compromettant, qu'il tint constamment 'à garder son indépendance vis-à-vis des philosophes'.[41] Tout le discours est construit sur ce mouvement de balancier: intégré au courant philoso-phique, Buffon en est aussitôt distingué par une série de traits signant son irréductibilité au groupe des meneurs qui, eux, ne surent pas garder la juste mesure: 'Sans doute il est de son temps; sans doute il serait facile de faire dans ses œuvres, surtout dans sa correspondance, la part des idées modernes. *Mais il n'aime pas le scandale.*'[42] Aux qualités pénétrantes du penseur, il sut ajouter celles d'un citoyen responsable: 'les utopies chimériques ne le tentent pas […] l'amour de l'ordre rendait suspect à Buffon l'esprit de réforme.'[43] Alors que la Troisième République commence à peine à se stabiliser, et tandis

36. Hémon, *Eloge*, p.24.
37. Hémon, *Eloge*, p.1.
38. Hémon, *Eloge*, p.2.
39. Hémon, *Eloge*, p.2.
40. Hémon, *Eloge*, p.23.
41. Hémon, *Eloge*, p.23.
42. Hémon, *Eloge*, p.28 (je souligne).
43. Hémon, *Eloge*, p.31-32.

qu'on commémore en cette année 1878 le centenaire de la mort de Voltaire, l'Académie célèbre en Buffon l'emblème d'une pratique mesurée de la philosophie, à bonne distance du patriarche de Ferney, tapageur et 'trop militant à son gré'.[44] Représentant des Lumières mais sans le bruit, le naturaliste, 'esprit libre, mais non pas indiscipliné',[45] incarnerait la face acceptable du courant philosophique. Au-delà du seul Buffon et quel que soit le régime en place, cet effort de différenciation caractérise la grande majorité des discours couronnés. Plus de vingt ans auparavant, Vauvenargues avait ainsi fait l'objet d'une appréciation en tous points concordante.[46]

Plus que des questions de caractère ou de tempérament, ce sont bien sûr des points de doctrine qui font office de critère discriminant. On devine sans peine la part faite à Rousseau dans cet inventaire critique au long cours. Si ses théories politiques le rendent évidemment irrécupérable, sa défense du sentiment religieux est en revanche mise en avant. Par sa recherche éperdue de solitude, Rousseau remplit mieux que personne la fonction de contraste que le concours assigne aux grands hommes du dix-huitième siècle. Le lauréat de 1868 lui sait gré d'avoir 'oppos[é] une digue à ce torrent de blasphème'[47] qui inondait alors l'espace public. Loin d'être l'indice d'une ténébreuse asocialité, son isolement condamne son siècle. Garde-fou salutaire, sa misanthropie est versée à son crédit parce qu'elle traduit une indépendance d'esprit sans équivalent: 'seul contre tous', Rousseau se montrait 'peu soucieux de plaire aux beaux esprits et aux gens à la mode, il heurtait de front ce qui faisait en son temps l'admiration des hommes'.[48] Pas dupe des succès de coteries ni des effets de mode, il sut mettre à nu les grandeurs factices de son temps. Comme Buffon

---

44. Hémon, *Eloge*, p.25.
45. Hémon, *Eloge*, p.29.
46. Désiré-Louis Gilbert, *Eloge de Vauvenargues qui a remporté le prix d'éloquence décerné par l'Académie française, dans sa séance publique annuelle du 28 août 1856* (Paris, 1856), p.15 (je souligne): 'Comme ces courants d'eau douce qui traversent, dit-on, l'Océan, sans rien prendre de son amertume, Vauvenargues traversera les passions et les luttes contemporaines, *sans y rien laisser de son calme et de sa douceur*. Dès le premier moment, il se *distinguera* par la gravité, par la tenue, dans un monde qui en avait souvent trop peu, et, de même que, dans les camps, parmi ses camarades, il avait conservé *son caractère propre*, il conservera parmi les écrivains d'alors *une place à part* et respectée.'
47. Charles Gidel, *Discours sur Jean Jacques Rousseau: discours qui a obtenu le prix d'éloquence décerné par l'Académie française dans sa séance publique annuelle du jeudi 20 août 1868* (Paris, 1868), p.45.
48. Gidel, *Discours sur Jean Jacques Rousseau*, p.2 et 5.

et Vauvenargues, mais pour d'autres raisons, lui aussi 's'est fait, au dix-huitième siècle, *une place à part*'.[49] En dépit de ses fautes, il aura surtout fait retentir la voix de la nature contre 'la sécheresse de la philosophie'.[50] De manière prévisible, et conformément aux vues de Victor Cousin mort un an avant la fin du concours, le discours primé célèbre la *Profession de foi du vicaire savoyard*, dont le grand mérite fut d''ameuter contre [Rousseau] les matérialistes et les athées'.[51]

Livrant une guerre aux matérialistes du passé comme du présent, l'Académie cherche, au cœur du dix-huitième siècle, les modèles d'un spiritualisme susceptible de montrer la voie. Chez Turgot, on discerne déjà des 'pressentiments spiritualistes'.[52] Cette session de 1846 est la dernière organisée sous le régime de Juillet. Avec l'éclatement de la révolution de Février puis les sanglantes journées de Juin, l'année 1848 diffuse une peur des mouvements insurrectionnels qui rejaillit aussitôt sur la lecture des Lumières. Dans ce contexte marqué par une ressaisie du dix-huitième siècle à des fins préventives, l'interprétation spiritualiste aura de plus en plus le vent en poupe. A l'image de Sainte-Beuve, dont l'attention s'oriente alors vers les Lumières 'pour bien montrer comment les révolutions arrivent, et [vers] les théoriciens du début du dix-neuvième siècle pour faire voir comment on peut les conjurer',[53] l'Académie fête successivement Bernardin de Saint-Pierre et Vauvenargues comme d'élégants avertisseurs d'incendie.

Au premier, le lauréat Prévost-Paradol assigne, comme il se doit, un 'rôle d'opposition contre l'esprit de son siècle'.[54] Tous les signes de dissidence sont ainsi mis en exergue. Introduit dans le salon de Mlle de Lespinasse, Bernardin s'y trouve rapidement en porte-à-faux. Cette société, insiste le lauréat, 'il ne la connut que pour s'en plaindre. Tout devait l'y blesser; on y traitait avec légèreté ce qu'il respectait le plus au monde, l'amour et la religion'.[55] C'est qu'il est

---

49. Gidel, *Discours sur Jean Jacques Rousseau*, p.45 (je souligne).

50. Gidel, *Discours sur Jean Jacques Rousseau*, p.32. Voir déjà Victor Cousin, *Philosophie populaire* (Paris, 1848), p.30.

51. Gidel, *Discours sur Jean Jacques Rousseau*, p.48.

52. Baudrillart, 'Turgot', p.1023. Plus loin, Turgot est encore classé dans 'cette grande école du spiritualisme que l'on retrouve partout où il s'agit de revendiquer les vrais principes de la science et de la société' (p.1032).

53. Roger Fayolle, *Sainte-Beuve et le XVIIIᵉ siècle, ou Comment les révolutions arrivent* (Paris, 1972), p.72.

54. Manuscrit de Lucien Anatole Prévost-Paradol, 'Eloge de Bernardin de Saint-Pierre', AI, 2D38, Ms.2, f.5.

55. Prévost-Paradol, 'Eloge de Bernardin de Saint-Pierre', f.14.

'moins [hostile] envers la religion que tout [son] siècle',[56] et 'l'into-
lérance des philosophes'[57] le blesse. Comme ses voisins de palmarès,
Bernardin incarne une philosophie du dix-huitième siècle acceptable
puisqu'elle intègre sa propre critique. Même après la Révolution
française, sa fonction demeure celle d'un vertueux contrepoids. Sous
le Directoire et le Consulat, en effet, 'sa position était difficile' au sein
de l'Institut. Sur tout sujet, des querelles l'opposaient à ses nouveaux
confrères. Au cœur du conflit entre 'la philosophie du XVIIIe siècle
et le spiritualisme chrétien',[58] Bernardin tint bon sans tomber dans
aucun excès, ne sacrifiant jamais son amour du bien public aux
nécessités du combat. En 1789, il avait d'ailleurs trouvé place 'parmi
les réformateurs sincères dans leur désir du progrès et dans leur
esprit de conciliation'.[59] Personne ne sut comme lui unir 'au désir du
progrès une inaltérable tolérance'.[60] Son vrai titre de gloire réside
dans l'incompréhension hargneuse qu'il éveilla toujours chez les
'esprits étroits et [les] cœurs emportés': 'Les uns ne lui pardonnent
pas encore d'avoir été trop respectueux envers la religion, les autres
de n'avoir pas répudié la raison et insulté la philosophie; les uns
d'avoir attaqué les abus, les autres de les avoir signalés avec une trop
patiente douceur.'[61] On ne parle pas encore de secondes Lumières
ni de Lumières tardives, mais c'est bien de cela qu'il s'agit. Restent
les célèbres bévues scientifiques de cet anti-newtonien notoire que
fut Bernardin. Comment les intégrer dans un éloge oratoire? Le
lauréat ne passe pas sous silence cette 'incompétence en matière
scientifique',[62] mais il en relativise la portée en déplaçant le questionnement. Au lieu de s'aventurer dans le détail des théories fantaisistes
dont regorgent les *Etudes de la nature*, Prévost-Paradol met l'accent sur
le besoin de croyance dont témoigne le succès populaire de l'ouvrage:
'qu'importaient au public [...] les objections des savants? Il ne
cherchait point dans ce livre une science nouvelle mais une nouvelle
croyance, une philosophie plus consolante et plus accessible que celle
du jour, un maître en l'art de croire et d'espérer.'[63] En substituant
l'analyse d'un succès de librairie à l'examen de l'œuvre elle-même,

---

56. Prévost-Paradol, 'Eloge de Bernardin de Saint-Pierre', f.16.
57. Prévost-Paradol, 'Eloge de Bernardin de Saint-Pierre', f.17.
58. Prévost-Paradol, 'Eloge de Bernardin de Saint-Pierre', f.33.
59. Prévost-Paradol, 'Eloge de Bernardin de Saint-Pierre', f.30.
60. Prévost-Paradol, 'Eloge de Bernardin de Saint-Pierre', f.41.
61. Prévost-Paradol, 'Eloge de Bernardin de Saint-Pierre', f.42.
62. Prévost-Paradol, 'Eloge de Bernardin de Saint-Pierre', f.22.
63. Prévost-Paradol, 'Eloge de Bernardin de Saint-Pierre', f.22.

Prévost-Paradol dénonce implicitement les effets pervers d'une philosophie desséchante à force d'analyse.

Honoré en 1856, Vauvenargues permet un pas supplémentaire dans la célébration d'un dix-huitième siècle irréductible aux Lumières. Mort prématurément en 1747 à l'âge de trente et un ans, le moraliste fournit l'occasion d'une réflexion sur ce qu'*aurait pu être* le dix-huitième siècle. Sans pousser l'hypothèse jusqu'à brosser un tableau contre-factuel, le lauréat n'en diffuse pas moins l'idée d'un autre dix-huitième siècle possible si Vauvenargues n'était pas mort si tôt. Au lieu de commémorer ce qui fut, l'éloge tourne à l'évocation, teintée d'amers regrets, de ce qui aurait dû advenir. Vauvenargues, croit-on savoir, n'aurait

> jamais donné dans les excès qui suivirent. Et même, ce triste spectacle de la philosophie qui s'égare aurait bientôt rebuté ce noble esprit, *spiritualiste par essence*, et, sans rien céder des droits de la raison humaine, il se serait réfugié de plus en plus vers ses maîtres et ses modèles, vers Pascal, Bossuet et Fénelon. A coup sûr, *il se serait séparé*, je ne dis pas seulement d'Helvétius et d'Holbach, mais de Voltaire lui-même: il l'aurait retenu, peut-être. On peut le dire, la mort de Vauvenargues fut un véritable malheur pour Voltaire.[64]

Le bon dix-huitième siècle, c'est donc un siècle qui n'a pas eu lieu. On n'en parle qu'à l'irréel du passé, en le centrant sur la fiction d'un Voltaire qui *aurait dû être* à la fois retenu et contenu.

Au service du juste milieu

En inscrivant le passé à l'ordre du jour, l'Académie cherche en priorité les modèles d'une modération susceptible d'étayer une politique du juste milieu. L'idéologie de la monarchie de Juillet, loin de s'éteindre avec le régime, semble avoir déteint sur la mémoire à long terme des Lumières. Elle trace un horizon d'attente rétrospectif qui marquera d'autant plus durablement la physionomie institutionnelle des Lumières que les régimes suivants ne la remettront guère en cause. C'est pourquoi les filtres mémoriels mis en place dans les concours des années 1830-1840 s'avèrent instructifs bien au-delà de cette seule séquence chronologique. Dès 1831, il revient à Malesherbes d'incarner l'harmonieuse fusion de l'esprit philosophique et de la foi chrétienne. Tout le concours sur Malesherbes, soutien déterminant

---

64. Gilbert, *Eloge de Vauvenargues*, p.31 (c'est moi qui souligne).

des philosophes mais condamné à l'échafaud après avoir défendu Louis XVI, tourne autour de cette épineuse conciliation. 'Que la philosophie réclame la première partie de cette vie, la religion se contentera de la dernière', avait écrit Chateaubriand. Pour le lauréat, tout au contraire, il n'y a pas lieu de répartir ainsi le legs de Malesherbes. Homme de transaction, le directeur de la Librairie se sera livré à un impossible exercice d'équilibriste, écartelé 'entre le fanatisme qui s'offensait de sa tolérance et des amours-propres qui n'étaient pas toujours modérés': 'Religion, philosophie, deux principes que les hommes ont fait ennemis, qu'ils inscrivent encore sur des bannières opposées, qu'ils osent accuser de leurs crimes ou de leurs folies, les voilà cette fois en présence, se donnant une main fraternelle, se prêtant l'un à l'autre une touchante assistance!'[65] La gloire de Malesherbes n'est pas éclatante, mais elle est pure. 'Elle ne divise pas les hommes par des ressentiments et des reproches; elle les invite au contraire à s'unir, à s'aimer.' Quelques mois après la révolution de Juillet, ces lignes sonnent comme un programme, une adresse au temps présent. Par son exemple douloureux, Malesherbes incite à s'élever au-dessus de la mêlée des opinions. Son souvenir, veut-on croire, est de nature à 'hâter parmi nous la réconciliation des partis'.[66] A l'autre extrémité du régime, en 1846, l'Académie récompense une interprétation analogue de Turgot, lequel incarne un principe modérateur au point d'offrir l'"image purifiée, image irréprochable'[67] d'un temps impur: dans un siècle d'excès, il se signale même comme le 'héros du bon sens'.[68] La bourgeoisie libérale du dix-neuvième siècle contemple en lui l'emblème d'une audacieuse prudence. Dévoué 'à l'ordre et au progrès, à la monarchie et à la liberté, il tenait au passé par ses mœurs, au siècle par ses idées'.[69] Pour mieux montrer qu'il 'se sépare'[70] du mouvement général, le discours multiplie les oppositions terme à terme ('homme de foi dans un siècle de scepticisme', il suivit 'sa pente encore plus que celle du temps').[71] Turgot rejoint ainsi la cohorte des grands hommes exfiltrés du dix-huitième siècle et célébrés *à part*. Sa grandeur fut de penser à côté de son siècle. Avec son indépendance d'esprit,

---

65. Bazin, *Eloge historique*, p.37.
66. Bazin, *Eloge historique*, p.40.
67. Baudrillart, 'Turgot', p.1021.
68. Baudrillart, 'Turgot', p.1021.
69. Baudrillart, 'Turgot', p.1048.
70. Baudrillart, 'Turgot', p.1033.
71. Baudrillart, 'Turgot', p.1049 et 1034. Idem pour les deux citations suivantes.

sa droiture et son sens de la nuance, 'il porte dans ses vues une impartialité que le siècle ne connaît pas' et qui l'expose à plus d'un danger. Turgot risque en effet 'de passer aux yeux de l'Eglise pour un penseur dangereux, aux yeux des philosophes pour un chrétien timoré'. Or cette figure de l'entre-deux scellant 'l'alliance des temps anciens et des temps nouveaux',[72] n'est-ce pas l'emblème doctrinaire par excellence? Quand il définit Turgot comme une 'figure placée au-dessus de la sphère des passions, et *doucement éclairée* du jour de la science et de la vertu',[73] le lauréat, qu'un commerce épistolaire lie à Victor Cousin depuis des mois, sait fort bien à qui il s'adresse. Son éloge de Lumières douces et tamisées laisse percer un réquisitoire contre des Lumières jugées aveuglantes par excès de véhémence.

Il n'est pas jusqu'à Voltaire qui ne soit mobilisé pour la promotion d'un climat doctrinal tempéré. Certes, admet le lauréat, le philosophe versa plus d'une fois dans de regrettables excès polémiques, mais il y fut contraint par les nécessités du moment. Sur le fond, son héritage ne laisse rien à craindre. Là encore, nous voyons ressurgir l'étendard d'une sage modération sous lequel s'avance le bon dix-huitième siècle de l'Académie. Voltaire joua un 'rôle double et difficile', celui de ces 'chefs de faction qui, après avoir excité des mouvements nécessaires, en combattent les conséquences désastreuses, et que préoccupent à la fois l'animosité de leurs adversaires et l'impatience de leurs partisans'.[74] Toujours ce même mouvement de balancier, dans la recherche d'un milieu réputé juste. Moteur d'une mobilisation de grande ampleur, Voltaire n'en fait pas moins office de garde-fou. Et le lauréat finit par s'incliner devant le 'déisme sincère' de celui qui, 's'il franchit l'irréligion, [...] recula épouvanté devant l'athéisme'.[75]

A la lecture d'hommages si raisonnables et si prudents, comment ne pas entériner le jugement d'Eugène Despois stigmatisant l''admiration peureuse' de l'Académie pour le dix-huitième siècle? Considérer l'envers du palmarès renforcerait le même constat: sans même parler d'Helvétius ou du baron d'Holbach, signalons que ni D'Alembert ni Diderot ne figurent au programme, ce qui fait une singulière lacune dans le tableau du siècle...[76] Quant aux figures célébrées, on a vu qu'elles soutenaient d'abord un projet de raccommodement et de

---

72. Baudrillart, 'Turgot', p.1048.
73. Baudrillart, 'Turgot', p.1022 (je souligne).
74. Harel, *Discours sur Voltaire*, p.16.
75. Harel, *Discours sur Voltaire*, p.16.
76. Diderot sera finalement inscrit au programme dans l'entre-deux-guerres.

pacification dépouillant les Lumières de leur caractère inquiétant. Passé au crible du genre épidictique dont la fonction de colmatage joue ici à plein régime, le dix-huitième siècle apporte des réponses au lieu d'attiser un questionnement.

Il est vrai que les discours des lauréats offrent, par définition, une version autorisée du passé. Ils reflètent parfois l'habileté de leur auteur bien plus que ses convictions profondes. A chaque session, l'intégrité du sujet ne pèse en effet pas lourd face à l'absolue nécessité de ne pas froisser le jury. Et quand le terrain devient glissant, l'autocensure reste le meilleur expédient pour ne pas annihiler toute chance de succès. Fût-ce au prix de la vérité historique, l'académiquement correct risque ainsi de l'emporter sur tout autre critère. Une confidence épistolaire de Prévost-Paradol, concurrent fébrile puis vainqueur contrit, éclaire bien ces méandres stratégiques. Pour justifier la teneur de son discours, il invoque 'la contrainte absolue du genre': 'j'ai dû glisser sur les questions sérieuses et me jouer longuement sur les banalités, pour plaire à l'Académie. Que la philosophie me le pardonne; j'espère lui donner un jour sa revanche.'[77] Il y a deux manières de lire cette indiscrétion qui, convenons-en, jette une lumière crue sur le fonctionnement des prix. On peut y voir une raison suffisante pour délaisser une fois pour toutes les corpus en question. Une autre attitude, selon nous préférable, implique d'inverser la perspective pour nous demander en quoi le déroulement du concours éclaire la dynamique plus générale de la consécration littéraire dans la France du dix-neuvième siècle. Car s'agissant des Lumières, la revanche annoncée par Prévost-Paradol n'eut, en réalité, jamais lieu. De plus, les discours primés forment un corpus dont on a longtemps sous-estimé la faculté de ruissellement. Leurs canaux de diffusion se révèlent en effet multiples. Ils sont reproduits et commentés dans la presse, avant d'être diffusés en brochures par la prestigieuse maison Firmin-Didot, imprimeur officiel de l'Institut. Mais leur circulation ne se borne pas à ces quelques promesses de visibilité. Bénéficiant de plusieurs vies éditoriales, les discours primés touchent en réalité plus d'une génération. On les retrouve régulièrement en tête des *Œuvres complètes* de l'auteur mis au programme. Souvent actifs sur le marché des manuels scolaires, les lauréats eux-mêmes n'hésitent pas à les recycler sans toujours en signaler l'origine. Le 'Rousseau' de Charles Gidel, couronné en 1868, se retrouve en substance dans l'*Histoire de*

---

77. Lettre à Ernest Havet (25 octobre 1852), citée d'après Octave Gréard, *Prévost-Paradol: étude suivie d'un choix de lettres* (Paris, 1894), p.200.

la littérature française que l'auteur, professeur puis proviseur de grands
lycées parisiens, publie chez Alphonse Lemerre, ouvrage maintes fois
réédité sous la République et disponible en librairie jusqu'au tournant
du vingtième siècle. De même, Auguste Laborde-Milaà ne tarde
pas à publier une version refondue de son 'Fontcncllc' dans la très
médiatisée série des *Grands Ecrivains français* dirigée par le diplomate
Jean-Jules Jusserand chez Hachette. D'autres exemples confirme-
raient une faculté de pénétration sociale non négligeable faisant de
ces exercices académiques le foyer méconnu d'une certaine vulgate
culturelle. Loin de se limiter au quart d'heure de célébrité offert au
lauréat, le concours articule deux temporalités distinctes, les écrits
de circonstances produits pour l'occasion s'inscrivant dans une durée
sans commune mesure avec celle d'un rite académique saisonnier.

De ce point de vue, les concours offrent un précieux laboratoire
d'analyse puisqu'ils donnent à voir de manière exemplaire les
distorsions à l'œuvre dans la canonisation officielle du dix-huitième
siècle. Le cas serait anecdotique s'il éclairait uniquement les formes
de consécration en vigueur dans le petit monde de la Coupole. Or
tel n'est pas le cas. En France, l'influence à long terme des partis
pris institutionnels du dix-neuvième siècle n'a de toute évidence pas
été suffisamment prise en compte. Parmi d'autres, les réflexions de
Catherine Volpilhac-Auger sur le filtre éditorial imposé aux Lumières
pendant le vingtième siècle n'en sont que plus précieuses. Elles
montrent comment un catalogue symboliquement central, celui de
la *Bibliothèque de la Pléiade*, a longtemps valorisé 'un dix-huitième
siècle édulcoré, construit sur des valeurs esthétiques qui ne sont pas
les siennes',[78] dont se trouvent exclus notamment les pans les plus
militants de l'histoire philosophique voltairienne. Par le choix des
auteurs comme par le tri pratiqué au sein des œuvres retenues, cette
collection emblématique de la mémoire littéraire nationale a de fait
pérennisé en plein vingtième siècle l'extrême prudence et les stratégies
d'évitement dont les institutions normatives du dix-neuvième siècle
avaient fourni le modèle. Au terme de sa démonstration (qui, au

---

78. Catherine Volpilhac-Auger, 'Une bibliothèque bleue: le siècle des Lumières en
    Pléiade', dans *La Bibliothèque de la Pléiade: travail éditorial et valeur littéraire*, éd.
    Joëlle Gleize et Philippe Roussin (Paris, 2009), p.103-15 (104). Voir aussi de la
    même auteure, 'Et les Lumières ne furent plus…?', *Fabula / Les Colloques* (2020),
    numéro thématique: *Accuser réception*, éd. Thierry Roger et Stéphane Zékian,
    https://www.fabula.org/colloques/document6567.php (date de dernière consul-
    tation le 20 avril 2023).

demeurant, ne méconnaît pas les audaces ponctuelles de la *Pléiade*), l'historienne évoque 'une collection qui semble éviter ce qui présenterait le dix-huitième siècle comme le lieu d'un bouillonnement d'idées et d'une remise en cause des cadres de pensée'.[79] Ces analyses attestent que les biais inhérents aux concours académiques ne sont pas propres à cette institution. En retracer l'horizon d'attente permet de mesurer son degré de convergence avec d'autres filières de consécration posthume comme l'Ecole, l'Université ou les divers panthéons éditoriaux. Dans l'ensemble, c'est bien la littérarisation du dix-huitième siècle qui paraît avoir favorisé, comme Despois l'avait pressenti, la neutralisation idéologique des Lumières. Si tel est le cas, il n'y a dès lors pas lieu d'envisager la mémoire académique comme une exception archaïque indigne de l'attention historienne: s'il n'y a pas d'anomalie mais, à l'inverse, une exemplarité académique dans l'art de désarmer le passé, les rouages de ces concours méritent autre chose que l'indifférence.

A titre programmatique, ajoutons pour finir que les palmarès constituent seulement la partie visible d'un continent discursif autrement plus tourmenté. Car sous la surface lisse des tableaux d'honneur se presse la foule des manuscrits écartés par le jury. Chaque session ouvre un large éventail de prises de parole sur les figures mises au programme. Aux yeux pressés de la postérité, les vitrines patrimoniales ont trop vite fait oublier ce continent englouti, véritable arrière-boutique de la mémoire officielle. On n'évalue pourtant pas un iceberg sur sa seule partie émergée. Paradoxalement, la volonté académique de surexposer certaines interprétations au détriment d'autres discours semble avoir été couronnée de succès: l'incuriosité de la postérité pour le linge sale des concours n'a que trop bien répondu aux souhaits du quai de Conti. Le temps est peut-être venu d'éclairer l'histoire des vainqueurs (au sens propre) à la lumière des discours non retenus. Dans l'architecture de la mémoire littéraire, la salle de réceptions jouxte un salon des refusés très peuplé quoique moins couru, et dont la visite pourrait s'avérer instructive.[80]

---

79. C. Volpilhac-Auger, 'Une bibliothèque bleue', p.112. Elle précise que 'les auteurs retenus sont d'abord ceux qui sont étrangers au mouvement de contestation politique et idéologique [...] ou qui restent en marge de ce mouvement' (p.107).
80. Pour plus d'éléments, je me permets de renvoyer, faute de place, à mon étude sur *La Littérature mise à prix: l'Académie française et son concours d'éloquence, XIXᵉ-XXᵉ siècles* (à paraître).

After Carlyle: 'Enlightenment' in Victorian Britain

BRIAN W. YOUNG

University of Oxford

Thomas Carlyle is occasionally associated with the 'Counter-Enlightenment', a loose movement of ideas made familiar by Isaiah Berlin, who frequently placed him as one of the few British figures within that doubtful pantheon, otherwise populated by the likes of de Maistre and, less persuasively, by Herder and other German thinkers critical of Kant.[1] We lack an authoritative foundational essay entitled 'Was ist Gegen-Aufklärung?', and students of nineteenth-century illiberal thought must make do with charting their way through a contesting series of reactionary moments even more challenging for the taxonomist of intellectual history than are the calmer waters navigated by students of a liberal Enlightenment. Alarmist histories of 'enemies of reason' – preludes to the irrationalism of fascism – frequently result, creating an anti-Whig theory of history in the process.[2] In such stormy seas Sturm und Drang turns nasty, Haydn's late symphonies modulating into the eerie wolf glen of Weber's *Freischütz* and the haunted memories of the *Dies irae* heard in Berlioz's opium-induced nightmares in his *Symphonie fantastique*. These are treacherously icy waters, where, whatever his faults as a historian of ideas, Berlin remains a solitary figure simultaneously sounding the depths of Enlightenment *and* the oceanic roots of Romanticism.[3]

---

1. Brian W. Young, 'The Counter-Enlightenments of Thomas Carlyle', in *Thomas Carlyle and the idea of influence*, ed. Paul Kerry, Albert D. Pionke and Megan Dent (Lanham, MD, 2018), p.193-223. I am grateful to Noël Sugimura and Joshua Bennett for criticism.
2. *Isaiah Berlin's Counter-Enlightenment*, ed. Joseph Mali and Robert Wokler (Philadelphia, PA, 2006).
3. *Isaiah Berlin and the Enlightenment*, ed. Laurence Brockliss and Ritchie Robertson (Oxford, 2016).

It is well to be metaphorically at sea when assessing the origins of nineteenth-century British studies of what came to be called the Enlightenment. Carlyle is, and was, a vigorously disorientating thinker. That was no small part of his value for his contemporaries and his immediate successors in the fluid forms of literary, historical and philosophical study that were uniquely the seas he chose to chart, and in which the likes of George Eliot, her partner George Henry Lewes, and John Stuart Mill similarly, if contrastingly, exercised their patently liberal influence over what they called the 'public mind' in Victorian Britain. Carlyle was educated in an Edinburgh that was about to historicise its own relations with the Enlightenment, a transitional moment of some complexity; if there was what John Gray has called with Joycean aplomb 'Enlightenment's wake', then the young Carlyle was in at the beginning.[4] But, as with anyone at a wake, he was intimately familiar with the recently deceased, and would come to offer his own addresses, sometimes as an *élogue*, more often as anathema.

As Carlyle grew older and yet more dyspeptic, repudiation was repeatedly the order of the day. Carlyle's love affair with all things German was not unique, but he embodied the 'German Idea' more powerfully and influentially than did any of his contemporaries.[5] As a 'maker', albeit through what Mill called the prose-poem of his *French Revolution* – which established Carlyle's reputation as a historian in the new regnal year of 1837 – he enjoyed an intellectual and cultural authority unique in the Victorian era. Defining himself against what he considered to be 'the poor bankrupt eighteenth century', Carlyle created an idea of the period that was to be creatively contested both by his near contemporaries and by the English generation born in the 1830s, the first decade of Reform, and which championed the second era of reform in the 1860s, but which came apart in the 1880s during the third era of political reform and the creation of mass democracy. British appreciation of its predecessor culture undertaken at any point from 1837 was conducted strictly and creatively 'after Carlyle'.[6]

It was also invariably conducted according to a Franco-German division of intellectual labour. Carlyle was indisputably on the German

4. John Gray, *Enlightenment's wake: politics and culture at the close of the modern age* (London, 1995).
5. See Rosemary Ashton, *The German Idea: four writers and the reception of German thought 1800-1860* (Cambridge, 1980).
6. See Brian W. Young, '"An epoch in the history of ones' mind": Gibbon, Carlyle, and the post-Reform generation' (forthcoming).

side of that divide, and on the other were the many followers of Auguste Comte, a pioneering *maître-penseur*, for whom Carlyle personally had no time. If Carlyle took forward and transformed what Mill called the 'Germano-Coleridgian' system, Mill and a host of Francophile writers engaged no less fundamentally with the 'Religion of Humanity'.[7] The former tendency of thought was in creative tension with the great majority of eighteenth-century ideas, taking both a Kantian and a post-Kantian turn; the latter saw itself as developing from and helping to evolve the liberal legacy of the eighteenth century, producing a post-revolutionary ethic of continuous reform. British studies of 'Enlightenment' took place within capacious, occasionally all-consuming continental shadows even as many of those studies sought to mark a distance between British and continental European thought. And while Mill was often claimed for the party of Comte, he was, of course, deeply indebted to the one figure all students of the eighteenth century agree to be a genuine figure of Enlightenment in Britain, Jeremy Bentham. However defined, and thence refined by Mill and others, Utilitarianism was an Enlightenment legacy to nineteenth-century Britain the importance of which cannot be overestimated, and it was not a purely secular inheritance. William Paley had promoted a Christian variant of Utilitarianism which proved especially dominant at Cambridge, where such figures as William Whewell, the polymath master of Trinity College and coiner of the word 'scientist', was the author not only of a *History of moral philosophy in England* in which Paley was critically appraised and Bentham berated in by far the longest and culminating section of the book, but also of a *History of the inductive sciences* that played its part in promoting the claims, albeit often critically, of Francis Bacon as the prime instigator of modern philosophy, ahead of both the immensely disliked Descartes and the totally despised Hobbes.[8]

7. John Stuart Mill, 'Coleridge', in *The Collected works of John Stuart Mill*, vol.10: *Essays on ethics, religion, and society*, ed. John M. Robson and Jack Stillinger (Toronto, 1969), p.117-63 (125); Terry R. Wright, *The Party of humanity: the impact of Comtean positivism on Victorian Britain* (Cambridge, 1986).

8. Niall O'Flaherty, *Utilitarianism in the age of Enlightenment: the moral and political philosophy of William Paley* (Cambridge, 2018); William Whewell, *Lectures on the history of moral philosophy in England* (London, 1852), p.14-35, 150-60, 163-68, 174-80, 199-265; William Whewell, *History of the inductive sciences, from the earliest to the present times*, 3 vols (London, 1837), vol.1, p.vii-xii; vol.2, p.127-29, 173-74, 296, 501; William Whewell, *Philosophy of the inductive sciences, founded upon their history*, 2 vols (London, 1840), vol.2, p.388-414; Richard Yeo, *Defining*

Insular though such accounts as those of Whewell undoubtedly were, Francis Bacon was beginning his long career in the history of ideas as an originator of a scientific revolution that would in its turn be seen by many historians as heralding the era of Enlightenment. Whewell described the Baconian epoch as an 'enlightened time', a phrase many had used in the eighteenth century of their own times.[9] The initial publication of Bacon's collected works, one of the most important contributions to the study of English intellectual history made in Victorian Britain, was effectively a cottage industry at Trinity College, Cambridge, its editors all having served their time as fellows of the college.[10] Macaulay, a generation or two ahead of those editors at Trinity, had earlier discussed Bacon equivocally in the *Edinburgh review*, an essay identified by Walter E. Houghton as 'the *locus classicus* of Victorian anti-intellectualism'.[11] For Macaulay, Bacon's was a living philosophy, the key words of which were unequivocally 'Utility and Progress'. Macaulay's all too infectious anti-intellectualism nonetheless led him to state that 'The inductive method has been practised ever since the beginning of the world by every human being. It is constantly practised by the most ignorant clown, by the most thoughtless schoolboy, by the very child at the breast.' So much for Bacon's contribution to philosophy, which Macaulay only cautiously proceeded to evaluate more positively; the characteristic cause of all this negativity was Macaulay's moralising, as he concluded regretfully that 'he who first treated legislation as a science was among the last Englishmen who used the rack, that he who first summoned philosophers to the great work of interpreting nature was among the last Englishmen who sold justice.'[12] It was, however, more than Trinity solidarity that led Whewell to praise Macaulay's essay as being 'of consummate eloquence and brilliancy'. He approvingly cited the essay on the twin ideals of 'utility' and 'progress', echoing his own plea in *The Philosophy of the inductive*

----

    science: William Whewell, natural knowledge, and polite debate in early Victorian Britain (Cambridge, 1993), p.9-10, 96-97, 106-107, 128-29, 166, 240.

9. Whewell, *Moral philosophy*, p.15.

10. Richard Yeo, 'An idol of the marketplace: Baconianism in nineteenth-century Britain', *History of science* 23 (1985), p.251-98.

11. Walter E. Houghton, 'Victorian anti-intellectualism', *Journal of the history of ideas* 13 (1952), p.291-313 (300).

12. Thomas Babington Macaulay, 'Lord Bacon', in *Critical and historical essays contributed to the Edinburgh review*, 3 vols (London, 1843), vol.2, p.280-429 (374, 406, 429).

sciences, that 'There is one very prominent feature in Bacon's speculations which we must not omit to notice; it is a leading and constant object with him to apply his knowledge to *Use*.'[13] Utility and progress were the guiding lights of these heirs to a Baconian legacy. What would later be called the 'Scientific Revolution' mattered more to many in nineteenth-century Britain than what would eventually become known as the Enlightenment.

For many deducible cultural reasons, English historians were long much more comfortable talking about the great instauration and the origins and progress of the Royal Society than they ever were writing about the Enlightenment, whether considered as European in nature or as having its own native variant. In an influential essay dating back to 1981, Roy Porter was a rare exception to this long-term trend, himself a student of the history of science by training, a meta-discipline that established itself earlier and more comfortably (if of late more precariously) than had intellectual history in Britain.[14] And it is notable how rarely English intellectual historians have talked about Hobbes specifically as a figure of the early Enlightenment. For them, he is predominantly a figure purely of the seventeenth century, and his eighteenth-century reception rarely concerns them. Indeed, in common with all too many nineteenth-century writers, they remain content in assuming that James Mill effectively recovered Hobbes as a mainstay of British philosophical thinking, thereby connecting him with a supposed tradition of English empiricism, a theme that grew up alongside the Victorian cult of Bacon. George Henry Lewes influentially insisted that it was James Mill who had rescued Hobbes as a political thinker from the *odium theologicum*.[15]

It is not accidental that these admirers of Bacon and Hobbes were also active participants in public life in the first half of the nineteenth century. With occasional exceptions such as Whewell, intellectual life in England was largely, but by no means exclusively, conducted outside its universities. Carlyle had wanted men of ideas (and, for him, they would have to have been men) to be active in public life. If Carlyle was

13. William Whewell, 'Spedding's complete edition of the works of Bacon', *Edinburgh review* 106 (1857), p.287-322 (290); Whewell, *Philosophy of the inductive sciences*, vol.2, p.409, 407.

14. Roy Porter, 'The Enlightenment in England', in *The Enlightenment in national context*, ed. Roy Porter and Mikuláš Teich (Cambridge, 1981), p.1-18.

15. George Henry Lewes, *The History of philosophy from Thales to Comte*, 3rd edn, 2 vols (London, 1867), vol.2, p.226.

interested in what became known as the Enlightenment, as he critically was, it was primarily through the place it had in the origins and progress of the French Revolution. And here this unbelieving promoter of 'natural supernaturalism' was decidedly critical of those qualities of the *philosophes* most celebrated by the likes of Jonathan Israel: their materialism, their atheism and their radical politics. Not that Carlyle was straightforwardly a metaphysical dualist, a Christian or anything remotely like a political or social conservative: he had absorbed enough from the Enlightenment to be plagued by doubts; but he had reacted against its reductive materialism, as he saw it, sufficiently to reject the consolations of a 'Radical' Enlightenment, albeit, in the case of Diderot, Carlyle expressed this sense of distance with some regret. He preferred men of action to thinkers, and it is notable how often he used moments in his monumental life of Frederick the Great, quintessentially his kind of hero, to vilipend the noxious influence of Voltaire, for whom the highest word of praise he could find was '*adroitness*', while regretting his scoffing mockery and contempt, although insisting that he did not wish to join in the post-revolutionary 'condemnatory clamour' against Voltaire, who was adjudged inferior by Carlyle both to Diderot and to Rousseau.[16]

Carlyle was most positive about Rousseau, one of the few eighteenth-century men to make it into his coterie of heroes as men of letters, alongside Samuel Johnson and, patriotically, Robert Burns. But the sexually ambiguous (if not ambivalent) Carlyle repudiated Rousseau's troubling sensuality; immediately pre-Victorian and Victorian propriety was appalled by Rousseau's sexual frankness, and this was as true of agnostics as it was of Christians, fervent or merely observant.[17] The fastidious agnostic John Morley was especially wary of what he called Rousseau's 'erotic mania', declaring with tremulous disgust of his relationship with Mme d'Houdetot, that 'the whole offers a scene of moral humiliation that half sickens, half appals, and we turn away with dismay as from a vision of the horrible loves of heavy-eyed and scaly shapes that haunted the warm primeval ooze.'[18] Victorian sexuality was terrified by Enlightenment sexuality, and

16. Thomas Carlyle, 'Diderot' and 'Voltaire', in *Critical and miscellaneous essays*, 5 vols (London, 1899), vol.3, p.177-248, vol.1, p.396-428; Brian W. Young, *The Victorian eighteenth century: an intellectual history* (Oxford, 2007), p.10-69.
17. Thomas Carlyle, *On heroes, hero-worship, and the heroic in history*, ed. Joel J. Brattin, Mark Engel and Michael K. Goldberg (Berkeley, CA, 1993), p.133-67.
18. John Morley, *Rousseau*, 2 vols (London, 1873), vol.1, p.xi, 263, 264.

even Walter Pater only went so far in his celebrations of Winckelmann's homoerotic variety of Hellenism, a cultivated ambivalence continued into the twentieth century by the work of Eliza M. Butler.

Pater silently blended Goethe with Mill in his contributions to eighteenth-century studies, which took the form of a chapter on Winckelmann in his *Renaissance studies* of 1873, and a fantasy biography of an aesthete princeling in *Imaginary portraits*, published in 1887. The chapter on Winckelmann was a deeply considered moment in the history of aesthetic theory and the revival of the 'Greek spirit', and it was at least as much about what Goethe owed the older German as it was about Winckelmann, both men contributing to what, in an echo of Mill, Pater called 'that note of revolt against the eighteenth century which we detect in Goethe' and which 'was struck by Winckelmann'.[19] German philhellenism mattered to Pater, both aesthetically and sexually, and something of that commitment entered the serious frivolity that animated 'Duke Carl of Rosenmold'.[20] Although early inclined to 'the somewhat questionable form of the contemporary French ideal, in matters of art and literature', of Apollo 'in the dandified costume of Lewis the Fourteenth', the purely imaginary Carl abjures all that for the true Greek ideal and, after a conversion to the Gothic at Cologne and Strasbourg directly ahead of the reality of that actually experienced by Goethe, he has a vision of his own place in the future. A religious sceptic, Duke Carl was his own Northern Apollo, a premature celebrant of what was yet to come, including naming that experience: 'With large belief that the *Eclaircissement*, the *Aufklärung* (he had already found the name for the thing) would indeed come, he had been in much bewilderment whence and how.' The greatest and most economical statement of the German recovery of ancient Greek ideals made in England before 1900 was declared not in a systematic treatise of intellectual history (or even in an essay by Carlyle), but in an aesthetic fiction, as Pater extolled the young duke's visionary journey:

> The spirits of distant Hellas would reawake in the men and women of little German towns. Distant times, the most alien thoughts, would come near together, as elements in a great historic symphony. A

19. Walter Pater, 'Winckelmann', in *Studies in the history of the Renaissance* (London, 1873), p.177-232.
20. See Stefano Evangelista and Katherine Harloe, 'Pater's "Winckelmann"', in *Pater the classicist*, ed. Charles Martindale, Stefano Evangelista and Elizabeth Prettejohn (Oxford, 2017), p.63-79.

kind of ardent, new patriotism awoke in him, sensitive for the first
time at the words *national* poesy, *national* art and literature, *German*
philosophy. To the resources of the past, of himself, of what was
possible for German mind, more and more his mind opens as he goes
on his way.[21]

Although he was a pronounced Francophile, Pater did not celebrate
the era of Voltaire, preferring the classical revival of the age of
Ronsard and Montaigne in France, as evoked in his unfinished
'romance' *Gaston de Latour*. He was, on the contrary, dismissive
of French eighteenth-century classicism, declaring in the essay on
Winckelmann that 'Voltaire belongs to that flimsier, more artificial,
classical tradition, which Winckelmann was one day to supplant, by
the clear ring, the eternal outline of the genuine antique.'[22] In common
with so many of his British contemporaries, Pater was animated by
the unfinished business for late-nineteenth-century Europeans of
what he called 'the *Enlightening*, the *Aufklärung*', initiated by 'Lessing
and Herder, brilliant precursors of the age of genius which centred
in Goethe, coming well within the natural limits of Carl's lifetime'.[23]
He was firmly on the German side in the British reception of an
enlightening age, the work of which continued into the nineteenth
century. As for Kant, so for Pater, *Aufklärung* was a continuous
process, not a historical moment.

Butler's iconoclastic study, *The Tyranny of Greece over Germany*,
appeared in 1935 when National Socialism was in control, and hers
was a critically revisionary account of what Pater had so enthusiastically evoked. Then a young fellow of Girton College, Cambridge,
she opened her much less adulatory account of Winckelmann with
an epigraph from Pater's chapter concerning him in *Studies in the
history of the Renaissance*. Herself queer, she regretted the 'emotional
rigidity of the convinced misogamist', along with his 'sterile loves
and fruitless passions'; this was not only literary history but also
an early exercise in the history of emotions, inspired by anger
at what was happening in a Germany she had known and been
ambivalent about since her Edwardian childhood.[24] It was, she

21. Walter Pater, 'Duke Carl of Rosenmold', in *Imaginary portraits* (London, 1887),
    p.117-53 (124, 144-45), original emphasis; Pater, 'Winckelmann', p.226.
22. Pater, 'Winckelmann', p.182.
23. Pater, 'Duke Carl of Rosenmold', p.152.
24. Eliza M. Butler, *Paper boats: an autobiography* (London, 1959), p.15-20, 26-29,
    42-53, 63, 81-99, 122-23, 126-28, 188-92.

insisted, Winckelmann's own actions, his own vision, that led to his death, drawing it out appropriately in the language of Greek drama: 'Winckelmann's death has that symbolical significance more often found in art than in life. It was Nemesis, and he brought it upon himself; a retribution for denying his gods and refusing to accomplish the task they had set him. He was killed by Arcangeli at Trieste; but he had annihilated his own future first.'[25] *The Tyranny of Greece over Germany* is a sort of 'Studies in the German Renaissance', but, whereas Pater in his *Studies in the history of the Renaissance* evoked a form of life thoroughly imbued by revivals of the Greek ideal, Butler argued that intellectually stifling tyranny, distorted by self-mythologising philhellenism, had annihilated any genuinely independent life in favour of the dangerous, death-dealing ideology of National Socialism. Her inclusive study of Lessing, Herder, Goethe, Schiller, Hölderlin and Heine, let alone of Nietzsche and Stefan Georg, was full of regret for what had followed in the tortured history of German philhellenism. What Butler began in the 1930s, Suzanne L. Marchand has continued in her 1996 study, *Down from Olympus*, bringing into consideration many other details of the compromised and compromising story of German classicism from 1750 into the 1970s.[26]

By the 1930s, not only the Germany that had inspired Carlyle but also Carlyle himself came under critical scrutiny, beginning in a lecture delivered at Manchester University in which Sir Herbert Grierson had publicly condemned him as an inspiration to the Nazis.[27] Hugh Trevor-Roper, who came of age in that politically turbulent decade, repeated the charge as recently as 1981.[28] Intellectual history is never politically neutral. Although it is written in a notably different register, not to say idiom, Butler cannot have been surprised at the appearance of Horkheimer and Adorno's *Dialectic of Enlightenment*; one surmises she was rather more suspicious of the deeply compromised call for a renewed *Goethezeit* in Friedrich Meinecke's immediately post-war apologia, *The German catastrophe*. Butler admired but she

25. Eliza M. Butler, *The Tyranny of Greece over Germany* (Cambridge, 1935), p.28, 31, 43.
26. Suzanne L. Marchand, *Down from Olympus: archaeology and philhellenism in Germany, 1750-1970* (Princeton, NJ, 1996).
27. Herbert J. C. Grierson, *Carlyle and Hitler* (Cambridge, 1933).
28. Hugh Trevor-Roper, 'The historical philosophy of Thomas Carlyle', in *History and the Enlightenment* (New Haven, CT, 2010), p.223-45.

did not love Germany; 'the German Idea' had come apart in Britain during the vicissitudes of the 1930s.[29]

But another philosopher than Goethe had directly prefigured the 'German Renaissance' for many a nineteenth-century British agnostic. The Spinoza who inspired his contemporary 'Sebastian van Storck' of Pater's *Imaginary portraits* to a determinedly solitary philosophical death in the Netherlands was an altogether more positive force for many of Pater's agnostic elders in Victorian intellectual life than was Winckelmann, though for many he was appreciated also as an inspiration to their equally beloved Goethe.[30] Both George Eliot and her partner George Henry Lewes separately lost their faith in Christianity when young, turning to continental thinking in helping them find their way in a new and unfamiliar world of ideas. Eliot had been involved in translating Feuerbach but then devoted a great deal of energy to a translation of Spinoza's *Ethics* which was finally published as recently as 2020.[31] Her own post-religious sensibility owed a lot to this work, in which she was encouraged by Lewes, who wrote about Spinoza admiringly in his own *History of philosophy from Plato to Comte*, in which the latter was very much preferred to the former.

And Lewes had originally made his name in 1855 with a well-received biography of Goethe, which he dedicated to Carlyle. In its pages, Lewes offered a condensed history of European thought as well as an intellectual biography. Without giving any name to the world of ideas into which his subject was born, Lewes apostrophised – in Carlylean mode – Goethe's birth in August 1749, thus:

> A momentous month in very momentous times. It was the middle of the eighteenth century: a period when the movement which had culminated in Luther was passing from religion to politics, and freedom was translating itself into liberty of action [...]. A period of deep unrest: big with events which would expand the conceptions of all men, and bewilder some of the wisest.

He developed the point by noting what was happening elsewhere at that very moment, mentioning Voltaire making his way to Berlin,

29. Brian W. Young, 'Intellectual history and *Historismus* in post-war England', in *A Companion to intellectual history*, ed. Richard Whatmore and Brian W. Young (Chichester, 2016), p.19-35.
30. Walter Pater, 'Sebastian van Storck', in *Imaginary portraits*, p.79-115.
31. *Spinoza's Ethics*, ed. Clare Carlisle, translated by George Eliot (Princeton, NJ, 2020).

Rousseau enjoying celebrity in brilliant circles in Paris, Samuel Johnson 'manfully toiling' on his dictionary, Gibbon suffering as a confusedly erudite schoolboy at Westminster, Goldsmith acting as a 'bear-leader' on the continent, Buffon and Haller producing experimental works, Hunter studying medicine, Mirabeau and Alfieri commencing 'tyrants in their nurseries', and the five-year-old Marat 'unmolested yet by the wickedness of "les aristocrates"'.[32] 'Enlightenment' was notably not inscribed in that moment in 1749 by Lewes, but he was ready much later in his biography to identify in Germany 'that brilliant error known as the Romantic School'. And he was also determined to see off that 'ungenerous party' which had assailed Goethe for lacking religion, when in fact he had combined 'deep religious sentiments, with complete scepticism on most religious doctrines'. Goethe's spiritual sensibility was a 'Hellenic' and poetical variant of Spinoza's pantheism.[33] Such religious seriousness appealed to earnest British agnostics rather more than did the scoffing widely attributed by them to the 'shallow' Voltaire. No Victorian British writer explicitly praised the 'age of Voltaire'.

Although Lewes devoted the first of his two lengthy volumes on the history of philosophy to Greek and Roman thought, it was clear that his treatment of the subject in the second volume was as a prelude to the vigorous exposition of Comte that he gave at its end. He was not uncritical of Comte, but it was evident from Lewes' exposition that this was the road to which all good philosophy had hitherto been leading.[34] Bacon is there, as are Descartes and Hobbes. Less expectedly, Lewes' treatment of eighteenth-century philosophy is largely in terms of the theory of the mind and the nervous system, in which Destutt de Tracy and David Hartley are more prominent than the Condorcet routinely celebrated by Comte and his followers. Indeed, considerable attention is given by Lewes to Gall (and Spurzheim and Combe), and to the physiological research that had led to the phrenology in which Lewes and Eliot had once invested heavily. Kant is subject to extended criticism, as is Hegel; Lewes preferred Fichte among German language philosophers, which would have intrigued Isaiah Berlin.[35] And Fichte's characterisation

32. George Henry Lewes, *The Life of Goethe*, 2nd edn (London, 1864), p.11-12.
33. Lewes, *Goethe*, p.402, 517, 518, 520.
34. Lewes, *History of philosophy*, vol.2, p.557-639.
35. Lewes, *History of philosophy*, vol.2, p.113-24, 160-88, 226-35, 305-79, 395-416, 440-556.

of Spinoza as a God-intoxicated man was noted approvingly by
Lewes, if without any citation.[36] German philosophical Hellenism was
also reproached by Lewes: parallels he drew between Alexandrian
philosophy and that of Schelling favoured neither mode of thought;
Plotinus' appeal to *'Ecstasy'* stood condemned alongside Schelling's to
'Intellectual Intuition'.[37]

Comtism inherited much from the French Enlightenment and
from the exponents of a 'science of man' who wrote in its immediate
wake. Living legacies are not always treated critically as histories by
their beneficiaries, and Comte's absorption of a version of Condorcet's
mental history of the progress of humanity is one such instance.
Crucially, however, there was no British equivalent of Victor Cousin,
the closest being Lewes, though himself a strong critic of Cousin's
Eclectic School of philosophy, which he saw as coming out of the
'reaction against the Philosophy of the Eighteenth Century', misiden-
tified by Cousin and others, according to Lewes, as pure materialism.[38]
With few exceptions, study of the history of philosophy in the
British Isles was not as totalising an experience as it was for Cousin
and his myriad followers.

Whewell, by contrast, had looked on with amazement as men of
what he considered to be the undoubted ability of Mill and Lewes
praised Comte, declared by him to be a thinker 'whose want of
knowledge and of temperate thought caused his opinions on the
philosophy and history of science to be of no value'. Comte, Whewell
regretted to say, was sometimes an 'absolutely puerile' thinker.[39] He
berated both Comte and de Maistre in his review of the complete
works of Bacon edited by Spedding and his erstwhile colleagues at
Trinity College, condemning the 'self-complacency' and obscurantism
of the one, and the risibly non-Baconian philosophy of the other, in
equally fervid tones.[40] Christianity in Victorian Britain, particularly
of the empirical variety to which Whewell was devoted, had little to
do with Counter-Enlightenment.

In contrast to this disavowal of Comte by Whewell, by far the
greater part of British writing on French eighteenth-century thought

---

36. Lewes, *History of philosophy*, vol.2, p.175.
37. Lewes, *History of philosophy*, vol.2, p.521.
38. Lewes, *History of philosophy*, vol.2, p.642-46.
39. William Whewell, 'Comte and positivism', *Macmillan's magazine* 13 (1866),
    p.353-62.
40. Whewell, 'Spedding's complete edition of the works of Bacon'.

was produced by men who idolised Mill as well as Comte. Two of the leading thinkers in this class were long lived: Frederic Harrison born in 1831 died as late as 1923, and John Morley, born in 1838, also died in 1923, patently a bad year for mid-Victorian men of letters. To the Bloomsbury generation they were Victorian fossils; as so often, Bloomsbury, a frequently self-obsessed and frankly immature group, ungenerously failed to acknowledge what they had inherited from their predecessor generations. When Lytton Strachey wrote admiringly about the French eighteenth century, it was as if the work of Harrison and Morley had never been published; Kingsley Martin, later the editor of *The New Statesman*, was more generous about them in his own early work on the French Enlightenment.[41]

Harrison was a devoted Comtist; Morley was severely ambivalent. As a devotee, Harrison was preoccupied by two eras of intellectual progress identified as epochal by Comte: the thirteenth century and the eighteenth century. Much of his voluminous writing was devoted to explicating the nature and progress of the French Revolution, the centenary of which in 1889 he piously celebrated in lengthy exploratory essays. He was also a qualified admirer of Gibbon, noting the sceptical detachment of the historian as a necessary moment in the evolution of the modern mind. An erstwhile enthusiast for Carlyle, he wrote critically of him at his death in 1881, though not as critically as Morley, who denounced him as an obscurantist hierophant, contrasting his mendacious pose as a seer and prophet with the altogether saner and more permanent contributions to Comte's science of sociology made by Mill, of whom Morley was one of the most fervent of his many younger disciples.[42] Utilitarianism was the living philosophy of the nineteenth century for Morley, and its fruitful fusion with Comte's new science of sociology was mediated in his account by the works of Turgot and Condorcet from the French eighteenth century, study of which preoccupied Morley's busy life as an editor of the *Fortnightly review* (initially edited by George Henry

41. Lytton Strachey, *Landmarks of French literature* (London, 1912), p.132-98; Kingsley Martin, *French liberal thought in the eighteenth century: a study of political ideas from Bayle to Condorcet* (London, 1929).

42. Frederic Harrison, *The Choice of books, and other literary pieces* (London, 1886); Frederic Harrison, *The Meaning of history* (London, 1894); Frederic Harrison, 'Thomas Carlyle', in *Studies in early Victorian literature* (London, 1902), p.43-63; Frederic Harrison, *Autobiographic memoirs*, 2 vols (London, 1911). The best study remains Martha S. Vogeler, *Frederic Harrison: the vocations of a positivist* (Oxford, 1984).

Lewes) and then as a Liberal MP who was to write the authorised biography of Gladstone precisely because his agnosticism would make him a suitably disinterested student of the Grand Old Man's potentially divisive Christianity.[43]

Morley produced studies of Voltaire and Rousseau as well as of Diderot and other *philosophes*, all written for the sort of reader who consulted the *Fortnightly review*, where many of his books had begun life as connected series of articles. They were histories of opinion written to aid living opinion, the history of ideas as a plastic and shaping element within the higher journalism. No less than for Pater and Kant before him, 'enlightening' continued as a process in and through Morley's histories of opinion. Morley's work on Rousseau merits rereading, not least as his interpretation of the citizen of Geneva as a proponent of dictatorial liberalism has much in common with what Isaiah Berlin would write about him. This approach to the history of thought was dominant until the late 1870s; thereafter the work of Leslie Stephen would mould the history of opinion more recognisably into modern intellectual history.

In a review of Stephen's study of eighteenth-century English thought published in Morley's *Fortnightly review* in 1877, Pattison delivered in heavily compressed form many of his thoughts about what he called the 'Age of Reason'. Aware of the importance of the French eighteenth century, he paid due, if slightly dismissive, reverence to the 'Voltairian era', but, as with Pater, he preferred to celebrate 'the "Aufklärung"', if admitting something of the 'flat and prosaic rationalism of the Aufklärung'. But the weakness of the era was evident rather more in France than it was in Germany – silently reversing here Lewes' judgement – as Pattison denounced, on the one hand, 'the self-complacency of the Age of Reason', while praising, on the other, 'the splendid period of German literature and speculation'.[44] A refugee from the Tractarian reaction against religious rationalism, he also transcended the Carlylean critique, declaring combatively that:

It is, perhaps, premature even in 1877 to speak of the epoch of the

---

43. John Morley, *Voltaire* (London, 1873); John Morley, *Diderot and the Encyclopædists*, 2 vols (London, 1878); John Morley, *Burke* (London, 1879); John Morley, *Critical miscellanies*, 4 vols (London, 1886-1908). David A. Hamer, *John Morley: liberal intellectual in politics* (Oxford, 1968), remains authoritative.

44. Mark Pattison, 'The age of reason', *Fortnightly review* 21 (1877), p.343-61 (344, 350, 351, 353).

romantic and catholic reaction as over. It is not ended; it is in many departments of life in full career; but it is doomed. It was a reaction, and nothing more. It was a just and necessary penalty which the human mind had to pay for the excesses and exaggeration of the eighteenth century.

Whereas the eighteenth century was a rationalistic era, a 'seculum rationalisticum', the nineteenth century was an age of realism ('realisticum'). Hegelian notions of progress had given way to those of Darwin, and progress had been made.[45]

And here is the reason that students of the Enlightenment rarely bother to read nineteenth-century English-language studies of the eighteenth century: before Stephen published his *History of English thought in the eighteenth century* in 1876, itself originally inspired by his reading a German study of English deism, there was no indigenous school of intellectual history.[46] There was literary history which sometimes explored ideas, but even Stephen's own many studies in this field were more concerned with personalities and controversies than they were with ideas. The histories of philosophy produced by Whewell and Lewes were teleological in character and interpretative purpose, and the eighteenth century mattered most for what was considered still living in its philosophy. And, as Mill influentially noted, Coleridge and the liberal Christians he inspired and who become so prominent in Victorian public life were part of the 'revolt against the eighteenth century'.[47] It was as a Francophile student of the French Revolution and the social sciences it spawned that Mill continued to be interested in the eighteenth century.[48]

As Morley observed, the French Revolution was still not over in the late nineteenth century, and much of its speculative energy continued to illuminate French thought, very much encompassing the work of Comte, about which he contributed a critical assessment for the *Encyclopaedia Britannica* in which he made the trenchant and telling observation that 'The Comtist system is utilitarianism

45. Pattison, 'The age of reason', p.350-51, 356.

46. Leslie Stephen, *History of English thought in the eighteenth century*, 2 vols (London, 1876).

47. John S. Mill, *The Collected works*, vol.1: *The Autobiography and literary essays*, ed. John M. Robson and Jack Stillinger (Toronto, 1981), p.160, 168-69, 212-23, 226-27, 270.

48. John S. Mill, *The Collected works*, vol.20: *Essays on French history and historians*, ed. John Cairns and John M. Robson (Toronto, 1985).

crowned by a fantastic decoration.'[49] Morley had no use for the religion of humanity, but he had for utilitarianism and philosophies of progress, for him closely allied living legacies of the eighteenth century. He and Harrison were the premier students of eighteenth-century French culture in Victorian England, but both were more formally students of the history of opinion than they were of intellectual history per se. In this regard they are less obviously exponents of intellectual history than was Stephen, whose centre of gravity was the eighteenth century, and hence the interest in his late studies in the history of British Utilitarianism, for him a living force in modern ethical life.[50]

Stephen is perhaps not conventionally thought of as a student of the Enlightenment because he specialised in eighteenth-century English intellectual history and is thereby doubly marginalised by those who continue to insist that, aside from Bentham, there was no English Enlightenment and that, even if there had been, it was an Enlightenment *'sans philosophes'*.[51] But this is a prejudice that Roy Porter initially exposed and which the work of John G. A. Pocock and others has done much to overcome.[52] Stephen had a model for his work in studies by Pattison, written largely as Stephen turned from being an Anglican clergyman into a pioneering agnostic layman.[53] In still highly important essays on religious rationalism in eighteenth-century England, as well as in allied studies of the history of scholarship, Pattison, who never renounced his own orders in the Church, served as the rector of Lincoln College, Oxford, shortly after Morley's studies there had ended in 1859. Pattison's pioneering studies in the history of scholarship demonstrated how much his absorption of the German Renaissance of the early nineteenth century, which had transformed classical and scriptural scholarship, had become a living resource in understanding the myriad processes of 'enlightening' of which Pattison was a witness as well as a practitioner.[54]

---

49. John Morley, 'Auguste Comte', in *Critical miscellanies*, vol.3, p.337-84 (378).
50. Leslie Stephen, *The English Utilitarians*, 3 vols (London, 1900).
51. See John Robertson, 'Franco Venturi's Enlightenment', *Past & present* 137 (1992), p.183-206.
52. See John G. A. Pocock, *Barbarism and religion*, 6 vols (Cambridge, 1999-2016), and Brian W. Young, *Religion and Enlightenment in eighteenth-century England: theological debate from Locke to Burke* (Oxford, 1998).
53. Young, *The Victorian eighteenth century*, p.104-47.
54. Mark Pattison, *Essays*, ed. Henry Nettleship, 2 vols (Oxford, 1881).

It was in a review of Pattison's *Memoirs* by Morley, in which he compared the rector's ego with that of Rousseau, that Morley revealed that, despite his Gallocentric view of the eighteenth century, he too considered a product of the *Aufklärung* to be superior to anything produced in France at that time. In a diversion initiated by reflections on the Goethe whom Pattison had, he claimed, insufficiently understood, Morley extolled the character and the art of Lessing: 'In art, in religion, in literature and drama, in the whole field of criticism, he launched ideas of sovereign importance, both for his own and for following times, and, in *Nathan the Wise*, the truest and best mind of the eighteenth century found its gravest and noblest voice.'[55] Highly critical as Morley was of Carlyle and his importation of allegedly German values, even his Francophilia gave way to the continuing importance of a German thinker to 'following times'. And Morley's critique of Carlyle also involved allusions to Rousseau, as it was the 'dangerous sophistry of the emotions' that Morley berated Carlyle as having continued, so much so that 'The Rousseau of these times for English-speaking people is Thomas Carlyle.' For Morley, things could not be any worse. Carlyle was better at the portrayal of the 'prominent men of the eighteenth century' such as Robespierre and Frederick the Great than he was as a student of the history of the opinions of that age, leading to the great paradox that informed Carlyle's collected works: 'The fact that to the eighteenth century belong the subjects of more than half of these thirty volumes, is a proof of the fascination of the period for an author who has never ceased to vilipend it.'[56] Morley was writing *after* Carlyle; he wanted future students of the eighteenth century to write *beyond* Carlyle.

It was a further paradox that Carlyle was a Scot who had repudiated Enlightenment. Scotland, more at least than England, had enjoyed its experience of Enlightenment, and it is, therefore, curious that little is made among modern students of intellectual history of Henry Thomas Buckle's incomplete *History of civilization in England*, in which intellectual progress in eighteenth-century Scotland – especially in chemistry and the medical sciences – was held up, in contrast with Catholic Spain (and by implication Anglican England)

---

55. John Morley, 'On Pattison's *Memoirs*', in *Critical miscellanies*, vol.3, p.133-73 (152, 156, 164). See Stuart Jones, *Intellect and character in Victorian England: Mark Pattison and the invention of the don* (Cambridge, 2007).
56. John Morley, 'Carlyle', in *Critical miscellanies*, vol.1, p.135-201 (147, 140, 158).

– as a major achievement in the hoped-for secularisation of European culture.[57] But Buckle's moment in the sun on the cusp of the 1850s and 1860s was short-lived, and Morley as a student of literature and opinion as well as of Comte (considered more positively) can have the last explanatory word on him: 'Buckle's crude and superficial notions about the history of civilisation pointed towards a true and complete conception of sociology.'[58]

Morley thought of himself as an exponent of exactly that 'complete conception', hence his immersion in the French Enlightenment out of which had emerged Comte. Even here, however, it is worth quoting from the close of his *Encyclopaedia Britannica* entry on Comte in explaining why the internal divisions of nineteenth-century English thought prevented it from creating anything like the evaluation of 'Enlightenment' made by contemporaneous French and German scholars: 'But the world has strong self-protecting qualities. It will take what is available in Comte, while forgetting that in his work which is as irrational in one way as Hegel is in another.'[59] Morley wrote after Carlyle but critically with Comte and against Hegel. Ambiguity and indeed ambivalence about 'Enlightenment' (and Counter-Enlightenment) left British thought about eighteenth-century 'enlightening' conceptually adrift in the patterns of nineteenth-century European intellectual history. What Franco Venturi said fifty years ago about the eighteenth century applies to study of it in the nineteenth: 'In England the rhythm was different.'[60] The efforts of Lewes, Pattison, Harrison and Morley notwithstanding, the North Sea and the English Channel isolated British attempts at channelling European thought into their own tidal waters; the spirit of Carlyle was still patrolling its shores.

57. Henry Thomas Buckle, *The History of civilization in England*, 2 vols (London, 1857-1861). More generally, see Brian W. Young, 'History', in *Historicism and the human sciences in Victorian Britain*, ed. Mark Bevir (Cambridge, 2017), p.154-85.
58. Morley, 'Carlyle', p.197.
59. Morley, 'Auguste Comte', p.384.
60. Franco Venturi, *Utopia and reform in the Enlightenment* (Cambridge, 1971), p.132.

Germanising the Enlightenment: Wilhelm Dilthey's *Aufklärung*

Avi Lifschitz

University of Oxford

One of the pillars of German philosophy in the late nineteenth century, Wilhelm Dilthey (1833-1911) is known today mostly for his writings on hermeneutics and the interpretation of history, especially after Heidegger and Gadamer's critical engagement with his work. If Dilthey's name is mentioned at all in eighteenth-century studies, it is usually found among the alleged critics of Enlightenment 'universality' and advocates of the historicist notion that each culture possesses its own unique centre of gravity, immeasurable by the standards of any other. Dilthey's distinction between the methods of interpretation in the humanities and those employed in the natural sciences has led Isaiah Berlin to identify him as a successor of Vico and Herder, who faithfully followed their theories of cultural pluralism and humanistic hermeneutics.[1] These were the hallmarks of what Berlin, following Friedrich Meinecke, saw as a mostly German movement, the so-called Counter-Enlightenment, which he opposed (quite misleadingly) to a monist, extremely rationalist Enlightenment.[2]

Once one delves, however, into Dilthey's sprawling output, this broad-brush portrait immediately becomes much more intricate.

---

1. Isaiah Berlin, *Three critics of the Enlightenment*, ed. Henry Hardy, 2nd edn (Princeton, NJ, 2013), p.25, 28, 58 (n.2), 149, 161-63. See also Charles Taylor, 'Understanding in human science', *The Review of metaphysics* 34:1 (1980), p.25-38.
2. Especially in the essay 'The Counter-Enlightenment', in *Against the current: essays in the history of ideas*, ed. Henry Hardy, 2nd edn (Princeton, NJ, 2013), p.1-32. Meinecke contrasted German proto-historicist thought with a mostly Franco-British Enlightenment in *Die Entstehung des Historismus* (1936). On Berlin's wholesale appropriation of this distinction, see Avi Lifschitz, 'Between Friedrich Meinecke and Ernst Cassirer: Isaiah Berlin's bifurcated Enlightenment', in *Isaiah Berlin and the Enlightenment*, ed. Laurence Brockliss and Ritchie Robertson (Oxford, 2016), p.51-66.

This article argues that Dilthey's view of the Enlightenment, like most other issues he seriously tackled, is characterised by a deep tension between opposing tendencies. Contrary to deprecating views of eighteenth-century philosophy around 1900, and despite his admiration of Schleiermacher and Goethe – whom he distinguished from the Enlightenment movement – Dilthey felt the need to vindicate a particular form of Enlightenment. While generally critical of the French Enlightenment, which he saw as a direct sequel of the seventeenth-century *âge classique*, he was capable of acknowledging some of its merits. Yet Dilthey's most appreciative account of the Enlightenment was dedicated to what he regarded as its German manifestation: a cluster of civil servants, educators, theologians and popular authors closely allied with the efforts of Frederick II to rebuild Brandenburg-Prussia in the aftermath of the Seven Years War.

In a series of long essays written in the first decade of the twentieth century, Dilthey elaborated his peculiar interpretation of Frederick II and the almost exclusively Prussian group of authors that he regarded as the German Enlightenment (*die deutsche Aufklärung*). It is in these essays, applying the Enlightenment moniker to a joint venture of the Prussian state and local intellectuals, that Dilthey 'germanised' what he had initially defined as a mostly French term. In these essays one can barely ignore the tensions between the local and the cross-European, between France and Prussia, and – most of all – between a teleological view of intellectual evolution and one that recognises the distinctive traits of a single author or a group of writers.

Tensions within the critique of historical reason

Such contrasts characterised not only Dilthey's work on the Enlightenment but also his broader oeuvre. On the one hand, his hermeneutics was rooted in the notion that all human phenomena, including the political, the cultural or the economic, must be examined within the context of lived experience (*Erlebnis*) and a specific life-nexus (*Lebenszusammenhang*) that has moulded itself through traditions, customs, language and shared history. At the same time, Dilthey's project was, to a large extent, a Kantian one. If Immanuel Kant had sought, in his *Critique of pure reason* (*Kritik der reinen Vernunft*, 1781), to outline the conditions for and the boundaries of the human understanding of natural phenomena, Dilthey extended this endeavour to all human artefacts while regarding reason itself as historically evolved and socially embodied.

Throughout his writings, Dilthey sought to develop a 'critique of historical reason': the delineation of the conditions of historical knowledge, accompanied by the historicisation of the concept of reason. Yet the awareness of the historicity of all forms of human life and thought threatened to undermine Dilthey's lifelong quest for a secure, scientific foundation for the human sciences, where individual facts and experience could be interpreted according to universal laws. His criticism of the abstract nature of Kant's concept of reason and his emphasis on lived experience clashed with a heartfelt craving for a law-based framework for the human sciences. As Max Horkheimer has suggested, Dilthey remained committed throughout his career to an ideal of scientific enquiry that was opposed to speculation, imaginative as the latter might be.[3]

This duality was also expressed in Dilthey's famous distinction between understanding or interpretation (*Verstehen*), the method of the human sciences, and explanation (*Erklären*), the task of the natural sciences. The entire distinction was meant to endow the humanities with scientific legitimacy and law-like character against stringent positivist and neo-Kantian criticism. Dilthey was adamant that this distinction reflected only different kinds of experience, based on the objects of enquiry: the human sciences dealt with inner experience, the reflective self-awareness of man-made artefacts, while the natural sciences explained our external experience of phenomena in nature, given to us through the senses.[4] This was not, however, an ontological divide between incommensurable entities. In some of his formulations, Dilthey seemed to prioritise unmediated awareness of human artefacts and history over conceptualisation and generalisation; on most occasions, however, he emphasised the conditions that rendered enquiry in the human sciences scientific and capable of generalisation from particular facts to universally valid laws.[5]

Criticising grand theories that ascribed a single purpose to human history as a whole, or what he saw as the irrationality of contemporary *Lebensphilosophie* that focused on the individual's emotion and

---

3. Max Horkheimer, 'The relation between psychology and sociology in the work of Wilhelm Dilthey', *Studies in philosophy and social science* 8 (1939), p.430-43.
4. This distinction plays a major role in the *Einleitung in die Geisteswissenschaften* (1883), in *Gesammelte Schriften* (henceforth *GS* followed by volume and page numbers), ed. Bernhard Groethuysen *et al.*, 26 vols (Stuttgart and Göttingen, 1922-2005), vol.1, p.8-14.
5. E.g. *GS*, vol.1, p.317; *GS*, vol.8, p.224-26; *GS*, vol.19, p.62.

spontaneous intuition, Dilthey sought a negotiated, psychologised sort
of empiricism that would replace its narrow, inflexible version ('Empirie,
nicht Empirismus').[6] Another tension existed between the professional
philosopher at the Friedrich Wilhelm University in Berlin, seeking to
vindicate the sound methods of the humanities against neo-Kantian
and positivist criticism, and the historicist thinker, acknowledging
the distinctiveness of all historical world views. As his critics pointed
out, Dilthey's historicism placed him on the edge of a relativist abyss
concerning values, systems and norms, a threat of which Dilthey was
fully aware.[7] Eventually, and as much as he embraced psychology and
imaginative hermeneutics, for Dilthey (as for Kant) philosophy could
never extend beyond the limits of possible human experience.[8]

   Even this all too brief account should indicate that Dilthey's
position within the historicist tradition was much more nuanced
than Isaiah Berlin's repeated references to him as a mere elaborator
of insights by Vico or an advocate of a quasi-artistic, non-
scientific intuition of different historical *Weltanschauungen*.[9] The

6.   *GS*, vol.19, p.17. See Hans-Ulrich Lessing, '"Empirie und nicht Empirismus":
     Dilthey und John Stuart Mill', in *Die Autonomie der Geisteswissenschaften: Studien
     zur Philosophie Wilhelm Diltheys*, vol.1 (Nordhausen, 2015), p.11-31.

7.   Especially in a retrospective assessment of his career upon his seventieth
     birthday (1903): 'The finitude of every historical phenomenon, be it a religion,
     an ideal or a philosophic system, hence the relativity of every sort of human
     conception of the connectedness of things, is the last word of the historical
     world view. All flows in process; nothing remains stable. On the other hand,
     there arises the need of thought and the striving of philosophy for universally
     valid cognition.' *GS*, vol.5, p.7-9. A modified version of Georg Iggers' translation
     in *The German conception of history: the national tradition of historical thought from
     Herder to the present*, 2nd edn (Middletown, CT, 1983), p.143-44.

8.   Frederick C. Beiser, *The German historicist tradition* (Oxford, 2011), esp. p.354-56;
     Charles Bambach, 'Hermeneutics and historicity: Dilthey's critique of historical
     reason', in *Interpreting Dilthey: critical essays*, ed. Eric S. Nelson (Cambridge,
     2019), p.82-102 (83-85).

9.   Berlin, *Three critics*, p.162: 'Vico virtually invented the concept of the
     understanding – of what Dilthey and others call *Verstehen*.' On some of
     the differences between Vico's theory of history and Dilthey's, see Howard
     N. Tuttle, 'The epistemological status of the cultural world in Vico and Dilthey',
     in *Giambattista Vico's science of humanity*, ed. Giorgio Tagliacozzo and Donald
     Phillip Verene (Baltimore, MD, 1976), p.241-50, esp. p.247-49. A corrective to
     such views as Berlin's can be found in Hans-Ulrich Lessing, *Wilhelm Dilthey*
     (Cologne, 2011), p.33-59, and Gudrun Kühne-Bertram, 'Zum Verhältnis von
     Naturwissenschaften und Geisteswissenschaften in der Philosophie Wilhelm
     Diltheys', in *Dilthey als Wissenschaftsphilosoph*, ed. Christian Damböck and

tension between deep historicist awareness and the search for a firm scientific foundation for the humanities, permeating Dilthey's entire oeuvre, is especially manifest in his work on the Enlightenment. On the one hand, Dilthey – the author of a monumental biography of Schleiermacher – saw the age of Goethe, Humboldt, Schleiermacher and Hegel as the time when the German spirit came into its own. This was in line with Dilthey's view that knowledge production depended on social, economic and political circumstances, as well as historically mutable national characteristics. It also reflected a strong teleological undercurrent in his works, where each intellectual development must play a role in the evolution of human civilisation. Nevertheless, Dilthey's essays on the eighteenth century are full of caveats against his own generalisations and teleological tendencies. Although his work is not free of excessive pride in the superiority of the German scholarship of his day and generalisations about the inner forces of the German *Geist* throughout history, Dilthey's views on the eighteenth century are more sophisticated than later distinctions between Enlightenment and its enemies.

Engaging with the Enlightenment, *c.*1900

Having published *Beiträge zum Studium der Individualität* (1896), Dilthey suspended his work on systematic philosophy for roughly a decade, which he dedicated mostly to research on historical themes. Initially he wanted to return to the life and work of Schleiermacher, whose substantial biography he had published in two volumes in the early 1870s. But the bicentenary of the Berlin Academy of Sciences, in 1900, accidentally led him in another direction. Dilthey was highly impressed by Adolf von Harnack's multi-volume history of the Academy, including a wealth of reproduced original documents:[10] he came to see the history of the Academy as an indispensable key to the reconstruction of the intellectual contexts of Schleiermacher's intellectual formation. Moreover, as noted by Dilthey's research assistant, Paul Ritter, it is through Harnack's history of the Berlin Academy that Dilthey gained an insight into the critical significance of

---

Hans-Ulrich Lessing (Freiburg and Munich, 2016), p.225-48. See also *Historical perspectives on Erklären and Verstehen*, ed. Uljana Feest (Dordrecht, 2010).

10. Carl Gustav Adolf von Harnack, *Geschichte der Königlich Preußischen Akademie der Wissenschaften zu Berlin* (Berlin, 1900) – still a major source for research on the Academy.

associations, institutions and the state for the production of knowledge and its transmission – a principle that would be plainly manifest in his writings on the eighteenth century.[11] Following in Harnack's footsteps while integrating the material into a broader account of intellectual life in eighteenth-century Prussia, Dilthey published six large essays in *Deutsche Rundschau* from June 1900 until September 1901. Two articles focused on Leibniz, founder and first president of the Berlin Academy, and the contexts of his own intellectual formation. The following couple of essays examined the Academy under Frederick II and its relationship with the Enlightenment in France and Germany, while the final two concentrated on history-writing in the eighteenth century.[12]

These somewhat occasional publications became the starting point of a much larger project on the history of German philosophy. Initially Dilthey envisaged the articles on Leibniz, the Berlin Academy and the Enlightenment under Frederick II as chapters in the first volume of a series covering intellectual developments from the late seventeenth century to the age of Goethe. Having signed a contract with a publisher, Dilthey delivered the manuscript in 1902 before withdrawing it from the printers. He now realised that the point of departure must be situated much earlier: Leibniz, the Academy and Prussian intellectual life under Frederick II could only be understood against the background of Luther and the German Reformation. Dilthey thus turned to reworking and expanding earlier essays on the philosophy of the fifteenth and sixteenth centuries, some of which had already been published in the 1890s.[13] But the intellectual chain reaction did not stop there: Dilthey decided that he had to research his way backwards to the poetry of the Middle Ages and on to the culture of the Germanic tribes invading the Roman Empire in late Antiquity, in order to cover the entire history of the German *Geist*. If this unfinished project was a case of *Gründlichkeit* undermining itself, the core articles of 1900-1901 provide a rare opportunity for an

---

11. Paul Ritter, 'Vorwort des Herausgebers', in *GS*, vol.3, p.v-x (vii). This section draws on the account provided in Ritter's preface.
12. 'Die Berliner Akademie der Wissenschaften, ihre Vergangenheit und ihre gegenwärtigen Aufgaben' (June and July 1900); 'Die deutsche Aufklärung im Staat und in der Akademie Friedrichs des Grossen' (April and May 1901); 'Das achtzehnte Jahrhundert und die geschichtliche Welt' (August and September 1901).
13. E.g. 'Auffassung und Analyse des Menschen im 15. und 16. Jahrhundert', *Archiv für Geschichte der Philosophie* 4 (1891), p.337-651, and 5 (1892), p.337-440.

examination of Dilthey's views on the Enlightenment.[14] It is in his essays on the Berlin Academy, Frederick the Great and the German Enlightenment – rather than in lecture notes on the grand trajectory of the history of philosophy or in essays on individual historians – that Dilthey painted a fuller portrait of this intellectual movement despite all his teleological tendencies.

The French Enlightenment and Frederick the Great

Unlike contemporary literary scholars such as Wilhelm Scherer (1841-1886), Dilthey did employ the term Enlightenment (*Aufklärung*) consciously, repeatedly and with a definite if not unitary sense.[15] His Enlightenment was on most occasions an intellectual trend or movement in, and of, the eighteenth century. Finding its clearest expression in France, it also drew on sources further afield and had important manifestations elsewhere. The roots of the Enlightenment were to be found, according to Dilthey, in the early and mid-seventeenth century, a time of increasing freedom from Church oversight of intellectual life, especially in Protestant countries. Authors such as Galileo and Descartes developed an ideal of a free and sovereign, self-confident human being, who believed in the progress of the intellect, toleration and improving manners. British ideas along these lines (especially Shaftesbury's) were received in France, according to Dilthey, following the sojourns of Voltaire and Montesquieu in England in the late 1720s.

Emphasising the links between intellectual production and political structures, Dilthey argued that the French Enlightenment was particularly moulded by court society (despite the prominence of authors who were anything but courtiers). Dilthey saw the French Enlightenment as a seamless continuation of the *âge classique*, whose great authors, in their turn, had been strongly influenced by the golden age of the late Roman Republic and the early Empire.

14. In his last years, Dilthey also completed a large essay on the General Legal Code of 1794 and the discussions that led to its promulgation, launched by Frederick before his death: Wilhelm Dilthey, 'Das Allgemeine Landrecht', in *GS*, vol.12, p.131-204.
15. For Scherer's attitude to the Enlightenment, see Paolo Panizzo, 'Aufklärung und Nation in der Germanistik um 1900', in *'Aufklärung' um 1900: die klassische Moderne streitet um ihre Herkunftsgeschichte*, ed. Georg Neugebauer, Paolo Panizzo and Christoph Schmitt-Maaß (Paderborn, 2014), p.125-46. On Hermann Hettner's stance, see Elisabeth Décultot's contribution in this volume.

Much of Dilthey's account of French literature around 1700 reflected common German views, around 1900, of the contrast between the allegedly frivolous French and the profound Germans.

> The unambivalent concept, the precisely regulated order of words, its logical, straightforward extension, but most of all the courtly narrowing down of the riches of language into the most decorous and graceful expression: these were the devices of the classical language in France. The sensual power of intuition, the impetuousness of passionate expression and the power of fantasy were sacrificed for exactness, rules and courtly decorousness.[16]

Style and content became identical, exuding the self-confidence of the new natural sciences. Enlightenment authors increasingly felt confident enough to pronounce judgement on politics and religion, advocating rational reform. As Dilthey put it, in the French Enlightenment 'reason feels sovereign over life itself' ('Sie fühlt sich dem Leben selbst gegenüber souverän').[17] But he also recognised that such presumptions were always accompanied by a sober recognition of the irony, or the tragicomedy, of the human condition: the fragility of the body and the questionable motives and consequences of human action. The literature of this period was, therefore, described by Dilthey as a heady mix of the following ingredients:

> Wit, *esprit*, feeling that extends all the way to sentimentality, reasoning as fragmentary as life itself, a mixture of enthusiasm and a sceptical sense of reality that results in irony. All this is bound together in a sparkling, glittering and scintillating whole in their [Enlightenment authors'] best writings: a portrayal of the agility of their mind, of the ambiguity of the world and the contradictory human condition.[18]

16. My translation, as in all subsequent cases unless otherwise noted. *GS*, vol.3, p.88: 'Das eindeutig bestimmte Wort, die genau regulierte Wortstellung, der logische, gradlinige Fortgang, der den Leser mühelos und unwiderstehlich mit sich zieht, vor allem aber eine höfische Einschränkung der lebendigen Sprachfülle auf die schicklichen und anmutigen Worte – das waren die Mittel dieser klassischen Sprache. Ihr entsprach der neue Stil. Die sinnliche Kraft der Anschauung, das Ungestüm des leidenschaftlichen Ausdrucks und die Macht der Phantasie wurden nun der Genauigkeit, der Regel und der höfischen Schicklichkeit geopfert.'

17. *GS*, vol.3, p.97.

18. *GS*, vol.3, p.98-99: 'Witz, Esprit, Gefühl, das bis zur Sentimentalität geht, Raisonnement, das fragmentarisch ist wie das Leben selbst, Mischung von Enthusiasmus und skeptischem Wirklichkeitssinn in der Ironie: all das ist

Voltaire and Diderot embodied this spirit perfectly, especially in their ease of composition in a broad range of genres – from drama to prose to philosophical dialogues and essays. Dilthey ascribed to Voltaire and the *encyclopédistes* tremendous power in the European public sphere, where they disseminated the *esprit philosophique* via popular means and forms. Royalty, aristocracy and high officialdom respected and feared the *philosophes*, which often led to their persecution. Yet, if things went wrong, Voltaire, D'Alembert and La Mettrie (among others) could always count on asylum in Berlin. It is here that Dilthey elaborated his account of Frederick the Great as philosopher, an author he was equally fascinated and puzzled by. He could have explained away Frederick's admiration of French culture and his notorious aversion to German literature by reference to his education, the conflict between Crown Prince Frederick and his father (Frederick William I), or youthful philosophical preferences that calcified into stubborn convictions. Dilthey opted, however, for a serious consideration of Frederick's writings and intellectual profile, trying to understand why a collaborator of Voltaire and D'Alembert could not simultaneously appreciate their German contemporaries.

The age of Enlightenment brought forth, according to Dilthey, four authors 'who covered the full gamut of life in poetry, philosophy and their stirring impact: in France, Voltaire and Diderot; in Germany, Frederick the Great and Lessing'.[19] Here Dilthey regarded Frederick as both author and monarch, an Enlightenment writer through and through rather than a royal protagonist who also happened to dabble in poetry. Frederick was, for Dilthey, an Enlightenment author in Germany rather than an author of the German Enlightenment. However reluctantly, he fully acknowledged that 'the greatest German between Luther and Goethe belongs – in his literary inclinations and most of all in essential traits of his intellectual constitution – to France.'[20] The earlier identification of some supposedly essential

---

zu einem funkelnden, schillernden, sprühenden Ganzen in ihren höchsten Produktionen verbunden: einem Abbilde der Beweglichkeit ihres Geistes, der Vieldeutigkeit der Welt, der widerspruchsvollen Situation des Menschen.'

19. *GS*, vol.3, p.100-101: 'Das Zeitalter der Aufklarung hat vier Große Schriftsteller hervorgebracht, welche so das Ganze des Lebens dichtend, philosophierend und in agitatorischem Wirken umfaßt haben: in Frankreich Voltaire und Diderot, in Deutschland Friedrich den Großen und Lessing.'

20. *GS*, vol.3, p.87: 'Der größte Deutsche zwischen Luther und Goethe gehört in seinen literarischen Neigungen und in wesentlichen Zügen seiner geistigen Verfassung überhaupt, Frankreich an.'

features of French literature allowed Dilthey to suggest why Frederick so intensely disliked the heightened sensitivity and Christian outlook of an author like Klopstock. Most German literature of the time, Dilthey argued, strove for an idealised representation of sentiment, abstracted from reality – while Frederick used literature, like Voltaire or even Diderot, to confront soberly the human condition as it actually was, with irony and wit as key instruments in his toolkit.

Frederick, Dilthey suggested, wrote in order to appropriate for himself the fullness of life in dazzling colours, from its uplifting episodes to the more frequent moments of frustration and futility. The point of the king's philosophy-making was not so much to establish new truths as to reframe ideas that could enhance his inner force, an ideal approximating the philosophical self-help methods of Seneca and Marcus Aurelius.[21] For Dilthey, Frederick's poetry expressed an omnivorous attitude to life, and his philosophy was characterised by the tension between consciousness of freedom and the causal nexus of action, an awareness of human dignity and a more mechanical materialism, the search for happiness and a sense of duty. No wonder, then, that Frederick felt close affinity with the great French authors of the seventeenth century. As D'Alembert reported to Mme Du Deffand from Sans-Souci in June 1763, Frederick claimed that he would have rather composed Jean Racine's tragedy *Athalie* (1691) than fought the recently concluded Seven Years War.[22] Such dramas seem to have powerfully resonated with the Prussian monarch. His reader Henri de Catt recounted that, following the Prussian defeat at the Battle of Hochkirch (14 October 1758), the king wished to listen to Racine's *Mithridate* (1673), relating the crushing defeat of the eponymous king of Pontus.[23] For Dilthey, great as the king's service to Prussia was on other fronts, Frederick was not interested in bridging the gap between Corneille and Racine, on the one hand, and Klopstock or the young Goethe on the other.

> He searched for formulations that would bring order and shed light on the unfathomable substance of things, and the German books which he happened to look up showed him only a struggle with the individual multifariousness of existence ('ein Ringen mit der individuellen Mannigfaltigkeit des Daseins'). In literature he sought

21. *GS*, vol.3, p.101.
22. Frederick II, *Œuvres de Frédéric le Grand*, ed. Johann David Erdmann Preuß, 30 vols (Berlin, 1846-1856), vol.25, p.305.
23. *GS*, vol.3, p.103.

sovereignty of the mind and self-confident joy, but he found in the poetry of his own nation only the dark severity of the life of the soul. As soon as his affairs allowed him to examine our literature, he immediately set aside its products, which were unbearable for him.[24]

This was, according to Dilthey, the 'tragic bipolarity' ('tragische Zwiespältigkeit') of Frederick's intellectual self-formation. The king of Prussia could not perceive the idiosyncratic powers of his own nation, which he promoted in other ways.

The German Enlightenment: a Prussian affair?

Dilthey was not, however, prepared to renounce Frederick as a German protagonist. The Seven Years War was the hinge on which his own bipolar account of the Prussian monarch turned. This major crisis, which Prussia barely survived, necessitated a programme of national reconstruction. Dilthey argued that it also changed Frederick completely: gone was the life-embracing, joyful author. He was replaced by a sombre, hard man who cared less about the broader reaches of philosophy and literature. Dilthey portrayed a new Frederick, focused more squarely on ethics and politics, and transforming his reflections directly into practical reforms. In these efforts, aimed at the reconstruction of the Prussian state, the German Enlightenment became the closest ally of the Prussian monarch.[25]

In Dilthey's account, this heterogeneous group of pastors, civil servants, journalists, lawyers and popular authors became the willing instrument of Frederick in educating and enlightening his *Volk*. Despite his substantial disagreements with Hegel on other issues, Dilthey shared his predecessor's postulation of a tight link between Reformation and Enlightenment.[26] For Hegel, the French Enlightenment was largely a substitute for an absent Reformation, and the *Aufklärung* an extension

24. *GS*, vol.3, p.109: 'Er suchte die Zusammenfassungen, welche in den unermeßlichen Stoff der Dinge Ordnung und Licht brächten, und die deutschen Bücher, die er aufschlug, zeigten ihm nur ein Ringen mit der individuellen Mannigfaltigkeit des Daseins. Er suchte Souveränität des Geistes und Heiterkeit in der Dichtung, und er fand in der Poesie seines Volkes hur die dunkle Schwere des Gemütslebens. So legte er bald, wenn die Geschäfte ihm Zeit für einen Blick in unsere Literatur gestatteten, ihre Produkte als ihm unerträglich zur Seite.'
25. *GS*, vol.3, p.128-31.
26. Georg Wilhelm Friedrich Hegel, *Lectures on the philosophy of history*, translated by John Sibree (London, 1894), p.460-64.

of Lutheran culture. Along similar lines, Dilthey's German Enlightenment was an outgrowth of Protestant principles. Accompanied by
a traditional Prussian emphasis on service to the state, the Lutheran
principle of the individual and unmediated interpretation of Scripture
gave rise to the deep convictions of local *Aufklärer* concerning human
dignity, the autonomy of the will and the duty to assume political and
social responsibility.[27] What Dilthey called the German Enlightenment
was an unabashedly Prussian affair. While it had initially been the
creation of the state, the German Enlightenment eventually moulded
the Prussian state in its own image by shaping the intellectual profile
of its main agents in the bureaucracy, the judiciary, the Church and all
educational institutions.

Schools and academies allowed this group, centred around civil
servants, to make Prussia the educator of its citizens – a task that
was, in Dilthey's eyes, all the more urgent in a small state without
abundant natural resources that wished to play a prominent role in
European affairs. Its human capital had to be honed and perfected,
and it is here that the German Enlightenment was smoothly aligned
with Frederick II's project of rebuilding his state after the crisis of the
Seven Years War. Schooling, while largely differentiated according to
class and estate, became increasingly focused on ethics and modern
topics. Educational reformers from Johann Bernhard Basedow
(1724-1790) to Johann Heinrich Pestalozzi (1746-1827) introduced
expedient teaching methods that were eagerly applied in Prussia.
Closely supervised by Frederick's ministers, especially Karl Abraham
von Zedlitz (1731-1793), Prussian civil servants and pastors launched
the development of what Dilthey saw as the 'great modern educational
apparatus' ('großes modernes Unterrichtswesen') for the bureaucratic
state (*Beamtenstaat*).[28]

Theology too became more squarely centred on moral conduct
in the here and now through a Wolffian emphasis on self-perfection.
Religious policy and Church life in Berlin were run by liberal, mostly
Wolffian, theologians such as August Friedrich Sack (1703-1786),
Johann Joachim Spalding (1714-1804) or Wilhelm Abraham Teller
(1734-1804), and the theology faculty at the University of Halle
became a centre of the rationalist criticism of Scripture following
the lead of Johann Salomo Semler (1725-1791). Members of the
Berlin Academy, particularly its classes of speculative philosophy and

27. *GS*, vol.3, p.135.
28. *GS*, vol.3, p.161.

belles-lettres, disseminated the same 'morally orientated rationalism' ('moralisch gerichteter Rationalismus'),[29] which Dilthey regarded as closely attuned to the educational and political agenda of the state. The same accent could be perceived in the more popular literature, philosophy and poetry of the time.

Dilthey's overall positive assessment of the contribution of the Enlightenment to the gradual evolution of a self-confident German spirit is, however, attenuated by his unmasked disdain for most of its literary manifestations, from popular treatises by Moses Mendelssohn (1729-1786) and Thomas Abbt (1738-1766) to novels by Friedrich Nicolai (1733-1811) and Johann Jakob Engel (1741-1802) – and even prints and paintings by Daniel Chodowiecki (1726-1801). What contemporary French authors like Diderot achieved with wit, lightness of touch and sober insight into the ambiguities of human life, their German peers (Lessing excepted) did in the most convoluted way. More than a century after their composition, Dilthey found these erstwhile admired works 'an immense spoilage, broad shallow waters through which the historian of literature wades only reluctantly'.[30] Nevertheless, the authors of the German Enlightenment shared the naturalism and optimism of the broader movement, and brought about the formation of modern literary German – no mean feat given the contemporary prominence of French and Frederick II's aversion to their Wolffian, metaphysical bent. While forging a practical alliance with such authors and officials, the king remained 'an aristocrat of the spirit' with a deep sense of reality that rendered him incapable of appreciating 'the raw forms' of this emerging national culture.[31]

The Berlin Academy and the German Enlightenment

The central organ of the alliance between the Prussian state and the German Enlightenment was, according to Dilthey, the Berlin Academy of Sciences and Belles-Lettres. Especially in its plenary meetings and in the festive sessions marking the king's birthday and his accession, the Academy facilitated direct contact between its members and such senior officials as ministers Zedlitz and Ewald Friedrich von Hertzberg (1725-1795), close collaborators of Frederick.

---

29. *GS*, vol.3, p.156.
30. *GS*, vol.3, p.174: 'eine unermeßliche Makulatur, weite, seichte Gewässer, durch die auch der Literaturhistoriker sich nur widerwillig hindurcharbeitet'.
31. *GS*, vol.3, p.134.

The speeches delivered on such occasions – written by the king himself, Zedlitz or Hertzberg, provided much-needed public articulation and clarification of the principles behind government policy. Such academic sessions fulfilled a significant mediating function, Dilthey argued, in the absence of a representative assembly similar to the British Parliament or an institution resembling the aristocratic legal courts (*parlements*) in France.[32]

Dilthey's appreciation of the eighteenth-century Berlin Academy should not be taken for granted. A proud holder of a philosophy chair at Berlin's renowned university, Dilthey could have looked back pitifully at an age when the Prussian capital possessed no institution of higher education or regarded the Frederician Academy as a foreign implant, detrimental to the evolution of German intellectual life.[33] Yet, as mentioned above, Harnack's history of the Academy, published on its bicentenary in 1900, provided Dilthey with the incentive to investigate eighteenth-century intellectual life in detail, independently from his work on Schleiermacher. Drawing on the documents published by Harnack, Dilthey argued that, throughout Frederick's reign and especially after the Seven Years War, the German element came to dominate the Berlin Academy. He perceived, for example, an increasing tendency to focus on ethics, pedagogy, aesthetics and politics among the topics the Academy set for its prize contests. The alliance between the local Enlightenment and the Prussian state overcame, according to Dilthey, even the king's reluctance to admit German authors as full members of the institution. While the prize contests attracted essays from foreign authors of the stature of D'Alembert, Condillac and Condorcet, the king resented the election of Lessing and Gellert as external members, thwarted the attempt to admit Mendelssohn and ignored recommendations by D'Alembert, his main academic adviser, to appoint German authors. Even Hertzberg's efforts, after Frederick's death, to admit a large number of German members into the Academy were countered by Frederick William II and his chief minister Wöllner. In 1795 Hertzberg's reforms were reversed, his cast of mind and allies deemed too liberal and Frederician.[34]

---

32. GS, vol.3, p.135.
33. On some of these views, see Avi Lifschitz, 'Les concours de l'Académie de Berlin, vecteurs de transferts intellectuels franco-allemands, 1745-1786', in *Les Échanges savants franco-allemands au XVIIIᵉ siècle: transferts, circulations et réseaux*, ed. Claire Gantet and Markus Meumann (Rennes, 2019), p.205-18.
34. *GS*, vol.3, p.139-41.

Dilthey's discussion of the Berlin Academy is not free of contradictions. On the one hand, he acknowledged Frederick's lack of interest in recruiting the best local minds to the institution, recognising that 'the Academy of the king of Prussia was a French society and wished to be considered as such.'[35] On the other hand, Dilthey repeatedly argued that the Berlin Academy was the main organ of the German Enlightenment, sometimes despite the king's own wishes and preferences. A case in point is Dilthey's vindication of the crowning of Mendelssohn (rather than Kant) with the prize for the 1763 contest on certainty in metaphysics. This was, for Dilthey, a strong expression of the moral rationalism that characterised much of the German Enlightenment. Unlike Mendelssohn's elaborate defence of Wolffian metaphysics, Kant's denial of the applicability of mathematics to metaphysics and his principled self-consignment to the realm of possible experience were 'a condemnation of the entire theoretical foundation of the *Weltanschauung* of the German Enlightenment', which the Berlin Academy represented and propagated.[36]

Another contrast can be perceived between the appreciation of the Academy as a venue for interaction between government officials, Academy members and the broader educated public, on the one hand, and Dilthey's own 'aristocracy of spirit', on the other. If the Academy had rightly denied the young Kant its first prize in 1763, it proved out of touch in the 1780s and 1790s, when it became a focal point of opposition to Kant's Critical Philosophy. Dilthey the expert philosopher blamed the public-facing character of the Berlin Academy. It was now the alliance between academics and the broader German Enlightenment, enthusiastically endorsed earlier, that ultimately prevented the Academy from acknowledging the genius of Kant's Critical Philosophy. Yet this reaction was, to a large extent, inevitable within Dilthey's framework: the domination of the German Enlightenment inside the Academy depended precisely on the maintenance of a robust consensus between professional academicians and the broader public of Prussian *Gebildete*.[37]

Despite these apparent contradictions, Dilthey's reflections on the Berlin Academy, prompted by Harnack's history, represent an

35. *GS*, vol.3, p.139: 'Die Akademie des Königs von Preußen war eine französische Gesellschaft und wollte als eine solche gelten.'
36. *GS*, vol.3, p.136: 'die Verurteilung des ganzen theoretischen Unterbaues der Weltanschauung der deutschen Aufklärung'.
37. *GS*, vol.3, p.157.

important element in his late work. The argument that the Academy was a major venue for the propagation of Enlightenment because it fostered the links between intellectuals and the state led him to further reflections on the interface between institutions and ideas. Dilthey realised that it was through its prize contests, proceedings, plenary meetings and public sessions that the Academy became a prominent institutional setting for knowledge production and its dissemination. For a professionally trained philosopher, this was not an obvious point to make. In fact, Dilthey's positive appraisal of the Berlin Academy extended to its endowment with quasi-human agency:

> Great institutions which mankind has formed for its common ends have an indestructible vitality that permits them to adapt to changing circumstances. Even when the fundamental laws of such an institution have proven inadequate, even if certain aspects of its purpose have become obsolete, its roots, reaching down to these common ends, continue to live; its legal foundations, its financial means, and the manifold relationships in which it has become involved guarantee its continued existence. The function it has served in one cultural situation is replaced by a new one in keeping with new needs. This is what happened with the Prussian Academy of Sciences.[38]

If this rhetoric comes close to fetishising the institution, we should still make an effort to appreciate Dilthey's emphasis on organisations as indispensable loci of philosophy-making. At least in his essays on the Enlightenment, composed in the first decade of the twentieth century, Dilthey tended to give institutions their due by contrast to later philosophers and historians of ideas.

---

38. Peter Paret's translation in Wilhelm Dilthey, 'Frederick and the Academy', in *Frederick the Great: a profile*, ed. Peter Paret (London, 1972), p.177-97 (180). *GS*, vol.3, p.113: 'Große Institutionen, welche sich die Tätigkeit der Menschheit für ihre Zweckzusammenhänge gebildet hat, passen sich mit unverwüstlicher Lebenskraft veränderten Verhältnissen an. Wenn die Verfassung einer solchen Institution sich unzureichend erwiesen hat, wenn so manches in ihren Zielen nicht mehr der Zeit entspricht: ihre Wurzeln leben fort, die in den Zweckzusammenhang selber hinabreichen; ihre rechtlichen Grundlagen, ihre Geldmittel, die mannigfachen Verhältnisse, in welche sie eingreift, sichern ihren Fortbestand. Die Funktion, die sie für eine gegebene Lage der Kultur erfüllt hat, wird nun ersetzt durch eine andere, welche den neu entstandenen Bedürfnissen entspricht. So ist es auch mit der preußischen Akademie der Wissenschaften gegangen.'

Enlightenment and the centralised *Rechtsstaat*

That a professor and civil servant in the Berlin of the Second Reich should postulate a tight link between intellectuals and the Prussian state may be unsurprising. And yet Dilthey's framework accounts for some noteworthy points of departure from common narratives about the Enlightenment around 1900. He chose to present Frederick and his ministers as the master builders of a modern constitutional monarchy characterised by the rule of law and welfare provision, both a *Rechtsstaat* and a *Wohlfahrtsstaat*. Dilthey saw the social contract, a central element in the natural law tradition, as 'endowing the authorities only with the function of realising the rule of law and the highest possible increase of the common good in the state'.[39] Enlightened reform, allowing citizens to realise their potential in the most secure manner, could only be accomplished in a hereditary monarchy, unencumbered by the friction of political parties and ruled by a bureaucracy orientated towards general welfare under a king who saw himself as the highest official (*oberster Beamter*, a reference to Frederick's self-presentation as the first servant of the state).

If this was a somewhat fanciful reading, projecting Dilthey's own notions of the Prussian *Rechtsstaat* back onto the eighteenth century, it also led him to relativise his enthusiasm for German critiques of the universalism of the French Enlightenment and natural law theory. This is particularly evident in Dilthey's subtle critique of Justus Möser (1720-1794), the Osnabrück jurist who emphasised the inner centre of gravity of each community in his attempt to counter enlightened absolutism and centralising reforms. Universal rights, political equality or the modernisation of traditional customs and laws were all anathema to Möser. Like other authors of the historicist school, Dilthey highly appreciated the uniqueness of Möser's corporative account of the state as a slowly evolving joint-stock company (*Aktiengesellschaft*) of property holders, assigning to non-proprietors subsidiary and subservient roles before the rise of early modern commerce and finance. Möser's theory ran deliberately

---

39. *GS*, vol.3, p.182-83: 'Und wenn nun der Unterwerfungsvertrag hinzutritt und das Untertanenverhältnis schafft, so empfängt in ihm die Obrigkeit nur die Funktion, die Herrschaft des Gesetzes im Staat und die höchste Steigerung des allgemeinen Wohles zu erwirken.' See also the introduction to *Frederick the Great's philosophical writings*, ed. Avi Lifschitz, translated by Angela Scholar (Princeton, NJ, 2021).

contrary to most early modern natural law theories, where the state originated in an original contract between largely equal individuals in a state of nature. Despite his admiration for the originality and rhetorical power of Möser's work, Dilthey thought that it ignored the achievements of modern reforming, centralised states, which were assisted and legitimised by natural law theory. In a brief remark in his essay 'The eighteenth century and the historical world' ('Das achtzehnte Jahrhundert und die geschichtliche Welt'), Dilthey went as far as arguing that the limitations of Möser's work had also marred the entire historical school of law, from Savigny onwards.[40] Dilthey seemed to suggest that sound research into medieval history might (and should) recover the customary law of traditional, closely knit communities; at the same time, he emphasised the pre-modern and largely obsolete nature of such ideas following the rise of the bureaucratised nation state.

Dilthey was also not too enthused by Möser's view of erudition as laziness that was only enhanced by Enlightenment or by the argument that 'the modern overestimation of the cultivation of reason and of the culture based upon it must no longer be allowed to influence the education of the young, the appointment and promotion of public officials, and all social political evaluation of man'.[41] While praising Möser's rejection of eighteenth-century standards as criteria for the assessment of earlier periods, Dilthey found his politics dubious. Conceived imaginatively and accompanied by a wealth of historical detail, Möser's theory of the state could still appear at first sight, around 1900, 'infinitely narrow and rigid' ('unendlich eng und starr'), displaying a wilful ignorance of the workings of large modern states and the contribution of natural law.[42] If Dilthey highly appreciated Möser's writings as launching the historicist tradition, on the political front the Berlin-based professor clearly embraced the

---

40. *GS*, vol.3, p.256. For different interpretations of Möser's thought, see Jonathan B. Knudsen, *Justus Möser and the German Enlightenment* (Cambridge, 1986), and Beiser, *German historicist tradition*, p.63-97.
41. Patricia Van Tuyls' translation in Wilhelm Dilthey, *Selected works*, vol.4: *Hermeneutics and the study of history*, ed. Rudolf A. Makkreel and Frithjof Rodi (Princeton, NJ, 1996), p.370. *GS*, vol.3, p.253: 'Ein Ende nehmen muß demnach die moderne überschätzung der Verstandesbildung und der darauf gegründeten Kultur, bei der Erziehung der Jugend, der Anstellung und Beförderung der Beamten, bei der ganzen sozialen und politischen Wertung des Menschen.'
42. *GS*, vol.3, p.256.

modern Prussian *Rechtsstaat*, which he saw as a product of the alliance between Frederick the Great and the German Enlightenment.

Within Dilthey's largely historicist essay on eighteenth-century history-writing, this critique of Möser was rather inconspicuous. It did not, however, escape the discerning eye of Dilthey's erstwhile student, Friedrich Meinecke, who begged to differ some thirty years later. In Meinecke's renowned work on the emergence of historicism, Möser was a pillar of the new German movement alongside Herder and Goethe. The critique of Möser, if any, is more attenuated in Meinecke's work, where Dilthey was explicitly taken to task for calling Möser a 'powerful autochton' ('gewaltiger Autochton'), and natural law was seen as a shallow, inflexible tradition incapable of grasping anything profound about human nature.[43] Indeed, Meinecke crowned Möser as a founding father of historicism precisely because of what he saw as the substitution of localism, historical right and 'creative individuality' for natural law theories that derived rights and duties from universal principles.[44]

Conclusion

Enlightenment authors were clearly not Dilthey's favourite writers, nor were their ideas equal, in his eyes, to those of Schleiermacher or Goethe. And yet Dilthey endowed the Enlightenment in its Prusso-German guise with specific content and a unique profile, while highlighting its contribution to the evolution of German intellectual life rather than regarding it as a trivial preface to Idealism or Romanticism. Instead of erecting an insuperable intellectual barrier between Enlightenment and German classicism, Dilthey emphasised continuities and shared legacies, explicitly defending some of the main endeavours of the Enlightenment: 'The German Enlightenment and its religious substance have long and often, until this day, been depicted from the perspective of the genius-besotted romantic critique or a venomous theological polemic. History will do it more justice.'[45]

43. Friedrich Meinecke, *Die Entstehung des Historismus*, ed. Carl Hinrichs (Munich, 1959), p.304; *GS*, vol.3, p.253. See Lifschitz, 'Between Meinecke and Cassirer', p.60. On this point I differ from Frederick Beiser's attempt to present Möser as adhering to the natural law tradition in significant ways. (Beiser, *German historicist tradition*, p.92-97.)

44. Meinecke, *Die Entstehung des Historismus*, p.330, 332.

45. *GS*, vol.3, p.142: 'Die deutsche Aufklärung und ihr religiöser Wahrheitsgehalt sind lange und vielfach noch bis auf diesen Tag von dem Gesichtspunkte der

His account of the German Enlightenment is, of course, not unprob-
lematic. It focuses on theological rationalism, education, ethics and an
updated Wolffianism while ignoring the radical edges. This not only
applies to marginal figures, so compellingly rescued from oblivion
recently by Martin Mulsow, but is also the case of authors such as
Lessing or Kant.[46] Dilthey's account has virtually no room for the
non-political writings of Frederick the Great, and it does not engage
with the intensive exchange of the ageing Frederick with D'Alembert
and Voltaire, with whom he continued to discuss metaphysical evil or
the human condition in general. Yet Dilthey's essays on the Enlightenment are more appreciative of the phenomenon than alternative
contemporary portraits. Unlike later polemicists, Dilthey engaged
closely with eighteenth-century authors, and was alert to the critical
tensions within their writings. He did not sweep aside the Enlightenment's ironic awareness of what Kant called the crooked timber of
humanity, and credited its authors with the legitimisation of reforms
that gave rise to the modern state, for better or worse.[47] If Dilthey's
Enlightenment is, like his entire oeuvre, deeply riven by duality

---

    genialitätsstolzen Kritik ihrer romantischen Gegner und einer gehässigen
    theologischen Polemik aufgefast worden. Die Geschichte wird gerechter
    urteilen.' See also p.145: 'So darf die Härte, mit welcher Niebuhr, die Grimm,
    Hegel und Ranke sich von dem theologischen Rationalismus abwandten,
    nicht darüber täuschen, da sie in der historischen Kritik die Nachfolger von
    Semler, Lessing und Spittler und in der Erfassung des Ewigen in der Gestalt
    des Geschichtlichen die Schüler von Lessing und Kant waren' ('The severity
    with which Niebuhr, the brothers Grimm, Hegel and Ranke turned away
    from theological rationalism should not deceive us. In historical criticism they
    were the successors of Semler, Lessing and Spittler, while in the recognition
    of the eternal in the mould of the historical, they were the students of Lessing
    and Kant').

46. See, most recently, Martin Mulsow, *Radikale Frühaufklärung in Deutschland
    1680-1720*, 2 vols (Göttingen, 2018). The first volume is an updated edition
    of *Moderne aus dem Untergrund* (Hamburg, 2002), translated into English by
    H. C. Erik Midelfort as *Enlightenment underground: radical Germany 1680-1720*
    (Charlottesville, VA, 2015).

47. 'Out of such crooked wood as the human being is made, nothing entirely
    straight can be fabricated.' From the sixth proposition of 'Idea for a universal
    history with a cosmopolitan aim', translated by Allen W. Wood, in *Anthropology,
    history, and education*, ed. Günter Zöller and Robert B. Louden (Cambridge,
    2011), p.108-20 (113). Immanuel Kant, 'Idee zu einer allgemeinen Geschichte in
    weltbürgerlicher Absicht' (1784), in *Akademie-Ausgabe*, vol.8 (Berlin and Leipzig,
    1923), p.15-31 (23): 'Aus so krummem Holze, als woraus der Mensch gemacht
    ist, kann nichts ganz Gerades gezimmert werden.'

and contrast, these features express a creative tension rather than a hopeless inconsistency or a contradiction in terms.[48]

48. This article was written during a research fellowship at the Excellence Cluster 'Temporal Communities' at the Freie Universität Berlin (EXC 2020, Project ID 390608380, funded by the Deutsche Forschungsgemeinschaft). I am grateful to the project directors, Anita Traninger and Andrew James Johnston, for their invitation, and to their entire team for the warm welcome and invaluable help.

Lumières in France: the contribution of Gustave Lanson and his pupils

Nicholas Cronk

University of Oxford

In 2006, the Bibliothèque nationale de France mounted an exhibition with the title 'Lumières! Un héritage pour demain'. A curious title, insofar as it contains a clear answer to the question it poses. But 'Lumières!', with its forceful exclamation mark, is certainly a confident assertion of the term, and of the values behind it. In a cartoon from 2014, Plantu uses the heading 'L'Europe des Lumières' to comment sardonically on the rise of the far right in the forthcoming European elections; and, more recently, President Macron has often invoked the values of *les Lumières* in the context of unrest arising from religious and racial tensions. The term is vividly present in modern French culture in a way that it was not even half a century ago. Much has been written on the use of the French term *Lumières*, and I propose in this article to begin by reviewing the terminological question and looking briefly at discussion of the term *lumière* in France, from the eighteenth century to the present. I will then explore a related institutional question and ask how the notion of *Lumières* was written about and taught, and when and how it entered the school and then university syllabus in France.

A concept in search of a term: from *lumière* to *Lumières*

There is a considerable literature on the use of the French term *Lumières*, and it may be useful to provide a brief (and inevitably selective) overview of these discussions. To begin with, the use of *Lumières* as a translation of *Aufklärung* is surprisingly recent. According to Diego Venturino's excellent study of this subject, the first occurrence of *le siècle des lumières* fully in its modern sense as a historicised concept to describe an object of academic study is found in Louis Réau's *L'Europe française au siècle des*

Lumières (1938), and he points out that the term has really only become current since the early 1960s.[1] The key starting point here is that from the late seventeenth century, and throughout the 1700s, French writers and intellectuals had a strong sense of belonging to a new age – even if they didn't know how exactly to describe it. Dan Edelstein argues that it is this new moment of self-consciousness, creating a self-reflexive historical narrative, that is the defining feature of what we now call the Enlightenment. In trying to find the right words to describe this new sense of moment, the image of light, *lumière*, is very common, as here in Fontenelle's 'Réponse à l'évêque de Luçon' (1732): 'Il s'est répandu depuis un temps un esprit philosophique presque tout nouveau, une lumière qui n'avait guère éclairé nos ancêtres.'[2] The metaphor of *les lumières* was already well established in the seventeenth century, but for it to acquire its 'enlightened' connotation, it was further necessary, as Céline Spector has argued, for there to be a receptive public and a sense of public opinion.[3]

Throughout the eighteenth century, the terminology remains slippery: we are speaking here of a metaphor, not a philosophical concept, and *lumière* can be expressed both in the singular and in the plural. Voltaire, in his fiction *Le Monde comme il va*, writes of a singular 'light of reason': 'Ils jugèrent bien, parce qu'ils suivaient la lumière de la raison';[4] while in his *Digression sur les Anciens et les Modernes*, Fontenelle writes of reasoning with *lumières* in the plural: 'Ainsi cet homme qui a vécu depuis le commencement du monde jusqu'à présent [...] est maintenant dans l'âge de la virilité, où il raisonne avec plus de force et a plus de lumières que jamais.'[5] Voltaire has a particular liking for the expression *siècle éclairé*: using the database *Tout Voltaire*, we find

1. Diego Venturino, 'L'historiographie révolutionnaire française et les Lumières, de Paul Buchez à Albert Sorel: suivi d'un appendice sur la genèse de l'expression "siècle des Lumières" (XVIIIe-XXe siècles)', in *Historiographie et usages des Lumières*, ed. Giuseppe Ricuperati (Berlin, 2002), p.21-84 (83).

2. Quoted by Anton M. Matytsin, 'Whose light is it anyway? The struggle for light in the French Enlightenment', in *Let there be Enlightenment: the religious and mystical sources of rationality*, ed. Anton M. Matytsin and Dan Edelstein (Baltimore, MD, 2018), p.62-85 (83).

3. See Céline Spector, 'The "lights" before the Enlightenment: the tribunal of reason and public opinion', in *Let there be Enlightenment*, ed. A. M. Matytsin and D. Edelstein, p.86-102.

4. *Œuvres complètes de Voltaire* (henceforth *OCV*), ed. Theodore Besterman *et al.*, 205 vols (Oxford, 1968-2022), vol.30B, p.59.

5. Fontenelle, *Entretiens sur la pluralité des mondes, Digression sur les Anciens et les Modernes*, ed. Robert Shackleton (Oxford, 1955), p.172.

eleven occurrences of the phrase in his writings; and, this time using *Electronic Enlightenment,* five further uses are to be found in Voltaire's letters.[6] This metaphor is of course as much visual as verbal, as Daniel Fulda has recently shown in his *Aufklärung fürs Auge.*[7] The frontispiece of Voltaire's *Eléments de la philosophie de Newton* (1738) depicts a writer, Voltaire, whose manuscript is illumined by a shaft of almost divine light descending from Newton himself, and reflected by a mirror held aloft by a bare-breasted muse, none other than Emilie Du Châtelet.[8] We may no longer sympathise with the gender stereotypes enshrined in this image (Du Châtelet was in fact a greater scientific thinker than Voltaire), but the quasi-divine metaphor of light descending from on high could hardly be more strident.

Crucially, however, the metaphor is treacherously multivalent. The biblical connotations of light are well known, beginning with Jesus' injunction to his disciples: 'I am the light of the world. Whoever follows me will never walk in darkness, but will have the light of life';[9] and we have only to think of the English Quakers and their 'inner light', where Voltaire finds echoes of the thinking of Malebranche.[10] So this is a metaphor with distinct religious undertones, one that can be used by writers who are ideologically opposed to the *philosophes,* as well as by other authors such as Dubos who are sceptical about the idea of progress.[11] Roland Mortier has produced evidence to suggest that the metaphor of light becomes increasingly secularised in the 1750s and 1760s,[12] but, even so, many contradictions remain.

6. Voltaire, *Correspondence and related documents,* ed. Theodore Besterman, in *OCV,* vol.85-135 (Oxford, 1968-1977), D1622, D11871, D13296, D15294 and D16525.
7. *Aufklärung fürs Auge: ein anderer Blick auf das 18. Jahrhundert,* ed. Daniel Fulda (Halle, 2020).
8. See *OCV,* vol.15, illustration 4, facing p.195.
9. John 8.12 (New International Version). See also Matthew 5.14: 'You are the light of the world. A city on a hill cannot be hidden. Neither do people light a lamp and put it under a bowl. Instead they put it on its stand, and it gives light to everyone in the house. In the same way, let your light shine before men, that they may see your good deeds and praise your Father in heaven' (NIV).
10. *Lettres sur les Anglais,* ed. N. Cronk, in *OCV,* vol.6B (Oxford, 2020), p.15. See also William H. Barber, 'Voltaire and Quakerism: Enlightenment and the inner light', *SVEC* 24 (1963), p.81-109.
11. On Dubos's views on the progress of *l'esprit philosophique,* see Dan Edelstein, *The Enlightenment: a genealogy* (Chicago, IL, 2010), p.24-28.
12. Roland Mortier, '*Lumière* et *lumières*: histoire d'une image et d'une idée au XVIIᵉ et au XVIIIᵉ siècle', in *Clartés et ombres du siècle des Lumières: études sur le XVIIIᵉ siècle littéraire* (Geneva, 1969), p.13-59.

As Anton Matytsin writes, 'the competing uses of the light metaphor reveal a complex spectrum of eighteenth-century views on the proper relationship between faith and reason.'[13]

To sum up the position in the eighteenth century, we can say that the metaphor of light is widely present, albeit ambiguously. The *Lumières* at this stage do not have a capital 'L', and the syntagm *siècle des lumières*, although it exists, is far from standard, and far from having a uniquely positive sense. Here is a notorious opponent of Voltaire, the abbé Nonnotte – this quotation comes from the article 'Préjugés' in his *Dictionnaire philosophique de la religion*: 'C'est un préjugé qui n'est ni excusable, ni tolérable, de prétendre que ce siècle est le siècle des véritables lumières, et que, jusqu'à nos jours, on n'avait pas su, ou que l'on n'avait pas osé penser.'[14] Even when Condorcet, a confirmed disciple of Voltaire, uses the expression, it is '*un* siècle de lumières' and not '*le* siècle…'. Here he is, writing at the end of the century on a quintessentially enlightened topic, the need for public education: 'Dans les siècles de préjugés, ceux qui ont éclairé les hommes ont diminué souvent le mal que leur faisaient ceux qui les gouvernaient, et dans un siècle de lumières toute vérité nouvelle devient un bienfait.'[15]

The nineteenth century inherits from the eighteenth the expression *siècle des lumières*, and inherits it with all its ambiguities. Tocqueville avoids the phrase,[16] as does Victor Cousin (notwithstanding his interest in Condorcet, who does use the expression).[17] Louis de Bonald speaks with irony in 1830 of 'cette bienheureuse époque, pompeusement décorée du nom de *siècle des lumières*';[18] and in the same vein there is this well-known passage from Taine, who sought to pin the blame of political instability in France on the Revolution: 'Aux approches de 1789, il est admis qu'on vit "dans le siècle des lumières", dans "l'âge de raison", qu'auparavant, le genre humain était dans l'enfance, qu'aujourd'hui il est devenu "majeur". Enfin la vérité s'est manifestée

---

13. Matytsin, 'Whose light is it anyway?', p.63.
14. Claude François Nonnotte, *Dictionnaire philosophique de la religion, nouvelle édition, corrigée et augmentée*, 4 vols (Besançon, J.-F. Charmet, 1774), vol.3, p.389. The article 'Préjugés' is absent from the 1772 edition of this work.
15. Condorcet, 'Sur l'instruction publique', quoted by Matytsin, 'Whose light is it anyway?', p.84.
16. See in this volume the article by Elisabeth Décultot, p.25.
17. See in this volume the article by Christian Helmreich, p.11.
18. See in this volume the article by Elisabeth Décultot, p.24.

et, pour la première fois, on va voir son règne sur la terre.'[19] This is a fascinating passage: the syntagm 'le siècle des lumières' is certainly used, but with a lower-case 'l', in inverted commas, and as a synonym for 'l'âge de raison'. The term exists, but hardly as the unique or principal designation of the period it refers to. And above all, what is striking here is Taine's almost disdainful use of the expression: he is anything but an advocate for this 'siècle des lumières'.

Diego Venturino has shown how the expression *le siècle des lumières* flourishes in the nineteenth century, not least in the writings of those hostile to the Revolution and the *philosophes*, and, in fact, the term gradually becomes historicised, in his phrase, precisely because of its polemical use by *opponents* of the Enlightenment. Two databases recently developed at the Sorbonne help confirm Venturino's findings:[20] the OBVIL *Critique* database (containing major works of French criticism spanning the period 1750-1925, with a particular emphasis on publications dating from the Third Republic), going through the interface *Obvie*, produces ten occurrences of 'siècle des lumières': not a large number, but still revealing some interesting and unexpected usages, including one by Albert Thibaudet in the 1930s. Most astonishingly, we discover that Emile Faguet (*En lisant Nietzsche*, 1904) uses 'le siècle des lumières' to refer to the nineteenth century! – a salutary reminder of just how slippery this term can be. If we run the same search in the *Très grande base (1801-1899)*, the results are more extensive: 'siècle des lumières' is widely found, but so are other expressions, including 'siècle éclairé' and 'siècle de Voltaire'. A more in-depth investigation of the expression *siècle des lumières* than is possible here would evidently need to include all the alternative expressions available, but here are some preliminary findings from the *Très grande base* that already suggest the wide variety of terminology in use in the nineteenth century:

encyclopédistes	2618 occurrences
siècle des lumières	739
siècle éclairé	352
siècle de Voltaire	131
siècle des philosophes	28

19. Hippolyte Taine, *Les Origines de la France contemporaine*, vol.1: *L'Ancien Régime* (Paris, 1875), book 3, ch.3. This work was reviewed critically by John Morley, who felt that Taine exaggerated the influence of Enlightenment writers on the course of the French Revolution.
20. I am very grateful to Glenn Roe for his advice concerning these databases.

It has been suggested that a critical point in the development of
the notion of Enlightenment was reached when the need was felt
in various European languages to find a translation of the German
Aufklärung. In this context we can say that, by the end of the nineteenth
century, the expression *siècle des lumières* is widely in use in French, yet
still not established as the standard translation of *Aufklärung*.

The *Lumières* as the subject of scholarly study

Another way to come at this question is to ask when the phenomenon
of the Enlightenment – whatever we choose to call it – first began to
be taught and studied as a subject. Giuseppe Ricuperati has pointed
to the importance of Gustave Lanson and his pupils,[21] whose significance is summed up by John Robertson in this way: 'Historical
distance entered studies of the Enlightenment only in the early
twentieth century. French literary historians, led by Gustave Lanson
and his pupils Daniel Mornet and Paul Hazard, were the first to
apply scholarship to the question of the Revolution's "intellectual
origins", and to set aside the simple equation of *philosophie* and revolution.'[22] This is an important insight. Just when we thought we were
moving away from a Francocentric view of the Enlightenment, John
Robertson is here giving priority to 'French literary historians'. And,
secondly, he is attributing this development to 'literary historians' and
not, as we might have expected, to philosophers or historians of ideas.
The very idea of talking about Lanson in the same breath as Franco
Venturi or Jürgen Habermas might once have seemed decidedly
eccentric, not to say reckless.

Gustave Lanson (1857-1934) was a historian of literature, a pupil
of Ferdinand Brunetière, the leading literary critic of his day. Lanson
taught in *lycées* in the 1890s, then in middle age made the transition
to university teaching: at the Ecole normale supérieure from 1894,
then as professor at the Sorbonne from 1904. He is usually now
remembered as the inventor of literary history in France; he rejected
the subjectivism and literary impressionism that characterised writing
about literature in the second half of the nineteenth century, and in

21. Giuseppe Ricuperati, 'Illuminismo e settecento dal dopoguerra ad oggi', in *La
     Reinvenzione dei lumi: percorsi storiografici del novecento*, ed. Giuseppe Ricuperati
     (Florence, 2000), p.201-22 (203-205).
22. John Robertson, *The Enlightenment: a very short introduction* (Oxford, 2015),
     p.9-10.

its place he wanted to create a form of literary criticism founded on erudition and precision that described as exhaustively as possible the sources of a given work of literature. A lecture delivered in Brussels in 1909, 'L'esprit scientifique et la méthode de l'histoire littéraire',[23] gives a flavour of his approach, which is now, needless to say, massively out of fashion. That said, Lanson's best-selling *Histoire de la littérature française*, first published in 1895, has been influential over a long period; a revised edition was published by Hachette as recently as 1985.

Antoine Compagnon, in his revisionist study *La Troisième République des lettres*, has done much to resurrect Lanson's reputation.[24] He shows how, at the turn of the twentieth century, at a time of huge upheaval at the Sorbonne, the dominant humanities discipline was history, including such prominent names as Ernest Lavisse. Literary study, in contrast, was viewed as a dilettantish subject and did not at all enjoy the same standing. Lanson set out to 'defend' literary study by giving it a clear methodology and purpose that historians could understand, and so he worked to establish the study of 'literary history' with its study of sources, and its mission to understand authors and their works in a historical, cultural and sociological context. The Lansonian 'method' has often been ridiculed, and we too easily forget that, influenced by his Sorbonne colleague Emile Durkheim, there was also a sociological aspect to Lanson's thinking about literature that was markedly innovative.[25]

Of particular interest here is to understand how Lanson came to focus on the study of the eighteenth century. In the 1890s he first made his name with a series of monographs on leading writers of the seventeenth century, producing books on Bossuet (1891), Boileau (1892) and Corneille (1898), the last two both appearing in the high-profile series *Les Grands Ecrivains français*, published by Hachette. The ideological bent here is clear: these were the authors that figured on *lycée* syllabuses in the 1890s, all of them part of the grand tradition of seventeenth-century literature viewed as

23. Gustave Lanson, *Méthodes de l'histoire littéraire* (Paris, 1925), ch.2.
24. Antoine Compagnon, *La Troisième République des lettres: de Flaubert à Proust* (Paris, 1983). See also Glenn H. Roe, *The Passion of Charles Péguy: literature, modernity, and the crisis of historicism* (Oxford, 2014).
25. See his essay 'L'histoire littéraire et la sociologie' (1904), in *Essais de méthode, de critique et d'histoire littéraire*, ed. Henri Peyre (Paris, 1965), p.61-80. See also Martine Jey, 'Gustave Lanson: de l'histoire littéraire à une histoire sociale de la littérature?', *Le Français aujourd'hui* 145 (2004), p.15-22.

the pinnacle of French (Catholic) culture. Stéphane Zékian shows
how the Académie was happy to celebrate the seventeenth century,
le grand siècle, but was far more cautious about celebrating the
eighteenth as an epoch (with just a partial exception for the case of
Voltaire).[26] Martine Jey has similarly shown how school syllabuses
of the nineteenth century are deeply mistrustful of Enlightenment
authors, and prefer the pedagogic security of *le siècle de Louis XIV*.[27]
There is an obvious irony of course in the fact that it was Voltaire
who gave currency to the expression *le siècle de Louis XIV*. Indeed,
the *Siècle de Louis XIV* is one of the few books of Voltaire's that could
safely be entrusted to schoolchildren, and it is a nice paradox that
Voltaire survives in schools up to the 1890s mainly on account of his
history of the seventeenth century.

Everything changes with the Dreyfus affair, in the late 1890s. The
facts are well known: on 13 January 1898, Zola published 'J'accuse',
an open letter to the president of the Republic, Félix Faure, on the
front page of *L'Aurore*, and the following day a petition was started,
calling for a revision of the decision concerning the officer Dreyfus.
Zola was the first to sign, Anatole France the second, and by the end
of the month the petition had collected over 3000 signatures. Lanson,
who added his name on 16 January, was an early signatory and
the only prominent teacher of literature at the Sorbonne to support
the cause (in contrast to the Sorbonne historians, who typically
identified as *dreyfusards*): as Compagnon puts it, 'Lanson fait figure
d'un dreyfusard de la première heure.'[28] The Dreyfus affair inevitably
recalled the Calas affair and memories of Voltaire's activism, and it
seems to have been the defining moment that turned Lanson into an
Enlightenment scholar, opening up for him also new career opportunities. Liberated once and for all from the conservative inheritance
of Brunetière, Lanson was appointed *maître de conférences* at the Ecole
normale in 1900, then professor at the Sorbonne in 1904, when he
announced that his inaugural course of lectures would be on Voltaire.

26. See the contribution by Stéphane Zékian in this volume, p.81-99.
27. See Martine Jey, 'The literature of the Enlightenment: an impossible legacy
    for the Republican school', *Yale French studies* 113 (2008), p.46-59. This is
    an interesting study, but it is misleading in treating the Third Republic as a
    whole, and in not recognising the watershed represented by the Dreyfus affair.
    See also, by the same author, *La Littérature au lycée: invention d'une discipline
    (1880-1925)* (Metz, 1998).
28. Compagnon, *La Troisième République des lettres*, p.63. The medievalist Joseph
    Bédier was a *dreyfusard*, but did not teach at the Sorbonne.

The political context here is all-important: following the victory of the Radicals in the elections of 1902, Emile Combes became the head of a government that in 1905 formally enacted the separation of Church and state: Voltaire's moment had come.

Previously, Brunetière had defended the literature of the seventeenth century, in particular the great Catholic writer Bossuet, but now the Third Republic looks to the eighteenth century, and to Voltaire, as its ideological guarantor. 'Bossuet ou Voltaire', writes Antoine Compagnon, 'c'est moins un choix littéraire qu'une alternative politique et idéologique inévitable, comme un nouveau clivage des anciens et des modernes, en l'occurrence des catholiques et des républicains.'[29] In an article of 1905, 'Dix-septième ou dix-huitième siècles?', Lanson denounces what he calls 'monarchical' literature, and explains why it is the writings of the *philosophes* (he does not use that term) that are most appropriate for the education of Third Republic students:

> C'est une absurdité de n'employer qu'une littérature monarchique et chrétienne à l'éducation d'une démocratie qui n'admet pas une religion d'Etat. [...] Des écrivains du règne de Louis XIV, de Boileau, de Racine, de La Fontaine, de Mme de Sévigné, on n'extrairait pas un grain de pensée patriotique ou sociale. [...] Nous reconnaissons dans [le dix-huitième siècle] les origines de l'ordre intellectuel et social où nous vivons. Nous y reconnaissons les sentiments qui sont encore aujourd'hui les moteurs de notre action. Voltaire, Montesquieu, Diderot, Rousseau, Buffon sont plus près de nous, instruisent mieux nos enfants à recueillir notre héritage et continuer notre effort, que Bossuet et Racine.[30]

Compagnon sums up the situation as follows: 'Autour de 1898, Voltaire est devenu la figure de proue de la littérature française. Mme de Maintenon perd tout crédit après la Séparation, Bossuet est relégué chez les cléricaux. Et Voltaire, c'est le XVIIIe siècle, les Lumières. Le témoignage de Lanson est d'autant plus éloquent qu'il avait d'abord choisi Bossuet et le XVIIe, la morale chrétienne.'[31] It is interesting that Compagnon uses here the term *Lumières* – that is his usage, not Lanson's. What Compagnon does not say is that after lecturing on

---

29. Compagnon, *La Troisième République des lettres*, p.98.
30. *Revue bleue* (30 September 1905), quoted by Compagnon, *La Troisième République des lettres*, p.110-11.
31. Compagnon, *La Troisième République des lettres*, p.110.

Voltaire, as a professor at the Sorbonne, Lanson effectively becomes a scholar of the Enlightenment. His lectures lead to the publication of a short but important book, *Voltaire*, published by Hachette in 1906 in the *Grands Ecrivains français* series. In this work, Lanson makes remarkable claims for Voltaire: not only is he 'le principal maître de style des Français lettrés', his ideological stance is already that of the modern-day radical: 'Nous continuons Voltaire, [...] nous faisons en notre temps ce qu'il a fait dans le sien.'[32] Lanson takes this line of argument further in his pioneering critical edition of the *Lettres philosophiques*, published in two volumes in 1909: this edition not only rescued from near oblivion a key Voltairean work that had been all but invisible for the previous hundred years, it also enshrined Voltaire as the moderate radical who was acceptable to the Third Republic.

Lanson was increasingly becoming interested in the broader movement of ideas in the eighteenth century, and, even in discussing Racine's *Athalie*, he adopts a Voltairean position in decrying the religious fanaticism of the priest Joad.[33] Already in 1903, he is asking the key question that would dominate early treatments of the Enlightenment – 'Quelle part faut-il faire à la littérature du XVIIIe siècle dans la Révolution française?'[34] – and, in a lecture delivered in 1907 to a body of *instituteurs*, he argued that they all shared with the eighteenth century a commitment to 'l'esprit critique et la tolérance'.[35] Lanson's teaching now seems to have been increasingly concerned with the eighteenth century, and what we can genuinely call 'Enlightenment' issues, and if this work is not now better known to us, that is because, in the manner of the times, his lecture courses were routinely published in the *Revue des cours et conférences*, a journal not now easily accessible. Over two years, Lanson taught first a course with the title 'Origines et premières manifestations de l'esprit philosophique dans la littérature française de 1675 à 1748', then the following year a course entitled 'Formation et développement de l'esprit philosophique du XVIIIe siècle';[36] his core conclusions

---

32. Gustave Lanson, *Voltaire* (1906; Paris, 1960), p.210, 217.
33. See Ralph Albanese, 'Critique universitaire et discours scolaire sous la Troisième République: le cas Racine', *Revue de l'histoire littéraire de la France* 109 (2009), p.645-59 (655-56).
34. 'Programme d'études sur l'histoire provinciale de la vie littéraire en France' (1903), in *Essais de méthode*, ed. H. Peyre, p.81-87 (85).
35. Compagnon, *La Troisième République des lettres*, p.110.
36. *Revue des cours et conférences* 16-17 (1907-1908) and 17-18 (1908-1910). There is a reprint of these two lecture courses, published in the *Burt Franklin research*

were summarised for a broader public in articles in the *Revue du mois*,[37] and in the *Revue de l'histoire littéraire de la France*.[38] Lanson was clearly engaged in what was a pioneering attempt to understand the movement of ideas that we would now call the Enlightenment; of course, as a professor of French literature, he confines his study to France, and his use of terminology is interesting, in that he refers not to *lumières*, as he might have done, but to *l'esprit philosophique*, a term that was more meaningful to his students and perhaps less polemical. Lanson subsequently extended his interests, lecturing on clandestine philosophical manuscripts, in the process defining a new subject, the importance of which has only become fully appreciated and exploited in recent years.[39]

Gustave Lanson went on to enjoy the rewards of institutional distinction: he succeeded Ernest Lavisse as director of the Ecole normale supérieure (1919-1927), and in 1923 was elected to a chair of eighteenth-century literary history, created especially for him, which he held until his retirement in 1928. When he died in 1934, Lanson was remembered above all as the inventor of French literary history, and posterity has not been kind. Sartre, a *normalien* during Lanson's time as director of the Ecole, was cruel about him, and, more generally, Lanson's famous method, including his positivist obsession with sources and his fetish for *fiches* (on which research students had to record their discoveries in orderly fashion) have been much mocked; it is hard to forget Péguy's description of Lanson's followers as 'fichomanes'. In recent years, Antoine Compagnon has resurrected Lanson's reputation as a literary scholar who defended literary study in the university when the subject was under threat, and critics like Alain Viala have remembered the significance of Lanson's early interest in the sociology of literature. However, and the omission is extraordinary, Lanson has not generally been remembered at all for his contribution to the study of the Enlightenment. Compagnon's otherwise excellent

and source works series under the title *Origines et premières manifestations de l'esprit philosophique dans la littérature française de 1675 à 1748* (New York, 1973).

37. Gustave Lanson, 'Le rôle de l'expérience dans la formation de la philosophie du XVIIIe siècle en France', *Revue du mois* 9:49 (1910), p.5-28, and 9:52 (1910), p.409-29.

38. Gustave Lanson, 'Questions diverses sur l'histoire de l'esprit philosophique en France avant 1750', *Revue de l'histoire littéraire de la France* 19 (1912), p.1-29 and 293-317.

39. See Geneviève Artigas-Menant, 'Cent ans de réponses aux "Questions diverses" de Lanson', *Problemata: revista internacional de filosofia* 4:3 (2013), p.21-49.

study has no discussion of this, nor does Jean-Thomas Nordmann's *Critique littéraire française au XIXe siècle (1800-1914).*[40] The reasons for this are easy to identify. Lanson's reputation as a literary historian passed so rapidly out of fashion that his intellectual contribution to eighteenth-century studies has not been taken seriously. To fully reconstruct Lanson's teaching of the Enlightenment, scholars need to piece together his ideas from a wide variety of sources, many of them no longer easily available. Lanson himself did not produce a major synthesis of his ideas, and no one has collected together his articles dealing with the Enlightenment in an easily accessible form.

His influence was exercised more through teaching than it was through publication, and we need to look more carefully therefore at the work of his pupils. Leaving to one side those pupils (such as Gustave Rudler, André Morize and Georges Ascoli) who were primarily literary scholars, there were three, Ely Carcassonne, Daniel Mornet and Paul Hazard, who became significant Enlightenment teachers and scholars in the period between the wars. The young Franco Venturi had to leave Italy with his family in the 1930s; when in 1939 he published *La Jeunesse de Diderot*, the teachers of eighteenth-century thought he had known in Paris were Lanson's pupils. It is interesting too that, like Lanson (and with the exception I will come to at the end of this article), his pupils all avoid using the term *Lumières*.

Ely Carcassonne, as well as writing on Fénelon, made a major contribution to Montesquieu studies with his thesis, published in 1927, *Montesquieu et le problème de la constitution française au XVIIIe siècle*. Carcassonne was later excluded from his university post by the Vichy government, and he died in 1941.

Daniel Mornet, Lanson's favoured pupil and successor, wrote both on literary topics and on the history of ideas. In *La Pensée française au XVIIIe siècle*, first published in 1926, and reaching an eleventh edition in 1965, he speaks of *l'esprit classique*, of *le rationalisme classique* and then of *l'esprit nouveau*. His best remembered book is *Les Origines intellectuelles de la Révolution française* (1933), a work that seeks to

---

40. Jean-Thomas Nordmann, *La Critique littéraire française au XIXe siècle (1800-1914)* (Paris, 2001). The one notable exception is Giuseppe Ricuperati, who writes that 'il distacco di Gustave Lanson da Fernand Brunetière è legato al superamento positivo dell'affaire Dreyfus e alla vittoria della giustizia et dalla ragione. Il Lanson riorienta la storia letteraria, di cui è ormai il protagonista, sul XVIII secolo. L'interesse si sposta da uno spirito classic come Bossuet a Voltaire' (*La Reinvenzione dei lumi*, p.vii).

connect the Enlightenment and the Revolution, though it is argued in a rather simplistic way.[41] His use of terminology is interesting: one chapter is entitled 'Les maîtres de l'esprit nouveau', and another, 'La diffusion des idées nouvelles parmi les gens de lettres': we find no mention anywhere of *les Lumières*.

Paul Hazard, a literary comparatist who cofounded the *Revue de littérature comparée*, was elected to the Académie française in 1939.[42] In *La Crise de la conscience européenne, 1680-1715*, first published in 1935, he has chapters such as 'La science et le progrès' and 'Vers un nouveau modèle d'humanité', which is opposed here to 'les croyances traditionelles' – again, we find no mention of *Lumières*. Hazard wrote a continuation of this work during wartime, in extremely challenging circumstances; he died in 1944, and this last work, *La Pensée européenne au XVIIIe siècle de Montesquieu à Lessing*, was published posthumously in 1946, appearing in the same series as Réau's *L'Europe française au siècle des Lumières*. In his final publication, Hazard does – at last – speak of *les lumières*, in a chapter 'La raison. Les Lumières':

> La lumière; ou mieux encore, les lumières, puisqu'il ne s'agissait pas d'un seul rayon, mais d'un faisceau qui se projetait sur les grandes masses d'ombre dont la terre était encore couverte, ce fut un mot magique que l'époque s'est plu à dire et à redire. [...] La lumière, les lumières, c'était la devise qu'ils inscrivaient sur leurs drapeaux, car pour la première fois, une époque choisissait son nom. Commençait le siècle des lumières; commençait l'Aufklärung.[43]

It may well be, as Diego Venturino argues, that Louis Réau is pioneering in his use of the phrase *siècle des Lumières*, in his book of 1938, *L'Europe française au siècle des Lumières*, even though, as Venturino concedes, the time frame that Réau ascribes to his '*siècle des Lumières*' is emphatically not one that we would now recognise. Yet it could be argued that it is Paul Hazard, Lanson's pupil, who plays the determining role in establishing the term *Lumières* in the

---

41. Lucien Febvre wrote a highly critical review in the *Annales* (1941), 'De Lanson à Mornet: un renoncement?', reprinted in *Combats pour l'histoire* (Paris, 1953), p.263-68.

42. On Hazard's career, see Giuseppe Ricuperati, 'Paul Hazard', *Belfagor* 23 (1968), p.564-95, and, by the same author, 'Paul Hazard e la storiografia dell'Illuminismo', *Rivista storica italiana* 86 (1974), p.372-404. See also in this volume the contribution by Elisabeth Décultot, p.36.

43. Paul Hazard, *La Pensée européenne au XVIIIe siècle de Montesquieu à Lessing*, 3 vols (Paris, 1946), vol.1, p.41-42.

French language. At a critical moment in European history, Hazard boldly proposes *Lumières* – firmly in the plural, with a capital 'L' – as the translation of *Aufklärung*. There is a direct line from Paul Hazard to that 2006 exhibition at the Bibliothèque nationale de France with which we began.

The theme of Enlightenment
in Russian historiography, 1860-1900

Andrew Kahn

University of Oxford

Discussions of Enlightenment in Russia inextricably attach to views on Catherine the Great. A revival of interest in her legacy in the last quarter of the nineteenth century occasioned the first substantial treatment of her reign in Russian historiography. In 1873 a statue was erected in the centre of St Petersburg to commemorate Catherine the Great.[1] *Russian antiquity*, one of the leading historical periodicals of the time, published in tandem the lengthy speech delivered at the unveiling of the monument. It frankly acknowledges that, while Catherine 'completed a great deal started by Peter, especially in the early years of her reign', nonetheless, 'since the empress' death over the course of more than a half century the memory of her has weakened significantly.'[2] In fact, the Catherine period had largely vanished from Russian historiography between her death in 1796 and the 1870s. The causes for the empress' eclipse were multiple. In the aftermath of the Napoleonic Wars, her grandsons Alexander I and Nicholas I capitalised on their glory abroad by consolidating their absolute control of a huge empire prone to unrest at the periphery. The hopes of the gentry for the liberal reforms, born from eighteenth-century Enlightenment ideals associated with Catherine's rule, were disappointed by Alexander I and then extinguished by Nicholas.[3]

---

1. The ceremonial protocol for the unveiling of the statue in the presence of the imperial family and attended by representatives of all the social estates was published in November 1873: *Vysochaishe utverzhdennyi tseremonial torzhestvennogo otkrytia pamiatnika Imperatritse Ekaterine II* (St Petersburg, 1873).
2. For the speech, also published as a separate pamphlet, 'Pamiatnik Ekaterine II: 24-ogo noiabria 1873', *Russkaia starina* (henceforth *RS*) 8 (1873), p.633-43. All translations are my own unless otherwise indicated.
3. Political history did not incline them to family affection. The assassination of their father Paul I, Catherine's son, followed the assassination of their

Nicholas' crushing of the Decembrist Rebellion in 1825 ushered in a reactionary period that ended in the disaster of the Crimean War (the region where Catherine had achieved military success).

Biographically, in the decades after her death, Catherine's reputation had been tainted by a lurid sexual element, the product largely of political caricature during the French Revolution when she was seen as a Russian Marie-Antoinette. The persistence of this sensationalist approach led to a form of cancellation in the Victorian atmosphere that permeated Nicholas' reign, with its emphasis on family values and the official state doctrine calling on writers to promote national values, populism and autocracy. In the 1830s, a culturally dispossessed gentry, searching for meaning and direction in history, turned inwards to a nostalgic, romantic vision of Russian history. Without the means to bring about reform, Slavophile cultural politics idealised the peasantry and countryside; newfound spiritual values were also mobilised to advocate the idea that the *Sonderweg* was Russia's modern destiny and set it on a path determined by its own indigenous institutions and practices rather than the Westernisation espoused by Catherine.[4]

These powerful factors began to abate in the late 1850s after Nicholas' death. Visions of Slavophile utopia waned at the end of his reign. In the cultural thaw that ensued, 'profound changes in the general intellectual climate [...] revolutionized social awareness.'[5] A greater pluralism in historical descriptions of nationality, the monarch and the nobility became possible. When the historian Vladimir Solovyov began publishing the initial volumes of his colossal *History of Russia* in the 1850s, a work that upset the Slavophiles because in their view it emphasised the role of the state at the expense of popular

---

grandfather, Peter III, her husband. See Simon Dixon, 'The posthumous reputation of Catherine II in Russia, 1797-1837', *The Slavonic and East European review* 77:4 (1999), p.646-79.

4. For a classic primary source on the distinct nature of Russian civilisation, see Ivan Kireevsky, 'On the nature of European culture and its relation to the culture of Russia', in *On spiritual unity: a Slavophile reader*, ed. and translated by Boris Jakim and Robert Bird (Hudson, NY, 1998), p.189-232. For important interpretations, see Andrzej Walicki, *The Slavophile controversy: history of a conservative utopia in nineteenth-century Russian thought* (Oxford, 1975), p.120-50, and V. S. Dubina, '"Osobyi put" teorii Sonderveg v interpretatsii natsional'noi istorii', in *'Osobyi put': ot ideologii k metodu*, ed. Andrei Zorin (Moscow, 2018), p.459-77.

5. Walicki, *The Slavophile controversy*, p.460.

culture, he espoused a belief in history as 'the science of national self-knowledge'.[6] In 1891, the historian Alexander Brückner felt it was time to take stock of the 'all-encompassing study of Russian history of the second half of the eighteenth century' conducted over the previous twenty years.[7] The degree to which this revival was regarded as an episode of the Enlightenment in Russia is the question to be addressed here. This chapter will argue that the emergence of an idea of Enlightenment in Russia was inseparable from the history of social thought.

The eighteenth century in an age of historicism

A new consciousness that the 'previous century has a special importance for the national history and history of Russian society'[8] is a striking feature of historiography immediately following the Great Reforms (and is overlooked in the scholarship). The rediscovery of Catherine's reign and accomplishments was inseparable, first, from the contemporary political context dominated by Tsar Alexander II – the Tsar Reformer – and, second, from the newfound prestige that history-writing acquired.

This has something in common with the method that Tolstoy applied in *War and peace* (1865). His original intention had been to study the psychology of the nobles who returned from exile in 1855. Uncovering the causes of their actions and explaining their corporate mentality and attitudes to the sovereign required, he found, a longer perspective dating two generations back to the Napoleonic period and even earlier. In the years when Tolstoy wrote his novel, one could also find the lives of an entire class of people in historical publications.

The 1860s saw the growth of historical writing. Attitudes and awareness of the period changed because of a larger cultural shift in the practice of history. The academic study of Russian history and law had been more a branch of philosophy than empirical investigation through the 1850s. The 1860s saw the flourishing of the 'thick journals'. These were the voluminous monthly periodicals in

6.   Edward C. Thaden, 'Friedrich Meinecke and Russian historicism', in *Interpreting history: collective essays on Russia's relations with Europe* (New York and Boulder, CO, 1990), p.53-72 (66).

7.   Brückner, quoted in the overview for the year's work in *RS* 7 (1891), p.726.

8.   Mikhail Shcherbatov, 'O povrezhdenii nravov v Rossii', *RS* 27 (1870), p.13-99 (14).

which the great nineteenth-century novels were serialised and much archival material was made public.[9] In the ensuing decades notable figures like Mikhail Semevsky, Alexander Pypin, Vasily Kliuchevsky and Sergei Solovyov put historical discourse and research on a new footing.[10] At the same time, amateur historians and history groups played an important part in finding and publishing vast documentation drawing on family papers and private archives. This material provided a wealth of evidence about the institutions of Catherine's reign, important individuals, her style of rule and the trajectory on which she had set the gentry.

Most important from a historical point of view were a number of publishing projects. They included the *Collection of the Imperial Russian Historical Society.* From 1867 until 1916 in 148 huge volumes this series published a vast amount of material, much of it the letters of Catherine the Great (single correspondences could be dispersed across many volumes).[11] In scale and scope this data dump about the governance of the Russian Empire was nearly unprecedented. Other outlets made available extensive material as published in a number of prominent periodicals. Chief among these were *Russian antiquity (Russkaia starina)* and *Russian archive (Russkii arkhiv).* Founded in 1870 by Semevsky, its long-term editor and an amateur historian with a great interest in the eighteenth century, *Russian antiquity* was a so-called thick journal published monthly until 1918. It contained numerous eighteenth-century sources, and added to the documentary record greatly by way of published diaries, correspondences, memoirs as well as analytical pieces. *Russian archive* was the enterprise of Peter Bartenev, an indefatigable archival historian.[12] This wealth of archival publications generated a wave of important editions of eighteenth-century writers and also a set of monographs that remain unrivalled for their command of the documentary evidence. Other important

9. On the term, see Robert Belknap, 'Survey of Russian journals, 1840-1880', in *Literary journals in imperial Russia*, ed. Deborah Martinsen (Cambridge, 1997), p.91-116 (109).

10. A. N. Shakhanov, *Russkaia istoricheskaia nauka vtoroi poloviny XIX-nachala XX veka: Moskovskii i Peterburgskii universitety* (St Petersburg, 2003).

11. For a brief but passionate defence of these historians as pioneers unjustly forgotten by later scholarship, see Michael Confino, 'The new Russian historiography, and the old – some considerations', *History and memory* 21:2 (2009), p.7-33, esp. p.11-12.

12. See Andrei Zaitsev, *Petr Ivanovich Bartenev i zhurnal 'Russkkii arkhiv'* (Moscow, 2001).

titles appeared, such as Mikhail Sukhomlinov's *History of the Russian Academy of Sciences* (founded by Peter the Great in 1722, the Academy was an important engine of new thought in Catherine's reign); the study *Novikov and the Moscow Martinists* (1867), an attempt to situate the publication and literary activities of Nikolai Novikov, one of the great protagonists in the period of the dissemination of new thinking, in the circles of Freemasonry and their philosophy of enlightened philanthropy; and Alexander Lappo-Danilevsky, *The Collection and compilation of the laws of the Russian Empire: a study in the internal politics of the empress* (1898). In addition, there were attempts at early history of the book in the catalogues and publications of Nikolai Guberti, *A Survey of rare books of the eighteenth century* published between 1878 and 1881.

The meaning of *prosveshchenie*

Discussion of an Enlightenment in Russia – its character, extent and institutions – has been sporadic. In recent scholarship, no consensus (or even real debate) has emerged on the character of the period. At one end of the spectrum there is a question as to whether it solely reflected Westernisation as a cultural phenomenon rather than intellectual trends; at the other end, the claim is that it did not exist at all. In *Russia's path toward Enlightenment: faith, politics, and reason, 1500-1801* (2016), the historian Gary Hamburg in effect equates the term with modernisation, placing a greater interest on technological change than on how Russian elites conceptualised their own historical period. In *The First epoch: the eighteenth century and the Russian cultural imagination* (2014), the literature scholar Luba Golburt, applying Reinhart Koselleck's model of conceptual history in which historical periods are seen as thresholds, argues that at the end of Catherine's reign contemporaries had become historically self-conscious, aware that her period was momentous because it set Russia on the path towards modernity. 'Enlightenment' does not figure in this paradigm, nor is it excluded. The historian Simon Dixon has approached the question by looking at the historical semantics of the term as used in Russian writing of the period. He casts doubt on the existence of an Enlightenment or Enlightenment in Russia by showing the narrow provenance of usage. The most common meanings of *prosveshchenie* are 'spiritual development', 'general knowledge' or 'education'.[13]

---

13. Simon Dixon, '"Prosveshchenie": Enlightenment in eighteenth-century Russia', *SVEC* 2008:01, p.228-49. Since the publication of this article, there has been

There would be good reason (and much evidence) to support
other conclusions, and the question could also be posed differently,
namely, given the term's traditional religious meanings, did contemporaries describe Enlightenment as they understood it through
other vocabulary and semantic fields? That said, the question of the
conceptual validity of the term in the eighteenth century, while a
rich one, is not the task of this chapter. The argument here concerns
the emergence of *prosveshchenie* as a concept that nineteenth-century
thinkers deemed to be a valid conceptual category for the eighteenth
century. Here, too, national institutions and the history of the
language complicate the picture. The shift in meaning reflected a
new political reality. Catherine's reign and legacy had been rapidly
forgotten: a word used to characterise the preceding period for
its progressive values was superfluous (*lishnee*). In the nineteenth
century the word *prosveshchenie* in the broad sense of 'education' is
applied not only as a matter of common parlance but because the
state's oversight was through the Ministry of National Education
(Ministerstvo narodnogo prosveshcheniia). Space for a different
discourse was occupied and controlled. Attempts to extend other
meanings occurred, and an argument for *prosveshchenie* as protected
by the autonomy of separate branches of knowledge was made but
discouraged. In 1896, a good half-century after his period of office
and forty years after his death, Sergey Uvarov, deputy minister of
National Education responsible for universities, is quoted as saying
that the problem with allowing a discourse of Enlightenment is that
one never knows where it will lead.[14]

The word *prosveshchenie* occurs repeatedly in the pages of the thick
journals. A shift in meaning can be dated to the 1870s when a set of
secondary meanings of 'Enlightenment', 'enlightened', 'enlightener'
is attested in historical writing. The vocabulary of Enlightenment
becomes a recurrent feature of the new assessments of Catherine's
reign. Even where newly published archival documents from the
eighteenth century do not explicitly talk about Enlightenment,

---

much scholarship on the place of religion in the Enlightenment that explores
how the terminology of Enlightenment, especially the vocabulary of *Lumières*,
works as both religious and secular and as an extenuation of religion as an
impediment. See now the essays in *Let there be Enlightenment: the religious
and mystical sources of rationality*, ed. Anton M. Matytsin and Dan Edelstein
(Baltimore, MD, 2018).

14. Leonid Maikov, 'Kak ponimat' basniu Krylova "Vodolazy"', *RS* 85 (1896),
p.267-83 (282).

the editorial language markedly favours this terminology. It can signify 'refined', 'polite', and therefore is roughly equivalent to 'Westernised', 'Europeanised' or sometimes 'educated' but as informed by a new episteme that is rational and secular. If it is only exceptionally used to denote a period meaning *Aufklärung*, in those instances the meaning seems unambiguous: 'St Petersburg' is referred to as a 'centre of Enlightenment', Russia is positioned as a country of Enlightenment in contrast with the Ottoman court.[15] Similarly, there are other unambiguous references associating Enlightenment with religion rather than superstition and with religious tolerance.[16] In a speech originally delivered to honour Nikolai Karamzin in 1820 and only published half a century later, Nikolai Turgenev, a physiocrat-inclined political economist, drew a distinction between 'the European Enlightenment' and 'our Enlightenment' but clearly saw them as distinct if equivalent.[17] Another publication in 1877 of the draft of an eighteenth-century official document approaches the question of how to control Freemasonry carefully, and argues that earlier attempts to curtail Freemasons' activities risked damaging Enlightenment and that reforms should be very gradual.[18] This article is only one of several to acknowledge that numerous members of the educated elite were Freemasons. Less frequent but of note is the claim made for Enlightenment for Russia on the grounds that in the eighteenth century the country's intellectual achievement owed much to the belated reception of classical Antiquity. The latter argument would find support in the paradigms of Enlightenment established by Peter Gay in *The Enlightenment: an interpretation* (1967-1970) and, more recently, in Dan Edelstein's *The Enlightenment: a genealogy* (2010).[19]

---

15. P. Maikov, 'Snosheniia Ekateriny II s Nekkerom i s Senak-de-Mel'ianom', *RS* 85 (1896), p.145-61 (157). ·
16. 'Po povodu prazdnovaniia Orlovskim dvoriatnstvom stoletiia so dniq pozhalovaniia dvorianskoi gramoty', *Russkii arkhiv* (henceforth *RA*) 5 (1890), p.133-75 (172); N. P. Durov, 'Fedor Vasil'evich Karzhavin, 1745-1812', *RS* 12 (1875), p.272-97.
17. Ivan Sreznevskii, 'A. I. Turgenev: otnoshenie k N. M. Karamzinu', *RS* 21 (1875), p.555-64 (563).
18. 'Unichtozhenie masonskikh lozh v Rossii v 1822: sekretnye zapiski i doneseniia senatora E. A. Kusheleva i drugie', *RS* 19 (1877), p.641-65 (643).
19. For an analogy of eighteenth-century Russia as Rome to France's Greece, see [Vospitannik Khar'kovsogo Universiteta 1820-kh gg], 'Vasilii Nazarovich Karazin, 1803', *RS* 12 (1875), p.334-37 (334).

Other articles attempt to be more precise: 'We think that the word "enlightenment" [*prosveshchenie*] is a concept [...] used not to refer to researcher-specialists, movers of science, but with reference to educated people, enlightened by the light of scientific knowledge.'[20] 'Enlightened Russia' or 'civilised Russia' is how certain people thought of their epoch, a time when 'enlightened people' found themselves 'like other peoples under the unlimited power of the autocrat'.[21] Moreover, discussions of national renovation accommodate both Peter the Great and Catherine: his mythic standing no longer overshadows her achievements specifically as an 'enlightener'. When the word *prosvetitel'* is used of Peter, it means narrowly an 'educator' or 'moderniser'; when it is used of Catherine, it signifies more broadly the moving force behind four areas where her reforms are associated with the civilising process.[22]

The vocabulary of Enlightenment appears consistently in four thematic categories that are mainstays of the treatment of the eighteenth century: (1) legal and judicial reforms affecting especially the landed gentry and the serfs; (2) advances in social welfare; (3) the ideal and reality of autocracy; and (4) measures taken to promote publishing and the intellectual and economic progressiveness of the gentry. What I hope to show, therefore, in this chapter is that, while the broader monolithic meaning of *prosveshchenie* to designate 'education/educated' remains in use, writers newly apply the meaning of Enlightenment as a project of reform. The impetus for reconceptualising the period clearly relates to the new historical situation. Other educated groups from the lower social estates, such as the sons of the parish clergy (the *popovichi*), who formed the non-noble intelligentsia were ambivalent about modernisation and

---

20. Maikov, 'Kak ponimat' basniu Krylova "Vodolazy"', p.275.
21. 'Zhurnal V. I. Zinov'eva', ed. N. P. Baryshnikov, *RS* 23 (1878), p.207-40.
22. Compare usage in 'Graf Nikitich Panin, 1771-1837', *RS* 8 (1873), p.338-73 (338), describing Peter the Great as 'prosvetitel'' to mean 'moderniser, civiliser' or even 'educator', to the references to the 'enlightened empress' ('prosvesh-chennaia Imperatritsa', p.4) by the eminent historian S. F. Platonov, *Stoletie konchiny Imperatritsy Ekateriny* (St Petersburg, 1897), a lecture he delivered at the graduation ceremony of the Higher Women's Courses in 1896; here as elsewhere the adjective attaches not only to a person but to the intellectual character of the period, one of 'enlightened reason' ('prosveshchennyi razum', p.6). Overall Platonov concludes that Catherine's government until the end of her reign was an enlightening force because 'she continued to illumine society' ('prodolzhaet svetit' obshchestvu', p.15).

Westernisation.[23] It is the nobility who see the Enlightenment period as a precursor to Alexander II's Great Reforms. The method in the body of the chapter will be to identify the motif of Enlightenment as a discourse in each of four areas: legislation, the status of the gentry, social welfare and corporate values, and enlightened despotism or autocracy.

The ruler as lawgiver

Before the 1870s, publications about Catherine remained largely biographical in character. An 1849 printing of Catherine's *Nakaz* (the famous *Instruction*) was part of a popular, cheap series. The centennial of the *Nakaz* in 1862, the year after the emancipation of the serfs, did not go entirely unnoticed. An 1862 pamphlet on the ruler as legislator marked the start of a surge of material on her legislation and judicial reforms.[24] The publication in 1862 of the diary of Catherine's private secretary A. V. Khrapovitsky was noteworthy evidence of both his and her reading and extensive reliance on a range of European sources in the production of numerous laws.[25] Starting with the *Nakaz*, the foundational document of her reign, Khrapovitsky names Montesquieu and Blackstone.[26] These sources were no secret since Catherine, working together with the drafting commission, openly cites them. More than a decade later a separate publication would cite Catherine commenting to D'Alembert in a letter, 'Montesquieu's *Esprit des lois* serves as my prayer book.' Khrapovitsky also goes on to note a few sources for the 1785 Charter to the Nobility, another key legislative act of her reign (in fact, the emancipation of the nobility from obligatory service happened in 1762 under Peter III, before being confirmed and enacted by Catherine).[27] His diary also sheds

23. See Laurie Manchester, *Holy fathers, secular sons: clergy, intelligentsia, and the modern self in revolutionary Russia* (De Kalb, IL, 2008).
24. P. N. Petrov, *Ekaterina II – zakonodatel'nitsa* (St Peterburg, 1863).
25. For a modern edition, see Aleksandr Khrapovitskii, *Pamiatnye zapiski A. V. Khrapovitskogo: stats-sekretaria imperatritsy Ekateriny vtoroi* (Moscow, 1990). The notes were first serialised with long gaps in *Otechestvennye zapiski* over more than a dozen instalments, then printed as a whole by the bibliographer Nikolai Gennadi, *Chteniia v Imperatorskom Obshchestve istorii i drevnostei'* (Moscow, 1862).
26. Khrapovitskii, *Pamiatnye zapiski*, esp. p.20, 23, 27.
27. The texts and essential commentary can be found in *The Laws of Russia*, series 2: *Imperial Russia*, vol.289: *April 21, 1785: Catherine II's charters of 1785 to the*

light on the empress' reading in relation to commercial legislation and
civil regulations (concerning the duel), and teaches posterity about her
working routines: 'What have I been doing', she is quoted as asking. 'I
have been exercising myself in legislation and history […]. I cannot do
any more on the laws, but I think that I can get started on history.'[28]

That position changes over the course of the 1870s, during which the
number of references to Catherine's legislation increases. Commentary
attributes Catherine's rationale to the application of reason and an
aspiration for progress. Insofar as reason is the enemy of crime,
the *Nakaz* aimed to educate, to reduce crime, especially corruption,
and to redress the 'weakness of popular justice' ('slabost' narodnogo
pravosudiia'). In 1873 an extensive article documented Catherine's
project on penal reform.[29] The commentator – the jurist and historian
Mikhail Filippov – claims that its passages on penal reform put the
Nakaz in the vanguard of European law-making, a point taken up by
another writer who identifies the borrowings from Beccaria's work on
crime and punishment as reference points for civilised conduct.[30]

Attention to the *Nakaz* situates Catherine's activities as a legislator
in the larger historical context of lawmakers, starting with Peter I.[31]
The author of an article on the history of advisory councils to the
monarch in the eighteenth century up to Catherine's accession
noted that the state had been weakened by poor management, that
justice was not dispensed in the lands, and that the standard of
living had dropped, all as a direct result of a failure to govern in
an enlightened way.[32] Discussions of the *Nakaz* are also informed by
some knowledge of her correspondence and court politics, since they
argue that her political style was to build consensus on law-making
in the Senate.[33] Certainly descriptions in the 1860s prominently

_____

   nobility and the towns, ed. and translated by David E. Griffiths and George
   E. Munro (Bakersfield, CA, 1991).
28. Khrapovitskii, *Pamiatnye zapiski*, p.213.
29. Mikhail Filippov, 'Tiur'my v Rossii: sobstvennoruchny proekt imperatritsy
   Ekateriny II', *RS* 8 (1873), p.60-86.
30. Filippov, 'Tiur'my v Rossii', p.63.
31. For examples of how sources treat administrators as enlighteners, see
   E. P. Karnovich, 'O polnom sobranii zakonov Rossiiskoi imperii', *RS* 10 (1874),
   p.408-40 (412-13).
32. Sergei Solov'ev, 'Imperatorskie sovety v Rossii v XVIII veka', *RS* 27 (1870),
   p.463-68 (467).
33. V. S. Ikonnikov, 'Pravitel'stviushchii Senat pri Ekaterine Vtoroi', *RA* 1 (1888),
   p.17-43 (19-22).

portrayed Catherine as a legislator, anticipating the revival of that image in the monument of 1873. These treatments, however, often focus on specific cases of justice and injustice and laws, and they also advance her vocabulary of citizenship, as in an article of 1878 that lists social welfare measures as aspects of law. Writing in 1851, the antiquarian and amateur historian Vukol Undolsky outlined his research ambition to write the history as 'an organic whole' of what he explicitly calls 'the Russian Enlightenment', by which he means a civilising process started in the eighteenth century anchored in the codification of law.[34] A cluster of articles published in 1885 adds a further conceptual note in describing legislation by seeing in the law, based on Catherine's learning, a didactic and moral instrument through which the 'gentry will be enlightened' ('prosvetitsia dvorianstvo').[35] The word choice here looks highly deliberate, because the verb 'to enlighten oneself' is construed as an active process that constitutes a civilising process achieved through obedience to law that is itself rooted in natural law.[36] This is not a familiar locution intended to signify 'become educated' in a vaguer sense, but specifically associated with a process based on reason and the internalisation of the law as a moral code. Or, to cite a 1887 article, what we have here is both 'education and enlightenment' ('obrazovanie i prosveshchenie').[37] Pieces published in the late 1880s, in a period of political turmoil when the historic context had changed after the assassination of Alexander II, continue to tout the significance of the *Nakaz* and also to let Catherine herself speak on the matter by quoting her writings, such as a letter to Baron Grimm about her law code's significance and also about her own place in the tradition of Peter the Great as a lawgiver who regards rules as the mark of an 'enlightened people'.[38]

The emergence of the legal ethos among officials under Nicholas I may have paved the way for later attention to Catherine as lawgiver

---

34. V. M. Undol'skii, 'Pis'ma Vukola Mikhailovicha Undol'skago k A. N. Popovu', *RA* 6 (1886), p.281-304 (285): 'For about a month now, having ordered a binding from the Lavra, I have been collecting and pasting different bits of the materials I have gathered for the history of the Russian Enlightenment.'
35. N. A. Ratynskii, 'Istoricheskaia spravka', *RA* 8 (1885), p.166-76 (172).
36. Aleksei Levshin, 'Dostopamiatnye minuty v moei zhizni: zapiska chelna Gosudarstvennogo Soveta A. I. Levshina', *RA* 8 (1885), p.475-558 (537).
37. V. E. Cheshikhin, 'Studenchesksiia bezchinstva v Derpte', *RA* 10 (1887), p.265-81 (269).
38. Ikonnikov, 'Pravitel'stviushchii Senat pri Ekaterine Vtoroi', p.31.

and in the balance of powers.[39] Recent legal historians have seen the need to point out what was already evident to thinkers from 1864: that reforms launched at the time represented continuity with the past institutional history of Russian law rather than a start de novo.[40] Interest in Catherine's laws was commensurate with Alexander II's legislation and a more widely held view that a modern state was governed by legal norms or *zakonnost'*. But the interest was more than theoretical since public opinion had come to value accountability and to condemn arbitrary rule (*proizvol*).[41] Both sides of autocracy, the law-abiding and the despotic, were amply attested in publications about the Catherine period. On the one hand, there is by way of example a highly laudatory piece on Catherine's penal reforms, putting her in the vanguard of legal practice in Europe as a follower of John Howard: 'the principles proclaimed by Catherine in her famous *Nakaz* in 1767 anticipated all European legislative codes practically by an entire century.'[42] Through the example of her own personal moderate behaviour, Catherine is also seen as ethical because she is shown to have made the connection between personal conduct and economic exploitation that resulted in the cruel excesses of serfdom. In a letter of 1782 to Tsarevich Paul published in 1890, Catherine castigates the French nobility. Dulled by the same love of luxury of which she faults Marie-Antoinette, the nobility do not see 'the abyss opening up under their feet by their insistence on medieval privileges'.[43] On the other hand, some articles exposed the decay of Catherine's rule into despotism. Under Catherine's progressive legislation, the nobility was protected against corporate punishments. Yet her final years were marked by the scandalous treatment of the gentry she had earlier favoured. *Russian antiquity* published a profile written by Pavel Radishchev of Stepan Sheshkovsky, the notorious torturer who had interrogated his father, among others, and made it his purpose to work over several court figures concerning their

39. Richard Wortman, *The Development of a Russian legal consciousness* (Chicago, IL, 1976), p.197-235.

40. See Tatiana Borisova and Jane Burbank, 'Russia's legal trajectories', *Kritika* 19:3 (2018), p.469-508 (471-72), and Elise Kimerling Wirtschafter, 'Russian legal culture and the rule of law', *Kritika* 7:1 (2006), p.61-70.

41. See W. Bruce Lincoln, *The Great Reforms: autocracy, bureaucracy, and the politics of change in imperial Russia* (De Kalb, IL, 1991), esp. p.159-89.

42. Filippov, 'Tiur'my v Rossii', p.60.

43. E. S. Shumigorskii, 'Imperatritsa Mariia Fedorovna: puteshestviie za granitsu 1781-1782', *RS* 5 (1890), p.17-78 (59).

caricatures and critical composition from the 1770s.[44] In order to subject Radishchev to interrogation, Catherine had him stripped by the Senate of his noble status. While the headnote comments that it is 'difficult to suppose that his name would have been unknown to any readers of *Russian antiquity*', discussions in print were a mark of the more liberal climate.[45] The piece about Sheshkovsky, containing a complete curriculum vitae, ends with an ironic comment. Pavel Radishchev notes that, nearby in the same cemetery where Sheshkovsky is buried, lie the playwrights Fonvizin and Lukin, both heroes of progress.[46]

Parallel histories: the gentry in the 1780s and 1860s

The Great Reforms began in 1861 with the Abolition of Serfdom, the Finance Reform (1863), the Reform of Higher Education (1863) and the Judicial Reform and Reform of the Zemstvo (both in 1864). The headline programmes included the relaxation of censorship and judicial changes, innovations to local government and the emancipation of nearly 23 million serfs. The impact of the 1861 emancipation reform on the gentry is a massive topic. For our purposes, the relevant fact is that parallels between the nineteenth and eighteenth centuries were evident to contemporary readers. In the Catherine period, autocracy relied on the aristocracy and service nobility for support, a position that was attenuated by the 1785 Rescript emancipating from obligatory service and granting the right in law to own private property, including serfs.[47] By the middle of the next century, a professional bureaucracy had supplanted this social base. In the

44. 'Sheshkovskii', *RS* 10 (1874), p.781-85 (782). This piece, while published anonymously, is thought to be the work of one of Radishchev's sons, Pavel, also the author of an 1857 biography of their father that did not clear censorship. That manuscript treats Sheshkovsky's role extensively and in similar terms. On attempts to restore his story to public view, with attention to the sentence that deprived Radishchev of his gentry status, see D. S. Babkin, 'Pervye biography A. N. Radishcheva', in *Biografiia A. N. Radishcheva napisannaia ego synoviami*, ed. D. S. Babkin (Moscow, 1959), p.2-36.

45. For a discussion of the liberal perspective, see Jörg Baberowski, *Autokratie und Justiz: zum Verhältnis von Rechsstaatlichkeit und Rückständigkeit im ausgehenden Zarenreich 1864-1917* (Frankfurt am Main, 1996), ch.1.

46. P. A. Efremov, 'Stepan Ivanovich Sheshkovskii, 1720-1794', *RS* 2 (1870), p.637-39 (637).

47. See Richard Pipes, 'Private property comes to Russia: the reign of Catherine II', *Harvard Ukrainian studies* 22 (1998), p.431-42.

words of one historian, the chief concern of the nobles had become
their declining economic and political position.[48] There was an
upside to this sense of decay. In Alexander II's Russia, the gentry
were only one segment of public opinion alongside the emancipated
masses, the between-states class that fed the radical intelligentsia.
Power in Catherine's Russia, as in Alexander II's Russia, was also
pyramidal. But, from the convening of her national assembly in 1767,
Catherine had created the strong sense that the collaboration of the
gentry was vital to her projects. Alexander II's reforms, carried out
by the bureaucracy, nonetheless required extensive consultation with
landowners, who supplied information about local economic and
social conditions. They prompted an interest in autocratic authority
and gentry institutions of Catherine's reign as a period that had set
a new precedent with its reforms to gentry culture, Russia's political
economy and the level of education of all classes.

The documentary material published in the 1870s and 1880s
about the eighteenth century is generically diverse, comprising
documentary, biographical, anecdotal and memoiristic writing.
Readers gained perspective on the present through the study of what
looked like a golden age under Catherine the Great. In the story that
emerges about the eighteenth century, the language of Enlightenment
has a conspicuous role. With the relaxation of censorship and greater
glasnost' of the post-Nikolaevan regime, readers could trace their
intellectual genealogy, cultural practices, legal privileges and sense of
civilisation to an earlier period. It is particularly relevant both in this
regard and with respect to discussions of the gentry, to consider the
belated publication in 1870 of a now classic essay by the nobleman
Mikhail Shcherbatov, *On the corruption of morals in Russia*, originally
written towards the end of Catherine's reign. Extensive treatment of
questions about the gentry in the eighteenth century historicised the
gentry's growth and the beginning of its decline. In his essay 'On the
corruption of morals in Russia', Shcherbatov lamented the decline of
the aristocracy brought about by the social mobility introduced by
Peter, complaining that the 'gentry were not revered clans but ranks
and rewards and services'.[49] A century after Catherine the Great
had fundamentally altered the status of this class with her legislation
of 1785, the gentry were once again in a position to consider their

48. Werner E. Mosse, 'Bureaucracy and nobility in Russia at the end of the
    nineteenth century', *The Historical journal* 24:3 (1981), p.605-28.
49. Shcherbatov, 'O povrezhdenii nravov v Rossii', p.35.

identity in relation to the state.[50] An article about 'Freethinkers in the reign of Catherine the Great' quotes a letter by Ivan Lopukhin about the crackdown against Alexander Radishchev, in which he notes that he is reading a work titled 'Qui peut être un bon citoyen'.[51] The same problem of defining civic virtue and loyalty, seen as a question of virtue and duty as long as absolute rule was reasonable, was faced a century later by the same class of people whose proximity to power was overtaken by professional bureaucrats.[52]

The relation between ruler and gentry was therefore one area of continuity and negative comparison. Although consensus had been building towards the abolition of serfdom, the emancipation of 1861 was handled in a top-down way. Local economic adjustments and land transfers, essential to the reform's success, were a matter for discussion by the gentry on the basis of every individual province, but the legal framework and basic terms had been set by the sovereign and bureaucracy. Readers of eighteenth-century materials in the 1870s and 1880s would have found evidence of at least a semblance of greater collaboration between the monarch and the gentry estate. Even in the ritualised language of a formal tribute to Catherine made in a speech on 11 February 1784, the Penza gentry characterised their genuine affection as reward for the 'peace, abundance, enlightenment and rule of law' that marked her reign.[53] Nikita Panin in a letter to Lemercier de La Rivière presented a Catherine who found that, far from demeaning her status, attention to representatives of the gentry was essential to the Legislative Commission, examples of

50. The literature on Catherine's class politics is enormous and beyond the scope of this article. A helpful overview can be found in S. V. Pol'skoi, '"Na raznye chiny razdeliaia svoi narod...": zakonodatel'noe zakreplenie soslovnogo statusa russkogo dvorianstva v seredine XVIII veka', *Cahiers du monde russe* 51:2-3 (2010), p.303-28.

51. 'Russkie vol'nodumtsy v tsarstvovanie Ekateriny II: Sekretno-Vskrytaia perepiska, 1790-1795', *RS* 9 (1874), p.259-76 (262).

52. For a suggestive albeit brief examination of the class mentality of the gentry based on honour codes rather than Enlightenment values, see V. S. Dubina and S. V. Pol'skoi, '"Osobyi put'": russkogo dvorianstva v otechestvennoi i zarubezhnoi istoriografii', *Izvestiia Samarskogo nauchnogo tsentra Rossiiskoi akademii nauk* 11 (2000), p.227-34.

53. 'Zhizn' Efima Petrovicha Chemesova, 1735-1801: zapiski dlia pamiati', *RS* 7 (1891), p.1-10 (5). Similarly, on Catherine's political allies who supported her cultural programme, see the biographies of Ekaterina Dashkova and Ivan Betskoi, among others, in the set of articles grouped in A. F. Bychkov, 'Spodvizhniki II', *RS* 8 (1873), p.691-734.

a group explicitly compared to nineteenth-century figures with the same values seen as 'high-standing, educated/enlightened [*prosvesh-chennye*] men constantly striving for social good'.[54]

Russian cultural politics after the heyday of Slavophilism was more historical but no less nationalist or conservative. The advocates of gentry liberalism were moved by immediate class interests, concerned as were the rulers with the post-reform economic realities. Historians in their camp, nationalist and anti-Western, rejected both the radicalism of ideas about popular utopia and its Enlightenment origins.[55] For that reason it is noteworthy that, in the many dozens of 'thick journal' articles on the Catherine period, the discourse of Western and anti-Western or Slavophile is absent. The historians engaged in recovering the history of the earlier period, many of whom were minor, amateur figures, remained aloof from contemporary ideological debates. Yet their project is profoundly responsive to a contemporary situation in which that 'science of self-knowledge' could help the gentry as a class consider its own position in relation to social progress.[56]

We find in the pages of the historical journals articles about forgotten figures who were once prominent reformers. The spotlight falls on a number of eighteenth-century writers who also thought of themselves as enlightened bureaucrats. They include the playwright Denis Fonvizin (1745-1792, secretary to Minister Nikita Panin), the poet Ivan Elagin (1725-1794), the author and polemicist Alexander Radishchev (in the Customs Office).[57] In their literary works, these writers explored for the Catherine period the economic problem of serf exploitation, the problem of corruption and ignorance, and the social responsibility of the gentry. They also used literature as a vehicle for social critique, a purpose that looked entirely at home alongside Russian literature written in the period.[58] Articles included new information, such as an account of Princess Dashkova's meeting

---

54. Vasilii Bil'basov, 'Nikita Panin i Mers'ie de la-Riv'er (1762-1767)', *RS* 72 (1891), p.283-324 (309); Ivan Mainov, 'Smolenskie dvoriane i obiazannye krest'iane', *RS* 8 (1873), p.910-39 (919).
55. Walicki, *The Slavophile controversy*, p.474.
56. See Thaden, 'Friedrich Meinecke and Russian historicism', p.66-72.
57. Of particular interest is M. N. Serdobin, 'Graf Nikita Petrovich Panin, russkii diplomat 1797 g.', *RS* 8 (1873), p.338-73, which treats him as one of a number of unjustly forgotten figures (esp. p.338).
58. Elise Kimerling Wirtschafter, *The Play of ideas in Russian Enlightenment theatre* (De Kalb, IL, 2003).

with the abbé Raynal and Prince D. A. Golitsyn's friendship with Helvétius, giving clear evidence of intellectual initiative as hallmarks of educated life in the period. If Catherine set the lead by sheer prominence of her example, other figures demonstrated their own autonomy as cultural agents.[59]

Many publications drew attention to the intellectual character of courtiers and their international networks. While the empress is a pivotal figure in establishing the ideals of Enlightenment, Enlightenment as a historically located movement depends on enlightened administrators and a growing class of educated elite.[60] The historiography encourages the view that the conditions for Enlightenment were laid down for other social groups not solely directed by government, allowing them to achieve a certain autonomy.

The use Fonvizin, Elagin and Radishchev made of literature as a vehicle for social critique looked suitable a century later in the new cultural context. The standing and economic position of the landed gentry was a staple of nineteenth-century Realist fiction, nowhere more important or memorable than in the novels of Turgenev and Tolstoy. Whether they lived on their estates or lived off rent, their heroes faced a combination of wrenching economic circumstances and challenges to a way of life established in the eighteenth century. Key aspects to their role in the running of the country, including terms of service to the state, their position in local governance and jurisprudence, and their relation to the monarch, were conditioned by new laws. The establishment of new schools and universities, the growth of travel abroad, the emergence of Moscow and St Petersburg as urban centres, the development of a new Russian literature, all affected their cultural identity and sense of self. This was not only a

---

59. D. D. Riabkin, 'Zapiski Professora Akademika T'ebo, 1765-1785', *RS* 9 (1874), p.575-93 (575).

60. For examples of how sources treat administrators as enlighteners, see Karnovich, 'O polnom sobranii zakonov Rossiiskoi imperii', p.412-14; N. M. Pavlov, *Nashe perekhodnoe vremia* (Moscow, 1888) (= supplement to *RA*, 1888), p.353-85; 'Biograficheskiia svedeniia o russkikh pisateliakh XVIII veka i bibliograficheskie izvestiia ob nikh proizvedeniiakh', *RS* 2 (1870), p.197-200, section dedicated to Ivan Perfil'evich Elagin. See also the biography of Dmitrii Vasil'evich Volkov (1718-1785): 'Dmitrii Vasil'evich Volkov, 1718-1785', *RS* 9 (1874), p.163-74. This research soon informed more popular studies at home and abroad such as Kazimierz Waliszewski, *Autour d'un trône: Catherine II de Russie, ses collaborateurs, ses amis, ses favoris* (Paris, 1894); F. G. Sideau and A. A. Kruglyi, *Dvor Imperatritsy Ekateriny II: ee sotrudniki i priblizhennye* (St Petersburg, 1899).

process of Westernisation since it involved questioning Russianness. Perhaps most importantly, seminal legislation for the first time conferred the right to own property, including serfs, on the landed gentry. At least in theory, the aim of these laws was to incentivise a return to the land with a view to promoting better stewardship, more inward investment, greater involvement in local governance and especially the regulation of provincial law courts.

Of consistent interest now to nineteenth-century historians were earlier figures who provided a form of critique of tsardom and the structure of state power. These are writers whose vocabulary is squarely in the semantic field of Enlightenment praxis, and who, if they use the term *prosveshchenie* at all, depart from the clerical meaning in order to convey a different set of meanings. Already a figure of interest to historical societies, Shcherbatov was an essayist of high intelligence with the outlook of a Roman senator and Stoic. He saw his own century in class terms, as the story of the rise of the gentry and decline of the aristocracy. The Table of Ranks, Peter I's mobility scheme for producing a new educated bureaucracy, had enlarged the gentry and made its fortunes dependent on the monarch. The result was that, even as manners improved under Peter, obsequiousness, in Shcherbatov's view, grew. Westernisation and luxury were signs of decay that troubled him as a cultural conservative. But the decline of the aristocracy was fundamentally more problematic. It eroded the position of a class whose responsibility was to counter absolutism. His intention, never objective, was to assert the decline of the nobility. Shcherbatov begins his essay, written ostensibly as a letter to his son, with reference to *prosveshchenie*: 'In contemplating the present century of my country, with such as a person can have who has been raised according to the old rules, whose passions have already, with the passage of years, declined, but whose experience has provided the requisite enlightenment [*prosveshchenie*] for the formation of judgement about matters'.[61] Shcherbatov casts his critique of Russian society and its power structure as a matter of judgement based on experience. The meaning of *prosveshchenie* here goes beyond the general sense of education to signify critical judgement worked out on the basis of experience and principle. If this classic use of the term is unusual in eighteenth-century Russian writing, the irony of its appearance

---

61. Shcherbatov, 'O povrezhdenii nravov v Rossii', p.13-16. A separate study might possibly reveal whether Shcherbatov was read by his contemporaries and contributed to the widespread disaffection that influenced the gentry.

here is important. However negative Shcherbatov will be on the character of his age for a moral decline brought about by secular values, materialism and unchecked despotism, he has internalised the procedure of formulating a rational critique in a self-conscious way. What Shcherbatov reproached was elsewhere viewed as marks of the polish of good manners that bespoke education and refinement or, in short, evidence of 'enlightened Russia' for which the gentry had to be standard-bearer.[62]

Accounts of Catherine's efforts to educate the nobility, sometimes by sending young nobles abroad, provide a counter-balance to the late lapse into unreason, as do articles on the visit to St Petersburg of Diderot and extensive publications from Catherine's correspondence with the *philosophes*.[63] Nonetheless, the clear sense that autocracy had turned into despotism by the early 1790s is striking as a juxtaposition with considerations of the consensual role of the gentry in governance issues, and especially in helping to reform the judicial system based on precepts of reason and virtue. Insofar as later commentators perceive progress in popular education (*narodnoe prosveshchenie*) of the eighteenth century, it is seen to depend on landowners or civil servants whose enlightenment operates at a higher level.[64] Other contributions consider debates in the period on forms of governance, showing that absolutism as a system was evolving, a point that mattered in the late-nineteenth-century understanding of the monarchy. Of particular note, as published in 1889, are documents concerning Panin's plan on governance in which he pondered the roles of branches of government as less centralised in order to achieve a balance of power; these are pieces in which there is a theme of debate and discord.[65]

The figures who brought an aspect of critique to political culture are also treated separately. In short biographical studies of eighteenth-century protagonists, the spotlight falls on high-profile government ministers like Ivan Betskoi and Ivan Elagin. Other articles put the spotlight on lesser-known civil servants such as Grigory Teplov, an enlightened bureaucrat, who drafted the crucial legislation of 1785 that

---

62. Mikhail Longinov, 'Mikhail Lomonosov: Vypiski iz zhurnalov Imperatorskoi Rossiiskoi Akademii', *RS* 8 (1873), p.563-84 (565).
63. Cheshikhin, 'Studencheskiia bezchinstva v Derpte', p.268.
64. F. V. Karazin, 'V. N. Karazin: pi'smo k doktory Remanu, 1810 g.', *RS* 12 (1875), p.750-57 (752).
65. Ikonnikov, 'Pravitel'stviushchii Senat pri Ekaterine Vtoroi', p.18-27.

transformed the status of the nobility by abolishing compulsory state service.[66] These biographies give emphasis to educational activities, civic projects and intellectual links. The prosopographies also help to give a sense of circles of like-minded individuals (some who may have been affiliated through Freemasonry) who had common ideals and possibly circulated ideas by sharing books. Who owned copies of Blackstone or the *Encyclopédie*, who bought textbooks for the Academy of Sciences, who read Beccaria is traced on these pages. The European connections of Catherine's advisers are also paid attention in the pages of these publications. Readers learned not only that Betskoi, an important adviser on education to Catherine, was her co-author with Diderot of *Les Plans et les statuts* (1775), but also that he, unlike Catherine, was an acolyte of Rousseau. There is a sense that Enlightenment as a process was from the bottom up as well as from the top down. The occasional hint of mockery at Catherine's 'intellectual vanity' in corresponding with Voltaire, Diderot, Grimm, Zimmermann can be detected, but it is tempered by the recognition that 'conversation with people of outstanding ability and education gave her great pleasure and was for her a necessity.'[67] That 'necessity' was not exclusive to the empress. Count Ivan Shuvalov in his letters to Voltaire about his love of philosophy speaks for other like-minded members of his generation. A new portrait of the age emerges through piecemeal evidence. Publications include the letters N. P. Rumiantsev wrote to the French Finance minister Jacques Necker about absolutism, as well as the letters Ivan Lopukhin wrote to A. M. Kutuzov, a fellow Freemason. Lopukhin expressed his fear that the prosecution of Alexander Radishchev in the darkest chapter of Catherine's reign was a betrayal of all that had been achieved: in seeking to defend the Enlightenment from the barbarism of the French Revolution, Catherine was destroying the legacy of the previous twenty-five years of openness.[68] The view that figures like Radishchev and Lopukhin were the first enlighteners, bearers of a radical message inspired by the likes of Tom Paine and enlightened because their message was about social justice, crystallised in the twentieth century. But even

66. See the section dedicated to Grigorii Nikolaevich Teplov in 'Biograficheskiia svedeniia o russkikh pisateliakh XVIII veka i bibliograficheskie izvestiia ob nikh proizvedeniiakh'.
67. De La Flise [*sic*], 'Ekaterina II i doctor M. I. Veikard', *RS* 72 (1891), p.531-64 (551).
68. 'Russkie vol'nodumtsy v tsarstvovanie Ekateriny II', p.262-64.

if we look at Mikhail Shcherbatov, a cultural conservative usually regarded as anti-Western and therefore not an enlightener, we find in his essays modes of rational argumentation and critical debate that are evidence of a sceptical, rational mentality consistent with Enlightenment critique. The Catherine period forged habits of mind that were shaped by the new discourses of progress of the previous thirty years of her reign.

A century later the gentry were beleaguered, often criticised by the new radical intelligentsia for disappointing democratic expectations. Oblomov, the famously inert hero of Goncharov's novel of 1859, had given his name to the phenomenon of idleness or Oblomovshchina. His name and the term became a byword for a gentry that had decayed in the countryside and largely failed to modernise their estates. By contrast, the articles collected in *Russian antiquity* even for the single year of 1878 portrayed a class capable of working together with the sovereign, open to new ideas and receptive to modern theories of pedagogy, and alert to the evils of serfdom, as in an account of the meeting of Princess Dashkova and the abbé Raynal, whose spiritual life, whether governed by Orthodoxy or influenced by a Masonic version of Pietism, was focused on secular good.

Social welfare and the gentry ethos

The moral case for the historic change had gathered head for some time among the gentry. The sovereign and government could not act on their own. The work to bring about the emancipation of 22 million peasant serfs (and an additional 1.6 million state peasants) had involved immensely complex negotiations at the gubernatorial level between landowners, the state and peasant representatives conducted by province.[69] The new economic system was a patchwork of changes; implementation of the emancipation from 1861 was slow. Nineteenth-century publications about historic serfdom under Catherine the Great were more concerned with principles than with economics. Looking back to Catherine's reign, the nineteenth-century publications historicised serfdom as a product of a phase in Russia's economic history rather than an ancient institution destined to survive into the modern period. Discussion focused on the role of the 'enlightened gentry' in improving the plight of the peasants, and posited a connection between the current emancipation of the serfs and enlightened

69. See Jerome Blum, *Lord and peasant in Russia* (Princeton, NJ, 1972).

thought as a civilising process. There was a common agreement about serf exploitation, something that was of course widely treated in nineteenth-century fiction in the plots of Turgenev, Tolstoy and many others. The comment of one historian seems a representative view of the consensus that was building up in the 1870s about the 1770s: 'A number of enlightened and highly placed men, in their constant drive for social good, sought out measures to secure landowners in the responsible acquittal owed to the peasants with whom they had made the agreements.' This long article provides an in-depth study of the causes of peasant unrest and economic underperformance in a single region in the recent period of 1846-1849. It is relevant here because its examination of the recent history of serfdom, including challenges like the enforcement of contracts and peasant morale, traces the causes for contemporary problems in the failures of the eighteenth century to instil a sense of mutual responsibility between landowners and the peasantry. Despite 'the rapid expansion in our country of enlightenment, encompassing the upper classes of the population', there was a failure to imbue the peasantry with 'a consciousness of the benefits of the well-ordered state'.[70]

The social and economic conditions that caused low productivity among peasants were in large part, Ivan Mainov, the compiler of the documents, argues, the fault of exploitative arrangements that left their mark on the 'character, intelligence and way of thinking of the highest class of society in the last reign'.[71] In faulting the social stagnation of the reign of Nicholas, he contrasts it explicitly with Catherine's attempts to instil in the nobility a more humane attitude to the serfs. This was a definite topos of the historiography. It is not surprising that writers of a popular and sometimes radical outlook on the left denounced serfdom as a 'dark stain' whose legality had to be questioned. One highlight in the historiography is an extended account of the notorious case of the landowner Darya Saltykova. Peasant rebellions even on a much lesser scale than the Pugachev Rebellion of 1774 were a frequent response to the cruelty of serf-owners, none worse than this woman popularly called Saltychikha or 'the woman cannibal', who tortured and murdered many of her female serfs. A lengthy article reconstructed the legal process in Catherine's handling of her arrest and life sentence, and how Catherine negotiated the tricky boundary between the gentry's corporate rights as political

70. Mainov, 'Smolenskie dvoriane i obiazannye krest'iane', p.919.
71. Mainov, 'Smolenskie dvoriane i obiazannye krest'iane', p.934.

necessity and a commitment enshrined in law to treat all humans with decency and an abolition of torture.[72] Patrimonial estates and property rights among the nobility, non-nobles and the servitor class of clerks became more extensive from the seventeenth century. But land regulation, in the word of Isabel de Madariaga, was 'chaotic', leading to much rural lawlessness, a situation that Catherine was determined to rectify.[73] Two decades later in the 1780s her legislation newly addressed the personal rights of the nobles and the collective rights of the nobility, defining property rights more extensively.[74] Discussions demonstrate awareness that her aim was not to shore up the system but to encourage landowners to show humanity and to manage the economic system better. There is also clear recognition in these publications that Catherine had abolitionist tendencies. While any wishes she had to end serfdom were checked, her management of state serfs and her attention to the better treatment of the serfs were noted. The expectation is that the gentry were encouraged by the empress to emulate the practices of the European Enlightenment in their management of land, treatment of the peasantry, obedience to the laws and pursuit of education.

The publication in 1874 of the correspondence between Senator Ivan Lopukhin (1756-1816), a Freemason and probably freethinker (said to have translated d'Holbach), and Aleksei Kutuzov, a fellow Freemason and dedicatee of Radishchev's work, sees a connection between positive social praxis and intellectual Enlightenment, and is just one statement of the much-repeated view that *prosveshchenie* had social uses.[75] Here, again, the meaning of the word goes well beyond the general sense of education. However, far from the reality that obtained for most of the population, the word refers to the procedures critical reasoning and a more modern set of assimilated progressive values guaranteed by good government and expectations of justice.

---

72. P. G. Kicheev, 'Saltychikha', *RA* 3 (1865), p.641-52.
73. See Isabel de Madariaga, *Russia in the age of Catherine the Great* (New Haven, CT, 1981), p.107-108.
74. De Madariga, *Russia in the age of Catherine the Great*, p.297-99; and for the Manifesto, 'Zhalovannaia Gramota Gosudaryni Imperatritsy Ekateriny Vtoroi na prava, vol'nosti i preiumshchestva blagorodnogo Rossiiskogo dvorianstva, 21 Aprelia 1785', *RA* 5 (1885), p.155-64, esp. the preamble which places an emphasis on these new rights as a reward, the product of Catherine's own rational thought process (*umstvovanie*), for the gentry's corporate sense of honour and virtue (p.157).
75. 'Russkie vol'nodumtsy v tsarstvovanie Ekateriny II', p.268-70.

The language of philanthropy, whether as individual good deeds or legislation, is common and provides a context for activities like the founding of the Society for Social Good (Soiuz obshchestvennogo blagodenstviia).[76]

The term in contemporary scholarship suited to this category would be 'pragmatic Enlightenment'. Numerous articles including a long piece listing specific initiatives described measures to improve public welfare that included urban redesign such as cleaning the Neva River,[77] the establishment of orphanages, the expansion of public education as its own good (as opposed to the Petrine use of education to create a functionary class)[78] and perhaps most prominently the persistent interest in penal reform. By the early 1890s publications of archival materials editorialised more overtly, drawing parallels between the past and present. In general, the nineteenth-century view of the eighteenth century as a philanthropic age associates the cultivation of civic virtues with a progressive Enlightenment fostered in the eighteenth century independent of the empress. Despite the continuing ban on the publication of works like Radishchev's *Journey from St Petersburg to Moscow* (only to be lifted in 1907), educated opinion was aware of links between the thinkers of the 1790s and later radical groups, starting with the Decembrists: both shared an interest in theories of political economy and, perhaps more significantly, in reforms to and limitation of monarchy, ideas that looked increasingly germane in the febrile atmosphere of the 1890s.

The credit is by no means confined to the empress herself. The many publications of private correspondences between members of the educated elite make clear how seriously noblemen, especially Freemasons, took the connection between intellectual Enlightenment and social welfare: in part this involves seeing the inner religious light, in part it acknowledges a connection between reason and virtue or in effect a commitment to practical enlightenment. Overall, the individual reforms are seen within new expectations of justice in which the vocabulary of citizenship is active. That is to say that within the period documents there is a new vocabulary of citizenship that carries with it expectations of justice, the public good and happiness. While

---

76. A. N. Sirotinina, 'K. F. Ryleev: istoriko-literaturnyj biograficheski ocherk', *RA* 6 (1890), p.113-209 (164-67); on Soiuz blagodenstviia, see p.139.

77. 'Ukaz Ekateriny II ob ochistke Nevy: 1-ogo maia 1775', *RS* 10 (1874), p.615-17.

78. Coverage of Catherine's promotion of schools for the nobility is given in Sirotinina, 'K. F. Ryleev', p.115.

archival publications of laws and acts dedicated to the enhancement of social welfare are frequent, more unusual is the republication of a forgotten play called *The Judicial act* by Zakhar Goriushkin, which opens with a speech by the judge on the debt virtue owes to enlightenment.[79] Excerpts from the empress' correspondence also burnish this positive assessment, apparent in the conclusion one article drew in 1888, that the significance of eighteenth-century Russian history lay in the new attitude that emerged to serfdom and the class system.[80]

In this same connection publications about the Academy of Sciences also credit it with disseminating Enlightenment; since the Academy did not have an explicit educational mission, the Enlightenment to which it belongs is by definition the world of science (given the abstract label of 'wisdom') and applied science, and one article expressly names the scientists who worked in Russia.[81] Another set of articles present the view that, while Russia's educated population was smaller than that of other European nations, the country can be counted among the 'enlightened peoples' or, in other words, among civilised nations governed by law, reason and progress.[82] While there is no doubt that the empress was the source of reason in her age, this body of evidence increasingly takes the view that her reforms produced a more civic-minded gentry that was not only Western in manners but also more European in mind-set.[83]

It can be seen that many eighteenth-century figures have ideas about the limits to state power but consider reform rather than a change of system to be the key to progress; this view is not diametrically opposed to religion, but the embrace of reason also encourages Christian feeling for humanity and religion as a useful institution of social progress. From a nineteenth-century perspective, it looked as

79. 'Sudebnoe deistvie v 1809, zrelishche sostavlennoe Goriushkiym', ed. Zakharii Goriushkin, *RS* 23 (1878), p.553-74 (553).
80. Pavlov, *Nashe perekhodnoe vremia*, p.389.
81. Mikhail Sukhomlinov, 'Piatidesiatiletnii i stoletnii iubilei S.-Peterburgskoi Akademii Nauk', *Russkaia starina* 18 (1877), p.1-20 (17). The biography of Teplov in 'Biograficheskiia svedeniia o russkikh pisateliakh XVIII veka i bibliograficheskie izvestiia ob nikh proizvedeniiakh' notes that, among his many improving activities such as gardening, music, agriculture, he did important work organising scientific knowledge in his *Catalogue of the Cabinet of Natural History* and also de facto managed the Academy between 1746 and 1762.
82. As noted in the travel diary of V. N. Zinov'ev: *Zhurnal Puteshestviia V. N. Zinov'eva po Germanii, Italii, Frantsii i Anglii v 1786-1790 gg.*, ed. N. P. Varyshnikov, *RS* 23 (1878), p.207-40, 399-440, 593-630 (612).
83. Bil'basov, 'Nikita Panin i Mers'ie de la-Riv'er', p.283-93.

though eighteenth-century gentry and bureaucracy demonstrated an ethos of civic responsibility they felt was to be expected of educated, progressive, enlightened administrators and jurists. This belief in incremental progress would not have satisfied the increasingly radical intelligentsia. By the 1880s, when Alexander Pypin compiled his massive volumes on the history of Russian literature, he found fault with Catherine's reign for failing to embrace the sort of democratic revolution the end of serfdom might have brought about nearly a century earlier. The insufficiency of gentry culture to the task of reform is a recurrent theme in the pages of his important historical writing: 'There needed to be a better-prepared foundation or at least from the side of power greater support extended to the best people in whose minds these ideas developed moral action. But this did not happen.'[84]

Autocracy as an ideal versus reality

In eighteenth-century political thought, insofar as it existed in Russia, the reinforcement of autocracy as the natural form of government for the country was an assumption. Yet, because the period took an interest in the evolution of Russia's historical institutions, the meaning of citizenship and public reason runs through work that documents how Catherine governed. What sort of 'enlightened despot' she was and whether comparable to Joseph II were the questions that naturally followed from the publication of massive amounts of her correspondence. There are also enquiries into her political philosophy, and the abiding question is whether she allowed a more consultative form of government that trained and encouraged enlightened bureaucrats.

In the pages of her correspondence, Catherine emerges as a managerial whirlwind. Her letters afford many apercus about power, but she is not a systematic thinker in the manner of Frederick II.[85] However, the picture that emerges from the new mass of evidence about legislation shifts the balance away from autocratic rule to the ways she sought consensus with the gentry and senatorial class (and in that respect may reflect the desperation of the liberal elite in the

---

84. Aleksandr Pypin, *Istoriia russkoi literatury* (1888), 4th edn, 4 vols (St Petersburg 1916), vol.4, p.16.
85. *Frederick the Great's philosophical writings*, ed. Avi Lifschitz, translated by Angela Scholar (Princeton, NJ, 2021).

1890s to find a way out of the crisis of tsardom that exploded in the 1905 Revolution). The workings of government and power structure at the court are seen from inside in a lengthy article treating the role of the Senate in her reign and another piece comparing Russia and Sweden's political structures.[86] Perspectives on Russia's international reputation as a civilised and civilising society accrue largely through the publication of correspondences and biographies of important figures. A long article by the historian Vasily Bilbasov on the influence of Lemercier de La Rivière on Catherine uses a wealth of archival sources to characterise Panin's (futile) efforts to achieve government with a better balance between the executive and other estates.

Chiefly remembered for his compendious biography of Catherine, Bilbasov offers this view on the origins of Panin's expectations. His analysis makes explicit use of certain Enlightenment premises that he clearly believes underlay Catherine's statecraft both early on and in her late assertions that monarchy remained the best way to preserve Enlightenment ideals against the barbarity of the French Revolution:

> Consistent with the rationalist philosophy of the eighteenth century, Catherine was convinced that reason and only reason could and ought to draft a new law code. [...] Educated in the Enlightenment ideas of French philosophy of the eighteenth century, Catherine had no idea that the laws of a nation are only the result of historical development; that they always correspond to the character of a nation; that in much they depend on the conditions of existence, the climate, the soil. One did not have to be a Russian, but one did have to know Russia and its past in order to compile for Russia the sort of law code that would make it possible 'to see the Russian people as happy and satisfied as human happiness and satisfaction could be encompassed on this earth' – for that, one had only to possess 'enlightened reason'.[87]

There is a lot of material to be found here that corroborates the language Catherine herself uses in letters when she speaks about 'le nouvel ordre des choses'.

By the end of the nineteenth century the equation of Catherine with a period of Enlightenment had crystallised in Russian historiography and life-writing. This view pervaded a new generation of biographical and political studies as well as popular literature.

---

86. Bil'basov, 'Nikita Panin i Mers'ie de la-Riv'er', p.324.
87. Bil'basov, 'Nikita Panin i Mers'ie de la-Riv'er', p.311.

Numerous pamphlets published in the late 1890s into the 1900s repeated the view that, through her support of publishing, legislation, enhancement of the sciences and literature, Catherine's application of 'enlightened measures' and 'enlightened ideas' had succeeded. Typical in this regard is the overview of the eighteenth century by Alexander Arkhangelsky, *The Empress Catherine II in the history of Russian literature and education.*[88] What is most instructive is its double use of *prosveshchenie* to mean both 'popular education' and 'Enlightenment': the two meanings of the single term form a double strand in a single civilising process. 'Popular education' was what Peter I achieved in laying the foundations of a secular culture enshrined institutionally from the start by the Academy of Sciences. And by the 1890s, 'popular education' was also a democratic priority for all but the most conservative writers, whether on the left or right.[89] Because Catherine's humane intentions relating to the serfs were regarded as 'enlightened', this intention counted more than her failure to emancipate them. Catherine promoted educational reforms for 'the lowest mass of people' and 'Enlightenment' as a more advanced form of progress and intellectual autonomy (the word 'ideas' figures large) among the elites. In 1873, Peter Pekarsky, a titan of eighteenth-century scholarship, published a set of materials by Mikhail Lomonosov in which the latter speaks about 'our enlightened age' ('v nashi prosveshchennye veki').[90] Seen within the norms of usage of his own period, Lomonosov's clear appropriation of the term to mean 'enlightened' rather than just 'educated' was making a statement. But when seen within its new provenance the phrase fits with the title of a public lecture given in Kyiv in 1874 by Professor I. N. Khrushchev: 'On the Enlightenment

88. Aleksandr Arkhangel'skii, *Imperatritsa II v istorii russkoi literatury i obrazovaniia* (Kazan, 1897).

89. How the intelligentsia's interest in socialism intersects with ideas about Enlightenment is a topic for further exploration in this context. What might be described in a longer discussion is how socialist thought catalysed the processes described here. The tension between utopian and pragmatic reform reverberated in the literature of the 1860s when Fyodor Dostoevsky published his *Notes from the underground* where the polemic with thinkers like Nikolai Chernyshevsky essentially caricatures the Enlightenment as a hyper-rational, utopian blueprint for a closed society. The general context was brilliantly set out in the classic work by Franco Venturi, *The Roots of revolution: a history of the populist and socialist movements in nineteenth-century Russia*, translated by Francis Haskell (London, 1960), with brief attention to the Enlightenment at p.243 and 296.

90. Petr Pekarskii, 'Mikhail Vasil'evich Lomonosov, "O razmnozhenii i sokhranenii rossiiskogo naroda" (1761)', *RS* 24 (1873), p.465-580 (565).

activity of Catherine II'.[91] Contemporary thinking about the period now placed its emphasis squarely on a meaning that in the period had been secondary and inconsistent. While Catherine herself regularly uses the French term *Lumières* to characterise the cultural milieu, eighteenth-century writers outlined modes of reasoning and feeling that they only inconsistently dubbed 'enlightened' because the term retained such strong ecclesiastic resonance. The practices of Enlightenment could be described by other names. By the last quarter of the eighteenth century, however, the Russian meaning of the loan word was aligned with the more general understanding of the original *Aufklärung* to describe a distinctive period.

***

The periodisation 'epoch of Enlightenment' became a fixture of Soviet literary and historical studies early in the scholarship of the new state. In Marxist-Leninist treatments, Catherine the Great was regularly reproved as a feudal ruler. In Soviet historiography, the period is cast as a battle between democratic enlighteners and Catherine as anti-Enlightenment. In the West, by an odd irony, she was also treated as an enemy of the Enlightenment. The nineteenth-century legacy of reappraisal was largely forgotten, as in these comments by Isaiah Berlin in an unpublished Harvard lecture: 'Why did the Russian intelligentsia become so interested in historical ideas? Largely because those were the ideas which were prevalent during the period during which Western ideas streamed into Russia, towards the end of the reign of Catherine the Great, who, despite repression, was not able to keep them out.'[92] In *The Enlightenment: history of an idea* (2017), Vincenzo Ferrone set out why one must think of the Enlightenment's legacies as historically specific rather than 'a kind of philosophia perennis'. In that spirit, the aim of this chapter has been to show how the term *prosveshchenie*, originally a diffuse concept in the eighteenth century, in two decades of the nineteenth century came to acquire a meaning comparable to *Aufklärung* and *Lumières*. We have seen that the meaning of the term is multi-faceted and dependent on later political contexts. In this treatment, the emphasis has been on Enlightenment

91. Quoted in V. S. [*sic*], 'Literatura Ekaterinskogo iubileia', *RS* 9 (1874), p.796-817 (797).
92. Isaiah Berlin, 'Four lectures on Russian historicism' (1962-1973), https://berlin. wolf.ox.ac.uk/published_works/singles/bib297.pdf (last accessed 24 April 2023).

as a value connected to the civic and intellectual profile of the gentry as seen retrospectively a century later. Between the 1880s and 1917 the story changed, as a different element of the intelligentsia authored a somewhat different narrative of the eighteenth century, one that was driven by a much more radical imperative as the shortcomings of the emancipation festered, exacerbated by the more illiberal reign of Alexander III. In the twentieth century, new paradigms for redescribing Russia's East-West relations from a twentieth-century perspective reflected another set of cultural forces and ideological positions. That history requires its own separate account.

The dilemma of Enlightenment: German, Jewish and antisemitic constructions of *Aufklärung* in the nineteenth century

MIKE ROTTMANN

Heinrich-Heine-Universität Düsseldorf

I.

Historians, philosophers, sociologists and literary scholars[1] are well aware that ideas, positions and concepts that were conceived, developed and communicated in the age of Enlightenment neither disappeared nor merely gathered dust in archives after the end of the epoch.[2] Later generations affirmed them, rejected them or became disillusioned with them, but never treated them with indifference. The persistence of Enlightenment after the end of its era has meanwhile been interpreted in several ways: as a philosophical programme, as a political project, as a literary movement or as the continuation of an unending historical epoch. Later circulations of Enlightenment ideas are particularly appealing and complex precisely because they are not abstract thought

---

1. I am grateful to William A. Theiss (Princeton) for his criticism and enormous help in preparing this text, and to Aleksandra Ambrozy (Halle) and Frederick Bellhoff (Düsseldorf) for their thoughtful reading and editing. Note on translations: original primary sources are quoted in English translation (with the original language given in parentheses or in a footnote). Quotations from secondary critical literature are given in English translation only.
2. Those who doubt the currency of the epoch and do not think highly of successors who defend the Enlightenment as a possible and meaningful programme or project have recently pleaded for 'archiving' the epoch, in other words, for its consistent historicisation. See e.g. Andreas Pečar and Damien Tricoire, *Falsche Freunde: war die Aufklärung wirklich die Geburtsstunde der Moderne?* (Frankfurt am Main and New York, 2015). A opposing programme comes from sociology: *Aufklärung als Aufgabe der Geistes- und Sozialwissenschaften: Beiträge für Günter Dux*, ed. Ulrich Bröckling and Axel T. Paul (Weinheim and Basel, 2019), esp. the essay by Günter Dux, 'Aufklärung als Aufgabe der Wissenschaft', p.23-25.

experiments, but attempts to intervene directly in society through scholarship, law or art. Alongside these clearly definable consequences of the age of Enlightenment for the shaping of modernity, there are also more diffuse reactions to the achievements of Enlightenment: the word itself is in many ways underdetermined and therefore susceptible to manipulation, distortion and political usurpation.[3]

I will justify the focus on the nineteenth century with reference to Bernhard Giesen's thesis, according to which 'the cultural identity of the Germans, carried by the educated bourgeoisie – the *Bildungsbürger* – and formulated by certain groups of intellectuals, arose within this time span of a "long" century [...] between the Enlightenment in the late eighteenth century and the founding of the Wilhelmine Empire in 1871'.[4] This article's first questions can be formulated as follows, informed by Georg Bollenbeck, who published an important essay on the 'Educated bourgeoisie's turning away from the Enlightenment' in the nineteenth century.[5] First, why, and through what linguistic forms (or semantics), was rejection or defence of Enlightenment ideas and values propagated in the second half of the nineteenth century? Since it is hardly possible to analyse the criticism and semantics of Enlightenment in the numerous debates of the *Vormärz* and the *Kaiserreich* comprehensively,[6] I will limit myself to one central conflict: the

3. See e.g. David Brooks, 'The Enlightenment project', *The New York Times* (28 February 2017); *Rethinking the Enlightenment: between history, philosophy, and politics*, ed. Geoff Boucher and Henry Martyn Lloyd (Lanham, MD, 2018); Nicolas Guilhot, 'Steven Pinker, *Enlightenment now: the case for reason, science, humanism, and progress*' (essay review), *H-Diplo commentary* (July 2018), https://networks.h-net.org/node/28443/discussions/1993064/h-diplo-commentary-1-enlightenment-now-case-reason-science (last accessed 25 April 2023).

4. Bernhard Giesen, *Intellectuals and the nation: collective identity in a German axial age* (Cambridge, 1998), p.10.

5. Georg Bollenbeck, 'Die Abwendung des Bildungsbürgertums von der Aufklärung: Versuch einer Annäherung an die semantische Lage um 1880', in *Nach der Aufklärung? Beiträge zum Diskurs der Kulturwissenschaften*, ed. Wolfgang Klein and Waltraud Naumann-Beyer (Berlin, 1995), p.151-62. This brief study refers to three important books by this author, which will be used to reconstruct his method and overarching theses: *Bildung und Kultur: Glanz und Elend eines deutschen Deutungsmusters*, 2nd edn (Frankfurt am Main, 1996); *Tradition, Avantgarde, Reaktion: deutsche Kontroversen um die kulturelle Moderne* (Frankfurt am Main, 1999); *Eine Geschichte der Kulturkritik: von Rousseau bis Günther Anders* (Munich, 2007).

6. Numerous references can be found, for example, in a monograph that focuses on the emergence of *Kulturkritik* in the eighteenth and early nineteenth centuries: Theo Jung, *Zeichen des Verfalls: semantische Studien zur Entstehung der Kulturkritik im 18. und frühen 19. Jahrhundert* (Göttingen, 2012), esp. p.315-82.

long-standing controversies that can be subsumed under the contemporary term 'Jewish question'. Hannah Arendt's panoramic definition of the 'Jewish question' is still valid:

> The modern Jewish question dates from the Enlightenment; it was the Enlightenment – that is, the non-Jewish world – that posed it. Its formulations and its answers have defined the behaviour and the assimilation of Jews. Ever since Moses Mendelssohn's genuine assimilation and Christian Wilhelm Dohm's essay 'On the Civic Improvement of Jews', the same arguments that found their chief representative in Lessing appear over and over in every discussion of Jewish emancipation.[7]

I therefore ask, secondly, how references to Enlightenment, both affirmative and negative, functioned in the context of this dispute. I am not aiming to reconstruct once again precisely why, from a historiographical perspective, it made perfect sense in the second half of the nineteenth and the first half of the twentieth centuries to explain the social situation of German Jews through the upheavals that took place in the eighteenth century. It suffices to point out that there was a debate throughout Jewish historiography of the nineteenth and twentieth centuries as to whether Judaism benefited from the Enlightenment or whether it lost its identity as a result of that period's transformations; we can contrast the assessments penned by the major historians Heinrich Graetz and Ismar Elbogen on the one hand,[8] and those by Martin

---

7.   Hannah Arendt, 'The Enlightenment and the Jewish question' (1932), in *The Jewish writings*, ed. Jerome Kohn (New York, 2007), p.3-18 (3). This was also the view of the antisemite Otto Bonhard (1893-1979) a few years earlier, in a book published under the pseudonym Otto Kernholt: *Vom Ghetto zur Macht: die Geschichte des Aufstiegs der Juden auf deutschem Boden*, 4th edn (Leipzig, 1923), p.49: 'So it went with Lessing, so with Dohm; they were later followed by the long succession of German campaigners for Judaism in the nineteenth century, who believed they owed it to their Enlightenment and liberalism to stand up for the supposedly oppressed Jewry' ('So war es bei Lessing, so bei Dohm; ihnen folgte dann später die lang Reihe von deutschen Vorkämpfern für das Judentum im 19. Jahrhundert, die es ihrer Aufklärung und ihrem Liberalismus schuldig zu sein glaubten, für das angeblich unterdrückte Judentum einzutreten'). See also Johannes Leicht, 'Otto Bonhard', in *Handbuch des Antisemitismus: Judenfeindschaft in Geschichte und Gegenwart*, ed. Wolfgang Benz, vol.8 (Berlin and Boston, MA, 2015), p.46-47.
8.   *Geschichte der Juden von den ältesten Zeiten bis auf die Gegenwart: aus den Quellen neu bearbeitet von Prof. Dr. H. Graetz*, vol.11: *Geschichte der Juden vom Beginn der Mendelssohn'schen Zeit (1750) bis in die neueste Zeit (1848)* (Leipzig, 1870), p.1-40,

Philippson or Salo Baron on the other.[9] But it is in fact misleading to describe the approval and criticism of the Enlightenment as a dispute between historical schools. In his *Geschichte der Juden*, Graetz already noted the tensions within Judaism that arose with the Enlightenment: 'Can a people be born in a single day?' ('Kann ein Volk in einem Tage geboren werden?'), Graetz asks his readers, in order to expose that the 'rejuvenation or rebirth of the Jewish people' ('Verjüngung oder Wiedergeburt des jüdischen Stammes') can be – 'and rightly so' ('mit Fug und Recht') – attributed to Moses Mendelssohn.[10] But Graetz also informs his readers that, 'with every step forward that the Berlin Enlightenment took', it stood 'against the entirety of Jews' ('jeder Schritt, den die Berliner Schule der Aufklärung vorwärts setzte, trat in Gegensatz gegen die Gesammtjudenheit').[11] The Enlightenment had created the fundamental tension between tradition and modernity, which still characterised the time in which Graetz lived and which he himself tried to describe.[12] This problem could be tentatively labelled an 'internal dilemma', since it resulted from the Enlightenment but was

146, 162-71, 371, 388, 413, 420, 443; Ismar Elbogen, *A Century of Jewish life* (Philadelphia, PA, 1944).

9. Martin Philippson, *Neueste Geschichte des jüdischen Volkes*, 2nd edn, vol.2 (Frankfurt am Main, 1930), p.8: 'The rich Jews mostly turned away from religion in superficial "Enlightenment" and frivolous gentility, while their fellow believers remained in the deepest old orthodoxy without participating in any way in the progress of general education. This behaviour, zealously encouraged by spiritual leaders, prevented them from striving for higher activity and gaining a better attitude to life' ('Die reichen Juden wandten sich zumeist in oberflächlicher "Aufklärung" und frivoler Vornehmheit von der Religion ab, während ihre Glaubensgenossen in der tiefsten Alt-Orthodoxie verblieben, ohne irgendwie an den Fortschritten der allgemeinen Bildung teilzunehmen. Dieses Verhalten, das von den geistlichen Führern mit Eifer gefördert wurde, verhinderte sie am Streben nach höherer Betätigung und an Gewinnung einer besseren Lebenshaltung'); Salo W. Baron, 'Ghetto and emancipation: shall we revise the traditional view?', *The Menorah journal* 14 (1928), p.515-26.

10. Graetz, *Geschichte der Juden*, vol.11, p.1, 3. See also Christoph Schulte, 'Die Zukunft des Judentums nach der Emanzipation: drei Modelle in der Berliner Haskala – Mendelssohn, Euchel, Friedländer', *Mendelssohn Studien* 20 (2017), p.11-24.

11. Graetz, *Geschichte der Juden*, vol.11, p.163.

12. Graetz, *Geschichte der Juden*, vol.11, p.v-vii. See also Shulamit Volkov, *Germans, Jews, and antisemites: trials in emancipation* (Cambridge, 2006), part 3: 'The German-Jewish project of modernity', p.159-286, and, by the same author, *Dilemma und Dialektik: zwei Jahrhunderte Aufklärung aus jüdischer Sicht* (Munich, 2002), p.28: 'The Jewish project of modernity was based on the intention to reform and to conserve at the same time.'

discussed at the end of the eighteenth century mostly within Judaism and with limited interactions with the Christian majority society.[13] Hannah Arendt rightly noted, moreover, that the arguments developed during this period would continue to be applied in the following century. It has also been repeatedly stressed in studies on nineteenth-century German-Jewish history that the significance of the Enlightenment and the movement to actualise it within German Jewry was extraordinarily extensive and meaningful, especially after the end of the epoch. Since it is hardly possible to consider the extensive literature on this point,[14] I quote a concise assessment by Werner E. Mosse:

> The political physiognomy of the German Jewry was shaped by the circumstances in which it first came to the stage of German politics, decisively and for all time.[15] This happened at the beginning of the nineteenth century, when, after the French Revolution, Europe was divided between 'authority' – meaning conservative, monarchical or clerical impulses – and a revolutionary democratic liberalism which stood for a general egalitarianism and which was a child of the Enlightenment. In this fight between the defenders of the old order and the advocates of the new, the Jewish position was unambiguous. The most important political question for the Jews

13. See Christoph Schulte, '"Diese unglückliche Nation": jüdische Reaktionen auf Dohms *Über die bürgerliche Verbesserung der Juden*', *Zeitschrift für Religions- und Geistesgeschichte* 54 (2002), p.352-65.
14. A selection of important research contributions: Hans Kohn, 'The multidimensional Enlightenment', *Journal of the history of ideas* 31 (1970), p.465-74; George L. Mosse, *German Jews beyond Judaism* (Bloomington, IN, and Cincinnati, OH, 1985); David Sorkin, *The Transformation of German Jewry, 1780-1840* (New York and Oxford, 1987); Jacob Katz, 'Varianten des jüdischen Aufklärungserlebnisses', in *Conditio Judaica: Judentum, Antisemitismus und deutschsprachige Literatur vom 18. Jahrhundert bis zum Ersten Weltkrieg*, ed. Hans Otto Horch and Horst Denkler, 2 vols (Tübingen, 1988), vol.1, p.1-9; Michael A. Meyer, 'Enlightenment: the powerful enticements of reason and universalism', in *Jewish identity in the modern world* (Seattle, WA, and Washington, DC, 1990), p.10-32; Zygmunt Baumann, 'Assimilation and Enlightenment', *Society* 27 (1990), p.71-81; David Sorkin, 'Jews, the Enlightenment and the sources of toleration: some reflections', *Leo Baeck Institute year book* 37 (1992), p.3-16; Arnold M. Eisen, 'Rethinking Jewish modernity', *Jewish social studies* 1 (1994), p.1-21; Paul Mendes-Flohr, *German Jews: a dual identity* (New Haven, CT, 1999); Volkov, *Dilemma und Dialektik*; Adam Sutcliffe, 'Judaism and the politics of Enlightenment', *American behavioral scientist* 49 (2006), p.702-15; Annelien de Dijn, 'The politics of Enlightenment: from Peter Gay to Jonathan Israel', *The Historical journal* 55:3 (2012), p.785-805.
15. Mosse refers to this important monograph: Rudolf Kaulla, *Der Liberalismus und die deutschen Juden* (Munich and Leipzig, 1928).

in Germany was at that time bourgeois equality, that is, the wish for full civil rights. In comparison with this goal, all other political problems appeared for the time being to be peripheral. [*Footnote in original*: As the doctrines of the Enlightenment spread among the Jews, their striving for bourgeois equality increasingly outweighed their attachment to tradition, their need for segregation and their fear of the consequences of assimilation.] But civil equality of the kind that the great majority of Jews strove for so passionately was a basic demand of the political ideology of the Enlightenment, which now [in the nineteenth century] went under the name 'Liberalism'. So it was natural, and indeed unavoidable, that the political sympathies of Jews in Germany and elsewhere lay with parties and groups that professed Liberalism. Moreover, it came to the point not only that Liberalism augured the achievement of civil equality, but that its adherents increasingly treated Jews as human and social equals even in private life. [...] The more Liberalism spread and the closer Jews identified themselves with its success, the stronger the mistrust and antipathy towards Jews became in the conservative camp.[16]

This article follows from Mosse's general schema. I am interested in the stakes with which German Jews, but also antisemites and *Bildungsbürger* who were neither Jewish nor members of the antisemitic party, processed references to Enlightenment in a specific set of texts. All three groups held positions on the Enlightenment as an epoch and on the long-term relevance of its meaning, I argue, and at the same time they used Enlightenment to put forward completely inconsistent political positions. Several paradoxes were the result of this multiplicity in the use of Enlightenment. German

16. Werner E. Mosse, 'Der Niedergang der Weimarer Republik und die Juden', in *Entscheidungsjahr 1932: zur Judenfrage in der Endphase der Weimarer Republik – ein Sammelband*, ed. Werner E. Mosse and Arnold Pauker, 2nd edn (Tübingen, 1966), p.3-4. See also Volkov, *Dilemma und Dialektik*, p.28: 'For more than a century, the majority of these modern Jews succeeded in maintaining their ambivalent position, namely to commit themselves to the Enlightenment, despite dilemmas and dialectics. The tolerance that underlies the Enlightenment, even its utopian-liberal political practice, opened the gateway to European society for the Jews'; and Sorkin, 'Jews, the Enlightenment and the sources of toleration', p.9: 'The Jews' regeneration was consequently a public issue. It was debated in the first half of the nineteenth century in respect to emancipation, in the last third of the century and during the Weimar Republic in terms of the "*Judenfrage*". In other words, it bedevilled Germans and German-Jews from the *Aufklärung* until the bitter end. And its companion piece was, of course, the German-Jewish cult of the *Aufklärung*: the more virulent the debate, the more energetic the celebration of the cult.'

Am Ende des Jahrhunderts

Rückschau auf 100 Jahre
geistiger Entwickelung

— Band III —

Dr. S. Bernfeld

Juden und Judentum im
neunzehnten Jahrhundert

Figure 1: Cover page from Dr. S[imon]. Bernfeld, *Am Ende des Jahrhunderts: Rückschau auf 100 Jahre geistiger Entwicklung*, vol.3: *Juden und Judentum im neunzehnten Jahrhundert* (Berlin, 1898).

Jews who sought civil equality (*Verbürgerlichung*) invoked the values of the Enlightenment in this process and counted on the acceptance of the term (Figure 1).[17] They appealed not only through the use of the term, but through symbolisations and interpretations, drawing, for

---

17. In Simon Bernfeld's recapitulation of the nineteenth century from a Jewish perspective, the Enlightenment and its ongoing relevance occupy an important place: *Am Ende des Jahrhunderts: Rückschau auf 100 Jahre geistiger Entwicklung*, vol.3: *Juden und Judentum im neunzehnten Jahrhundert* (Berlin, 1898). But in Bernfeld's book, as in the works of Graetz and others, the 'internal dilemma' becomes part of the discussion; see p.8, 10-11, 25, 30-40, 78-79, 100-105, 125, 158.

instance, on the paradigmatic relationship of Moses Mendelssohn and Lessing (Figure 2), from which they derived a specific cultural code.[18] Antisemites, meanwhile, did not deny that Jewish emancipation was based on the Enlightenment and was supported by liberalism; indeed, they affirmed it, if only to then attack it exhaustively. In that second step they discredited the Enlightenment as a whole or reinterpreted the term, even turning it against the Jews; they demanded 'Enlightenment about Jewish mismanagement' ('Aufklärung über die jüdische Mißwirtschaft') and 'Enlightenment about the true nature of Judaism' ('Aufklärung über die wahre Natur des Judenthums') (Figures 3 and 4).[19] By this, of course, they did not mean the banishment of prejudices about Judaism, but expressed the view that the liberal advancement of Jewish emancipation was based on false assumptions that were now to be enlightened. The antisemitic 'concept' of Enlightenment nevertheless remained connected to the epoch, invoking not only the word but also the wider semantic field – they, too, referenced 'Humanität' and 'Bildung' (Figure 5). In addition, antisemites were able to make use of another 'internal dilemma', namely the less-than-Jewish-friendly positions of the Enlightenment thinkers themselves. Certain statements made by thinkers such as Voltaire did not require much caricature to be read as antisemitic.[20] At the same time, once

18. Since this aspect has already been very well explored, I refer to exemplary sources and the most important literature: for the Jewish perspective see Gabriel Riesser, *Einige Worte über Lessing's Denkmal an die Israeliten Deutschlands gerichtet* (Frankfurt am Main, 1838), and Immanuel Heinrich Ritter, *Mendelssohn und Lessing: nebst einer Gedächtnisrede auf Moses Mendelssohn zu dessen 100jährigen Todestage, gehalten im akademischen Vereine für jüdische Geschichte und Literatur*, 2nd edn (Berlin, 1886); for a Judeophobic perspective see Wilhelm Marr: *Lessing contra Sem* (1883), 2nd edn (Leipzig, 1885). See the superb studies from Markus Fauser, 'Deutsch-jüdische Gedächtniskultur: das Jubiläumsjahr 1879', in *Lessing und das Judentum*, ed. Dirk Niefanger, Gunnar Och and Birka Siwczyk (Hildesheim, 2015), p.183-204, and Christhard Hoffmann, 'Constructing Jewish modernity: Mendelssohn jubilee celebrations within German Jewry, 1829-1929', in *Towards normality? Acculturation and modern German Jewry*, ed. Rainer Liedtke and David Rechter (Tübingen, 2003), p.27-52.

19. Or once again, in terms of conspiracy theory, from Kernholt [Bonhard], *Vom Ghetto zur Macht*, p.215: 'Among these officially supported cover-up efforts, we can further obtain the necessary enlightenment about Judaism in all its branches only through self-help' ('Bei diesen amtlich unterstützten Vertuschungsbestrebungen kann uns natürlich nur Selbsthilfe fördern, um auch weiterhin die nötige Aufklärung über das Judentum in allen seinen Zweigen zu erhalten').

20. See Kernholt [Bonhard], *Vom Getto zur Macht*, p.40-50, 251. But he also uses manipulation when he speaks of the 'antisemitism of outstanding people'

Leſſing-Mendelsſohn-Gedenkbuch.

Zur hundertfünfzigjährigen Geburtsfeier

von

Gotthold Ephraim Leſſing und Moſes Mendelsſohn,

ſowie zur Säcularfeier von Leſſing's „Nathan".

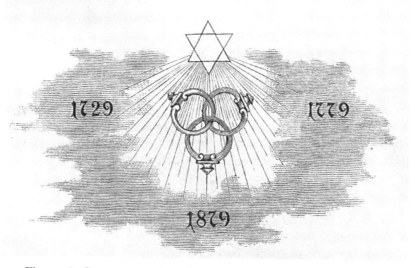

Figure 2: Cover page from *Lessing-Mendelssohn-Gedenkbuch: zur hundertfünfzigjährigen Geburtsfeier von* Gotthold Ephraim Lessing *und* Moses Mendelssohn, *sowie zur Säcularfeier von Lessing's 'Nathan'*, ed. Deutsch-Israelitischer Gemeindebunde (Leipzig, 1879).

Billige Flugblätter
zur
Aufklärung über die jüdische Mißwirthschaft.

25 Stück 30 Pfge.   100 Stück für 1 Mark.
1000 Stück 8 Mark, auch gemischt.

Figure 3: 'Billige Flugblätter zur Aufklärung über die jüdische Mißwirthschaft', advert in *Statistik des Judenthums: Sonder-Abdruck aus dem Antisemiten-Katechismus von Theodor Fritsch (Thomas Frey)* (Leipzig, 1892).

Wenige Bücher können sich rühmen, mit solchem Interesse vom Publikum aufgenommen zu sein, wie der

Antisemiten-Katechismus.
16. Auflage. Taschen=Format. Preis geb. 1 Mk.

Die immer brennender werdende **Judenfrage** und die immer weitere Kreise ergreifende **Aufklärung über die wahre Natur des Judenthums** sind die Ursachen des lebhaften An=theils, den das Publikum an dieser Schrift nimmt.

Der **Antisemiten-Katechismus** enthält in knapper Form eine **erdrückende Fülle thatsächlichen Materials,** welches die gegnerischen Angriffe schlagend widerlegt.

Figure 4: 'Antisemiten-Katechismus', advert in *Statistik des Judenthums: Sonder-Abdruck aus dem Antisemiten-Katechismus von Theodor Fritsch (Thomas Frey)* (Leipzig, 1892).

Das geiftige Bindemittel unter allen denjenigen, die ernft-
lich auf eine Löfung der Judenfrage hinftreben, find die

Deutfch-Sozialen Blätter.

Herausgegeben von **Theod. Fritfch.**
Mit der Beilage:
Antifemitifche Partei Nachrichten.
Das Blatt hat in allen Welttheilen, wo Deutfche wohnen,
Anhänger gefunden und zählt die einflußreichften Stände zu
feinen Lefern.

**Wer für die wahre Aufklärung und Freiheit unferes
Volkes, für wahre Humanität und Bildung wirken will,
der verbreite die „Deutfch-Sozialen Blätter" und helfe
feinen Brüdern die Augen öffnen über den modernen
Juden-Unfug.**

Figure 5: 'Deutsch-soziale Blätter', advert in *Antisemiten-Katechismus:
eine Zusammenstellung des wichtigsten Materials zum Verständnis der
Judenfrage von Theodor Fritsch*, 25th edn (Leipzig, 1893).

bourgeois-liberal and Jewish organisations were founded before 1900
that explicitly set themselves the task of combating antisemitism (and
pushing for equal rights),[21] their publications used the word *Aufklärung*
with a high frequency.[22]

('Antisemitismus hervorragender Menschen') and cites a long list of such authors:
'Tacitus, Pascal, Voltaire, Herder, Goethe, Kant, Jean Paul, Schopenhauer,
Grillparzer, Wagner' (p.246).

21. The Verein zur Abwehr des Antisemitismus was founded in 1890, the Central-
Verein deutscher Staatsbürger jüdischen Glaubens (abbreviated CV) in 1893.
See Arnold Paucker, *Der jüdische Abwehrkampf gegen Antisemitismus und Nationalsozialismus in den letzten Jahren der Weimarer Republik* (Hamburg, 1968), esp.
p.29-50; Barbara Suchy, 'The Verein zur Abwehr des Antisemitismus (I):
from its beginnings to the First World War', *Leo Baeck Institute year book* 28:1
(1983), p.205-39; Barbara Suchy, 'The Verein zur Abwehr des Antisemitismus
(II): from the First World War to its dissolution in 1933', *Leo Baeck Institute
year book* 30:1 (1985), p.67-100; Avraham Barkai, *'Wehr dich!': der Centralverein
deutscher Staatsbürger jüdischen Glaubens (C.V.) 1893-1938* (Munich, 2002), esp.
p.185-91.
22. See e.g. Ludwig Holländer, 'Aufklärung und immer wieder Aufklärung', *Central-
Verein-Zeitung: Blätter für Deutschtum und Judentum* 5 (3 March 1926), p.112-13.

All this leads to a general question: to what extent is it possible to expose antisemitic references to Enlightenment as false or untrue? In other words, is it possible to argue, with reference to historical knowledge of the eighteenth century, that antisemitic writers spread a false idea of the historical Enlightenment? Of course, one would like to say: if antisemites called their 'Enlightenment' 'medicine',[23] we call it poison. These two questions inevitably lead to another problem: do Jewish and anti-Jewish writers refer at all to the historical event 'Enlightenment' in their writings, or do they think of 'Enlightenment' as a project on which they themselves actively continue to work? Are they speaking as historical interpreters or politically engaged intellectuals? And is it possible to define the timeless project of Enlightenment with criteria that match the rigour of the understanding of the historical Enlightenment? In this respect, the distinction between politics and scholarship seems to be relevant not only for a differentiated analysis of the positioning of historical actors. In our own present moment, too, it is crucial to be able to determine whether scholarly or political motives lie behind approvals and criticisms of Enlightenment.

II.

I would therefore like to formulate the main question raised in this article in a more pointed way. Is it reasonable and possible to combat references to the Enlightenment which one rejects as populist and non-objective through weapons offered by historically inspired scholarship? Again and again, one observes the Enlightenment instrumentalised to justify positions that one rejects out of one's own understanding of the epoch. But do we reject in fact, or merely out of political difference? Phrased oversimply: is it appropriate, or even effective, to respond to politics with science? After Donald Trump's election, many intellectuals expressed concern (rightly, I think) about the cultural changes suggested by his politics with repeated reference to the achievements of the Enlightenment.[24] Yet nineteenth- and

23. Kernholt [Bonhard], *Vom Ghetto zur Macht*, p.vi: 'My book is intended to serve the investigation of truth even where it is unpleasant for us and does not accommodate the tendency towards self-righteousness. To remain with my first metaphor: it is concerned with the activity of medical enlightenment' ('Mein Buch soll der Ermittelung der Wahrheit dienen auch da, wo sie uns unangenehm ist und der Neigung zur Selbstgerechtigkeit nicht entgegenkommt. Um bei meinem ersten Vergleiche zu bleiben: es handelt sich um ärztliche Aufklärungstätigkeit').
24. The internet preserves a mass of blog posts, newspaper articles and scholarly

twentieth-century intellectual history is replete with debates in which Enlightenment was a point of reference, and the study of these debates can be highly instructive. In this context, I would like to suggest that the connection between Judaism and the Enlightenment by no means only took place in the nineteenth and early twentieth centuries, but has gained new topicality through recently political developments (although no longer under the banner of the 'Jewish question'). At the same time, it is striking that the debate on the emancipation of the Jews is taken as a paradigm for interpreting contemporary questions of integration and their political framing.[25]

In 2017, David Biale[26] published an essay which impressively demonstrates how relevant interpretations of Enlightenment can be. This is already very clearly emphasised by the title of the essay, when Biale asks: 'The end of Enlightenment?'[27] As becomes obvious, Biale framed his contribution, which he wrote as a politically committed intellectual and at the same time as a historian of Judaism, in reaction to Donald Trump's election and because of his confusion about support for Trump among Jewish voters. Biale wants to explain a contradiction, which he describes as follows: 'These Jewish Trump supporters, many of them Orthodox, evidently do not fear that the Jews will be imperilled by his victory. If he does embody an anti-Enlightenment politics (one hesitates to call his incoherent tweets an ideology), these voters are apparently not concerned that a reversal

---

papers on this topic. The arguments span a wide field, from connecting Trump to the Counter-Enlightenment, invoking the Enlightenment as 'medicine' against his policies, or assessing that the Enlightenment has already established forms that Trump can access (albeit ignorantly). See e.g. Suzanne Nossel, 'Donald Trump's assault on the Enlightenment', *Foreign policy* (25 January 2017); Andrew Clark, 'The Enlightenment – Donald Trump may represent its final days', *Financial review* (27 January 2017); Robert Darnton, 'To deal with Trump, look to Voltaire', *The New York Times* (27 December 2018).

25. See Felix Axster, Mathias Berek and Stefanie Schüler-Springorum, 'Verschenkte Potenziale: marginalisierte Ideen über gesellschaftlichen Zusamenhalt im Kaiserreich und in der Nachwendezeit', in *Gesellschaftlicher Zusammenhalt: ein interdisziplinärer Dialog*, ed. Nicole Deitlhoff, Olaf Groh-Samberg and Matthias Middell (Frankfurt am Main, 2020), p.152-73, and Christoph Schulte, 'Integration durch Haskala? Ein Paradigma für Minoritäten-Integration heute?', in *Das Prinzip Aufklärung zwischen Universalismus und partikularem Anspruch*, ed. Christina-Monika Hinneburg and Grażyna Jurewicz (Paderborn, 2014), p.25-36.

26. Since 1999, Biale has been serving as Emanuel Ringelblum Distinguished Professor of Jewish History at the University of California at Davis.

27. David Biale, 'The end of Enlightenment?', *Jewish social studies* 22 (2017), p.141-45.

of universalist and rationalist values endangers the Jews.'[28] The essay culminates in a sustained appeal to Trump's Jewish voters, for whom – 'as for all children of the Enlightenment' – 'a clarion call to action has been sounded before the lights go out all over the civilised world.'[29] In the following, I want to linger on the particularities of Biale's argument, which, it seems to me, goes far beyond the general debate about 'Trump and Enlightenment' or 'Trump as counter-enlightener'. This is because Biale connects a historical interpretation of the Enlightenment with an analysis of contemporary politics, which, as already quoted, culminates in a call for political action. The essay gains its persuasive power insofar as all three elements – history, analysis and activism – merge and support each other. First of all, it is important that Biale once again justifies why he considers Jews in particular to be 'children of the Enlightenment':

> It is a truism, but one worth repeating, that modern Jews are all products of the Enlightenment, regardless of whether they endorse its precepts. Even ultra-Orthodox Jews are products of the Enlightenment, which serves primarily as a foil for their own equally modern antimodernism. And Jews of the Middle East and North Africa were also, willingly or not, products of the Enlightenment's colonialist project. The Enlightenment was not always an unmitigated blessing for the Jews, but their success in integrating into modern societies as a minority was predicated on the Enlightenment's promise to erase religious and ethnic barriers. This was a hard-won battle that took the better part of two centuries. [...] [T]he point should be clear: the Enlightenment project did not end with the French Revolution but continued, contested, until recent times.[30]

This position, as well as the historical portrait cited below, corresponds not only for the most part to the latest historical scholarship,[31] but also to the self-perception of Jews in the nineteenth century:

28. Biale, 'The end of Enlightenment?', p.142-43.
29. Biale, 'The end of Enlightenment?', p.144. He accuses Trump's Jewish voters of the following assessment, which he considers gravely false, not only for historical reasons: 'Their thinking must run like this: Jews are now part of the economic elite of America, the very elite Trump has installed in his cabinet [...]. This right-wing Jewish embrace of Trump, which goes beyond traditional Jewish Republicanism, seems to be predicated on the idea that Jews no longer need the Enlightenment' (p.143).
30. Biale, 'The end of Enlightenment?', p.142.
31. Biale's comment on the attitude of Orthodoxy is also accurate. See Mordechai Breuer, 'Das Bild der Aufklärung bei der deutsch-jüdischen Orthodoxie',

The French Revolution's creation of the category of citizen meant that the Jews had to be emancipated. Conversely, the Nazi revolt against the democratic and egalitarian ideals of the Enlightenment necessarily entailed the reversal of Jewish emancipation, whether as a prelude to genocide or otherwise. And finally, the defeat of Nazism led directly or indirectly to the defeat of antisemitism and to Jewish sovereignty.[32]

Following this historical panorama, which begins with the positive Enlightenment event (French Revolution) and, despite catastrophe (the Holocaust), leads to a positive outcome (the founding of the State of Israel), Biale asks two questions: is this historical panorama true, and, secondly, does Trump's election 'portend an epochal turning point in Jewish history'? His tentative answer to both questions is: 'yes'.[33] Biale identifies 'family resemblances' between the 'turn to nativism and authoritarianism akin to the fascist and quasi-fascist regimes of the 1930s' and the rejection of universal values of science and human rights that exist today: '[I]n both cases, the embrace of ethnonationalism and disdain for democratic norms have deep historical roots in the rejection of the rationalism of the Enlightenment and the politics of the French Revolution.'[34] Biale's political analyses are astute and anything but docile, especially when he points out that authoritarian and, in his view, always anti-Enlightenment politicians only 'maintain the veneer of democracy'.[35] He also makes a prescient comment on a case that has become even more serious since 2017: 'If we want to see a possible future, we need only look to Vladimir Putin's Russia, so admired by Trump.'[36] He identifies a 'dialectic of Enlightenment' operating in many countries which, as 'products of the Enlightenment' itself, exist 'in reaction to Enlightenment globalism';[37] and he observes nationalists in many countries for whom 'Enlightenment is passé' as 'a vestige of a false universalism

---

in *Aufklärung und Haskala in jüdischer und nichtjüdischer Sicht*, ed. Karlfried Gründer and Nathan Rotenstreich (Heidelberg, 1990), p.131-42, and Rainer Kampling, 'Die Neo-Orthodoxie des 19. Jahrhunderts und die Haskala: Randbemerkungen zu übersehenen Nähen', in *Was war deutsches Judentum? 1870-1933*, ed. Christina von Braun (Berlin, 2015), p.61-70.

32. Biale, 'The end of Enlightenment?', p.141.
33. Biale, 'The end of Enlightenment?', p.141.
34. Biale, 'The end of Enlightenment?', p.141-42.
35. Biale, 'The end of Enlightenment?', p.142.
36. Biale, 'The end of Enlightenment?', p.142.
37. Biale, 'The end of Enlightenment?', p.142.

and rationality'.[38] While the Trump administration's world view espouses a 'version of Western civilisation' that 'does not include the Enlightenment',[39] Biale lets his readers know that, on the one hand, 'Zionism was an Enlightenment project' and, on the other hand, '[t]he success of Israeli democracy, with all its faults, is a remarkable testimony to this Enlightenment legacy.'[40]

It is certainly noteworthy that Biale firmly couples all the major events of modern Jewish history to the Enlightenment in order to increase leverage on Trump's Jewish voters: he claims that, by approving authoritarian policies, they are putting all their achievements at risk. Although Biale does not hide the fact that Enlightenment 'was not always an unmitigated blessing for the Jews', his image of Enlightenment is nevertheless overwhelmingly affirmative. Emphasising the benefits of Enlightenment is here not just a historical argument, because, if it were, we would no doubt be more critical of the Enlightenment.[41] In a state of crisis, it is no longer a matter of reconstructing a historical period in its fullness and subtlety down to the last detail, but of diminishing ambiguity; for it is this clarity that makes the political appeal possible. One last aspect that Biale brings into the field, meanwhile, should help us to find a connection back to the German nineteenth century, namely, what Biale calls a 'perverse confirmation'. One such perverse confirmation, in the nineteenth century, has already been mentioned: German Jews invoked the Enlightenment and its values, and antisemites confirmed that modern Judaism was indeed properly rooted in those values, a first step in the destruction or at least the reinterpretation of them. According to Biale, in today's America, Jews consider this country their 'natural home': because they identify themselves with its values, they are economically successful and stand firmly on the side of the West in the war against Islam.[42] Propagandists discursively include Jews in their nationalist camps by pitting the '"Judeo-Christian West" [...] at war with global Islam' (Stephen Bannon).[43] At the

---

38. Biale, 'The end of Enlightenment?', p.144.
39. Biale, 'The end of Enlightenment?', p.143.
40. Biale, 'The end of Enlightenment?', p.143. See also Georges Bensoussan, 'Le sionisme, un enfant de l'Europe des Lumières', *Cités* 47-48 (2011), p.141-53, and Fania Oz-Salzberger, 'Enlightenment, Haskalah, and the State of Israel', *The European legacy* 25 (2020), p.801-25.
41. See de Dijn, 'The politics of Enlightenment'.
42. Biale, 'The end of Enlightenment?', p.143.
43. Biale, 'The end of Enlightenment?', p.143. See e.g. Scott Shane, 'Stephen Bannon in 2014: we are at war with radical Islam', *The New York Times*

same time, the right-wing camp mobilises against 'global capitalism', terminology that refers in a classic antisemitic trope – here I also agree with Biale – to Jewish bankers. This again raises a serious paradox and dilemma: when Jews accept this world view, which may be attractive in some respects, and thus help to establish it, they destabilise their own situation.

In another respect, Biale's essay is important for the overarching question that this article formulates. Especially when analysing controversies concerning Enlightenment, and, in doing so, seeking the positions of different factions, it is important to identify those central points of intersection where opinions converge. These ironic convergences are the keys to understanding the points of conflict.

III.

References to Enlightenment in debates that were culturally and politically relevant in the nineteenth, twentieth and twenty-first centuries have so far been explored only in a rudimentary way. It is obvious, but cannot yet be considered as sufficiently analysed, that the semantics of the Enlightenment were activated particularly intensively in times of crisis and transition. But, in 1995, the literary and cultural historian Georg Bollenbeck published a remarkable essay, whose provocative thesis is already contained in the title of his paper: 'Die Abwendung des Bildungsbürgertums von der Aufklärung' ('The educated bourgeoisie's turn away from the Enlightenment'). Bollenbeck's observation was that the German *Bildungsbürgertum* had turned away from the values and ideals of the European Enlightenment as a whole, and he dated this rejection to the late nineteenth and early twentieth centuries.[44] But, far from diminishing the relevance of Enlightenment in general, this 'Abwendung', which is not the same as rejection, only left the concept even more discursively charged.[45] Bollenbeck argues

---

(1 February 2017); Tom McCarthy, 'Steve Bannon's Islamophobic film script just one example of anti-Muslim views', *The Guardian* (3 February 2017); in a broader context, Michael Hirsh, 'Team Trump's message: the clash of civilizations is back', *Politico* (20 November 2016), and Brandon W. Hawk, 'Why far-right nationalists like Steve Bannon have embraced a Russian ideologue', *The Washington Post* (16 April 2019).

44. Bollenbeck, 'Abwendung', p.151.
45. See Stefan-Ludwig Hoffmann, 'Brothers and strangers? Jews and Freemasons in nineteenth-century Germany', *German history* 18:2 (2000), p.143-61 (156):

that a positive 'line of continuity' broke off around 1880, and that values and ideals which were previously highly esteemed then became devalued: education and culture, the rule of law and the public sphere, the individual and humanity, people and nation, general wellbeing and progress.[46] The term 'Enlightenment' gained a 'negative content'.[47] Bollenbeck distinguishes (and at this point his approach is particularly innovative) between what has been 'thought on the philosophical high ground', on the one hand, and the 'collective knowledge of a society' on the other hand.[48] The interest, then, consists in adopting a 'discourse-historical perspective' in order to gain further insight into 'communicative practices and collective stocks of knowledge' as distinct from the history of theory and exclusive academic disputes.[49] His aim is to capture the maximum 'social scope' of Enlightenment in the nineteenth century.

Bollenbeck begins by pointing out what is 'sufficiently well known', namely that 'towards the end of the eighteenth century [...] the great thinkers and poets moved away from the Enlightenment without breaking with it.'[50] This refers above all to Romanticism's critique of the Enlightenment, a thoroughly complex process that Bollenbeck masterfully conveys. He then turns to what has 'remained almost unknown', namely the 'underestimated actuality of the Enlightenment in the nineteenth century':

> Until the end of the nineteenth century, the self-appointed *Gebildeten* [educated], those typical German pioneers of modernisation, understood Enlightenment as a current aim, as an outcome, a process and a goal. Only after 1880 does the *Bildungsbürgertum* turn away from Enlightenment. That suggests a fundamental and consequential, though hitherto underrated, semantic revolution in German history. With it, the great political vision of 'egalitarian civil society' loses its attraction, and an anti-Enlightenment, anti-liberal and antidemocratic thinking gains in influence accordingly, a thinking that undoes any idea that presents itself as humanistic and antidogmatic, and that

---

'Nevertheless, these concepts underwent a process of *re*-interpretation that continued to draw on their original meaning, rather than entirely repudiating them.'

46. Bollenbeck, 'Abwendung', p.153.
47. Bollenbeck, 'Abwendung', p.153, 159.
48. Bollenbeck, 'Abwendung', p.154.
49. Bollenbeck, 'Abwendung', p.154.
50. Bollenbeck, 'Abwendung', p.151; Bollenbeck, *Geschichte der Kulturkritik*, p.111-22, 155.

lays the ground for authoritarian solutions, up until the acceptance of National Socialism as the presumed 'lesser evil'.[51]

Bollenbeck is concerned with demonstrating the 'unbroken presence of the Enlightenment in the basic semantics of the bourgeoisie', a phenomenon that cannot be classified as a mere reception phenomenon,[52] but rather makes visible an 'unbroken line of continuity'.[53] His thesis is therefore not only that the Enlightenment in the nineteenth century unfolds 'possible effects', but that Enlightenment ideas and 'political concepts of emancipation' in the nineteenth century entered 'a new kind of scope'.[54] Through the category of semantics, he seeks to describe phenomena that cannot be grasped with the conventional frameworks.[55] The fundamental point is that the semantic field cannot be limited to Enlightenment/enlightener/ enlightened or similar metaphors, but is instead placed in a 'pejorative conceptual field': 'Rationalism – West – Utilitarianism – Civilisation'.[56] He concludes that in this 'uncoupling from Western European semantics [...] lies the specifically German semantic innovation'.[57]

51. Bollenbeck, 'Abwendung', p.151. See also p.153-56, and Bollenbeck, *Geschichte der Kulturkritik*, p.14, 143-47, 155. This perspective finds support in Reinhart Siegert, 'Enlightenment in the 19th century – "overcoming" or diffusion?', translated by David Paisey, in *Volksaufklärung: biobibliographisches Handbuch zur Popularisierung aufklärerischen Denkens im deutschen Sprachraum von den Anfängen bis 1850*, ed. Holger Böning and Reinhart Siegert, vol.3 (Stuttgart-Bad Cannstatt, 2016), p.lxxix-cxv.

52. See Bollenbeck, 'Abwendung', p.153: 'In the nineteenth century, the Enlightenment was not only perceived, but also perpetuated in relation to the interpretative pattern of "Bildung und Kultur" and the liberal ideology of emancipation. Their emancipative ideas shape the basic semantics of the German educated middle classes, those patterns of interpreting the world that are built into language with a loosened, but still not entirely non-committal connection to action.'

53. Bollenbeck, 'Abwendung', p.153.

54. Bollenbeck, 'Abwendung', p.153.

55. Bollenbeck, 'Abwendung', p.152, mentions three dimensions of 'Enlightenment': '"Enlightenment" as the self-interpretation of the Enlightenment thinkers', '"Enlightenment" as a structural epochal concept' and '"Enlightenment" as a universal concept'.

56. Bollenbeck, *Geschichte der Kulturkritik*, p.155. See also Bollenbeck, 'Abwendung', p.153, 160. This is supported by the results of Jörn Leonhard, *Liberalismus: zur historischen Semantik eines europäischen Deutungsmusters* (Munich, 2001), p.254-61, 344-45, 375, 415, 434.

57. Bollenbeck, *Bildung und Kultur*, p.164.

Bollenbeck concludes that Enlightenment in the nineteenth century 'continues to be understood as a current project and not as a completed and overcome epoch'.[58] The problem of the epoch boundary (e.g. around 1780) is consequently that the 'historical impact of the Enlightenment in the nineteenth century is hastily narrowed down'.[59] However, the 'end' of the Enlightenment epoch in terms of the history of ideas cannot be 'reinterpreted as a finding in the history of mentality'.[60]

Bollenbeck's argument could be summarised as follows: in the late nineteenth and early twentieth centuries, a large breadth of society processed basic programmes and ideas of the Enlightenment. The ideas of the Enlightenment thinkers, originally formulated by an elite, gradually seeped into the lifeworld of the bourgeoisie and led to the 'bürgerlichen Wertehimmel' ('bourgeois value system'),[61] albeit with increasing controversy. The political and social questions and challenges of the century were placed in terms of Enlightenment. The ideas of the Enlightenment did not persist in 'pure form' – they were not historically frozen – but were negotiated through the prism of the present, that is affirmed, rejected and perhaps modified. Systematically, it is important that the actualising concepts of Enlightenment were linked not only to the epoch alone, but also to liberalism:

> Political claims of liberalism are also to be found in the conception of the currency of the Enlightenment as a process and a goal. But, above all, there is, bound up with the idea that the Enlightenment is current, an optimistic anthropology and conception of the past, without which liberalism – in its conviction that it represents the basic tendencies of the age in inexorable progress towards reason and freedom – is unthinkable.[62]

58. Bollenbeck, *Bildung und Kultur*, p.155.
59. Bollenbeck, 'Abwendung', p.153.
60. Bollenbeck, *Geschichte der Kulturkritik*, p.154-55.
61. Manfred Hettling and Stefan-Ludwig Hoffmann, 'Der bürgerliche Wertehimmel: zum Problem individueller Lebensführung im 19. Jahrhundert', *Geschichte und Gesellschaft* 23 (1997), p.333-59; *Der bürgerliche Wertehimmel: Innenansichten des 18. Jahrhunderts*, ed. Manfred Hettling and Stefan-Ludwig Hoffmann (Göttingen, 2000).
62. Bollenbeck, 'Abwendung', p.155-56. See *Liberalismus als Feindbild*, ed. Ewald Grothe and Ulrich Sieg (Göttingen, 2014); Ulrich Wyrwa, *Juden in der Toskana und in Preußen im Vergleich: Aufklärung und Emanzipation in Florenz, Livorno, Berlin und Königsberg i. Pr.* (Tübingen, 2003), esp. p.205-414; Shulamit Volkov,

Bollenbeck is able not only to draw the link between the Enlightenment and liberalism from the relevant articles in important literary encyclopaedias, but also to identify these positions in the writings of the cultural critic Julius Langbehn and the ethnic (*völkisch*) literary historian Adolf Bartels.[63] German liberalism was a 'child of the Enlightenment', because German liberal 'faith' was based on ideas that could be attributed without ambiguity to the eighteenth century: 'reason, progress and modernity'.[64] Insofar as this 'faith' in liberal progress no longer seems tenable due to the processes of social change, the 'heritage' of the Enlightenment also becomes questionable: 'In the nineteenth century, the Enlightenment promise of emancipation remains present within liberalism, but, with the loss of social integration and possibilities of reform, the Enlightenment too, around the end of the century, lost its attraction and currency. [...] The old liberal stance, with its Enlightenment call for emancipation, seemed to go on the defensive.'[65] It has frequently been noted that Enlightenment had a difficult standing in Germany; on this point, studies in the history of science, culture and mentalities agree. So overwhelmingly bad was the reputation of Enlightenment in Germany that it has had to be pointed out that amidst 'the long tradition of Enlightenment criticism in Germany [...] [it] should not be overlooked that there was also a thinner, but also existing branch of factual analysis [...] and explanatory-historical approach to the Enlightenment'.[66] As early

---

'Nochmals zum Antimodernismus im Kaiserreich', in *Das Deutsche Kaiserreich in der Kontroverse*, ed. Sven Oliver Müller and Cornelius Torp (Göttingen, 2009), p.66-76.

63. Bartels applauds the 'break of the German Volk with liberalism' and considers this development more important than 'all war and any other events'. His writings are praised by Bonhard as 'excellent enlightening work' ('treffliche Aufklärungsarbeit'). Kernholt [Bonhard], *Vom Ghetto zur Macht*, p.192. Langbehn, for his part, appreciates that the 'flat, disintegrating spirit of Enlightenment and liberalism' is contradicted by the conservative side. Bollenbeck, 'Abwendung', p.156.

64. Bollenbeck, 'Abwendung', p.157, 158-59.

65. Bollenbeck, 'Abwendung', p.159.

66. Winfried Müller, *Die Aufklärung* (Munich, 2002), p.67-68. See Wolfgang Hardtwig, 'Wie deutsch war die deutsche Aufklärung', in *Nationalismus und Bürgerkultur in Deutschland 1500-1914: ausgewählte Aufsätze* (Göttingen, 1994), p.55-78 (55): 'In German political culture of the nineteenth and twentieth centuries and within the undisputed *Sonderweg* of German historiography, especially in the twentieth century, the tradition of the German Enlightenment had a difficult status. It was at times forgotten, at times marginalised, in

as 1843, a well-known encyclopaedia conspicuously took a stand in favour of the Enlightenment, but in doing so it only confirmed that it had barely any defenders: 'Enlightenment is a concept whose meaning and truth are so great, and so illuminating, that it is hardly comprehensible how it could have come into disrepute. But that is exactly what has happened in many ways since the middle of the eighteenth century' ('Aufklärung ist ein Begriff, dessen Bedeutung und Wahrheit so groß und so einleuchtend ist, daß man kaum begreift, wie er habe in übeln Ruf kommen können. Dennoch ist dieses seit der Mitte des 18. Jahrh. vielfach geschehen').[67]

IV.

Although several methodological issues require further discussion, the observation formulated at the beginning of this article has now been defended: ideas attributed to the Enlightenment were not treated with indifference after 1800, but nor were they universally accepted. Bollenbeck's thesis, according to which *Bildungsbürger* (as interpretive elites) distanced themselves from the Enlightenment without banning its references from their discourses, can also be confirmed. The following section shows that another constellation of ideas, born in the late eighteenth century, also persisted throughout the nineteenth century.[68] This was the debate about the 'true and false Enlightenment' ('wahre und falsche Aufklärung'), and it provided a stabilising force for the centrality of Enlightenment in social discourse.[69]

---

many cases systematically fought and discredited'; and Alexander Mitscherlich, 'Neuerliches Nachdenken über die Aufklärung', *Merkur* 31:345 (1977), p.101-13 (101): 'Enlightenment has never really been recognised here alongside the philosophical systems indigenous to Germany. In the overall historical record of the last 200 years, we have bitterly lacked rational dryness. We might otherwise have been spared the arrogance of imperial Germany and the *Afterglauben* of National Socialism. And even at the moment, interest in enlightenment remains poor.' See also Joachim Whaley, 'German studies: where is the *Aufklärung* now?', *Journal for eighteenth-century studies* 34:4 (2011), p.487-93.

67. *Allgemeine deutsche Real-Encyklopädie für die gebildeten Stände: Conversations-Lexikon*, 9th edn, 15 vols (Leipzig, 1843), vol.1, p.622.

68. See Horst Stuke, 'Aufklärung', in *Geschichtliche Grundbegriffe: historisches Lexikon zur politisch-sozialen Sprache*, ed. Otto Brunner, Werner Conze and Reinhart Koselleck, vol.1 (Stuttgart, 1972), p.243-342 (341-42).

69. See Werner Schneiders, *Die wahre Aufklärung: zum Selbstverständnis der deutschen Aufklärung* (Freiburg and Munich, 1974).

In an 1864 pamphlet, the Catholic professor of philosophy and later bishop of Mainz Paul Leopold Haffner (1829-1899) stated the following: 'The light of the true and false Enlightenment shows itself most fully in the effects which both of them bring about on the social level' ('Das Licht der wahren und falschen Aufklärung unterscheidet sich am vollständigsten in den Wirkungen, welche beide auf socialem Gebiete hervorbringen').[70] Haffner applied not only the word 'Enlightenment', but also the entire arsenal of relevant metaphors ('light', 'sun', 'shade' and 'darkness', or 'Licht', 'Sonne', 'Schatten' and 'Finsternis').[71] And he assumed that Enlightenment brought about its effects in the 'social sphere' ('socialem Gebiete'). Haffner sought to establish a supra-temporal, 'true' ('wahre') understanding of Enlightenment, but, because the term 'Enlightenment' was bound to the postulates of the eighteenth century, he had to distinguish his apologetic project and his concept of Enlightenment from the 'false' ('falsche') historical epoch. The history of Enlightenment on the one hand 'must begin with God, and end with God' ('müßte mit Gott beginnen und mit Gott aufhören').[72] His basic formulation of the programme of 'Enlightenment', on the other hand, was even more clear: 'Enlightenment means illumination of the spirit through truth, liberation from the shadows of error, ignorance, doubt. In its deepest meaning, Enlightenment is the transfiguration of reason' ('Aufklärung heißt Erleuchtung des Geistes durch die Wahrheit, Befreiung von den Schatten des Irrthums, der Unwissenheit, des Zweifels. Aufklärung ist in seiner tiefsten Bedeutung Verklärung der Vernunft').[73] The interesting aspect of Haffner's text is the following paradox: obviously, the term 'Enlightenment' was firmly bound to the eighteenth century and thus to a series of ideas that Haffner (and certainly not only he) considered antireligious. So why could Haffner, a bishop of the Catholic Church, not resign the period to the historical past and keep silent about its aims? For him, the term 'Enlightenment' was indeed of such importance, and so appealing, that he felt compelled to rescue and redefine it for his own aims: 'I would have to speak of

---

70. Paul Leopold Haffner, *Die deutsche Aufklärung: eine historische Skizze*, 3rd edn (Mainz, 1864), p.103. The first chapter of the first lecture is entitled: 'Die wahre und die falsche Aufklärung', p.1-11.
71. See Haffner, *Die deutsche Aufklärung*, p.iv, 2-4, 10, 121, 143 ('Licht'), 29, 35, 77 ('Sonne'), iv, 1-4, 10-11, 28, 79, 131 ('Schatten'), 10 ('Finsternis').
72. Haffner, *Die deutsche Aufklärung*, p.2.
73. Haffner, *Die deutsche Aufklärung*, p.1.

the shining of the divine light, or of our walking in the light of God, if I wanted to give the word back its meaning and present a history of true Enlightenment' ('Von den Leuchten des göttlichen Lichtes oder von unserem Wandel im Lichte Gottes müßte ich reden, wenn ich dem Worte seine Bedeutung wiedergeben und eine Geschichte der wahren Aufklärung vortragen wollte').[74] On the other side, even such a second declared opponent of the eighteenth-century Enlightenment as the pugnacious, nationalist, conservative historian Georg von Below (1858-1927) could not simply pass over 'the Enlightenment' with indifference. He needed it precisely because he held it responsible for almost all the evils of the present,[75] and, in 1916, he opted for 'Romanticism'[76] as a *Weltanschauung* and principle of scholarship: 'For us, the Enlightenment is a position that has been superseded' ('Die Aufklärung ist für uns ein überwundener Standpunkt'), Below stated with reference to the Protestant Church historian Adolf von Harnack,[77] and any 'attempt to canonise the Enlightenment' ('Versuch der Kanonisierung der Aufklärung')[78] had to be prevented precisely for this reason and vigorously rejected. In order to bring about the 'overcoming of the Enlightenment in the fields of science and politics' ('Überwindung der Aufklärung auf dem Gebiet der Wissenschaften und der Politik'),[79] Below first had to prove its damaging influence on all areas of life (academia, culture, religion, politics and the economy) and to contrast the promises of 'Romanticism' as an alternative.[80] Below was certain not only that there was 'an' Enlightenment that was concretely realised in the eighteenth century, but also that there

---

74. Haffner, *Die deutsche Aufklärung*, p.2.
75. Georg von Below, *Die deutsche Geschichtsschreibung von den Befreiungskriegen bis zu unseren Tagen* (1916), 2nd edn (Munich and Berlin, 1924). Below opposes Enlightenment as a whole. This entirety of Enlightenment manifests, Below believes, in a series of cultural and political 'inventions', all of which he rejects: cultural history, rationalism, cosmopolitanism, pacifism, individualism, subjectivism, democratic historiography, etc. See Hans Cymorek, *Georg von Below und die deutsche Geschichtswissenschaft um 1900* (Stuttgart, 1998).
76. Below, *Die deutsche Geschichtsschreibung*, p.87, 159; Georg von Below, *Die Ursachen der Reformation* (Munich and Berlin, 1917), p.163.
77. Below, *Die Ursachen der Reformation*, p.170. Below approvingly quotes a statement by Harnack from a conference given in 1896, 'Das Christentum und die Geschichte', published in Adolf von Harnack, *Reden und Aufsätze*, vol.2 (Giessen, 1904), p.1-22 (5).
78. Below, *Die Ursachen der Reformation*, p.171.
79. Below, *Die deutsche Geschichtsschreibung*, p.87.
80. Below, *Die deutsche Geschichtsschreibung*, p.1-2, 12, 14, 16-18, 157.

were 'Enlightenment tendencies' ('Aufklärungstendenzen') that had existed since then.[81]

As a convinced étatist, Below maintained three fixed principles throughout his life: the German *Staat*, the German *Nation* and the German *Volk*.[82] The term *Volk* comes from the Enlightenment, and the modern coinage of the term *Nation* also comes from the Enlightenment.[83] As an explicitly political historian, he wanted to stabilise the unity of these entities at all costs and defend them against possible challenges. Therefore, he had to 'cleanse' them of everything that, in his view, represented faulty interpretation. Below regarded Reformation and Romanticism as historical models, since those movements had pioneered *Staat*, *Nation* and *Volk* in religious, spiritual and cultural terms. The Enlightenment, like other 'countries' and foreign *Völker*, was considered a disruptive factor or threat to this unity. In Germany, Below advocated the disintegration of tendencies in cultural history, sociology and individualism, all of which he suspected of having their origin in the Enlightenment. Below concluded his work, which was actually 'only' a recapitulation of historical scholarship in the nineteenth century, with a comprehensive, thoroughly emotional manifesto against the Enlightenment in all areas of social life and the disciplines of its interpretation. It represents a catalogue of political demands:

> Against the cosmopolitanism of the Enlightenment we oppose state and national consciousness, against the free trade doctrine of Manchesterism we oppose a view free of such dogmatism, namely the economic autarky of the nation state and the right of the state to regulate economic conditions with the flexibility of the system as demanded by historical development. We take account of the 'Haupt-und Staatsaktionen' despised by the Enlightenment by recognising 'the primacy of external politics over all internal needs [...]'. We understand the concept of culture more deeply than the Enlightenment did. [...] We are unable to think of culture without a commitment to our own *Volkstum*. We do not believe, as the Enlightenment did, in natural law and in a state constitution that is valid for

---

81. Below, *Die Ursachen der Reformation*, p.169.
82. See Ulrich Herrmann, 'Volk – Nation – Vaterland: ein Grundproblem deutscher Geschichte', in *Volk – Nation – Vaterland*, ed. Ulrich Herrmann (Hamburg, 1996), p.11-18, and Giesen, *Intellectuals and the nation*.
83. Bollenbeck, 'Abwendung', p.160-61. See also Reinhart Koselleck *et al.*, 'Volk, Nation, Nationalismus, Masse', in *Geschichtliche Grundbegriffe*, ed. O. Brunner, W. Conze and R. Koselleck, vol.7 (Stuttgart, 1992), p.141-431.

all peoples; constitutional law and historiography in Germany have worked to eliminate the prevalence of unhistorical revolutionary ideas, to eliminate the foreign, French, radical element from German blood; they have helped us to possess a state with its own institutions, to be able to set German freedom against Welsh freedom.[84]

It is striking that Below hardly quotes any texts from the eighteenth century. He mainly refers to the opinions of prominent figures, which he sometimes distorts and abbreviates, thus creating a suggestive chain of plausibility and forming a political corridor of opinion.

Below is considered to be the paragon of German historiography in the second half of the *Kaiserreich* and the first half of the Weimar Republic. His positions already made many of his contemporaries uncomfortable. One can find Below's position repugnant and find fault with his polemics, resentment and lack of methodological rigour, but it is difficult to dismiss his remarks on the Enlightenment epoch as wrong *tout court* or as a misunderstanding. One could object that he overstates individual aspects and that he shifts too much of 'the whole Enlightenment' to France, but one would have to bear in mind that his interpretation of the epochs was in line with the scholarship of his time. Ernst Troeltsch, who as a theologian had a more positive view of the Enlightenment,[85] took Below's work seriously. Criticising Below

---

84. 'Wir setzen dem Kosmopolitismus der Aufklärung das staatliche und nationale Bewußtsein, der Freihandelslehre des Manchestertums eine von solchem Dogmatismus freie Anschauung, die wirtschaftliche Autarkie des National-staats, das Recht des Staats zur Regelung der wirtschaftlichen Verhältnisse, mit der Beweglichkeit des Systems, wie sie durch die historische Entwicklung verlangt wird, entgegen. Wir tragen den von der Aufklärung verachteten "Haupt- und Staatsaktionen" Rechnung durch die Anerkennung "des Primats der äußeren Politik vor allen innern Bedürfnissen [...]". Wir fassen den Begriff der Kultur tiefer, als die Aufklärung tat. [...] Wir vermögen uns Kultur ohne das Bekenntnis zum eigenen Volkstum nicht zu denken. Wir glauben nicht wie die Aufklärung an ein Naturrecht und an eine für alle Völker gültige Staatsverfassung; Staatsrechtswissenschaft und Geschichtswissenschaft in Deutschland haben daran gearbeitet, das Vorwalten der ungeschichtlichen revolutionären Ideen zu beseitigen, das fremde, französische, radikale Element aus dem deutschen Blut auszuscheiden; sie haben uns dazu verholfen, einen Staat mit eigenen Einrichtungen zu besitzen, deutsche Freiheit gegen welsche Freiheit setzen zu können.' Below, *Die deutsche Geschichtsschreibung*, p.159.

85. Ernst Troeltsch, 'Aufklärung', in *Realencyklopädie für protestantische Theologie und Kirche*, ed. Albert Hauck, 3rd edn, vol.2 (Leipzig, 1897), p.225-41; Trutz Rendtorff, 'Theologische Orientierung im Prozeß der Aufklärung: eine Erinnerung an Ernst Troeltsch', *Aufklärung* 2 (1987), p.19-34.

becomes possible if one is prepared to make a different assessment of the achievements of the Enlightenment and thus, like Below, to position oneself politically. This is a dilemma. Nothing protects the word 'Enlightenment' from being politically instrumentalised. A correction could not be achieved through academic dialogue alone. Below, who is ostensibly writing as a historian, has opened up a semi-discursive field that invites political dispute while undermining scholarly dispute. This is precisely why Below was rejected by scholars during his lifetime, even though he was influential. The point remains that Below cannot be disproven through any 'better' interpretations of the Enlightenment. However, it is possible to use exactly the same terms, as Troeltsch did, and to argue that the ideas enclosed in these terms are supra-temporally positive and should be the foundation of cultural, social development.

V.

Controversies are the main manifestation of dissent about the historical Enlightenment and competing conceptions of Enlightenment. Differences always become visible when disputes arise and when cultural and political battles are fought. Conflicts and crises materialise in language.[86] Keywords are activated, revitalised and reinterpreted in specific contexts.[87] It could certainly be possible to thoroughly examine the extensive political literature of the nineteenth century and to analyse how the keyword 'Enlightenment' was deployed in controversies. In the third volume of his *Deutsche Geschichte im Neunzehnten Jahrhundert* (1885), the historian Heinrich von Treitschke (1834-1896) felt compelled to point out that 'the Germans' ('die Deutschen') had long allowed themselves to be 'deceived' ('getäuscht') about the 'corrosive and inflammatory efficacy of radical Judaism' ('zerreibende und verhetzende Wirksamkeit des radicalen Judenthums'), because they had unsuspectingly taken this 'new literary power [...] for German Enlightenment and German liberalism [...] which in reality was Jewish hatred of Christianity and Jewish cosmopolitanism. [...] Only at a much later time did the nation

---

86. See Reinhart Koselleck, 'Social history and conceptual history', *International journal of politics, culture and society* 2 (1989), p.308-25.
87. See Rolf Reichardt, 'Light against darkness: the visual representations of a central Enlightenment concept', *Representations* 61 (1998), special issue: *Practices of Enlightenment*, p.95-148.

realise that since the end of the twenties [of the nineteenth century]
a foreign drop had entered its blood' ('die Deutschen [täuschten]
sich über den Charakter dieser neuen literarischen Macht [...] [und
hielten] arglos für deutsche Aufklärung und deutschen Freisinn [...]
was in Wahrheit jüdischer Christenhaß und jüdisches Weltbür-
gerthum war. [...] Erst in einer weit späteren Zeit erkannte die Nation,
daß seit dem Ende der zwanziger Jahre [des 19. Jahrhunderts] ein
fremder Tropfen in ihr Blut gerathen war').[88] Among the numerous
debates that took place in the public sphere of the empire, I will
now single out the so-called 'Jewish question'.[89] Antisemites stylised
the 'Jewish question' as the 'social question' par excellence; from the
1870s onwards, antisemitism can be described as a *Weltanschauung* or
at least as part of one.[90] References to Enlightenment can be found
in publications on the 'Jewish question' as late as the 1930s.[91] The
link between the 'Jewish question' and Enlightenment was eminently
political because the emancipation of the Jews, their legal equality
and cultural integration remained political issues.[92] The dilemma

88. Heinrich von Treitschke, *Deutsche Geschichte im Neunzehnten Jahrhundert*, 5 vols
    (Leipzig, 1879-1894), vol.3, p.705.
89. *Die 'Judenfrage': Schriften zur Begründung des modernen Antisemitismus 1789 bis 1914
    | The 'Jewish question': literature on the roots of modern antisemitism 1780 until 1918*,
    ed. Wolfgang Benz (Munich, 2003); Reinhard Rürup, *Emanzipation und Antisemi-
    tismus: Studien zur 'Judenfrage' der bürgerlichen Gesellschaft* (Göttingen, 1975); Jacob
    Toury, '"The Jewish question": a semantic approach', *The Leo Baeck Institute
    year book* 11:1 (1966), p.85-106; Arndt Kremer, *Deutsche Juden – deutsche Sprache:
    jüdische und judenfeindliche Sprachkonzepte und -konflikte 1893-1933* (Berlin, 2007).
90. See Moshe Zimmermann, 'Die "Judenfrage" als "die soziale Frage": zu
    Kontinuität und Stellenwert des Antisemitismus vor und nach dem National-
    sozialismus', in *Deutsch-jüdische Vergangenheit: der Judenhaß als Herausforderung*
    (Paderborn, 2005), p.289-301, and Volkov, *Germans, Jews, and antisemites*, part
    2: 'Antisemitism as a cultural code', p.67-144.
91. See e.g. Gottfried Feder, Ferdinand Werner and Graf Ernst Reventlow, *Das
    neue Deutschland und die Judenfrage: des Diskussionsbuches erster Teil* (Leipzig, 1933):
    on the one hand, 'Enlightenment' about Judaism is demanded (p.38, 185),
    on the other hand, the 'false doctrines of the Enlightenment and the French
    Revolution' (p.117) are to be shown, and with quotations from prominent Jews
    (such as Nahum Goldmann) it is to be proven that the Jews were driving forces
    in the restructuring of society and modernisation following the Enlightenment
    (p.89).
92. See Julius H. Schoeps, 'Aufklärung, Judentum und Emanzipation', in *Judentum
    im Zeitalter der Aufklärung*, ed. Lessing-Akademie (Wolfenbüttel, 1977), p.75-102;
    Moshe Zimmermann, 'Aufklärung, Emanzipation, Selbstemanzipation', in
    Aufklärung und Haskala, ed. K. Gründer and N. Rotenstreich, p.143-52; Leon
    Botstein, 'Emanzipation und Assimilation: die Auswirkung der aufklärerischen

already mentioned pervades the entire debate, insofar as arguments are repeatedly presented 'with' Enlightenment: 'The emancipation of the Jews is to be abolished; they are to be placed under special foreign law (Jewish law). [...] With the progress of enlightenment, everyone will eventually learn to regard it as shameful to be in any kind of relationship with Jews' ('Die Emancipation der Juden ist aufzuheben; dieselben sind unter besonderes Fremden-Gesetz (Judenrecht) zu stellen. [...] Mit der fortschreitenden Aufklärung wird es schließlich ein Jeder als beschämend empfinden lernen, in irgend welchen Beziehungen zu Juden zu stehen').[93] One can, indeed, reject the linking of anti-Jewish agitation and Enlightenment as a monstrous mesalliance; however, Enlightenment was an influential political *Kampfbegriff* within the debate about the social position of Jews in German society. Antisemites criticised 'the Enlightenment' for promising Jews social participation through emancipation. But the educated and liberal *Bürger* of the present were also attacked for upholding this promise. Enlightenment had a double reference, historical and contemporary at once. This can be seen, for example, in the pamphlet of the antisemite Paul Köhler: 'All education, all Enlightenment will not protect us from this fate. Our pompous "Gebildeten", the enlightened bourgeoisie, the progressive aristocracy – have they not mainly fallen prey to Judaism?' ('Alle Bildung, alle Aufklärung werden vor diesem Geschick nicht bewahren. Unsere großsprecherischen "Gebildeten", das aufgeklärte Bürgerthum, der fortschrittliche Adel – sind sie nicht hauptsächlich der Verjudung verfallen?').[94] He criticised the eighteenth-century epoch as follows:

Tradition im 19. Jahrhundert', in *Judentum und Modernität: Essays zur Rolle der Juden in der deutschen und österreichischen Kultur 1848 bis 1938* (Vienna and Cologne, 1991), p.21-29. Comprehensive accounts of the emancipation era are: Andreas Gotzmann, *Eigenheit und Einheit: Modernisierungsdiskurse des deutschen Judentums der Emanzipationszeit* (Leiden, 2002), and Marion Kaplan, 'As Germans and as Jews in imperial Germany', in *Jewish daily life in Germany, 1618-1945*, ed. Marion Kaplan (Oxford and New York, 2005), p.173-270, esp. p.214. See also the current contribution to the debate by Simone Lässig, 'A "Jewish Sattelzeit"? Recasting an era of upheaval and transformation', *Central European history* 51:4 (2018), p.656-61.

93. Thomas Frey [i.e. Theodor Fritsch], *Antisemiten-Katechismus: eine Zusammenstellung des wichtigsten Materials zum Verständnis der Judenfrage*, 25th edn (Leipzig, 1893), p.24.

94. Paul Köhler, *Die Verjudung Deutschlands und der Weg zur Rettung: noch einmal ein Wort für und wider 'W. Marr: Der Sieg des Iudenthums über das Germanenthum'* (Stettin, 1880), p.51.

Like Lessing, the whole age of Enlightenment with its undermining of the Christian faith, the French Revolution with its undermining of the Christian state and social order, is a trailblazer for Judaism. And the clever people well understood its advantage. It was convenient for the Jews that the Christians themselves threw away their eternal ideals and limited their aspirations to this world of the senses, its order and exploitation! This was the Jews' first domain. There they were experienced. There they could take up the competition against the goyim and hope to remain victors. How the 'young Germany', led by Jewish writers, shook up Christian faith and morals! How it preached the emancipation of the flesh! How the Jews knew how to make Christians loathe their holy religion, the Gospel, as a rigid and unbearable fetter! 'Since 1848', Marr rightly says, 'the successful thirty-year war of the Jews against us has begun.'[95]

It should be emphasised that Köhler considered the Young Germany (Junges Deutschland) to be an extended branch of the Enlightenment in the nineteenth century; Heinrich von Treitschke had also interpreted the authors of the *Vormärz* epoch in this way.[96] Treitschke's

95. 'Wie Lessing ist das ganze Zeitalter der Aufklärung mit seiner Untergrabung des christlichen Glaubens, die Französische Revolution mit ihrer Untergrabung der christlichen Staats- und Gesellschaftsordnung ein Bahnbrecher für das Judenthum. Und das schlaue Volk hat seinen Vortheil wohl begriffen. Das paßte den Juden, daß die Christen selbst ihre Ewigkeitsideale wegwarfen und ihr Trachten aus diese Sinnenwelt, ihre Ordnung und Ausnutzung beschränkten! Das war der Juden eigenstes Gebiet. Da waren sie erfahren. Da konnten sie die Concurrenz gegen die Gojim aufnehmen und hoffen, Sieger zu bleiben. Wie rüttelte das "junge Deutschland", jüdische Schriftsteller voran, an christlichem Glauben und Sitte! Wie predigte es die Emancipation des Fleisches! Wie wußten die Juden den Christen ihre heilige Religion, das Evangelium zum Ekel zu machen als eine starre und unerträgliche Fessel! "Seit 1848", sagt Marr mit Recht, "beginnt nun der erfolgreiche dreißigjährige Krieg der Juden gegen uns." Köhler, *Die Verjudung Deutschlands und der Weg zur Rettung*, p.24.
96. Treitschke, *Deutsche Geschichte im Neunzehnten Jahrhundert*, vol.3, p.714: 'Along with Börne and Heine, with the incursion of Judaism, a new literary epoch was heralded, the ugliest and most barren period of our new literary history, which fortunately was not to last long. Since the days of Lessing, no German school of poetry has sown so much discord and created so little that lasts as the radical feuilleton poetry of the 1830s' ('Mit Börne und Heine, mit dem Einbruch des Judenthums, kündigte sich eine neue literarische Epoche an, die zum Glück nicht lange währen sollte, die häßlichste und unfruchtbarste Zeit unserer neuen Literaturgeschichte. Seit Lessing's Tagen hat keine deutsche Dichterschule so viel Unfrieden gesät und so wenig Dauerndes geschaffen wie die radicale Feuilleton-Poesie der dreißiger Jahre'). These passages were taken up by Paul Nerrlich, *Herr von Treitschke und das junge Deutschland* (Berlin, 1890).

scrutiny of the 'old Enlightenment' (of the eighteenth century) and his efforts to establish a new, pro-religious Enlightenment (for the nineteenth century) would have to be examined separately. In his view, the 'old Enlightenment' also included the 'democratic Enlightenment', of which he qualified the Jewish writer Fanny Lewald as a follower: 'In the tendentious novel Jenny, she championed the emancipation of her fellow Jews, not without skill, but also not without manufactured and stilted Jewish pain; she possessed the talent of seeing all things from only one side, – that dangerous gift which makes Jews such useful lawyers' ('In dem Tendenzromane Jenny verfocht sie die Emancipation ihrer Stammgenossen, nicht ohne Geschick, aber auch nicht ohne gemachten und gezierten Judenschmerz; sie besaß das Talent, alle Dinge nur von einer Seite zu sehen, – jene gefährliche Gabe, welche die Juden zu so brauchbaren Rechtsanwälten macht').[97] In the course of the 'Berliner Antisemitismusstreit' in 1879/1880, the liberal historian Theodor Mommsen (1817-1903) expressed a decidedly political standpoint for the Enlightenment and for the continued emancipation of the Jews. Responding to Heinrich von Treitschke's essay *Unsere Aussichten*,[98] Mommsen addressed the audience, asking: 'Is the empire of Kaiser Wilhelm really the country of Frederick the Great, the country of Enlightenment and tolerance, and the country in which one asked about character and quality of mind, rather than religious confession and nationality?' ('Ist das Reich Kaiser Wilhelms wirklich noch das Land Friedrichs des Großen, das Land der Aufklärung und der Toleranz, das Land, in dem nach Charakter und Geist, und nicht nach Konfession und Nationalität gefragt wird?').[99] Mommsen's question proves, as it were by

97. Treitschke, *Deutsche Geschichte im Neunzehnten Jahrhundert*, vol.5, p.887.

98. Treitschke is also highly praised in Kernholt [Bonhard], *Vom Ghetto zur Macht*, p.261: 'Powerful was the enlightenment that had emanated from Treitschke's description of the decline in Jewish activities since the beginning of the nineteenth century. Even more powerful was the personal impact he had on thousands of students as a university educator' ('Gewaltig war die Aufklärung, die von Treitschkes Schilderung der jüdischen Zersetzungstätigkeit seit Beginn des 19. Jahrhunderts ausging, gewaltiger noch die persönliche die er als Hochschullehrer auf Tausende von Schülern ausübte').

99. Theodor Mommsen, 'Rede vom 18. März 1880 zur Vorfeier des Geburtstages des Kaisers in der Königlich Preußischen Akademie der Wissenschaften', in *Reden und Aufsätze*, 2nd edn (Berlin, 1905), p.89-103 (92). In 1866, a Prague publicist expressed himself even more optimistically when he saw the validity of the previously mentioned values defended by Christian fellow citizens: ['R'], 'Ein Zeichen der Zeit', *Das Abendland: Central-Organ für alle zeitgemäßen Interessen*

implication, that the ideals of the Enlightenment were no longer a
self-evident part of the 'bürgerlichen Wertehimmel' at the end of
the nineteenth century.[100] Although Enlightenment, strictly speaking,
is not a single value, Mommsen was able to name achievements
of the Enlightenment that had a prominent value for him in this
debate: tolerance, interdenominational acceptance and the lack of
national partisanship. The word 'Enlightenment' was often used as a
matrix for a whole range of values and norms: tolerance, humanity,
equality, freedom, freedom of expression and many more. More
than twenty-five years after the 'Antisemitismusstreit', the left-liberal
member of the Reichstag Adolf Neumann-Hofer (1867-1925) participated in a questionnaire on the 'solution to the Jewish question'
posed by the German-Jewish doctor, politician and newspaper editor
Julius Moses. Neumann-Hofer, a political scientist and journalist by
profession, introduced his vote with the following statement: 'Is there
a Jewish question? As a strictly personal question for the modern,
enlightened, liberal Kulturmenschen, certainly not. But since this
type of person today, although we live in the twentieth century,
still makes up a small fraction of humanity, even only a small

---

des Judenthums 3 (29 November 1866), p.177: 'If, in spite of enlightenment and
morality, we are frequently in a position to complain about the still rampant
hatred of Jews, it is all the more pleasant for us to register deeds of humanity
and true human love on the part of our Christian fellow citizens. Despite all
the still widespread prejudices in confessional matters, it cannot be denied
that the trend of our time is generally a humane one, progressing in the
spirit of love and fraternisation of all people without distinction of class and
faith, and we could cite innumerable proofs of a non-prejudiced and loving
encounter on the Christian side' ('Wenn wir trotz Aufklärung und Gesittung
öfters in der Lage sind über den noch immer stark wuchernden Judenhaß zu
klagen , so ist es uns eine um so angenehmere Pflicht Akte der Humanität
und wahrer Menschenliebe von Seiten unserer christlichen Mitbürger zu
registrieren. Es läßt sich bei allen noch immer viel verbreiteten Vorurtheilen
in konfessionellen Angelegenheiten nicht in Abrede stellen, daß die Richtung
der Zeit im Allgemeinen eine humane, im Geiste der Liebe und Verbrüderung
aller Menschen ohne Unterschied des Standes und des Glaubens fortschreitende
sei, und wir könnten unzählige Beweise einer vorurtheilsfreien und liebevollen
Begegnung christlicherseits anführen').

100. See Stefan Rebenich, 'Eine Entzweiung: Theodor Mommsen und Heinrich von
Treitschke', in *Berlins wilde Energien: Porträts aus der Geschichte der Leibnizischen
Wissenschaftsakademie*, ed. Stefan Leibfried *et al.* (Berlin and Boston, MA, 2015),
p.262-85, and *Der 'Berliner Antisemitismusstreit' 1879-1881: eine Kontroverse um
die Zugehörigkeit der deutschen Juden zur Nation. Kommentierte Quellenedition*, ed.
Karsten Krieger, 2 vols (Munich, 2003).

fraction of so-called educated humanity, that is not decisive' ('Gibt es eine Judenfrage? Als rein persönliche Frage für den modernen, aufgeklärten, liberalen Kulturmenschen ganz gewiss nicht. Da dieser Typus des Menschen heute aber, obwohl wir im 20. Jahrhundert leben, immer noch einen kleinen Bruchteil der Menschheit, ja sogar nur einen kleinen der sogenannten gebildeten Menschheit ausmacht, ist das nicht ausschlaggebend').[101] Neumann-Hofer thus clarifies that, for modern, enlightened, liberal *Kulturmenschen*, the Jewish question does not exist in the form presented by the antisemitic party. However, because only a small fraction of mankind is of this enlightened kind, one cannot simply refer to the Enlightenment and expect the matter to be settled. The fact that Mommsen and Neumann-Hofer were ultimately disillusioned (or powerless) in their efforts to uphold the values of the Enlightenment suggests that both of them realised exactly this.

Antisemites also made their own extensive use of the figure of 'true and false Enlightenment'; more than that, they demanded 'Enlightenment' about Judaism and used the basic slogan of the Enlightenment for their own purposes, just as the bishop of Mainz, Haffner, had done. Or they took up the vocabulary of the despised

101. Quoted after *Die Lösung der Judenfrage: eine Rundfrage von Julius Moses im Jahre 1907 mit Antworten von Eduard Bernstein, Otto Julius Bierbaum, Arthur Fitger [...] und 90 weiteren Persönlichkeiten des öffentlichen Lebens,* ed. Gesellschaft für Deutsche Presseforschung zu Bremen (Bremen, 2010), p.234. A little over twenty years earlier, the playwright and poet Richard Schmidt-Cabanis contributed a similar assessment to a survey on the same topic: 'It is the quite natural and sincere embarrassment that must be awakened again and again in the offspring of the nineteenth century, that is: in our so-called "age of Enlightenment", not only the discussion is still open about medieval nocturnal creatures such as hatred of faith and religious persecution, but that "legendary" dragon dynasty even comes to light again visibly and tangibly, breathing fire and poison, and challenges the crowd of Georgsritter des Humanismus to a hard fight in the ranks' ('[E]s ist das ganz natürliche und aufrichtige Beschämung, welches immer wieder im Sprösslinge des 19. Jahrhunderts wach werden muss: dass über mittelalterliche Nachtgestalten, wie Glaubenshass und Religions-verfolgung, in unserem sogenannten "Zeitalter der Aufklärung" nicht nur die Discussion noch offen zu halten ist, sondern dass jenes "sagenhafte" Drachen-geschlecht sogar wieder sichtbar und greifbar, feuerspeiend und gifthauchend zu Tage kommt und die Schaar der Georgsritter des Humanismus zu hartem Kampfe in die Schranken fordert'); *Briefe berühmter christlicher Zeitgenossen über die Judenfrage: nach Manuscripten gedruckt und mit Autorisation der Verfasser zum ersten Male herausgegeben, mit biographischen Skizzen der Autoren und einem Vorworte versehen von I[sidor] Singer* (Vienna, 1885), p.126-27.

'German "liberal" Bildungsphilister'[102] and converted it, sarcastically and polemically, into the language of their own defence. This can be seen particularly succinctly in a polemic by the influential antisemite Wilhelm Marr: *Lessing contra Sem: allen 'Rabbinern' der Juden- und Christenheit, allen Toleranz-Duselheimern aller Parteien, allen 'Pharisäern und Schriftgelehrten' tolerantest gewidmet.* Marr wanted to 'prove' ('beweisen') that Lessing had not been an 'unconditional apostle of Jewish emancipation' ('bedingungslose[r] Apostel der Judenemancipation'), but rather had written his objections to Judaism into his drama *Nathan der Weise.*

VI.

Enlightenment was also a term of protection and a frame of reference for German Jews who had turned to the project of *Verbürgerlichung* and made German culture a part of their identity.

> We Jews do not fight our battle with the sword of iron, we do not use bludgeons and other instruments of murder to help us to our rights, we fight with the weapons of a free man, no less with the only weapons worthy of our century of humanity and Enlightenment, the weapons of the spirit and of intelligence.[103]

> Do we need to mention the many Semitic pens that are working diligently on a daily basis to spread education and enlightenment among the German people?[104]

Following Georg Bollenbeck, it is useful to examine the semantic field and the content of the concepts of Enlightenment that circulated in the broader context of this acrimonious nineteenth-century debate. This raises the question of whether representatives of the educated

102. Marr, *Lessing contra Sem*, p.29.
103. 'Wir Juden kämpfen unsern Kampf nicht mit dem Schwert aus Eisen, wir gebrauchen nicht Knüttel und andere Mordwerkzeuge, um uns zu unserem Rechte zu verhelfen, wir kämpfen mit den eines freien Mannes, nicht minder den unseres Jahrhunderts der Humanität und Aufklärung allein würdigen Waffen, den Waffen des Geistes und der Intelligenz.' Isidor Singer, *Presse und Judenthum*, 2nd edn (Vienna, 1882), p.182-83.
104. 'Brauchen wir an die vielen semitischen Federn zu erinnern, die in emsiger Tagesarbeit redlich bemüht sind, Bildung und Aufklärung zu verbreiten im deutschen Volke?' *Kulturdefizit am Ende des 19. Jahrhunderts von Dr. med. Marcus Hirsch* (Frankfurt am Main, 1898), p.127.

bourgeoisie held on to Enlightenment after all, but also whether our findings allow for conclusions to be drawn about how great, or small, the trust in Enlightenment values actually was.[105] After all, it is not only Catholics and Protestants who belong to the educated middle class. Jewish citizens in particular have repeatedly been described as *Bildungsbürger* par excellence.[106] The connection between Enlightenment and liberalism mentioned by Bollenbeck can also be examined in this context. This is not only the nexus of Enlightenment and liberalism that can be reconstructed in terms of intellectual history,[107] but also the polemical connection between the two currents, especially when it is related to the Jewish minority.[108] In fact, another word was added to the pejorative conceptual field ('Judenliberalen' and 'Jüdischer Liberalismus'), claiming that the starting point for the alleged phenomenon of 'Jewish liberalism' was the Enlightenment or the French Revolution. 'Our time is so fond of "liberty, equality and fraternity", these immortal postulates of the great French Revolution whose programme was the exact opposite of that of today's "Jewish

105. Volkov, *Germans, Jews, and antisemites*, does, however, cite some Jewish intellectuals whose confidence in the Enlightenment faltered in the last third of the nineteenth century and around the turn of the century, but did not disappear completely: Nahum Sokolov (p.15), Theodor Herzl, Max Nordau and Bernard Lazare (p.29-31).

106. Gunilla Budde, Eckart Conze and Cornelia Rauh, 'Einleitung: Bürgertum und Bürgerlichkeit nach 1945', in *Bürgertum nach dem bürgerlichen Zeitalter: Leitbilder und Praxis nach 1945*, ed. Gunilla Budde *et al.* (Göttingen, 2010), p.7-25 (9). Recent research has gone so far as to state that the failure of emancipation can be attributed to an excess of *Bürgerlichkeit*, that Jews were too committed to bourgeois cultural models: in the eyes of their critics, *Bürgerlichkeit* had virtually become a Jewish way of life. See Simone Lässig, *Jüdische Wege ins Bürgertum: kulturelles Kapital und sozialer Aufstieg im 19. Jahrhundert* (Göttingen, 2004), and *Juden als Träger bürgerlicher Kultur in Deutschland*, ed. Julius H. Schoeps (Stuttgart and Bonn, 1989).

107. See Rudolf Vierhaus, 'Liberalismus und deutsches Bürgertum', in *Vergangenheit als Geschichte: Studien zum 19. und 20. Jahrhundert*, ed. Hans Erich Bödecker, Benigna von Krusenstjern and Michael Matthiesen (Göttingen, 2003), p.171-82, and Jörn Leonhard, 'Politisches Gehäuse und ideologische Sprache des Fortschritts: Verfassung, Verfassungsstaat und Liberalismus im 19. Jahrhundert', in *Durchbruch der Moderne? Neue Perspektiven auf das 19. Jahrhundert*, ed. Birgit Aschmann (Frankfurt am Main, 2019), p.218-51.

108. See Ullrich Sieg, 'Antisemitismus und Antiliberalismus im Deutschen Kaiserreich', in *Liberalismus als Feindbild*, ed. E. Grothe and U. Sieg, p.93-112, and Thomas Gräfe, 'Der Hegemonieverlust des Liberalismus: die "Judenfrage" im Spiegel der Intellektuellenbefragungen 1885-1912', *Jahrbuch für Antisemitismusforschung* 25 (2016), p.73-100.

liberalism", in that it expressed a purely Christian principle in its very basic ideas' ('Unsere Zeit schwärmt so sehr für "Freiheit, Gleichheit und Brüderlichkeit", diese unsterblichen Postulate der grossen französischen Revolution deren Programm das genaue Gegentheil von demjenigen des heutigen "jüdischen Liberalismus" war, indem es in seinen ebengenannten Grundgedanken ein rein christliches Princip aussprach').[109] Here it is clear that the vocabulary of liberalism had gradually degenerated into a semantic emblem; increasingly, it was a term that did not so much denote a precisely definable philosophical concept, as articulate, in terms of a slogan, the affiliation to a faction. One could ask whether the defenders of the Enlightenment had simply given up on entering into debates about the past. It soon becomes apparent not only that the term 'Enlightenment' is very compelling in this respect, but also – like everything that is articulated in language – that it has no robust powers of resistance to prevent misuse.

VII.

This article was an attempt to explain the use of the word 'Enlightenment' in a specific context: a controversy that was of great importance for the German nineteenth century, and not only because of its relationship to the catastrophe of the twentieth century. I have deliberately left out more complex interpretations, such as those of Hannah Arendt, Theodor W. Adorno and Max Horkheimer, and Zygmunt Baumann, in order to be able to draw somewhat more freely from the sources. Certainly, the examples chosen may have left behind a certain ambiguity, but I am convinced that this ambiguity does justice to the way in which 'Enlightenment' was received after the end of the age of Enlightenment. On the one hand, the word was used without any deeper historical dimension behind it; on the other hand, several parties took a stake, driven by political and cultural intentions, in attributing new meanings to the word and distinguishing it from its eighteenth-century use. Although the texts of very different actors (a bishop, several historians, politicians and journalists) have been analysed, other highly relevant kinds of texts have been excluded, such as sermons and novels. Well-informed philosophical and historical texts, such as circulated in the nineteenth

109. M[oritz von] Reymond, *Wo steckt der Mauschel? Oder Jüdischer Liberalismus und wissenschaftlicher Pessimismus: ein offener Brief an W. Marr* (Bern and Leipzig, 1879), p.27.

century (Moritz Lazarus, Hermann Cohen) and increasingly from the 1920s onwards (Ernst Cassirer, Karl Mannheim), have also been excluded. In general, this article has adopted Bollenbeck's useful suggestion to examine not just the *Höhenkamm.*

It should also be emphasised again at this point that I do not want to suggest that the three groups (*Bildungsbürger,* Jewish Germans and antisemites) were internally homogeneous, nor that they each represented a consistent concept of Enlightenment. Of course, Jewish intellectuals of all kinds also argued intensively amongst themselves about the question of whether the Enlightenment of the eighteenth century was – to put it simply – good or bad for the development of Judaism. The multiple valences of Enlightenment in this regard were brilliantly interpreted by Hannah Arendt in her 1932 essay. It would be worth examining separately how the interpretation not only of the Enlightenment, but also of its consequences, changed from a Jewish perspective in precisely the period that can be described, following Werner Mosse, as the 'end of emancipation'. It seems to me that the modern epoch of Jewish history not only ends there, but also brought with it a kind of final reckoning with the Enlightenment, and with liberalism.

Finally, a question remains open that I have repeatedly alluded to: can interpretations of Enlightenment be corrected? Can they be corrected scientifically and finally, or does there come a point at which it is no longer possible to present complex historical arguments in the public sphere and at which even academics must say: it is time to adopt a political position? I do not mean to suggest that dispassionate academic work should be banished from public discourse. Theodor Mommsen's involvement in the 'Antisemitismusstreit' proves that it is possible to argue with political clarity and at the same time bring the historian's knowledge to bear. David Biale's essay is also a model. To be sure, Biale simplifies the Enlightenment, and one could raise many objections. But, because Biale has also written substantial books and because his analyses of political culture are convincing, one can assess and accept the outline of his image of the Enlightenment. After all, we understand that he is concerned not solely with the historical epoch, but also with an application of the Enlightenment as an argument intended to contribute to an understanding of the present.

Nihilism, Enlightenment and the 'new failure of nerve': arguments about Enlightenment in New York and Los Angeles, 1941-1947

JAMES SCHMIDT

Boston University

On 10 November 1941, Theodor W. Adorno wrote to Max Horkheimer to confirm arrangements for the journey that would take him to Los Angeles, where they would begin the long-anticipated and much-delayed collaboration that resulted, three years later, in the *Philosophische Fragmente*, the first draft of *Dialectic of Enlightenment*. He would travel by train from Manhattan to Cleveland, spend the night there and proceed to Chicago where, on the evening of Sunday 16 November, he would set out 'for the wild west', arriving at Los Angeles' Union Station three days later. Summarising the tasks he had been completing during his final weeks in New York he mentioned an 'unusually encouraging lunch with MacDonald and one of his colleagues' at which it became evident that 'his circle is so taken with our things that they would publish every sentence.' Concluding that it would have been 'too unsympathetic' to brush off the offer from 'these people, who really had something to do with us', he informed Horkheimer that he had explained 'as sincerely as possible that collaboration with us is impossible'.[1]

Adorno's account of his meeting with these two American admirers is the only surviving evidence of one of the more intriguing missed connections during the American exile of the Institute for Social Research. For the 'MacDonald' with whom Adorno met was the American cultural critic Dwight Macdonald. His meeting with Adorno took place in the midst of a protracted struggle with

---

1.   Theodor W. Adorno, *Briefe und Briefwechsel*, ed. Theodor W. Adorno Archive, vol.4.2: Theodor W. Adorno and Max Horkheimer, *Briefwechsel, 1938-1944*, ed. Christoph Gödde and Henri Lonitz (Frankfurt am Main, 2004), p.286.

his fellow editors at *Partisan review* over the future direction of the journal that would climax two years later in Macdonald's resignation after a heated exchange of articles in the journal published under the collective title 'The new failure of nerve'. Horkheimer followed these exchanges as he worked with Adorno and, in September 1943, began to sketch a response to the salvo of articles by Sidney Hook, John Dewey and Ernest Nagel that launched the debate. For the rest of the year he worked fitfully on his 'Hook article'[2] and eventually used an edited version of it as the second chapter of *Eclipse of reason*, his 1947 attempt to present the argument of *Dialectic of Enlightenment* to an Anglophone audience.

In retrospect, Adorno's conclusion that collaboration with Macdonald would be impossible fits neatly into the received narrative of the Frankfurt School's disengagement from American intellectual life.[3] Offered the opportunity to present their work to Anglophone readers, Adorno demurred and, joining Horkheimer in Los Angeles, began the collaboration that produced a notoriously enigmatic German text. But Horkheimer's interest in the 'New failure of nerve' exchanges complicates this narrative. For not only did Horkheimer follow the debate; he eventually found a way to join it. But the summary of his work with Adorno that he offered in *Eclipse of reason* lent support to an American reception of *Dialectic of Enlightenment* that saw the book as mounting a critique of the Enlightenment that echoed the views of its conservative critics.

Enlightenment, nihilism and National Socialism

The January-February 1943 issue of *Partisan review* featured a trio of articles by the philosophers Sidney Hook, John Dewey and Ernest Nagel published under the title 'The new failure of nerve, part I'.[4] The

---

2. Max Horkheimer, 'Hook', a paper bound document housed in the Max Horkheimer Archive in Frankfurt (henceforth MHA), https://sammlungen.ub. uni-frankfurt.de/horkheimer/content/pageview/6622310 (last accessed 26 April 2023).

3. For critiques of this line of interpretation, see Thomas Wheatland, *The Frankfurt School in exile* (Minneapolis, MN, 2009), and David Jenemann, *Adorno in America* (Minneapolis, MN, 2007).

4. Sidney Hook, 'The new failure of nerve', *Partisan review* 10:1 (January-February 1943), p.2-23; John Dewey, 'Anti-naturalism in extremis', *Partisan review* 10:1 (January-February 1943), p.24-39; Ernest Nagel, 'Malicious philosophies of science', *Partisan review* 10:1 (January-February 1943), p.40-57.

series, which continued in the journal for the next few months, was the brainchild of Hook, who had taken its title from the classicist Gilbert Murray's account of the rise of asceticism, mysticism and pessimism during the Hellenistic period.[5] Hook argued that while the new failure of nerve employed 'a modern idiom' it too was marked by a 'flight from responsibility, both on the plane of action and on the plane of belief'. Symptoms of that flight included the recent 'recrudescence of beliefs in the original depravity of human nature', the ubiquity of 'prophecies of doom for western civilization [...] dressed up as laws of social dynamics', the 'frenzied search' for a moral foundation that 'transcends human interests', a general pessimism about 'prospects for social reform', the 'refurbishing of theological and metaphysical dogmas' and an ongoing 'campaign to "prove" that without a belief in God and immortality, democracy – or even plain moral decency – cannot be reasonably justified.'[6]

The immediate provocation for the series was the philosopher Mortimer Adler's notorious address to a September 1940 conference at the Jewish Theological Seminary in New York. Sponsored by the Conference on Science, Philosophy and Religion in their Relation to the Democratic Way of Life, Inc., this energetically promoted event sought 'to rally our intellectual and spiritual forces' against the rising tide of 'totalitarian thinking'. The press release sketching the group's plans emphasised the pluralistic character of the undertaking and insisted that the convenors sought neither to deprive philosophy and science of their 'genuine autonomy' nor to suggest that 'it is possible or desirable that Western religions be reduced to a common denominator'. Nevertheless, it expressed the conviction that 'our common background gives us a broad basis for a united, democratic American way of life'. Fundamental to that way of life was 'the religious principle of the Fatherhood of God and the worth and dignity of Man when regarded as a child of God'.[7]

Whatever hope the convenors may have had for a collegial exploration of common commitments was shattered by Adler's caustic

5. Gilbert Murray, *Four stages of Greek religion* (New York, 1912), p.103, 109-10, 120, 133, 141.
6. Hook, 'The new failure of nerve', p.2-3.
7. For the aims of the conference, see Van Wyck Brooks, 'Conference on science, philosophy and religion in their relation to the democratic way of life', in *Science, philosophy, and religion: a symposium* (New York, 1941), p.1-11, and the article '79 leaders unite to aid democracy', *The New York Times* (1 June 1940), p.10.

talk, which charged that the greatest danger to 'the democratic way of life' came not from foreign enemies but from forces closer to home. He insisted that

> the most serious threat to Democracy is the positivism of the professors, which dominates every aspect of modern education and is the central corruption of modern culture. Democracy has much more to fear from the mentality of its teachers than from the nihilism of Hitler. It is the same nihilism in both cases, but Hitler's is more honest and consistent, less blurred by subtleties and queasy clarifications, and hence less dangerous.[8]

Adler asserted that 'the professors' were, at bottom, hypocrites. Though they favoured religious toleration and gave lip service to the idea that religious belief played a central role in society, they neither recognised that 'religion rests on supernatural knowledge' nor acknowledged that 'it is superior to both philosophy and science.' That refusal, he charged, paved the way for catastrophe: 'The mere toleration of religion, which implies indifference to or denial of its claims, produces a secularized culture as much as militant atheism or Nazi nihilism.' Indeed, Adler found Nazi nihilism preferable to the academic variety. It was possible, he suggested, that by 'preparing the agony through which our culture will be reborn' Hitler could be viewed as part of 'the Divine plan to bless man's temporal civilization with the goodness of Democracy'.[9] But academics were so thoroughly complicit in the crisis engulfing modern culture that, 'until the professors and their culture are liquidated, the resolution of modern problems [...] will not even begin.'[10]

Adler's rhetoric was extreme, but the connection he drew between National Socialism and a pervasive cultural nihilism was hardly unique. The Thomist philosopher Jacques Maritain had made much the same point, arguing that democracy ultimately rested on an 'organic hierarchy of liberties', and an understanding of their proper ordering demanded the metaphysical and theological insights that modern science and technology had eroded.[11] For this

8. Mortimer J. Adler, 'God and the professors', in *Science, philosophy, and religion*, p.120-38 (127-28).
9. Adler, 'God and the professors', p.136, 138.
10. Adler, 'God and the professors', p.134.
11. Jacques Maritain, 'Science, philosophy, and faith', in *Science, philosophy, and religion*, p.162-83 (178-79).

reason, 'an education in which the sciences of phenomena and the corresponding techniques take precedence over philosophical and theological knowledge is already, potentially, a Fascist education' based on 'biology, hygiene and eugenics'.[12]

The historian Carlton J. H. Hayes offered a similar diagnosis. Every civilisation, he argued, builds upon 'a particular religious profession and upon the popular *mores* emanating from it'. That foundation had been shattered by the 'secularizing of religion and the universities', the 'atomizing of society' that resulted from liberalism's 'warfare on privileged corporations', and the dislocations produced by the Industrial Revolution, which sparked a movement of masses across Europe in search of work that was 'almost Gypsy-like'. He doubted that the 'religious void' that had opened could be filled by appeals to 'humanity' or 'science' – concepts that were 'too abstract and intellectual' as well as 'a bit stale'. The masses found their programme either 'in materialistic communism or in nationalistic deification of blood and soil'.[13] And the political theorist John Hallowell charged that the growing prestige of science and 'the infiltration of positivism into all realms of thought' had so eroded the moral presuppositions on which liberalism rested that even those prominent German intellectuals who, prior to 1933, had professed to be 'liberals' were able 'to accept, and even in many cases actively to acclaim' the National Socialist regime. 'Like the National Socialists', he concluded, 'they were nihilists. They had neither the standards nor the will to declare this despotism wrong or evil.'[14]

The association of National Socialism with nihilism owed much of its currency to Hermann Rauschning's *Revolution of nihilism*, first published in German in 1938 (*Die Revolution des Nihilismus*) and available in English within a year. One of the first insider accounts of the Third Reich, the book sought to warn those conservatives who, like Rauschning, had initially supported Hitler in the hope that he might curb what they viewed as the revolutionary excesses of the Weimar Republic. Chastened by what he had seen in Germany, Rauschning maintained that the course pursued by the new regime

12. Maritain, 'Science, philosophy, and faith', p.182.
13. Carlton J. H. Hayes, 'The novelty of totalitarianism in the history of Western civilization', *Proceedings of the American Philosophical Society* 82:1 (23 February 1940), p.95-96, and, by the same author, 'The challenge of totalitarianism', *The Public opinion quarterly* 2:1 (January 1938), p.21-26.
14. John H. Hallowell, 'The decline of liberalism', *Ethics* 52:3 (April 1942), p.345-46.

dashed any hope that Nationalism Socialism could forge an alliance between 'middle-class nationalism and monarchist conservatism'. The regime that had come to power in 1933 was 'no longer a nationalist but a revolutionary movement', and its policies sought nothing less than 'the abolition of the existing elements of order'. It was, in short, 'possessed incurably with the devil of nihilism'.[15]

During the 1941-1942 academic year, Rauschning's book served as the focus for a faculty seminar conducted by the émigrés who had come to New York to join the University in Exile at the New School for Social Research.[16] Among the topics explored was the rise of illiberal and anti-Enlightenment ideas in Germany, concerns that occupied a central place in the lecture on 'German Nihilism' delivered in February 1942 by the recently arrived émigré political philosopher Leo Strauss.[17] Examining how a cluster of ideas that was not 'nihilistic in itself, and perhaps even not entirely unsound [...] led however to nihilism in post-war Germany', Strauss' lecture traced the response of 'a few very intelligent and very decent, if very young, Germans' who – disgusted by the 'communist-anarchist-pacifist future' that they saw as the implicit aim of the Weimar Republic and influenced by a group of teachers (including Oswald Spengler, Carl Schmitt, Ernst Jünger and Martin Heidegger) 'who knowingly or ignorantly paved the way for Hitler' – had been moved to reject the 'ideas of modern civilization'.[18]

Strauss maintained that 'The idea of *modern* civilization is of English and French origin; it is not of German origin' and characterised 'modern civilization' an attempt 'to lower the moral standards, the moral claims, which had previously been made by all responsible teachers' while, at the same time, aggressively enforcing these now-diminished ideals. Morality had been reduced to a defence of individual rights, a pursuit of 'enlightened self-interest', a defence of honesty on the grounds that it is 'the best policy', and a hope that the conflict between 'common interest and private industry' could be solved economically. To its 'lasting honour', German thought opposed this 'debasement of morality, and [...] the concomitant decline of a truly

15. Hermann Rauschning, *The Revolution of nihilism: warning to the West*, translated by Ernest W. Dickes (New York, 1939), p.xi-xv, 16-17.

16. For a discussion of the seminar and its activities, see Peter M. Rutkoff and William B. Scott, *New School: a history of the New School for Social Research* (New York, 1986), p.137-43.

17. Leo Strauss, 'German nihilism', ed. David Janssens and Daniel Tanguay, *Interpretation* 26:3 (spring 1999), p.353-78.

18. Strauss, 'German nihilism', p.359-63.

philosophical spirit'. But the sole alternative it could provide was the 'only unambiguously unutilitarian value': courage. By the end of the nineteenth century it was clear that the attempted German synthesis of the 'modern' ideal of material wellbeing and the 'pre-modern' ideal of military virtue could not hold: 'it was overrun by Western positivism, the natural child of the enlightenment'. And so Strauss' 'very intelligent and very decent, if very young, Germans' found themselves left with no alternative but to follow the path blazed by Nietzsche. Cutting their ties with the Anglo-French ideal of modern civilisation, they held fast to the sole 'pre-modern ideal' they could still salvage: martial virtue. This ideal would find its 'most vulgar' exemplification in National Socialist militarism.[19]

Though Strauss was not alone in arguing that National Socialism was the bitter fruit of 'Enlightenment rationalism', his lecture offers one of the more concise versions of a narrative that saw the Enlightenment as an irresistible force that undermines the established order, corrodes all moral values and produces a world in which the sole remaining standard was instrumental efficacy.[20] The work Horkheimer and Adorno were commencing in California is sometimes seen as yet another contribution to this line of argument. But that interpretation misses some important differences.

Myth, Enlightenment and mimesis

Dialectic of Enlightenment opens with a sentence that invites misunderstandings: 'Enlightenment, understood in the widest sense as progressive thought, has always aimed at liberating human beings from fear and installing them as masters. Yet the wholly enlightened earth is radiant with triumphant calamity.'[21] In a single gesture, Horkheimer and Adorno offer a sweeping definition of enlightenment (which ought to dispel the illusion that the book was concerned with the historical period known as 'the Enlightenment') and an

19. Strauss, 'German nihilism', p.370-72.
20. For discussions of Strauss' debts to earlier versions of this narrative, see William H. F. Altman, 'Exotericism after Lessing: the enduring influence of F. H. Jacobi on Leo Strauss', *Journal of Jewish thought and philosophy* 15:1 (2007), p.59-83, and David Janssens, 'The problem of the Enlightenment: Strauss, Jacobi, and the pantheism controversy', *The Review of metaphysics* 56:3 (March 2003), p.605-31.
21. Max Horkheimer and Theodor W. Adorno, *Dialectic of Enlightenment*, ed. Gunzelin Schmid Noerr, translated by Edmund Jephcott (Stanford, CA, 2007), p.1.

equally sweeping summary of its consequences: a world illuminated by 'triumphant calamity'. It does not help matters that the passage is cast in the form that Albert O. Hirschman characterised as 'the single most popular and effective weapon in the annals of reactionary rhetoric': the so-called 'perversity thesis', which argues that attempts to improve society invariably produce effects that are the opposite of those intended.[22]

What is most memorable about *Dialectic of Enlightenment* is those pithy formulations (e.g. the three words: 'Enlightenment is totalitarian') that appear to confirm what readers are ready to assume: that Horkheimer and Adorno viewed the foundations of the Nazi terror as having been laid by the Enlightenment.[23] It is all too easy to overlook Horkheimer and Adorno's failure to draw the conclusion to which the perversity thesis typically leads: the admonition that, since efforts at enlightenment yield perverse results, the project should be abandoned. In intent, if not always in execution, *Dialectic of Enlightenment* pursued an argument of a different sort. As Adorno suggested in *Minima moralia*, 'Not least among the tasks now confronting thought is that of placing all the reactionary arguments against Western culture in the service of progressive enlightenment.'[24] But such a strategy was not without its risks and, in their attempt to thwart the perverse effects of an enlightenment gone awry, Horkheimer and Adorno wound up writing a book that produced a perverse effect of its own: the conviction among some readers that the book was a rejection of 'the Enlightenment project' root and branch, rather than an attempt to rescue it from what it threatened to become.

Part of the problem is that Horkheimer's most forceful explanations of his position tend to be the most misleading. For example, in a 1939 letter to Adler's mentor Robert Maynard Hutchins he wrote, 'If one had to give a quick rough characterization of the complicated process of the breakdown of culture in recent decades – its ultimate causes in every field will be found to go back to the Renaissance – one might say that passionate and unconditional interest in truth has

---

22. Albert O. Hirschman, *The Rhetoric of reaction: perversity, futility, jeopardy* (Cambridge, MA, 1991), p.11-19.
23. See, among many possible examples, Jeffrey Herf, *Reactionary modernism: technology, culture, and politics in Weimar and the Third Reich* (Cambridge, 1984), p.233-34.
24. Theodor W. Adorno, *Minima moralia: reflections from damaged life* (London, 1978), p.192.

been replaced by an interest in "success".'[25] By framing his 'rough characterization' as a narrative of decline (i.e. from the Renaissance onwards, success trumps truth), it would appear that Horkheimer saw the Enlightenment as setting in motion a process of critique that not only undermines traditional values, but ultimately eliminates any alternative standard of evaluation. In short: the Enlightenment breeds nihilism.

But the fulcrum around which the opening chapter of *Dialectic of Enlightenment* turns had less to do with the opposition between myth and enlightenment than with a philosophical anthropology that sketched an account of the development of human relationships with nature in which mimetic interactions were supplanted by efforts at conceptualisation and categorisation that were fundamental both to mythological forms of thought and to modern, scientific approaches to nature. Drawing on Walter Benjamin's account of the weakening of the 'mimetic faculty', Marcel Mauss's studies of magical practices and Roger Caillois's discussion of mimetic forms of adaptation, the opening chapter of *Dialectic of Enlightenment* traced a 'subterranean history' in which mute, bodily reactions to the overwhelming force of nature were gradually channelled into magical practices that controlled and ritualised these spontaneous forms mimetic adaptation.

Had Horkheimer and Adorno been content to view myth and enlightenment as polar opposites, *Dialectic of Enlightenment* would have offered the argument that a fair number of its readers assume it provides. For, if the book traced the pathologies that result from the triumph of 'formal' modes of rationality over 'substantive' forms, then the remedy for these pathologies required a retreat to a form of reasoning that had yet to be contaminated by the baleful impact of formal rationality. In such an account, 'the Enlightenment' marks the point where things begin to turn incomparably worse: hence the need to resuscitate earlier forms of reasoning. Yet, by pushing their account of enlightenment well beyond the boundaries of the eighteenth century and locating its origins deep in human prehistory, Horkheimer and Adorno cut off any hope of finding, in an earlier age, an escape from the 'irresistible' force of enlightenment. Conservative critics of the Enlightenment might entertain the hope that a retreat to earlier modes of thought – for Adler, the 'medieval synthesis', for

25. Max Horkheimer to Robert Maynard Hutchins (7 January 1939), in Max Horkheimer, *Gesammelte Schriften*, vol.16: *Briefwechsel 1937-1940*, ed. Gunzelin Schmid Noerr (Frankfurt am Main, 1995), p.536-37.

Strauss, 'classical' political philosophy – would cure the woes that had befallen the modern world. But, for Horkheimer and Adorno, there was no going back.[26]

Political struggles at the *Partisan review*

While Horkheimer and Adorno were untangling the dialectic of myth and enlightenment in Los Angeles, Dwight Macdonald's relations with his fellow editors at *Partisan review* had reached breaking point. The most politically engaged of the editors, from 1939 onwards, he had opposed American entry into the war, arguing that by increasing the power of the state it would constitute a setback for the labour movement. At the same time, he avidly followed debates on whether the Nazi state constituted a new economic order.[27] His offer to publish whatever works by members of the Institute for Social Research Adorno could provide would appear to have been part of his attempt to expand the journal's offerings beyond its traditional concern with literature and the arts. These efforts led to increased tensions with his fellow editors William Philips and Phillip Rahv, who had directed the journal since its founding. As early as the summer of 1940 Macdonald explored the possibility of removing Philips from the editorial board and expanding it to include the cultural critics Clement Greenberg and Harold Rosenberg.[28] These tensions would leave their mark on the trajectory of the 'New failure of nerve' exchanges.

In his contribution to the initial trio of articles that launched the dispute, Hook focused on the attempts by Adler and others

---

26. For a less compressed discussion of Horkheimer and Adorno's argument, see my 'What, if anything, does *Dialectic of Enlightenment* have to do with "the Enlightenment"?', in *Aufklärungs-Kritik und Aufklärungs-Mythen*, ed. Sonja Lavaert and Winfried Schröder (Berlin and Boston, MA, 2018), p.11-27.

27. See e.g. his exchanges with James Burnham: James Burnham, 'The theory of the managerial revolution', *Partisan review* 8:3 (May-June 1941), p.181-97; Dwight Macdonald, 'The end of capitalism in Germany', *Partisan review* 8:3 (May-June 1941), p.198-220; Dwight Macdonald, 'The Burnhamian revolution', *Partisan review* 9:1 (January-February 1942), p.76-84.

28. Dwight Macdonald, 'War and the intellectuals: act two', *Partisan review* 6:3 (spring 1939), p.3-20; Dwight Macdonald, 'National defense: the case for socialism', *Partisan review* 7:4 (July-August 1940), p.250-66; Dwight Macdonald, 'Notes on a strange war', *Partisan review* 7:3 (May-June 1940), p.170-75; Dwight Macdonald, 'Political notes', *Partisan review* 9:6 (November-December 1942), p.476-82. For a discussion, see Michael Wreszin, *A Rebel in defense of tradition: the life and politics of Dwight Macdonald* (New York, 1994), p.86-94.

to attribute the maladies that plagued the modern world to the triumph of scientific modes of reasoning. He dismissed such views as bordering on 'fantasy'. They viewed a world in which scientific rationality reigned triumphant, but Hook argued that the 'scientific method has until now been regarded as irrelevant in testing the values embodied in social institutions'. And, conceding that 'liberal, labor, and socialist movements' had 'prided themselves on being scientific', he noted that they had 'lost one social campaign after another' and were incapable of providing 'a positive philosophy, that would weld emotion and scientific intelligence, as a new rallying ground'. Though the nineteenth century may have witnessed an 'enthusiasm for the bare results of the physical sciences', Hook stressed that this enthusiasm should not be confused with 'an acceptance of a scientific or experimental philosophy of life in which all values are tested by their causes and consequences'.[29] While Adler saw himself as confronting a world that had been laid waste by a triumphant enlightenment, Hook surveyed a world in which attempts at enlightenment had scarcely begun.

The series continued with four articles in the March-April issue that betrayed an uncertainty as to what was ultimately at stake. The first was an article on Kierkegaard (who had figured, in passing, in Hook's essay) by Norbert Guterman, a Polish writer who had studied in Paris during the 1920s, where he moved in Surrealist and Marxist circles before coming to the United States as an associate of the Institute for Social Research.[30] He argued that those 'modern "existentialist" philosophers' who claimed to be Kierkegaard's heirs had much in common with the 'rationalists' they claimed to denounce: 'they accept and sanction the dualism expressed in such oppositions as Reason-Faith, Theory-Practice, Knowledge-Instinct, Real-Ideal, Essence-Existence' and differed from the 'rationalists' only in that they preferred a more abstract version of these oppositions.[31] Guterman's article was followed by a brief contribution from Richard Chase, a literary critic and close friend of Lionel Trilling, who – drawing on recent writings by Aldous Huxley and Gerald Heard – was content to second Hook's critique of the resurgence of irrationalism, and an

---

29. Hook, 'The new failure of nerve', p.8-10.
30. For a brief discussion of the essay and Guterman's relationship to the Institute for Social Research, see Wheatland, *The Frankfurt School in exile*, p.128-29.
31. Norbert Guterman, 'Neither-nor', *Partisan review* 10:2 (March-April 1943), p.134-42 (139).

essay by the anthropologist Ruth Benedict rejecting the idea (which none of the participants in the debate had advanced) that the 'social disorders of the world' could be traced to the fundamental 'belligerency of human nature'.[32]

The second set of articles closed with the continuation of Hook's initial article, which, 'for reasons of space', had been 'held over' from the previous issue. Expanding the scope of the debate considerably, it argued that the 'failure of nerve' was by no means restricted to conservatives: the same 'atmosphere of mysticism, of passionate, sometimes sacrificial, unrealism, and of hysterical busywork' could also be found on the political left.[33] From this point onwards, the discussion of the 'new failure of nerve' concentrated on political questions, with heated exchanges between Hook and Meyer Schapiro and a response from Dwight Macdonald that, submitted at the moment when disagreements with his fellow editors Rahv and Philips had become irreconcilable, has been aptly characterised by Michael Wreszin as Macdonald's 'rhetorical resignation' from the journal.[34]

Macdonald began by noting that Hook's account of the 'rising tide of obscurantism' had failed to explain '*Why* is the tide rising?' and instead was content to assume that 'if only people would get some sense into their heads and act rationally, our problems would be well on the road to solution.' But such an assumption failed to note that the 'Failure of nerve' posed 'an historical rather than a logical question'. As a result, Hook was unable to understand that this alleged 'failure' relied on 'an adaptation to a certain historical situation'.[35]

For Macdonald the origins of the alleged 'failure of nerve' could be traced to what he characterised as the 'increasingly unconscious

---

32. Richard V. Chase, 'The Huxley-Heard paradise', *Partisan review* 10:2 (March-April 1943), p.143-58; Ruth Benedict, 'Human nature is not a trap', *Partisan review* 10:2 (March-April 1943), p.159-64.

33. Sidney Hook, 'The failure of the left', *Partisan review* 10:2 (March-April 1943), p.165-77 (165).

34. Wreszin, *A Rebel in defense of tradition*, p.121. Schapiro's contributions were published under the pseudonym 'David Merian': David Merian, 'The nerve of Sidney Hook', *Partisan review* 10:3 (May-June 1943), p.248-57; Sidney Hook, 'The politics of Wonderland', *Partisan review* 10:3 (May-June 1943), p.258-62; Dwight Macdonald, 'The future of democratic values', *Partisan review* 10:4 (July-August 1943), p.321-44; David Merian and Sidney Hook, 'Socialism and the failure of nerve: the controversy continued', *Partisan review* 10:5 (September-October 1943), p.473-81. For Macdonald's formal letter of resignation, see 'Letters', *Partisan review* 10:4 (July-August 1943), p.382-83.

35. Macdonald, 'The future of democratic values', p.321.

character of the war' in Europe and the realisation that the policies of the allies amounted to 'an opportunistic adaptation to a reactionary status quo'.[36] Contrasting the entry of Napoleon's armies into Italy with the Allies' recent victory in North Africa, he noted,

> When Bonaparte entered Milan in 1796, the Marquis del Dongo fled to his country estate; when Eisenhower entered Algiers in 1942, the men of Vichy entertained his officers at their clubs. Bonaparte brought along a young artist who gave the delighted Milanese the first political cartoon they had ever seen: a drawing of a French soldier slitting the belly of a rich landowner, from which poured not blood but wheat. Eisenhower brought along Col. Darryl F. Zanuck, late of Hollywood.[37]

While the armies of revolutionary France sought to 'politicize the struggle', Macdonald maintained that the forces engaged in the battle against Hitler's armies made every effort to play down the ideological stakes: 'Some weeks ago, the Office of War Information issued directives to its propagandists on "the nature of the enemy". He was described as a bully, a murderer, a thief, a gangster, etc., but only once in the lengthy document as a fascist.'[38] Concluding that what had been lost was something more than just the 'old optimism of progress', Macdonald saw the pursuit of the war as increasingly marked by 'a scepticism about basic values and ultimate ends, a refusal to look too far ahead'.[39] This scepticism, he concluded, was part of a broader retreat from the principles that had been 'painfully built up since the end of the middle ages', had gained 'general assent since the eighteenth century' and finally 'achieved political reality in the American and French Revolutions'.[40] In the ensuing conflict between these values and the development of capitalist economies 'it is the values and not the productive system which are giving way.' The forces that had once been viewed as laying the foundations for a more humane society had now become its executioners.

> Man has learned to master nature so well that we use the most advanced technology to blast to bits the fabric of culture. Art museums, hospitals, vast industrial works, ancient churches and

36. Macdonald, 'The future of democratic values', p.325.
37. Macdonald, 'The future of democratic values', p.323.
38. Macdonald, 'The future of democratic values', p.324.
39. Macdonald, 'The future of democratic values', p.325.
40. Macdonald, 'The future of democratic values', p.326.

modernistic housing projects, whole historic cities like Warsaw, Coventry, Cologne, and Nuremberg – all are being destroyed with the most admirable efficiency week after week, month after month. Every one can read and write, popular education is a reality – and so the American masses read pulp fiction and listen to soap operas on that triumph of technology, the radio, and the German and Russian masses are the more easily indoctrinated with a lying and debased official culture.[41]

We now live, Macdonald concluded, in 'pretty much the kind of world Marx and Engels thought we should be living in, failing socialist revolution: a world of wars, crises, mass unemployment, centralized power and general instability'.[42]

The letter Adorno sent to Horkheimer immediately before leaving New York to join him in Los Angeles characterised 'MacDonald' and his unnamed colleague as people 'who really had something to do with us'. The extent of the agreement between the exiting editor of *Partisan review* and the exiled director of the Institute for Social Research may have become clearer to Horkheimer as he and Adorno struggled to bring their account of the 'self-destruction of enlightenment' to completion. In September 1943 an already overburdened Horkheimer decided to enter the fray with a critique of Sidney Hook.

Horkheimer contra Hook

The earliest indication that Horkheimer intended to join the 'Failure of nerve' debate appears in letters sent to Herbert Marcuse and Leo Lowenthal on 11 September 1943. The letter to Marcuse characterises the text as 'some notes' on the articles by Hook, Dewey and Nagel, while the letter to Lowenthal describes it as an 'almost finished' article.[43] Two weeks later the 'article on Hook' turns up in a letter to Lowenthal, though Horkheimer notes that, working with Adorno 'night and day' on what would become the *Dialectic of Enlightenment*'s

---

41. Macdonald, 'The future of democratic values', p.327-28.
42. Macdonald, 'The future of democratic values', p.329-31.
43. For the letter to Marcuse, see Max Horkheimer, *Gesammelte Schriften*, vol.17: *Briefwechsel 1941-1948*, ed. Gunzelin Schmid Noerr (Frankfurt am Main, 1996), p.470-71; for the letter to Lowenthal, see MHA, http://sammlungen.ub.uni-frankfurt.de/horkheimer/content/pageview/6329012 (last accessed 26 April 2023).

chapter on the culture industry, he has not had the time to finish 'the last few pages'.[44] There is no further mention of the article until a 28 March 1944 letter to Lowenthal reporting that arrangements with the sociologist Benjamin Nelson to translate the German text into English had broken down. At this point Horkheimer had recently returned from a visit to Columbia University where he had given the series of lectures on 'Society and reason' that would be revised and published the following spring as *Eclipse of reason*. In the course of these revisions, Horkheimer's article on Hook became the basis for the book's second chapter: 'Conflicting panaceas'.

The Hook manuscript had originally opened with a discussion of the 'transitory and futile role' of 'systems of thought' in the transformation of American views on the war in Europe. Before the war, 'there was hardly a political conviction more generally shared [...] than a rigid pacifism' that sought to avoid 'foreign entanglements' and viewed the goal of 'making the world safe for Democracy' as 'a silly, mendacious, obsolete ideology'. But rather rapidly 'a superior leadership has accomplished so complete a change of attitude that the people today are fighting under a charter whose aim is the acceptance of democratic principles all over the globe.' A similar transformation could be seen in American attitudes towards the Soviet Union.

> Up to 1940, the average man, for instance a bank clerk, thought of Russia as a dark power of evil, a symbol of crime, vice, and corruption, the deadly enemy of Western Civilization; in 1941 he was instructed that in America the accounts of practically all European aliens, with only the Russians excepted, had to be frozen. In 1943 he is perhaps dying on a battlefield for a cause which unites his country with Russia.[45]

Such rapid transformations of belief could be observed even in 'the highest, most general intellectual patterns'. 'Today the pursuit of individual happiness, security, success and profits is exalted to a lesser extent by the agencies responsible for the propagation of the right spirit. Such ideas are superseded by devotion to a common cause, postponement of each and every private business, and willingness to

---

44. Horkheimer to Lowenthal (29 September 1943), MHA, http://sammlungen. ub.uni-frankfurt.de/horkheimer/content/pageview/6328994 (last accessed 26 April 2023).
45. Horkheimer, 'Hook', p.1.

die for a national ideal.'[46] These rapid transformations of beliefs were not confined to the United States; a similar transformation had taken place in Mussolini's Italy and Hitler's Germany. In all three cases, 'changeability with regard to ideas is universally accompanied by its opposite, fanatic adherence to them.'[47]

Words had been transformed into 'counters' and, ultimately, into 'fetishes'. In the process, they took on an almost magical power.

> In the very era of relativism, the time when each child looks at an idea as either an advertisement or rationalization, the very fear that language might still harbour mythological residue has endowed words with a mythological character. As in the days of magic, each word is regarded as a dangerous force which possibly could destroy society, and for which the speaker must be held responsible.[48]

That Horkheimer took such concerns to heart in his revisions of his own text can be seen in the modification of a passage that initially observed that

> All the processes of enlightenment have not cured men of their inclination to follow any false prophet, if only he promises an outlet for the fear and rage of which larger parts of all nations seem to be obsessed. In this respect, change, as compared with the Middle Ages, does not go very deep. The difference is that now there are other victims. Witches, sorcerers, and heretics have been replaced by Negroes or reds or Zoot-Suiters, while the Jews are still the Jews.[49]

The parallel passage in *Eclipse of reason* kept the allusion to attacks on Mexican Americans (the targets of the 1943 'Zoot Suit Riots' in Los Angeles), but eliminated the now politically suspect reference to the persecution of 'Negroes' and 'reds'.

In both the 'Hook manuscript' and *Eclipse of reason* Horkheimer maintained that, like the neo-Thomists they attacked, Hook and his fellow 'neo-Positivists' were compelled to fall back on self-evident principles. But, while neo-Thomists did so consciously, 'positivism is completely naive about them.'[50] And neo-Thomists – no less than their 'neo-Positivist' critics – ultimately would end up reconciling

46. Horkheimer, 'Hook', p.2.
47. Horkheimer, 'Hook', p.3.
48. Horkheimer, 'Hook', p.7.
49. Horkheimer, 'Hook', p.9-10.
50. Horkheimer, 'Hook', p.29.

individual thinking to modern forms of mass manipulation. But, while Horkheimer found both positions unpalatable, it was less clear what he offered as an alternative.

This should hardly be surprising. He commenced work on the lectures that would become *Eclipse of reason* at the very moment when work on the *Dialectic of Enlightenment* had been broken off and, as a result, found himself forced to provide what his collaboration with Adorno had been unable to produce: an account of how enlightenment might be rescued from the catastrophe that had befallen it. It is clear that he had reservations about the alternative *Eclipse of reason* had sketched. In a letter to Lowenthal written in January 1946, he noted,

> the book, as it is, opposes the concept of nature so directly to that of spirit, and the idea of object to that of subject, that our philosophy appears as much too static and dogmatic. We have accused the others, both Neo-Thomists and Positivists, of stopping thought at isolated and therefore contradictory concepts and, as it is, it would be only too easy for them to accuse us of doing the same thing.[51]

It was hardly surprising, then, that sympathetic (albeit puzzled) readers of *Eclipse of reason* might conclude that Horkheimer sought, in place of the 'formal reason' criticised in the book's opening chapters, to rehabilitate a new form of 'objective reason'.

An example of such a misreading can be seen in the enthusiastic letter that the philosopher and editor Ruth Nanda Anshen sent to Horkheimer after the book's publication. She praised its defence of 'objective reason', that 'concrete unity of experience, whereby every abstract entity derives its vitality'.[52] Her subsequent suggestion, in a review of Erich Fromm's *Man for himself*, that moral life must 'correspond to the ontological and metaphysical virtues which include both the *lumen naturale* and the *lumen supernaturale*' finally drove Horkheimer to draft a rejoinder aimed at distinguishing Anshen's interpretation of his work from what he understood it to be arguing: 'In spite of my critique of "subjective reason" and its relapse into a second mythology – a critique bearing only a superficial resemblance to certain antipathies nourished by Dr. Anshen – I have never

51. Horkheimer to Lowenthal (10 January 1946), Cambridge, MA, Harvard University, Houghton Library, Leo Lowenthal papers, bMS Ger 185 (47), f.20.
52. Ruth Nanda Anshen to Horkheimer (23 July 1947), in Horkheimer, *Gesammelte Schriften*, vol.17, p.867-78.

advocated a return to an even more mythological "objective reason" borrowed from history. [...] I have attacked enlightenment in the spirit of enlightenment, not of obscurantism.'[53] He was fighting a losing battle. By replacing the chiasmus of enlightenment and myth that had been fundamental to the argument of *Dialectic of Enlightenment* with the stark demarcation between formal and substantive types of reasoning, *Eclipse of reason* invited readings that saw Horkheimer (and, by association, Adorno) as engaged in a project that sought to find a path that would lead back from the difficulties that plagued the project of enlightenment to the certainties of a less troubled time.

That misunderstanding remains with us today, especially in America, where *Dialectic of Enlightenment* tends to be read as yet another example of the 'failure of nerve' it sought to remedy.

---

53. Horkheimer, draft of a letter to the editor of *Philosophical review* (April 1949), in Max Horkheimer, *Gesammelte Schriften*, vol.18: *Briefwechsel 1949-1973*, ed. Gunzelin Schmid Noerr (Frankfurt am Main, 1996), p.23. Since the letter was never printed in the *Philosophical review*, it is possible that Horkheimer never sent it.

Ideas in action: Franco Venturi's *Settecento*

RUGGERO SCIUTO

University of Oxford

'moy j'écris pour agir'

Voltaire to Jacob Vernes, 15 April 1767[1]

The year 1931 is still remembered today as one of the lowest and darkest in the history of Italian academia.[2] At the suggestion of Giovanni Gentile, the then minister of Education Balbino Giuliano required that all professors teaching at an Italian higher institution swear an oath of allegiance to the Fascist Party.[3] Some gladly did so. Others did so begrudgingly: warned by Benedetto Croce and Palmiro Togliatti, they resolved to sign solely out of consideration that to resign would be to let the Italian youth fall into the clutches of someone whose views would indeed align with those of the ruling party. Only a handful of academics refused to swear, retiring early or even opting for self-exile. Among the latter was Lionello Venturi, professor of art history at the University of Turin specialising in investigating the Venetian School and French modernism.[4]

---

1. Voltaire, *Correspondence and related documents*, ed. Theodore Besterman, in *Œuvres complètes de Voltaire*, vol.85-135 (Oxford, 1968-1977), D14117.

2. The research for this article was made possible by a Leverhulme Early Career Fellowship. I am extremely grateful to Professor Nicholas Cronk, who first drew my attention to Venturi's scholarship, as well as to Professor Daniel Fulda and Professor John Robertson for their feedback on the presentation that forms the basis of the present contribution. All translations are mine unless otherwise indicated.

3. See Roberto Pertici, 'Giuliano, Balbino', in *Dizionario biografico degli Italiani*, vol.56 (2001), https://www.treccani.it/enciclopedia/balbino-giuliano_(Dizionario-Biografico) (last accessed 26 April 2023).

4. See Marco Cavenago, 'Venturi, Lionello', *Dizionario biografico degli Italiani*,

Born in Rome on 16 May 1914, Lionello's son, Franco Venturi, lived in Turin until 1932 when, jailed for his anti-Fascist views and swiftly released thanks to the intervention of his grandfather Adolfo, also an influential academic, he joined his father in his Parisian exile. Enrolled at the Sorbonne, Franco studied under economic historian Henri Hauser, political historian Charles Seignobos and literature scholar Daniel Mornet.[5] As was also the case with Theodor Adorno, it was exile and the experience of the rise of totalitarianism that drew the young Venturi to the study of the eighteenth century. But it was importantly for a solution to the impending threats posed by Nazi Fascism, and not for the origins of totalitarianism itself, that he was looking when he first approached French Enlightenment texts.

The first authors to spark Venturi's attention were accordingly those who put politics at the core of their intellectual enquiry: those whose novels and poems 'are politics' and whose thoughts are 'opposition to dictatorship', as Venturi eloquently said of Miguel de Unamuno's writings in an article that appeared in the anti-Fascist journal *Quaderni di giustizia e libertà*.[6] In dom Deschamps's *Le Vrai Système*, which he edited with Diderot scholar Jean Thomas in 1939, Venturi discerned, as he later wrote with tangible enthusiasm, 'the historical and ideological basis of that political and social ideal [Communism] that held sway in the years between the two world

---

vol.98 (2020), https://www.treccani.it/enciclopedia/lionello-venturi_%28Dizionario-Biografico%29/ (last accessed 26 April 2023).

5.   For a short biography of Franco Venturi we refer the reader to Adriano Viarengo's entry in the *Dizionario biografico degli Italiani*, vol.98 (2020), https://www.treccani.it/enciclopedia/franco-venturi_%28Dizionario-Biografico%29/ (last accessed 26 April 2023). A more extensive study is Adriano Viarengo, *Franco Venturi: politica e storia nel Novecento* (Rome, 2014). For more on Daniel Mornet's attitudes towards the Enlightenment, see Nicholas Cronk's contribution in this volume.

6.   Quoted by Giuseppe Giarrizzo, 'Venturi e il problema degli intellettuali', in *Il coraggio della ragione: Franco Venturi intellettuale e storico cosmopolita*, ed. Luciano Guerci and Giuseppe Ricuperati (Turin, 1998), p.9-59 (11). In Venturi's eyes, political affinities often take precedence over literary merits. Speaking of Italian anti-Fascist historian Gaetano Salvemini, for instance, in the *Trevelyan lectures*, i.e. his essay *Utopia and reform in the Enlightenment* (Cambridge, 1971), p.6, Venturi writes: 'I remember how astonished and puzzled I felt, though, of course I did not dare say so, that he, Salvemini, could love the poet of the age of Augustus. How could a man of such independent and frank character, whose political ideas were so emancipated, whose social conscience so acute and modern, how could a scholar of his stamp venerate Horace, politically and socially so different, even his opposite?'

wars'.[7] In Diderot he similarly saw an author who succeeded at giving a political twist to Enlightenment philosophy.[8] Dismissive of his literary and philosophical achievements ('Trop nouveau dans ses idées et trop fort dans ses paroles pour être considéré comme un littérateur, Diderot n'est pas un philosophe au véritable sens du mot, ni un poète, au sens profond'), Venturi hails in the chief editor of the *Encyclopédie* the man who endured imprisonment at Vincennes following the publication of the *Lettre sur les aveugles* and the intellectual who raised his voice in defence of the abbé de Prades first, and against Frederick the Great's refutation of d'Holbach's *Essai sur les préjugés* later.[9] With his *Jeunesse de Diderot* of 1939, to this day a seminal source for the study of the intellectual development of the young *philosophe*, Venturi offered his readers 'une "Histoire politique de Denis Diderot"', a political history of Denis Diderot.[10] And, from that moment onwards, political history became Venturi's primary field of enquiry.

7. Franco Venturi, 'La fortuna di dom Deschamps', *Cahiers Vilfredo Pareto* 5:11 (1967), p.47-55 (50): 'Ricordo ancora lo stupore che mi colse leggendo e trascrivendo alla Bibliothèque Nationale di Parigi i preziosi manoscritti suoi, provenienti da Poitiers: sembrava di vedere messa a nudo, in tutta la sua cruda primitività, la base storica e ideologica dell'ideale politico e sociale che dominava l'orizzonte degli anni tra le due guerre mondiali.' The full reference for Venturi's edition of *Le Vrai Système* is Léger-Marie Deschamps, *Le Vrai Système, ou le Mot de l'énigme métaphysique et morale*, ed. Jean Thomas and Franco Venturi (Paris, 1939). For a study of Venturi's attitudes towards Communism, see Manuela Albertone, 'Illuminismo e comunismo', in *Comunismo e socialismo: storia di un'idea*, ed. Manuela Albertone *et al.* (Turin, 2014), p.93-109. See also Giarrizzo, 'Venturi e il problema degli intellettuali', p.13.

8. Franco Venturi, *Jeunesse de Diderot (1713-1753)* (Paris, 1939), p.8 (emphasis added): '[Il] doit être considéré comme *un des plus importants parmi les hommes qui surent donner un sens politique à la philosophie française des lumières.* [...] Diderot est [...] l'une des forces essentielles qui amenèrent [l']insertion des idées et des rêves des philosophes des lumières dans l'histoire de la France et de l'Europe.'

9. Venturi, *Jeunesse de Diderot*, p.8-9. Venturi published Diderot's response to Frederick the Great's refutation of d'Holbach's *Essai sur les préjugés* under the eloquent title of *Pages inédites contre un tyran* (Paris, 1937). He then returned to Diderot in Franco Venturi, *Settecento riformatore*, 7 vols (Turin, 1969-1990), vol.4.1: *La caduta dell'Antico Regime: i grandi stati dell'Occidente*. A comprehensive study of Diderot's late political thought is Anthony Strugnell, *Diderot's politics: a study of the evolution of Diderot's political thought after the Encyclopédie* (The Hague, 1973).

10. Venturi, *Jeunesse de Diderot*, p.8-9. For more on the *Jeunesse de Diderot*, see Roland Mortier, 'Franco Venturi et sa *Jeunesse de Diderot*', *Rivista storica italiana* 108 (1996), p.751-54.

But does the notion of 'political history' truly capture the complexity of Venturi's method? To the eyes of a non-continental historian, Venturi's scholarship may rather resemble that of a social or economic historian. His publications are often concerned with overpopulation and commerce, economic growth and labour, latifundia and changes in agricultural practices. In the *Trevelyan lectures* that he delivered in Cambridge in 1969, Venturi accordingly points to the weakness of any interpretations of *Aufklärung* which, like Ernst Cassirer's, fail to pay sufficient attention to 'the state, the land, or commerce'.[11] Anna Maria Rao has observed, however, that, in Italy, Venturi's books were received with more than a hint of bewilderment by heavy-duty social historians, who disparagingly dismissed them as cultural history.[12] This criticism (because indeed it was meant as one) is not entirely out of place. Venturi's interest was not in economic crises and famines as such; it went to the books, pamphlets and newspaper articles that they occasioned. Famines and economic crises were not nefarious events impacting on the lives of many and the geopolitical status quo as much as triggers for intellectual discussion that could lead, in turn, to social improvement. Venturi is, in many respects, a historian of ideas, and the articles that he published in the *Rivista storica italiana* on the genesis and diffusion of such words and phrases as 'Sapere aude', 'Barocco' or 'Despotismo orientale' are obvious cases in point in this respect.[13] The primary focus of Venturi's many publications is no doubt on the individuals and their ideas.[14] Better still, it is on those individuals who managed to turn their ideas into practice or at least set their minds to solving concrete problems. After all, as perceptively noted by Venturi's English translator, Robert Burr Litchfield, 'thought was intimately associated with action' in Venturi's

---

11. Venturi, *Utopia and reform*, p.2.
12. Anna Maria Rao, 'Enlightenment and reform: an overview of culture and politics in Enlightenment Italy', *Journal of modern Italian studies* 10:2 (2005), p.142-67 (147).
13. Franco Venturi, 'Contributi ad un dizionario storico: Was ist Aufklärung? Sapere aude!', *Rivista storica italiana* 71 (1959), p.119-28 (also available in English as 'Was ist Aufklärung? Sapere aude!', in *Italy and the Enlightenment: studies in a cosmopolitan century*, ed. Stuart Woolf, translated by Susan Corsi, London, 1972, p.33-41); Franco Venturi, 'Contributi ad un dizionario storico: despotismo orientale', *Rivista storica italiana* 72 (1960), p.117-26 (also available in English as 'Oriental despotism', in *Italy and the Enlightenment*, ed. S. Woolf, p.41-51).
14. Biographical sketches play an important role in Venturi's historiography. For more on this topic, see Marino Berengo, 'Franco Venturi e la biografia', *Rivista storica italiana* 108 (1996), p.717-26.

mind, and '"doing" was a necessary consequence of "knowing".'[15] How ideas circulated was also key to Venturi.[16] What is, after all, his monumental *Settecento riformatore* if not a global history of the eighteenth century explored and recounted through the prism of understudied eighteenth-century Italian sources, be they newspapers like the *Notizie del mondo*, letters or travel journals?[17] And yet, Venturi could not have been more explicit in his rejection of that quest for intellectual genealogies which he thought was specific to historians of ideas, or 'philosophers' as he dubs them: 'we must not follow the ideas back to their origins', he writes in the *Trevelyan lectures*, 'but examine their *function* in the history of the eighteenth century. Philosophers are tempted to push upstream until they arrive at the source. Historians must tell us *how* the river made its way, among what obstacles and difficulties.'[18] Blinded by their obstinacy to draw everything back to previous sources, Venturi reasons, historians of ideas end up missing what is specific and innovative about individual thinkers and social actors. This is a criticism that Venturi addresses not only to Cassirer, but also to Peter Gay and Carl Becker. Of the latter's *Heavenly city of the eighteenth-century philosophers*, in particular, he writes that 'it derives from an effort to find in the thought of Diderot, or d'Holbach, Voltaire and Hume, not what was new, historically important and fruitful, but

15. Robert Burr Litchfield, 'Franco Venturi's "crisis" of the Old Regime', *Journal of modern Italian studies* 10:2 (2005), p.234-44 (235).

16. See Franco Venturi, 'La circolazione delle idee', *Rassegna storica del Risorgimento* 41 (1954), p.203-22.

17. Many scholars have criticised Venturi's approach, which looks at European as well as global events through the prism of Italian sources such as gazettes and diaries. See John Robertson, 'Franco Venturi's Enlightenment', *Past & present* 137 (1992), p.183-206 (194): 'For all the remarkable detail of their news coverage, the Italian journals hardly provide the basis for a general narrative of European history. By its nature their evidence is partial and (for the modern historian) at least second-hand: even when their content was not subject to censorship (or self-censorship), it was often derived from other journals, not necessarily those of the country which the news concerned. The Italian journals thus cannot substitute for the domestic sources of the individual countries, or even for the diplomatic dispatches of which Venturi was once so dismissive.'

18. Venturi, *Utopia and reform*, p.2-3 (emphasis added). And again (p.2): 'A careful examination shows that the philosophical interpretation of the *Aufklärung*, from Kant to Cassirer and on to present-day scholars, may well be a misleading factor in various ways.' For more on this, see Rao, 'Enlightenment and reform', p.160: '[Venturi's] was a "political history of ideas" that could not be cast as philosophical or literary history, and which indeed took on polemical terms when confronting these themes.'

what substantially coincided with the fundamental ideas of the past.'
Becker's, he continues, 'is retrospective history, told with great charm
and scholarship, as always happens with intelligent conservatives.
They are sceptical about everything, except their own determination
not to yield to the new, the unexpected, to anything outside their
heavenly city.'[19] Historians of ideas, Venturi reasons, should not be
on the lookout for previous instances of a given concept, but rather
study how ideas adapt to the constantly changing historical, social
and intellectual context.

Even this claim ought in fact to be duly tempered. While sensitive
to questions of readership and reception, Venturi proved somewhat
sceptical of scholarship centred on specific schools or intellectual
circles (of scholarship '[starting] from society and not from ideas,
from groups and not from individuals, from climates of opinion and
not from elements in the thought', as he puts it).[20] He was accordingly
disapproving of the then still nascent sociability and network studies,
and of an article by Daniel Roche on the Académie de Châlons-
sur-Marne he wrote: 'If one takes a modest and peaceful French
provincial academy of the eighteenth century, and draws a multitude
of arrows shooting off in all directions into Europe just because one
of its members happened to live in Florence or elsewhere; [...] one is
obviously using a cyclotron to crack a nut.'[21] To scholarship in this
vein, Venturi opposed, as we have seen, what often feels like a very
fragmented approach, with single thinkers and their ideas at its core.
As Robert Burr Litchfield puts it: 'For Venturi, "texts" were events in
the life-experience biographies of the authors, a part of the syndrome
of "knowing" and "doing". The question for him might have been
less whether Louis-Sébastien Mercier's *L'An 2440* was typical of
clandestine books published in the 1770s, as what the relationship this
work had to the life experience and other works of Mercier.'[22] More
than history of ideas, Venturi's is therefore intellectual history (or even
'history of intellectuals', as Vincenzo Ferrone dubs it).[23] It is, even
better, political intellectual history, where the word 'political' should

---

19. Venturi, *Utopia and reform*, p.3-4. For more on Carl Becker's views on the
    Enlightenment, see Gregory Brown's contribution in this volume.
20. Venturi, *Utopia and reform*, p.9.
21. Venturi, *Utopia and reform*, p.9-10. See also Rao, 'Enlightenment and reform',
    p.150.
22. Litchfield, 'Franco Venturi's "crisis" of the Old Regime', p.240.
23. Vincenzo Ferrone, *The Enlightenment: history of an idea* (Princeton, NJ, and
    Oxford, 2017), p.89.

be taken as meaning 'pertaining to government'. It is, as will become clearer in later pages, politically engaged political intellectual history drawing extensively on social as well as economic history.[24]

From a politically engaged political intellectual historian of the eighteenth century who studied under Mornet and whose first intellectual outputs took shape in the age of totalitarianism one would arguably expect a great emphasis on the events of the late 1780s and early 1790s. But the reality is that the French Revolution almost disappears in an eventful temporal continuum such as Venturi's *Settecento* – and rather literally so, for *Settecento riformatore* ends exactly in 1789.[25] Italocentrism and cosmopolitanism, which interestingly coexist within Venturi's historiography, are no doubt important factors in this partial eclipse of the French Revolution. But they are not the only ones.

In a paper delivered in 1979 at the fifth conference of the International Society for Eighteenth-Century Studies in Pisa, Venturi introduced a notion that he significantly developed in volume 3 of *Settecento riformatore*: the notion of the 'first crisis of the *Ancien Régime*'.[26] Under this name, Venturi brings together a wide variety of distant and apparently unrelated destabilising events taking place across the Western world between 1768 and 1776, including the famines of the 1760s, Pasquale Paoli's insurrection in Corsica, the arrival of the Russian fleet in the Mediterranean Sea, the subsequent revolt of Greece against Ottoman control, the first partition of Poland of 1772, the Cossack Rebellion lead by Pugachev in the early 1770s

24. See Venturi, *Utopia and reform*, p.2: 'What is lacking [from contemporary scholarship, and the reference is specifically to Nicolao Merker's *L'Illuminismo tedesco: l'età di Lessing* of 1968] is "le gouvernement", as Diderot said – concrete political action.' See also Franco Venturi, 'The European Enlightenment', in *Italy and the Enlightenment*, ed. S. Woolf, p.3-32 (3): 'Our interest is in the relationship between [...] the Enlightenment and political, social and economic life in the eighteenth century.'

25. Rao, 'Enlightenment and reform', p.144: 'Another major issue in the Italian studies of the 1950s and 1960s was the place of the French Revolution in eighteenth-century Italian history as part of European history. Cantimori, and then Saitta, Berengo, Villani, Galasso and Giarrizzo, all shared a strong interest in this crucial theme of Italian historiography in that period. Venturi, for his part, had started out with the problem of revolution, but he had largely left it as the distant background to his *Settecento riformatore*, even if he returned to it in his great fresco entitled *L'Italia fuori d'Italia* (1973), that appeared in the Einaudi *Storia d'Italia*.'

26. Franco Venturi, 'La prima crisi dell'Antico Regime: 1768-1776', *SVEC* 190 (1980), p.63-80.

and of course the American Declaration of Independence of 1776. Venturi's insistence on the notion that the *Ancien Régime* was already under significant pressure in the late 1760s and early 1770s is in keeping with scholarship carried out by Albert Sorel, Jean Jaurès and Robert Roswell Palmer, among others, but was forcefully opposed by British scholars.[27] Crucially, it also puts into perspective the events of 1789-1794. As Venturi himself writes in his 'Preface' to the English translation of volume 4, part 1, of *Settecento riformatore*, 'the French Revolution seems increasingly less alone and isolated and increasingly a part of a general process that one is tempted, with Gibbon's formula, to call the decline and fall of the Old Regime.'[28]

With the French Revolution now deprived of at least some of its former prestige, the position of defining factor of the eighteenth century was left up for grabs, and it was the gentler and softer notion of *riforma* (reform) that was to take it up. The word *riforma*, which we find in the titles of many of the eighteenth-century sources used by Venturi, including Carlantonio Pilati's vehemently anticlerical *Di una riforma in Italia* of 1767 and Filippo Buonarroti's *Riforma dell'Alcorano*, reappears almost obsessively in Venturi's textual corpus.[29] It is not just his *magnum opus*, *Settecento riformatore*; it is also his *Trevelyan lectures*, known in Italy as *Utopia e riforma nell'Illuminismo*, or the three volumes that he edited for the series *Letteratura italiana: storia e testi* published by Riccardo Ricciardi Editore: *Riformatori lombardi, piemontesi e toscani* of 1958, *Riformatori napoletani* of 1962 and *Riformatori delle antiche repubbliche, dei ducati dello Stato pontificio e delle isole* of 1965, this last one coedited with Giuseppe Giarrizzo and Gianfranco Torcellan.

Reform, in Venturi's eyes, was everywhere in the eighteenth century. The *combats des Lumières*, the campaigns that Enlightenment

---

27. Venturi, *Settecento riformatore*, vol.4.1, p.xi. See also Litchfield, 'Franco Venturi's "crisis" of the Old Regime', p.237: 'In the *Times higher education supplement*, Jeremy Black, who had written extensively about eighteenth-century international relations, attacked the very notion of a "general crisis" in the years 1768-89: "this entails the amalgamation of some very disparate problems and developments, and a tendency to exaggerate signs of conflict or to see them all as aspects of a common crisis"'.

28. Franco Venturi, *The End of the Old Regime in Europe, 1768-1776*, vol.4.1: *The Great states of the West*, translated by Robert Burr Litchfield (Princeton, NJ, 1991), p.x.

29. A large section of the second volume of *Settecento riformatore* (p.250-93) is dedicated to jurist and historian Carlantonio Pilati. The full reference for Venturi's edition of Buonarroti's text is Filippo Buonarroti, *La Riforma dell'Alcorano*, ed. Alessandro Galante Garrone and Franco Venturi (Palermo, 1992).

thinkers fought, were many and diverse. In order, Venturi lists as the most important d'Holbach's against religion, Rousseau's for democracy, a widespread one against feudalism, Beccaria's against torture and the death penalty, and Voltaire's for tolerance. But beyond this mesmerising plurality of visions, Venturi – a truly Diderotian scholar, in this respect – sees unity: the Enlightenment as a whole had 'Change!' or 'Reform!' as its motto. 'Wouldn't it be better', he writes in the *Trevelyan lectures*, 'to return to the interpretation of the encyclopaedists as *philosophers* and reformers, as people who lived for their ideas, and who found a way of changing the reality which surrounded them?'[30] For better or worse, the line separating the greatest minds of the century and any provincial individual committed to the idea of bettering suddenly disappears: anyone who is determined to changing the status quo becomes a reformer.[31]

Together with the idea that the Old Regime had already undergone a significant crisis in the 1760s and 1770s, Venturi's emphasis on reform shields the Enlightenment from the accusation of having generated the events of 1793-1794 while also contributing to a reconsideration of the place and importance of the French Revolution. Eighteenth-century reforms are not, or at least not primarily, steps towards the outbreak of the Revolution, as one would be prone to believe; they are political initiatives that, had they only been successful, would have made a revolution utterly unnecessary. As Venturi puts it in his discussion of the first crisis of the Old Regime:

> the conservative fortresses did resist the first revolutionary waves of the second half of the eighteenth century, they outlived the first crisis of the *Ancien Régime*. They resisted precisely because they were

30. Venturi, *Utopia and reform*, p.14.
31. In this respect, Venturi's view of the Enlightenment appears to be very close to Tocqueville's who, as mentioned by Elisabeth Décultot in her contribution in this volume, thought that what brought together eighteenth-century French thinkers was their fascination with politics and the art of government. See Alexis de Tocqueville, *L'Ancien Régime et la Révolution* (Paris, 1856), p.211-12: '[Les gens de lettres en France] ne demeuraient pas, comme la plupart de leurs pareils en Allemagne, entièrement étrangers à la politique, et retirés dans le domaine de la philosophie pure et des belles-lettres. Ils s'occupaient sans cesse des matières qui ont trait au gouvernement; c'était là même, à vrai dire, leur occupation propre. On les entendait tous les jours discourir sur l'origine des sociétés et sur leurs formes primitives, sur les droits primordiaux des citoyens et sur ceux de l'autorité, sur les rapports naturels et artificiels des hommes entre eux, sur l'erreur ou la légitimité de la coutume, et sur les principes mêmes des lois.'

both conservative and reformist [...]. The result is well known: two decades had to elapse before the problems that had emerged between 1768 and 1776 could arise again, though profoundly changed, in revolutionary France.[32]

As this quotation makes rather clear, to replace 'revolution' with 'reform' as the key concept at the heart of the Enlightenment is also to make a strong political and theoretical statement. In the *Trevelyan lectures*, Venturi attacks Marxist historians for taking for granted the bourgeois nature of the Enlightenment: 'I believe', he writes, 'that [...] the relations between the bourgeois forces, however active or static, and the movement of the Enlightenment, must remain a problem; they cannot be taken for granted or used as an historical presupposition.'[33] Venturi's Enlightenment, by contrast, is almost indissolubly connected to conservative forces, be they the nobility or the monarchy (or both).[34] As he points out, all but one of the members of the Accademia dei Pugni, the Milanese learned society revolving around Cesare Beccaria and the Verri brothers, were noblemen – the exception being Paolo Frisi, a clergyman. Sure enough, Diderot was no nobleman: he was the son of a cutler. But he sat at Catherine the Great's table towards the end of his life, and rumour has it that he would pound the empress' knees while talking politics. Most of the readers of his late works published in the *Correspondance littéraire* wore a more or less sparkly crown, and while he may have of course voiced strong democratic feelings – suffice it to think of the famous incipit to the *Observations sur le Nakaz* ('Il n'y a point de vrai souverain que la nation; il ne peut y avoir de vrai législateur que le peuple') – Diderot

32. Venturi, *Settecento riformatore*, vol.3: *La prima crisi dell'Antico Regime*, p.xiv-xv. The Italian original reads: 'le fortezze conservatrici resistettero alle prime ondate rivoluzionarie del secondo Settecento, fecero fronte alla prima crisi dell'Antico Regime. Resistettero proprio perché erano insieme conservatrici e riformatrici [...]. Il risultato è notissimo: un ventennio dovette trascorrere perché i problemi che si erano affacciati tra il 1768 e il 1776 potessero imporsi di nuovo, anche se ormai profondamente mutati, trovando nella Francia della rivoluzione il loro nuovo e decisivo punto focale.'

33. Venturi, *Utopia and reform*, p.11.

34. Venturi, 'The European Enlightenment', p.9: 'It cannot be stressed enough that that truth about the French Revolution, perceived by a few of the best historians of the nineteenth century and later studied in depth and defined by Mathiez and Lefebvre, the fact, that is, that it was the nobles' rebellion which gave rise to the Revolution proper, is applicable to the whole of the French eighteenth century and to the initial formation of the ideas of the Enlightenment.'

was clear that change, in the East as in the West, had to come from above: it was Catherine's duty, he suggested, to ensure that absolutism in Russia end at her death.[35]

The Enlightenment *sensu* Venturi was therefore indissolubly connected to the ruling classes, to the aristocracy, to the monarchy and even to absolute monarchies – and this is an aspect of Venturi's scholarship that many historians, most notably Giuseppe Giarrizzo, have often contested.[36] Despite the partial failure of the reforms he sought to implement, Joseph II holds a special place in Venturi's account of the eighteenth century, and so do Maria Theresa and Catherine the Great.[37] Perhaps more curious is Venturi's barely concealed fascination with the marquis de Pombal, the de facto ruler of Portugal from 1750 to 1777, who exercised autocratic power and violently repressed political opposition, while also fighting the power of the nobility, introducing extensive liberal reforms, abolishing the auto-da-fé, expelling the Jesuits from the country, boosting its economic growth, and rebuilding its capital in the aftermath of that disastrous 1755 earthquake which inspired, among other works, Voltaire's *Poème sur le désastre de Lisbonne*.

Venturi's Enlightenment is doubly bound to absolutism: if on the one hand absolutism can promote and sponsor socio-political reforms, on the other it can also induce change in spite of itself, through censorship and repression. Where there was no strong monarchical power, Venturi reasons, Enlightenment struggled to take root. In fact, he goes as far as to argue that the very Enlightenment that emerged at the turn of the eighteenth century was a by-product of the aggressive foreign policy of the Sun King:

> The coalition among the enemies of Louis XIV created a common spirit among men and states of differing creeds and mentality, between

35. Denis Diderot, *Observations sur le Nakaz*, in *Œuvres complètes*, ed. Laurent Versini, 5 vols (Paris, 1994-1997), vol.3, p.501-78 (507). See also Rao, 'Enlightenment and reform', p.159.

36. Giuseppe Giarrizzo, 'L'Illuminismo e la società italiana: note di discussione', in *L'età dei Lumi: studi storici sul settecento europeo in onore di Franco Venturi*, ed. Lester G. Crocker, 2 vols (Naples, 1985), vol.1, p.165-89, esp. p.168-69. For more on Venturi's attitudes towards absolute monarchy, see Cecilia Carnino, 'Rereading Franco Venturi's eighteenth century: absolutist monarchy between reform and revolt', *History of European ideas* 35 (2009), p.11-23.

37. On Venturi's attitudes towards Joseph II, in particular, see Derek Beales, 'Franco Venturi and Joseph II's *grande progetto*', *Rivista storica italiana* 108 (1996), p.742-50.

the Empire and England, Holland and the Duchy of Savoy. There was already a group of people inclined not only towards interpreting this new spirit but also towards acting on it and spreading it. [...] One name sums up this group: it is, of course, that of Pierre Bayle.[38]

In the *Trevelyan lectures* as well as in *Settecento riformatore*, Venturi often insists on the idleness and backwardness of eighteenth-century republics. Geneva, the Dutch Republic, Venice and Genoa all entered in the eighteenth century 'a phase of irreversible decline' that relegated them to 'the fringe of history itself', Venturi contends. Convinced that 'they existed outside and beyond the hard contingencies which caused strife and internal transformation in other European states', eighteenth-century republics proved fundamentally incapable of carrying out extensive reform plans.[39] As Venturi writes in a paper on 'The European Enlightenment' given at the eleventh conference of the International Committee of Historical Sciences:

> In sharp contrast [...] to the impatience and reforming improvisations of the Habsburg sovereign [...] stood the passivity, the complete incapacity for reform of the oligarchic states. [...] Even the greatest, richest, most vigorous of the countries governed constitutionally by a noble ruling class, England, proved incapable of reform through the means and instruments of the eighteenth century. [...] It was not propaganda, or only propaganda, which made Voltaire, Diderot and the other men of the Enlightenment believe that reforms could not be born in the land of the *liberum veto*. This was the practical truth.[40]

Having withered in their homelands, republican virtues and ideals blossomed, perhaps unexpectedly, in the bosom of absolutism.[41] 'La

---

38. Venturi, 'The European Enlightenment', p.3-4.
39. Venturi, *Utopia and reform*, p.70.
40. Venturi, 'The European Enlightenment', p.30-31.
41. See also Venturi, *Utopia and reform*, p.70-71: 'the word "republic" found an echo in the minds of many people, but as a form of life, not as a political force. [...] There survived a republican friendship, a republican sense of duty, a republican pride, even though the world had changed. These may even have existed in the very heart of a monarchical state, in the innermost self of those who seemed fully integrated in the world of absolutism.' For more on Venturi and republicanism, see Silvia Berti, 'Repubblicanesimo e Illuminismo Radicale nella storiografia di Franco Venturi', in *Il repubblicanesimo moderno: l'idea di repubblica nella riflessione storica di Franco Venturi*, ed. Manuela Albertone (Naples, 2006), p.155-75, esp. p.172.

liberté naîtra du sein de l'oppression', Encyclopaedist Alexandre Deleyre wrote in his 1774 *Tableau de l'Europe,* and a large number of intellectuals, including high-profile members of the French administration such as the marquis d'Argenson, minister of Foreign Affairs in the mid-1740s, appeared to share in his faith, Venturi remarks.[42]

But why would Venturi, an intellectual whose interest in the Enlightenment developed in response to the rise of totalitarianism, place so much emphasis on the decline of eighteenth-century republics and on the link between Enlightenment and absolutism?

An engaged intellectual who saw in writing a powerful means to engage politically and change the status quo, Venturi may have thought of his own scholarship as a way of warning his contemporary and future readers of the political calamities that could befall them. To say that Venturi reconsidered the link between Enlightenment and Revolution (and, incidentally, the link between Enlightenment and Risorgimento, and between Russian Populism and Russian Revolution, too), to say that he interpreted eighteenth-century attempts at reform as initiatives that are worthy of interest in themselves and not because of their putative links to the Revolution, is not to say that his historiography escapes the trap of teleology. Quite the contrary: Venturi's Enlightenment is the smithy in which our modern world was forged. Apprehended by the Francoists in 1941 and later extradited to Italy, Venturi was interrogated by the Fascists, sent to an internment camp in Monteforte Irpino, and eventually imprisoned in Avigliano.[43] Questioned about his studies at the Sorbonne, he answered that they aimed 'to cast light on the origins of modern democracies and the men who are generally taken to be their forerunners'.[44] By pointing to the idleness of eighteenth-century republics, to their lack of reform spirit and ruinous decline, Venturi may have therefore attempted to warn us of the dangers that mature democracies often face, of that intellectual apathy and torpor that could eventually lead to the rise of counter-Enlightenment forces such as populism and obscurantism.[45]

---

42. Alexandre Deleyre, *Tableau de l'Europe pour servir de supplément à l'Histoire philosophique et politique des établissements et du commerce des Européens dans les deux Indes* (Amsterdam, n.n., 1774), p.54. See also Venturi, *Utopia and reform,* p.73.

43. Viarengo, 'Venturi, Franco'.

44. Quoted by Leo Valiani, 'Una testimonianza', *Rivista storica italiana* 108 (1996), p.507-49 (516). The Italian original reads 'Ammetto che la mia attività di studioso in Francia abbia avuto carattere politico mettendo in luce le origini e gli uomini che sono considerati come i precursori dei regimi democratici.'

45. See Berti, 'Repubblicanesimo e Illuminismo Radicale', p.157: 'Fare luce su

Much like Cicero's, Venturi's history is *magistra vitae*; it is a history of engaged intellectuals, written by an engaged intellectual, and hoping to form engaged intellectuals. It is a history written to be always actual, and one that is worth rediscovering today, and not just because of its political merits.

A most attentive reader of Venturi's work, intellectual historian Jonathan Israel also conceives of his own scholarship on the so-called 'Radical Enlightenment' as an antidote against rampant intellectual and political apathy. The similarities between Israel's approach and Venturi's do not end there. Israel fully shares Venturi's scepticism about social history, and, while the Italian scholar avowedly turned his back on any routes that may have taken him to Mount Parnassus, leaving out such towering literary figures of the Italian Enlightenment as Parini and Goldoni, the author of *Democratic Enlightenment* is hardly less critical of literature-driven interpretations.[46] Arguing against the existence of different national Enlightenments, both Venturi and Israel offer their readers a grand, global perspective, which allows lesser-known cultural realities to emerge and enables the reader to detect otherwise unsuspected connections and resonances. Indeed, given his interest in republicanism and in-depth knowledge of authors such as Diderot, dom Deschamps, Boulanger, Buonarroti and Pilati, Venturi is often taken to be a forerunner of post-1980s scholarship on the Radical Enlightenment such as that of Margaret Jacobs and Israel himself.

Yet, Israel's method differs from Venturi's in important ways.[47] While Venturi sees in the French Revolution merely one in a long series of socio-economically and geopolitically destabilising events that punctuated the second half of the eighteenth century, Israel places the Revolution back at the centre of the Enlightenment project.

---

quel coacervo di problemi significava non solo far avanzare le conoscenze storiografiche, ma anche non sbagliare – o comunque sbagliare di meno – nell'azione politica. Significava valorizzare l'elemento libertario gravido di ideali democratici e socialisti, e riuscire a comprendere, ma anche a isolare, l'elemento totalitario che concettualmente faceva la sua prima apparizione in scena nel mondo settecentesco.'

46. Franco Venturi, *Settecento riformatore*, vol.1: *Da Muratori a Beccaria*, p.xiii.
47. For more on this point, see Keith M. Baker, 'Venturi's "Utopia and reform in the Enlightenment"', in *Il repubblicanesimo moderno*, ed. M. Albertone, p.33-58, and John Robertson, 'Enlightenment without "origins"? From *Radicati di Passerano* to *Utopia e riforma*', in *Il repubblicanesimo moderno*, ed. M. Albertone, p.131-54.

The opposition between Venturi and Israel becomes starker still if we look at the genesis of the French Revolution and its connections to Enlightenment culture. As this article hopes to have shown, Venturi interprets the Enlightenment as a top-down reform project that had the potential to prevent the outbreak of the Revolution. Following his mentor Mornet, he accordingly argues that, while the Russian October Revolution was almost unambiguously a product of the intellectual framework in which it developed, the notions of Enlightenment and French Revolution should be kept distinct. Israel, by contrast, writes disparagingly of socio-political factors, and identifies the primary (if not the sole) direct cause of the French Revolution in the philosophical ideas of those eighteenth-century materialist, and for the most part atheist, thinkers who make up his 'Radical Enlightenment':

> the Radical Enlightenment – and not the Enlightenment as such – is the only important direct cause of the French Revolution understood as a total transformation of the political, legal, cultural, and educational framework of French life, administration, and society. Everything else, the financial difficulties that brought the French *ancien régime* monarchy crashing down, discontent of the peasantry, pre-1789 legal politics, and the French nobility's tenacious promotion of its power and privileges, however crucial to the mechanics of the historical process that made the Revolution possible, was entirely secondary, in fact tertiary, in shaping the revolutionary outcome.[48]

Sure enough, Venturi also emphasised the French Enlightenment's debt to unorthodox thinkers such as Pierre Bayle or John Toland. But, unlike Israel's Spinoza, Venturi's Toland is not a solidly radical figure; he is a convinced deist, and so are many of Venturi's intellectual heroes – Radicati, for one, but also the young Diderot, at least until 1749. As Silvia Berti has rightly observed, Venturi's Enlightenment may be anticlerical, but it is not for that necessarily antireligious.[49] While Israel's political engagement prompts him to present his Radical Enlightenment as a perfectly coherent set of ideas, all consistently deriving from one-substance metaphysics (i.e. materialistic monism), Venturi offers of the various intellectuals whom we are now accustomed to viewing as participants in the Radical Enlightenment project a vastly more nuanced and unprejudiced interpretation. Perhaps

48. Jonathan Israel, *Democratic Enlightenment: philosophy, revolution, and human rights 1750-1790* (Oxford, 2011), p.16.
49. Berti, 'Repubblicanesimo e Illuminismo Radicale', p.162.

more fragmented than Israel's, Venturi's Enlightenment is also, at one and the same time, much more cohesive. If Israel is prepared to distinguish two diametrically opposed wings within eighteenth-century culture, Venturi tends to see a 'reformer' in each and every participant in the Enlightenment project. One might think that this interpretation does not do justice to the diversity of Enlightenment actors. And yet, it is in fact hardly disputable that even some of the most prominent figures in Israel's Radical Enlightenment advocated gradual, unhurried reform. Baron d'Holbach, who is widely taken to be a solid, even monolithic radical thinker, was no exception:

> ce n'est point par des convulsions dangereuses, ce n'est point par des combats, des régicides et des crimes inutiles que les plaies des nations pourront se refermer. Ces remèdes violents sont toujours plus cruels que les maux que l'on veut faire disparaître. C'est à l'aide de la vérité que l'on peut faire descendre Astrée parmi les habitants de la terre. La voix de la raison n'est ni séditieuse ni sanguinaire. Les réformes qu'elle propose, pour être lentes, n'en sont que mieux concertées. En s'éclairant, les hommes s'adoucissent; ils connaissent le prix de la paix; ils apprennent à tolérer les abus que, sans danger pour l'Etat, on ne peut anéantir tout d'un coup. Si l'équité permet aux nations de mettre fin à leurs peines, elle défend au citoyen isolé de troubler la patrie et lui ordonne de sacrifier son intérêt à celui de la société. C'est en rectifiant l'opinion, en combattant le préjugé, en faisant connaître aux princes et aux peuples le prix de l'équité, que la raison peut se promettre de guérir les maux du genre humain, et d'établir solidement le règne de la liberté.[50]

By placing the idea of reform as opposed to revolution at the core of the Enlightenment project, by providing us with an image of the Enlightenment that is at one and the same time nuanced and coherent, Venturi's work, with all its limits, can help us to problematise and enrich recent scholarship on the eighteenth century while also acting as a reassuring guide at a time when the political legacy of the Enlightenment figures again very prominently in public discourse.

---

50. [Paul-Thiry d'Holbach], *Système social, ou Principes naturels de la morale et de la politique, avec un examen de l'influence du gouvernement sur les mœurs*, 3 vols (London [Amsterdam], [Marc-Michel Rey], 1773), vol.2, p.34. For more on d'Holbach's view on the individual's right of resistance against the authority, see Ruggero Sciuto, 'Bringing together the *Essay* and the *Second treatise*: d'Holbach interpreter of Locke', *Studi Lockiani: ricerche sull'età moderna* 3 (2022), p.61-86.

The question of Peter Gay's Enlightenment: between 'heavenly city' and the 'brute facts of political life' (1948-1956)

GREGORY S. BROWN

University of Nevada, Las Vegas

Peter Gay's *Enlightenment: an interpretation* represents both a culmination and a point of departure for contemporary Enlightenment scholarship. The two volumes, published in 1965 and 1969, are generally read as the culmination of fifteen years of research and methodological and interpretive analysis. But, while the strengths and shortcomings of the volumes have been widely discussed, less attention has been paid to the genesis of the project, and the context in which it was undertaken. Viewed as a whole, Gay's work of the 1950s and 1960s set the standard for the study of the Enlightenment in the English-speaking world at the time, and played a central role in the establishment of the field of eighteenth-century studies as we know it. But, if we consider this work not as a whole but as a process of intellectual development, we can set aside preconceptions about Gay and look instead at his early work as a window into the genealogy of the origins of contemporary American scholarship on the Enlightenment.

Those who have read *The Enlightenment* and inferred from it Gay's method as an intellectual historian have tended, since the second volume appeared in 1969, to question the originality of his approach, his sources and thus his conclusions. This critical reading of Gay as 'conventional intellectual history' was made, most influentially, by Robert Darnton in his *Journal of modern history* review essay published in 1971; Darnton situated Gay's work in the German Idealist tradition, incarnated by the eminent philosopher Ernst Cassirer and his classic, *Die Philosophie der Aufklärung*.[1] This

---

1. Robert Darnton, 'In search of the Enlightenment: recent attempts to create a social history of ideas', *Journal of modern history* 43:1 (1971), p.113-32; Ernst Cassirer, *Die Philosophie der Aufklärung*, 2 vols (Tübingen, 1932).

reading, which has remained influential, presents Gay's work as indicative of early-twentieth-century, idealist historiography, which remained largely impervious to the methods of social history until the 1970s.[2]

This article seeks to resct the origins of Gay's project, and by extension of the American scholarly engagement with the Enlightenment in the post-war years. My contention here is that Gay, in taking up the topic in the years between 1952 and 1955, brought a much more complicated – and intellectually much more interesting – series of concerns to his topic, which arose from the particularities of post-war American political and intellectual culture. By considering Gay not only as a historian but also as a historical figure, as documented in his correspondence and manuscripts (and by drawing on work by previous scholars who conducted interviews with him), this article will present Gay's entry into the field in the 1950s as an important moment in the series of 'inventions of Enlightenment' under study in this volume.

This article argues that Gay's approach, while both admiring of and in the tradition of Cassirer, nevertheless represents a significant break from, and challenge to, the Kantian Idealist tradition. I argue instead that the influences on Gay came from a variety of German intellectual traditions, with a focus on social scientific and social psychological methods. We shall see that his interests in political theory and in social psychology informed his work on the Enlightenment – and, by extension, the field of eighteenth-century studies – from the beginning. At the same time, Gay's turn to the Enlightenment reflected a response to specific problems in American liberal thought of the early to mid-1950s. Thus, it will argue that Gay's 'invention' of the

---

2. Johnson Kent Wright, 'Foreword', in Carl Becker, *The Heavenly city of the eighteenth-century philosophers*, 2nd edn (New Haven, CT, 2003), p.i-xii; Annelien de Dijn, 'The politics of Enlightenment from Peter Gay to Jonathan Israel', *The Historical journal* 55:3 (2012), p.785-805; Al Coppola, 'Enlightenolatry from Peter Gay to Steven Pinker: mass marketing Enlightenment and the thick eighteenth century', *The Eighteenth century: theory and interpretation* 62:4 (winter 2021), p.412-31. On intellectual history as impervious to social historiography until the 1970s, see e.g. Daniel Wickburg, 'Intellectual history vs. the social history of intellectuals', *Rethinking history* 5:3 (2001), p.383-95. For a more nuanced narrative of this evolution, see Anthony La Vopa, 'Finding meaning in the Enlightenment', in *Enlightenment past and present: essays in a social history of ideas*, Oxford University Studies in the Enlightenment (Liverpool, Liverpool University Press / Voltaire Foundation, 2022), p.1-30.

Enlightenment both arose from and contributed to important transformations in the social organisation and methodologies of the discipline of history and of humanities scholarship more broadly.

The American tradition of Enlightenment scholarship, 1910-1952

Before turning to Gay's 'invention' of Enlightenment, let us begin by considering briefly the tendencies in Enlightenment scholarship which emerged in the American academy prior to 1945. The first tradition emerged, at the turn of the twentieth century, in the discipline of philosophy, exemplified by John Grier Hibben, who was the first to use 'the Enlightenment' in an American scholarly work. For Hibben, and other philosophers influenced directly by Hegel, the term signified the period of the eighteenth century.[3]

The other tradition of Anglo-American interpretation, which would be influential in philology and history, sought to find in the work of the French *philosophes* what John Morley called in 1878 the 'literary preparation for the French Revolution'. This approach explicitly framed the history of eighteenth-century ideas in terms of the outbreak of the French Revolution; it emerged in American scholarship with Morley's contemporary and fellow liberal, Andrew Dickson White, the founding president of the American Historical Association, and was advanced into the early twentieth century by James Harvey Robinson.[4]

After 1918, this tradition took two distinct paths, in French and in history respectively. In departments of Romance languages, influenced by Gustave Lanson and Paul Hazard (who both served as visiting lecturers at Columbia), a sympathetic version of this

---

3.   John Grier Hibben, *The Philosophy of the Enlightenment* (New York, 1910). See also David Beveridge Tomkins, 'The individual and society: a comparison between the views of the enlightenment and those of the nineteenth century', doctoral dissertation, New York University, 1914. On this point in greater depth and breadth, see James Schmidt, 'Inventing the Enlightenment: anti-Jacobins, British Hegelians, and the *Oxford English dictionary*', *Journal of the history of ideas* 64:3 (July 2003), p.421-43.

4.   John Morley, *Diderot and the Encyclopædists*, 2 vols (London, 1878), vol.1, p.i. On White and Robinson, see Gregory S. Brown, 'Andrew Dickson White and America's unfinished (French) Revolution', *Age of revolutions* (14 September 2020), https://ageofrevolutions.com/2020/09/14/andrew-dickson-white-and-americas-unfinished-french-revolution/ (last accessed 27 April 2023).

interpretive tradition emerged; Norman Torrey, in his anthology *Voltaire and the age of Enlightenment* published in 1931, made clear the meaning in his first line: 'The Age of Enlightenment is a term applied to a definite revolution in the history of thought which took place in the eighteenth century.'[5] However, in the discipline of history, the successors to Robinson in the 'New History' turned that interpretation on its head, retaining the link of the history of ideas to the French Revolution but finding therein evidence of the naivety, superficiality and impracticality of the intellectual movement. This tradition took a much more sceptical view of the practical value of the Enlightenment for the contemporary era, culminating in Crane Brinton's 1963 American Historical Association presidential address, in which he presented the Enlightenment as largely ideological, and culturally conservative – a 'new religion, certainly related to, descended from, and by many reconciled with, Christianity'.[6] In this inversion, we see of course the influence of Carl Becker.

Becker had been hired as professor of modern European history at Cornell in 1919; though without training in continental European history or literature, he became a leader in the field primarily through his students, to whom he introduced the extensive primary source holdings of the Andrew Dickson White collection. Becker's presidential lecture for the American Historical Association, the now-classic 'Everyman his own historian', applied principles of philosophical pragmatism to historiography, arguing that a democratic society required professional historians to address not only the facts of the past but also the understanding and memory of the public about the meaning of the past. This approach represented a significant break from Hegelian philosophy of history and from Germanic documentary methods.[7]

The next year, Becker delivered a series of lectures at Yale Law School, which were published as *The Heavenly city of the eighteenth-century philosophers*; this essay argued against the Hegelian legacy, against the French literary historiographical tradition and against the empirical work of Robinson. Becker presented the European

5. Norman Torrey, *Voltaire and the age of Enlightenment* (New York, 1931), p.1. Although he did not use the term 'Enlightenment', Ira O. Wade, *The Clandestine organization and diffusion of philosophic ideas in France from 1700 to 1750* (Princeton, NJ, 1938), represented an innovative and influential strand of this tradition.
6. Crane Brinton, 'Many mansions', *American historical review* 69:2 (January 1964), p.309-26.
7. Carl Becker, 'Everyman his own historian', *American historical review* 37:2 (January 1932), p.221-36.

Enlightenment as a continuity from medieval and early modern Thomist Christian thought. It argued, most strikingly, that the confidence of the *philosophes* in rationalism and empirical natural philosophy was as much 'an act of faith' as medieval scholasticism placed in the Scriptures. In the final lecture, Becker likened this 'new religion' to the 'sacred principles of the Revolution', and then, in an astonishing leap of logic, drew a line from the 'democratic faith of the eighteenth century' to the *Communist manifesto* and the 'Russian Revolution which menaces us in the name of "liberty and equality"'.[8]

Heavenly city had a significant impact in the United States academy; in the decades after its publication, it became widely adopted in historiography and in history classrooms as the standard account of 'the Enlightenment'. Even Gay, to whose trenchant criticism of the work we shall turn shortly, called it a 'masterpiece of persuasion that has done more to shape the current image of the Enlightenment than any other book [...]. [I]ts witty formulations have been accepted by a generation of students and borrowed in textbook after textbook.'[9] Becker reasserted the tendency of American historians of ideas to view the significance of the eighteenth century primarily as a matter of political thought, and to assess its significance primarily through the political events of the American and French Revolution. At the same time, Becker took a sceptical view of that political impact, and diminished the importance of the Enlightenment as a usable past for secular culture within liberal democracy. The Enlightenment, as presented in *Heavenly city*, is fundamentally ideological and, as a result, antithetical to Becker's own pragmatism; he worried that its lack of concern for empirical society and the people who lived in it would accelerate the threat to democracy which he perceived in the spread of Bolshevism. Becker's influence contributed significantly to the relative neglect, and negative assessment, of eighteenth-century European thought by American historians from the 1930s to the 1950s.

***

This brings us to Peter Gay, in 1952, when he would take up the study of the Enlightenment. He did so with no training in either the discipline of history or the study of the eighteenth century, and,

---

8.   Becker, *Heavenly city*, p.155, 161-64.
9.   Peter Gay, 'Carl Becker's *Heavenly city*', *Political science quarterly* 72:2 (June 1957), p.182-99.

consequently, Gay did *not* approach the issue as had many of his Anglophone predecessors, from the standpoint of the relationship of the Enlightenment to the French Revolution. Nor did he approach it from the German Idealist philosophical paradigm. Gay did however approach the topic from his own significant and timely intellectual commitments, which were in the study of political theory, the historical application of social psychology, and the pertinence of both those questions for understanding the contemporary United States.

Gay's prior work to that point, which had been in the field of politics and on the topic of social democracy, has been little considered in the context of his subsequent work on the Enlightenment; however, as I argue here, there were significant continuities. I build this argument on two previous, insightful studies of Gay's intellectual evolution, both of which correctly emphasise the importance of his views on contemporary American culture and politics, as a German immigrant, for the evolution of his approach to, and on, the European Enlightenment.[10] Gay's former student Helmut Smith draws primarily on his published work but also conducted interviews by correspondence, and Merel Leeman explored Gay's career until 1970 in a doctoral thesis, based on extensive in-person interviews as well as some of the archival sources consulted here.[11] Leeman makes the case for a link from his study of Bernstein to his study of Voltaire almost too directly: 'Both Bernstein and Voltaire represented his answers to the rise of ideologies.'[12] Both Smith and Leeman brilliantly weave together Gay's writings on the topic over fifteen years, but are inclined towards what Gay referred to as the 'rage for coherence'. My approach, in contrast to that of Smith and Leeman, emphasises the intellectual, political and socio-political context of the years 1952-1956 to the form in which Gay reinvented the Enlightenment for post-war America.

---

10. On his early life in Germany and his immigration to, and maturation in, the United States, see Peter Gay, *My German question: growing up in Nazi Berlin* (New Haven, CT, 1999).
11. Helmut Walser Smith, 'Reluctant return: Peter Gay and the cosmopolitan work of the historian', in *The Second generation: émigrés from Nazi Germany as historians*, ed. Andreas Daum (New York, 2015), p.210-28; Merel Leeman, 'Transatlantic Enlightenment: Peter Gay and the drama of German history in the United States, 1930-1970', doctoral dissertation, Amsterdam University, 2017.
12. Leeman, 'Transatlantic Enlightenment', p.81.

German immigrant intellectuals in American intellectual culture, 1948-1952: political theory and historiographical practice

While many American liberal intellectuals of the early 1950s held a sanguine view of the national political culture, and while Gay expressed a consistent optimism about American culture, he also held preoccupations that made him anxious. His writings from the years 1952-1956 indicate a concern with prospects for democracy in the United States, with the direction of Cold War American foreign policy, with the domestic influence of McCarthyism, and with what he characterised as a tendency among American academics not to engage with the important political and intellectual challenges of the day. His concerns tracked less with neo-Kantian or post-war American liberalism than with the concerns of German refugee intellectuals – and those of his intellectual mentor, Franz Neumann.

Neumann's intellectual, political and professional trajectory was both characteristic of his generation and utterly remarkable. Though rarely cited today, his contributions to the disciplines of legal theory and political science have long been noted, with the best-known work being Stuart Hughes' essay, which situated Neumann 'between liberalism and social democracy'.[13] The most recent major work, *Learning from Franz L. Neumann*, highlights both the breadth and the depth of his erudition as well as his lucidity as a student of the 'brute facts of political life'.[14] Neumann came of age in imperial Germany, and after 1918 became an activist in the Social Democratic Party and then a leading labour lawyer for German trade unions as well as a Weimar-era public intellectual, defending constitutional democracy in debates with Carl Schmitt in the early 1930s. In March 1933, he fled Germany and, to establish residency in England, enrolled as a doctoral student at the London School of Economics (LSE) under Harold Laski, the left-leaning political theorist and influential Labour Party intellectual. By the time he completed his thesis in 1936, Neumann had given up on the prospects of a restoration of democracy in Germany and migrated to the United States as an

13. H. Stuart Hughes, 'Franz Neumann between liberalism and social democracy', in *The Intellectual migration: Europe and America, 1930-1960*, ed. Donald Fleming and Bernard Bailyn (Cambridge, MA, 1969), p.446-62.
14. David Kettler and Thomas Wheatland, *Learning from Franz L. Neumann: law, theory, and the brute facts of political life* (London, 2019).

affiliate of the Institute for Social Research (the 'Frankfurt School') in exile in New York, working on the Institute's externally funded research projects and lecturing in law at Columbia. In this period, he drew upon both his background in political theory and his deep understanding of the practical operation of German politics and civil society in his highly influential study of Nazi rule, *Behemoth*. During the war, he worked for the US government, including the Office of Strategic Services, and, immediately after the war, he served as a lead researcher on the American prosecutorial team at the international war-crimes tribunal in Nuremberg. In 1948, Neumann returned to New York and took up a full-time appointment in the Columbia University Department of Public Law and Government.

From his return to Columbia until his sudden death in 1954, Neumann exerted considerable influence on post-war political scientific research and theory in both Germany and the United States. Although the Frankfurt School's most widely referenced writers considered him insufficiently 'critical' in his approach to politics, Herbert Marcuse and Otto Kirchheimer both praised him as the stand-out thinker of the group for his lucidity and comprehensiveness. In posthumous tributes, Marcuse described him as having a 'rare sense as a political scholar'; Kirchheimer praised his 'excelling brilliance' and 'daring'.[15] More recent work has noted the evident, if indirect, influence of Neumann on Hannah Arendt.[16] Yet Neumann's contribution to Enlightenment scholarship has not been adequately considered – either in its own right or in his influence on Gay and, *ipso facto*, the field of eighteenth-century studies. Neumann, for our argument, provides the most evident vector for the influence of the thought of left-leaning German intellectual immigrants on post-war American Enlightenment scholarship.

This claim is based, in part, on the historical specificity of the migration of intellectuals from Germany to the United States during and after the war; this group, as Neumann himself noted, stood apart from other intellectual migrations, due to the particularities of his generation's intellectual and cultural background in relation to the opportunities

15. Herbert Marcuse, 'Preface', in Franz Neumann, *The Democratic and the authoritarian state: essays in political and legal theory*, ed. Herbert Marcuse (Glencoe, IL, 1957), p.vii-x (vii); Otto Kirchheimer, 'Franz Neumann: an appreciation', *Dissent* 4 (autumn 1957), p.382-87 (382-83).

16. Vicky Iokavou, 'Totalitarianism as a non-state: on Hannah Arendt's debt to Franz Neumann', *European journal of political theory* 8:4 (2009), p.29-47; Samantha Rose Hill, *Hannah Arendt* (London, 2021), p.120-30.

they perceived in the post-war American academy. In his own reflection on this 'cultural migration', Neumann underscored the contrast between the limitations imposed on innovative German scholars (many but not all Jewish) in the hierarchical and rigid university environment of Germany (even before 1932), which he contrasted to the dynamism and vibrancy he perceived in the United States, but it remains to be demonstrated how essential this group, including Neumann, was to the reemergence of the Enlightenment in the Anglophone world.[17]

The preoccupation of many of these left-leaning German immigrant scholars was to rethink the concept of the 'state', in the context of liberal political theory and practice. Neumann had become interested in the history and concept of the *Rechtsstaat* during the Weimar period, and he elaborated on this during his study as a refugee in England in the mid-1930s. His 1936 doctoral thesis, 'Governance and the rule of law', focused particularly on the role of the judiciary.[18] For Neumann, the liberal conception of the state had to be defined by the universality and rationality of the rule of law, yet not separated from the question of equity, and this inflection would clearly be evident in Neumann's legal writings – and his influence on Gay.

Those concerns informed the establishment in 1949 of an interdisciplinary research group on 'the state' as one of the first three of the Columbia Seminars; Neumann quickly emerged as an influential figure in that group.[19] Neumann's prominence was due, in part, to

---

17. Franz Neumann, 'The social sciences', in *The Cultural migration: the European scholar in America*, ed. W. Rex Crawford (Philadelphia, PA, 1953), p.4-26. On the influence of German émigré scholars on historical scholarship, and in particular Renaissance studies, see Kay Schiller, 'Paul Oskar Kristeller, Ernst Cassirer and the "humanistic turn" in American emigration', in *Exile, science and Bildung: the contested legacies of German émigré intellectuals*, ed. David Kettler and Gerhard Lauer (New York, 2005), p.125-38, and more specifically on émigré historians, see *Dynamics of emigration: émigré scholars and the production of historical knowledge in the twentieth century*, ed. Stefan Burger and Phillip Müller (New York, 2022), and the unpublished thesis by Iryna Mykhailova, 'Humanism in exile: German scholars of Renaissance in the United States', oral presentation, Göttingen, 17 May 2019.
18. Franz Neumann, 'The governance of the rule of law: an investigation into the relationship between the political theories, the legal system, and the social background in competitive society', doctoral dissertation, London School of Economics, 1936.
19. Ira Katznelson, 'A Seminar on the State', in *Desolation and Enlightenment: political knowledge after total war, totalitarianism, and the Holocaust* (New York, 2003), p.102-37.

Behemoth, which made clear the need for further analysis than the classical definitions set forth by Hegel or Weber. Neumann had introduced, in his writings on Nazi Germany, the idea of a 'non-state' – better understood as an anti-state. In his post-war writings, however, Neumann moved beyond this question to look in depth at the concept of 'political freedom' in terms other than the natural law tradition, which defined it largely as the limited authority of the state over the individual. Indeed, his major works after 1948 addressed freedom, notably 'Concept of political freedom' (first presented in 1949) as well as 'Intellektuelle und politische Freiheit' and 'Recht und Staat' (1954), both translated posthumously from German by Gay.[20]

One concept Neumann did not address directly in this work, but which came to hold particular interest for his contemporaries, was 'totalitarianism'. 'Totalitarianism', as a term and a concept, was not newly coined in the post-war period, but, in the late 1940s and early 1950s, it took on a particular significance for scholarship on eighteenth-century thought – most notably in some passages of Arendt's *Origins of totalitarianism* and, in a much less nuanced fashion, with the publication of the first volume of Jacob Talmon's *Origins of totalitarian democracy*. In retrospect, another link that is often made is the publication of the work by Theodor Adorno and Max Horkheimer, due to the title associated with the 1947 second edition, *Dialektik der Aufklärung* (and the 1972 translation, *Dialectic of Enlightenment*).[21] It would be both tempting and logical to assume that Neumann – and then Gay – took up the study of political theory of the Enlightenment in the early 1950s either to extend or to refute this theory of the Enlightenment as the origin of totalitarianism. Yet none of these works, as frequently cited as they are today, seems to have provoked either man directly, at least not in these years. Neumann published nothing directly on any of these works, and, while Gay would express his dissatisfaction and impatience with all of the above approaches, it is not clear he had read any of them during this period when he entered into the field of Enlightenment

20. Both essays are reprinted as 'Intellectual and political freedom' and 'Anxiety and politics' in *The Democratic and the authoritarian state*, ed. H. Marcuse, p.160-215 and 270-300.
21. On the now-lost first edition, self-published in 1944 as *Philosophische Fragmente*, and the second edition, published in a limited print run in Amsterdam, see James Schmidt, 'Language, mythology, and Enlightenment: historical notes on Horkheimer and Adorno's *Dialectic of Enlightenment*', *Social research* 65:4 (1998), p.807-38.

scholarship in the early 1950s.[22] Rather than see their interest as a direct response to totalitarian theory, in any of its guises, we may more usefully understand their interest as having arisen from a concern with more fundamental problems, the concepts of the liberal state and of personal freedom. Neumann, as noted, had explored this historical tendency of state bureaucracy and large social structures to impose cultural and social-psychological constraints on the thought and action of the individual across his body of work; indeed, his final essay, entitled 'Recht und Staat', delivered at the Freie Universität in 1954, considered this problem in explicitly social-psychological terms, drawing from Hegel, Marx, Freud and Gustave Le Bon, to reach a conclusion which framed the conflicts inherent in American religious tolerance, labour relations and race relations in terms of 'conspiracy theory' and 'collective anxiety, identification and guilt'. In translating this essay in the mid-1950s, Gay would entitle it 'Anxiety and politics'.

***

It is in this context that we can approach Neumann's most direct writing on eighteenth-century thought, his introduction written in early 1949 to a translation he edited for the Hafner Library of Classics, of Montesquieu's *Spirit of the laws*.[23] The text itself was not new; the volume reprinted the first English translation, produced by Thomas Nugent in 1756. Nor was Montesquieu new material for Neumann; in his 1930 essay on the German concept of *Reichstaat*, he had invoked Montesquieu's concept of separation of constitutional powers as meaningful only if accompanied by a 'balance of social powers'. His 1936 thesis on the 'rule of law' referenced Montesquieu twenty-six times, attributing profound influence to his discussions of the judiciary, the principle of separation of powers and the power of the state. But the 1949 essay offered a much more sustained discussion; this essay represented only the second significant interpretation of the

22. The only reference to any of these texts or interpretations in his earliest work, discussed below, was a passing mention, without reference, of the 'fashionable' description of Rousseau as 'totalitarian' in his introduction to his translation of Cassirer. It is also not clear that Gay had read Cassirer on the Enlightenment prior to translating his Rousseau essay.
23. Charles de Secondat de Montesquieu, *Spirit of the laws*, ed. Franz Neumann, translated by Thomas Nugent (New York, 1949); Franz Neumann, 'Editor's introduction', in Montesquieu, *Spirit of the laws*, ed. F. Neumann, p.ix-lxiv.

Spirit of the laws in English in half a century and broke with the main thrust of previous American interpretations of Montesquieu.[24]

In this essay, Neumann sought to clarify a widely stated but rarely examined *doxa* of American intellectual and political culture, that Montesquieu's advocacy for the 'separation of powers' in book 11 had found its practical application in the Constitution of the United States. Indeed, Neumann's essay on Montesquieu was far more than merely an introduction for general interest readers; it was an essay on both political thought and intellectual history. Neumann here deployed a rich array of references to early modern political theory and works of history, to raise his two central preoccupations of the time: (1) the social and cultural basis of the state as a functional political entity and (2) the challenge posed to liberalism and democracy by the state. Neumann went to great lengths to argue against what he called 'constitutional fetishism' – that is, mistaking a theoretical justification for a given structure for the social and psychological factors which drive political action of those who live within that structure, clearly in reference to the concept of the separation of powers. Consistent with the general tendency in mid-twentieth-century progressive legal theory, Neumann considered the 'impartiality' of the judiciary to be a highly problematic assumption. He praised Montesquieu's insight into the necessity of a judiciary conscious of its (aristocratic) social standing and its legal and social autonomy from the executive power of the state (monarch). His presentation of *Spirit of the laws* to an American audience made an important innovation in breaking with previous American readings of Montesquieu as having recapitulated Locke; anticipating the progressive direction of American jurisprudence of the 1950s and 1960s, he called for a more progressive approach to federalism, which would not only divide power within the state but also balance 'social power'.

These questions about whether and how the state could be reconciled to liberal constitutional order set the foundation for what would become Gay's interest in eighteenth-century political thought. Neumann's interest in the issue of the state, in Montesquieu's legal theory and more broadly in Enlightenment political theory is important for understanding Gay's turn to the Enlightenment in 1952. Understanding the relationships among personal freedom, law,

---

24. Franz Neumann, 'Montesquieu', in *The Democratic and the authoritarian state*, ed. H. Marcuse, p.96-148.

social equality and the operation of the state was – for both men – not just a theoretical question; it was an essential problem of modern democracy, the answer to which was rooted in the eighteenth century; as Smith put it, 'the Enlightenment belonged nowhere if not at the very center of modern history. Getting it right was [...] crucial.'[25]

Cassirer and Rousseau: gateways to 'the Enlightenment'

Gay arrived at Columbia to study political theory in 1949 and found in Neumann his intellectual mentor. Neumann provided Gay bibliographic and theoretical insights which informed his interest in the history of social democracy, first in England and then in Germany. Following the completion of his doctorate, Gay became an instructor in government and attended the faculty Seminar on the State. Here he encountered the questions and problems which set the context for his entry into the field of the Enlightenment. In 1952, Gay had just completed his first book on Bernstein and German social democracy and, concerned with his prospects in political science, was seeking a larger theme for his next research project. His stated interest was to explore the failure of social democracy to emerge in American politics. Neumann suggested he read one of Cassirer's last works written prior to the collapse of the Weimar Republic, on a topic which at first seemed far from his concerns – an essay on the political theory of Jean-Jacques Rousseau. 'It was Franz Neumann [...] who first called my attention to Cassirer's articles of 1932 on Rousseau, which I then translated.'[26] Gay's translation, with his own introduction, was published as *The Question of Jean-Jacques Rousseau* by Columbia University Press in 1954. The book appeared in a special series, edited by Jacques Barzun, celebrating the university's bicentennial with scholarly works intended for the general public which would highlight the importance of intellectual 'freedom'.[27]

25. Smith, 'Reluctant return', p.217.
26. Peter Gay, 'The social history of ideas: Ernst Cassirer and after', in *The Critical spirit: essays in honor of Herbert Marcuse*, ed. Kurt Wolff and Barrington Moore (Boston, MA, 1967), p.106-21 (116). Neumann had also referenced the Cassirer text (in German) in his 1948 'Montesquieu' essay (p.123, n.31), to support the point that 'civil society', and social hierarchy, must be considered in any theory of justice.
27. Ernst Cassirer, *The Question of Jean-Jacques Rousseau*, ed. and translated by Peter Gay (New York, 1954), the 'General editor's preface' at p.v-vi. The essay had first been delivered as a lecture in 1932 and then published the

The choice of this text and of the topic of Rousseau as political theorist is significant for multiple reasons to our consideration of what, in the context of the moment, the Enlightenment may have represented for Gay. Within the German intellectual tradition, Rousseau held a particular importance, from Sturm und Drang through to the Hegelian legacy, which in turn provided the foundation for most Anglophone writing on the Enlightenment up to the 1930s. In *Die Philosophie der Aufklärung* Cassirer had devoted less attention to Rousseau than other writers of the era, but, in the article which Gay translated, written after the larger work, Cassirer engaged more fully with Rousseau and presented the political writings as conveying more cogency than had most previous interpretations, in German or English. Cassirer's reading of Rousseau did resemble that of a contemporary work, Alfred Cobban's *Rousseau and the modern state*, and Neumann, while preparing his LSE thesis, had recognised this comparison (even if Cobban, in his first edition, had not). To underscore the point, Neumann draws on Cobban in defending Rousseau from the claim of being a 'state-absolutist', and he notes the interest of Cobban, among others, in the 'social and political factors as constitutive elements' of Rousseau's thought, which render 'extremely problematical [...] every idealistic interpretation of Rousseau [...] even that of Cassirer, which starts from the specific problematic of Kantian idealism'. Gay, in his own introduction to Cassirer, likewise praised Cobban as one of the few commentators, other than Cassirer, to read Rousseau as having written a coherent body of moral and political thought which sought to provide a basis for personal freedom.

That Gay's first foray into Enlightenment scholarship was inspired by reading Cassirer might not seem surprising, considering the standard reading of Gay's work as, to an extent, warmed-over Cassirer. However, Gay (following the direction indicated by Neumann in his thesis) took a quite different approach, adopted a quite different focus and reached quite different conclusions from Cassirer. In so doing, he initiated a new direction in post-war Anglophone Enlightenment scholarship.

---

same year as 'Das Problem Jean Jacques Rousseau', *Archiv für Geschichte der Philosophie* 41:2-3 (1932), p.117-213, 479-513, and in French as 'Le problème Jean-Jacques Rousseau', *Bulletin de la Société française de philosophie* 32:2 (June 1932), p.46-66. It has been republished more recently in an edition presented by Jean Starobinski: Ernst Cassirer, *Le Problème Jean-Jacques Rousseau*, translated by Marc B. de Launay (Paris, 2012).

Methodologically, Gay recalled in a 1988 reminiscence, he established his intention to find his own intellectual path from the outset of his work with Neumann, whom he described, affectionately, as a 'rigid, philosophical left-wing Marxist', but an 'intellectual democrat'. But Gay situated himself neither in the Idealist tradition associated with Cassirer nor in the positivist tradition then dominant in the department, under the influence of Paul Lazarsfeld. He recalled drawing inspiration from aspects of the 'German intellectual tradition' which could be synthesised with the approach of 'empirical, practical-minded Americans'. His interest was drawn to the work of those who sought to incorporate the social experience and social psychology of the author under study to the historical interpretation of that author's work, such as Neumann, Irwin Panofsky, Paul Tillich and Erich Auerbach – as well, of course, as Freud. Gay attributed this heteroclite set of intellectual influences to the guidance of Neumann; he also attributed to Neumann the legacy of an intellectual ethos, 'to bring to bear the legacy of European culture in American universities' – 'a most varied legacy' united primarily by the experience of all these authors of having become intellectual refugees from Nazism. Although Gay often downplayed the importance of his own exile experience, there is significant evidence he was influenced by other German émigré scholars in the early 1950s.[28]

With respect to Cassirer, Gay made clear his relationship in a 1967 essay in honour of Herbert Marcuse: 'Cassirer's work as a historian was a great achievement but a flawed one.' Indeed, Gay questioned Cassirer on precisely the point for which he himself would later be challenged, the claim of conceiving intellectual history as a field in which the goal is to demonstrate positive truths about the flow of ideas. Gay emphasised here that methods of interpretation, especially those imported from other disciplines, 'liberated' the historian to employ a 'creative function' or imagination, with 'method and delicacy'. He used, significantly, two examples to illustrate this claim, first 'the literature on Rousseau', citing his own translation of Cassirer, and, second, Marcuse's interpretation of Hegel's ideas of the state. Both examples for Gay demonstrated that an intellectual historian

---

28. Peter Gay, 'The German-Jewish legacy and I: some personal reflections', *The American Jewish Archives journal* 40:2 (1988), p.203-10 (209-10). See also Gay, *My German question*. On the particularly interesting case of Auerbach as a German immigrant intellectual, see Kadar Kanuck, *East-West mimesis: Auerbach in Turkey* (Palo Alto, CA, 2010).

could read the same texts quite differently from previous scholars, by attending to differences in context. Gay credited Cassirer with finding 'coherence […][,] a vital center, a core' in Rousseau's political writings by understanding different contexts in which he wrote at separate times. At the same time, Gay found Cassirer's 'rage for coherence' limiting, because it created interpretive discomfort with 'discordant desires and conflicting traditions' present in the same text, leading the historian to risk minimising tensions and reducing ambiguities. For Gay, however, the 'really serious difficulty in Cassirer's conception of intellectual history' is his 'failure to do justice to the social dimensions of ideas', since after all Cassirer himself wrote as a philosopher.[29]

To distinguish his own work from what he called Cassirer's 'unpolitical Idealism' in his 1967 essay on Cassirer, and to describe the 'varied legacy' on which he drew, Gay would come by the early 1960s to describe his approach as 'The social history of ideas'. From the beginning of his work as an intellectual historian, Gay considered himself interested in methodologies that would incorporate the methods of the social sciences, in particular psychology. In the early 1950s, he aligned himself with a particular variant of German intellectual historiography proposed by another German immigrant historian, Hajo Holborn, whom Gay had encountered in Neumann's seminar. Holborn had described it as 'German Idealism in a social history perspective'; Gay, when he described the method, in the 1960s, allied it, tellingly, with 'Freud's theories of human nature and growth'. Indeed, it is frequently overlooked that Gay, not Darnton, coined the very phrase 'Social history of ideas' as a third 'type of intellectual history', distinct from the work of both the 'historians of ideas' and the 'political sociologists of ideas', in the preface to his *Party of humanity*.[30]

Substantively, Gay took issue with one of Cassirer's main claims about the Enlightenment, that the *philosophes* lacked interest in political theory – and especially the issue of 'the state'. In his final book,

29. Gay, 'The social history of ideas', p.106-21.
30. Gay first used the term in two texts written in 1964, the prefaces to his *Party of humanity: essays in the French Enlightenment* (New York, 1964), p.ix-xii (x), and to the second edition of *Voltaire's politics: the poet as realist* (1959; New York, 1965), p.vi-ix (viii). He explained it as a method more fully in 'The social history of ideas'; Hajo Holborn, 'Der deutsche Idealismus in sozialgeschichtlicher Beleuchtung', *Historische Zeitschrift* 174 (1952), p.359-84. Holborn also published a series of essays, in English, on methodology, in the *Journal of the history of ideas* between 1948 and 1951, formative years for Gay in Neumann's seminar.

written in English and posthumously published, *The Myth of the state*, Cassirer included a chapter on 'The philosophy of the Enlightenment and its Romantic critics', which asserted that, despite expressing 'a keen interest in all political problems', the age of Enlightenment 'did not develop a new political philosophy'. For Cassirer, the great achievement of the era, of course, was Kant's *Critique of pure reason*, and he asserted here that significant advances in political thought beyond natural right came only in the next generation.[31] Gay, by contrast, entered into the field, starting in 1952, to pursue his primary interest in political theory; indeed, his focus in the introduction to *Question* engages immediately with Rousseau as a political thinker.[32]

This interest in questions of political theory and approach to the Enlightenment as a source for understanding the origins and meaning of the liberal state would inform the work Gay took up in the months and years following his translation of *Question*. In the 1953-1954 academic year, he wrote his first article on the Enlightenment for *Political science quarterly*, a review of recent scholarship on eighteenth-century constitutional and political theory, which assessed this work as demonstrating 'neglect, characterized by misconceptions' and concluded that 'unfamiliarity breeds contempt.' He identified two misleading tendencies in these interpretations, both of which he considered the result of ahistorical misuse of the Enlightenment – 'radicals [...] concerned with debunking Enlightenment theorists as bourgeois ideologists' to dismiss its significance, and 'so-called "new conservatives" [...] perpetuating clichés [...] to construct [their] conservative world view' in opposition to straw men. Gay defended Rousseau, drawing on Cassirer and Cobban (and, at least indirectly, on Neumann), from criticisms he considered irrational and illiberal; he defended Voltaire from claims he produced 'propaganda' for absolutist monarchy; and he defended Montesquieu (drawing here explicitly on Neumann) from charges of being naive in his advocacy for constitutional and political reform. Moreover, he ranged beyond political theory strictly speaking, to defend Enlightenment moral, social and epistemological discourse, by linking it to present concerns, both its philosophical scepticism and in social psychology; indeed, Gay explicitly suggested a goal of reconciling the Enlightenment to Freud, noting this topic 'deserves lengthier treatment'. The final section of

---

31. Ernst Cassirer, *The Myth of the state* (New Haven, CT, 1946), p.176-77.
32. Peter Gay, 'Introduction', in Cassirer, *The Question of Jean-Jacques Rousseau*, ed. P. Gay, p.3-32 (4).

the essay, tellingly entitled 'The Enlightenment and contemporary politics', called for further study of precisely those aspects of Enlightenment thought to have the most value for contemporary society, which he identified as 'the right to free thought and expression', 'diversity' and 'secular' values. Here he attached to the Enlightenment, for the first time, a moniker borrowed from Morley, the 'party of humanity'.[33] By the summer of 1955, which Gay spent researching in Oxford, he described his project in a letter to Theodore Besterman in Geneva, as a work on 'the political theory of the Enlightenment'.[34]

In January 1956, Gay participated in a colloquium sponsored by the American Council for Learned Societies, on 'The present-day relevance of eighteenth-century thought'. The opening session, devoted to 'The origins of the American state', included a lengthy open discussion on whether Enlightenment political theory retained relevance to contemporary constitutional and political culture. Gay is not recorded in the published proceedings as having intervened in this discussion, but, years later, he would present his own interpretation, as the conclusion to volume 2 of *The Enlightenment*. In preparing that chapter, Gay recalled that he took away from the 1956 colloquium an important insight, that the leading scholars of American constitutional history at that time assumed the 'uniqueness of American experience, that America grew in an ideological vacuum'. He recalled that he realised then, at his first academic conference on the subject, his personal perspective would be essential to his contribution to American culture; he must 'take [his] stand against the "uniqueness" interpretation'. His own interest in contemporary American political culture compelled him to demonstrate the limited nature of American eighteenth-century constitutional thought, restricted largely to 'natural right' theory, in contrast to a wider array of questions and issues being asked in Europe at the time, informed by 'utilitarianism'.[35]

Speaking at the colloquium on a different panel, devoted to 'Theories of man', Gay defended Enlightenment thought from criticisms of it as naively believing in a linear progression through history and

33. Peter Gay, 'The Enlightenment in the history of political theory', *Political science quarterly* 69:3 (September 1954), p.374-89 (375).

34. Geneva, Institut et Musée Voltaire archives (henceforth IMV), Fonds Besterman, Dossier Gay, 1955-1967, MS TB 8530 (Gay's letter to Besterman, 16 August 1955).

35. New York, Columbia University Archives (henceforth CUA), Series IV, 18th Century Seminar papers, #0118, 18 January 1967. Gay spoke to the seminar on this occasion on the topic of 'European and American Enlightenments'.

suggested the much more nuanced writings on historical progress were 'by no means irrelevant today'. His formal presentation, 'Light on the Enlightenment', distinguished the 'heritage' of the Enlightenment, which he suggested had been 'grossly misunderstood', from 'the century itself'. Here again he explicitly linked Voltaire, Diderot and Rousseau to Freud, to suggest the specific critical spirit of Enlightenment rationalism to have been 'sophisticated rather than naive' and the much-noted 'optimism' of eighteenth-century rationalist thought to have been 'tempered by a realistic appreciation' of the inertial impact of culture and tradition. The particular 'light' Gay proposed to have come from the Enlightenment was in social science, the origins of 'present-day psychology, sociology [...] legal procedure, theories of punishment, of democratic theory and practice'. In the ensuing discussion he noted his goal to be 'not just to describe' but to 'understand' the values of the Enlightenment; 'the world is quite full of textbooks that are quite wrong' on this point.[36] He had clearly set his sights on writing a new history of the Enlightenment, broader in perspective and in method than what had been produced to that point.

The intellectual politics of Peter Gay's approach to 'the Enlightenment'

Between 1952 and 1956, as the Enlightenment thus became Gay's primary research topic, he remained actively engaged as a scholar and teacher in political thought and became actively engaged as a citizen in contemporary American affairs. With a group of Columbia colleagues, including the historian Richard Hofstadter, he advocated in 1952 on behalf of Adlai Stephenson's presidential campaign, and, with Hofstadter, organised a counter-petition in *The New York Times* against the Columbia administration's evident support for Stephenson's opponent and Columbia's president, Dwight Eisenhower. For Gay and Hofstadter, the election of Eisenhower foreclosed the prospect of any social democratic movement in the USA, and, moreover, raised concerns that it would empower the growing authoritarianism represented by McCarthy.[37]

36. Peter Gay, 'Light on the Enlightenment', in *The Present-day relevance of eighteenth-century thought*, ed. Roger McCutcheon (Washington, DC, 1956), p.41-52 (41-43, 51-52).
37. CUA, Peter Gay papers 1954-2003, box 11, f.7, undated. Another manuscript for this period outlined a lecture on 'The prospects for social democracy', from

Gay also participated actively in academic circles, at Columbia and more broadly, which were concerned with what they considered an intellectually shallow tendency to accept American democratic culture as free from ideology and history.[38] Hofstadter, in this moment, began his first work on American anti-intellectualism, which he first considered in the context of Tocqueville's theories of the civic tradition of American democracy; in April 1953, Hofstadter delivered a lecture at the University of Michigan, 'Democracy and anti-intellectualism in America'.[39] Gay provided comment to Hofstadter on these early ideas; while criticising Hofstadter's application of social psychology, he agreed that 'anti-intellectualism' must be addressed as a problem in American culture, including among intellectuals themselves.[40] Gay, for his part, wrote in the spring of 1954 a letter to the editor of *The American scholar*, supporting the critique made by the sociologist David Riseman of fellow American intellectuals on multiple fronts. Supporting Riseman's call for a balance of 'loyalty and freedom', Gay criticised liberal intellectuals who, he believed, used anti-Stalinism to justify a lapidary response to McCarthy; he criticised the pessimism and sentimentalism of those on the left for their 'gloomy anti-McCarthyite' sentiments, borne of 'intellectual conformism'; and, thirdly, he criticised the 'apologetic conservatism' of right-leaning intellectuals for buying into a 'conspiracy theory of history'.[41] He also drafted, in 1953 or 1954, and perhaps in response to Eisenhower's first State of the Union address, a lengthy essay, 'On American irresponsibility'. Citing a range of historical and sociological works, Gay laid out what he considered the underlying reasons for the shortcomings he perceived in contemporary American

---

1848 to the present. See also the discussion of his conversations in this period with Hofstadter, described in David Brown, *Richard Hofstadter: an intellectual biography* (Chicago, IL, 2007), p.84 and *passim*.

38. See Brown, *Hofstadter*, p.87-88, 165-66. See also Leeman, 'Transatlantic Enlightenment', p.91-109: based on interviews with Gay conducted in 2009, Leeman positions him among the so-called 'West Side *kibbutz*' of left-leaning German émigré intellectuals and the overlapping 'Columbia School' of émigré academics, who distinguished themselves from the better-known 'New York Intellectuals' in their belief in the importance of social scientific and historical research on American culture and society, informed by the German intellectual heritage and methodologies.

39. *Michigan alumnus quarterly review* 59:21 (August 1953), p.281-95.

40. Brown, *Hofstadter*, p.110-30.

41. Gay's letter to the editor, in Peter Gay *et al.*, 'More about freedom and loyalty', *American scholar* 23:3 (summer 1954), p.376-78 (377-78).

political and intellectual culture, including the rightward turn in post-war US social and foreign policy, in the 'antics' of McCarthy and Cohn, in the anti-immigrant sentiment reflected in the passage of the 1952 McCarran–Walter Act and in the naivety of left-leaning intellectuals about the Soviet Union. Gay shared the essay with Hofstadter, who provided handwritten comments; however, it was apparently set aside and never published.[42]

As he pursued these questions of contemporary political affairs, Gay made his pivot definitively into the Enlightenment. Although the years 1953 to 1956 clearly constituted an inflection point for Gay, personally and professionally, his intellectual trajectory into the Enlightenment should be seen as a continuity in his intellectual concerns, more than a break. Years later, in personal correspondence, he would acknowledge, 'The jump was not so great as it might seem.'[43] What occurred in 1954 to 1956 was a series of circumstances that offered him an opportunity to pursue his concerns in a new context. In the summer of 1954, Neumann died tragically in an automobile accident in Switzerland; in January 1955, Gay's own father passed away prematurely. In that same year, the Department of History recruited him into a tenured academic position, but, before he began at the Department of History, he spent an academic year at Princeton on a fellowship from the Council of the Humanities. There he entered in close contact with two scholars deeply immersed in the intellectual history of eighteenth-century France – and whose scholarly precision appealed to him as an alternative to the heady world of German émigré intellectuals – Robert R. Palmer and Ira O. Wade.

In the course of his year at Princeton, he began work on what he hoped would be an original study on the political theory of the Enlightenment; however, by his own admission, he embarked without much of a clear sense of the topic or sources he would explore. During that year, Gay read Becker for the first time – and took significant issue with him. A critique of Becker provided Gay with a vector to link his concerns with conservatism in American culture to his

---

42. CUA, Peter Gay papers 1954-2003, box 6, f.2, 'American irresponsibility' (undated). Affixed to the typescript is a newspaper clipping of Eisenhower's remarks at a 1954 press conference. This same theme of political 'irresponsibility' informed another, undated, manuscript of Gay's lecture notes, entitled 'Anti-intellectualism'.

43. CUA, Peter Gay papers 1954-2003, box 6, f.1. Quoted as well in Leeman, 'Transatlantic Enlightenment', p.121.

concerns with the reduced state of the Enlightenment in American historiography.

Gay intended not only to revisit Becker's interpretation but to revise and replace it with a more sympathetic portrayal, framed in the context of questions about morality and political theory; he also intended the new version to be more relevant to the contemporary concerns of his time, focused on religious tolerance, secularism, intellectual freedom and political reformism. He first delivered his criticism at a conference held in 1956 at Colgate University, organised by Becker's former students, to commemorate the twenty-fifth anniversary of *Heavenly city*; he then published a more fully developed version in *Political science quarterly* in 1957 (before the publication of the conference proceedings).[44]

***

Another important aspect of Gay's evolution into a historian of the Enlightenment was his first engagement, during his research leave at Princeton, with primary source materials outside of the contemporary civilisation curriculum. He encountered a then-obscure Voltaire text, the anonymously published political pamphlet *Idées républicaines*; this text drew Gay's interest for its argument against the political influence of the Calvinist clergy in Geneva. His first insight, however, was contextual; by reading it against other pamphlets, he concluded that previous scholars had misdated the drafting to 1762 and as a result misapprehended the intent and meaning of the text in the context of Genevan politics. Gay, seeking to stake a claim in the field, sent a sixty-page manuscript to Besterman for his newly established annual, *Travaux sur Voltaire et le dix-huitième siècle*.[45]

Gay, evidently unaware of the large collection of microfilmed reproductions of Voltaire correspondence at the American Philosophical

---

44. Gay, 'Carl Becker's *Heavenly city*'. The conference version is in *Carl Becker's Heavenly city revisited*, ed. Raymond Rockwood (Ithaca, NY, 1958), p.27-51.
45. Geneva, IMV, Fonds Besterman, Dossier Gay, MS TB 8532 (Gay's letter to Besterman, 14 January 1957). The essay was published as Peter Gay, 'Voltaire's "Idées républicaines": a study in bibliography and interpretation', *SVEC* 6 (1958), p.69-108; an excerpt also appears as an appendix to *Voltaire's politics: the poet as realist* (Princeton, NJ, 1959), p.346-51. The critical edition, edited by John Renwick, adopts Gay's dating of the work to 1765; see Voltaire, *Œuvres de 1764-1766*, ed. Marie-Hélène Cotoni *et al.*, in *Œuvres complètes de Voltaire*, vol.60B (Oxford, 2018), p.105-69.

Library in Philadelphia, enquired of Besterman about the anticipated progress of the edition of Voltaire's *Correspondence*, of which the first volumes had appeared in 1954. Gay hoped to draw upon what he now represented as a study of 'Voltaire's political ideas'. In response, Besterman sent him transcriptions of letters related to the Genevan 'revolution', which Gay used to develop his analysis and argument in what became *Voltaire's politics*. Besterman, although known for his cantankerous relations with other academics, welcomed Gay's interest and invited Gay to visit Les Délices, which he did in July 1958 – and, in 1961, Gay was among the first whom Besterman invited to the International Congress on the Enlightenment.[46] The former had been for over ten years actively cultivating academic allies in the United States; he seems to have perceived in the latter a kindred spirit. The men shared an experience of having emigrated as assimilated, secular young men of Jewish heritage to Anglophone cultures; they also shared a penchant for building socio-professional networks into formal organisations; and both retained a self-conscious sense of being outsiders to major academic institutions. This relationship, on which much more could be written from available documentation, would in the 1960s have significant influence on the organisation of eighteenth-century studies.

Thus, by the late 1950s, Gay had not only found his topic and his argument; he had also found his ambition as a historian. He began to contemplate a much broader, more comprehensive interpretation of the Enlightenment, which would transcend the evident limitations of approaches he perceived to be dominant – both the philosophical readings of canonical texts, which he associated with political theorists such as Laski (rather than Cassirer), and the textual and manuscript-focused work associated with Wade.

His inclination as a scholar, significantly, remained closely aligned with the collaborative, interdisciplinary and applied approach Neumann had modelled in the Seminar on the State and which characterised other German immigrant schools, including the influential school of medievalists and Renaissance scholars around Aby Warburg at Princeton. As he began to work out the scope and form of his major work on the Enlightenment, and now established in his own right at Columbia, Gay sought to engage his work with the extant scholarly literature by rewriting the 'heavenly city' and to

46. Geneva, IMV, Fonds Besterman, Dossier Gay, MS TB 8542 (Gay's letter to Besterman, 8 October 1957) and MS TB 8557 (Gay's letter to Besterman, 30 October 1961).

revise the established corpus of readings in the Columbia contemporary civilisation curriculum. He also sought to engage with the methods raised by innovative literary scholarship and by the social sciences.

In 1962, Gay – now promoted to professor at Columbia – and his English department colleague James Clifford convinced the Columbia administration to support a new Columbia faculty seminar, under the name 'Eighteenth-century European culture'.[47] Gay intended this nomenclature to emphasise the breadth of topics and the interdisciplinary approaches which he sought to bring together. In an undated manuscript from the early 1960s, he made clear that 'The Enlightenment and the 18th century were not synonymous', and distinguished between 'The Enlightenment of the *Philosophes* and the larger atmosphere'. The context of 'the eighteenth century' offered support for the progressive tendencies of the *philosophes* and also served as 'a tension with their time'. Of the former, he highlighted 'the Scientific Revolution, medical progress, advances in food production, transportation, technology, the arts of government', and of the latter he noted in particular 'religious questions'.[48]

At the seminar's first substantive meeting, on 28 November 1962, Gay presented a four-page outline of the work he was undertaking – on 'The Enlightenment', which the group would discuss directly for the first two meetings and periodically over the next several years. Even during his year of leave spent at Stanford in 1965-1966, Gay closely oversaw the schedule and the participants; he eagerly sought out, and became frustrated by his inability to attract, colleagues not only from the various humanities departments, but also from political science, economics, psychology and law. He also, from the beginning, drew upon the body of thought he had encountered with Neumann; the argument and structure of the study, from its first version, were constructed on a historical dialectic, a thesis of pre-Christian paganism, and an antithesis of medieval science, to produce the synthesis of the 'science of freedom'.[49]

47. Elizabeth Powers, 'Critiquing the Enlightenment: *The Seminar on eighteenth-century European culture (#417)*', in *A Community of scholars: seventy-five years of the University seminars at Columbia*, ed. Thomas Vinciguerra (New York, 2020), p.16-29.
48. CUA, Peter Gay papers 1954-2003, box 11, f.1, document 6: 'Progress in the Enlightenment' (undated manuscript), p.2.
49. CUA, Series IV, #0118, 28 November 1962, p.2.

Also evident from the beginning was an interest in another synthesis, which he had first encountered in Neumann's seminar, that of social materialist analysis (though Gay had rejected Neumann's Marxism) and of social psychology, drawn of course from Freud. In that initial outline of 'The Enlightenment', twenty-five years before he would set out Freud as the culmination of the bourgeois culture of the nineteenth century, Gay built out the implications of his interest in applying Freud to the intellectual historical method, first raised in his essay on Cassirer and Rousseau. The outline presented, in explicitly Freudian terms, the conclusion which 'The Enlightenment' would reach. Gay proposed that the story of the Enlightenment should culminate in neither Kant nor the French Revolution, but rather in a specific form of personal freedom and psychological self-regulation, the 'domestication of pleasure [and] growth of the collective superego'. 'The goal of the Enlightenment', as he proposed it here, was to create humanity's 'genital personality'.[50] In 1964, he would describe the narrative of 'The Enlightenment' as the story of a 'psychological progression [... on the part of the *philosophes*], using antiquity to battle their way out of Christianity'.[51] For Gay, this was clearly not an Idealist history; it would be a psycho-social and dialectical story of the Enlightenment, a story of its subjects' own self-awareness and of their inner conflict with the dominant culture of their era.

Conclusion: the continuing relevance of Gay's Enlightenment in American intellectual culture

By 1969, Gay (after several years of entertaining outside offers) decided to leave Columbia – and, with his project finished, to leave the Enlightenment. In May of that year, he presented a final paper to the seminar, addressing 'Some unfinished business in eighteenth-century studies'.

He also remained actively engaged, through Clifford and Besterman, in the formation of ASECS in 1969, following the creation of an International Society in 1967. Gay's contributions included the idea of an organisation that would truly be 'interdisciplinary', not only in structure but also in spirit. To Gay, interdisciplinary meant

---

50. CUA, Series IV, #0118, 28 November 1962, p.4.
51. CUA, Series IV, #0118, 18 November 1964.

involving not only literary scholars and historians but also social scientists, and an intellectual agenda actively engaged with contemporary philosophical and political issues. Gay also contributed, with Donald Greene, the moniker 'eighteenth-century studies'; in 1967, he had already prevailed upon Besterman to bestow the International Society with this name, to ensure the object of study would be the broader context and would include social and political developments, not merely textual analysis of 'the Enlightenment'.[52]

***

In 1996, more than twenty-five years after he had last published on the topic, Gay delivered a lecture in a series called 'Human values', entitled 'The living Enlightenment'. He began by restating the central thesis of his interpretation, the Enlightenment as a 'secular revolution' in thought, and distinguished his interpretation from those which viewed it through the prism of the excesses of the French Revolution. He paid homage to Cassirer, and then proceeded to a defence of the '*philosophes*' from those 'who write obituaries for the Enlightenment'. He attributed these critical readings, much as he had in his 1950s articles, to two different traditions: conservatives defending 'dogmatism' and 'piety', and those who consider the Enlightenment legacy to be a naive 'political monomania'. Here, unlike in his earlier writings, he responded directly to the totalitarian critique of the post-war years. He described Horkheimer and Adorno in terms similar to his critique of Becker, as 'brilliant, aphoristic and [...] perverse'; 'The *Dialektik der Aufklärung*', he continued, 'with its dazzling acrobatics, is wholly innocent of empirical material to support its conclusions.' Talmon, for Gay, offered a more substantive engagement with the sources but chose them selectively, to support a 'tendentious' interpretation, one 'tone deaf' to context.

Gay then turned his fire on the critics who considered the Enlightenment to be inattentive to the importance of values and belief, ranging from the 'conservative' Michael Oakshott to the 'pragmatist' Richard Rorty to the 'post-modernist' Jean-François Lyotard. Gay restated his central claim, which he had first laid out in the mid-1950s, that the Enlightenment could be defined, and admired, as a theory about human nature, sufficiently nuanced to provide 'a practicable

52. Gay to Besterman, March 1967, Oxford, Voltaire Foundation, Besterman Collection, carton 12, dossier 1; CUA, Series IV, #0118, 13 February 1969.

basis for politics', in its own time – and for ours, over two centuries later. Gay, however, warned against a superficial adoption of the Enlightenment as a platform for the eve of the third millennium; 'we have learned', he stated, referring to survey data demonstrating the widespread and growing belief in contemporary American culture, as of 1996, in claims not supported by evidence or consistent with rational analysis, 'that secular superstitions can be as deadly as the most fervent sectarian faith'.

He did not believe, by any stretch of the imagination, that the 'party of humanity' had carried the day. He remained 'optimistic' that it could provide an opportunity for further thought within contemporary intellectual debate. For Gay, the living Enlightenment that he had done so much to invent in the post-war moment, remained – and remains – a basis for engaged humanistic scholarship, an opportunity for thinkers in the here and now to engage with our own contemporary cultural and political concerns. 'The Enlightenment remains', he concluded, 'an invitation' to adopt the 'intellectual stance of choice'.[53]

53. Peter Gay, 'The living Enlightenment', https://tannerlectures.utah.edu/_resources/documents/a-to-z/g/Gay98.pdf (last accessed 27 April 2023).

'Die Zeit der Aufklärung ist wieder da': activist appropriations of the Enlightenment in the Hegelian Left and in eighteenth-century studies in the GDR

Daniel Fulda

Martin-Luther-Universität Halle-Wittenberg

Translated by Gita Rajan

What are 'activist appropriations of the Enlightenment'?

Semantically, an activist conception of the Enlightenment focuses on its programme of criticism leading to reform, a founding principle of the concept of the historical Enlightenment since it emerged as a force around 1700. In German the word *Aufklärung* implies a dynamic process of advances in both knowledge and moral lifestyle. By contrast, the *pragmatics* of activism highlights the role of protagonists who typically regard themselves as champions of Enlightenment, resolved to realise the Enlightenment project by practical means, be it through writing, or political actions and public campaigning. This innate desire to have an impact derives from a view of one's own time as being not only particularly in need of Enlightenment, but also capable of progressive reform.

For the activist the Enlightenment project is the order of the day, so to speak, which takes precedence over everything else. One might argue that this is an all-too-common approach, with its belief that Enlightenment will eventually bring about a change for the better. However, there is also a second, more flexible variant that allows such change to be imagined without needing overt personal commitment and, to that extent, it represents a more passive stance reflecting the original meteorological meaning of *Aufklärung*: 'the clouds are dispelled, the sky becomes clear.'[1] A third variant, an anti-activist stance that stems from opposition or scepticism, sometimes even sympathy, has not lost its relevance either. This variant rejects Enlightenment activism altogether, aware of the risk it carries of becoming ideological. Reinhart Koselleck delivers an example of this last stance in both *Kritik und Krise* (*Critique and crisis*, originally published in 1959, translated in 1988) and his studies on the history of concepts in *Sattelzeit*.

Enlightenment activism along the continuum characterised above can be observed not only among a number of thinkers and actors of the eighteenth century, but also in later generations who saw parallels with their own struggles, invoked the historical idea of Enlightenment and claimed the mantle of responsibility for carrying the project forward. This tendency prevailed even in some areas of Enlightenment studies, although such activism risked blurring the boundaries between the scholar's commitment to objectivity and the outcome desired by a partisan champion. In what follows, I will present examples of these three activist approaches to Enlightenment.

Nicolaus Hieronymus Gundling, jurist, philosopher and historian at the University of Halle, represents the historical Enlightenment (see below, p.287). Arnold Ruge and other Hegelians on the left wing of the political spectrum belong to a later generation who revisited the questions and contentions of the historical Enlightenment and took upon themselves the mission to see it through to fruition (p.289). Finally, the Enlightenment research pursued in the German Democratic Republic (GDR) is an example of scholarly work that was never entirely devoid of political activism pursued in the service of the socialist state and the Communist Party (p.293), sometimes even becoming involved in undercover operations on behalf of the *Staatssicherheitsdienst* (commonly known as the Stasi), the GDR's infamous state security service (p.298).

How the study of the Enlightenment came to be forged and fashioned in the GDR will be analysed in greater detail because it is

---

1.   Kaspar von Stieler, *Der Deutschen Sprache Stammbaum und Fortwachs, oder Teutscher Sprachschatz* (Nuremberg, Hofmann, 1691), col.968-69: 'nubes dissipantur, cœlum fit serenum. [...] Aufklärung'. All translations are my own unless otherwise indicated. On the emergence of the term 'enlightenment', referring not to weather events but to cognitive activities, see Daniel Fulda, 'Identity in diversity: programmatic pictures of the Enlightenment', *Journal for eighteenth-century studies* 45:1 (2022), p.43-62 (51).

closest to us in at least two respects: *temporally*, as very recent history, and *conceptually*, as it is an academic approach to the Enlightenment like our own. That said, the three stages analysed here show a pattern of steady intensification: from the pre-March period (i.e. preceding the March 1848 Revolution in the German Confederation) to the post-World War II era, Enlightenment activism increasingly took on the appearance of an ideology, with the activism of the GDR Enlightenment scholars proving to be the most outspoken.

Gundling 1715

One of the earliest exhibits of an Enlightenment programme are the frontispiece and preface to *Gundlingiana*, Gundling's essay collection that appeared in forty-five volumes from 1715 onwards. The frontispiece exemplifies what *Aufklärung* primarily signified around 1700, namely, the clearing up or brightening of the sky, especially as the sun breaks through the clouds (Figure 6).

In regard to the categorical proclamation '*dispellam*', which sets a combative tone, the preface offers this explanation: 'The truth is a light that enlightens everyone: it dispels all darkness: its motto, as I have had it set on the title page, is therefore "*dispellam*".'[2] The anthropomorphising figure of the sun that inherently wields the power to disperse the clouds suggests that, for Gundling, the acuity of his mind represented a critical force for advancing the Enlightenment project.

As described in the preface, he sees himself partaking of and operating in a historical movement that begins with Grotius and Pufendorf, and in time attracts 'many other brave men'. Although in that process 'the world' has become 'wiser to some extent', the caveat, '[t]he dark clouds of error cannot be dissipated all at once',[3] suggests that, in terms of both its duration and its scope, Gundling understands the Enlightenment as a process of historic proportions set into motion by *actions* of brave champions and not through merely waiting. Such

2. [Nicolaus Hieronymus Gundling], *Gundlingiana, darinnen allerhand zur Jurisprudentz, Philosophie, Historie, Critic, Litteratur und übrigen Gelehrsamkeit gehörige Sachen abgehandelt werden*, vol.1 (Halle, Rengerische Buchhandlung, 1715), 'Vorrede', non paginated [p.)(4r]: 'Dann die Wahrheit ist ein Licht, welches alle erleuchtet: Sie vertreibet alle Finsternüß: Ihre Devise, wie ich auf das Titelblat setzen lassen, ist deßhalb *dispellam*.'
3. [Gundling], *Gundlingiana*, 'Vorrede', [p.)(4v]: 'Die Welt ist in einigen Stücken schon klüger als vor 100. Jahren. Die trübe Irrthums-Wolcken werden nicht auf einmahl zertheilet.'

Figure 6: Title page of [Nicolaus Hieronymus Gundling],
*Gundlingiana, darinnen allerhand zur Jurisprudentz, Philosophie,
Historie, Critic, Litteratur und übrigen Gelehrsamkeit gehörige Sachen
abgehandelt werden*, vol.1-45 (Halle, Rengerische Buchhandlung,
1715-1732), vol.1. Source: Universitäts- und Landesbibliothek
Sachsen-Anhalt, Halle (Saale).

activism, however, demands not only a high degree of self-assurance but also a combative attitude towards adversaries, at least verbally, through proclamations asserting that irrational attitudes like pedantry or superstition that oppose the truth should 'finally be beaten down and kicked to the ground'.[4] Gundling intensifies his attacks on the personal 'enemies' of those championing the Enlightenment when he claims that the former will have 'died of the poisonous ulcer of their envy and taken their boils with them'.[5]

Arnold Ruge and the Hegelian Left in the 1840s

From the very start, one strand of Enlightenment thought was thus avowedly activist. Its force is palpable again 125 years later, when the Enlightenment is powerfully invoked in Germany's pre-March 1848 era, the *Vormärz*, marking the beginning of a new phase in the history of the reception of the Enlightenment in Germany. Opponents of the Restoration sought to recover a positive view of the Enlightenment, after it had been challenged by the Romantics and religious conservatives as well as by Hegel. For the first time the Enlightenment is understood as a historical forerunner of one's own efforts: on the one hand, it is historicised, on the other, it is presented as excitingly groundbreaking and topical.

A sympathetic invocation of the Enlightenment in the *Vormärz* can already be found in Friedrich Christoph Schlosser's *Geschichte des achtzehnten Jahrhunderts und des neunzehnten bis zum Sturz des französischen Kaiserreichs*, published in seven thick volumes between 1836 and 1848, particularly in the sections on the literary history of the late seventeenth and eighteenth centuries.[6] It is worth mentioning that Schlosser's extremely popular work was quickly translated into

---

4. [Gundling], *Gundlingiana*, 'Vorrede', [p.)(4r]: 'Die Pedanterey, der Aberglaube [...] muß doch endlich unten liegen, und zu Boden getretten werden.'
5. [Gundling], *Gundlingiana*, 'Vorrede', [p.)(4r]: 'Feinde [...] an dem gifftigen Geschwür ihres Neides gestorben, und ihre Eiterbeulen mit sich genommen'.
6. See Friedrich Christoph Schlosser, *Geschichte des achtzehnten Jahrhunderts und des neunzehnten bis zum Sturz des französischen Kaiserreichs: mit besonderer Rücksicht auf geistige Bildung*, vol.1 (Heidelberg, 1836), p.3, 22, 388, 571-72, 578-79, 640. In the first volume, the authors from whose works Schlosser derives his concept of Enlightenment are: Christian Thomasius, Johann Christoph Gottsched, Voltaire, Ewald von Kleist, Karl Wilhelm Ramler, Gotthold Ephraim Lessing and Johann Wilhelm Ludwig Gleim. In the ensuing volumes, the frequency with which 'Enlightenment' is mentioned increases.

English.[7] Scholars of the history of ideas have notably overlooked the fact that, in this text, 'enlightenment' appears many dozens of times as a translation of *Aufklärung*, albeit in lower case and mainly as a noun without an article.[8] By contrast, the term *Aufklärung* is not mentioned in the shorter preliminary version of Schlosser's book, published as early as 1823.[9] As a moderate liberal who was critical of the French *philosophes*, Schlosser saw himself as an adherent of the Enlightenment, insofar as it was not atheistically radicalised. Schlosser's understanding of the Enlightenment cannot be called activist, for this Heidelberg historian saw himself as educator of a bourgeoisie defined primarily by its moral standards, not by its political activism.[10]

Compared with that, the self-image of Arnold Ruge is shaped by a much stronger identification with the – generally so apostrophised – Enlightenment, and by an activist will to push ahead with the Enlightenment project. In a letter to Moritz Fleischer, a contributor to the *Rheinische Zeitung*, which famously also published Karl Marx's journalistic writings, Ruge cheered: 'The time of Enlightenment is here again.'[11] A few months later, Ruge, in a letter to Adolf Stahr, his coeditor for the Hegelian Left's most important journal, *Hallische Jahrbücher* (*Halle yearbooks*), again put the spotlight on the present time: 'Our time is the most foundational period of Enlightenment to have ever existed, rendering it necessary that we write like Voltaire and

---

7.   See F[riedrich] C[hristoph] Schlosser, *History of the eighteenth century and of the nineteenth till the overthrow of the French Empire: with particular reference to mental cultivation and progress*, translated, with a preface and notes, by D[avid] Davison, vol.1-8 (London, 1843-1852).

8.   The extent to which translations from German contributed to the coinage and popularisation of the noun 'enlightenment' in English has already been examined by James Schmidt: 'Inventing the Enlightenment: anti-Jacobins, British Hegelians, and the *Oxford English dictionary*', *Journal of the history of ideas* 64:3 (July 2003), p.421-43. The Schlosser translation, however, predates the Hegel translations examined by Schmidt.

9.   See Friedrich Christoph Schlosser, *Geschichte des achtzehnten Jahrhunderts in gedrängter Uebersicht: mit steter Beziehung auf die völlige Veränderung der Denk- und Regierungsweise am Ende desselben*, 2 vols (Heidelberg, 1823), vol.1, p.273.

10. See Michael Gottlob, *Geschichtsschreibung zwischen Aufklärung und Historismus: Johannes von Müller und Friedrich Christoph Schlosser* (Frankfurt am Main, 1989), p.213-15.

11. Arnold Ruge's letter to Moritz Fleischer (23 February 1841), in *Der Redaktionsbriefwechsel der Hallischen, Deutschen und Deutsch-Französischen Jahrbücher*, ed. Martin Hundt, 3 vols (Berlin, 2010), vol.1, p.688: 'Die Zeit der Aufklärung ist wieder da.'

Rousseau.' Ruge justifies this emphatic view of his own time by citing the political developments in 'all of Europe' as indicative that the 'correct interpretation of Hegel's philosophy' had finally been afforded by the Hegelian Left and the critics of the Christian faith, namely David Friedrich Strauss, Ludwig Feuerbach and Bruno Bauer.[12] In a letter written a little later, he also refers to Marx.[13] But in his view the reactionary forces had also gained momentum: 'The police are getting nasty and the opposition is already there.' Nevertheless, Ruge is convinced that he is on the right side of a historical trend that must and will prevail: 'The progress is incredibly robust.' To ride that wave as a writer, however, one would have to write along the lines of 'Rousseau and Sieyès', who were champions of the Revolution of 1789: 'These men write swords and daggers; they are more powerful than cannons and bayonets.'[14]

A more elaborate justification for the parallel between the pre-1789 and the post-revolutionary period is rendered in a review of Schlosser's *Geschichte des achtzehnten Jahrhunderts* in Ruge's journal, now renamed because of censorship *Deutsche Jahrbücher für Wissenschaft und Kunst* (*German yearbooks for scholarship and the arts*). At the dawn of the Enlightenment, it went, the true light finally shone into the world: 'Just as Christ was born during the reign of Augustus, so too was the Enlightenment during the time of the modern Augustus, Louis XIV, in order to send out its apostles all over the world under the reign of his successors. It is nothing but philosophy itself, but in a folksy, popular way, espousing people's consciousness, even world consciousness.'[15]

---

12. Ruge's letter to Adolf Stahr (7 November 1841), in *Der Redaktionsbriefwechsel*, vol.2, p.864: 'Unsre Zeit ist die fundamentalste Aufklärungsperiode, die es je gegeben hat, und es wird nöthig, wie Voltaire und Rousseau zu schreiben.'
13. See Ruge's letter to Robert Prutz (9 January 1842), in *Der Redaktionsbriefwechsel*, vol.2, p.931.
14. Ruge's letter to Adolf Stahr (7 November 1841), in *Der Redaktionsbriefwechsel*, vol.2, p.864: 'Die Polizei wird eklig, und die Opposition ist es schon geworden'; 'Die Entwicklung ist riesenstark'; 'Die Kerle schreiben Schwerter und Dolche, sie sind mächtiger als Kanonen und Bajonette.'
15. [Karl Friedrich Köppen], '[Review of] *Geschichte des 18. Jahrhunderts und des 19. bis zum Sturz des französischen Kaiserthums [Kaiserreichs]: von F. C. Schlosser*', *Deutsche Jahrbücher für Wissenschaft und Kunst* 5:2-6 (1841), p.5-7, 9-12, 13-14, 17-20, 21-23 (18): 'Wie zur Zeit des Augustus Christus geboren wurde, so zur Zeit des modernen Augustus, Ludwig's XIV., die Aufklärung, um unter seinen Nachfolgern Apostel auszusenden in alle Welt. Sie ist nichts Anderes, als die Philosophie selbst, aber als populäre, als volksthümliche, als Volksbewußtsein, ja als Weltbewusstsein.'

According to Ruge's interpretation of the Hegelian idea, only with the advent of the Enlightenment does humankind become conscious of what is necessary, both intellectually and historically. Just as important in the view of the Hegelian Left is the practical realisation of what is theoretically necessary: 'But it [Enlightenment] still has to be realised, because it is still confronted with the enduring presence of the old monarchy and the Church.'[16] The French Revolution was only the 'first [...] victory' of the Enlightenment, incomplete and of only limited impact, especially outside France.[17] For the 'eighteenth century', 'our interest' – as the reviewer explains in an address to his readers in 1841 – 'could not just be scholarly, historical, but also direct, practical', 'since we are still completely caught up in its struggle'.[18]

Based on my reflections, on the one hand, about Schlosser's *Geschichte* and, on the other, about Ruge and the Hegelian Left, it should be clear that Schlosser's *Geschichte*, although sympathetic to the Enlightenment, does not meet the standards of the anonymous reviewer of the *Jahrbücher*, who sees Schlosser as one of the 'old rationalists' 'whose time is, of course, over', for, although he 'substantially promoted the cause of reason, at least in Germany',[19] he lacked the 'real philosophical insight', or the consistency of insight, into the progress of history. In what follows, that sense of superiority will reemerge among those who believe, with ever more conviction, that they can demonstrate the necessary laws of history.

Much more could be said about the propensity of the pre-March 1848 radicals to parallel their own era with the previous century. Karl Friedrich Köppen, who wrote the Schlosser review,[20] dedicated an entire book to that parallel. On the face of it, the book is a eulogy

16. [Köppen], '[Review of] *Geschichte*', p.18: 'Noch aber hat sie [die Aufklärung] sich erst zu verwirklichen, denn noch steht ihr als Positives die alte Monarchie und die Kirche gegenüber.'

17. [Köppen], '[Review of] *Geschichte*', p.18: 'erster [....] Sieg'.

18. [Köppen], '[Review of] *Geschichte*', p.19: 'zum achtzehnten Jahrhundert [...], das nicht bloß ein wissenschaftliches, historisches, sondern ein unmittelbares, praktisches Interesse für uns hat, da wir noch selbst ganz und gar in dessen Kampf befangen sind'.

19. [Köppen], '[Review of] *Geschichte*', p.19: Schlosser 'gehört zu jenem muskelkräftigen Schlage der alten Rationalisten, [...] deren Zeit freilich vorüber ist, die aber die Sacher Vernunft, wenigstens in Deutschland, wesentlich gefördert haben'.

20. As Ruge notes in his letter to Robert Prutz (9 January 1842), in *Der Redaktionsbriefwechsel*, vol.2, p.931. Köppen was one of the most active contributors to the yearbooks.

for Frederick the Great in commemoration of the one hundredth anniversary of his accession to the throne in 1740. But packaged within Prussian patriotism is a resounding call to resume and realise the Enlightenment project, whose 'intrinsic purpose' the author considers 'a revolution', namely, to overthrow Christianity as well as the monarchical principle.[21] 'Aurora rises; piercing wind blowing; but gloomy night clouds still lingering on the waters. When will we see the sun?'[22] As this quote on the very first page of Köppen's book vividly demonstrates, the meteorological imagery originally accompanying the term *Aufklärung* was again taken up during the pre-March 1848 period.

In the tradition of the Hegelian Left: Enlightenment studies in the GDR

A good one hundred years later, most GDR Enlightenment scholars agreed with the stance of the Hegelian Left on the Enlightenment in many respects, including their call for its revitalisation. Also apparent is the reappearance of their sense of superiority over less radical contemporaries or predecessors, who were cast deprecatingly as 'mere' liberals. As before, the Enlightenment was conceived as both a historical epoch and a 'mission' one saw oneself called to fulfil during one's own time, and in that sense it was both an object of study and a guiding principle.[23] Thus, although rooted in the past, it had lost none of its topicality,[24] and continued to function as a signpost to the future.[25]

---

21. A passage from Köppen's Schlosser review that was abridged by the censors and that Ruge quotes in the same letter to Prutz (*Der Redaktionsbriefwechsel*, vol.2, p.931).

22. Carl Friedrich Köppen, *Friedrich der Grosse und seine Widersacher: eine Jubelschrift* (Leipzig, 1840), p.1: 'Morgenroth steigt herauf; scharfe Lüfte wehen; aber noch lagern düstre Nachtwolken auf den Gewässern. Wann werden wir die Sonne sehen?'

23. Winfried Schröder *et al.*, *Französische Aufklärung: bürgerliche Emanzipation, Literatur und Bewußtseinsbildung* (Leipzig, 1974), p.748 (author of this part: W. Schröder).

24. See Werner Bahner, 'Übergreifende und spezifische Aspekte der europäischen Aufklärung (unter besonderer Berücksichtigung der romanischen Länder)', in *Aufklärung als europäisches Phänomen: Überblick und Einzeldarstellungen* (Leipzig, 1985), p.5-110 (5).

25. See Schröder *et al.*, *Französische Aufklärung*, p.672, with a quote from [Köppen], '[Review of] *Geschichte*', p.5. That quote was also used by Bahner, 'Übergreifende und spezifische Aspekte der europäischen Aufklärung', p.7.

Nevertheless, this identification with the historical Enlightenment era was not entirely unqualified, either among the Hegelian Left of the 1840s, or among the Enlightenment scholars of the GDR. Both claimed to be superior and more advanced. The *Vormärz* radicals believed that they had benefited from the philosophical acuity of the Hegelian dialectic, in particular from a deeper insight into Hegel's understanding of historical necessity, an advantage the Enlightenment thinkers did not have. Scholars in the GDR shared this belief, but with an added reservation. Even as they recognised the foundational beginnings of materialistic thinking in the Enlightenment and among the Hegelian Left, they reserved their highest praise for Marx, for taking a decisive step towards a materialistic theory of history and society.[26]

The history of the reception of the Enlightenment thus includes a series of assertions that it has been superseded by a newer and more scientific world view. The Hegelian Left invoked the Enlightenment to claim a superior understanding of the world even as they accused the German Enlightenment in particular of having remained trapped in moralistic-idealistic reformism they themselves had overcome. A century later, the GDR Enlightenment scholars added their Marxist-Leninist critique to that, distancing themselves from the Hegelian Left. However, the most prominent GDR Enlightenment scholars occasionally departed from the logic of constant overcoming, when they interpreted and evaluated the humanistic ideas within Enlightenment philosophy and literature as more than 'superstructures' (*Überbau*), reflecting the concerns and interests of the rising bourgeois class. According to Werner Krauss, 'the benefit derived from the

---

26. See Schröder *et al.*, *Französische Aufklärung*, p.673, and the extensive criticism of the Hegelian Left in Werner Krauss, 'Karl Marx im Vormärz', in *Das wissenschaftliche Werk*, vol.1: *Literaturtheorie, Philosophie und Politik*, ed. Manfred Naumann (Berlin and Weimar, 1987), p.433-84, furthermore, with reference to Enlightenment, Werner Krauss, 'Die französische Aufklärung und die deutsche Geisteswelt', in *Das wissenschaftliche Werk*, vol.7: *Aufklärung III: Deutschland und Spanien*, ed. Martin Fontius, with a note from Renate Petermann and Peter-Volker Springborn (Berlin and New York, 1996), p.231-49 (233-38). There is also a French translation of this essay, 'L'ère française des Lumières et les intellectuels allemands', which appeared in the Communist-influenced Parisian magazine *La Pensée* 123 (October 1965), p.78-92. From a critical distance, see Horst Möller, 'Die Interpretation der Aufklärung in der marxistisch-leninistischen Geschichtsschreibung', *Zeitschrift für historische Forschung* 4 (1977), p.438-72 (441), on the propensity of GDR Enlightenment studies to refer to the Enlightenment, while also distancing itself from it.

powerful ideological superstructure of the Enlightenment created by the aspiring bourgeoisie exceeded not only the limited possibilities of their own time, but also the future reality of bourgeois society.'[27] Such departures from the Marxist interpretation of history, however, did not change the teleologisation towards socialism. Only socialism could realise the humanistic utopias of the historical Enlightenment. The high esteem in which the Enlightenment was held was a consequence of the central role it was assigned in the Marxist rendering of the historical process, but, as we can see, there were unhistorical 'jumps' into the eighteenth century, too.[28]

The biases and points of emphasis of the Hegelian Left can also be found at the core of the GDR's Enlightenment interpretation. Here as there, the French Enlightenment thinkers were greatly revered for having turned against the aristocrats, or the 'feudal' political order, displaying with their revolutionary consistency a form of activism that won acclaim for resorting to militancy[29] and engaging in a resolute criticism of religion, while the Germans came across as naive and tame in comparison. Accordingly, Romance studies became the leading discipline in GDR Enlightenment research. Another commonality is the sympathy for the French materialists, whom the Hegelian Left saw primarily as critics of religion and the GDR Marxists as the forerunners of their own brand of 'materialism'. In any case, both their normative contempt and their historiographic disregard for religion are characteristic of GDR scholarship on the Enlightenment. With religious belief cast per se as superstition, the world-historical task of the Enlightenment was to overcome it.

This attitude of celebrating but in part also reproaching the Enlightenment does not represent a contradiction for the Hegelian

27. Werner Krauss, 'Einführung in das Studium der französischen Aufklärung', in *Das wissenschaftliche Werk*, vol.6: *Aufklärung II: Frankreich*, ed. Werner Bahner *et al.* (Berlin and Weimar, 1987), p.5-20 (6): 'Der Vorsprung des von dem aufstrebenden Bürgertum geschaffenen machtvollen ideologischen Überbaus der Aufklärung ging nicht nur über die beschränkten Möglichkeiten der eigenen Zeit hinaus, sondern auch über die künftige Wirklichkeit der bürgerlichen Gesellschaft.'

28. For the 'suspension' of the basis-superstructure theory that was connected to it, see Möller, 'Die Interpretation der Aufklärung in der marxistisch-leninistischen Geschichtsschreibung', p.447-52.

29. Bahner, 'Übergreifende und spezifische Aspekte der europäischen Aufklärung', p.6; see Werner Krauss, 'Über die Konstellation der deutschen Aufklärung', in *Das wissenschaftliche Werk*, vol.7, ed. W. Bahner, p.5-99 (8-10).

Left or the GDR Marxists. The progressivist concept of history that they espoused both paved the way for later epochs and demanded that they overcome the deficits of earlier ones. In this concept of history, historical knowledge forms the basis of, and thus is closely related to, the justification of one's own convictions. Only a correct understanding of history would allow its course – as presented – to culminate in the ideological point upheld by the historian. However, this line of thinking did not stem only from Enlightenment studies. The authoritative Marxist-Leninist or historical materialist world view had pervaded the state, society and science, and it consequently underpinned the understanding of every programmatic text of the humanities. The guiding principle of research was that of legitimising the state ideology; thus Enlightenment studies had to empirically prove that the progressive activists of the eighteenth century were precursors of socialism. As a result, the strain of activism that the GDR Enlightenment scholars typically espoused, in alignment with their enlightened self-image and their socialist convictions, also willy-nilly legitimised the dictatorship in which they lived and worked. Even an extremely competent and innovative scholar like Werner Krauss, who privately criticised the situation in the GDR,[30] could not escape this trap.

Since socialism in the GDR had, by definition, drawn the right conclusions from the preceding course of history, the socialist order would now certainly result from the 'correctly' reconstructed history.[31] As a consequence, research was tasked with closing the circle twice: the philosophy of history would have to coincide with historical empiricism, just as all academic research had to coincide with the ideology of the wider society. In the GDR this applied to the humanities and the social sciences in general, but especially to Enlightenment studies, which was held in particularly high esteem. Consequently, research and scholarship were only considered successful if they aptly closed both circles.[32] Failure to achieve this

30. See Werner Krauss, *Briefe 1922 bis 1976*, ed. Peter Jehle in collaboration with Elisabeth Fillmann and Peter-Volker Springborn (Frankfurt am Main, 2002), p.648, 650, 652-53, 805, 827, 854 (1957-1967).
31. In Marxist terminology, Krauss explains this in his 1950 foreword to a volume of essays that was not published at the time: 'Kurze Vorbemerkung über eine parteiliche Wissenschaft', in *Das wissenschaftliche Werk*, vol.1, ed. M. Naumann, p.5-6.
32. Also according to Möller, 'Die Interpretation der Aufklärung in der marxist-isch-leninistischen Geschichtsschreibung', p.471-72.

double closure spelled scientific weakness, but not attempting to do so represented an indefensible break with premises that were non-negotiable. This paved the way for a fundamentally antiplu-ralistic premise to take root in GDR Enlightenment studies until 1989/1990, which meant that research could not acknowledge contingency, nor the possibility of multiple outcomes. No ambiguity could be allowed to permeate the interpretation of the course of history, given that the 'task' of the Enlightenment was predefined. However, some changes could be observed in the 1980s. The ideological bias towards the sources gradually weakened, simple base-superstructure derivations declined and a certain degree of methodological pluralism – within the confines of the Marxist framework – came to be accepted.[33]

One further point needs to be emphasised: there is a considerable difference between the Hegelian Left, a minority acting in opposition to the state but which claimed sole possession of the truth, and the GDR Enlightenment activists, who were generally in agreement with the ruling party that controlled every facet of the state and society, as laid down in the GDR constitution adopted in 1968 (article 1, paragraph 1). Supported by the state, Enlightenment studies in the GDR was allowed to set up working groups at the prestigious Berlin Academy of Sciences.[34] Those who did not subordinate their research to the permissible ideological premises, however, were silenced or pushed into niches. A well-known example is the historian Günter Mühlpfordt, who lost his professorship in 1958 and was rehabilitated only in 1990. Even fervent Marxists Winfried Schröder and Manfred Naumann, who dared to doubt the system, faced long prison sentences or the loss of their professorships.

33. As summarised by Jens Saadhoff, *Germanistik in der DDR: Literaturwissenschaft zwischen 'gesellschaftlichem Auftrag' und disziplinärer Eigenlogik* (Heidelberg, 2007), p.396-98, from his studies relating to Germanistics.
34. See Wolfgang Klein, 'Romanisten am Zentralinstitut für Literaturgeschichte: eine institutions- und politikgeschichtliche Betrachtung', *Osnabrücker Beiträge zur Sprachtheorie* 45 (1991), p.13-26.

An Enlightenment scholar in the service of the
GDR's *Staatssicherheitsdienst*

As an activist approach to the Enlightenment and Enlightenment
studies in the GDR was required by the official ideology and was
shaped by it, it is difficult to assess whether particular scholars'
commitment to activism was motivated by personal conviction or
merely represented the unavoidable fulfilment of a social contract,
especially since that was the measure of academic success. However,
even those forced to partake in the 'activism game' without deep
conviction effectively affirmed its norms.

Ulrich Ricken (1926-2011) was exceptionally active, politically and
academically, and it is mainly owing to his tireless efforts that the
Halle Centre for Enlightenment Studies (Interdisziplinäres Zentrum
für die Erforschung der Europäischen Aufklärung – IZEA) was
founded.[35] In 1951, while still a student of Romance languages and
literatures, he wrote in his curriculum vitae, presumably included
in his application for admission to the Socialist Unity Party of
Germany (Sozialistische Einheitspartei Deutschlands – SED), on the
anniversary of Goethe's birth: 'It is clear to me that we will have to
revolutionise our so-called humanities to such a great extent as to
allow them to fully serve a progressive development.'[36] Party members,
in particular, were expected to 'actively participate', as stated in an
'investigative report' of the Ministry for State Security (Ministerium
für Staatssicherheit – MfS, for which *Staatssicherheitsdienst* or *Stasi*
are common abbreviations) prior to Ricken's recruitment as so-called
Geheimer Mitarbeiter (GM) or secret collaborator[37] (literally: 'immer

35. See Daniel Fulda, 'Aufklärung(sforschung) im Sozialismus: ideologische
    Bedingungen und ihre Überwindung in der Gründungsphase des hallischen
    Aufklärungszentrums', in *Revolution trifft Aufklärungsforschung: 1989/90,
    DDR-Erbe und die Gründung des hallischen Aufklärungszentrums*, ed. Daniel Fulda
    (Halle, 2021), p.61-107.
36. Ulrich Ricken's curriculum vitae, 28 August 1951, Halle (Saale), Bundesarchiv –
    Stasi-Unterlagen-Archiv (German Federal Archives – Stasi Records Archives),
    Ministerium für Staatssicherheit (henceforth MfS) (Ministry for State Security),
    Bezirksverwaltung (henceforth BV) Halle (Saale) (District Administration Halle
    (Saale)), Abt. II VIII 1244/75, vol.1, p.22-23: 'Es ist mir klar, dass wir gerade
    unsere sogennanten Geisteswissenschaften in besonders starkem Maße revolu-
    tionieren müssen, um sie voll einer fortschrittlichen Entwicklung dienen zu
    lassen.'
37. 10 June 1959, MfS, BV Halle, Abt. II VIII 1244/75, vol.1, p.31. Unsurprisingly,
    SED members made up a good third of the Stasi's unofficial collaborators. See

gesellschaftlich aktiv tätig',[38] or permanently socially active and involved; the pleonasm of German and foreign words here obviously suggesting greater emphasis). A GM was an undercover informer assigned to spy on people or organisations classified by the MfS as hostile.[39] In the hierarchy of importance, the GM was above another category of secret informers, namely the *Geheimer Informator* (GI), later designated as unofficial collaborators (*Inoffizieller Mitarbeiter* – IM). Ricken's mentor Krauss was briefly an unofficial collaborator, a GI (1959/1960).[40]

Ricken's Stasi files, running to more than 800 pages, leave no doubt about his involvement as a GM and IM from 1959 to 1989. Initially, he operated in those capacities with prolonged interruptions; however, from 1975 onwards his involvement was permanent. Ricken had taken on that responsibility voluntarily, without any pressure or coercion, in line with his image as an active socialist.[41] His task was to gain the trust of his French contact points in France (where he had been assigned to keep an eye on persons employed at the universities he visited, including those involved in the Communist Party and GDR citizens teaching in France)[42] as well as in Halle and Berlin (where the focus was mainly on university teachers from France or the French cultural attachés and councils).[43] The MfS considered unofficial collaborators as the 'main weapon in the fight against the enemy'.[44] While the GM/IM reports primarily served as information sources, their underlying purpose was to exert pressure on people who may have been potential recruits for the MfS, or its opponents. Fortunately, it is arguable that Ricken's reports would probably not

---

Jens Gieseke, *The History of the Stasi: East Germany's secret police, 1945-1990* (New York, 2014), p.87.

38. 'Auskunft' about Ricken from the Mfs district administration, Leipzig, Dept. XV, 24 June 1959, MfS, BV Halle, Abt. II VIII 1244/75, vol.1, p.40.

39. See Gieseke, *The History of the Stasi*, p.79.

40. See Hans Ulrich Gumbrecht, *Vom Leben und Sterben der großen Romanisten: Karl Vossler, Ernst Robert Curtius, Leo Spitzer, Erich Auerbach, Werner Krauss* (Munich and Vienna, 2002), p.201-202.

41. See MfS, BV Halle, Abt. II VIII 1244/75, vol.1, p.33 (report on Ricken's recruitment dated 19 June 1959) and p.68 (MfS information about Ricken from 21 August 1965).

42. See e.g. the 'travel itinerary', 28 July 1959, MfS, BV Halle, Abt. II VIII 1244/75, vol.1, p.46-50.

43. See the 'Einsatz- und Entwicklungskonzeption für den IMV "Roman"', 22 June 1978, MfS, BV Halle, Abt. II VIII 1244/75, vol.1, p.136-38.

44. Gieseke, *The History of the Stasi*, p.78-79.

have served this latter purpose. As a rule they paint a positive, even harmonious, picture of the situation which he had to explore.[45] He rarely expressed critical assessments of third parties – exceptions were when he considered someone to be academically incompetent,[46] or when someone's personal problems were already well-known.[47] Ricken was not a know-it-all spy seeking to harm others, not a true 'Chekist', as his officers-in-charge noted with regret.[48] His continued association with the Stasi as an informant was a consequence and expression of the activist and totalitarian claim of the Marxist-Leninist system, which established the bounds of an acceptable world view and exploited individuals to that end.

   In Ricken's Stasi files, the keyword *Aufklärung* appears to mean two different things. On the one hand, it signifies that the information gained through 'secret-intelligence gathering' about the categories of persons just mentioned was not available in the ordinary course of events and certainly not approved for public access.[49] In that sense, Ricken was an active *Aufklärer* even as an informant. On the other hand, *Aufklärung* appears in his Stasi files increasingly frequently as the term we are familiar with for an epoch that remains topical, for

45. See e.g. Ricken's 'Bericht über die Studienreise nach Frankreich', 14 March 1978, MfS, BV Halle, Abt. II VIII 1244/75, vol.2, p.98, or the information he provided about a French language assistant, p.163.

46. See Ricken's 'Bericht' (tape transcript), 16 March 1976, MfS, BV Halle, Abt. II VIII 1244/75, vol.2, p.9-10.

47. See the report on the meeting, 23 December 1982, MfS, BV Halle, Abt. II VIII 1244/75, vol.3, p.68.

48. See 'Beurteilung über IMS "Roman"', 13 December 1983, MfS, BV Halle, Abt. II VIII 1244/75, vol.1, p.194. Chekists were the members of the first Communist secret service in the Soviet Union and were regarded by the Stasi as role models for ideological determination and unhesitating severity.

49. MfS, BV Halle, Abt. II VIII 1244/75, vol.1, p.43 ('Auskunft' about Ricken from the Mfs district administration, Leipzig, Dept. XV, 24 June 1959): 'aufklären', and p.123 ('Perspektivplan' for Ricken as IM, 8 July 1976): 'Aufklärung der Pläne und Absichten der französischen Botschaft im Bereich der Kultur-politik sowie [...] Kontrolle der Aktivitäten und Kontakte zu den an der Uni tätigen französischen Staatsbürgern'); vol.2, p.151 ('Treffbericht' of the officer-in-charge): 'Aufklärung der an die Universität Lille delegierten Mitarbeiterin der MLU – [name blacked out] – Arbeits-, Lebens- und Wohnbedingungen, Umgangskreis, Verhalten'; vol.2, p.157-58, 164-65; vol.3, p.39, 42, 113; vol.3, p.271, one of the targets here is the future French cultural attaché. This terminology corresponds to the official language regulations of the MfS. See *Das Wörterbuch der Staatssicherheit: Definitionen zur 'politisch-operativen Arbeit'*, ed. Siegfried Suckut, 2nd edn (Berlin, 1996), p.60-61.

Ricken's activities as an unofficial collaborator in the 1980s allowed him to closely pursue his academic goals in the field of Enlightenment studies. After Krauss' death in 1976, Ricken was the GDR's most active and recognised Enlightenment scholar on the international stage.[50] Since 1979 he had been active in the major congresses of the International Society for Eighteenth-Century Studies; he became a member of the Society's Executive Committee in 1987, after his candidacy as an elected member in 1979 had been unsuccessful. His reports portray Enlightenment scholars in Western countries, and especially in France, as mostly progressive and open to the GDR, that is, as potential 'political allies'.[51] Adversaries – whose existence was inherent to an activist understanding of the Enlightenment – include not only the so-called imperialist enemies of peace and detente (on the political level)[52] but also emergent trends in the academic field, most probably postmodernism and poststructuralism, which came to be dubbed 'irrational'.[53] In promoting Enlightenment studies in cross-bloc cooperation, Ricken puts forth the argument that this would serve to counteract a conservative relapse in the international political climate.

At first glance, the thrust of Ricken's line of argument was rather

50. Ricken's first book after his habilitation thesis was in French. See Ulrich Ricken, *Grammaire et philosophie au siècle des Lumières: controverses sur l'ordre naturel et la clarté du français* (Villeneuve-d'Ascq, 1978). His next book on eighteenth-century theories of language was translated into English: *Linguistics, anthropology and philosophy in the French Enlightenment: language theory and ideology*, translated by Robert W. Norton (London and New York, 1994).

51. MfS, BV Halle, Abt. II VIII 1244/75, vol.2, p.184-85, 189 [1979]; vol.3, p.116-20 (autumn 1983), the quote is from p.120. See also Ricken's report on the joint collaboration with Lille dated 10 December 1981, vol.3, p.46, and 4 March 1986, vol.3, p.160. Ricken regularly emphasises that the political attitude of his contacts in the West is 'progressive'.

52. See also the report, apparently written by Ricken, about his and the rector's trips to France, December 1986, MfS, BV Halle, Abt. II VIII 1244/75, vol.3, p.180-200, esp. p.196. Against 'US nuclear missiles': report on a trip to West Germany, undated [autumn 1983], see vol.3, p.116-20 (119).

53. See also Ricken's report, 10 May 1988, MfS, BV Halle, Abt. II VIII 1244/75, vol.3, p.227-36 (236). Ricken never specifies what he means by 'irrational currents'. His source is the Frankfurt political scientist Iring Fetscher (see p.229), who at a symposium in West Germany attended by Ricken vaguely warned against Peter Sloterdijk as a 'postmodern' author and 'poststructural thinker'. See the published version, Iring Fetscher, 'Aufklärung und Gegenaufklärung in der Bundesrepublik', in *Aufklärung und Gegenaufklärung in der europäischen Literatur, Philosophie und Politik von der Antike bis zur Gegenwart*, ed. Jochen Schmidt (Darmstadt, 1989), p.522-47 (546).

diffuse. Firstly, it claims a certain relevance of GDR Enlightenment
studies ideologically and for the state's foreign policy. Secondly, this
added legitimacy to Ricken's numerous and long sojourns in Western
countries. In 1987, he began to pursue a more specific goal: inspired
by his visits to the Herzog August Bibliothek (HAB) at Wolfenbüttel in
West Germany, he came up with a visionary plan to build an Enlightenment research centre in Halle. The idea was to put Halle's extensive
library holdings on the eighteenth century on display and to use them
in a manner comparable to the HAB. Ideologically, the most delicate
points of contention in this plan were the cooperation offered by Paul
Raabe, director of the HAB, and the need for the financial support
promised by the Volkswagen Foundation. This would make the West
German strand of Enlightenment studies, once regarded as deficient
and historically regressive, as hostile and needing to be pushed
back,[54] both a partner and indeed a role model. Yet that problem
could be resolved discursively by tweaking the friend–foe scheme.
While not contradicting that scheme, Ricken's reports portrayed
West German Enlightenment research no longer as adversarial but,
instead, as an ally in the fight against 'politically conservative forces
and irrational currents'.[55] This shift also mirrored the change in
spirit of Honecker's visit to Bonn in 1987, which heralded a general
surge in the willingness to cooperate.[56] Indeed, even the department
head of counter-espionage of the MfS district administration was so
persuaded by Ricken's arguments that he incorporated them almost
verbatim into the reports which he sent to the headquarters in Berlin
and the SED head of the Halle district, and he expressed support
for his unofficial collaborator's plans to establish a research centre at
Martin Luther University (MLU) and cooperate with West German
institutions.[57]

Additional arguments that Ricken put to the MfS officer included
the claim that the Enlightenment was 'an important theoretical
source of Marxism' and 'a legacy to which the humanistic forces in

54. See MfS, BV Halle, Abt. II VIII 1244/75, vol.2, p.190.
55. Ricken's report, 10 May 1988, MfS, BV Halle, Abt. II VIII 1244/75, vol.3,
    p.227-36 (236): 'politisch konservative Kräfte und irrationale Strömungen'.
56. See the 'Operative information' for the MfS, signed by Lieutenant Colonel
    Kittler, which was forwarded to the first secretary of the SED district adminis-
    tration, 5 July 1988, MfS, HA XX, no.6121, p.24.
57. See Kittler, 'Operative information', 5 July 1988, MfS, HA XX, no.6121, p.23,
    and his preceding cover letter, p.19. Kittler's source is Ricken's report, 10 May
    1988, MfS, BV Halle, Abt. II VIII 1244/75, vol.3, p.227-36.

many countries today refer'.[58] With their insistence on the continued pertinency of the Enlightenment, especially where its ideals had not yet been realised, Ricken and his officer were arguing within the activist paradigm in advocating for an Enlightenment Centre that would establish 'very favourable opportunities to be academically and politically effective' and support the GDR's foreign policy.[59] The Stasi files provide a strong indication that the Enlightenment Centre in Halle could not have been founded during the GDR era without the support of the MfS. Ricken's secret-intelligence activities probably contributed both to his research policy activism and to achieving that goal. What conclusions should be drawn today from this hitherto unknown backstory of the IZEA is another question, and one that deserves a chapter of its own.

Ideology versus pluralism

How much activism can Enlightenment studies endure without sacrificing academic integrity? Placing oneself in the service of a dictatorship as a secret-service agent surely crosses the line; it reduces Enlightenment activism to mere self-contradiction. Ricken's case represents an extreme example, although he was by no means the only unofficial collaborator among the philology professors in the GDR (a whole slew of them are known to have been active as IMs).[60] In itself, an activist approach to one's own research topic is not necessarily problematic – although it can distort the methods and results. Yet research is never completely value-free. Rather, it is a matter of methodically controlling and self-critically reflecting on one's own unavoidable perspective. In addition, there are still good reasons today – which few would dispute – to continue seeing the Enlightenment as a mission worthy of civic and scholarly attention.

A problem arises when ideological constructions of history claim that their world view is exclusively appropriate or legitimate. By 'ideology' I mean a 'closed' world view that pervades 'everything',

58. Kittler, 'Operative information', 5 July 1988, MfS, HA XX, no.6121, p.22: 'machte die Aufklärung zu einer wichtigen theoretischen Quelle des Marxismus und gleichzeitig zu einem Erbe, auf das sich heute die humanistischen Kräfte in vielen Ländern berufen'.

59. Kittler, 'Operative information', 5 July 1988, MfS, HA XX, no.6121, p.23: 'sehr günstige Möglichkeiten für wissenschaftspolitische Wirksamkeit'.

60. See Joachim Walther, *Sicherungsbereich Literatur: Schriftsteller und Staatssicherheit in der Deutschen Demokratischen Republik* (Berlin, 1996), p.318-20, 493-96, 582-90.

especially social theory, politics, philosophy and the very concept of history.[61] Marxism in the GDR incorporated a state-approved understanding of the Enlightenment, and inevitably that ideological lens was brought to bear on Enlightenment studies. As described above, Enlightenment studies had to be stretched to close the circle twice, between the philosophy of history and historical empiricism on the one hand, and between research and society on the other. Given their claim to a totality, ideologies contradict the premise of pluralism on which open societies are founded, neither allowing substantial criticism nor recognising other world views as equal in principle. As already indicated, that is not to say that research in countries with a pluralistic democracy is free from political bias. However, ideology in the sense just defined is generally not imposed by (state) authorities in democratic societies, and it runs counter to the principle of falsification, according to which theories must be falsifiable in order to be considered scientific.

At Halle, the establishment of the Enlightenment Centre finally brought about a breakthrough in pluralism, ending the previous commitment to Marxism-Leninism because that would have been unacceptable to the partners in the West. Both the March 1989 cooperation agreement with the Herzog August Library and the application for the Volkswagen Foundation funding, written shortly before the fall of the Berlin Wall, remained silent about the 'Marxist-Leninist Enlightenment research' being carried out in Halle, which Ricken's first concept paper from 1987 heralded and other documents in his Stasi file confirmed.[62] Once the inevitable point of reference

61. See Hannah Arendt, *Totalitarianism: part three of The Origins of totalitarianism* (New York, 1968), p.166-69.
62. 'Kooperationsvereinbarung über vergleichende interdisziplinäre Aufklärungsforschung zwischen dem interdisziplinären Forschungszentrum "Europäische Aufklärung" der Martin-Luther-Universität Halle-Wittenberg und der Herzog August Bibliothek Wolfenbüttel' ('Cooperation agreement on comparative interdisciplinary research on the Enlightenment between the interdisciplinary research center "European Enlightenment" at MLU Halle-Wittenberg and the HAB') (I would like to thank Prof. Dr. Klaus Bochmann very much for providing me with a photocopy of the contract); Ulrich Ricken, 'Das interdisziplinäre Forschungszentrum "Europäische Aufklärung" der Martin-Luther-Universität Halle-Wittenberg: Voraussetzungen, geplante Aufgaben, Struktur' ('Requirements, planned tasks, structure'), draft proposal of 11 August 1989, Halle (Saale), IZEA Archive. See also Ulrich Ricken, 'Probleme, Verpflichtungen, Voraussetzungen der zukünftigen Aufklärungsforschung an der Martin-Luther-Universität' ('Problems, obligations, preconditions of future

for Enlightenment research, in 1989 socialism was supplanted by 'the diversity of the scientific and cultural currents of the Enlightenment movement', a new direction or point of orientation signalled in Ricken's most recent papers.[63] Referring back to the starting point of this article, we can conclude that this decisive move to redefine the mission of the Enlightenment Centre finally restored the 'freedom [...] to dissent', which Gundling had demanded as early as 1715.[64]

Enlightenment research at the MLU'), 9 December 1987, MfS, BV Halle, Abt. II VIII 1244/75, vol.3, p.238-59 (248 and 259).

63. Ricken, 'Das interdisziplinäre Forschungszentrum "Europäische Aufklärung"', p.5: 'die Vielfalt der wissenschaftlichen und kulturellen Strömungen der Aufklärungsbewegung'. This formulation is found for the first time in a paper written shortly after the contract was signed in Wolfenbüttel. See Ulrich Ricken, 'Vorlage für den Rektor der MLU' ('Template for the rector'): 'Voraussetzungen, Aufgabe, Struktur, Entwicklungsperspektiven des interdisziplinären Forschungszentrums', 28 April 1989, Halle (Saale), IZEA Archive, p.7.

64. [Gundling], *Gundingliana*, 'Vorrede', p.[)(6r]: 'Freyheit [...] zu dissentiren'.

Bibliography

'79 leaders unite to aid democracy', *The New York Times* (1 June 1940), p.10.

Achella, Stefania, 'The dark side of thought: the body, the unconscious and madness in Hegel's philosophy', in *The Owl's flight: Hegel's legacy to contemporary philosophy*, ed. Stefania Achella *et al.* (Berlin, 2021), p.23-36.

Adler, Mortimer J., 'God and the professors', in *Science, philosophy, and religion: a symposium* (New York, 1941), p.120-38.

Adorno, Theodor W., *Briefe und Briefwechsel*, ed. Theodor W. Adorno Archive, vol.4.2: Theodor W. Adorno and Max Horkheimer, *Briefwechsel, 1938-1944*, ed. Christoph Gödde and Henri Lonitz (Frankfurt am Main, 2004).

–, *Minima moralia: reflections from damaged life* (London, 1978).

Albanese, Ralph, 'Critique universitaire et discours scolaire sous la Troisième République: le cas Racine', *Revue de l'histoire littéraire de la France* 109 (2009), p.645-59.

Albertone, Manuela, 'Illuminismo e comunismo', in *Comunismo e socialismo: storia di un'idea*, ed. Manuela Albertone *et al.* (Turin, 2014), p.93-109.

Allgemeine deutsche Real-Encyklopädie für die gebildeten Stände: Conversations-Lexikon, 9th edn, 15 vols (Leipzig, 1843).

Altman, William H. F., 'Exotericism after Lessing: the enduring influence of F. H. Jacobi on Leo Strauss', *Journal of Jewish thought and philosophy* 15:1 (2007), p.59-83.

Arendt, Hannah, 'The Enlightenment and the Jewish question' (1932), in *The Jewish writings*, ed. Jerome Kohn (New York, 2007), p.3-18.

–, *Totalitarianism: part three of The Origins of totalitarianism* (New York, 1968).

Arkhangel'skii, Aleksandr, *Imperatritsa II v istorii russkoi literatury i obrazovaniia* (Kazan, 1897).

Artigas-Menant, Geneviève, 'Cent ans de réponses aux "Questions diverses" de Lanson', *Problemata: revista internacional de filosofia* 4:3 (2013), p.21-49.

Ashton, Rosemary, *The German Idea: four writers and the reception of German thought 1800-1860* (Cambridge, 1980).

Axster, Felix, Mathias Berek and Stefanie Schüler-Springorum, 'Verschenkte Potenziale: marginalisierte Ideen über gesellschaftlichen Zusammenhalt im Kaiserreich und in der Nachwendezeit', in *Gesellschaftlicher Zusammenhalt: ein interdisziplinärer Dialog*, ed. Nicole Deitlhoff, Olaf Groh-Samberg and Matthias Middell (Frankfurt am Main, 2020), p.152-73.

Baberowski, Jörg, *Autokratie und Justiz: zum Verhältnis von Rechtsstaatlichkeit und Rückständigkeit im ausgehenden Zarenreich 1864-1917* (Frankfurt am Main, 1996).

Babkin, D. S., 'Pervye biography A. N. Radishcheva', in *Biografiia A. N. Radishcheva napisannaia ego synoviami*, ed. D. S. Babkin (Moscow, 1959), p.2-36.

Bahner, Werner, 'Übergreifende und spezifische Aspekte der europäischen Aufklärung (unter besonderer Berücksichtigung der romanischen Länder)', in *Aufklärung als europäisches Phänomen: Überblick und Einzeldarstellungen* (Leipzig, 1985), p.5-110.

Baker, Keith M., 'Venturi's "Utopia and reform in the Enlightenment"', in *Il repubblicanesimo moderno: l'idea di repubblica nella riflessione storica di Franco Venturi*, ed. Manuela Albertone (Naples, 2006), p.33-58.

Baldensperger, Fernand, 'Romantique, ses analogues et ses équivalents: tableau synoptique de 1650 à 1810', *Harvard studies and notes in philology and literature* 19 (1937), p.13-105.

Bambach, Charles, 'Hermeneutics and historicity: Dilthey's critique of historical reason', in *Interpreting Dilthey: critical essays*, ed. Eric S. Nelson (Cambridge, 2019), p.82-102.

Barber, William H., 'Voltaire and Quakerism: Enlightenment and the inner light', *SVEC* 24 (1963), p.81-109.

Barkai, Avraham, *'Wehr dich!': der Centralverein deutscher Staatsbürger jüdischen Glaubens (C.V.) 1893-1938* (Munich, 2002).

Barnikol, Ernst, 'Bauers Kulturgeschichte des 18. Jahrhunderts und seine These von der Säkularisation des Pietismus', in *Bruno Bauer: Studien und Materialien* (Assen, 1972), p.274-90.

–, *Bruno Bauer: Studien und Materialien* (Assen, 1972).

–, *Das entdeckte Christentum im Vormärz: Bruno Bauers Kampf gegen Religion und Christentum und Erstausgabe seiner Kampfschrift* (Jena, 1927).

Baron, Salo W., 'Ghetto and emancipation: shall we revise the traditional view?', *The Menorah journal* 14 (1928), p.515-26.

Baryshnikov, N. P. (ed.), 'Zhurnal V. I. Zinov'eva', *Russkaia starina* 23 (1878), p.207-40.

Battistoni, Giulia, 'Implications of mental derangement in moral and juridical context starting from Hegel', in *Philosophy and madness from Kant to Hegel and beyond*, ed. Francesca Iannelli and Mariannina Failla (Milan, in press).

Baudrillart, Henri, 'Turgot', *Revue des deux mondes* 15:6 (1846), p.1019-49.

Bauer, Bruno, *Briefwechsel zwischen Bruno Bauer und Edgar Bauer während der Jahre 1839-1842* (Berlin, 1844).

–, *Geschichte der Politik, Cultur und Aufklärung des achtzehnten Jahrhunderts*, 4 vols (Berlin, 1843-1845).

–, 'Die Posaune des Jüngsten Gerichts', in *Die Hegelsche Linke: Dokumente zu Philosophie und Politik im deutschen Vormärz*, ed. Heinz and Igrid Pepperle (Leipzig, 1985), p.235-372.

Bauer, Nancy, *et al.*, 'Debating Hegel's legacy for contemporary feminist politics', in *Hegel's philosophy and feminist thought: beyond Antigone?*, ed. Kimberly Hutchings and Tuija Pulkinnen (New York, 2010), p.233-52.

Baumann, Zygmunt, 'Assimilation and Enlightenment', *Society* 27 (1990), p.71-81.

Bazin, Anaïs, *Eloge historique de Chrétien-Guillaume Lamoignon de Malesherbes: discours qui a remporté le prix d'éloquence décerné par l'Académie française, dans sa séance du 9 août 1831* (Paris, 1831).

Beales, Derek, 'Franco Venturi and Joseph II's *grande progetto*', *Rivista storica italiana* 108 (1996), p.742-50.

Becker, Carl, 'Everyman his own historian', *American historical review* 37:2 (January 1932), p.221-36.

–, *The Heavenly city of the eighteenth-century philosophers*, 2nd edn (New Haven, CT, 2003).

Becker, Karin E., 'Licht – (L)lumière(s) – siècle des Lumières: von der Lichtmetapher zum Epochenbegriff der Aufklärung in Frankreich', doctoral dissertation, University of Cologne, 1994.

Beiser, Frederick C., *The German historicist tradition* (Oxford, 2011).

Belknap, Robert, 'Survey of Russian journals, 1840-1880', in *Literary journals in imperial Russia*, ed. Deborah Martinsen (Cambridge, 1997), p.91-116.

Below, Georg von, *Die deutsche Geschichtsschreibung von den Befrei-ungskriegen bis zu unseren Tagen* (1916), 2nd edn (Munich and Berlin, 1924).

–, *Die Ursachen der Reformation* (Munich and Berlin, 1917).

Benedict, Ruth, 'Human nature is not a trap', *Partisan review* 10:2 (March-April 1943), p.159-64.

Benhabib, Seyla, 'Hegel, die Frauen und die Ironie', in *Denken der Geschlechterdifferenz*, ed. Herta Nagl-Docekal and Herlinde Pauer-Studer (Vienna, 1990), p.19-36.

Bensoussan, Georges, 'Le sionisme, un enfant de l'Europe des Lumières', *Cités* 47-48 (2011), p.141-53.

Benz, Wolfgang (ed.), *Die 'Judenfrage': Schriften zur Begründung des modernen Antisemi-tismus 1789 bis 1914 | The 'Jewish question': literature on the roots of modern antisemitism 1780 until 1918* (Munich, 2003).

Berengo, Marino, 'Franco Venturi e la biografia', *Rivista storica italiana* 108 (1996), p.717-26.

Berlin, Isaiah, 'The Counter-Enlightenment', in *Against the current: essays in the history of ideas*, ed. Henry Hardy, 2nd edn (Princeton, NJ, 2013), p.1-32.

–, 'Four lectures on Russian historicism' (1962-1973), https://berlin.wolf.ox.ac.uk/published_works/singles/bib297.pdf (last accessed 24 April 2023).

–, *Three critics of the Enlightenment*, ed. Henry Hardy, 2nd edn (Princeton, NJ, 2013).

Bernfeld, Simon, *Am Ende des Jahrhunderts: Rückschau auf 100 Jahre geistiger Entwicklung*, vol.3: *Juden und Judentum im neunzehnten Jahrhundert* (Berlin, 1898).

Berti, Silvia, 'Repubblicanesimo e Illuminismo Radicale nella storiografia di Franco Venturi', in *Il repubblicanesimo moderno: l'idea di repubblica nella riflessione storica di Franco Venturi*, ed. Manuela Albertone (Naples, 2006), p.155-75.

Biale, David, 'The end of Enlightenment?', *Jewish social studies* 22 (2017), p.141-45.

Bil'basov, Vasilii, 'Nikita Panin i Mers'ie de la-Riv'er (1762-1767)', *Russkaia starina* 72 (1891), p.283-324.

'Biograficheskiia svedeniia o russkikh pisateliakh XVIII veka i bibliograficheskie izvestiia ob nikh proizvedeniiakh', *Russkaia starina* 2 (1870), p.197-200.

Birkert, Alexandra, *Hegels Schwester: auf den Spuren einer ungewöhnlichen Frau um 1800* (Ostfildern, 2008).

Blum, Jerome, *Lord and peasant in Russia* (Princeton, NJ, 1972).

Blumenberg, Hans, *Aspekte der Epochenschwelle: Cusaner und Nolaner* (Frankfurt am Main, 1976).

Bollenbeck, Georg, 'Die Abwendung des Bildungsbürgertums von der Aufklärung: Versuch einer Annäherung an die semantische Lage um 1880', in *Nach der Aufklärung? Beiträge zum Diskurs der Kulturwissenschaften*, ed. Wolfgang Klein and Waltraud Naumann-Beyer (Berlin, 1995), p.151-62.

–, *Bildung und Kultur: Glanz und Elend eines deutschen Deutungsmusters*, 2nd edn (Frankfurt am Main, 1996).

–, *Eine Geschichte der Kulturkritik: von Rousseau bis Günther Anders* (Munich, 2007).

–, *Tradition, Avantgarde, Reaktion: deutsche Kontroversen um die kulturelle Moderne* (Frankfurt am Main, 1999).

Bonald, Louis de, 'De la chrétienté et du christianisme', in *Œuvres de M. de Bonald*, vol.12 (Paris, 1830), p.317-48.

–, 'Démonstration philosophique du principe constitutif de la société', in *Œuvres de M. de Bonald*, vol.12 (Paris, 1830), p.1-254.

Borchmeyer, Dieter, *Weimarer Klassik: Portrait einer Epoche* (1994; Weinheim, 1998).

Borisova, Tatiana, and Jane Burbank, 'Russia's legal trajectories', *Kritika* 19:3 (2018), p.469-508.

Botstein, Leon, 'Emanzipation und Assimilation: die Auswirkung der aufklärerischen Tradition im 19. Jahrhundert', in *Judentum und Modernität: Essays zur Rolle der Juden in der deutschen und österreichischen Kultur 1848 bis 1938* (Vienna and Cologne, 1991), p.21-29.

Boucher, Geoff, and Henry Martyn Lloyd (ed.), *Rethinking the Enlightenment: between history, philosophy, and politics* (Lanham, MD, 2018).

Bourdin, Jean-Claude, *Hegel et les matérialistes français du XVIIIᵉ siècle* (Paris, 1992).

Brauer, Oscar Daniel, 'Hegels Aufklärung der Aufklärung', in *Hegels Phänomenologie des Geistes: ein kooperativer Kommentar zu einem Schlüsselwerk der Moderne*, ed. Klaus Vieweg and Wolfgang Welsch (Frankfurt am Main, 2008), p.474-88.

Breuer, Mordechai, 'Das Bild der Aufklärung bei der deutsch-jüdischen Orthodoxie', in *Aufklärung und Haskala in jüdischer und nichtjüdischer Sicht*, ed. Karlfried Gründer and Nathan Rotenstreich (Heidelberg, 1990), p.131-42.

Briese, Olaf, 'Vom Gottesgericht zum Weltgericht: apokalyptische Motive in Aufklärung und Vormärz', in *Der nahe Spiegel: Vormärz und Aufklärung*, ed. Wolfgang Bunzel, Norbert Otto Eke and Florian Vaßen (Bielefeld, 2008), p.51-78.

Brinton, Crane, 'Many mansions', *American historical review* 69:2 (January 1964), p.309-26.

Bröckling, Ulrich, and Axel T. Paul (ed.), *Aufklärung als Aufgabe der Geistes- und Sozialwissenschaften: Beiträge für Günter Dux* (Weinheim and Basel, 2019).

Brockliss, Laurence, and Ritchie Robertson (ed.), *Isaiah Berlin and the Enlightenment* (Oxford, 2016).

Brooks, David, 'The Enlightenment project', *The New York Times* (28 February 2017).

Brooks, Van Wyck, 'Conference on science, philosophy and religion in their relation to the democratic way of life', in *Science, philosophy, and religion: a symposium* (New York, 1941), p.1-11.

Brown, David, *Richard Hofstadter: an intellectual biography* (Chicago, IL, 2007).

Brown, Gregory S., 'Andrew Dickson White and America's unfinished (French) Revolution', *Age of revolutions* (14 September 2020), https://ageofrevolutions.com/2020/09/14/andrew-dickson-white-and-americas-unfinished-french-revolution/ (last accessed 27 April 2023).

Brugère, Fabienne, *et al.* (ed.), *Lumières* 8 (2006), special issue: *Foucault et les Lumières*.

Bubenik-Bauer, Iris, and Ute Schalz-Laurenze (ed.), *Frauen in der Aufklärung: '... ihr werten Frauenzimmer, auf!'* (Frankfurt am Main, 1995).

Bubert, Marcel, 'Aufklärerisches Denken im Mittelalter? Alteuropäische Anläufe zu Differenzierung, Vernunftkult und Religionskritik', in *Bildung als Aufklärung:*

historisch-anthropologische Perspektiven, ed. Anne Conrad, Alexander Maier and Christoph Nebgen (Vienna, 2020), p.159-74.

Buckle, Henry Thomas, *The History of civilization in England*, 2 vols (London, 1857-1861).

Budde, Gunilla, Eckart Conze and Cornelia Rauh, 'Einleitung: Bürgertum und Bürgerlichkeit nach 1945', in *Bürgertum nach dem bürgerlichen Zeitalter: Leitbilder und Praxis nach 1945*, ed. Gunilla Budde *et al.* (Göttingen, 2010), p.7-25.

Bunzel, Wolfgang, 'Zurück in die Zukunft: die Junghegelianer in ihrem Verhältnis zur Aufklärung', in *Der nahe Spiegel: Vormärz und Aufklärung*, ed. Wolfgang Bunzel, Norbert Otto Eke and Florian Vaßen (Bielefeld, 2008), p.31-49.

Buonarroti, Filippo, *La Riforma dell'Alcorano*, ed. Alessandro Galante Garrone and Franco Venturi (Palermo, 1992).

Burger, Stefan, and Phillip Müller (ed.), *Dynamics of emigration: émigré scholars and the production of historical knowledge in the twentieth century* (New York, 2022).

Burnham, James, 'The theory of the managerial revolution', *Partisan review* 8:3 (May-June 1941), p.181-97.

Butler, Eliza M., *Paper boats: an autobiography* (London, 1959).

–, *The Tyranny of Greece over Germany* (Cambridge, 1935).

Bychkov, A. F., 'Spodvizhniki II', *Russkaia starina* 8 (1873), p.691-734.

Carlyle, Thomas, 'Diderot', in *Critical and miscellaneous essays*, 5 vols (London, 1899), vol.3, p.177-248.

–, *On heroes, hero-worship, and the heroic in history*, ed. Joel J. Brattin, Mark Engel and Michael K. Goldberg (Berkeley, CA, 1993).

–, 'Voltaire', in *Critical and miscellaneous essays*, 5 vols (London, 1899), vol.1, p.396-428.

Carnino, Cecilia, 'Rereading Franco Venturi's eighteenth century: absolutist monarchy between reform and revolt', *History of European ideas* 35 (2009), p.11-23.

Cassirer, Ernst, *The Myth of the state* (New Haven, CT, 1946).

–, *Die Philosophie der Aufklärung*, 2 vols (Tübingen, 1932).

–, *La Philosophie des Lumières*, ed. and translated by Pierre Quillet (Paris, 1966).

–, 'Das Problem Jean Jacques Rousseau', *Archiv für Geschichte der Philosophie* 41:2-3 (1932), p.117-213, 479-513.

–, 'Le problème Jean-Jacques Rousseau', *Bulletin de la Société française de philosophie* 32:2 (June 1932), p.46-66.

–, *Le Problème Jean-Jacques Rousseau*, ed. Jean Starobinski, translated by Marc B. de Launay (Paris, 2012).

–, *The Question of Jean-Jacques Rousseau*, ed. and translated by Peter Gay (New York, 1954).

Cavenago, Marco, 'Venturi, Lionello', *Dizionario biografico degli Italiani*, vol.98 (2020), https://www.treccani.it/enciclopedia/lionello-venturi_%28Dizionario-Biografico%29/ (last accessed 26 April 2023).

Chartier, Roger, *Les Origines culturelles de la Révolution française* (Paris, 2000).

Chase, Richard V., 'The Huxley-Heard paradise', *Partisan review* 10:2 (March-April 1943), p.143-58.

Cheshikhin, V. E., 'Studenchesksiia bezchinstva v Derpte', *Russkii arkhiv* 10 (1887), p.265-81.

Clark, Andrew, 'The Enlightenment – Donald Trump may represent its final days', *Financial review* (27 January 2017).

Clark, Jonathan C. D., 'The Enlightenment: catégories, traductions et objets sociaux', *Lumières* 17/18 (2011), special issue: *Les Lumières dans leur siècle*, ed. Didier Masseau and Gérard Laudin, p.19-39.

Cobban, Alfred, *Rousseau and the state* (London, 1934).

Compagnon, Antoine, *La Troisième République des lettres: de Flaubert à Proust* (Paris, 1983).

Confino, Michael, 'The new Russian historiography, and the old – some considerations', *History and memory* 21:2 (2009), p.7-33.

Conrad, Anne, 'Aufklärung(en), Bildung, Religion – und Gender?', in *Bildung als Aufklärung: historisch-anthropologische Perspektiven*, ed. Anne Conrad, Alexander Maier and Christoph Nebgen (Vienna, 2020), p.379-402.

Coppola, Al, 'Enlightenolatry from Peter Gay to Steven Pinker: mass marketing Enlightenment and the thick eighteenth century', *The Eighteenth century: theory and interpretation* 62:4 (winter 2021), p.412-31.

Cousin, Victor, *Cours de l'histoire de la philosophie: histoire de la philosophie du XVIIIe siècle*, 2 vols (Paris, 1829).

–, *Cours de philosophie: introduction à l'histoire de la philosophie* (Paris, 1828).

–, *Cours d'histoire de la philosophie moderne pendant les années 1816 et 1817* (Paris, 1841).

–, *Cours d'histoire de la philosophie morale au dix-huitième siècle professé à la Faculté des lettres en 1819 et 1820*, 4 vols (Paris, 1839-1842).

–, *Fragmens philosophiques* (Paris, 1826).

–, *Fragmens philosophiques*, 2nd edn (Paris, 1833).

–, *Fragments et souvenirs*, 3rd edn (Paris, 1857).

–, *Philosophie populaire* (Paris, 1848).

–, *Premiers essais de philosophie*, 3rd edn (Paris, 1855).

Cymorek, Hans, *Georg von Below und die deutsche Geschichtswissenschaft um 1900* (Stuttgart, 1998).

Daled, Pierre F., *Le Matérialisme occulté et la genèse du sensualisme: écrire l'histoire de la philosophie en France* (Paris, 2005).

D'Alembert, Jean, 'Discours préliminaire des éditeurs', in *Encyclopédie, ou Dictionnaire raisonné des sciences, des arts et des métiers*, ed. Denis Diderot and Jean D'Alembert, vol.1 (Paris, Briasson, David l'aîné, Le Breton, Durand, 1751), p.i-xlix.

–, 'Essai sur les élémens de philosophie, ou sur les principes des connaissances humaines, avec les éclaircissemens', in *Œuvres complètes* (1821-1822), 5 vols (Geneva, 1967), vol.1, p.115-348.

Darnton, Robert, 'In search of the Enlightenment: recent attempts to create a social history of ideas', *Journal of modern history* 43:1 (1971), p.113-32.

–, 'To deal with Trump, look to Voltaire', *The New York Times* (27 December 2018).

David, Pascal, 'Lumière', in *Vocabulaire européen des philosophies: dictionnaire des intra-duisibles*, ed. Barbara Cassin (Paris, 2004), p.742-46.

de Dijn, Annelien, 'The politics of Enlightenment: from Peter Gay to Jonathan Israel', *The Historical journal* 55:3 (2012), p.785-805.

De La Flise [*sic*], 'Ekaterina II i doctor M. I. Veikard', *Russkaia starina* 72 (1891), p.531-64.

Deleyre, Alexandre, *Tableau de l'Europe pour servir de supplément à l'Histoire philosophique et politique des établissements et du commerce des Européens dans les deux Indes* (Amsterdam, n.n., 1774).

Delon, Michel, 'Les Lumières: travail d'une métaphore', *SVEC* 1552 (1976), p.527-41.

De Madariaga, Isabel, *Russia in the age of Catherine the Great* (New Haven, CT, 1981).

Demier, Francis, *La France de la Restauration (1814-1830)* (Paris, 2012).

Deschamps, Léger-Marie, *Le Vrai Système, ou le Mot de l'énigme métaphysique et morale*, ed. Jean Thomas and Franco Venturi (Paris, 1939).

Despois, Eugène, *Les Lettres et la liberté* (Paris, 1865).

Dewey, John, 'Anti-naturalism in extremis', *Partisan review* 10:1 (January-February 1943), p.24-39.

[d'Holbach, Paul-Thiry], *Système social, ou Principes naturels de la morale et de la politique, avec un examen de l'influence du gouvernement sur les mœurs*, 3 vols (London [Amsterdam], [Marc-Michel Rey], 1773).

Diderot, Denis, *Observations sur le Nakaz*, in *Œuvres complètes*, ed. Laurent Versini, 5 vols (Paris, 1994-1997), vol.3, p.501-78.

Dilthey, Wilhelm, 'Das achtzehnte Jahrhundert und die geschichtliche Welt', in *Wilhelm Diltheys gesammelte Schriften*, vol.3 (Leipzig and Berlin, 1927), p.209-75.

–, 'Das Allgemeine Landrecht', in *Gesammelte Schriften*, ed. Bernhard Groethuysen *et al.*, 26 vols (Stuttgart and Göttingen, 1922-2005), vol.12, p.131-204.

–, 'Auffassung und Analyse des Menschen im 15. und 16. Jahrhundert', *Archiv für Geschichte der Philosophie* 4 (1891), p.337-651, and 5 (1892), p.337-440.

–, *Einleitung in die Geistes-wissenschaften* (1883), in *Gesammelte Schriften*, ed. Bernhard Groethuysen *et al.*, 26 vols (Stuttgart and Göttingen, 1922-2005), vol.1, p.8-14.

–, 'Frederick and the Academy', in *Frederick the Great: a profile*, ed. Peter Paret (London, 1972), p.177-97.

–, *Gesammelte Schriften*, ed. Bernhard Groethuysen *et al.*, 26 vols (Stuttgart and Göttingen, 1922-2005).

–, *Selected works*, vol.4: *Hermeneutics and the study of history*, ed. Rudolf A. Makkreel and Frithjof Rodi (Princeton, NJ, 1996).

Dixon, Simon, 'The posthumous reputation of Catherine II in Russia, 1797-1837', *The Slavonic and East European review* 77:4 (1999), p.646-79.

–, '"Prosveshchenie": Enlightenment in eighteenth-century Russia', *SVEC* 2008:01, p.228-49.

'Dmitrii Vasil'evich Volkov, 1718-1785', *Russkaia starina* 9 (1874), p.163-74.

Dubina, V. S., '"Osobyi put" teorii Sonderveg v interpretatsii natsional'noi istorii', in *'Osobyi put": ot ideologii k metodu*, ed. Andrei Zorin (Moscow, 2018), p.459-77.

–, and S. V. Pol'skoi, '"Osobyi put"': russkogo dvorianstva v otechestvennoi i zarubezhnoi istoriografii', *Izvestiia Samarskogo nauchnogo tsentra Rossiiskoi akademii nauk* 11 (2000), p.227-34.

Durov, N. P., 'Fedor Vasil'evich Karzhavin, 1745-1812', *Russkaia starina* 12 (1875), p.272-97.

Dux, Günter, 'Aufklärung als Aufgabe der Wissenschaft', in *Aufklärung als Aufgabe der Geistes- und Sozialwissenschaften: Beiträge für Günter Dux*, ed. Ulrich Bröckling and Axel T. Paul (Weinheim and Basel, 2019), p.23-25.

Dziudzia, Corinna, and Sonja Klimek (ed.), *Gelehrte Frauen der Frühaufklärung: einsame 'Wunderthiere' oder vernetzte Akteurinnen?* (Berlin, 2022).

Eberhard, Johann August, 'Vermuthungen über den Ursprung der heutigen Magie: ein historischer Versuch', *Berlinische Monatsschrift* 10 (1787), p.6-33.

Eckermann, Johann Peter, *Gespräche mit Goethe in den letzten Jahren seines Lebens* (Berlin, 1982).

Edelstein, Dan, *The Enlightenment: a genealogy* (Chicago, IL, 2010).

Efremov, P. A., 'Stepan Ivanovich Sheshkovskii, 1720-1794', *Russkaia starina* 2 (1870), p.637-39.

Eichner, Hans (ed.), *Romantic and its cognates: the European history of a word* (Toronto, 1972).

Eisen, Arnold M., 'Rethinking Jewish modernity', *Jewish social studies* 1 (1994), p.1-21.

Elbogen, Ismar, *A Century of Jewish life* (Philadelphia, PA, 1944).

Essbach, Wolfgang, *Die Junghegelianer: Soziologie einer Intellektuellengruppe* (Munich, 1988).

Evangelista, Stefano, and Katherine Harloe, 'Pater's "Winckelmann"', in *Pater the classicist*, ed. Charles Martindale, Stefano Evangelista and Elizabeth Prettejohn (Oxford, 2017), p.63-79.

Falkenstern, Rachel, 'On the uses and abuses of doing feminist philosophy with Hegel', *Verifiche* 2 (2021), p.111-32.

Fauquet, Eric (ed.), *Victor Cousin, homo théologico-politicus: philologie, philosophie, histoire littéraire* (Paris, 1997).

Fauser, Markus, 'Deutsch-jüdische Gedächtniskultur: das Jubiläumsjahr 1879', in *Lessing und das Judentum*, ed. Dirk Niefanger, Gunnar Och and Birka Siwczyk (Hildesheim, 2015), p.183-204.

Fayolle, Roger, 'Le XVIIIe siècle jugé par le XIXe: à propos d'un concours académique sous le premier Empire', in *Approches des Lumières: mélanges offerts à Jean Fabre* (Paris, 1974), p.181-96.

–, *Sainte-Beuve et le XVIIIe siècle, ou Comment les révolutions arrivent* (Paris, 1972).

Febvre, Lucien, 'De Lanson à Mornet: un renoncement?' (1941), *Combats pour l'histoire* (Paris, 1953), p.263-68.

Feder, Gottfried, Ferdinand Werner and Graf Ernst Reventlow, *Das neue Deutschland und die Judenfrage: des Diskussionsbuches erster Teil* (Leipzig, 1933).

Feder, Johann Georg Heinrich, *Der neue Emil oder von der Erziehung nach bewährten Grundsätzen*, 2 vols (Erlangen, Walther, 1768-1775).

Feest, Uljana (ed.), *Historical perspectives on Erklären and Verstehen* (Dordrecht, 2010).

Ferrone, Vincenzo, *The Enlightenment: history of an idea* (Princeton, NJ, and Oxford, 2017).

Fetscher, Iring, 'Aufklärung und Gegenaufklärung in der Bundesrepublik', in *Aufklärung und Gegenaufklärung in der europäischen Literatur, Philosophie und Politik von der Antike bis zur Gegenwart*, ed. Jochen Schmidt (Darmstadt, 1989), p.522-47.

Filippov, Mikhail, 'Tiur'my v Rossii: sobstvennoruchny proekt imperatritsy Ekateriny II', *Russkaia starina* 8 (1873), p.60-86.

Fontenelle, *Entretiens sur la pluralité des mondes, Digression sur les Anciens et les Modernes*, ed. Robert Shackleton (Oxford, 1955).

Frederick II, *Œuvres de Frédéric le Grand*, ed. Johann David Erdmann Preuß, 30 vols (Berlin, 1846-1856).

Frey, Thomas [i.e. Theodor Fritsch], *Antisemiten-Katechismus: eine Zusammenstellung des wichtigsten Materials zum Verständnis der Judenfrage*, 25th edn (Leipzig, 1893).

Fulda, Daniel (ed.), *Aufklärung fürs Auge: ein anderer Blick auf das 18. Jahrhundert* (Halle, 2020).

–, 'Aufklärung(sforschung) im Sozialismus: ideologische Bedingungen und ihre Überwindung in der Gründungsphase des hallischen Aufklärungszentrums', in *Revolution trifft Aufklärungsforschung: 1989/90, DDR-Erbe und die Gründung des hallischen Aufklärungszentrums*, ed. Daniel Fulda (Halle, 2021), p.61-107.

–, 'Identity in diversity: programmatic pictures of the Enlightenment', *Journal for eighteenth-century studies* 45:1 (2022), p.43-62.

Garve, Christian, 'Versuch über die Prüfung der Fähigkeiten', *Neue Bibliothek der schönen Wissenschaften und der freyen Künste* 8:1 (1769), p.1-44.

Gay, Peter, 'Carl Becker's *Heavenly city*', *Political science quarterly* 72:2 (June 1957), p.182-99; conference version in *Carl Becker's Heavenly city revisited*, ed. Raymond Rockwood (Ithaca, NY, 1958), p.27-51.

–, 'The Enlightenment in the history of political theory', *Political science quarterly* 69:3 (September 1954), p.374-89.

–, 'The German-Jewish legacy and I: some personal reflections', *The American Jewish Archives journal* 40:2 (1988), p.203-10.

–, 'Introduction', in Ernst Cassirer, *The Question of Jean-Jacques Rousseau*, ed. and translated by Peter Gay (New York, 1954), p.3-32.

–, 'Light on the Enlightenment', in *The Present-day relevance of eighteenth-century thought*, ed. Roger McCutcheon (Washington, DC, 1956), p.41-52.

–, 'The living Enlightenment', https://tannerlectures.utah.edu/_resources/documents/a-to-z/g/Gay98.pdf (last accessed 27 April 2023).

–, *My German question: growing up in Nazi Berlin* (New Haven, CT, 1999).

–, *The Party of humanity*: essays in the French Enlightenment (New York, 1964).

–, 'The social history of ideas: Ernst Cassirer and after', in *The Critical spirit: essays in honor of Herbert Marcuse*, ed. Kurt Wolff and Barrington Moore (Boston, MA, 1967), p.106-21.

–, 'Voltaire's "Idées républicaines": a study in bibliography and interpretation', *SVEC* 6 (1958), p.69-108.

–, *Voltaire's politics: the poet as realist* (1959; New York, 1965).

–, *et al.*, 'More about freedom and loyalty', *American scholar* 23:3 (summer 1954), p.376-78.

Gennadi, Nikolai, *Chteniia v Imperatorskom Obshchestve istorii i drevnostei'* (Moscow, 1862).

Gesellschaft für Deutsche Presseforschung zu Bremen (ed.), *Die Lösung der Judenfrage: eine Rundfrage von Julius Moses im Jahre 1907 mit Antworten von Eduard Bernstein, Otto Julius Bierbaum, Arthur Fitger [...] und 90 weiteren Persönlichkeiten des öffentlichen Lebens* (Bremen, 2010).

Gethmann-Siefert, Annemarie, 'Arte e religione: un effetto sinergetico nella questione "Illuminismo"', in *Arte, religione e politica in Hegel*, ed. Francesca Iannelli (Pisa, 2013), p.59-68.

Giarrizzo, Giuseppe, 'L'Illuminismo e la società italiana: note di discussione', in *L'età dei Lumi: studi storici sul settecento europeo in onore di Franco Venturi*, ed. Lester G. Crocker, 2 vols (Naples, 1985), vol.1, p.165-89.

–, 'Venturi e il problema degli intellettuali', in *Il coraggio della ragione: Franco Venturi intellettuale e storico cosmopolita*, ed. Luciano Guerci and Giuseppe Ricuperati (Turin, 1998), p.9-59.

Gidel, Charles, *Discours sur Jean Jacques Rousseau: discours qui a obtenu le prix d'éloquence décerné par l'Académie française dans sa séance publique annuelle du jeudi 20 août 1868* (Paris, 1868).

Gieseke, Jens, *The History of the Stasi: East Germany's secret police, 1945-1990* (New York, 2014).

Giesen, Bernhard, *Intellectuals and the nation: collective identity in a German axial age* (Cambridge, 1998).

Gilbert, Désiré-Louis, *Eloge de Vauvenargues qui a remporté le prix d'éloquence décerné par l'Académie française, dans sa séance publique annuelle du 28 août 1856* (Paris, 1856).

Godel, Rainer, *et al.*, 'Aufklärungen', in *Handbuch Europäische Aufklärung: Begriffe – Konzepte – Wirkung*, ed. Heinz Thoma (Stuttgart, 2015), p.86-122.

Goriushkin, Zakharii (ed.), 'Sudebnoe deistvie v 1809, zrelishche sostavlennoe Goriushkiym', *Russkaia starina* 23 (1878), p.553-74.

Gottlob, Michael, *Geschichtsschreibung zwischen Aufklärung und Historismus: Johannes von Müller und Friedrich Christoph Schlosser* (Frankfurt am Main, 1989).

Gotzmann, Andreas, *Eigenheit und Einheit: Modernisierungsdiskurse des deutschen Judentums der Emanzipationszeit* (Leiden, 2002).

Graetz, Heinrich, *Geschichte der Juden von den ältesten Zeiten bis auf die Gegenwart: aus den Quellen neu bearbeitet von Prof. Dr. H. Graetz*, vol.11: *Geschichte der Juden vom Beginn der Mendelssohn'schen Zeit (1750) bis in die neueste Zeit (1848)* (Leipzig, 1870).

Gräfe, Thomas, 'Der Hegemonieverlust des Liberalismus: die "Judenfrage" im Spiegel der Intellektuellenbefragungen 1885-1912', *Jahrbuch für Antisemitismusforschung* 25 (2016), p.73-100.

'Graf Nikitich Panin, 1771-1837', *Russkaia starina* 8 (1873), p.338-73.

Gray, John, *Enlightenment's wake: politics and culture at the close of the modern age* (London, 1995).

Gréard, Octave, *Prévost-Paradol: étude suivie d'un choix de lettres* (Paris, 1894).

Grierson, Herbert J. C., *Carlyle and Hitler* (Cambridge, 1933).

Griffiths, David E., and George E. Munro (ed. and trans.), *The Laws of Russia*, series 2: *Imperial Russia*, vol.289: *April 21, 1785: Catherine II's charters of 1785 to the nobility and the towns* (Bakersfield, CA, 1991).

Grothe, Ewald, and Ulrich Sieg (ed.), *Liberalismus als Feindbild* (Göttingen, 2014).

Guilhot, Nicolas, 'Steven Pinker, *Enlightenment now: the case for reason, science, humanism, and progress*' (essay review), *H-Diplo commentary* (July 2018), https://networks.h-net.org/node/28443/discussions/1993064/h-diplo-commentary-1-enlightenment-now-case-reason-science (last accessed 25 April 2023).

Guizot, François, *Cours d'histoire moderne: histoire générale de la civilisation en Europe, depuis la chute de l'empire romain jusqu'à la Révolution française* (Paris, 1828).

Gumbrecht, Hans Ulrich, 'Persuader ceux qui pensent

comme vous: les fonctions du discours épidictique sur la mort de Marat', *Poétique* 79 (1979), p.363-84.

–, *Vom Leben und Sterben der großen Romanisten: Karl Vossler, Ernst Robert Curtius, Leo Spitzer, Erich Auerbach, Werner Krauss* (Munich and Vienna, 2002).

[Gundling, Nicolaus Hieronymus], *Gundlingiana, darinnen allerhand zur Jurisprudentz, Philosophie, Historie, Critic, Litteratur und übrigen Gelehrsamkeit gehörige Sachen abgehandelt werden,* vol.1 (Halle, Rengerische Buchhandlung, 1715).

Guterman, Norbert, 'Neither-nor', *Partisan review* 10:2 (March-April 1943), p.134-42.

Habermas, Jürgen, *Die Moderne – ein unvollendetes Projekt: philosophisch-politische Aufsätze 1977-1990* (Leipzig, 1990).

Habib, M. A. R., *Hegel and the foundations of literary theory* (Cambridge, 2019).

Haffner, Paul Leopold, *Die deutsche Aufklärung: eine historische Skizze,* 3rd edn (Mainz, 1864).

Hallowell, John H., 'The decline of liberalism', *Ethics* 52:3 (April 1942), p.345-46.

Hamer, David A., *John Morley: liberal intellectual in politics* (Oxford, 1968).

Hardtwig, Wolfgang, 'Wie deutsch war die deutsche Aufklärung', in *Nationalismus und Bürgerkultur in Deutschland 1500-1914: ausgewählte Aufsätze* (Göttingen, 1994), p.55-78.

Harel, Charles-Jean, *Discours sur Voltaire, qui a remporté le prix d'éloquence décerné par l'Académie française, dans sa séance publique du jeudi 29 août 1844* (Paris, 1844).

Harnack, Carl Gustav Adolf von, 'Das Christentum und die Geschichte', in *Reden und Aufsätze,* vol.2 (Giessen, 1904), p.1-22.

–, *Geschichte der Königlich Preußischen Akademie der Wissenschaften zu Berlin* (Berlin, 1900).

Harrison, Frederic, *Autobiographic memoirs,* 2 vols (London, 1911).

–, *The Choice of books, and other literary pieces* (London, 1886).

–, *The Meaning of history* (London, 1894).

–, 'Thomas Carlyle', in *Studies in early Victorian literature* (London, 1902), p.43-63.

Hawk, Brandon W., 'Why far-right nationalists like Steve Bannon have embraced a Russian ideologue', *The Washington Post* (16 April 2019).

Hayes, Carlton J. H., 'The challenge of totalitarianism', *The Public opinion quarterly* 2:1 (January 1938), p.21-26.

–, 'The novelty of totalitarianism in the history of Western civilization', *Proceedings of the American Philosophical Society* 82:1 (23 February 1940), p.95-96.

Hazard, Paul, *La Pensée européenne au XVIIIe siècle de Montesquieu à Lessing,* 3 vols (Paris, 1946).

Hegel, Georg Wilhelm Friedrich, *Frühe Exzerpte,* ed. Friedhelm Nicolin, in *Gesammelte Werke,* vol.3 (Hamburg, 1991).

–, *Frühe Schriften I,* ed. Nicolin Friedhelm and Gisela Schüler, in *Gesammelte Werke,* vol.1 (Hamburg, 1989).

–, *Frühe Schriften II*, ed. Walter Jaeschke, in *Gesammelte Werke*, vol.2 (Hamburg, 2014).

–, *Grundlinien der Philosophie des Rechts*, ed. Klaus Grotsch and Elisabeth Weisser-Lohmann, in *Gesammelte Werke*, vol.14.1 (Hamburg, 2009).

–, *Grundlinien der Philosophie des Rechts: Anhang*, ed. Klaus Grotsch and Elisabeth Weisser-Lohmann, in *Gesammelte Werke*, vol.14.3 (Hamburg, 2011).

–, *Grundlinien der Philosophie des Rechts: Beilagen*, ed. Klaus Grotsch and Elisabeth Weisser-Lohmann, in *Gesammelte Werke*, vol.14.2 (Hamburg, 2010).

–, *Hegel: the letters*, translated by Clark Butler and Christiane Seiler (Bloomington, IN, 1984).

–, *Jenaer kritische Schriften*, ed. Otto Pöggeler and Hartmund Buchner, in *Gesammelte Werke*, vol.4 (Hamburg, 1968).

–, *Jenaer Schriften, 1801-1807*, ed. Eva Moldenhauer and Karl Markus Michel, in *Werke in zwanzig Bänden: auf der Grundlage der Werke von 1832-1845 neu edierte Ausgabe*, vol.2 (Frankfurt am Main, 1970).

–, *Lectures on the philosophy of history*, translated by John Sibree (London, 1894).

–, *Phänomenologie des Geistes*, ed. Wolfgang Bonsiepen and Reinhard Heede, in *Gesammelte Werke*, vol.9 (Hamburg, 1980).

–, *The Phenomenology of spirit*, translated by Terry Pinkard (Cambridge, 2018).

–, 'Sekundäre Überlieferungen', in *Gesammelte Werke*, vol.25.2,

ed. Christoph Johannes Bauer (Hamburg, 2011), p.919-1117.

–, *Vorlesungen über die Geschichte der Philosophie III*, ed. Eva Moldenhauer and Karl Markus Michel, in *Werke in zwanzig Bänden: auf der Grundlage der Werke von 1832-1845 neu edierte Ausgabe*, vol.20 (Frankfurt am Main, 1979).

–, *Vorlesungen über die Philosophie der Kunst I: Nachschriften zu den Kollegien der Jahre 1820/21 und 1823*, ed. Niklas Hebig, in *Gesammelte Werke*, vol.28.1 (Hamburg, 2015).

–, *Vorlesungen über die Philosophie des subjektiven Geistes I: Nachschriften zu den Kollegien der Jahre 1822 und 1825*, ed. Christoph Johannes Bauer, in *Gesammelte Werke*, vol.25.1 (Hamburg, 2008).

Hémon, Félix, *Eloge de Buffon* (Paris, 1878).

Herf, Jeffrey, *Reactionary modernism: technology, culture, and politics in Weimar and the Third Reich* (Cambridge, 1984).

Herrmann, Ulrich, 'Volk – Nation – Vaterland: ein Grundproblem deutscher Geschichte', in *Volk – Nation – Vaterland*, ed. Ulrich Herrmann (Hamburg, 1996), p.11-18.

Hettling, Manfred, and Stefan-Ludwig Hoffmann (ed.), *Der bürgerliche Wertehimmel: Innenansichten des 18. Jahrhunderts* (Göttingen, 2000).

–, 'Der bürgerliche Wertehimmel: zum Problem individueller Lebensführung im 19. Jahrhundert', *Geschichte und Gesellschaft* 23 (1997), p.333-59.

Hettner, Hermann, 'Die Kämpfe der Aufklärung', in *Literatur-geschichte des 18. Jahrhunderts: in drei Theilen*, vol.1: *Geschichte der englischen Literatur von der Wiederherstellung des Königthums bis in die zweite Hälfte des achtzehnten Jahrhunderts, 1660-1770* (1856; Braunschweig, 1881), p.3-10.

–, *Literaturgeschichte des 18. Jahrhunderts: in drei Theilen* (1856-1869), 4th edn (Braunschweig, 1881).

–, *Die romantische Schule in ihrem inneren Zusammenhange mit Göthe und Schiller* (Braunschweig, 1850).

Hibben, John Grier, *The Philosophy of the Enlightenment* (New York, 1910).

Hill, Samantha Rose, *Hannah Arendt* (London, 2021).

Hinchman, Lewis P., *Hegel's critique of the Enlightenment* (Gainesville, FL, 1984).

Hirsch, Marcus, *Kulturdefizit am Ende des 19. Jahrhunderts von Dr. med. Marcus Hirsch* (Frankfurt am Main, 1898).

Hirsh, Michael, 'Team Trump's message: the clash of civilizations is back', *Politico* (20 November 2016).

Hirschman, Albert O., *The Rhetoric of reaction: perversity, futility, jeopardy* (Cambridge, MA, 1991).

Hodge, Joanna, 'Women and the Hegelian state', in *Women in Western political philosophy*, ed. Ellen Kennedy and Susan Mendus (New York, 1987), p.127-58.

Hoffmann, Christhard, 'Constructing Jewish modernity: Mendelssohn jubilee celebrations within German Jewry, 1829-1929', in *Towards normality? Acculturation and modern German Jewry*, ed. Rainer Liedtke and David Rechter (Tübingen, 2003), p.27-52.

Hoffmann, Stefan-Ludwig, 'Brothers and strangers? Jews and Freemasons in nineteenth-century Germany', *German history* 18:2 (2000), p.143-61.

Hofstadter, Richard, 'Democracy and anti-intellectualism in America', *Michigan alumnus quarterly review* 59:21 (August 1953), p.281-95.

Holborn, Hajo, 'Der deutsche Idealismus in sozialgeschichtlicher Beleuchtung', *Historische Zeitschrift* 174 (1952), p.359-84.

Holländer, Ludwig, 'Aufklärung und immer wieder Aufklärung', *Central-Verein-Zeitung: Blätter für Deutschtum und Judentum* 5 (3 March 1926), p.112-13.

Hook, Sidney, 'The failure of the left', *Partisan review* 10:2 (March-April 1943), p.165-77.

–, 'The new failure of nerve', *Partisan review* 10:1 (January-February 1943), p.2-23.

–, 'The politics of Wonderland', *Partisan review* 10:3 (May-June 1943), p.258-62.

Horkheimer, Max, *Gesammelte Schriften*, vol.16: *Briefwechsel 1937-1940*, ed. Gunzelin Schmid Noerr (Frankfurt am Main, 1995).

–, *Gesammelte Schriften*, vol.17: *Briefwechsel 1941-1948*, ed. Gunzelin Schmid Noerr (Frankfurt am Main, 1996).

–, *Gesammelte Schriften*, vol.18: *Briefwechsel 1949-1973*, ed. Gunzelin Schmid Noerr (Frankfurt am Main, 1996).

–, 'The relation between psychology and sociology in the work of Wilhelm Dilthey', *Studies in philosophy and social science* 8 (1939), p.430-43.

–, and Theodor W. Adorno, *Dialectic of Enlightenment*, ed. Gunzelin Schmid Noerr, translated by Edmund Jephcott (Stanford, CA, 2007).

Houghton, Walter E., 'Victorian anti-intellectualism', *Journal of the history of ideas* 13 (1952), p.291-313.

Hughes, H. Stuart, 'Franz Neumann between liberalism and social democracy', in *The Intellectual migration: Europe and America, 1930-1960*, ed. Donald Fleming and Bernard Bailyn (Cambridge, MA, 1969), p.446-62.

Hundt, Martin (ed.), *Der Redaktionsbriefwechsel der Hallischen, Deutschen und Deutsch-Französischen Jahrbücher*, 3 vols (Berlin, 2010).

Iannelli, Francesca, 'Hegel's constellation of the feminine between philosophy and life: a tribute to Dieter Henrich's *Konstellationsforschung*', in *The Owl's flight: Hegel's legacy to contemporary philosophy*, ed. Stefania Achella *et al.* (Berlin, 2021), p.239-55.

–, 'Die Kunst der ästhetischen Bildung bei Hegel', in *Objektiver und absoluter Geist nach Hegel*, ed. Thomas Oehl and Arthur Kok (Leiden, 2018), p.481-503.

–, 'Die Omnipräsenz von Hegels Philosophie und insbesondere seiner Ästhetik: ein Kabinett hegelianischer Kuriositäten', in *Das Beste von Hegel*, ed. Klaus Vieweg (Berlin, 2023), p.307-26.

–, and Alain P. Olivier, 'En traduisant Hegel – traducendo Hegel: aesthetic theory and/ in translation practice', *Studi di estetica* 1 (2022), p.157-98.

Iggers, Georg, *The German conception of history: the national tradition of historical thought from Herder to the present*, 2nd edn (Middletown, CT, 1983).

Ikonnikov, V. S., 'Pravitel'stviushchii Senat pri Ekaterine Vtoroi', *Russkii arkhiv* 1 (1888), p.17-43.

Iokavou, Vicky, 'Totalitarianism as a non-state: on Hannah Arendt's debt to Franz Neumann', *European journal of political theory* 8:4 (2009), p.29-47.

Israel, Jonathan, *Democratic Enlightenment: philosophy, revolution, and human rights 1750-1790* (Oxford, 2011).

–, *Radical Enlightenment: philosophy and the making of modernity, 1650-1750* (Oxford, 2001).

Jamme, Christoph, '"Jedes Lieblose ist Gewalt": der junge Hegel, Hölderlin und die Dialektik der Aufklärung', in *Der Weg zum System: Materialien zum jungen Hegel*, ed. Christoph Jamme and Helmut Schneider (Frankfurt am Main, 1990), p.130-70.

Janet, Paul, *Victor Cousin et son œuvre* (Paris, 1885).

Janssens, David, 'The problem of the Enlightenment: Strauss,

Jacobi, and the pantheism controversy', *The Review of metaphysics* 56:3 (March 2003), p.605-31.

Jenemann, David, *Adorno in America* (Minneapolis, MN, 2007).

Jey, Martine, 'Gustave Lanson: de l'histoire littéraire à une histoire sociale de la littérature?', *Le Français aujourd'hui* 145 (2004), p.15-22.

–, 'The literature of the Enlightenment: an impossible legacy for the Republican school', *Yale French studies* 113 (2008), p.46-59.

–, *La Littérature au lycée: invention d'une discipline (1880-1925)* (Metz, 1998).

Jones, Stuart, *Intellect and character in Victorian England: Mark Pattison and the invention of the don* (Cambridge, 2007).

Jung, Theo, *Zeichen des Verfalls: semantische Studien zur Entstehung der Kulturkritik im 18. und frühen 19. Jahrhundert* (Göttingen, 2012).

Kampling, Rainer, 'Die Neo-Orthodoxie des 19. Jahrhunderts und die Haskala: Randbemerkungen zu übersehenen Nähen', in *Was war deutsches Judentum? 1870-1933*, ed. Christina von Braun (Berlin, 2015), p.61-70.

Kant, Immanuel, 'An answer to the question: what is Enlightenment?', in *Kant's political writings*, ed. Hans S. Reiss, translated by Hugh Barr Nisbet (Cambridge, 1970), p.54-60.

–, 'Idea for a universal history with a cosmopolitan aim', translated by Allen W. Wood, in

Anthropology, history, and education, ed. Günter Zöller and Robert B. Louden (Cambridge, 2011), p.108-20.

–, 'Idee zu einer allgemeinen Geschichte in weltbürgerlicher Absicht' (1784), in *Akademie-Ausgabe*, vol.8 (Berlin and Leipzig, 1923), p.15-31.

–, 'What is orientation in thinking?', in *Critique of practical reason and other writings in moral philosophy*, ed. and translated by White Beck Lewis (Chicago, IL, 1949), p.295-305.

Kanuck, Kadar, *East-West mimesis: Auerbach in Turkey* (Palo Alto, CA, 2010).

Kaplan, Marion, 'As Germans and as Jews in imperial Germany', in *Jewish daily life in Germany, 1618-1945*, ed. Marion Kaplan (Oxford and New York, 2005), p.173-270.

Karazin, F. V., 'V. N. Karazin: pi'smo k doktory Remanu, 1810 g.', *Russkaia starina* 12 (1875), p.750-57.

Karnovich, E. P., 'O polnom sobranii zakonov Rossiiskoi imperii', *Russkaia starina* 10 (1874), p.408-40.

Katz, Jacob, 'Varianten des jüdischen Aufklärungserlebnisses', in *Conditio Judaica: Judentum, Antisemitismus und deutschsprachige Literatur vom 18. Jahrhundert bis zum Ersten Weltkrieg*, ed. Hans Otto Horch and Horst Denkler, 2 vols (Tübingen, 1988), vol.1, p.1-9.

Katznelson, Ira, 'A Seminar on the State', in *Desolation and*

*Enlightenment: political knowledge
after total war, totalitarianism, and
the Holocaust* (New York, 2003),
p.102-37.

Kaulla, Rudolf, *Der Liberalismus
und die deutschen Juden* (Munich
and Leipzig, 1928).

Kernholt, Otto [i.e. Otto Bonhard],
*Vom Ghetto zur Macht: die
Geschichte des Aufstiegs der Juden
auf deutschem Boden*, 4th edn
(Leipzig, 1923).

Kettler, David, and Thomas
Wheatland, *Learning from Franz
L. Neumann: law, theory, and the
brute facts of political life* (London,
2019).

Khrapovitskii, Aleksandr,
*Pamiatnye zapiski A. V. Khrapo-
vitskogo: stats-sekretaria imperatritsy
Ekateriny vtoroi* (Moscow, 1990).

Kicheev, P. G., 'Saltychikha',
Russkii arkhiv 3 (1865), p.641-52.

Kimerling Wirtschafter, Elise, *The
Play of ideas in Russian Enlightenment theatre* (De Kalb, IL,
2003).

–, 'Russian legal culture and the
rule of law', *Kritika* 7:1 (2006),
p.61-70.

Kirchheimer, Otto, 'Franz
Neumann: an appreciation',
Dissent 4 (autumn 1957),
p.382-87.

Kireevsky, Ivan, 'On the nature of
European culture and its relation
to the culture of Russia', in *On
spiritual unity: a Slavophile reader*,
ed. and translated by Boris Jakim
and Robert Bird (Hudson, NY,
1998), p.189-232.

Klein, Wolfgang, 'Romanisten am
Zentralinstitut für Literaturgeschichte: eine institutions- und

politikgeschichtliche Betrachtung', *Osnabrücker Beiträge zur
Sprachtheorie* 45 (1991),
p.13-26.

Knudsen, Jonathan B., *Justus Möser
and the German Enlightenment*
(Cambridge, 1986).

Köhler, Paul, *Die Verjudung
Deutschlands und der Weg zur
Rettung: noch einmal ein Wort
für und wider 'W. Marr: Der
Sieg des Iudenthums über das
Germanenthum'* (Stettin, 1880).

Kohn, Hans, 'The multidimensional Enlightenment', *Journal
of the history of ideas* 31 (1970),
p.465-74.

Köppen, Carl Friedrich, *Friedrich
der Grosse und seine Widersacher:
eine Jubelschrift* (Leipzig, 1840).

[Köppen, Karl Friedrich],
'[Review of] *Geschichte des 18.
Jahrhunderts und des 19. bis zum
Sturz des französischen Kaiserthums
[Kaiserreichs]: von F. C. Schlosser*',
*Deutsche Jahrbücher für Wissen-
schaft und Kunst* 5:2-6 (1841),
p.5-7, 9-12, 13-14, 17-20, 21-23.

Koselleck, Reinhart, 'Das 18.
Jahrhundert als Beginn der
Neuzeit', in *Epochenschwelle
und Epochenbewußtsein*, ed.
Reinhart Herzog and Reinhart
Koselleck (Munich, 1987),
p.269-82.

–, 'Social history and conceptual
history', *International journal of
politics, culture and society* 2 (1989),
p.308-25.

–, *et al.*, 'Volk, Nation, Nationalismus, Masse', *Geschichtliche
Grundbegriffe: historisches Lexikon
zur politisch-sozialen Sprache*, ed.
Otto Brunner, Werner Conze

and Reinhart Koselleck, vol.7 (Stuttgart, 1992), p.141-431.

Kottman, Paul, *Love as human freedom* (Stanford, CA, 2017).

Krauss, Werner, *Briefe 1922 bis 1976*, ed. Peter Jehle in collaboration with Elisabeth Fillmann and Peter-Volker Springborn (Frankfurt am Main, 2002).

–, 'Einführung in das Studium der französischen Aufklärung', in *Das wissenschaftliche Werk*, vol.6: *Aufklärung II: Frankreich*, ed. Werner Bahner *et al.* (Berlin and Weimar, 1987), p.5-20.

–, 'L'ère française des Lumières et les intellectuels allemands', *La Pensée* 123 (October 1965), p.78-92.

–, 'Die französische Aufklärung und die deutsche Geisteswelt', in *Das wissenschaftliche Werk*, vol.7: *Aufklärung III: Deutschland und Spanien*, ed. Martin Fontius, with a note from Renate Petermann and Peter-Volker Springborn (Berlin and New York, 1996), p.231-49.

–, 'Der Jahrhundertbegriff im 18. Jahrhundert: Geschichte und Geschichtlichkeit in der französischen Aufklärung', in *Die Innenseite der Weltgeschichte: ausgewählte Essays über Sprache und Literatur*, ed. Helga Bergmann (Leipzig, 1983), p.109-54.

–, 'Karl Marx im Vormärz', in *Das wissenschaftliche Werk*, vol.1: *Literaturtheorie, Philosophie und Politik*, ed. Manfred Naumann (Berlin and Weimar, 1987), p.433-84.

–, 'Kurze Vorbemerkung über eine parteiliche Wissenschaft', in *Das wissenschaftliche Werk*, vol.1: *Literaturtheorie, Philosophie und Politik*, ed. Manfred Naumann (Berlin and Weimar, 1987), p.5-6.

–, 'Siècle im 18. Jahrhundert', *Beiträge zur romanischen Philologie* 1 (1961), p.83-98.

–, 'Über die Konstellation der deutschen Aufklärung', in *Das wissenschaftliche Werk*, vol.7: *Aufklärung III: Deutschland und Spanien*, ed. Martin Fontius, with a note from Renate Petermann and Peter-Volker Springborn (Berlin and New York, 1996), p.5-99.

–, 'Zur Periodisierung Aufklärung, Sturm und Drang, Weimarer Klassik', in *Sturm und Drang*, ed. Manfred Wacker (Darmstadt, 1985), p.67-95; first published in *Sinn und Form* 12:1-2 (1961), p.376-99.

Kremer, Arndt, *Deutsche Juden – deutsche Sprache: jüdische und judenfeindliche Sprachkonzepte und -konflikte 1893-1933* (Berlin, 2007).

Krieger, Karsten (ed.), *Der 'Berliner Antisemitismusstreit' 1879-1881: eine Kontroverse um die Zugehörigkeit der deutschen Juden zur Nation. Kommentierte Quellenedition*, 2 vols (Munich, 2003).

Kühne-Bertram, Gudrun, 'Zum Verhältnis von Naturwissenschaften und Geisteswissenschaften in der Philosophie Wilhelm Diltheys', in *Dilthey als Wissenschaftsphilosoph*, ed. Christian Damböck and Hans-Ulrich Lessing (Freiburg and Munich, 2016), p.225-48.

Laborde-Milaà, Auguste, *Fontenelle* (Paris, 1905).

Lacretelle, Charles, *Testament philosophique et littéraire*, vol.1 (Paris, 1840).

Lambrecht, Lars, 'Zur Rezeption der Französischen Revolution bei den Junghegelianern', in *Der nahe Spiegel: Vormärz und Aufklärung*, ed. Wolfgang Bunzel, Norbert Otto Eke and Florian Vaßen (Bielefeld, 2008), p.205-18.

Lamennais, Félicité de, 'Influence des doctrines philosophiques sur la société' (1815), in *Œuvres complètes de F. de Lamennais*, 12 vols (Paris, 1836-1837), vol.6, p.119-52.

–, *Réflexions sur l'état de l'Eglise en France pendant le dix-huitième siècle, et sur sa situation actuelle* (Paris, 1808).

Landrin, Xavier, 'Genèse et activités du groupe doctrinaire (1815-1821): contribution à une sociologie historique du libéralisme', in *Les Formes de l'activité politique: éléments d'analyse sociologique (18ᵉ-20ᵉ siècle)*, ed. Antonin Cohen, Philippe Riutort and Bernard Lacroix (Paris, 2006), p.211-26.

Lanson, Gustave, 'L'histoire littéraire et la sociologie' (1904), in *Essais de méthode, de critique et d'histoire littéraire*, ed. Henri Peyre (Paris, 1965), p.61-80.

–, *Méthodes de l'histoire littéraire* (Paris, 1925).

–, *Origines et premières manifestations de l'esprit philosophique dans la littérature française de 1675 à 1748*, *Burt Franklin research and source works series* (New York, 1973).

–, 'Programme d'études sur l'histoire provinciale de la vie littéraire en France' (1903), in *Essais de méthode, de critique et d'histoire littéraire*, ed. Henri Peyre (Paris, 1965), p.81-87.

–, 'Questions diverses sur l'histoire de l'esprit philosophique en France avant 1750', *Revue de l'histoire littéraire de la France* 19 (1912), p.1-29 and 293-317.

–, 'Le rôle de l'expérience dans la formation de la philosophie du XVIIIᵉ siècle en France', *Revue du mois* 9:49 (1910), p.5-28, and 9:52 (1910), p.409-29.

–, *Voltaire* (1906; Paris, 1960).

Lässig, Simone, 'A "Jewish Sattelzeit"? Recasting an era of upheaval and transformation', *Central European history* 51:4 (2018), p.656-61.

–, *Jüdische Wege ins Bürgertum: kulturelles Kapital und sozialer Aufstieg im 19. Jahrhundert* (Göttingen, 2004).

La Vopa, Anthony, 'Finding meaning in the Enlightenment', in *Enlightenment past and present: essays in a social history of ideas*, Oxford University Studies in the Enlightenment (Liverpool, Liverpool University Press / Voltaire Foundation, 2022), p.1-30.

Leeman, Merel, 'Transatlantic Enlightenment: Peter Gay and the drama of German history in the United States, 1930-1970', doctoral dissertation, Amsterdam University, 2017.

Leicht, Johannes, 'Otto Bonhard', in *Handbuch des Antisemitismus: Judenfeindschaft in Geschichte und Gegenwart*, ed. Wolfgang Benz, vol.8 (Berlin and Boston, MA, 2015), p.46-47.

Leonhard, Jörn, *Liberalismus: zur historischen Semantik eines europäischen Deutungsmusters* (Munich, 2001).

–, 'Politisches Gehäuse und ideologische Sprache des Fortschritts: Verfassung, Verfassungsstaat und Liberalismus im 19. Jahrhundert', in *Durchbruch der Moderne? Neue Perspektiven auf das 19. Jahrhundert*, ed. Birgit Aschmann (Frankfurt am Main, 2019), p.218-51.

Lescure, Adolphe de, *Etude sur Beaumarchais: discours qui a obtenu le prix d'éloquence décerné par l'Académie française dans sa séance publique annuelle du 25 novembre 1886* (Paris, 1887).

Lessing, Hans-Ulrich, '"Empirie und nicht Empirismus": Dilthey und John Stuart Mill', in *Die Autonomie der Geisteswissenschaften: Studien zur Philosophie Wilhelm Diltheys*, vol.1 (Nordhausen, 2015), p.11-31.

–, *Wilhelm Dilthey* (Cologne, 2011).

Levshin, Aleksei, 'Dostopamiatnye minuty v moei zhizni: zapiska chelna Gosudarstvennogo Soveta A. I. Levshina', *Russkii arkhiv* 8 (1885), p.475-558.

Lewes, George Henry, *The History of philosophy from Thales to Comte*, 3rd edn, 2 vols (London, 1867).

–, *The Life of Goethe*, 2nd edn (London, 1864).

Lifschitz, Avi, 'Between Friedrich Meinecke and Ernst Cassirer: Isaiah Berlin's bifurcated Enlightenment', in *Isaiah Berlin and the Enlightenment*, ed. Laurence Brockliss

and Ritchie Robertson (Oxford, 2016), p.51-66.

–, 'Les concours de l'Académie de Berlin, vecteurs de transferts intellectuels franco-allemands, 1745-1786', in *Les Echanges savants franco-allemands au XVIIIe siècle: transferts, circulations et réseaux*, ed. Claire Gantet and Markus Meumann (Rennes, 2019), p.205-18.

– (ed.), *Frederick the Great's philosophical writings*, translated by Angela Scholar (Princeton, NJ, 2021).

Lilti, Antoine, *L'Héritage des Lumières: ambivalences de la modernité* (Paris, 2019).

Lincoln, W. Bruce, *The Great Reforms: autocracy, bureaucracy, and the politics of change in imperial Russia* (De Kalb, IL, 1991).

Litchfield, Robert Burr, 'Franco Venturi's "crisis" of the Old Regime', *Journal of modern Italian studies* 10:2 (2005), p.234-44.

Longinov, Mikhail, 'Mikhail Lomonosov: Vypiski iz zhurnalov Imperatorskoi Rossiiskoi Akademii', *Russkaia starina* 8 (1873), p.563-84.

Lough, John, 'Reflections on *Enlightenment* and *Lumières*', *British journal for eighteenth-century studies* 8:1 (1985), p.1-15.

Lovejoy, Arthur O., 'The meaning of "romantic" in early German Romanticism', *Modern language notes* 31 (1916), p.385-96, and 32 (1917), p.65-77.

Macaulay, Thomas Babington, 'Lord Bacon', in *Critical and historical essays contributed to the*

Edinburgh review, 3 vols (London, 1843), vol.2, p.280-429.

McCarthy, Tom, 'Steve Bannon's Islamophobic film script just one example of anti-Muslim views', *The Guardian* (3 February 2017).

Macdonald, Dwight, 'The Burnhamian revolution', *Partisan review* 9:1 (January-February 1942), p.76-84.

–, 'The end of capitalism in Germany', *Partisan review* 8:3 (May-June 1941), p.198-220.

–, 'The future of democratic values', *Partisan review* 10:4 (July-August 1943), p.321-44.

–, 'Letters', *Partisan review* 10:4 (July-August 1943), p.382-83.

–, 'National defense: the case for socialism', *Partisan review* 7:4 (July-August 1940), p.250-66.

–, 'Notes on a strange war', *Partisan review* 7:3 (May-June 1940), p.170-75.

–, 'Political notes', *Partisan review* 9:6 (November-December 1942), p.476-82.

–, 'War and the intellectuals: act two', *Partisan review* 6:3 (spring 1939), p.3-20.

Macherey, Pierre, 'Les débuts philosophiques de Victor Cousin', *Corpus: revue de philosophie* 18 (1991), p.29-49.

McMahon, Darrin, *Enemies of the Enlightenment: the French counter-Enlightenment and the making of modernity* (Oxford and New York, 2002).

Maikov, Leonid, 'Kak ponimat' basniu Krylova "Vodolazy"', *Russkaia starina* 85 (1896), p.267-83.

Maikov, P., 'Snosheniia Ekateriny II s Nekkerom i s Senak-de-Mel'ianom', *Russkaia starina* 85 (1896), p.145-61.

Mainov, Ivan, 'Smolenskie dvoriane i obiazannye krest'iane', *Russkaia starina* 8 (1873), p.910-39.

Mali, Joseph, and Robert Wokler (ed.), *Isaiah Berlin's Counter-Enlightenment* (Philadelphia, PA, 2006).

Manchester, Laurie, *Holy fathers, secular sons: clergy, intelligentsia, and the modern self in revolutionary Russia* (De Kalb, IL, 2008).

Marchand, Suzanne L., *Down from Olympus: archaeology and philhellenism in Germany, 1750-1970* (Princeton, NJ, 1996).

Marcuse, Herbert, 'Preface', in Franz Neumann, *The Democratic and the authoritarian state: essays in political and legal theory*, ed. Herbert Marcuse (Glencoe, IL, 1957), p.vii-x.

Maritain, Jacques, 'Science, philosophy, and faith', in *Science, philosophy, and religion: a symposium* (New York, 1941), p.162-83.

Marr, Wilhelm, *Lessing contra Sem* (1883), 2nd edn (Leipzig, 1885).

Martin, Kingsley, *French liberal thought in the eighteenth century: a study of political ideas from Bayle to Condorcet* (London, 1929).

Mascat, Jamila, *Hegel a Jena: la critica dell'astrazione* (Lecce, 2011).

Matytsin, Anton M., 'Whose light is it anyway? The struggle for light in the French Enlightenment', in *Let there be Enlightenment: the religious and mystical sources of rationality*, ed. Anton M. Matytsin and Dan Edelstein (Baltimore, MD, 2018), p.62-85.

–, and Dan Edelstein (ed.), *Let there be Enlightenment: the religious and mystical sources of rationality* (Baltimore, MD, 2018).

Meinecke, Friedrich, *Die Entstehung des Historismus*, ed. Carl Hinrichs (Munich, 1959).

Mendelssohn, Moses, 'Über die Frage: was heißt aufklären?', *Berlinische Monatsschrift* 4 (1784), p.193-200.

Mendes-Flohr, Paul, *German Jews: a dual identity* (New Haven, CT, 1999).

Merian, David [i.e. Shapiro], 'The nerve of Sidney Hook', *Partisan review* 10:3 (May-June 1943), p.248-57.

–, and Sidney Hook, 'Socialism and the failure of nerve: the controversy continued', *Partisan review* 10:5 (September-October 1943), p.473-81.

Meyer, Michael A., 'Enlightenment: the powerful enticements of reason and universalism', in *Jewish identity in the modern world* (Seattle, WA, and Washington, DC, 1990), p.10-32.

Michaut, Narcisse, *Eloge de Buffon, précédé d'une notice par M. Emile Gebhart* (Paris, 1878).

Mill, John Stuart, 'Coleridge', in *The Collected works of John Stuart Mill*, vol.10: *Essays on ethics, religion, and society*, ed. John M. Robson and Jack Stillinger (Toronto, 1969), p.117-63.

–, *The Collected works*, vol.1: *The Autobiography and literary essays*,

ed. John M. Robson and Jack Stillinger (Toronto, 1981).

–, *The Collected works*, vol.20: *Essays on French history and historians*, ed. John Cairns and John M. Robson (Toronto, 1985).

Mirabeau, comte de, *De la monarchie prussienne sous Frédéric le Grand*, 8 vols (London, n.n., 1788).

Mitscherlich, Alexander, 'Neuerliches Nachdenken über die Aufklärung', *Merkur* 31:345 (1977), p.101-13.

Moggach, Douglas, *Philosophie und Politik bei Bruno Bauer* (Frankfurt am Main, 2009).

Möller, Horst, 'Die Interpretation der Aufklärung in der marxistisch-leninistischen Geschichtsschreibung', *Zeitschrift für historische Forschung* 4 (1977), p.438-72.

Mommsen, Theodor, 'Rede vom 18. März 1880 zur Vorfeier des Geburtstages des Kaisers in der Königlich Preußischen Akademie der Wissenschaften', in *Reden und Aufsätze*, 2nd edn (Berlin, 1905), p.89-103.

Montesquieu, Charles de Secondat de, *Spirit of the laws*, ed. Franz Neumann, translated by Thomas Nugent (New York, 1949).

Moreau, Pierre-François, 'Victor Cousin, la philosophie et son histoire', *Le Télémaque* 54:2 (2018), p.57-66.

Morley, John, 'Auguste Comte', in *Critical miscellanies*, 4 vols (London, 1886-1908), vol.3, p.337-84.

–, *Burke* (London, 1879).

–, 'Carlyle', in *Critical miscellanies,*
4 vols (London, 1886-1908), vol.1,
p.135-201.

–, *Critical miscellanies,* 4 vols
(London, 1886-1908).

–, *Diderot and the Encyclopædists,*
2 vols (London, 1878).

–, 'On Pattison's *Memoirs*', in *Critical
miscellanies,* 4 vols (London,
1886-1908), vol.3, p.133-73.

–, *Rousseau,* 2 vols (London,
1873).

–, *Voltaire* (London, 1873).

Mortier, Roland, 'Franco Venturi
et sa *Jeunesse de Diderot*', *Rivista
storica italiana* 108 (1996),
p.751-54.

–, '*Lumière* et *lumières*: histoire d'une
image et d'une idée au XVIIe
et au XVIIIe siècle', in *Clartés
et ombres du siècle des Lumières:
études sur le XVIIIe siècle littéraire*
(Geneva, 1969), p.13-59.

–, *Le 'Tableau littéraire de la France
au XVIIIe siècle': un épisode de la
'guerre philosophique' à l'Académie
française sous l'Empire, 1804-1810*
(Brussels, 1972).

Mosse, George L., *German Jews
beyond Judaism* (Bloomington, IN,
and Cincinnati, OH, 1985).

Mosse, Werner E., 'Bureaucracy
and nobility in Russia at the
end of the nineteenth century',
The Historical journal 24:3 (1981),
p.605-28.

–, 'Der Niedergang der Weimarer
Republik und die Juden', in
*Entscheidungsjahr 1932: zur
Judenfrage in der Endphase
der Weimarer Republik – ein
Sammelband,* ed. Werner E. Mosse
and Arnold Pauker, 2nd edn
(Tübingen, 1966), p.3-4.

Müller, Ernst, *Kunstreligion und
ästhetische Religiosität* (Berlin,
2004).

Müller, Winfried, *Die Aufklärung*
(Munich, 2002).

Mulsow, Martin, *Enlight-
enment underground: radical
Germany 1680-1720,* translated
by H. C. Erik Midelfort
(Charlottesville, VA, 2015).

–, *Moderne aus dem Untergrund*
(Hamburg, 2002).

–, *Radikale Frühaufklärung in
Deutschland 1680-1720,* 2 vols
(Göttingen, 2018).

Murray, Gilbert, *Four stages of Greek
religion* (New York, 1912).

Nagel, Ernest, 'Malicious philosophies of science', *Partisan review*
10:1 (January-February 1943),
p.40-57.

Nardelli, Elena, and Saša Hrnjez,
'Is it possible to speak about a
Hegelian theory of translation?
On Hegel's *Übersetzungsbegriff*
and some paradigmatic practices
of translation', *Verifiche* 49:1-2
(2020), p.v-xxvii.

Nerrlich, Paul, *Herr von Treitschke
und das junge Deutschland* (Berlin,
1890).

Neumann, Franz, 'Anxiety and
politics', translated by Peter Gay,
in *The Democratic and the authoritarian state: essays in political and
legal theory,* ed. Herbert Marcuse
(Glencoe, IL, 1957), p.270-300.

–, 'Editor's introduction', in Charles
de Secondat de Montesquieu,
Spirit of the laws, ed. Franz
Neumann, translated by Thomas
Nugent (New York, 1949),
p.ix-lxiv.

–, 'The governance of the rule of law: an investigation into the relationship between the political theories, the legal system, and the social background in competitive society', doctoral dissertation, London School of Economics, 1936.

–, 'Intellectual and political freedom', translated by Peter Gay, in *The Democratic and the authoritarian state: essays in political and legal theory*, ed. Herbert Marcuse (Glencoe, IL, 1957), p.160-215.

–, 'Montesquieu', in *The Democratic and the authoritarian state: essays in political and legal theory*, ed. Herbert Marcuse (Glencoe, IL, 1957), p.96-148.

–, 'The social sciences', in *The Cultural migration: the European scholar in America*, ed. W. Rex Crawford (Philadelphia, PA, 1953), p.4-26.

Nicolai, Friedrich, *Beschreibung einer Reise durch Deutschland und die Schweiz, im Jahre 1781: nebst Bemerkungen über Gelehrsamkeit, Industrie, Religion und Sitten*, 12 vols (Berlin and Stettin, Friedrich Nicolai, 1783-1796).

Nicolin, Friedhelm (ed.), *Hegel in Berichten seiner Zeitgenossen* (Hamburg, 1970).

Nonnotte, Claude François, *Dictionnaire philosophique de la religion, nouvelle édition, corrigée et augmentée*, 4 vols (Besançon, J.-F. Charmet, 1774).

Nordmann, Jean-Thomas, *La Critique littéraire française au XIXᵉ siècle (1800-1914)* (Paris, 2001).

Nossel, Suzanne, 'Donald Trump's assault on the Enlightenment', *Foreign policy* (25 January 2017).

O'Flaherty, Niall, *Utilitarianism in the age of Enlightenment: the moral and political philosophy of William Paley* (Cambridge, 2018).

Oz-Salzberger, Fania, 'Enlightenment, Haskalah, and the State of Israel', *The European legacy* 25 (2020), p.801-25.

'Pamiatnik Ekaterine II: 24-ogo noiabria 1873', *Russkaia starina* 8 (1873), p.633-43.

Panizzo, Paolo, 'Aufklärung und Nation in der Germanistik um 1900', in *'Aufklärung' um 1900: die klassische Moderne streitet um ihre Herkunftsgeschichte*, ed. Georg Neugebauer, Paolo Panizzo and Christoph Schmitt-Maaß (Paderborn, 2014), p.125-46.

Pascal, Jean-Noël, 'Les débuts du procès des Lumières: Barante et son *De la littérature française pendant le XVIIIᵉ siècle* (1809)', *Orages: littérature et culture 1760-1830* 2 (2003), p.177-90.

Pater, Walter, 'Duke Carl of Rosenmold', in *Imaginary portraits* (London, 1887), p.117-53.

–, 'Sebastian van Storck', in *Imaginary portraits* (London, 1887), p.79-115.

–, 'Winckelmann', in *Studies in the history of the Renaissance* (London, 1873), p.177-232.

Pattison, Mark, 'The age of reason', *Fortnightly review* 21 (1877), p.343-61.

–, *Essays*, ed. Henry Nettleship, 2 vols (Oxford, 1881).

Paucker, Arnold, *Der jüdische Abwehrkampf gegen Antisemitismus und Nationalsozialismus in den letzten Jahren der Weimarer Republik* (Hamburg, 1968).

Pavlov, N. M., *Nashe perekhodnoe vremia* (Moscow, 1888).

Pečar, Andreas, and Damien Tricoire, *Falsche Freunde: war die Aufklärung wirklich die Geburtsstunde der Moderne?* (Frankfurt am Main and New York, 2015).

Pekarskii, Petr, 'Mikhail Vasil'evich Lomonosov, "O razmnozhenii i sokhranenii rossiiskogo naroda" (1761)', *Russkaia starina* 24 (1873), p.465-580.

Perelman, Chaïm, and Lucie Olbrechts-Tyteca, *La Nouvelle Rhétorique: traité de l'argumentation*, vol.1 (Paris, 1958).

Pertici, Roberto, 'Giuliano, Balbino', in *Dizionario biografico degli Italiani*, vol.56 (2001), https://www.treccani.it/enciclopedia/balbino-giuliano_(Dizionario-Biografico) (last accessed 26 April 2023).

Petrov, P. N., *Ekaterina II – zakonodatel'nitsa* (St Peterburg, 1863).

Philippson, Martin, *Neueste Geschichte des jüdischen Volkes*, 2nd edn, vol.2 (Frankfurt am Main, 1930).

Pinkard, Terry, *Hegel: a biography* (Cambridge, 2000).

Pipes, Richard, 'Private property comes to Russia: the reign of Catherine II', *Harvard Ukrainian studies* 22 (1998), p.431-42.

Platonov, S. F., *Stoletie konchiny Imperatritsy Ekateriny* (St Petersburg, 1897).

Pocock, John G. A., *Barbarism and religion*, 6 vols (Cambridge, 1999-2016).

Pöggeler, Otto, 'Hegel, der Verfasser des ältesten Systemprogramms des deutschen Idealismus', *Hegel-Studien* 4 (1969), p.17-32.

Pol'skoi, S. V., '"Na raznye chiny razdeliaia svoi narod...": zakonodatel'noe zakreplenie soslovnogo statusa russkogo dvorianstva v seredine XVIII veka', *Cahiers du monde russe* 51:2-3 (2010), p.303-28.

Pommier, Jean, 'L'évolution de Victor Cousin', *Revue d'histoire de la philosophie* [1st series] (1931), p.172-203.

'Po povodu prazdnovaniia Orlovskim dvoriatnstvom stoletiia so dniq pozhalovaniia dvorianskoi gramoty', *Russkii arkhiv* 5 (1890), p.133-755.

Porter, Roy, 'The Enlightenment in England', in *The Enlightenment in national context*, ed. Roy Porter and Mikuláš Teich (Cambridge, 1981), p.1-18.

Powers, Elizabeth, 'Critiquing the Enlightenment: *The Seminar on eighteenth-century European culture (#417)*', in *A Community of scholars: seventy-five years of the University seminars at Columbia*, ed. Thomas Vinciguerra (New York, 2020), p.16-29.

Pypin, Aleksandr, *Istoriia russkoi literatury* (1888), 4th edn, 4 vols (St Petersburg 1916).

['R'], 'Ein Zeichen der Zeit', *Das Abendland: Central-Organ für alle zeitgemäßen Interessen des*

Judenthums 3 (29 November 1866), p.177.

Rao, Anna Maria, 'Enlightenment and reform: an overview of culture and politics in Enlightenment Italy', *Journal of modern Italian studies* 10:2 (2005), p.142-67.

Ratynskii, N. A., 'Istoricheskaia spravka', *Russkii arkhiv* 8 (1885), p.166-76.

Rauschning, Hermann, *The Revolution of nihilism: warning to the West*, translated by Ernest W. Dickes (New York, 1939).

Ravaisson, Félix, *La Philosophie en France au XIXe siècle* (Paris, 1868).

Rebenich, Stefan, 'Eine Entzweiung: Theodor Mommsen und Heinrich von Treitschke', in *Berlins wilde Energien: Porträts aus der Geschichte der Leibnizischen Wissenschaftsakademie*, ed. Stefan Leibfried *et al.* (Berlin and Boston, MA, 2015), p.262-85.

Reichardt, Rolf, 'Light against darkness: the visual representations of a central Enlightenment concept', *Representations* 61 (1998), special issue: *Practices of Enlightenment*, p.95-148.

Rendtorff, Trutz, 'Theologische Orientierung im Prozeß der Aufklärung: eine Erinnerung an Ernst Troeltsch', *Aufklärung* 2 (1987), p.19-34.

Rey, Lucie, 'Victor Cousin et l'instrumentalisation de l'histoire de la philosophie', *Le Télémaque* 54:2 (2018), p.43-55.

Reymond, M[oritz von], *Wo steckt der Mauschel? Oder Jüdischer*

Liberalismus und wissenschaftlicher Pessimismus: ein offener Brief an W. Marr (Bern and Leipzig, 1879).

Riabkin, D. D., 'Zapiski Professora Akademika T'ebo, 1765-1785', *Russkaia starina* 9 (1874), p.575-93.

Ricken, Ulrich, *Grammaire et philosophie au siècle des Lumières: controverses sur l'ordre naturel et la clarté du français* (Villeneuve-d'Ascq, 1978).

–, *Linguistics, anthropology and philosophy in the French Enlightenment: language theory and ideology*, translated by Robert W. Norton (London and New York, 1994).

Ricuperati, Giuseppe (ed.), *Historiographie et usages des Lumières* (Berlin, 2002).

–, 'Illuminismo e settecento dal dopoguerra ad oggi', in *La Reinvenzione dei lumi: percorsi storiografici del novecento*, ed. Giuseppe Ricuperati (Florence, 2000), p.201-22.

–, 'Paul Hazard', *Belfagor* 23 (1968), p.564-95.

–, 'Paul Hazard e la storiografia dell'Illuminismo', *Rivista storica italiana* 86 (1974), p.372-404.

Riesser, Gabriel, *Einige Worte über Lessing's Denkmal an die Israeliten Deutschlands gerichtet* (Frankfurt am Main, 1838).

Ripalda, José Maria, 'Aufklärung beim frühen Hegel', in *Der Weg zum System: Materialien zum jungen Hegel*, ed. Christoph Jamme and Helmut Schneider (Frankfurt am Main, 1990), p.112-29.

Ritter, Immanuel Heinrich, *Mendelssohn und Lessing: nebst*

einer Gedächtnisrede auf Moses Mendelssohn zu dessen 100jährigen Todestage, gehalten im akademischen Vereine für jüdische Geschichte und Literatur, 2nd edn (Berlin, 1886).

Ritter, Joachim, *Hegel und die Französische Revolution* (Cologne and Opladen, 1957).

Ritter, Paul, 'Vorwort des Herausgebers', in Wilhelm Dilthey, *Gesammelte Schriften*, ed. Bernhard Groethuysen *et al.*, 26 vols (Stuttgart and Göttingen, 1922-2005), vol.3, p.v-x.

Robertson, John, *The Enlightenment: a very short introduction* (Oxford, 2015).

–, 'Enlightenment without "origins"? From *Radicati di Passerano* to *Utopia e riforma*', in *Il repubblicanesimo moderno: l'idea di repubblica nella riflessione storica di Franco Venturi*, ed. Manuela Albertone (Naples, 2006), p.131-54.

–, 'Franco Venturi's Enlightenment', *Past & present* 137 (1992), p.183-206.

Roe, Glenn H., *The Passion of Charles Péguy: literature, modernity, and the crisis of historicism* (Oxford, 2014).

Rosenkranz, Karl, *Georg Wilhelm Friedrich Hegel's Leben* (Berlin, 1844).

Rózsa, Erzsébet, 'Besonderheit und Selbstbestimmung: einführende Gedanken in Hegels Grundlegung seiner Theorie der modernen Freiheit in der *Einleitung* zur *Rechtsphilosophie* von 1820', in *Hegel's logic and politics: problems, legacies, and*

perspectives, ed. Gregor Schäfer (Lanham, MD, in press).

–, 'Liebe und Freiheit bei Hegel', in *Morale, etica, religione tra filosofia classica tedesca e pensiero contemporaneo*, ed. Luca Illetterati *et al.* (Padua, 2020), p.365-77.

–, 'Von Antigone zur anständigen Frau: Hegels Frauenbild im Spannungsfeld zwischen der Phänomenologie des Geistes und der Rechtsphilosophie von 1820', in *The Owl's flight: Hegel's legacy to contemporary philosophy*, ed. Stefania Achella *et al.* (Berlin, 2021), p.259-76.

Rürup, Reinhard, *Emanzipation und Antisemitismus: Studien zur 'Judenfrage' der bürgerlichen Gesellschaft* (Göttingen, 1975).

'Russkie vol'nodumtsy v tsarstvovanie Ekateriny II: Sekretno-Vskrytaia perepiska, 1790-1795', *Russkaia starina* 9 (1874), p.259-76.

Rutkoff, Peter M., and William B. Scott, *New School: a history of the New School for Social Research* (New York, 1986).

Saadhoff, Jens, *Germanistik in der DDR: Literaturwissenschaft zwischen 'gesellschaftlichem Auftrag' und disziplinärer Eigenlogik* (Heidelberg, 2007).

Salaün, Franck, and Jean-Pierre Schandeler, *Enquête sur la construction des Lumières* (Ferney-Voltaire, 2018).

Schalk, Fritz, 'Aufklärung', in *Historisches Wörterbuch der Philosophie*, ed. Joachim Ritter, vol.1 (Basel, 1971), col.620-33.

Scheliha, Arnulf von, 'Der Entzug von Bruno Bauers *venia docendi* und die Argumente der gutachtenden theologischen Fakultäten', in *Bruno Bauer: ein 'Partisan des Weltgeistes'?*, ed. Klaus-Michael Kodalle and Tilman Reitz (Würzburg, 2010), p.63-73.

Schiller, Kay, 'Paul Oskar Kristeller, Ernst Cassirer and the "humanistic turn" in American emigration', in *Exile, science and Bildung: the contested legacies of German émigré intellectuals*, ed. David Kettler and Gerhard Lauer (New York, 2005), p.125-38.

Schlosser, Friedrich Christoph, *Geschichte des achtzehnten Jahrhunderts in gedrängter Uebersicht: mit steter Beziehung auf die völlige Veränderung der Denk- und Regierungsweise am Ende desselben*, 2 vols (Heidelberg, 1823).

–, *Geschichte des achtzehnten Jahrhunderts und des neunzehnten bis zum Sturz des französischen Kaiserreichs: mit besonderer Rücksicht auf geistige Bildung*, vol.1 (Heidelberg, 1836).

–, *History of the eighteenth century and of the nineteenth till the overthrow of the French Empire: with particular reference to mental cultivation and progress*, translated, with a preface and notes, by D[avid] Davison, vol.1-8 (London, 1843-1852).

Schmidt, James, 'Inventing the Enlightenment: anti-Jacobins, British Hegelians, and the *Oxford English dictionary*', *Journal of the history of ideas* 64:3 (July 2003), p.421-43.

–, 'Language, mythology, and Enlightenment: historical notes on Horkheimer and Adorno's *Dialectic of Enlightenment*', *Social research* 65:4 (1998), p.807-38.

–, 'What, if anything, does *Dialectic of Enlightenment* have to do with "the Enlightenment"?', in *Aufklärungs-Kritik und Aufklärungs-Mythen*, ed. Sonja Lavaert and Winfried Schröder (Berlin and Boston, MA, 2018), p.11-27.

Schneiders, Werner, *Die wahre Aufklärung: zum Selbstverständnis der deutschen Aufklärung* (Freiburg and Munich, 1974).

Schoeps, Julius H., 'Aufklärung, Judentum und Emanzipation', in *Judentum im Zeitalter der Aufklärung*, ed. Lessing-Akademie (Wolfenbüttel, 1977), p.75-102.

– (ed.), *Juden als Träger bürgerlicher Kultur in Deutschland* (Stuttgart and Bonn, 1989).

Schröder, Winfried, *et al.*, *Französische Aufklärung: bürgerliche Emanzipation, Literatur und Bewußtseinsbildung* (Leipzig, 1974).

Schubert, Alexander, *Phänomenologie des Zeitgeistes: mit Hegel durchs 21. Jahrhundert* (Vienna, 2022).

Schulte, Christoph, '"Diese unglückliche Nation": jüdische Reaktionen auf Dohms *Über die bürgerliche Verbesserung der Juden*', *Zeitschrift für Religions- und Geistesgeschichte* 54 (2002), p.352-65.

–, 'Integration durch Haskala? Ein Paradigma für Minoritäten-Integration heute?', in *Das Prinzip Aufklärung zwischen Universalismus und partikularem Anspruch*, ed. Christina-Monika Hinneburg and Grażyna Jurewicz (Paderborn, 2014), p.25-36.

–, 'Die Zukunft des Judentums nach der Emanzipation: drei Modelle in der Berliner Haskala – Mendelssohn, Euchel, Friedländer', *Mendelssohn Studien* 20 (2017), p.11-24.

Serdobin, M. N., 'Graf Nikita Petrovich Panin, russkii diplomat 1797 g.', *Russkaia starina* 8 (1873), p.338-73.

Shakhanov, A. N., *Russkaia istoricheskaia nauka vtoroi poloviny XIX-nachala XX veka: Moskovskii i Peterburgskii univer-sitety* (St Petersburg, 2003).

Shane, Scott, 'Stephen Bannon in 2014: we are at war with radical Islam', *The New York Times* (1 February 2017).

Shcherbatov, Mikhail, 'O povrezhdenii nravov v Rossii', *Russkaia starina* 27 (1870), p.13-99.

'Sheshkovskii', *Russkaia starina* 10 (1874), p.781-85.

Shumigorskii, E. S., 'Imperatritsa Mariia Fedorovna: puteshestviie za granitsu 1781-1782', *Russkaia starina* 5 (1890), p.17-78.

Sideau, F. G., and A. A. Kruglyi, *Dvor Imperatritsy Ekateriny II: ee sotrudniki i priblizhennye* (St Petersburg, 1899).

Sieg, Ullrich, 'Antisemitismus und Antiliberalismus im Deutschen Kaiserreich', in *Liberalismus als Feindbild*, ed. Ewald Grote and Ulrich Sieg (Göttingen, 2014), p.93-112.

Siegert, Reinhart, 'Enlight-enment in the 19th century – "overcoming" or diffusion?', translated by David Paisey, in *Volksaufklärung: biobibliographisches Handbuch zur Popularisierung aufklärerischen Denkens im deutschen Sprachraum von den Anfängen bis 1850*, ed. Holger Böning and Reinhart Siegert, vol.3 (Stuttgart-Bad Cannstatt, 2016), p.lxxix-cxv.

Simon, Jules, *Victor Cousin* (Paris, 1887).

Singer, I[sidor] (ed.), *Briefe berühmter christlicher Zeitgenossen über die Judenfrage: nach Manuscripten gedruckt und mit Autorisation der Verfasser zum ersten Male herausgegeben, mit biographischen Skizzen der Autoren und einem Vorworte versehen von I[sidor] Singer* (Vienna, 1885).

–, *Presse und Judenthum*, 2nd edn (Vienna, 1882).

Sirotinina, A. N., 'K. F. Ryleev: istoriko-literaturnyj biograficheski ocherk', *Russkii arkhiv* 6 (1890), p.113-209.

Smith, Helmut Walser, 'Reluctant return: Peter Gay and the cosmopolitan work of the historian', in *The Second generation: émigrés from Nazi Germany as historians*, ed. Andreas Daum (New York, 2015), p.210-28.

Solov'ev, Sergei, 'Imperatorskie sovety v Rossii v XVIII veka', *Russkaia starina* 27 (1870), p.463-68.

Sorkin, David, 'Jews, the Enlight-enment and the sources of toleration: some reflections', *Leo Baeck Institute year book* 37 (1992), p.3-16.

–, *The Transformation of German Jewry, 1780-1840* (New York and Oxford, 1987).

Spector, Céline, 'The "lights" before the Enlightenment: the tribunal of reason and public opinion', in *Let there be Enlightenment: the religious and mystical sources of rationality*, ed. Anton M. Matytsin and Dan Edelstein (Baltimore, MD, 2018), p.86-102.

Spinoza, Baruch, *Spinoza's Ethics*, ed. Clare Carlisle, translated by George Eliot (Princeton, NJ, 2020).

Spitzer, Alan B., *The French generation of 1820* (Princeton, NJ, 1987).

Sreznevskii, Ivan, 'A. I. Turgenev: otnoshenie k N. M. Karamzinu', *Russkaia starina* 21 (1875), p.555-64.

Stephen, Leslie, *The English Utilitarians*, 3 vols (London, 1900).

–, *History of English thought in the eighteenth century*, 2 vols (London, 1876).

Stieler, Kaspar von, *Der Deutschen Sprache Stammbaum und Fortwachs, oder Teutscher Sprach-schatz* (Nuremberg, Hofmann, 1691).

Strachey, Lytton, *Landmarks of French literature* (London, 1912).

Strauss, Leo, 'German nihilism', ed. David Janssens and Daniel Tanguay, *Interpretation* 26:3 (spring 1999), p.353-78.

Strugnell, Anthony, *Diderot's politics: a study of the evolution of Diderot's political thought after the Encyclopédie* (The Hague, 1973).

Stuke, Horst, 'Aufklärung', in *Geschichtliche Grundbegriffe: historisches Lexikon zur politisch-sozialen Sprache*, ed. Otto Brunner, Werner Conze and Reinhart Koselleck, vol.1 (Stuttgart, 1972), p.243-342.

Suchy, Barbara, 'The Verein zur Abwehr des Antisemitismus (I): from its beginnings to the First World War', *Leo Baeck Institute year book* 28:1 (1983), p.205-39.

–, 'The Verein zur Abwehr des Antisemitismus (II): from the First World War to its dissolution in 1933', *Leo Baeck Institute year book* 30:1 (1985), p.67-100.

Suckut, Siegfried (ed.), *Das Wörterbuch der Staatssicherheit: Definitionen zur 'politisch-operativen Arbeit'*, 2nd edn (Berlin, 1996).

Sukhomlinov, Mikhail, 'Piatide-siatiletnii i stoletnii iubilei S.-Peterburgskoi Akademii Nauk', *Russkaia starina* 18 (1877), p.1-20.

Sulzer, Johann Georg, *Kurzer Begriff aller Wissenschaften [...]: zweyte ganz veränderte und sehr vermehrte Auflage* (Leipzig, bey Johann Christian Langenheim, 1759).

Sutcliffe, Adam, 'Judaism and the politics of Enlightenment', *American behavioral scientist* 49 (2006), p.702-15.

Taine, Hippolyte, *Les Origines de la France contemporaine*, vol.1: *L'Ancien Régime* (Paris, 1875).

Taylor, Charles, 'Understanding in human science', *The Review of metaphysics* 34:1 (1980), p.25-38.

Testa, Italo, *Hegel critico e scettico: Illuminismo, repubblicanesimo e antinomia alle origini della dialettica* (Padua, 2002).

Thaden, Edward C., 'Friedrich Meinecke and Russian historicism', in *Interpreting history: collective essays on Russia's relations with Europe* (New York and Boulder, CO, 1990), p.53-72.

Theis, Laurent, *François Guizot* (Paris, 2008).

Thoma, Heinz, 'Aufklärung', in *Handbuch Europäische Aufklärung: Begriffe – Konzepte – Wirkung*, ed. Heinz Thoma (Stuttgart, 2015), p.67-85.

Thomas, François, 'Introduire le sauvage allemand dans le beau monde parisien: l'enjeu éthique et politique de la traduction dans le débat entre les Lumières et le romantisme allemand', in *La Traduction: philosophie et traduction – interpréter/traduire*, ed. Christian Berner and Tatiana Milliaressi (Villeneuve d'Asc, 2011), p.148-62.

Tocqueville, Alexis de, *L'Ancien Régime et la Révolution* (Paris, 1856).

–, *L'Ancien Régime et la Révolution*, ed. J.-P. Mayer (Paris, 1967).

Tomba, Massimilano, 'Bruno Bauers kritische Auseinandersetzung mit der französischen Revolution: Historiographie, Politik, Geschichtsphilosophie', in *Bruno Bauer: ein 'Partisan des Weltgeistes'?*, ed. Klaus-Michael Kodalle and Tilman Reitz (Würzburg, 2010), p.251-62.

–, *Krise und Kritik bei Bruno Bauer* (Frankfurt am Main, 2005).

Tomkins, David Beveridge, 'The individual and society: a comparison between the views of the enlightenment and those of the nineteenth century',

doctoral dissertation, New York University, 1914.

Torrey, Norman, *Voltaire and the age of Enlightenment* (New York, 1931).

Toury, Jacob, '"The Jewish question": a semantic approach', *The Leo Baeck Institute year book* 11:1 (1966), p.85-106.

Treitschke, Heinrich von, *Deutsche Geschichte im Neunzehnten Jahrhundert*, 5 vols (Leipzig, 1879-1894).

Trevor-Roper, Hugh, 'The historical philosophy of Thomas Carlyle', in *History and the Enlightenment* (New Haven, CT, 2010), p.223-45.

Troeltsch, Ernst, 'Aufklärung', in *Realencyklopädie für protestantische Theologie und Kirche*, ed. Albert Hauck, 3rd edn, vol.2 (Leipzig, 1897), p.225-41.

Tuttle, Howard N., 'The epistemological status of the cultural world in Vico and Dilthey', in *Giambattista Vico's science of humanity*, ed. Giorgio Tagliacozzo and Donald Phillip Verene (Baltimore, MD, 1976), p.241-50.

'Ukaz Ekateriny II ob ochistke Nevy: 1-ogo maia 1775', *Russkaia starina* 10 (1874), p.615-17.

Undol'skii, V. M., 'Pis'ma Vukola Mikhailovicha Undol'skago k A. N. Popovu', *Russkii arkhiv* 6 (1886), p.281-304.

'Unichtozhenie masonskikh lozh v Rossii v 1822: sekretnye zapiski i doneseniia senatora E. A. Kusheleva i drugie', *Russkaia starina* 19 (1877), p.641-65.

Valentini, Francesco, 'Hegel critico dell'Illuminismo', in *Individuo e modernità: saggi sulla filosofia di Hegel*, ed. Marcella D'Abbiero and Paolo Vinci (Milan, 1995), p.63-74.

Valiani, Leo, 'Una testimonianza', *Rivista storica italiana* 108 (1996), p.507-49.

Venturi, Franco, 'La circolazione delle idee', *Rassegna storica del Risorgimento* 41 (1954), p.203-22.

–, 'Contributi ad un dizionario storico: despotismo orientale', *Rivista storica italiana* 72 (1960), p.117-26; English translation: 'Oriental despotism', in *Italy and the Enlightenment: studies in a cosmopolitan century*, ed. Stuart Woolf, translated by Susan Corsi (London, 1972), p.41-51.

–, 'Contributi ad un dizionario storico: Was ist Aufklärung? Sapere aude!', *Rivista storica italiana* 71 (1959), p.119-28; English translation: 'Was ist Aufklärung? Sapere aude!', in *Italy and the Enlightenment: studies in a cosmopolitan century*, ed. Stuart Woolf, translated by Susan Corsi (London, 1972), p.33-41.

–, *The End of the Old Regime in Europe, 1768-1776*, vol.4: *The Great states of the West*, translated by Robert Burr Litchfield (Princeton, NJ, 1991).

–, 'The European Enlightenment', in *Italy and the Enlightenment: studies in a cosmopolitan century*, ed. Stuart Woolf, translated by Susan Corsi (London, 1972), p.3-32.

–, 'La fortuna di dom Deschamps', *Cahiers Vilfredo Pareto* 5:11 (1967), p.47-55.

–, *Jeunesse de Diderot (1713-1753)* (Paris, 1939).

–, *Pages inédites contre un tyran* (Paris, 1937).

–, 'La prima crisi dell'Antico Regime: 1768-1776', *SVEC* 190 (1980), p.63-80.

–, *The Roots of revolution: a history of the populist and socialist movements in nineteenth-century Russia*, translated by Francis Haskell (London, 1960).

–, *Settecento riformatore*, 7 vols (Turin, 1969-1990).

–, *Utopia and reform in the Enlightenment* (Cambridge, 1971).

Venturino, Diego, 'L'historiographie révolutionnaire française et les Lumières, de Paul Buchez à Albert Sorel: suivi d'un appendice sur la genèse de l'expression "siècle des Lumières" (XVIIIe-XXe siècles)', in *Historiographie et usages des Lumières*, ed. Giuseppe Ricuperati (Berlin, 2002), p.21-84.

Vermeren, Patrice, *Victor Cousin: le jeu de la philosophie et de l'Etat* (Paris, 1995).

Viarengo, Adriano, *Franco Venturi: politica e storia nel Novecento* (Rome, 2014).

–, 'Venturi, Franco', in *Dizionario biografico degli Italiani*, vol.98 (2020), https://www.treccani.it/enciclopedia/franco-venturi_%28Dizionario-Biografico%29/ (last accessed 26 April 2023).

Vierhaus, Rudolf, 'Liberalismus und deutsches Bürgertum', in *Vergangenheit als Geschichte: Studien zum 19. und 20. Jahrhundert*, ed. Hans Erich Bödecker, Benigna von Krusenstjern and Michael Matthiesen (Göttingen, 2003), p.171-82.

Vieweg, Klaus, *Das Denken der Freiheit* (Munich, 2012).

–, *Hegel: der Philosoph der Freiheit* (Munich, 2019).

–, 'Warum Hegel kein Rassist war', *Die Welt* (24 December 2020), p.28.

Villemain, Abel-François, *Cours de littérature française: tableau du XVIII* *siècle*, 4 vols (Paris, 1838).

–, *Tableau de la littérature au XVIII* *siècle*, 2nd edn, 4 vols (Paris, 1840).

Vincent, Julien, '"Maudit soit le talent qui n'a pas la vertu pour compagne": l'abbé Grégoire face à la lâcheté des hommes de lettres (1789-1839)', in *'La Modernité dure longtemps': penser les discordances des temps avec Christophe Charle*, ed. François Jarrige and Julien Vincent (Paris, 2020), p.19-41.

Vogeler, Martha S., *Frederic Harrison: the vocations of a positivist* (Oxford, 1984).

Volkov, Shulamit, *Dilemma und Dialektik: zwei Jahrhunderte Aufklärung aus jüdischer Sicht* (Munich, 2002).

–, *Germans, Jews, and antisemites: trials in emancipation* (Cambridge, 2006).

–, 'Nochmals zum Antimodernismus im Kaiserreich', in *Das Deutsche Kaiserreich in der Kontroverse*, ed. Sven Oliver Müller and Cornelius Torp (Göttingen, 2009), p.66-76.

Volpilhac-Auger, Catherine, 'Une bibliothèque bleue: le siècle des Lumières en Pléiade', in *La Bibliothèque de la Pléiade: travail éditorial et valeur littéraire*, ed. Joëlle Gleize and Philippe Roussin (Paris, 2009), p.103-15.

–, 'Et les Lumières ne furent plus...?', *Fabula / Les Colloques* (2020), special issue: *Accuser réception*, ed. Thierry Roger and Stéphane Zékian, https://www.fabula.org/colloques/document6567.php (last accessed 20 April 2023).

Voltaire, *Correspondence and related documents*, ed. Theodore Besterman, in *Œuvres complètes de Voltaire*, vol.85-135 (Oxford, 1968-1977).

–, *Lettres sur les Anglais*, ed. N. Cronk, in *Œuvres complètes de Voltaire*, vol.6B (Oxford, 2020).

–, *Œuvres complètes de Voltaire*, ed. Theodore Besterman et al., 205 vols (Oxford, 1968-2022).

–, *Œuvres de 1764-1766*, ed. Marie-Hélène Cotoni et al., in *Œuvres complètes de Voltaire*, vol.60B (Oxford, 2018).

[Vospitannik Khar'kovsogo Universiteta 1820-kh gg], 'Vasilii Nazarovich Karazin, 1803', *Russkaia starina* 12 (1875), p.334-37.

Vosskamp, Wilhelm, 'Klassisch/Klassik/Klassizismus', in *Ästhetische Grundbegriffe: historisches Wörterbuch in sieben Bänden*, ed. Karlheinz Barck et al., 7 vols (Stuttgart and Weimar, 2001-2005), vol.3, p.289-305.

V. S., 'Literatura Ekaterinskogo iubileia', *Russkaia starina* 9 (1874), p.796-817.

Vysochaishe utverzhdennyi tseremonial torzhestvennogo otkrytia pamiatnika Imperatritse Ekaterine II (St Petersburg, 1873).

Wade, Ira O., *The Clandestine organization and diffusion of philosophic ideas in France from 1700 to 1750* (Princeton, NJ, 1938).

Walicki, Andrzej, *The Slavophile controversy: history of a conservative utopia in nineteenth-century Russian thought* (Oxford, 1975).

Waliszewski, Kazimierz, *Autour d'un trône: Catherine II de Russie, ses collaborateurs, ses amis, ses favoris* (Paris, 1894).

Walther, Joachim, *Sicherungsbereich Literatur: Schriftsteller und Staatssicherheit in der Deutschen Demokratischen Republik* (Berlin, 1996).

Waszek, Norbert, '1789, 1830 und kein Ende: Hegel und die Französische Revolution', in *Französische Revolution und Pädagogik der Moderne*, ed. Ulrich Herrmann and Jürgen Oelkers (Weinheim and Basel, 1989), p.347-59.

–, *The Scottish Enlightenment and Hegel's account of civil society* (Boston, MA, and London, 1988).

–, 'The Scottish Enlightenment in Germany, and its translator Christian Garve (1742-1798)', in *Scotland in Europe*, ed. Tom Hubbard and R. D. S. Jack (Amsterdam and New York, 2006), p.55-71.

–, 'Zwischen Vertrag und Leidenschaft – Hegels Lehre von der Ehe und die Gegenspieler: Kant und die Frühromantiker

(Schlegel, Schleiermacher)', in *Gesellschaftliche Freiheit und vertragliche Bindung in Rechtsgeschichte und Philosophie*, ed. Jean-François Kervégan and Heinz Mohnhaupt (Frankfurt am Main, 1999), p.271-99.

Wellek, René, 'The term and concept of classicism in literary history', in *Discriminations: further concepts of criticism* (New Haven, CT, and London, 1970), p.55-89.

Whaley, Joachim, 'German studies: where is the *Aufklärung* now?', *Journal for eighteenth-century studies* 34:4 (2011), p.487-93.

Wheatland, Thomas, *The Frankfurt School in exile* (Minneapolis, MN, 2009).

Whewell, William, 'Comte and positivism', *Macmillan's magazine* 13 (1866), p.353-62.

–, *History of the inductive sciences, from the earliest to the present times*, 3 vols (London, 1837).

–, *Lectures on the history of moral philosophy in England* (London, 1852).

–, *Philosophy of the inductive sciences, founded upon their history*, 2 vols (London, 1840).

–, 'Spedding's complete edition of the works of Bacon', *Edinburgh review* 106 (1857), p.287-322.

Wickburg, Daniel, 'Intellectual history vs. the social history of intellectuals', *Rethinking history* 5:3 (2001), p.383-95.

Wolfe, Jean-Claude, 'Bruno Bauers Posaune des Jüngsten Gerichts', in *Utopie und Apokalypse in der Moderne*, ed. Stefan Bodo Würffel *et al.* (Paderborn, 2010), p.119-28.

Wortman, Richard, *The Development of a Russian legal consciousness* (Chicago, IL, 1976).

Wreszin, Michael, *A Rebel in defense of tradition: the life and politics of Dwight Macdonald* (New York, 1994).

Wright, Johnson Kent, 'Foreword', in Carl Becker, *The Heavenly city of the eighteenth-century philosophers*, 2nd edn (New Haven, CT, 2003), p.i-xii.

Wright, Terry R., *The Party of humanity: the impact of Comtean positivism on Victorian Britain* (Cambridge, 1986).

Wyrwa, Ulrich, *Juden in der Toskana und in Preußen im Vergleich: Aufklärung und Emanzipation in Florenz, Livorno, Berlin und Königsberg i. Pr.* (Tübingen, 2003).

Yeo, Richard, *Defining science: William Whewell, natural knowledge, and polite debate in early Victorian Britain* (Cambridge, 1993).

–, 'An idol of the marketplace: Baconianism in nineteenth-century Britain', *History of science* 23 (1985), p.251-98.

Young, Brian W., 'The Counter-Enlightenments of Thomas Carlyle', in *Thomas Carlyle and the idea of influence*, ed. Paul Kerry, Albert D. Pionke and Megan Dent (Lanham, MD, 2018), p.193-223.

–, '"An epoch in the history of ones' mind": Gibbon, Carlyle, and the post-Reform generation' (forthcoming).

–, 'History', in *Historicism and the human sciences in Victorian Britain*, ed. Mark Bevir (Cambridge, 2017), p.154-85.

–, 'Intellectual history and *Historismus* in post-war England', in *A Companion to intellectual history*, ed. Richard Whatmore and Brian W. Young (Chichester, 2016), p.19-35.

–, *Religion and Enlightenment in eighteenth-century England: theological debate from Locke to Burke* (Oxford, 1998).

–, *The Victorian eighteenth century: an intellectual history* (Oxford, 2007).

Zaitsev, Andrei, *Petr Ivanovich Bartenev i zhurnal 'Russkkii arkhiv'* (Moscow, 2001).

Zékian, Stéphane, *La Littérature mise à prix: l'Académie française et son concours d'éloquence, XIXᵉ-XXᵉ siècles* (forthcoming).

–, 'Vie et mort d'un concours: le prix d'éloquence à l'Académie française (XIXᵉ-XXᵉ siècle)', *Recherches & travaux* 99 (2001), http://journals.openedition.org/recherchestravaux/4082 (last accessed 20 April 2023).

'Zhalovannaia Gramota Gosudaryni Imperatritsy Ekateriny Vtoroi na prava, vol'nosti i preiumshchestva blagorodnogo Rossiiskogo dvorianstva, 21 Aprelia 1785', *Russkii arkhiv* 5 (1885), p.155-64.

'Zhizn' Efima Petrovicha Chemesova, 1735-1801: zapiski dlia pamiati', *Russkaia starina* 7 (1891), p.1-10.

Zimmermann, Moshe, 'Aufklärung, Emanzipation,

Selbstemanzipation', *Aufklärung und Haskala in jüdischer und nichtjüdischer Sicht*, ed. Karlfried Gründer and Nathan Rotenstreich (Heidelberg, 1990), p.143-52.

–, 'Die "Judenfrage" als "die soziale Frage": zu Kontinuität und Stellenwert des Antisemitismus vor und nach dem Nationalsozialismus', in *Deutschjüdische Vergangenheit: der Judenhaß als Herausforderung* (Paderborn, 2005), p.289-301.

Zinov'ev, V. N., *Zhurnal Puteshestviia V. N. Zinov'eva po Germanii, Italii, Frantsii i Anglii v 1786-1790 gg.*, ed. N. P. Varyshnikov, *Russkaia starina* 23 (1878), p.207-40, 399-440, 593-630.

Žižek, Slavoj, *Hegel in a wired brain* (London and New York, 2020).

Index

This index was prepared by Dominique Lussier.

Aaron, 33
Abbt, Thomas, 131
Abel, Jacob Friedrich, 60
absolutism, 18-19, 135, 173-74,
    251-53, 273
Académie française, 81-85, 89-99,
    148, 153
Adler, Mortimer J., 225, 230-33
    'God and the professors', 226
Adorno, Theodor W., 1, 220, 223-24,
    232, 236, 240, 242
    Briefe und Briefwechsel, 223
    Minima moralia, 230
–, and Max Horkheimer
    Dialectic of Enlightenment, 109,
        223-24, 229-32, 236, 239-40, 266
    Dialektik der Aufklärung, 266, 282
agnostics, 106, 110-11, 114, 116
Alexander I, emperor of Russia, 155
Alexander II, emperor of Russia, 157,
    163, 165-66, 168
Alexander III, emperor of Russia,
    184
Alfieri, Vittorio, 111
*Allgemeine deutsche Real-Encyklopädie
    für die gebildeten Stände*, 206
American Revolution, 235, 261
Anshen, Ruth Nanda, 239
antisemitism, 187n, 190, 192, 195-96,
    199-201, 212-13, 217-18, 221
Arendt, Hannah, 1, 189, 220, 264
    'The Enlightenment and the Jewish
        question', 187, 221
    Origins of totalitarianism, 266
Argenson, René-Louis de Voyer,
    marquis d', 253

Aristotle, 5
Arkhangelsky, Alexander, *The Empress
    Catherine II in the history of Russian
    literature and education*, 182
Arnim, Bettina von, 76
Ascoli, Georges, 152
atheism, 17, 18n, 28, 45, 92, 96, 106,
    226, 255
Auerbach, Erich, 271
Aufklärung, see concepts of Enlight-
    enment, etc.
Augustus, Roman emperor, 291

Bach, Johann Sebastian, 50
Bacon, Francis, 103-105, 111-12
Bannon, Stephen, 200
Barante, Amable Guillaume Prosper
    Brugière, baron de, 82
Barnikol, Ernst, 44
Baron, Salo W., 'Ghetto and
    emancipation: shall we revise the
    traditional view?', 188
Bartels, Adolf, 205
Bartenev, Peter, 158
Basedow, Johann Bernhard, 130
Baudrillart, Henri, 'Turgot', 86, 88,
    92, 95-96
Bauer, Bruno, 1, 37-40, 291
    *Briefwechsel zwischen Bruno Bauer
        und Edgar Bauer während der Jahre
        1839-1842*, 45
    Christianity revealed, 37, 46
    *Documents on the negotiations on
        the confiscation of the 'History of
        politics, culture and Enlightenment
        of the eighteenth century'*, 46

*History of Germany and of the
French Revolution under the rule of
Napoleon*, 51
*History of politics, culture and Enlight-
enment of the eighteenth century*, 37,
39-42, 44-46, 48-55
*History of the French Revolution until
the founding of the Republic* (with
Edgar Bauer and Ernst Jungnitz),
51
'The trumpet of the Last
Judgement on Hegel: an
ultimatum', 43
Bauer, Edgar, 37, 45
*Library of German enlighteners of the
eighteenth century*, 38
*The Political literature of the Germans
in the eighteenth century*, 38
Baumann, Zygmunt, 220
Bayle, Pierre, 3n, 252, 255
Bazin, Anaïs, *Eloge [...] de
Malesherbes*, 29, 95
Beaumarchais, Pierre Augustin
Caron de, 82, 87
Beccaria, Cesare, 164, 174, 249-50
Becker, Balthazar, 44
Becker, Karin Elizabeth, 24n
Becker, Karl, 245, 260, 277, 282
'Everyman his own historian', 260
*The Heavenly city of the eighteenth-
century philosophers*, 245-46,
260-61, 278
Bédier, Joseph, 148n
Beethoven, Ludwig van, *Fidelio*, 77
Beiser, Frederick, 137n
Below, Georg von
*Die deutsche Geschichtsschreibung von
den Befreiungskriegen bis zu unseren
Tagen*, 208-11
Die Ursachen der Reformation, 208
Benedict, Ruth, 'Human nature is
not a trap', 234
Benjamin, Walter, 231
Bentham, Jeremy, 103, 116
Berlin, Isaiah, 101, 111, 114
Four lectures on Russian historicism,
183
Three critics of the Enlightenment,
119, 122
Berlin Academy of Sciences, 123-25,
130-34, 297

Berlioz, Hector, *Symphonie fantastique*,
101
Bernardin de Saint-Pierre,
Jacques-Henri, 82, 92-93
Etudes de la nature, 93
Bernfeld, Simon, *Am Ende des
Jahrhunderts: Rückschau auf
100 Jahre geistiger Entwicklung*, 191
Bernstein, Eduard, 262, 269
Berry, Charles Ferdinand, duc de, 11
Berti, Silvia, 'Repubblicanesimo
e Illuminismo Radicale nella
storiografia di Franco Venturi',
253n-254n, 255
Besterman, Theodore, 274, 278-79,
281-82
Betskoi, Ivan, 173-74
Biale, David, 'The end of Enlight-
enment?', 197-201, 221
Bible (New Testament)
John, 143
Matthew, 143n
Bibliothèque nationale de France,
141, 153, 243
Biedermann, Karl, *Germany in the
eighteenth century*, 47
Bilbasov, Vasily, 'Nikita Panin i
Mers'ie de la-Riv'er', 181
Black, Jeremy, 248n
Blackstone, William, 163, 174
Blow, Susan E., 75
Blumenberg, Hans, 22
Bodmer, Johann Jacob, 48
Boileau-Despréaux, Nicolas, 147, 149
Bollenbeck, Georg, 218-19, 221
'Die Abwendung des Bildungsbür-
gertums von der Aufklärung',
186, 201-206, 209
Bildung und Kultur, 186n, 203-204
*Eine Geschichte der Kulturkritik: von
Rousseau bis Günther Anders*, 186n,
202n-203n, 204
*Tradition, Avantgarde, Reaktion:
deutsche Kontroversen um die
kulturelle Moderne*, 186n
Bonald, Louis de, 24, 29, 144
Bonhard, Otto [Otto Kernholt], *Vom
Ghetto zur Macht: die Geschichte des
Aufstiegs der Juden auf deutschem
Boden*, 187n, 192n, 196n, 205n
Bonnet, Jean-Claude, 82

Borgondio, Gentile, 77
Börne, Ludwig, 214n
Bossuet, Jacques Bénigne, bishop of
  Meaux, 94, 147, 149, 152n
Boulanger, Nicolas-Antoine, 254
Bourdin, Jean-Claude, *Hegel et les
  matérialistes français*, 70n
Brauer, Oscar Daniel, 68
Breitinger, Johann Jacob, 48
Brinton, Crane, 'Many mansions',
  260
Brückner, Alexander, 157
Brunetière, Ferdinand, 146, 148-49,
  152n
Buckle, Henry Thomas, *History of
  civilization in England*, 117-18
Buffon, Georges-Louis Leclerc, comte
  de, 82, 86, 90-91, 111, 149
Bunzel, Wolfgang, 38
Buonarroti, Filippo, 254
  Riforma dell'Alcorano, 248
Burns, Robert, 106
Butler, Eliza M., 107, 109-10
  Paper boats, 108
  The Tyranny of Greece over Germany,
  108-109

Caillois, Roger, 231
Calas affair, 148
Campe, Joachim Heinrich
  Kleine Seelenlehre für Kinder, 59
  Theophron, 64
Cantimori, Delio, 247n
Carcassonne, Ely, 152
  *Montesquieu et le problème de la consti-
  tution française au XVIIIᵉ siècle*, 152
Carlyle, Thomas, 101-103, 105-107,
  109-10, 113-14, 117-18
  'Diderot', 106
  *On heroes, hero-worship, and the heroic
  in history*, 106
  'Voltaire', 106
Cart, Jean-Jacques, *Vertrauliche Briefe
  über das vormalige staatsrechtliche
  Verhältnis des Waadtlandes (Pays de
  Vaud) zur Stadt Bern* (transl. Hegel),
  66-67
Cassirer, Ernst, 1, 221, 244-45,
  271-73, 279, 282
  The Myth of the state, 273
  Die Philosophie der Aufklärung,

36, 257-58, 270; transl. Pierre
  Quillet, *La Philosophie des
  Lumières*, 36
  The Question of Jean-Jacques Rousseau,
  ed. and transl. Peter Gay, 267n,
  269-71, 273, 281
Catalani, Angelica, 77
Catherine the Great, empress of
  Russia, xi, 155-60, 162-71, 173-83,
  250-51
  Nakaz, 163-66
  Les Plans et les statuts, 174
Catholicism, 14, 17n, 29, 45, 115,
  148-49, 207, 219
Catt, Henri de, 128
Chase, Richard V., 'The
  Huxley-Heard paradise', 234
Chateaubriand, François-René,
  vicomte de, 95
Chénier, André, 82
Chénier, Marie-Joseph, 82
Chernyshevsky, Nikolai, 182n
Chodowiecki, Daniel, 131
Christianity, xi, 27, 29, 42, 54, 93-94,
  103, 106, 110, 112, 114-15, 128,
  179, 189, 211, 214, 215n-216n, 220,
  260-61, 281, 291, 293
Cicero, 254
classicism, 3, 30-31, 34, 47-48,
  108-109, 137
Clifford, James, 280-81
Cobban, Alfred, *Rousseau and the
  modern state*, 270, 273
Cohen, Hermann, 221
Cohn, 277
Coleridge, 115
*Collection of the Imperial Russian
  Historical Society*, 158
Combe, George, 111
Combes, Emile, 149
Compagnon, Antoine, *La Troisième
  République des lettres*, 147-51
Comte, Auguste, 103, 111-13, 115, 118
concepts of Enlightenment, etc.
  Aufklärung, xi, 1-4, 21-23, 31-32,
  35-36, 39, 46-49, 51-55, 57-73,
  79, 107-108, 114, 117, 120, 123,
  125-27, 129-31, 133-38, 141, 146,
  153-54, 161, 183, 188-90, 191n,
  192, 195-96, 202-21, 244, 245n,
  285, 286n, 287, 290-95, 300

Counter-Enlightenment, 101, 112,
    118-19, 253
Enlightenment, xi, 1-4, 21-23,
    32-33, 38, 40, 42-44, 101-106,
    111, 115-20, 123-27, 142, 145-46,
    148, 150-53, 155, 160-61, 170,
    177, 183, 185-89, 196-201, 205,
    211, 229-31, 247n, 249-62,
    264-66, 268-70, 272-75, 277-83,
    285-87, 289-90, 292-98, 301-305
    Italian, 254
    Radical, 254-56
    Russian (*prosveshchenie*), 155, 157,
        159-63, 164-65, 168-84
    Scottish, 59, 102, 117
enlightenment, 229-31, 233,
    238-40, 290
lumière, 141-44, 153
Lumières, xi, 1-4, 6-7, 11, 14, 17n,
    21-25, 27, 29, 32-34, 35n, 36,
    69-70, 81-82, 85-88, 91-94,
    96-99, 112-13, 118, 125-26, 129,
    135, 141, 149, 152-54, 160n, 183,
    242-43, 248, 255, 295
lumières, 25n, 87-88, 142, 144-46,
    151, 153
Condillac, Etienne Bonnot de, 16-17,
    19, 85, 132
Condorcet, Marie Jean Antoine
    Nicolas de Caritat, marquis de,
    111, 113, 132
    *Esquisse d'un tableau historique des
        progrès de l'esprit humain*, 16
    'Sur l'instruction publique', 144
Corneille, Pierre, 128, 147
Costa, Andrea, 77
Counter-Enlightenment, *see* concepts
    of Enlightenment, etc.
Cousin, Victor, 1, 5-7, 10-12, 13n,
    18-19, 86, 92, 96, 112, 144
    *Cours de l'histoire de la philosophie:
        histoire de la philosophie du XVIIIe
        siècle*, 6, 8-9, 12-16, 18-19
    *Cours de l'histoire de la philosophie
        morale au XVIIIe siècle*, 11
    *Cours de philosophie: introduction à
        l'histoire de la philosophie*, 16-17
    *Cours d'histoire de la philosophie
        moderne pendant les années 1816 et
        1817*, 16, 20n
    Fragments et souvenirs, 67-68

Fragments philosophiques, 10-11,
    18-19
*Histoire de la philosophie morale
    du XVIIIe siècle*, 11
*Introduction à l'histoire de la
    philosophie*, 6
Premiers essais de philosophie, 20
Croce, Benedetto, 241

D'Alembert, Jean, xi, 96, 127-28, 132,
    138, 163
    'Discours préliminaire des éditeurs'
        (*Encyclopédie*), 22
    'Tableau de l'esprit humain au
        milieu du dix-huitième siècle', 22
Dante (Durante Alighieri), 68
Darnton, Robert, 272
    'In search of the Enlightenment:
        recent attempts to create a social
        history of ideas', 257-58
Darwin, Charles, 115
Dashkova, Ekaterina Romanova,
    Princess, 170, 175
David, Pascal, 57n
Degérando, Joseph Marie, *Histoire
    comparée des systèmes de philosophie*,
    19n
deism, 44-45, 71, 96, 115, 255
Deleyre, Alexandre, *Tableau de
    l'Europe*, 253
Descartes, René, 8n, 13-14, 16, 17n,
    20, 22n, 103, 111, 125
    Discours de la méthode, 14
    Méditations métaphysiques, 14
Deschamps, Dom Léger-Marie, *Le
    Vrai Système* (ed. Franco Venturi
    and Jean Thomas), 242, 254
Despois, Eugène, *Les Lettres et la
    liberté*, 82-83, 96, 99
Desrais, Claude Louis, xi
Destutt de Tracy, Antoine Louis
    Claude, 111
Dewey, John, 224, 236
d'Holbach, Paul-Thiry, 69, 71, 94,
    96, 177, 245, 249
    Le Christianisme dévoilé, 46
    Essai sur les préjugés, 243
    Système social, 256
Diderot, Denis, 15, 26n, 96, 106,
    127-28, 131, 149, 173-74, 243, 245,
    247n, 249-50, 252, 254-55, 275

Lettre sur les aveugles, 243
Observations sur le Nakaz, 250-51
Dilthey, Wilhelm, 1, 22, 119-25
  Gesammelte Schriften, 122, 125n,
  126-38
Dippel, Johann Conrad, 44
Dixon, Simon, "'Prosveshchenie'":
  Enlightenment in eighteenth-
  century Russia', 159
Dohm, Christian Wilhelm, 'On the
  Civic Improvement of Jews', 187
Dostoevky, Fyodor, *Notes from the
  underground*, 182n
Dreyfus affair, 148, 152n
Dubos, Jean-Baptiste, 143
Du Châtelet, Emilie Le Tonnelier de
  Breteuil, marquise, 143
Du Deffand, Marie de Vichy de
  Chamrond, marquise, 128
Durkheim, Emile, 147

Eberhard, Johann August, 70
  'Vermuthungen über den Ursprung
  der heutigen Magie', 59
Eckermann, Johann Peter, *Gespräche
  mit Goethe in den letzten Jahren seines
  Lebens*, 12n
eclecticism, 5, 8, 10, 18-19
Edelmann, Johann Christian, 37,
  44-46
Edelstein, Dan, 142
  The Enlightenment: a genealogy,
  161
*Einleitung in die Schönen Wissen-
  schaften: nach dem Französischen
  des Herrn Batteux, mit Zusätzen
  vermehrt von Karl Wilhelm Ramler*,
  58n
Eisenhower, Dwight, 235, 275-76,
  277n
Eisenmenger, Johann Andreas,
  Judaism revealed, 46
Elagin, Ivan, 170-71, 173
Elbogen, Ismar, 187
Eliot, George, 102, 110-11
Encyclopédie, 174, 243
encyclopédistes, 11, 127, 145, 249, 253
Engel, Johann Jakob, 131
Engelhard, Philippine, 76
Engels, Georg Wilhelm Friedrich,
  40, 236

Enlightenment, *see* concepts of
  Enlightenment, etc.
Essbach, Wolfgang, *Die Junghegelianer:
  Soziologie einer Intellektuellengruppe*,
  43-44

Faguet, Emile, *En lisant Nietzsche*, 145
fatalism, 17, 18n
Faure, Félix, 148
Fayolle, Roger
  'Le XVIIIe siècle jugé par le
  XIXe', 81-82
  Sainte-Beuve et le XVIIIe siècle, 92
Febvre, Lucien, 153n
Feder, Johann Georg Heinrich, *Der
  neue Emil oder von der Erziehung
  nach bewährten Grundsätzen*, 59
Fénelon, François de Salignac de La
  Mothe, 94, 152
Ferguson, Adam, 59, 67
  An Essay on the history of civil society,
  59; transl. Christian Garve,
  *Versuch über die Geschichte der
  bürgerlichen Gesellschaft*
Ferrone, Vincenzo, *The Enlightenment:
  history of an idea*, 183, 246
Feuerbach, Ludwig, 30, 40, 110, 291
Fichte, Johann Gottlieb, 19, 111
Filippov, Mikhail, 164, 166
Fleischer, Moritz, 290
Fontenelle, Bernard Le Bovier de, 3n,
  82, 86-88
  *Digression sur les Anciens et les
  Modernes*, 142
  'Réponse à l'évêque de Luçon', 142
Fonvizin, Denis, 167, 170-71
Forkel-Liebeskind, Meta Dorothea,
  76
Forster, Georg, 67
Fortnightly review, 113-14
France, Anatole, 148
Franklin, Benjamin, xi
Frederick II the Great, king of
  Prussia, 41, 106, 117, 120, 124-25,
  127-33, 135, 137-38, 180, 215, 243,
  293
Freemasons, 161, 174-75, 177-78
French Revolution, 7, 14-16, 24-25,
  28-29, 38-40, 47, 51-54, 63, 66-69,
  72, 89, 93, 102, 106, 113, 115,
  144-46, 150, 153, 156, 174, 181,

189, 198-99, 212n, 214, 219-20,
235, 247-50, 253-55, 259-62,
281-82, 291-92
Freud, Sigmund, 267, 271-73, 275,
281
Friedrich Wilhelm I, king of Prussia,
40, 127
Friedrich Wilhelm II, king of Prussia,
132
Friedrich Wilhelm III, king of
Prussia, 77
Frisi, Paolo, 250
Fritsch, Theodor, *Antisemiten-Kate-chismus: eine Zusammenstellung des wichtigsten Materials zum Verständnis der Judenfrage*, 213
Fröbel, Friedrich Wilhelm August, 75
Fromm, Erich, *Man for himself*, 239
Fromm, Maria Magdalena Louisa
(Hegel's mother), 58, 66, 74
Fulda, Daniel (ed.), *Aufklärung fürs Auge*, 143

Gadamer, Hans-Georg, 119
Galasso, Giuseppe, 247n
Galileo Galilei, 125
Gall, Franz Joseph, 111
Garat, Dominique-Joseph, 82
Garve, Christian, 'Versuch über die
Prüfung der Fähigkeiten', 59
Gay, Peter, 1, 245, 261-72, 274-81
'Carl Becker's *Heavenly city*', 261,
278
The Enlightenment: an interpretation,
161, 257-58, 274, 281
'The Enlightenment in the history
of political theory', 274
'The German-Jewish legacy and I:
some personal reflections', 271
'Light on the Enlightenment', 275
'The living Enlightenment', 282-83
'On American irresponsibility', 276
Party of humanity: essays in the French Enlightenment, 272
'The social history of ideas: Ernst
Cassirer and after', 269, 272
Voltaire's politics: the poet as realist,
272n, 279
Gellert, Christian Fürchtegott, 132
'gens de lettres', 25-27, 83, 153, 249n
Gentile, Giovanni, 241

Geoffrin, Marie-Thérèse, 73
Georg, Stefan, 109
Gervinus, Gottfried, 47
Giarrizzo, Giuseppe, 247n-248n, 251
Gibbon, Edward, 111, 113, 248
Gidel, Charles
    Discours sur Jean Jacques Rousseau,
    91-92, 97
    Histoire de la littérature française, 97
Gieseke, Jens, *The History of the Stasi*,
299
Gieson, Bernhard, *Intellectuals and the nation*, 186
Gilbert, Désiré-Louis, *Eloge de Vauvenargues*, 91n, 94
Giuliano, Balbino, 241
Gladstone, William Ewart, 114
Gleim, Johann Wilhelm Ludwig,
289n
Goethe, Johann Wolfgang von, 12n,
32, 38, 47, 49-50, 52, 107-11, 117,
120, 123-24, 127-28, 137, 195n,
298
    Werther's sorrows, 51
    Wilhelm Meister, 49
Golburt, Luba, *The First epoch: the eighteenth century and the Russian cultural imagination*, 159
Goldmann, Nathan, 212n
Goldoni, Carlo, 254
Goldsmith, Oliver, 111
Golitsyn, Prince Dmitri Alekseievich,
171
Goncharov, Ivan, 175
Goriushkin, Zakhar, *The Judicial act*,
179
Gottsched, Johann Christoph, 48,
289n
Graetz, Heinrich, *Geschichte der Juden*,
187-88
Gray, John, 102
Gréard, Octave, *Prévost-Paradol*, 97
Greenberg, Clement, 232
Greene, Donald, 282
Grierson, Herbert J. C., 109
Grillparzer, Franz, 195n
Grimm, Friedrich Melchior, 165, 174
    Correspondance littéraire, 250
Grimm, Jacob, 138n
Grimm, Wilhelm, 138n
Grotius, Hugo, 287

Guberti, Nikolai, *A Survey of rare books of the eighteenth century*, 159
Guizot, François, 7n, 11-12, 15, 86
  Cours d'histoire moderne, 13n
Gumbrecht, Hans Ulrich, 84
Günderrode, Karoline von, 76
Gundling, Nicolaus Hieronymus, 286
  Gundlingiana, 287, 289, 305
Guterman, Norbert, 'Neither-nor', 233

Habermas, Jürgen, 69n, 146
Habsburg dynasty, 252
Haffner, Paul Leopold, *Die deutsche Aufklärung: eine historische Skizze*, 207-208, 217
Haller, Albrecht von, 111
Hallische Jahrbücher, 290
Hallowell, John H., 'The decline of liberalism', 227
Hamburg, Gary, *Russia's path toward Enlightenment: faith, politics, and reason, 1500-1801*, 159
Handel, George Frideric, 50
Hardt, Hermann von der, 44
Hardtwig, Wolfgang, *Nationalismus und Bürgerkultur in Deutschland 1500-1914*, 205n-206n
Harel, Charles-Jean, *Discours sur Voltaire*, 86-87, 96
Harnack, Carl Gustav Adolf von
  Geschichte der Königlich Preußischen Akademie der Wissenschaften zu Berlin, 123-24, 132-33
  Reden und Aufsätze, 208n
Harrison, Frederic, 113, 116, 118
Hartley, David, 111
Hauser, Henri, 242
Havet, Ernest, 97n
Haydn, Joseph, 77, 101
Hayes, Carlton J. H., 'The novelty of totalitarianism in the history of Western civilization', 227
Hazard, Paul, 146, 152-54, 259
  La Crise de la conscience européenne, 1680-1715, 153
  La Pensée européenne au XVIIIe siècle de Montesquieu à Lessing, 36, 153
Heard, Gerald, 233
Hegel, Christiane Louise, 63, 74-75

Hegel, Georg Wilhelm Friedrich, 8n, 34, 38-40, 43, 45, 48n, 49, 51, 57-60, 62-63, 66-69, 73-79, 111, 115, 118, 123, 129, 138n, 259-60, 266-67, 271, 289, 291, 294
  Aesthetics, 77
  Encyclopaedia, 75
  Frühe Exzerpte, 59n, 67n
  Frühe Schriften I, 58n, 60-65, 69, 70n
  Frühe Schriften II, 66
  Grundlinien der Philosophie des Rechts, 59, 72, 76, 78-79
  Hegel: the letters, 75n
  Jenaer kritische Schriften, 69
  Jenaer Schriften, 1801-1807, 70
  Lectures on the philosophy of history, 129
  Lectures on the philosophy of religion, 39
  Phänomenologie des Geistes, 70-72
  'Über einige Vortheile, welche uns die Lektüre der alten klassischen Griechischen und Römischen Schriftsteller gewährt', 59n
  'Ueber einige charakteristische Unterschiede der alten Dichter', 59n
  Vorlesungen über die Geschichte der Philosophie III, 35n, 70
  Vorlesungen über die Philosophie der Kunst I, 77
  Vorlesungen über die Philosophie des subjektiven Geistes I, 74-75
  –, Schelling and Hölderlin, *Das älteste Systemprogramm des deutschen Idealismus*, 66-67
Heidegger, Martin, 119, 228
Heine, Heinrich, 109, 214n
  On the history of religion and philosophy in Germany, 48
Helvétius, Claude-Adrien, 17, 70, 94, 96, 171
Hémon, Félix, *Eloge de Buffon*, 86, 90-91
Herder, Johann Gottfried, 101, 108-109, 119, 137, 195n
Hermersdorf, Charlotte Wilhelmine von, 74
Hertzberg, Ewald Friedrich von, 131-32

Herzl, Theodor, 219n
Hettner, Hermann Julius Theodor,
  1, 23, 47
  Literaturgeschichte des 18.
    Jahrhunderts, 30-36
  Die romantische Schule in ihrem
    inneren Zusammenhange mit Göthe
    und Schiller, 30-31
Heyne, Christian Gottlob, 67
Hibben, John Grier, *The Philosophy of*
  the Enlightenment, 259
Hinchman, Lewis P., *Hegel's critique of*
  the Enlightenment, 71
Hippel, Theodor Gottlieb, *Über die*
  bürgerliche Verbesserung der Weiber, 76
Hirsch, Marcus, *Kulturdefizit am Ende*
  des 19. Jahrhunderts von Dr. med.
  Marcus Hirsch, 218
Hirschman, Albert O., *The Rhetoric of*
  reaction, 230
Hitler, Adolf, 226-28, 235, 238
Hobbes, Thomas, 103, 105, 111
Hoffmann, Stefan-Ludwig,
  'Brothers and strangers? Jews and
  Freemasons in nineteenth-century
  Germany', 201n-202n
Hofstadter, Richard, 275-77
  'Democracy and anti-intellec-
    tualism in America', 276
Holborn, Hajo, 272
Hölderlin, Friedrich, 63, 65, 109
Honecker, Erich, 302
Hook, Sidney, 236
  'The failure of the left', 234
  'The new failure of nerve', 224-25,
    232-34
Horace, 242n
Horkheimer, Max, 1, 109, 121, 220,
  223-24, 236-37
  Eclipse of reason, 224, 237-40
  Gesammelte Schriften, vol.16:
    Briefwechsel 1937-1940, 230-31
  Gesammelte Schriften, vol.17:
    Briefwechsel 1941-1948, 236, 239
  Gesammelte Schriften, vol.18:
    Briefwechsel 1949-1973, 240
  'Hook', 237-38
Hotho, Heinrich Gustav, 77
Houdetot, Elisabeth de La Live de
  Bellegarde, comtesse d', 106
Houghton, Walter E., 104

Howard, John, 166
Huber, Therese, 76
Hughes, Stuart, 'Franz Neumann
  between liberalism and social
  democracy', 263
Humboldt, Alexander von, 75, 123
Hume, David, 245
Hunter, William, 111
Hutchins, Robert Maynard, 230
Huxley, Aldous, 233

Idealism (German), 19, 31, 70, 79,
  137, 257-58, 262, 270-72, 281
Iffland, August Wilhelm, 52
Islam, 200
Israel, Jonathan, 3n, 106, 254-56
  Democratic Enlightenment, 254-55

Jacobi, Friedrich Heinrich, 69n
Jacobs, Margaret, 254
Janet, Paul, *Victor Cousin et son œuvre*,
  8n
Jaurès, Jean, 248
Jean Paul, Johann Paul Friedrich
  Richter, *known as*, 49, 195n
Jeremiah, 45
Jesuits, 251
Jesus Christ, 143, 291
Jey, Martine, 148
Johnson, Samuel, 106, 111
Joseph II, Holy Roman emperor,
  180, 251
Joyce, James, 102
Judaism, 187-92, 195-201, 211-21,
  238
July Revolution (1830), 6, 12, 68, 95
Jünger, Ernst, 228
Jusserand, Jean-Jules (ed.), *Grands*
  Ecrivains français, 98

Kant, Immanuel, 8n, 11, 19-20, 36,
  38, 62, 64, 69, 72, 78, 101, 108,
  111, 114, 121-22, 133, 138, 195n,
  245n, 258, 270, 281
  'Beantwortung der Frage: was ist
    Aufklärung?', 57; 'An answer to
    the question: what is Enlight-
    enment?', 70
  Critique of practical reason and other
    writings in moral philosophy, 69n
  Critique of pure reason, 120, 273

'Idea for a universal history with a cosmopolitan aim', 138n
Metaphysik, 76
Karamzin, Nikolai, 161
Kaulla, Rudolf, *Der Liberalismus und die deutschen Juden*, 189n
Kettler, David, and Thomas Wheatland, *Learning from Franz L. Neumann*, 263
Khrapovitskii, A. V., *Pamiatnye zapiski*, 163-64
Khrushchev, I. N., 'On the Enlightenment activity of Catherine II', 182-83
Kierkegaard, Søren Aabye, 233
Kirchheimer, Otto, 264
Kleist, Ewald von, 289n
Klett, Christoph August, 66
Kliuchevsky, Vasily, 158
Klopstock, Friedrich Gottlieb, 128
Knutzen, Martin, 44
Köhler, Paul, *Die Verjudung Deutschlands und der Weg zur Rettung*, 213-14
Köppen, Karl Friedrich, 291-92
 Friedrich der Grosse und seine Widersacher: eine Jubelschrift, 293
Koselleck, Reinhardt, 22, 159
 Kritik und Krise, 286
 Sattelzeit, 286
Kotzebue, August von, 52
Krauss, Werner, 22, 299
 Briefe 1922 bis 1976, 296
 'Einführung in das Studium der französischen Aufklärung', 295
Kutuzov, Aleksei M., 174, 177

Laborde-Milaà, Auguste, 'Fontenelle', 87-88, 98
Lacretelle, Charles, *Testament philosophique et littéraire*, 85
Lafontaine, August, 49, 52
La Fontaine, Jean de, 149
Lamennais, Félicité de
 'Influence des doctrines philosophiques sur la société', 27n
 Réflexions sur l'état de l'Eglise en France, 27
La Mettrie, Julien Offray de, 127
Langbehn, Julius, 205

Lanson, Gustave, 1, 146-52, 259
 'L'esprit scientifique et la méthode de l'histoire littéraire', 147
 'Formation et développement de l'esprit philosophique du XVIIIe siècle', 150
 Histoire de la littérature française, 147
 'L'histoire littéraire et la sociologie', 147n
 'Origines et premières manifestations de l'esprit philosophique dans la littérature française de 1675 à 1748', 150
 'Programme d'études sur l'histoire provinciale de la vie littéraire en France', 150
 'Questions diverses sur l'histoire de l'esprit philosophique en France avant 1750', 151
 'Le rôle de l'expérience dans la formation de la philosophie du XVIIIe siècle en France', 151
 Voltaire, 150
Lappo-Danilevsky, Alexander, *The Collection and compilation of the laws of the Russian Empire: a study in the internal politics of the empress*, 159
Laski, Harold, 263, 279
Lavisse, Ernest, 147, 151
Lazarsfeld, Paul, 271
Lazarus, Moritz, 221
Le Bon, Gustave, 267
Leeman, Merel, 'Transatlantic Enlightenment: Peter Gay and the drama of German history in the United States, 1930-1970', 262, 276n
Lefebvre, Georges, 250n
Leibniz, Gottfried Wilhelm, 8, 124
Lemercier de La Rivière, Paul-Pierre, 169, 181
Lescure, Adolphe de, *Etude sur Beaumarchais*, 87
Lespinasse, Julie de, 92
Lessing, Gotthold Ephraim, 38, 41, 69, 108-109, 117, 127, 131-32, 138, 187, 192, 214, 218, 289n
 Nathan the Wise, 59, 117, 218
Le Tellier, Charles François, *Le Tombeau de Voltaire foudroyé*, xi

Levachez, Charles François Gabriel, xi
Lewald, Fanny, 214
Lewes, George Henry, 102, 105, 110-14, 118
  History of philosophy from Plato to Comte, 110-12, 115
  The Life of Goethe, 111
liberalism, 47, 101-103, 114, 155, 167, 170, 180, 187n, 189-90, 192, 203n, 204-205, 211, 219-20, 227, 258, 263, 267-68, 273
Librairie, 95
Litchfield, Robert Burr, 'Franco Venturi's "crisis" of the Old Regime', 244-46, 248n
Locke, John, 6, 8, 16-17, 18n, 268
  Essai sur l'entendement humain, 17
Loeffler (Hegel's teacher), 58n
Lomonosov, Mikhail, 182
Lonzi, Carla, *Sputiamo su Hegel*, 78
Lopukhin, Ivan, 169, 174, 177
Louis XIV, king of France, 12n, 89, 107, 148-49, 251, 291
Louis XVI, king of France, 95
Louis-Philippe Ier, king of France, 86
Lowenthal, Leo, 236-37, 239
Lukin, Vladimir, 167
Lumières, see concepts of Enlightenment, etc.
Luther, Martin, 35, 41, 110, 124, 127, 130
Lyotard, Jean-François, 282

Macaulay, Thomas Babington, 33, 104
  'Lord Bacon', 104
McCarthy, Joseph Raymond, 263, 275-77
Macdonald, Dwight, 223-24, 232, 234, 236
  'The future of democratic values', 234-36
Macron, Emmanuel, 141
Madariaga, Isabel de, *Russia in the age of Catherine the Great*, 177
Mainov, Ivan, 'Smolenskie dvoriane i obiazannye krest'iane', 170, 176

Maintenon, Françoise d'Aubigné, marquise de, 149
Maistre, Joseph de, 101, 112
Malebranche, Nicolas, 143
Malesherbes, Chrétien Guillaume de Lamoignon de, 82, 85, 87, 94-95
Mannheim, Karl, 221
Marat, Jean-Paul, 111
Marchand, Suzanne L., *Down from Olympus*, 109
Marcus Aurelius, 128
Marcuse, Herbert, 236, 264, 271
Maria Theresa, empress of Austria, 251
Marie-Antoinette Joseph Jeanne de Lorraine, queen of France, 156, 166
Maritain, Jacques, 'Science, philosophy, and faith', 226-27
Marivaux, Pierre Carlet de Chamblain de, 82
Marr, Wilhelm, *Lessing contra Sem*, 218
Martignac, Jean-Baptiste Sylvère Gay, comte de, 11
Martin, Kingsley, *French liberal thought in the eighteenth century*, 113
Marx, Karl, 40, 236, 267, 290-91, 294
materialism, 17, 18n, 20, 92, 106, 112, 128, 173, 227, 255, 281, 294-95
Mathiez, Albert, 250n
Matytsin, Anton, 'Whose light is it anyway?', 142n, 144
Mauss, Marcel, 231
Meinecke, Friedrich, 119
  Die Entstehung des Historismus, 137
  The German catastrophe, 109
Mendelssohn, Fanny, 77
Mendelssohn, Felix, 77
Mendelssohn, Moses, 60, 69n, 131-33, 187-88, 192
  Phädon oder über die Unsterblichkeit der Seele, in drey Gesprächen, 58
  'Über die Frage: was heisst aufklären?', 57, 62
Mercier, Louis-Sébastien, *L'An 2440*, 246
Merker, Nicolao, *L'Illuminismo tedesco: l'età di Lessing*, 247n

Michaut, Narcisse, 86-87
Milder-Hauptmann, Pauline Anna, 77
Mill, James, 105, 107, 112-13
Mill, John Stuart, 102-103, 115
  'Coleridge', 103
Mirabeau, Honoré Gabriel Riqueti, comte de, 111
  De la monarchie prussienne sous Frédéric le Grand, 28
Mommsen, Theodor, 'Rede vom 18. März 1880 zur Vorfeier des Geburtstages des Kaisers in der Königlich Preußischen Akademie der Wissenschaften', 215-17, 221
Montaigne, Michel de, 108
Montesquieu, Charles de Secondat, baron de La Brède et de, 15-16, 26n, 69, 125, 149, 163, 273
  De l'esprit des lois, 163, 267-68; transl. Thomas Nugent, *Spirit of the laws*, 267
Moreau, Pierre-François, 6
Morellet, André, 82
Moritz, Karl Philipp, *Anton Reiser*, 51
Morize, André, 152
Morley, John, 113, 116, 118, 145n, 274
  'Auguste Comte', 115-16, 118
  'Carlyle', 117-18
  Diderot and the Encyclopædists, 114, 259
  'On Pattison's *Memoirs*', 117
  Rousseau, 106, 114
  Voltaire, 114
Mornet, Daniel, 146, 152, 242, 247, 255
  Les Origines intellectuelles de la Révolution française, 152-53
  La Pensée française au XVIII⁰ siècle, 152
Mortier, Roland, 82, 143
Möser, Justus, 135-37
Moses, 33
Moses, Julius, 216
Mosse, Werner E., 'Der Niedergang der Weimarer Republik und die Juden', 188-89, 221
Mühlpfordt, Günter, 297

Müller, Winfried, *Die Aufklärung*, 205
Mulsow, Martin, 138
Murray, Gilbert, *Four stages of Greek religion*, 225
Mussolini, Benito, 238

Nagel, Ernest, 224, 236
Naigeon, Jacques André, 82
Napoleon Ist (Napoléon Bonaparte), 40, 68, 78, 235
Naumann, Manfred, 297
Necker, Jacques, 174
Nelson, Benjamin, 237
Neumann, Franz Leopold, 263-65, 269, 271-73, 277, 279-81
  Behemoth, 264, 266
  'Concept of political freedom', 266
  'Editor's introduction', in Montesquieu, *Spirit of the laws*, 267-68
  'Governance and the rule of law', 265, 267, 270
  'Intellektuelle und politische Freiheit', 266
  'Montesquieu', 268, 269n
  'Recht und Staat', 266-67
Neumann-Hofer, Adolf, 216-17
Newton, Isaac, 93, 143
Nicholas I, emperor of Russia, 155-56, 165, 176
Nicolai, Christoph Friedrich, 28n, 70, 131
  Beschreibung einer Reise durch Deutschland und die Schweiz, im Jahre 1781, 59n
Niebuhr, Barthold Georg, 138n
Nietzsche, Friedrich, 109, 229
nihilism, 226-28, 231
Nonnotte, Claude François, *Dictionnaire philosophique de la religion*, 144
Nordau, Max, 219n
Nordmann, Jean-Thomas, *La Critique littéraire française au XIX⁰ siècle (1800-1914)*, 152
Novikov, Nikolai, 159

Oakshott, Michael, 282
Olbrechts-Tyteca, Lucie, 84

Paine, Tom, 174
Paley, William, 103
Palmer, Robert Roswell, 248, 277
'Pamiatnik Ekaterine II: 24-ogo
    noiabria 1873', 155
Panin, Nikita, 169-70, 173, 181
Panofsky, Irwin, 271
Paoli, Pasquale, 247
Paret, Peter, 134
Parini, Giuseppe, 254
Parny, Evariste de Forges de, 82
Partisan review, 224-25, 232-33, 236
Pascal, Blaise, 84, 195n
Pascal, Jean-Noël, 82n
Pater, Walter, 107-108, 114
    Imaginary portraits, 107-108, 110
    *Studies in the history of the
    Renaissance*, 107-109
Pattison, Mark, 116-18
    'The age of reason', 114-15
Paul I, emperor of Russia, 155n, 166
Paulus, Caroline, 77
Pečar, Andreas, 3n
Péguy, Charles, 151
Pekarskii, Petr, 'Mikhail Vasil'evich
    Lomonosov, "O razmnozhenii i
    sokhranenii rossiiskogo naroda"
    (1761)', 182
Perelman, Chaïm, 84
Pestalozzi, Johann Heinrich, 75, 130
Peter I, emperor of Russia (Peter the
    Great), 40, 155, 159, 162, 164-65,
    172, 182
Peter III, emperor of Russia, 156n,
    163
Philippson, Martin, *Neueste Geschichte
    des jüdischen Volkes*, 187-88
Philips, William, 232, 234
philosophes, 11, 13-14, 24-26, 29, 35,
    64, 90, 93, 95-96, 106, 114, 116,
    127, 143, 145, 149, 173, 243, 249,
    259, 261, 272, 280-82, 290
Pietism, 41-44, 46, 175
Pilati, Carlantonio, *Di una riforma
    in Italia*, 248, 254
Pinel, Philippe, 75
Pinkard, Terry, *Hegel*, 60, 63
Plantu, 141
Plato, 17n
Platonov, S. F., 162n

Plotinus, 112
Pocock, John G. A., 116
Pöggeler, Otto, 65n
Pombal, Sebastião Jose de Carvalho
    e Melo, marquis de, 251
Porter, Roy, 105, 116
Prades, Jean-Martin, abbé de, 243
Prévost-Paradol, Lucien Anatole, 97
    'Eloge de Bernardin de
    Saint-Pierre', 92-94
Prometheus, 45
Protestantism, 45, 51, 125, 130, 208,
    219
Prutz, Robert, 291n-293n
Pufendorf, Samuel, baron von, 287
Pugachev Rebellion, 176, 247
Putin, Vladimir, 199
Pypin, Alexander, 158
    Istoriia russkoi literatury, 180

['R'], 'Ein Zeichen der Zeit', *Das
    Abendland: Central-Organ für alle
    zeitgemäßen Interessen des Judenthums*,
    215n-216n
Raabe, Paul, 302
Racine, Jean, 149
    Athalie, 128, 150
    Mithridate, 128
Radishchev, Alexander, 166-67,
    169-71, 174, 177
    Journey from St Petersburg to Moscow,
    178
Radishchev, Pavel, 166-67
Rahv, Phillip, 232, 234
Ramler, Karl Wilhelm, 289n
Ranke, Leopold von, 138n
Rao, Anna Maria, 'Enlightenment
    and reform: an overview of
    culture and politics in Enlight-
    enment Italy', 244, 245n, 247n
Rauschning, Hermann, *Revolution of
    nihilism*, 227-28
Ravaisson, Félix, *La Philosophie en
    France au XIXe siècle*, 5
Raynal, Guillaume-Thomas, 171,
    175
Réau, Louis, *L'Europe française au
    siècle des Lumières*, 141-42, 153
Reformation, the, 47, 124, 129, 209
Reid, Thomas, 20

religious sects
Anabaptists, 28n
Moravians, 28n
Quakers, 28n, 143
Rey, Lucie, 18n
Reymond, M[oritz von], *Wo steckt der Mauschel? Oder Jüdischer Liberalismus und wissenschaftlicher Pessimismus*, 220
Rheinische Zeitung, 290
Ricken, Ulrich, 298-305
Ricuperati, Giuseppe, 146
La Reinvenzione dei lumi, 152n
Riseman, David, 276
Ritter, Joachim, 67
Ritter, Paul, 123, 124n
Robert, Friederike, 77
Robertson, John
The Enlightenment, 146
'Franco Venturi's Enlightenment', 245n
Robespierre, Maximilien Marie Isidore de, 117
Robinet, Jean-Baptiste, 71
Robinson, James Harvey, 259-60
Roche, Daniel, 246
Romanticism, 3, 30-31, 38, 48, 101, 111, 115, 137, 202, 208-209, 289
Ronsard, Pierre de, 108
Rorty, Richard, 282
Rosenberg, Harold, 232
Rosenkranz, Karl, *Georg Wilhelm Friedrich Hegel's Leben*, 59, 63
Rosenzweig, Franz, 66
Rossini, Gioachino, 77
Rousseau, Jean-Jacques, xi, 11, 15, 26n, 60, 63, 66, 71, 82-83, 91-92, 106, 111, 117, 149, 174, 249, 270-73, 275, 291
Du contrat social, 24
Profession de foi du vicaire savoyard, 92
Royal Society, 105
Rudler, Gustave, 152
Ruge, Arnold, 37, 38n, 286, 290-91
Rumiantsev, N. P., 174
Russian antiquity, 155, 158, 166-67, 175
Russian October Revolution, 253, 255, 261

Sack, August Friedrich, 130
Sainte-Beuve, Charles-Augustin, 92
Salieri, Antonio, 77
Saltykova, Daria, 176
Salvandy, Narcisse-Achille de, 86
Salvemini, Gaetano, 242n
Sartre, Jean-Paul, 151
Savigny, Friedrich Karl von, 136
scepticism, 10, 12, 18, 20, 95, 107, 111, 113, 175, 235, 246, 254, 261, 273, 286
Schalk, Fritz, 24n
Schapiro, Meyer, 234
Schelling, Caroline, *née* Michaelis, 76
Schelling, Friedrich Wilhelm Joseph von, 63, 65, 112
Scherer, Wilhelm, 125
Schiller, Friedrich von, 50, 60, 109
Schleiermacher, Friedrich, 67, 120, 123, 132, 137
Schlosser, Friedrich Christoph, 32
Geschichte des achtzehnten Jahrhunderts in gedrängter Uebersicht, 31, 290
Geschichte des achtzehnten Jahrhunderts und des neunzehnten bis zum Sturz des französischen Kaiserreichs, 31, 289-92; English transl. David Davison, 290
Schlözer, Dorothea, 76
Schmitt, Carl, 228, 263
Scholem, Gershom, 1
Schopenhauer, Arthur, 195n
Schröder, Winfried, 297
Seignobos, Charles, 242
Semevsky, Mikail, 158
Semler, Johann Salomo, 130, 138n
Seneca, 128
sensualism, 17-20, 30
sentimentalism, 48-49, 276
Sévigné, Marie de Rabutin-Chantal, marquise de, 149
Shaftesbury, Anthony Ashley Cooper, 3rd earl of, 125
Shcherbatov, Mikhail, 157, 175
On the corruption of morals in Russia, 168, 172-73
Sheshkovsky, Stepan, 166-67
Shuvalov, Count Ivan, 174
Sieyès, Emmanuel Joseph, 291

Singer, Isidor, *Presse und Judenthum*, 218

Smith, Helmut Walser, 'Reluctant return: Peter Gay and the cosmopolitan work of the historian', 262, 269

Sokolov, Nahum, 219n

Solov'ev, Sergei, 164

Solovyov, Vladimir, 158
   History of Russia, 156

Sontag, Henriette, 77

Sorbonne, 6, 12, 17, 145-48, 150, 242, 253

Sorel, Albert, 248

Sorkin, David, 'Jews, the Enlightenment and the sources of toleration', 190n

Spalding, Johann Joachim, 130

Spector, Céline, 142

Spener, Philipp, 28n

Spengler, Oswald, 228

Spinoza, Baruch, 3n, 44, 110-12, 255
   Ethics (transl. George Eliot), 110

Spittler, Ludwig Timotheus, 138n

Spurzheim, Johann, 111

Staël-Holstein, Germaine de (Mme de Staël), 76

Stahr, Adolf, 290-91

Stalin, Joseph, 276

Stephen, Leslie, 115
   The English Utilitarians, 116
   History of English thought in the eighteenth century, 114-15

Stephenson, Adlai, 275

Stieler, Kaspar von, *Der Deutschen Sprache Stammbaum und Fortwachs, oder Teutscher Sprachschatz*, 285-86

Stone, Alison, 79

Strachey, Lytton, *Landmarks of French literature*, 113

Strauss, David Friedrich, 1, 39, 291

Strauss, Leo, 'German nihilism', 228-29, 232

Stuke, Horst, 57n

Suard, Jean-Baptiste Antoine, 82

Sukhomlinov, Mikail, *History of the Russian Academy of Sciences*, 159

Sulzer, Johann Georg, *Kurzer Begriff aller Wissenschaften*, 59

Tableau littéraire de la France au XVIIIe siècle, 81-82

Tacitus, 195n

Taine, Hippolyte, *Les Origines de la France contemporaine*, 24, 144-45

Talmon, Jacob, *Origins of totalitarian democracy*, 266

Teller, Wilhelm Abraham, 130

Teplov, Grigory, 173

Tetens, Johannes Nikolaus, 70

Thaden, Edward C., 157

theism, 18n

Thibaudet, Albert, 145

Thoma, Heinz, 82

Thomasius, Christian, 289n

Tillich, Paul, 271

Tocqueville, Alexis de, 1, 23, 27-28, 33, 144, 276
   L'Ancien Régime et la Révolution, 25-30, 36, 249n

Togliatti, Palmiro, 241

Toland, John, 255

Tolstoy, Leo, 171, 176
   War and peace, 157

Torcellan, Gianfranco, 248

Torrey, Norman, *Voltaire and the age of Enlightenment*, 260

Treitschke, Heinrich von
   Deutsche Geschichte im Neunzehnten Jahrhundert, 211-12, 214-15
   Unsere Aussichten, 215

Trevor-Roper, Hugh, 109

Tricoire, Damien, 3n

Trilling, Lionel, 233

Troeltsch, Ernst, *Realencyklopädie für protestantische Theologie und Kirche*, 210-11

Trump, Donald, 196-200

Tucher, Marie Helena Susanne von (Hegel's wife), 74-75, 78

Turgenev, Ivan, 171, 176

Turgenev, Nikolai, 161

Turgot, Anne Robert Jacques, 82, 86, 88, 92, 95-96, 113

Unamuno, Miguel de, 242

Undolskii, Vukol, 'Pis'ma Vukola Mikhailovicha Undol'skago k A. N. Popovu', 165

utilitarianism, 103, 113, 115-16, 203, 274
Uvarov, Sergey, 160

Valentini, Francesco, 70n
Valiani, Leo, 'Una testimonianza', 253n
Van Dale, Anton, 44
Vauvenargues, Luc de Clapiers, marquis de, 82, 91-92, 94
Venturi, Adolfo, 242
Venturi, Franco, 1, 146, 152, 242, 244, 254-56
 'Contributi ad un dizionario storico: despotismo orientale', 244n
 'Contributi ad un dizionario storico: Was ist Aufklärung? Sapere aude!', 244n
 The End of the Old Regime in Europe, 1768-1776 (English transl. Robert Burr Litchfield), 248
 'The European Enlightenment', 247n, 250-52
 'La fortuna di dom Deschamps', 242-43
 L'Italia fuori d'Italia, 247n
 La Jeunesse de Diderot, 152, 243
 Pages inédites contre un tyran, 243n
 'La prima crisi dell'Antico Regime: 1768-1776', 247
 Riformatori delle antiche repubbliche, 248
 Riformatori lombardi, piemontesi e toscani, 248
 Riformatori napoletani, 248
 The Roots of revolution, 182n
 Settecento riformatore, 243n, 245, 247-50, 252
 Utopia and reform in the Enlightenment, 118, 242n, 244-46, 247n, 248-50, 252
Venturi, Lionello, 241-42
Venturino, Diego
 'L'historiographie révolutionnaire française et les Lumières', 85, 88, 141-42, 145
Vernes, Jacob, 241
Verri, Alessandro, 250
Verri, Pietro, 250

Viala, Alain, 151
Vico, Giambattista, 119, 122
Vieweg, Klaus, *Hegel: der Philosoph der Freiheit*, 58n-60n, 63n, 67n-68n
Villemain, Abel-François, 11-12, 13n, 15, 32, 86
 Cours de littérature française: tableau du XVIIIᵉ siècle, 12n-13n
 Tableau de la littérature au XVIIIᵉ siècle, 31
Vincent, Julien, 89
Volkov, Shulamit
 Dilemma und Dialektik, 188n, 190n
 Germans, Jews, and antisemites: trials in emancipation, 219n
Volney, Constantin François de Chasseboeuf, comte de, 82
 Les Ruines, 76
Volpilhac-Auger, Catherine, 'Une bibliothèque bleue', 98-99
Voltaire, xi, 11, 15-16, 26n, 27, 43, 69-71, 82-83, 86, 91, 94, 96, 98, 106, 108, 110-11, 114, 125, 127-28, 138, 143-45, 148-50, 152n, 174, 192, 195n, 241, 245, 249, 252, 262, 273, 275, 278, 289n, 291
 Correspondence, 278-79
 Eléments de la philosophie de Newton, 143
 Idées républicaines, 278
 Lettres philosophiques (ed. Lanson), 150
 Lettres sur les Anglais, 143
 Le Monde comme il va, 142
 Poème sur le désastre de Lisbonne, 251
 Siècle de Louis XIV, 148

Wade, Ira O., 277, 279
 The Clandestine organization and diffusion of philosophic ideas in France from 1700 to 1750, 260n
Wagner, Richard, 195n
Walicki, Andrzej, *The Slavophile controversy*, 156
Walpole, Horace, 33
Warburg, Aby, 279
Weber, Carl Maria von, *Der Freischütz*, 101
Weber, Max, 41, 266

Whewell, William, 103-105, 115
  'Comte and positivism', 112
  *History of moral philosophy in
    England*, 103-104
  History of the inductive sciences, 103
  *The Philosophy of the inductive
    sciences*, 104-105
White, Andrew Dickson, 259-60
Wieland, Christoph Martin, 52
Wilhelm II, German emperor, 215
Winckelmann, Johann Joachim,
  107-10

Wolff, Christian, 130-31, 133, 138
Wöllner, Johann Christoph von,
  132
Wreszin, Michael, *A Rebel in defense of
  tradition*, 234

Zanuck, Darryl F., 235
Zedlitz, Karl Abraham von, 130-32
Zékian, Stéphane, 148
Zimmermann, Johann Georg, 174
Zola, Emile, 'J'accuse', 148